BIOTECHNOLOGY DESKBOOK

William L. Anderson, Nancy S. Bryson,
William M. Cohen, Robert C. Davis Jr.,
Philip Katz, Richard J. Mannix,
Steven P. Quarles, and Richard E. Schwartz

An ELI Deskbook

Environmental Law Reporter
Environmental Law Institute
Washington, D.C.

BIOTECHNOLOGY DESKBOOK

Table of Contents

About the Authors . . .

William L. Anderson practices in civil litigation involving product liability, toxic tort, and environmental matters. His specialty is complex health and life science cases arising from alleged health and plant injury from exposure to chemical products. He is experienced in litigating matters involving specialized scientific knowledge such as developmental toxicology (birth defects), genetic syndromes and causation, toxicology, pharmacokinetics, and epidemiology. Mr. Anderson's work has extended to regulatory matters related to science litigation, including classification and marketing of products under the European Union's complex directives governing dangerous substances and plant protection products. He is also part of Crowell & Moring's growing Biotechnologies practice group. Mr. Anderson received his J.D. from the University of Minnesota Law School in 1988, and his B.A. degree from Hendrix College in 1975.

Nancy S. Bryson is a partner in Crowell & Moring's Natural Resources and Environment group and co-chair of the firm's Biotechnologies practice. Her practice concentrates on the major federal laws regulating the health, safety, and environmental release of consumer and commercial products. Her clients have included major chemical producers, consumers, personal care and commercial product manufacturers, utility companies, the forest products industry, farms, and national trade associations. She has represented them in proceedings and initiatives in the various federal agencies of jurisdiction, as well as in federal district court and appellate litigation and legislative matters. Prior to entering private practice, Ms. Bryson was a staff attorney and Assistant Counsel for Appellate Litigation in the Occupational Safety and Health Division of the Solicitor's Office in the U.S. Department of Labor and a trial attorney and Assistant Chief of the Land and Natural Resources Division's Environmental Defense Section at the U.S. Department of Justice. Ms. Bryson has lectured and written extensively on many aspects of environmental law. Ms. Bryson received her law degree from the Georgetown University Law Center in 1975, and her undergraduate degree *summa cum laude* from Boston University in 1972.

Bill Cohen is an adjunct professor at the Washington College of Law, American University, Washington, D.C. There he teaches courses on: EIA and NEPA; and biotechnology and environmental regulations. Also, he is Of Counsel, Perkins Coie, Washington, D.C. He had been a trial lawyer and Section Chief, Environment and Natural Resources Division, U.S. Department of Justice. He co-chairs the American Law Institute-American Bar Association (ALI-ABA) program on NEPA/EIA.

Robert C. Davis Jr. is a partner specializing in environmental litigation, with particular emphasis on hazardous waste issues. He has represented clients in both administrative and judicial proceedings under the Resource Conservation and Recovery Act, Superfund, the Clean Air Act, the Clean Water Act, the Toxic Substances Control Act, the National Environmental Policy Act, and other federal and state statutes and regulatory programs. Robert has extensive experience dealing with environmental compliance issues at government-owned, contractor-operated federal facilities and applying environmental laws to mining sites. He has handled many cases involving insurance coverage issues related to chemical companies, oil refineries, service stations, pipeline companies, dry cleaning facilities, municipal landfills, hazardous waste disposal sites, and various manufacturing companies. Through his pro bono work, Robert has handled numerous matters before the U.S. Court of Veterans Appeals. Mr. Davis is a frequent lecturer and has published a variety of manuals and articles concerning a wide range of environmental issues. Mr. Davis received his LL.M. (Environmental), with Highest Honors, from George Washington University National Law Center in 1984, his J.D. from Oklahoma City University School of Law in 1978, and his B.B.A. from the University of Oklahoma in 1974. He previously served as Vice-Chair, ABA Special Committee on Environmental Litigation Techniques.

Philip Katz is a partner in Crowell & Moring's Health Care and Biotechnology groups who advises companies, trade associations, and individuals in matters arising under regulation by the Food and Drug Administration, Federal Trade Commission, and Consumer Product Safety Commission. He counsels clients on matters of regulatory compliance, strategic planning, and public policy, and advocates on their behalf before federal agencies, in court and other forums. Mr. Katz's clients include manufacturers and distributors of prescription and over-the-counter drugs, medical devices, foods, and cosmetics. He helps them anticipate and address regulatory issues in their day-to-day business operations and long-range decisionmaking, and represents them in administrative and judicial enforcement proceedings and competitor challenges. Mr. Katz also helps clients participate in the debate on public policy issues before government agencies and with Congress. He is a frequent speaker on a range of topics, and has served on the faculty of seminars conducted by the Food and Drug Law Institute. Mr. Katz graduated from Georgetown University Law Center *magna cum laude* and received a B.A. with distinction from the University of Virginia. Before practicing law, he was a staff member in the U.S. House of Representatives, and a lobbyist.

Richard J. Mannix is Special Counsel at Crowell & Moring. His practice is devoted to occupational safety and health and environmental issues, and to legislative developments affecting health, safety, and environmental law. In the area of health and safety, Mr. Mannix has conducted comprehensive health and safety audits of major manufacturing facilities and has prepared various site-specific self-audit materials. He counsels clients with respect to the development of on-site health and safety programs, compliance strategies, and their relationships with state and federal Occupational Safety and Health Administration (OSHA) offices. He has successfully petitioned federal OSHA for clarification of OSHA standards and provides regular counseling to clients on the progress of new and revised workplace standards. Mr. Mannix participated on behalf of several clients in the development of OSHA's ergonomics rulemaking and counsels clients with respect to impending regulatory initiatives, including potential revisions to the permissible exposure limits and the development of a comprehensive health and safety program rule. He is also periodically called upon to provide training sessions for clients' in-house regulatory compliance specialists and to conduct "shadow audits" to audit company audit systems. Prior to joining Crowell & Moring in 1988, Mr. Mannix served as Director of Legislative and Regulatory Affairs for a major public utility. Mr. Mannix holds an M.A. degree and a Ph.D. degree from New York University, and a J.D. degree *cum laude* from Brooklyn Law School, where he was Senior Editor of the *Brooklyn Law Review*.

Steven P. Quarles is chair of Crowell & Moring's Natural Resources and Environment group. His practice includes counseling, litigation, and legislative representation for a wide range of forest products, mining, agricultural and land development associations and companies, and state and local governments. He addresses issues concerning wildlife and endangered species, federal lands (including mineral, forestry, and access law), and water and air quality (including matters involving nonpoint source controls and point source permitting, impaired waters and total maximum daily loads, and wetlands regulation). Mr. Quarles represents clients in federal courts in all the federal circuits and the U.S. Supreme Court. He is chief litigation counsel to the American Forest and Paper Association and the National Pork Producers Council. He also litigates on behalf of the National Association of Homebuilders, a coalition of silvicultural and agricultural interests, and others on Clean Water Act and Endangered Species Act issues. Mr. Quarles graduated from Princeton University, where he was awarded the Herrick Prize, and Yale Law School. He received a Fulbright Scholarship to Aligarh Muslim University, India. Prior to his government service, Mr. Quarles was a program coordinator for the Ford Foundation in Rio de Janeiro, Brazil.

Richard E. Schwartz has specialized in environmental law since 1973, primarily working with the Clean Water Act (CWA), Clean Air Act, Resource Conservation and Recovery Act (RCRA), Occupational Safety and Health Act, and the Superfund Act. In 1974, Mr. Schwartz represented the steel industry in the U.S. Environmental Protection Agency's (EPA's) first toxic pollutant hearings under the CWA. From 1974 to 1984, he argued industry's position on numerous occasions during the many stages of the ensuing litigation over the "Flannery toxic pollutant consent decree." He represented the steel industry in three lawsuits challenging EPA's effluent discharge limitations for that industry. A successful 1983 settlement of one of these suits was praised by the *Washington Post* as a "creative solution" to a difficult dispute. For the leather tanning industry, Mr. Schwartz won its first effluent discharge limitations suit in 1975; convinced EPA to abandon proposed pretreatment standards in 1979; obtained delisting under RCRA of its solid wastes in 1980; and obtained a favorable settlement in its second effluent discharge limitations case in 1983. Mr. Schwartz received his J.D. from the University of Michigan in 1973, and his B.A. from Yale University in 1970.

Foreword

Few topics are as controversial as the use of genetically modified organisms in agriculture, forestry, environmental remediation, and other industrial applications. Genetically engineered enzymes, biopesticides, plants that express their own insect repellants or are engineered to survive herbicides, trees and bacteria designed for bioremediation, transgenic fish that grow faster or quicker, plants and animals capable of producing pharmaceuticals, and foods modified to provide greater nutrient value are only some of the examples. The *Biotechnology Deskbook* is an accessible and understandable guide that leads you through the maze of federal laws and regulations, describing how the various requirements apply to different intended uses. It begins with an extensive discussion that offers the insights and expertise of attorneys who specialize in biotechnology and are familiar with the issues. They lay out those issues in plain English, discussing various laws and rules and how they fit into the "big picture" of biotechnology regulation.

The *Biotechnology Deskbook* provides extensive analysis of the *Coordinated Framework for the Regulation of Biotechnology* and the *Policy on Planned Introductions of Biotechnology Products*. The substantial body of regulation and guidance for particular types of organisms is discussed, as are recent case studies that provide examples of the application of these requirements. The role of the National Environmental Policy Act in assuring full consideration of the environmental effects of releases is examined. Current regulatory programs of the U.S. Department of Agriculture, the U.S. Environmental Protection Agency, the U.S. Department of the Interior, and the Food and Drug Administration are described, as are other applicable statutes. Liability and enforcement issues are also examined in this up-to-date book.

The *Biotechnology Deskbook* was edited by *ELR*® Editor-in-Chief John Turner. In addition, *ELR*® Managing Editor Linda Johnson did an excellent job preparing the book, and thanks go to Carolyn Fischer, our copy editor, and Bill Straub, our desktop publisher.

The *Biotechnology Deskbook* joins a long list of other Environmental Law Institute (ELI) publications that provide similarly comprehensive reviews of environmental law and policy. Please visit our website, www.eli.org, for a complete description and for ordering information, including online ordering. Or you may call us at 1-800-433-5120 or (202) 939-3844 or contact us by e-mail at orders@eli.org. As a national environmental research and publishing organization dedicated to the development of more effective and efficient environmental protection efforts, ELI is pleased to present the *Biotechnology Deskbook*. We hope those involved in addressing the challenging and complex issues associated with biotechnology will find it invaluable.

—J. William Futrell, President
Environmental Law Institute

CHAPTER 1

I. The Federal Framework for the Regulation of Biotechnology

A. Scope

This deskbook is designed to provide a comprehensive overview of the federal laws and regulations that apply to those genetically modified organisms produced through recombinant deoxyribonucleic acid (rDNA) technology which are not drugs. These organisms are being designed for use in agriculture (food and materials production), forestry, environmental remediation, and a variety of industrial applications. Examples include genetically engineered enzymes, biopesticides, plants that either express their own insect repellents or are engineered to survive herbicide application, trees and bacteria designed for bioremediation, transgenic fish that grow faster and quicker, plants or animals capable of producing pharmaceuticals, and foods modified to provide greater nutrient value.

As commercialized, most of these organisms will live, grow, and perform their intended function outside of the scientific laboratory or traditional manufacturing plant. All present issues relating to their potential to create unreasonable risk for human health or the environment. There is, however, no single comprehensive U.S. biotechnology law that provides a uniform process for evaluating such risks or a uniform standard for risk management decisions prior to commercialization. A number of different federal laws apply, depending on the intended use of the organism. This means that commercialization will likely trigger the jurisdiction of several different agencies, most commonly including the U.S. Department of Agriculture (UDSA), the U.S. Environmental Protection Agency (EPA), or the Food and Drug Administration (FDA). Where release into the environment raises potential issues for endangered species, or for migratory birds, the U.S. Department of the Interior (DOI) will also have a significant role.

The relationship and coordination of these authorities is governed by the policy statements contained in the 1986 *Coordinated Framework for the Regulation of Biotechnology (Framework)*[1] and the 1992 *Policy on Planned Introductions of Biotechnology Products Into the Environment (Planned Introductions)*.[2] Both of these policy statements were developed by an interagency task force working under the direction of the White House Office of Science and Technology Policy (OSTP). The individual and collective experience of the primary agencies of jurisdiction has also been translated into a substantial body of regulation and guidance for particular types of organisms.[3] Recent case studies of the path to commercialization for a variety of genetically modified organisms provide additional examples of the application of these laws within the *Framework* umbrella. These case studies also highlight the increasing complexity of federal reviews and the implication of more and more of the primary environmental and natural resources laws.

This chapter will provide an overview of the *Framework* and subsequent guidance on the planned release of genetically modified organisms into the environment. The next chapter will describe the role of the National Environmental Policy Act (NEPA) in assuring full consideration of environmental effects of releases. Chapters 3 through 7 will deal with the current regulatory programs of the FDA, the USDA, and EPA. Chapter 8 will address liability and enforcement issues.

This deskbook will not address the numerous other legal topics in the field of biotechnology. These include ethics, patents, and international law, each of which could be the subject of a separate deskbook.[4]

B. The Coordinated Framework for the Regulation of Biotechnology

The 1986 *Framework* is the product of a series of discussions in the early 1980s about the legal rules which should apply to the commercialization of products of biotechnology. In 1980, the U.S. Supreme Court held for the first time that a living bacteria, engineered by human invention to do a better job of cleaning up oil, could be patented.[5] This decision opened the door to expansive intellectual property rights in genetically engineered organisms. Other new applications of biotechnology to produce new and improved

---

1. Coordinated Framework for Regulation of Biotechnology, 51 Fed. Reg. 23302 (June 26, 1986).

2. Exercise of Federal Oversight Within Scope of Statutory Authority: Planned Introductions of Biotechnology Products Into the Environment, 57 Fed. Reg. 6753 (Feb. 27, 1992).

3. Each of the primary federal regulatory agencies has a website providing historic and current information on its activities with relation to the regulation of biotechnology. These include: http://www.aphis. usda.gov/bbep (USDA); http://fda.gov/biotechn.html (FDA); and http://www.epa.gov/pesticides/biopesticides and http://www.epa. gov/opptintr/biotech/index.html (EPA) (last visited July 20, 2001).

4. Ethical issues play a major role in the formulation of biotechnology policy, the use of biotechnology to create living organisms, and the need for privacy in genetic testing. Several excellent websites addressing ethical issues include http://www.ethics.ubc.ca/brynw/ (The Centre for Applied Ethics, University of British Columbia (last visited July 20, 2001) and http://www.ajobonline.com/beginners. php (The American Journal of Bioethics Online) (last visited July 20, 2001). Patent law developments have opened the door to new intellectual property rights in intergeneric bacteria, plants, and animals. An important and unresolved constitutional issue relates to how much human genetic material will render a transgenic animal unpatentable under the Thirteenth Amendment. *See, e.g.*, Animal Legal Defense Fund v. Quigg, 932 F.2d 920 (Fed. Cir. 1991); Richard Maulsby, Facts on Patenting Life Forms Having a Relationship to Humans (unpublished manuscript), *available at* http://uspto.gov/web/offices/com/speeches/98-06.htm (last visited July 20, 2001). An excellent introduction to the developing area of international law in this field can be found in Jim Chen, *Diversity and Deadlock: Transcending Conventional Wisdom on the Relationship Between Biological Diversity and Intellectual Property*, 31 ELR 10625 (June 2001). The website of the European Union, http://www.europa.eu.int/index-en.htm (last visited July 20, 2001) provides a good source of up-to-date information on the regulation of biotechnology in Europe.

5. Diamond v. Cakrabarty, 447 U.S. 303 (1980).

drugs, enhance plant and animal productivity, and convert biomass to energy were rapidly appearing. The technology was viewed as vitally important to U.S. competitiveness. It also appeared to promise opportunities to reduce the environmental impact of many existing practices, such as the extensive use of chemical pesticides.

At the same time, legitimate safety concerns were being raised associated with the movement of genetically modified organisms out of the laboratory and into the environment. The National Institutes of Health's (NIH's) *Guidelines for Research Involving Recombinant DNA Molecules (Guidelines)*[6] had, as published in 1976, listed environmental release as a prohibited form of experimentation, although this provision had been liberalized to allow for such research with approvals.[7] What was the effect of the genetic manipulation on the potential virulence of the altered organisms? Would the new organisms obtain a selective advantage? Was there an adequate safety net in place to assure appropriate safeguards for human health and the environment?

1. The 1984 Proposal

In response to these issues, an interagency working group was formed under the White House Cabinet Council on Natural Resources and the Environment to evaluate the adequacy of the health and environmental safety review in the regulatory processes applicable to the variety of new organisms.[8] The workgroup's evaluation and recommendations were published in late 1984 as a *Proposal for a Coordinated Framework for Regulation of Biotechnology*.[9] This proposal included:

- A 19-page index matrix of existing federal laws applicable to licensing and other premarketing requirements, post-marketing requirements (safety, manufacturing, reporting requirements, transportation, and disposal), export controls, research and information-gathering authorities, patents, air and water emissions, and requirements applicable to federal agencies[10];
- Proposed regulatory policies of the FDA,[11] EPA,[12] and the USDA[13] on the review of research and products of biotechnology;
- A proposed scientific advisory mechanism for coordinating responses to scientific questions raised by applications received by the various involved agencies (establishment of agency-specific advisory committees on biotechnology)[14]; and

- A proposal for interagency coordination of regulatory activities related to biotechnology.[15]

The legal matrix, as suggested by the comprehensive nature of the categories described above, is a cradle-to-grave approach to coverage. Of particular interest for this deskbook are three of the seven categories—licensing and premarketing review, post-marketing requirements, and requirements for federal agencies. The laws identified include:

- *Licensing and Premarket Review*: The Federal Food, Drug, and Cosmetic Act (FFDCA) (drugs, medical devices, food and color additives, and human drugs)[16]; the Public Health Service Act (PHS) (licensing requirements for human biologics and clinical laboratories engaged in interstate commerce)[17]; the Virus-Serum-Toxin Act) (licenses for products used in the treatment of animals shipped interstate or imported)[18]; the Toxic Substances Control Act (TSCA) (premanufacture review of new chemical substances and authorizes regulation of new and existing substances)[19]; and the Federal Insecticide, Fungicide, and Rodenticide Act (FIFRA) (premarket registration of all pesticides).[20]
- *Post-Marketing Requirements*: The Occupational Safety and Health Act (OSH Act)[21]; worker protection regulations and guidances; hazardous substance and waste management laws including the Comprehensive Environmental Response, Compensation, and Liability Act (CERCLA)[22]; the Resource Conservation and Recovery Act (RCRA)[23]; the Marine Protection, Research, and Sanctuaries Act (Ocean Dumping)[24]; and other containment laws such as the Federal Meat Inspection Act (FMIA)[25]; the Poultry and Poultry Products Inspection Act (PPIA)[26]; the Federal Plant Pest Act (FPPA)[27]; the Plant Quarantine Act (PQA)[28]; the Animal Quarantine Laws,[29] and the Hazardous Materials Transportation Act (HMTA).[30]
- *Requirements for Federal Agencies*: Two key laws are identified in this section. These are NEPA,[31] which requires all agencies to conduct environmental impact statements on "major federal actions significantly affecting the environment."

---

6. Guidelines for Research Involving Recombinant DNA Molecules, 51 Fed. Reg. 16958 (May 7, 1986) (originally published at 41 Fed. Reg. 27902 (July 7, 1976)).

7. For a history of the maturation of these *Guidelines* as they apply to environmental releases, see the discussion in Foundation on Econ. Trends v. Heckler, 756 F.2d 143, 15 ELR 20248 (D.C. Cir. 1985).

8. Proposal for a Coordinated Framework for Regulation of Biotechnology, 49 Fed. Reg. 50856 (Dec. 31, 1984).

9. *Id.*

10. *Id.* at 50858-77.

11. *Id.* at 50878-80.

12. *Id.* at 50888-97.

13. *Id.* at 50897-904.

14. *Id.* at 50905.

15. *Id.*

16. 21 U.S.C. §301 et seq.

17. 42 U.S.C. §§262, 263a.

18. 21 U.S.C. §151 et seq.

19. 15 U.S.C. §2601 et seq.

20. 7 U.S.C. §§136-136y, ELR STAT. FIFRA §§2-34.

21. 29 U.S.C. §651 et seq.

22. 42 U.S.C. §§9601-9675, ELR STAT. CERCLA §§101-405.

23. *Id.* §§6901-6992k, ELR STAT. RCRA §§1001-11011.

24. 33 U.S.C. §1401 et seq.

25. 21 U.S.C. §601 et seq.

26. *Id.* §451 et seq.

27. 7 U.S.C. §§150aa-jj.

28. 39 U.S.C. §3014.

29. 21 U.S.C. §101 et seq. and 19 U.S.C. §1306.

30. 49 U.S.C. §5101 et seq.

31. 42 U.S.C. §§4321-4370d, ELR STAT. NEPA §§2-209.

The second is the Endangered Species Act (ESA).[32] This legislation requires federal agencies to ensure that their activities or programs will not jeopardize the continued existence of a listed species. Consultation is required with the DOI or the National Marine Fisheries Service (NMFS).

In general, the sense of the proposal offered for comment was that existing authorities were sufficient to address the potential risks presented by products of biotechnology. These should be evaluated on a case-by-case basis drawing on the expertise of the particular agency involved in the area, and new or revised authorities developed as needed. Several key themes in the *Framework* include the reminder that biological manipulation in agriculture is well known and understood; it was important not to hobble innovation through unreasonably restrictive regulatory measures; and that interagency coordination could ease the difficulty of dealing with multiple agencies.

2. Establishment of the Biotechnology Science Coordinating Committee (BSCC) and Finalization of the Statutory Matrix

The proposed *Framework* was finalized in two installments. The first, which occurred on November 15, 1985, finalized the legal matrix.[33] It also identified the agency-specific advisory committees which would advise on biotechnology issues. And it established the BSCC, as an interagency coordinating committee. In order to assure independence from any individual agency, the BSCC was created as a committee to the Federal Coordinating Council for Science, Engineering, and Technology (FCCSET). The FCCSET is the statutory interagency coordinating mechanism housed within the OSTP. The BSCC's charter provides that it would:

- Serve as a coordinating forum for addressing scientific problems, sharing information, and developing consensus;
- Promote consistency in the development of federal agencies' review procedures and assessments;
- Facilitate continuing cooperation among federal agencies on emerging scientific issues; and
- Identify gaps in scientific knowledge.[34]

3. The 1986 *Framework*

In 1986, the remainder of the *Framework* was finalized, including the general principles for its application, and statements of agency policy from the FDA, the USDA, EPA, the Occupational Safety and Health Administration (OSHA), and NIH. The essential policy finding of the *Framework* is

that commercialization could safely proceed under the framework of existing law because:

- The biotechnology methods by which the new products are created do not themselves create special risks;
- Use of existing laws provides more immediate regulatory protection and certainty for the industry than possible with the implementation of new laws; and
- No alternative, uniform statutory approach appears reasonable since the broad spectrum of regulated products cuts across many product uses regulated by different agencies.[35]

The *Framework* is designed to accommodate and harmonize the differing legal authorities of the agencies, create common terminology, and assure similarly protective reviews.

a. Definition of "Intergeneric" and "Pathogen"

The *Framework* proposed that the types of products deserving special evaluation under the *Framework* should be those which are "intergeneric" and "pathogenic." Intergeneric organisms are those formed by "deliberate combination of genetic material from sources in different genera."[36] Intergeneric materials that are well-characterized and contain only noncoding regulatory regions would be exempt from this definition. A "pathogen" is a virus or microorganism (including its viruses and plasmids, if any) that has the ability to cause disease in other living organisms (humans, animals, plants, microorganisms).[37] Nonpathogenic strains of a species which contains pathogenic strains would be exempt (such as *Escherichia coli* (e. coli) K-12).

In addition the *Framework* notes that a definition of "release into the environment" was needed and that a working group on greenhouse containment and small field trials had been established. The group was tasked with exploration of both physical and biological "containment" mechanisms.[38]

4. Agency Statements of Policy

a. FDA Statement of Policy for FFDCA-Regulated Foods

The FDA stated that its administrative review of the products of biotechnology under the FFDCA[39] would be conducted in light of the intended use of products on a case-by-case basis. Although the FDA noted that the rDNA technology was capable of producing foods and food additives with new structural features or could introduce new contaminants affecting safety, efficacy, and stability, these could all be addressed within its current procedures. New administrative procedures based on generic concerns about biotechnology were not considered to be necessary. The

32. 16 U.S.C. §§1531-1544, ELR Stat. ESA §§2-18.

33. Coordinated Framework for Regulation of Biotechnology; Establishment of Biotechnology Science Coordinating Committee, 50 Fed. Reg. 47174, 47177 (Nov. 14, 1985). The regulatory matrix is found at Appendix II. Individual statutes are discussed in detail in Chapters 3-8.

34. *Id.* at 47174-75. Under the Clinton Administration, the FCCSET became the National Science and Technology Council (NSTC). The Committee on Science of NSTC has a subcommittee which addresses biotechnology issues. *See* http://www.ostp.gov/NSTC/html/nstc_comm.html (last visited July 20, 2001).

35. 51 Fed. Reg. at 23303.

36. *Id.* at 23307.

37. *Id.*

38. *Id.* at 23308.

39. 21 U.S.C. §§301-397.

FDA further noted the application of NEPA to any of its major actions significantly affecting the environment.[40]

b. EPA Statement of Policy for FIFRA and TSCA

EPA's jurisdiction over products of biotechnology is derived from FIFRA and TSCA. In its statement of policy, EPA announced that it would focus its authorities under both laws on microorganisms which are (1) used in the environment, (2) are pathogenic or contain genetic material from pathogens, or (3) contain new combinations of traits.[41] EPA also announced the following requirements for microbial products subject to FIFRA or TSCA jurisdiction:

- Deliberately formed intergeneric microorganisms will be subject to review before any environmental releases (including small-scale field testing and other environmental research and development);
- Other microorganisms formed by genetic engineering will be subject to pre-release review under FIFRA or TSCA if any source organism is a pathogen; and
- Reporting requirements under TSCA substantial risk and FIFRA unreasonable risk information provisions are applicable.

c. USDA Statement of Policy

The USDA's policy statement essentially provides its view that agriculture and forestry products developed through biotechnology will not differ fundamentally from conventional products and that the existing framework will be adequate. It is noted that its guidelines for research paralleled those of NIH. It also announced new regulations on notifications for biotechnology products which were published as a companion rule.[42]

d. OSHA Statement of Policy

OSHA determined in its statement of policy that its existing statutory authorities and implementing regulations were sufficient to address any occupational safety and health issues that might arise for workers dealing with products of biotechnology. These authorities included the general duty provision of the law, which provides that employers have a general duty to provide a workplace "free from recognized hazards that are causing or are likely to cause death or serious physical harm."[43] In addition, OSHA expressed the view that any particular hazards were likely to arise from chemicals involved in the production of genetically modified organisms and not the organisms themselves. OSHA identified a series of specific standards in place to protect against specific workplace problems, including

- Specific air contaminants,
- Access to employee exposure and medical records,
- Hazard communication,
- Exposure to toxic chemicals in laboratories,
- Respiratory protection, and
- General safety standards.

e. NIH Statement of Policy

NIH's statement of policy relates to the application of the *Guidelines*. The *Guidelines*, originally developed in 1976, apply to research using rDNA technology which is funded in whole or in part by NIH. They provide definitions of physical and biological containment (Biosafety Levels 1–4) and a risk-based hierarchical procedure for approval of experiments, ranging from experiments that are exempt to those for which notification simultaneous with initiation are required, to experiments requiring preapproval by an Institutional Biosafety Committee (IBC) to those requiring review by the NIH Recombinant DNA Advisory Committee (RAC) and approval by NIH and the IBC and publication in the *Federal Register*.

The *Guidelines*, although legally applicable only to NIH-sponsored research, were widely used as guides for research. The regulations at the time placed experiments involving the "deliberate release into the environment of any organism containing recombinant DNA, except [certain listed] plants" in III-A-2, a category requiring RAC review and NIH/IBC approval to the extent conducted with federal funds.[44] NIH's policy statement notes that if such experiments are submitted to other agencies for review and NIH is notified, it may determine that the other agency's review serves the same purpose and waive its review.[45]

C. Field Research: The 1992 OSTP Planned Introductions

Almost immediately upon the conclusion of the *Framework*, the OSTP turned its attention to the issue of standardizing requirements for planned introduction where the implementing legislation left such decisions to the discretion of the administering agency. The *Principles for Federal Oversight of Biotechnology: Planned Introduction Into the Environment of Organisms With Modified Hereditary Traits* were announced on July 31, 1990.[46] These provide that planned introductions into the environment of organisms which deliberately modified hereditary traits should *not* be subject to oversight (defined as notification to, approval by, or other review by a federal agency), unless information concerning the risk posed by the introduction indicates that oversight is necessary.[47]

Introductions are considered similar to those previously made when the level of risk of the introduction is comparable. Based on experience with introduction, the principles encourage agencies to develop categories of introductions for exclusion from oversight. Six categories were suggested, several based on the type of modifications, e.g., selective breeding, transformation, deletions, and use of noncoding marker genes, and one based on risk (risk no greater than that of unmodified parent organisms).

---

40. 51 Fed. Reg. at 23313.

41. *Id.* at 23315.

42. *Id.* at 23302.

43. 29 U.S.C. §654(a)(1); 51 Fed. Reg. at 23348.

44. As appears in 51 Fed. Reg. 16958 (May 7, 1986).

45. 51 Fed. Reg. at 23350.

46. Planned Introduction Into the Environment of Organisms With Modified Hereditary Traits, 55 Fed. Reg. 31118 (July 31, 1990).

47. *Id.* at 31120.

Risk-based factors for evaluation for both organisms and the target environment are identified.[48] In 1992, the OSTP issued a final policy incorporating these principles with minor revisions.[49] The final policy announced three fundamental scope principles. These are:

- A decision to exercise oversight within the scope of discretion afforded by statute should not turn on the fact that an organism has been modified or modified by a particular process or technique, because such fact is not alone a sufficient indication of risk.
- A decision to exercise oversight in the scope of discretion afforded by statute should be based on evidence that the risk presented by introduction of an organism in a particular environment used for a particular type of application is unreasonable.
- Organisms with new phenotypic traits conferring no greater risk to the target environment than the parental organisms should be subject to a level of oversight no greater than that associated with the unmodified organisms.[50]

The primary changes made to the final policy included the recognition that a number of different types of oversight were available—ranging from no action to full pre-release approval processes. In addition, examples of categories for exclusion were taken out of the policy—and development of appropriate exclusions left to the agencies. The standard given to the agencies was described as follows:

Unreasonable risk is the threshold for exercising oversight within the scope of discretion afforded by statute. The term does not denote a fixed absolute number. Rather, a risk is "unreasonable" where the environmental benefits achieved by oversight measures to reduce the risk are greater than the social cost of those oversight measures.[51]

D. The National Research Council (NRC) 2000 Report: Genetically Modified Pest-Protected Plants

The NRC revisited issues in implementation of the *Framework* in a report issued in 2000.[52] The report notes that hundreds of decisions concerning environmental releases of genetically engineered products have now been made. It evaluates the operation of the *Framework* with respect to one particular type of product—plants that are engineered to express bT toxins to protect themselves from insects. Such plants are considered to be "pest-protected plants" and trigger the jurisdiction of the three major regulatory agencies, EPA, the USDA, and the FDA. EPA has jurisdiction to review the incorporated protectant as a pesticide under FIFRA. The USDA has jurisdiction to review the plant to assure that it is not a plant pest. The FDA has jurisdiction over the food produced by the plant to assure that it is safe and not adulterated.

The subject of how the agencies discharge their substantive reviews of these products is discussed in detail in the following chapters. In general, the NRC finds that toxicity, allergenicity, effects of gene flow, development of resistant pests, and effects on nontarget species are of concern for both conventional and transgenic pest-protected plants and encourages additional and comparable research on both. The NRC reaffirms the fundamental principles of the *Framework* and finds that EPA, the USDA, and the FDA have successfully applied existing statutes to address risks of introduction of new products of biotechnology. General recommendations for improvement include the following:

- The quantity, quality, and public accessibility of information on the regulation of products should be expanded;
- Ready access to information on product reviews and approvals and a meaningful opportunity for stakeholder participation are critical to the credibility of the regulatory process;
- A joint memorandum of understanding which provides guidance on the regulatory issues that are the purview of each agency and which may be joint issues (such as gene transfer for the USDA and EPA and allergenicity for EPA and the FDA) and provides a process for the timely exchange of information would be useful;
- A joint guidance document from the agency identifying common date and information needed to characterized products would be helpful;
- Nonregulatory mechanisms should be used to accomplish federal goals wherever possible;
- Greater process flexibility is desirable; and
- Work remains to be done to fill in gaps in the existing framework which become apparent as new issues emerge.

E. The OSTP/Council on Environmental Quality (CEQ) Case Studies

On May 3, 2000, President William J. Clinton directed the CEQ and the OSTP to "conduct a six-month interagency assessment of Federal environmental regulations pertaining to agricultural biotechnology and, if appropriate, make recommendations to improve them."[53] The assessment was intended to focus on environmental regulation—an area perceived to be not well understood. The case studies provide excellent descriptions of the regulatory path to market for a

---

48. For *organisms*, these include fitness, infectivity, virulence, pathogenicity, and toxicity; host range, the type of substrate or resources utilized; environmental limits to growth or resources utilized; environmental limits to growth or reproduction (habitat or microhabitat); susceptibility to control by antibiotics, biocides, by substrate or by mechanical means; and whether and how introduced traits are expressed.

   For the *target environment*, the factors include selection pressure for the introduced trait; presence of wild, weedy, or feral relatives within dispersal capability of the organism or its genes; presence of vectors or agents of dissemination or dispersal (e.g., mites, insects, rodents, birds, humans, machines, wind, and water); direct involvement in basic ecosystem process (e.g., nutrients cycling); whether there are alternative hosts or partners (e.g., the organism is involved in symbiosis or mutualism); range of environments for testing or use in light of potential geographic range; and effectiveness of confinement, monitoring, and migration plans.

49. 57 Fed. Reg. 6753 (Feb. 27, 1992).

50. *Id.* at 6757.

51. *Id.*

52. NATIONAL RESEARCH COUNCIL, GENETICALLY MODIFIED PEST PROTECTED PLANTS: SCIENCE AND REGULATION (2000).

53. COUNCIL ON ENVIRONMENTAL QUALITY AND THE OFFICE OF SCIENCE & TECHNOLOGY POLICY, CEQ/OSTP ASSESSMENT: CASE STUDIES OF ENVIRONMENTAL REGULATION FOR BIOTECHNOLOGY 1 (2001).

variety of products, some of which have made it and some which are in early stage development. The term "agricultural biotechnology" is defined to include "the use in the environment of any organism that has been genetically modified using [rDNA] techniques." The term "environmental regulations" is defined to include certain aspects of confinement, as well as introduction into the environment without confinement.

There are six case studies, reprinted in the Appendix of this text, and four sidebars.[54] These are:

● *Salmon*: This case study involves the potential aquaculture production or importation of Atlantic salmon genetically engineered to contain an additional fish growth hormone gene that will make it grow faster. The genetic engineering causes the fish to contain a new animal drug which is regulated by the FDA, the agency with lead drafting authority for the case study. Net pen aquaculture provides a high opportunity for escape of fish into the wild, triggering concerns under the ESA and NEPA. Other applicable statutes include the Lacey Act, the Non-Indigenous Aquatic Nuisance Prevention and Control Act, and the §10 provisions of the Rivers and Harbors Act. A sidebar discussion of the commercialization of ornamental goldfish accompanies this case study. EPA's authorities under TSCA replace the FDA/FFDCA role in this sidebar.[55] Petitions seeking a thorough assessment of risks associated with commercialization of this species have recently been filed with both the FDA and the USDA.[56]

● *Bt (Bacillus thuringiensis)-Maize*: Bt-maize is in widespread use in the United States, and there has been much debate on its possible effects on nontarget species. Food safety issues have also been associated with the BtCry9D protein found in StarLink™ corn but that issue is not addressed in this case study. The primary statutes involved are FIFRA, the FFDCA, and the Plant Protection Act (PPA). The Migratory Bird Treaty Act (MBTA) and the ESA are also addressed. EPA was the lead drafting agency, with assistance from the Animal and Plant Health Inspection Service (APHIS) and the DOI. Sidebars evaluating biocontrol using a virus and genetically modified arthropods are also included. The FFDCA is not a relevant statute in this analysis.[57]

● *Herbicide-Tolerant Soybean:* This plant is also currently grown widely in the United States and has the potential to change the way in which herbicides are used to control weeds. The principle statutes involved here are the PPA, FIFRA, the FFDCA, and the ESA. APHIS was the drafting team leader, assisted by EPA and the DOI. A hypothetical pharmaceutical producing plant is included as a sidebar for comparison of different environmental exposure issues. This plant is evaluated under the Virus-Serum-Toxin Act (VSTA), the PHS, the FFDCA, the PPA, and NEPA. The FDA and APHIS prepared the case study.[58]

● *Animals Producing Human Drugs*: This hypothetical example evaluates a genetically engineered goat whose primary use is to produce pharmaceuticals. Primary statutes include the PHS, the FFDCA, and NEPA. The FDA, APHIS, and the Food Safety and Inspection Service (FSIS) drafted the study. A sidebar for animals used to produce animal biologics discusses the VSTA, the Animal Quarantine Laws, TSCA, and the Animal Welfare Act. APHIS, the FDA, and the FSIS drafted this case study.[59]

● *Bioremediation Using Poplar Trees*: This case study evaluates a poplar tree genetically modified to detoxify trichloroethylene (TCE), a common and widespread environmental contaminant. This tree is currently in research and development but is used to describe the environmental regulation and oversight of a perennial plant. The principle statutes involved are the PPA and TSCA. The role of compliance with remedy selection requirements of CERCLA are also discussed. The U.S. Forest Service, APHIS, EPA, and the DOI were on the drafting team.[60]

● *Bioremediation and Biosensing Using Bacteria*: This case study describes a TSCA premanufacture notice (PMN) filed in 1995 for a genetically modified bacteria used to detect and destroy concentrations of polycyclic aromatic hydrocarbons. The process resulted in a consent order defining terms under which the bacteria could be released in the field for developmental testing purposes at a single site and identified the outstanding risk questions that would need to be addressed prior to commercialization. The primary statute discussed in the case study is TSCA. EPA, the DOI, and APHIS were on the drafting team.[61]

54. These case studies are discussed in greater detail in subsequent chapters, in the context of the specific legal authorities involved. Each of the case studies is reproduced in the Appendix.

55. *Case Study No. I: Growth-Enhanced Salmon, at* http://www.ostp. gov/html/012201.html (last visited July 10, 2001).

56. *See Foes of Genetically Engineered Salmon Call for Close FDA Scrutiny of Risks*, WALL ST. J., May 10, 2001, at A20.

57. *Case Study No. II: Bt-Maize, at* http://www.ostp.gov/html/012201. html (last visited July 20, 2001).

58. *Case Study No. III: Herbicide-Tolerant Soybean, at* http://www.ostp.gov/html/012201.html (last visited July 20, 2001).

59. *Case Study No. IV: Farm Animal (Goat) That Produces Human Drugs, at* http://www.ostp.gov/html/012201.html (last visited July 20, 2001).

60. *Case Study No. V: Bioremediation Using Poplar Trees, at* http://www.ostp.gov/html/012201.html (last visited July 20, 2001).

61. *Case Study No. VI: Bioremediation and Biosensing Using Bacteria, at* http://www.ostp.gov/html/012201.html (last visited July 20, 2001).

CHAPTER 2

I. The Umbrella Function of NEPA

The 1986 *Framework*, as described in Chapter 1, identified two laws containing requirements applicable to all agencies reviewing biotechnology products. These laws are NEPA[1] and the ESA.[2] Litigation under NEPA has been instrumental in identifying critical issues of risk associated with the release of products of biotechnology into the environment. This chapter will provide a review of the NEPA process followed by an analysis of the NEPA case law dealing with biotechnology. It will also summarize the key provisions of the ESA and current issues arising under that law which relate to the commercialization of products of biotechnology, such as growth-enhanced salmon.

A. The Role of NEPA

NEPA requires that federal agencies publicly address the environmental impact of any of their proposals for action that may significantly affect the environment. Section 102 of NEPA compels agencies to develop methods and procedures that will ensure that "unquantified environmental amenities and values may be given appropriate consideration in decisionmaking."[3] Section 102 requires that, for "every recommendation or report on proposals for legislation and other major Federal actions significantly affecting the quality of the human environment," the responsible federal official must prepare a "detailed statement" covering five specific issues, including impacts, effects, and alternatives.[4] This detailed statement is commonly referred to as an environmental impact statement (EIS). It is typically preceded by a "rough-cut" assessment, or environmental assessment (EA), to determine whether a full-fledged EIS is necessary.

The EIS serves as both an aid in decisionmaking for the agency and as a source of information for other interested parties. It provides environmental source material for evaluating the benefit of the proposed project in light of its environmental risks and for comparing these to the environmental risks presented by alternative courses of action.[5] As the Supreme Court has stated:

> NEPA has twin aims. First, it places upon an agency the obligation to consider every significant aspect of the environmental impact of a proposed action. Second, it ensures that the agency will inform the public that it has indeed considered environmental concerns in the decisionmaking process.[6]

1. The CEQ

Section 202 of NEPA created the CEQ which consists of three members appointed by the president with advice and consent of the Senate.[7] The CEQ has a variety of functions. These include gathering and analyzing information concerning the quality of the environment, review and appraisal of federal programs and activities, development of recommendations for improving environmental quality, reviewing the adequacy of systems for monitoring environmental changes, and assisting efforts of federal agencies to develop programs related to environmental quality.[8]

2. NEPA Regulations

The regulations adopted by the CEQ for implementing NEPA are codified at 40 C.F.R. Parts 1500-1508. These regulations implement the EIS requirement and other NEPA requirements and generally address the way in which environmental considerations should be included in agency decisionmaking. Because NEPA does not give the CEQ authority to impose regulations on other federal agencies, some courts have held that the CEQ's regulations are not binding on agencies which have not expressly adopted them,[9] although courts are likely to pay substantial deference to the CEQ's interpretation of NEPA.[10] Moreover, almost all federal agencies have expressly adopted the CEQ's regulations.[11]

3. The Role of EPA

EPA reviews and comments upon all draft EIS officially filed with EPA and has established procedures governing this review and evaluation.[12] EPA seeks to participate early in the NEPA compliance efforts of other federal agencies in order to identify matters of concern at the earliest possible moment. Agencies are under a special obligation to provide draft EIS to EPA where the proposed action relates to air or water quality, noise abatement or control, pesticide regulation, solid waste disposal, radiation criteria and standards, or other areas in which EPA has jurisdiction. For example, §309 of the Clean Air Act (CAA) requires that EPA comment in writing on EIS and refer to the CEQ any matter determined to be unsatisfactory from a standpoint of public health or welfare or environmental quality. Thus, EPA comments on virtually every draft EIS.

---

1. 42 U.S.C. §§4321-4370d, ELR Stat. NEPA §§2-209.

2. 16 U.S.C. §§1531–1544, ELR Stat. ESA §§2-18.

3. 42 U.S.C. §4332, ELR Stat. NEPA §102.

4. *Id.* §4332(2)(C), ELR Stat. NEPA §102(2)(C).

5. *See* Massachusetts v. Andrus, 594 F.2d 872, 883, 9 ELR 20162, 20168 (1st Cir. 1979).

6. Baltimore Gas & Elec. Co. v. Natural Resources Defense Council, 462 U.S. 87, 97, 13 ELR 20544, 20546 (1983).

7. 42 U.S.C. §4342, ELR Stat. NEPA §202.

8. *Id.* §4344, ELR Stat. NEPA §204.

9. *See, e.g.,* Limerick Ecology Action v. NRC, 869 F.2d 719, 19 ELR Digest 20907 (3d Cir. 1989).

10. Robertson v. Methow Valley Citizens Council, 490 U.S. 332, 19 ELR 20743 (1989).

11. NEPA regulations adopted by the USDA are codified at 7 C.F.R. pt. 1b; those adopted by the FDA are codified at 21 C.F.R. pt. 25; and those adopted by EPA are codified at 40 C.F.R. pt. 6.

12. U.S. EPA, Policies and Procedures for the Review of Federal Actions Impacting the Environment (1984).

EPA also has its own procedures for compliance with CEQ regulations.[13] Congress has expressly exempted numerous EPA activities from NEPA. Thus, the Agency prepares an EIS when specifically required to do so—as in the case of Clean Water Act new source national pollutant discharge elimination system (NPDES) permits—or when it chooses to do so. Courts have also granted implied exemptions to EPA for many of its regulatory functions on the theory that EPA's adherence to the procedural mandates of its statutes is the "functional equivalent" of an EIS and provides adequate assurance that environmental factors are given appropriate consideration.[14]

4. The EIS Process

The first step in the EIS process is to determine whether a particular action is a major federal action "significantly affecting the quality of the human environment." Responsibility for making this determination rests with the agency that will undertake the action. CEQ regulations require agencies to identify those types of actions for which an EIS is not necessary.[15] These are called "categorical exclusions."[16] If the contemplated action does not fall within a categorical exclusion, the agency must prepare an EA. The EA is a "rough-cut" assessment to determine whether a full-fledged EIS is necessary.[17]

The decision on whether to prepare an EIS is governed by the rule of reason. The agency must make a rational decision that its planned action is "major" and that it will have a "significant" impact on the environment. Courts recognize that this decision "implicates substantial agency expertise" and will give deference to agency expertise; there are, however, many instances in which courts have overturned an agency decision that was arbitrary and capricious or involved a clear error in judgment.[18]

If the agency decides, based on the EA, that an EIS is not required, it must then issue a finding of no significant impact (FONSI).[19] The FONSI may be a simple document that briefly explains the finding. It will typically include the EA or a summary of the EA and may reference related documents. This is intended to ensure that the agency understood the NEPA requirements and gave the problem adequate consideration, and it provides the courts with a basis for review.

If the decision is to proceed with an EIS, the agency must publish a notice of intent and begin to determine, within the scope of the EIS, the range of actions, alternatives, and impacts to be considered. This "scoping process" is a preliminary step intended to encourage participation and to focus the EIS.[20] It provides an early opportunity to affect the subject matter of the EIS.

A draft EIS must be made available for comment to the CEQ, to other federal agencies, and to identifiable outside interest groups.[21] The draft statement is subject to comment for 45 days.[22] In addition, federal agencies are required to consult with state and local environmental agencies in preparing the EIS. Other federal statutes impose specific consultation responsibilities in addition to the NEPA requirements.[23] The CEQ rarely comments. As noted above, EPA comments on virtually every draft EIS, by virtue of the statutes it administers and pursuant to §309 of the CAA, which applies generally to the environmental impact of any matter relating to its duties and responsibilities.[24]

After comments have been reviewed and any new issues have been incorporated into the EIS, a final EIS must be circulated to each agency and individual who made substantive comments on the draft and to any other agency with jurisdiction or special expertise in the area in which environmental impacts have been identified.[25] If there are significant changes to the project or the analysis, the EIS may have to be recirculated as a draft. Unless there are compelling reasons, no decision on a proposed action may be made until 90 days after publication of notice of the filing of a draft EIS or 30 days after publication of notice of the filing of a final EIS.[26]

NEPA requires that the EIS accompany the proposal through the remaining agency review procedures. This has been interpreted to mean that the EIS must be considered "at every stage where an overall balancing of environmental and nonenvironmental factors is appropriate and where alterations might be made in the proposed action to minimize environmental costs."[27]

5. When Is an EIS Required?

EPA requires agencies to prepare an EIS for all "major Federal actions significantly affecting the quality of the human environment."[28] This phrase has been difficult to define and has been the subject of much litigation. A majority of the courts have found that the proposed action must be both "major" and have a "significant impact" on the environment, but others have found an EIS is necessary if the action has significant impacts and must, therefore, be considered major.[29] CEQ regulations state that the term "major ... reinforces but does not have a meaning independent of 'significant.'"[30]

The term "action" has been construed broadly to include not only actual construction of facilities, but also project proposals, proposals for new legislation, regulations, policy

13. 40 C.F.R. pt. 6, subpt. J.

14. *See Limerick Ecology Action*, 869 F.2d at 729 n.7, 19 ELR Digest at 20907.

15. 40 C.F.R. §1507.3.

16. *Id.* §1508.4.

17. *Id.* §1508.9.

18. *See, e.g.*, Marsh v. Oregon Natural Resources Council, 490 U.S. 360, 19 ELR 20749 (1989).

19. 40 C.F.R. §1508.13.

20. *Id.* §1501.7.

21. 42 U.S.C. §4332(2)(C), ELR Stat. NEPA §102(2)(C); 40 C.F.R. §§1502.19, 1503.1.

22. 40 C.F.R. §1506.10(c).

23. *See, e.g.*, Fish and Wildlife Coordination Act, 16 U.S.C. §661 et seq.; National Historic Preservation Act, 16 U.S.C. §470 et seq.; ESA; Department of Transportation Act, 49 U.S.C. §1653(f).

24. 42 U.S.C. §7609, ELR Stat. CAA §309. *See* Arnold W. Reitze Jr., Clean Air Act: Compliance and Enforcement (Envtl. L. Inst. 2001).

25. 40 C.F.R. §1502.19.

26. *Id.* §1506.10.

27. Calvert Cliffs Coordinating Comm., Inc. v. Atomic Energy Comm'n, 449 F.2d 1109, 1 ELR 20346 (D.C. Cir. 1971).

28. 42 U.S.C. §4332(2)(C), ELR Stat. NEPA §102(2)(C).

29. *Compare* River Rd. Alliance, Inc. v. Corps of Eng'rs, 764 F.2d 445, 15 ELR 20518 (7th Cir. 1985), *cert. denied*, 475 U.S. 1055 (1986), *with* Minnesota Pub. Interest Research Group v. Butz, 498 F.2d 1314, 4 ELR 20700 (8th Cir. 1974).

30. 40 C.F.R. §1508.18.

statements, or expansion or revision of ongoing programs.[31] An action is "federal" if it is directly undertaken by a federal agency. Federal action also includes a federal agency's decision to grant its required approval of the activity of others. This may occur where the agency's authority is essentially supervisory, e.g., rate increases, discharge permits, licenses.[32] An EIS may also be required when the federal agency possesses the power to control a nonfederal activity, although it is not required where the agency has the option, but not the duty, to control nonfederal action.[33]

The term "significant" requires consideration of both the context of the impact and its intensity. For example, "[a]ny action that substantially affects, beneficially or detrimentally, the depth or course of streams, plant life, wildlife habitats, fish and wildlife, and the soil and air 'significantly affects the quality of human environment.'"[34] When coupled with an effect on the physical environment, socio-economic impacts, such as changes in commuter traffic patterns, the loss of job opportunities, or environmental justice concerns may also have to be considered, although economic and social effects alone do not require an EIS.[35]

6. The Preparation of an EIS

Under NEPA, the official responsible for the proposed federal action has the duty to prepare the EIS.[36] This can create a problem where there are two or more federal agencies involved. To address this situation, the CEQ has developed the "lead" agency concept under which the agencies will designate one of their number to prepare the EIS, based on the degree of involvement and other factors.[37] The other agencies act as cooperating agencies.[38] Where both federal and state agencies are involved, a federal and state agency may act as joint lead agencies.[39] In general, the federal agency is responsible for preparation of the EIS, although there are circumstances under §102(2)(D) of NEPA, or under other statutes, in which responsibility can be transferred to states.[40] Private persons may not prepare an EIS, but they may supply the information to be used. The federal agency must independently evaluate the information and is responsible for its accuracy.[41]

The range of impact to be considered in the EIS can be extremely broad. In general, NEPA requires that the EIS address the following five issues:

- The environmental impact of the proposed action;

- Any adverse environmental effects which cannot be avoided if the proposal is implemented;
- Alternatives to the proposed action;
- The relationship between local short-term uses of man's environment and the maintenance and enhancement of long-term productivity; and
- Any irreversible or irretrievable commitments of resources which would be involved in the proposed action if it is implemented.

When information is unavailable regarding reasonably foreseeable and significant impacts, the regulation requires that the agency prepare an evaluation of such impacts based on theoretical approaches or research methods generally accepted in the scientific community.[42]

The EIS should provide "a detailed and careful analysis of the relative environmental merits and demerits of the proposed action and possible alternatives."[43]

7. Judicial Review

NEPA requires agencies to "take a 'hard look' at the environmental consequences before taking a major action."[44] The role of the courts on judicial review of NEPA decisions is "to ensure that the agency has adequately considered and disclosed the environmental impact of its actions and that its decision is not arbitrary or capricious."[45] In most situations, judicial review takes place under the Administrative Procedure Act.[46] Other statutes may specifically provide for judicial review and a NEPA challenge may be undertaken under those statutes.

B. Application of NEPA to Biotechnology

NEPA challenges have been used extensively by plaintiffs to challenge federal decisions relating to biotechnology research and development, the *Framework* itself, and approval of environmental release activities. This case law and the general principles which have emerged from it are described below.

1. EIS for the NIH *Guidelines* Satisfied NEPA Requirements for Laboratory Research

One of the early federal actions on biotechnology was taken by NIH when it issued its *Guidelines*.[47] At the time of publication, NIH announced that it was preparing a draft EIS, which was published for comment in 1976 and finalized in 1977.[48] A research project to test the biological properties of polyoma DNA cloned in bacterial cells in a guideline-compliant laboratory at the Fort Detrick, Maryland, Cancer Research Center was thereafter sought to be en-

31. S. Rep. No. 91-296, at 20 (1969).

32. *See, e.g.*, Natural Resources Defense Council v. EPA, 859 F.2d 156, 19 ELR 20016 (D.C. Cir. 1988).

33. Sierra Club v. Hodel, 848 F.2d 1068, 18 ELR 21237 (10th Cir. 1988).

34. Natural Resources Defense Council v. Grant, 341 F. Supp. 356, 357, 2 ELR 20185, 20189 (E.D.N.C. 1972).

35. *See* Town of Groton v. Laird, 353 F. Supp. 344, 3 ELR 20316 (D. Conn. 1972); Tongass Conservation Soc'y v. Cheney, 924 F.2d 1137, 21 ELR 20558 (D.C. Cir. 1991).

36. 42 U.S.C §4332(2)(C), ELR Stat. NEPA §102(2)(C).

37. 40 C.F.R. §1501.5.

38. *Id.* §1501.6.

39. *Id.* §1501.5(b).

40. 42 U.S.C. §4332(2)(D), ELR Stat. NEPA §102(2)(D).

41. 40 C.F.R. §1506.5(a).

42. *Id.* §1502.22(b).

43. Natural Resources Defense Council v. Callaway, 524 F.2d 79, 92, 5 ELR 20640, 20647 (2d Cir. 1975).

44. Kleppe v. Sierra Club, 427 U.S. 390, 410 n.21, 6 ELR 20532, 20537 n.21 (1976).

45. Baltimore Gas & Elec. Co. v. Natural Resources Defense Council, 462 U.S. 87, 97-98, 13 ELR 20544, 20546 (1983).

46. 5 U.S.C. §706(2)(A), *available in* ELR Stat. Admin. Proc.

47. 41 Fed. Reg. 27902 (July 7, 1976).

48. *Id.* 38426 (Sept. 9, 1976); 42 Fed. Reg. 6532 (Feb. 2, 1977).

joined for insufficient NEPA compliance.[49] The plaintiff asserted that this experiment could result in the release to the environment of organisms that would present a threat to life and health which had been inadequately considered.

The reviewing court rejected the claim. It held that NIH had appropriately recognized that the issuance of the *Guidelines* constituted a major federal action, as they laid down criteria for safe research in this new area of science, including detailed requirements for both physical and biological containment to prevent environmental release. The court also found that the EIS prepared by NIH met the requisite "hard-look" standard. The court found that the experiment at issue presented no substantial risk to human health or the environment because:

- There is little likelihood that the materials will escape from the maximum containment of the highly secure laboratory (P4) in which it would be conducted;
- If such an escape did occur, the rDNA molecules would not survive but would self-destruct outside the laboratory environment; and
- The particular virus being used had never been implicated in human disease.[50]

2. Deliberate Release Into the Environment Decisions Require an Additional Hard Look

In subsequent litigation, the Foundation on Economic Trends (Foundation) sought to enjoin NIH's approval of an experiment at the University of California involving the deliberate release into the environment of genetically altered bacteria.[51] The plan was to apply these bacteria to plots of potatoes, tomatoes, and beans to determine whether they could increase the crop's frost resistance.[52] NIH had approved this experiment on the basis of an EA. The court considered the facts and enjoined the experiment. NIH was sent back to the drawing board to complete an EIS.

At the time of issuance of the original NIH *Guidelines*, deliberate release experiments were prohibited.[53] The EIS accompanying the *Guidelines* noted:

> Should organisms containing recombined DNA be dispersed into the environment, they might, depending on their fitness relative to naturally occurring organisms, find a suitable ecological niche for their own reproduction. A potentially dangerous organism might then multiply and spread. Subsequent cessation of experiments would not stop the diffusion of the hazardous agent.[54]

Changes to the *Guidelines* in 1978 allowed NIH to waive the prohibition against deliberate release experiments.[55] Such decisions were to be made by the NIH Director with the RAC in order to determine that no significant risk to the environment would be presented. A need for definitive stan-

dards to guide the exercise of such discretion was suggested. No such standards were forthcoming. The deliberate release experiments were approved by NIH in September 1983, on the basis of a limited review and the Foundation lawsuit followed. A federal district court enjoined the experiment pending conduct by NIH of further NEPA review.

On appeal, the D.C. Circuit affirmed. It noted that NIH's consideration of the experiment fell far short of NEPA requirements.[56] The court stressed that although the original NIH EIS described the possibility of dispersion of genetically modified organisms as a major environmental concern, NIH completely failed to address the issue. It held that NIH "must attempt to evaluate seriously the risk that emigration of such organisms from the test site will create ecological disruption."[57] Until NIH completed that evaluation, no judgment could be made as to whether an EIS would be required.

3. The Federal *Framework* Is Not a Major Federal Action

The Foundation also sought to challenge the *Framework* itself as invalid for lack of compliance with NEPA.[58] The gravamen of this complaint was that the *Framework* constituted rulemaking fraught with such environmental risk that an EIS was required. The court rejected this argument on a number of grounds.

First, the court held that the *Framework* was not a rule but rather, "a first effort to aid in formulation of agency policy with respect to control of microorganisms developed by genetic engineering techniques."[59] Second, the court held that the plaintiffs had no standing to bring the action. The injury presented was based on a hypothetical construction of how the *Framework* might operate, which was insufficient to establish distinct and palpable injury. The plaintiffs also failed to establish the causation and redressability elements of standing based on failure to properly allege any connection between the *Framework* and any future approval for use of genetically engineered products.[60]

4. When NEPA Does Not Dictate Outcome—The "Hard Look"

With the maturation of the *Framework*, jurisdiction over many environmental release experiments shifted to the major regulatory agencies of jurisdiction, EPA, the USDA, and the FDA. NEPA challenges to enjoin projects became less successful as these agencies applied their risk assessment processes and expertise to the substantive risk issues associated with deliberate release of organisms to the environment.

49. Mack v. Califano, 447 F. Supp. 668, 8 ELR 20347 (D.D.C. 1978).

50. *Id.* at 671, 8 ELR at 20347-48.

51. Foundation on Econ. Trends v. Heckler, 756 F.2d 143, 15 ELR 20248 (D.C. Cir. 1985).

52. *Id.* at 149, 15 ELR at 20251.

53. *Id.* at 148, 15 ELR at 20250.

54. *Id.* at 148-49, 15 ELR at 20250.

55. *Id.* at 149, 15 ELR at 20250-51(citing 43 Fed. Reg. 33042 (July 28, 1978)).

56. *Id.* at 153, 15 ELR at 20253.

57. *Id.* at 154, 15 ELR at 20254.

58. Foundation on Econ. Trends v. Johnson, 661 F. Supp. 107, 17 ELR 21148 (D.D.C. 1986).

59. *Id.* at 109, 17 ELR at 21148-49.

60. *Id.*, 17 ELR at 21149. Further development of the standing issues presented in this case is provided in a companion case decided on the same date. Foundation on Econ. Trends v. Thomas, 661 F. Supp. 713, 17 ELR 21149 (D.D.C. 1986) (EPA not required to adopt financial responsibility standards under FIFRA for holders of experimental use permits for genetically modified organisms).

One of the first of these cases presented a challenge to EPA's decision under FIFRA to approve an experimental use permit for field testing of the frost-resistant genetically modified strains of *Pseudomonas Syringae* and *Pseudomonas Flourescens*.[61] This decision was based on an extensive administrative record which included evaluation by EPA scientists of extensive information of the characteristics of the altered bacteria, analysis of risks to humans, dissemination of mutant bacteria from the test site, survivability and colonization abilities of the bacteria, and possible effects from its release on precipitation patterns. EPA's internal evaluation and decisions on these risk issues was presented to a group of independent scientists sitting on EPA's FIFRA Scientific Advisory Panel (SAP) for review. EPA's conclusion that no unreasonable risk would be presented by the experiment was also reviewed by the USDA, the FDA, and NIH. Notice of the application was also published in the *Federal Register*.

The court reviewed EPA's decision to grant the permit on the same grounds as those applied to NEPA review—was there a procedural defect or was the agency's decision arbitrary and capricious on the basis of the record before it. The court found the decision was neither and approved it as well-reasoned and focused on all of the critical issues. The court also rejected the Foundation's NEPA arguments as applied to EPA on the now-familiar ground that EPA's analysis was the functional equivalent of NEPA review.[62]

5. New Sorts of Activities, Such as Bioprospecting, Trigger NEPA Review

In an interesting case describing the "integral relationship" between natural resource law and the Federal Technology Transfer Act (FTTA),[63] the court evaluated the role of NEPA in the development of a bioprospecting Cooperative Research and Development Agreement (CRADA) between Diversa Corporation, the National Park Service (NPS), and Yellowstone National Park.[64] The FTTA is designed to encourage and enhance technological innovation for commercial and public purposes. To accomplish this, the FTTA authorizes government-operated laboratories to enter into CRADAs with nonfederal parties. The bioprospecting CRADA provides a set of rules for cooperative research into the biological resources of Yellowstone secured through specimen collection permits and the commercialization of inventions and products developed from those specimens by the parties. Among other things, the CRADA grants royalty fees and licensing rights to Yellowstone in connection with all such inventions and products developed by Diversa.

The CRADA was challenged on a number of grounds, including the failure of the NPS to prepare an EA. The NPS argued that "the activities performed under the CRADA fall under a categorical exclusion for 'day-to-day resource management and research activities,'" and "approval of the CRADA was not a 'major federal action.'"[65] The reviewing

court disagreed, pointing out as a matter of fact that the NPS provided no evidence that such a determination was made before the CRADA was finalized. The court also observed that the "commercial exploitation of natural resources does not strike the Court as logically equivalent to 'day-to-day resource management and research activities.'"[66]

The court also noted that the DOI's own department manual identifies several exceptions applicable to all categorical exclusions, including:

Actions that may "[h]ave adverse effects on such unique geographic characteristics as ecologically significant or critical areas . . . have highly controversial environmental effects, . . . have highly uncertain and potentially significant environmental effects or involve unique or unknown environmental risks, . . . [e]stablish a precedent for future action or represent a decision in principle about future actions with potentially significant environmental effects, . . . [or that are] directly related to other actions with individually insignificant but cumulatively significant environmental effects.[67]

The court thus held that the NPS "could not reasonably have found none of [these] exceptions . . . to apply" because "the Yellowstone-Diversa CRADA is a precedent setting agreement within the National Park System and the DOI in general."[68] In arriving at these conclusions, the court focused squarely on the effects of the CRADA—commercial exploitation of a very broad range of natural resources. As the court noted, "the [Yellowstone-Diversa] CRADA, on its face, allows for a tremendously broad range of activities spanning a broad range of ecosystems" including thermal features, alpine tundra ecosystems, subalping forests, riparian habitats, sedge marshes, bogs, swamps, streams, and lakes.[69]

In the end, it was the court's judgment that "[t]he novel legal and factual issues raised by bioprospecting in Yellowstone require an intensive deliberation by the defendants, ideally with public input—precisely the deliberation mandated by Congress through the NEPA."[70]

C. The Role of the ESA

Congress enacted the ESA in 1973 in recognition of the fact that many of the nation's, and the world's, animal and plant species were disappearing. The ESA applies to all "species"[71] of "fish or wildlife"[72] and "plants."[73] It is intended "to provide a means whereby the ecosystems upon which endangered species and threatened species depend may be conserved."[74]

1. Listing and Critical Habitat Designation

Section 4 of the ESA sets forth a procedure to designate species as "endangered" or "threatened." A species is considered to be endangered if it is in danger of extinction

61. Foundation on Econ. Trends v. Thomas, 637 F. Supp. 25, 16 ELR 20632 (D.D.C. 1986); See discussion of the details of this EPA authority *infra* at Chapter 5.

62. *Foundation on Econ. Trends*, 637 F. Supp. at 28, 16 ELR at 20634.

63. 15 U.S.C. §3701 et seq.

64. Edmonds Inst. v. Babbitt, 42 F. Supp. 2d 1, 17-20, 29 ELR 21154, 21160-61 (D.D.C. 1999).

65. *Id.* at 18, 29 ELR at 21160.

66. *Id.*

67. *Id.* at 18-19, 29 ELR at 21161.

68. *Id.* at 19, 29 ELR at 21161.

69. *Id.*

70. *Id.*

71. 16 U.S.C. §§1531, 1532(16), ELR Stat. ESA §§2, 3(16).

72. *Id.* §1532(8), ELR Stat. ESA §3(8).

73. *Id.* §1532(14), ELR Stat. ESA §3(14).

74. *Id.* §1531(b), ELR Stat. ESA §2(b).

throughout all or a significant portion of its range. A threatened species is one that is likely to become an endangered species within the foreseeable future throughout all or a significant portion of its range.[75] A number of factors are considered in making this determination, including: "the present or threatened destruction, modification, or curtailment of its habitat or range"; "overutilization for commercial, recreational, scientific, or educational purposes"; "disease or predation"; "the inadequacy of existing regulatory mechanisms"; or "other natural or manmade factors affecting its continued existence."[76]

In addition, §4 requires, when "prudent and determinable," the designation of "critical habitat" for any listed species.[77] Critical habitat includes geographic areas where "those physical or biological features essential to the conservation of the species" are found and "which may require special management consideration or protections."[78] This includes areas essential to the conservation of the species, but not otherwise occupied by the species at the time of listing.[79]

2. Prohibition on Unauthorized "Take" of a Listed Species

Once a fish, wildlife, or plant species is listed under the ESA, §9 of the statute proscribes all prohibited acts relative to all such species that apply to "any persons subject to the jurisdiction of the United States."[80] These prohibitions are the principle means by which species are protected under the ESA (and they are reinforced by both civil and criminal penalties).[81]

The most notable among these prohibitions is the one making it unlawful for any person to "take" a listed species. The term "take" means "to harass, harm, pursue, hunt, shoot, wound, kill, trap, capture, or collect, or to attempt to engage in any such conduct."[82] By regulation, the word "harm" is further defined to mean "an act which actually kills or injures wildlife. Such act may include significant habitat modification or degradation where it actually kills or injures wildlife by significantly impairing essential behavioral patterns, including breeding, feeding, or sheltering."[83]

3. Agency Jurisdiction and the Consultation Process

The two federal agencies with primary responsibility for the administration of the ESA are the U.S. Fish and Wildlife Service (FWS), located within the DOI, and the NMFS, located within the U.S. Department of Commerce. Generally speaking, the FWS is responsible for terrestrial and freshwater species and migratory birds, while the NMFS is responsible for marine species and anadromous fish.[84] USDA's APHIS is re-sponsible for overseeing import and export activities involving terrestrial plants listed under the ESA.

Under ESA §7, all federal agencies are required to consult with the FWS or the NMFS, to ensure that "any action authorized, funded or carried out" by the agency will not jeopardize endangered or threatened species or adversely modify its designated or proposed critical habitat.[85] If it is determined that an action is likely to adversely affect a listed species, the FWS or the NMFS, as the case may be, issues a biological opinion (BO). If the BO finds that the action is not likely to jeopardize the species' continued existence or adversely modify its designated critical habitat, the document may, among other things, make an incidental take statement. That statement provides immunity from the take provisions to both the agency and the regulated party. If jeopardy or adverse modification is found, the BO offers reasonable and prudent alternatives to the action.[86] If consultation has not occurred because there was no triggering action or if the FWS/NMFS refrain from issuing an incidental take statement, the federal agency is liable.

Section 7 also sets forth a procedure under which "agency actions" may be exempted from the restrictions of the ESA if a cabinet-level "Endangered Species Committee" decides, among other things, that "the benefits of such actions clearly outweigh the benefits of alternative courses of action consistent with conserving the species or its critical habitat, and such action is in the public interest."[87] This procedure, however, has been used sparingly.

4. Habitat Conservation Plans (HCPs)

Section 10 of the ESA provides a somewhat similar incidental take safe harbor provision for other parties such as private landowners, corporations, state or local governments, or other nonfederal landowners, by permitting "incidental takes" of listed species. To obtain such an "incidental take" permit, one must develop, obtain approval of, and implement a "conservation plan," otherwise known as an HCP.[88] An HCP, which is intended to offset the harmful effects the proposed activity might have on a listed species, must set forth "the impact which will likely result from such taking"; the "steps the applicant will take to minimize and mitigate such impacts"; the "alternative actions to such taking" considered by the applicant; "the reasons why such alternatives are not being utilized"; and "such other measures" that may be required "as being necessary or appropriate for purposes of the plan."[89]

Under §10, therefore, and in concert with an approved HCP, parties may seek to use and develop land inhabited or used by a listed species, and any resulting "take" of that species, to the extent it "will not appreciably reduce the likelihood of the survival and recovery of the species in the wild,"[90] is allowed as "incidental to, and not the purpose of, the carrying out of an otherwise lawful activity."[91]

---

75. *Id.* §1533(a)(1)-(2), ELR Stat. ESA §4(a)(1)-(2).

76. *Id.* §1533(a)(1)(A)-(E), ELR Stat. ESA §4(a)(1)(A)-(E).

77. *Id.* §1533(a)(3)(A), ELR Stat. ESA §4(a)(3)(A).

78. *Id.* §1532(5)(A)(i), ELR Stat. ESA §3(5)(A)(i).

79. *Id.* §1532(5)(A)(ii), ELR Stat. ESA §3(5)(A)(ii).

80. *See id.* §1538(a)(1)-(2), ELR Stat. ESA §9(a)(1)-(2).

81. *Id.* §1540(a)-(b), ELR Stat. ESA §11(a)-(b).

82. *Id.* at §1532(19), ELR Stat. ESA §3(19).

83. 50 C.F.R. §17.3.

84. *See generally* the FWS' and the NMFS' websites, http://www.fws.gov and http://www.nmfs.noaa.gov (last visited July 20, 2001).

85. 16 U.S.C. §§1531, 1536(a)(2), (a)(4), ELR Stat. ESA §§2, 7(a)(2), (a)(4).

86. *Id.* §1536(b), ELR Stat. ESA §7(b).

87. *Id.* §1536(e)-(h), ELR Stat. ESA §7(e)-(h).

88. *Id.* §1539(a), ELR Stat. ESA §10(a).

89. *Id.* §1539(a)(2)(i)-(iv), ELR Stat. ESA §10(a)(2)(i)-(iv).

90. *Id.* §1539(a)(2)(B)(iv), ELR Stat. ESA §10(a)(2)(B)(iv).

91. *Id.* §1539(a)(1)(B), ELR Stat. ESA §10(a)(1)(B).

D. Biotechnology and Endangered and Threatened Species

The following current examples best illustrate the interplay between biotechnology and the regulation of endangered or threatened species.

1. EPA's FIFRA Endangered Species Protection Program (ESPP)

One regulatory program that warrants mention in connection with any discussion of biotechnology and the federal agency consultation process under the ESA is EPA's ESPP. EPA is required to ensure that the pesticides it registers for use will not harm or otherwise negatively affect listed species, or species proposed for listing, or designated critical habitat, or proposed critical habitat. To assist it in this process, EPA's Office of Pesticide Programs (OPP), Field and External Affairs Division, developed the ESPP, a voluntary initiative that relies on cooperation between the FWS, EPA regional offices, states, and pesticide users.[92]

The stated goals of the ESPP are to protect listed species from the use of pesticides and to minimize the impact of the program on pesticide users.[93] To implement the ESPP, EPA assesses the risk of pesticide use to species listed under the ESA, consults with the FWS where there are unavoidable concerns relating to pesticide uses and listed species or their habitats, and implements use limitations either specified in BOs by the FWS or developed from such opinions.[94]

To implement the use limitations, the OPP, among other things, encourages the addition of generic label statements to pesticides directing users to county-by-county information and maps (county bulletins) that illustrate the location of species and their habitats, and provides relevant recommended pesticide use practices in consideration thereof.[95] The program also provides tips on how to reduce the runoff and drift of pesticides during and after use.

2. Bt-Maize and Nontarget Endangered or Threatened Species

As discussed in more detail in Chapter 5, EPA has granted a number of companies, including the Monsanto Company and Novartis, five-year product registrations under FIFRA to commercially plant corn genetically engineered to produce a bacterial toxin known as Bt. The toxin is genetically added to the corn to kill harmful pests such as the European corn borer that destroys corn crops ("target" species). Since that initial planting, however, considerable debate has arisen as to whether the pollen from the Bt-maize is harming or could harm "nontarget" species such as monarch butterflies. (Monarch butterflies feed on milkweed, which typically is located in and around cornfields. The concern is that the milkweed becomes "dusted" with Bt-maize pollen, which is then digested by the monarchs during feeding.)

Monarch butterflies are not currently a listed species under the ESA. However, some groups are now expressing a similar concern for the 19 or so other nontarget butterfly and moth species, including the Karner Blue butterfly, that are listed as endangered or threatened under the ESA, and that also may eat plants in and around Bt cornfields. As a result, and in anticipation of the expiration of the initial wave of Bt-maize registrations this year, a number of environmental and other groups have already notified EPA of their intent to sue if it fails, during the reregistration process, to consult with the FWS under the ESA on the potential effects of Bt-maize on all nontarget endangered and threatened butterfly and moth species.

3. Transgenic Salmon Versus Wild Endangered Salmon

In addition to the possible impacts of genetically modified plant organisms on nontarget endangered or threatened species, another rising area of concern involves the impact of genetically modified animal species on their wild endangered or threatened cousins. On November 17, 2000, the FWS and the NMFS jointly listed the native Atlantic salmon population in Maine as an endangered species under the ESA[96] That listing implicates the aquaculture production of transgenic salmon in open water net pens or other "contained" conditions in or near the critical habitat waters of the newly listed endangered salmon population as discussed in OSTP Case Study No. I: Growth-Enhanced Salmon. "Transgenic fish are fish that have been modified to contain copies of new genetic constructs introduced into their genome by modern techniques (specifically, recombinant DNA techniques)."[97] The impetus behind the genetic modification of salmon is to produce a faster growing salmon at less cost than is currently possible with nontransgenic, farm-raised hybrid salmon.

The chief concern regarding transgenic salmon is their propensity to escape from their open water containment systems into the surrounding waters. Escape can occur as a result of storms, seal attacks, or human error. Escaped transgenic salmon may disturb the newly listed endangered salmon's habitat through, among other things, predation, competition for resources, and the spread of disease, or by breeding with the endangered salmon, altering their genetic makeup forever. And while plans are to raise only reproductively sterile female transgenic salmon, science currently cannot guarantee 100% reproductive sterility, leaving open the possibility that a reproductively active female transgenic salmon could be released.

The FWS and the NMFS already have been working with the state of Maine and other interested stakeholders and agencies to address the potential impacts of nontransgenic, farm-raised hybrid salmon on the endangered salmon population and critical habitat. More recently, the FDA spearheaded the first of a reported series of case studies into the potential impacts of transgenic Atlantic salmon raised in net pens in or near both the Atlantic and Pacific coastal waters of the United States. The purpose of the FDA case study is to illustrate "the types of environmental safety considerations that would go into a U.S. government evaluation of a request

92. *See generally* EPA's website, http://www.epa.gov (last visited July 20, 2001).

93. *Id.*

94. *Id.*

95. *Id.*

96. 65 Fed. Reg. 69459 (Nov. 17, 2000).

97. *Case Study No. I: Growth-Enhanced Salmon, supra* Chapter 1, note 55, at 2. Traditional aquaculture production of nontransgenic, farm-raised hybrid salmon is also implicated by the listing of the native Atlantic salmon population in Maine as an endangered species.

for approval of a transgenic Atlantic salmon variety for use in aquaculture, and the government agencies and authorities involved."[98]

Although it is reported that no "complete application [has yet been] submitted to FDA for use of a transgenic fish,"[99] when and if such an application is made, the procedures, namely the federal agency consultation process, and prohibitions of the ESA certainly will be implicated.

E. Other U.S. Wildlife Laws

In addition to the ESA, a number of other U.S. laws also are intended to protect wild fauna and flora and related habitat. As a result, they too could be implicated by biotechnology applications. These include the Marine Mammal Protection Act (MMPA),[100] the MBTA,[101] the Anadromous Fish Conservation Act,[102] the Lacey Act,[103] and the Magnuson-Stevens Fishery Conservation and Management Act (Magnuson-Stevens Act),[104] as amended by the 1996 Sustainable Fisheries Act.

---

98. *Id.* at 2. The federal regulatory agencies with some kind of authority or responsibility over transgenic salmon farming operations include the FDA, the U.S. Army Corps of Engineers, the FWS, the NMFS, and EPA.

99. *Id.*

100. 16 U.S.C. §§1361-1421h, ELR Stat. MMPA §§2-409.

101. *Id.* §§703-712.

102. *Id.* §§757a-757g.

103. 18 U.S.C. §42 et seq.

104. 16 U.S.C. §§1801-1883.

For example, the MMPA, which the NMFS is responsible for implementing, regulates the "taking" of marine mammals, e.g., whales, dolphins, porpoises, seals, and seal lions, which includes anything that may harm, harass, or kill a marine mammal. The MMPA also proscribes protection, conservation, and recovery programs for marine mammals.

The Lacey Act, prohibits the importation into, or the shipment among, the United States, including any territory or possession, of certain categories of wild animal species determined to be "injurious to human beings, to the interest of agriculture, horticulture, forestry, or to wildlife or the wildlife resources of the United States."[105] Another part of the Lacey Act, generally speaking, makes it a federal crime for any person to import, export, transport, sell, receive, acquire, possess, or purchase any fish, wildlife, or plant taken, possessed, transported, or sold in violation of any federal, state, foreign, or Indian tribal law, treaty, or regulation.[106]

Finally, the Magnuson-Stevens Act, also administered by the NMFS, applies when designated "essential fish habitat" is present. Any activities that might adversely affect designated essential fish habitat, which is defined as "those waters and substrate necessary to fish for spawning, breeding, feeding or growth to maturity,"[107] must be assessed and measures taken to avoid, minimize, mitigate, or compensate for such impacts. Failing that, the lead federal agency must explain why such measures will not be taken.[108]

---

105. 18 U.S.C. §42.

106. *Id.* §3372(1), (2)(A), (4).

107. 16 U.S.C. §1802(10).

108. *See Case Study No. I: Growth-Enhanced Salmon, supra* Chapter 1, note 55, at 12.

CHAPTER 3

I. The Role of the USDA for Plants and Animals

A. The Role of the USDA

Within the framework of federal regulation of agricultural biotechnology, the USDA is responsible for ensuring that new varieties of plants and genetically altered organisms are safe to grow. As it indicated in a 1984 policy statement: "The mandate of [the] USDA, simply stated, is to protect and enhance agriculture and forestry in the United States."[1]

B. Statutory Authorities

1. The PPA

For many years, the USDA derived its authority with respect to genetically altered plants from the FPPA of 1957, formerly 7 U.S.C. §§150aa-150jj, and the PQA of 1912, formerly 7 U.S.C. §§151-167. These laws provided the department with regulatory authority over the movement into, within, or through the United States of plants, plant products, plant pests, and any product or article which may contain a plant pest at the time of movement. Effective June 22, 2000, those statutes were repealed and replaced by the PPA[2] which currently provides the basis for the USDA's authority over genetically engineered organisms. The PPA consolidated and enhanced the USDA's authority to

> prohibit or restrict the importation, entry, exportation, or movement in interstate commerce of any plant, plant product, biological control organism, noxious weed, article, or means of conveyance, if the Secretary determines that the prohibition or restriction is necessary to prevent the introduction into the United States or the dissemination of a plant pest or noxious weed within the United States.[3]

A "plant pest" is defined as any living stage of a protozoan, nonhuman animal, parasitic plant, bacterium, fungus, virus, infectious agent or pathogen, or similar or allied article that can injure or cause disease or damage plants or plant products.[4] The USDA views this concept broadly. The definition of "plant pest" covers "direct or indirect injury, disease, or damage not just to agricultural crops, but also to plants in general, for example, native species, as well as to organisms that may be beneficial to plants, for example, honeybees."[5]

2. The VSTA

The VSTA governs viruses, serums, toxins, and other analogous products used to treat domestic animals.[6] The VSTA re-

quires a license for the preparation of a virus, serum, toxin, or analogous product to be sold, bartered, exchanged, or shipped in the United States and intended for use in the treatment of domestic animals.[7] The Act grants the government the right to conduct inspections of establishments that prepare such viruses, serums, toxins, or analogous products.[8] An establishment will be exempt from the licensing requirement when preparing a virus, serum, toxin, or analogous product solely for administration to the establishment's animals, or solely for administration to animals under a veterinarian-client-patient relationship, or solely for distribution within a state when that state has granted a USDA-approved license for such distribution.[9] The VSTA prohibits the preparation, sale, barter, exchange, or shipment of a "worthless, contaminated, dangerous, or harmful virus, serum, toxin, or analogous product intended for use in the treatment of domestic animals."[10]

The VSTA also requires a permit for the importation of a "virus, serum, toxin, or analogous product for use in the treatment of domestic animals."[11] All viruses, serums, toxins, and analogous products will be inspected before importation is permitted.[12] The Act prohibits the importation into the United States of any "worthless, contaminated, dangerous, or harmful virus, serum, toxin, or analogous product for use in the treatment of domestic animals."[13]

3. Animal Pest Act

The Animal Pest Act[14] grants the USDA authority to issue regulations and take such measures as needed to prevent the import or interstate transport of "any contagious, infectious, or communicable disease of animals and/or live poultry from a foreign country into the United States or from one State or Territory of the United States or the District of Columbia to another."[15] Nonhuman animal pathogens that are not veterinary biologics are regulated by means of a permit and quarantine system. The system applies to organisms which are defined as "all cultures or collections of organisms or their derivatives which may introduce or disseminate any contagious or infectious disease of animals (including poultry)."[16] It also applies to vectors which are

> all animals (including poultry) such as mice, pigeons, guinea pigs, rats, ferrets, rabbits, chickens, dogs, and the like, which have been treated or inoculated with organisms, or which are diseased or infected with any

---

1. 49 Fed. Reg. 50897, 50898 (Dec. 31, 1984).

2. 7 U.S.C. §§7701-7772.

3. Id. §7712(a).

4. Id. §7702(14); 7 C.F.R. §340.1.

5. 62 Fed. Reg. 63312 (Nov. 28, 1997).

6. 21 U.S.C. §§151-159.

7. See id. §§151, 154.

8. See id. §157.

9. See id. §154a.

10. Id. §151.

11. Id. §§152, 155.

12. See id. §153.

13. Id. §152.

14. Id. §§111-149.

15. Id. §111.

16. 9 C.F.R. §122.1(d).

contagious, infectious, or communicable disease of animals or poultry or which have been exposed to any
such diseases.[17]

Permit applications are reviewed by APHIS to determine
whether the organism requires safety testing to ensure that it
is free from livestock pathogens. If such testing is required,
the applicant must enter into a Cooperative Trust Fund
Agreement with the agency and pay for the testing.

4. The FMIA

The FMIA[18] requires that the FSIS of the USDA inspect
meat products that are intended for use as human food to ensure that they are wholesome, not adulterated, and properly
labeled. The statute gives that agency authority to inspect
cattle, sheep, swine, goats, horses, mules, and other equines.
Where meat and other products are commingled, jurisdiction is shared with the FDA. The USDA does not exercise
jurisdiction over products that contain less than 3% meat.
Regulation is by means of inspection of establishments for
sanitation, inspection of animals before and after slaughter,
product inspection, labeling, disposal of condemned materials, and laboratory inspection.

5. The PPIA

The PPIA[19] provides similar authority with respect to poultry products, including chickens, ducks, turkeys, geese,
guineas, and other domesticated birds, whether alive or
dead. The USDA exercises jurisdiction over poultry products containing more than 2% poultry.

C. APHIS

APHIS primarily administers the USDA program for biotechnology.[20] APHIS has 10 program offices: animal care;
wildlife services; international services; plan protection and
quarantine; veterinary services; legislative and public affairs; marketing and regulatory programs business services;
investigative and enforcement services; organization and
professional development; and policy and program development.[21] Its mission is to protect the nation's animal and
plant resources by: (1) safeguarding resources from exotic
invasive pests and diseases, (2) monitoring and managing
agricultural pests and diseases existing in the United States,
(3) resolving and managing trade issues related to animal or
plant health, and (4) ensuring the humane care and treatment
of animals.[22]

APHIS Plant Protection and Quarantine safeguards agriculture and natural resources from the risks associated with
the entry, establishment, or spread of animal and plant pests
and noxious weeds.[23] The Veterinary Services program pro-

tects and improves the health, quality, and marketability of
U.S. animals, animal products, and veterinary biologics by:
(1) preventing, controlling, and/or eliminating animal diseases, and (2) monitoring and promoting animal health and
productivity.[24]

D. Other USDA Offices

1. Grain Inspection, Packers, and Stockyards Administration (GIPSA)

The GIPSA facilitates the marketing of livestock, poultry,
meat, cereals, oilseeds, and related agricultural products and
promotes fair and competitive trading practices for the overall benefit of American agriculture.[25] The GIPSA's Federal
Grain Inspection Service (FGIS) establishes the Official
Standards for Grain, which are used each and every day by
sellers and buyers to communicate the type and quality of
grain bought and sold. The FGIS also establishes standard
testing methodologies to accurately and consistently measure grain quality. The program provides for the impartial
application of these grades and standards through a network
of federal, state, and private inspection agencies known as
the official system.

2. The FSIS

The FSIS protects consumers by ensuring that meat, poultry,
and egg products are safe, wholesome, and accurately labeled.[26] Under the FMIA, the PPIA, and the Egg Products
Inspection Act, the FSIS inspects all meat, poultry, and egg
products sold in interstate commerce and reinspects imported products, to ensure that they meet U.S. food safety
standards. In slaughter plants, inspection involves examining, before and after slaughter, birds and animals intended
for use as food. In egg processing plants, inspection involves examining, before and after breaking, eggs intended
for further processing and use as food.

The FSIS also sets requirements for meat and poultry labels and for certain slaughter and processing activities, such
as plant sanitation and thermal processing, that the industry
must meet. The FSIS tests for microbiological, chemical,
and other types of contamination and conducts epidemio-
logical investigations in cooperation with the Centers for
Disease Control and Prevention based on reports of
foodborne health hazards and disease outbreaks. In addition, the agency conducts enforcement activities to address
situations where unsafe, unwholesome, or inaccurately labeled products have been produced or marketed. The FSIS
regulates the slaughter of livestock and poultry involved in
biotechnology experiments.[27]

3. Agricultural Research Service (ARS)

The ARS is the principal in-house research agency of the
USDA.[28] The goal of ARS research is higher production and

17. *Id.* §122.1(e).
18. 21 U.S.C. §§601-695.
19. *Id.* §§451-471.
20. *See* http://www.aphis.usda.gov (last visited July 20, 2001).
21. *See* http://www.aphis.usda.gov/oa/orgchart.html (last visited July 20, 2001).
22. **APHIS, S**TRATEGIC **P**LAN (2000-2005), *available at* http://www.aphis.usda.gov/oa/aphissp/spmiss20.html (last visited July 20, 2001).
23. *See* http://www.aphis.usda.gov/ppq (last visited July 20, 2001).
24. *See* http://www.aphis.usda.gov/vs/who_we_are.htm (last visited July 20, 2001)
25. *See* http://www.usda.gov/gipsa (last visited July 20, 2001).
26. *See* http://www.fsis.usda.gov (last visited July 20, 2001).
27. 9 C.F.R. §§309.17, 381.75.
28. *See* http://www.nps.ars.usda.gov (last visited July 20, 2001).

more environmentally sensitive farming techniques. ARS research into improvement of crops and livestock included modern adaptations of traditional breeding methods and new biotechnology techniques. For example, the ARS recently released to industry cattle germplasm with high breeding value for twinning. Developed through intensive selection, this twinning technology has the potential to increase efficiency of beef production by 25%. On the biotech side, ARS scientists have mapped two clusters of chicken genes that may facilitate location of economically important genes.

4. Cooperative State Research, Education, and Extension Service (CSREES)

The CSREES seeks to advance a global system of research, extension, and higher education in the food and agricultural sciences and related environmental and human sciences to benefit people, communities, and the nation. The CSREES' mission emphasizes partnerships with the public and private sectors. Its programs provide access to scientific knowledge; strengthen the capabilities of land grant and other institutions in research, extension, and higher education; increase access to and use of improved communication and network systems; and promote informed decisionmaking by producers, families, communities, and other customers. This includes research programs on value-added product development, plant and animal genome, integrated pest management, water quality, human nutrition, food safety, and animal and plant systems.

E. The USDA and NEPA

Courts have provided an exception to the requirement that federal agencies must prepare an EIS. The exception has come to be known as the "functional equivalency doctrine." It states that "where a federal agency is engaged primarily in an examination of environmental questions, and where substantive and procedural standards ensure full and adequate consideration of all environmental issues, then formal compliance with NEPA is not necessary, functional compliance being sufficient."[29] Thus, EPA's regulation of genetically modified organisms as pesticides, discussed elsewhere in this deskbook, does not require preparation of an EIS.

There is a minority view that the doctrine could also apply in the context of environmental releases regulated by the USDA. Statutes administered by the USDA, such as the PPA, are designed to prevent environmental harm and clearances granted under their authority could be described as the functional equivalent of an EIS. However, the USDA continues to require at least an EA. APHIS prepares an EA for permit applications and petitions for nonregulated status discussed below and, if necessary, will develop an EIS. To date, however, the EAs for all permit applications to field test genetically modified organisms and for all petitions for nonregulated status have resulted in FONSIs.[30]

F. Plants

1. Field Testing and Movement Permits

Under authorities provided in the PPA, APHIS issues field test permits for new plants that have the potential to create pest problems in domestic agriculture. This could apply to plants, plant products, and other articles developed through biotechnological processes if such plants, plant products, or articles present a risk of plant pest introduction, spread, or establishment. The APHIS regulations specifically applicable to genetically modified organisms were first promulgated in 1987 and are codified at 7 C.F.R. Part 340. They control the introduction of a class of organisms referred to as "regulated articles."

A regulated article is defined as "any organism which has been altered or produced through genetic engineering, if the donor organism, recipient organism, or vector or vector agent belongs to any genera or taxa designated in §340.2 [of the regulation]" and meets the definition of a plant pest, or any organism or product which APHIS determines or has reason to believe is a plant pest.[31] Organisms that are not classified may become regulated articles if there is reason to believe that they are plant pests. Regulated article status has been applied to most of the genetically modified plants that have been developed to date.[32]

The regulations, as issued in 1987, provided procedures for obtaining an APHIS permit for the "introduction" of a regulated article. "Introduction" includes the importation, interstate movement, or "release into the environment" of a regulated article. Regulated articles are "released into the environment" when they are used outside the confinement of a laboratory, greenhouse, or other contained structure.

To obtain a permit, a plant breeder must provide detailed information including scientific details relating to the development and identity of the regulated article, the purposes for introduction of the regulated article, and the procedures, processes, and safeguards that will be employed to prevent escape and dissemination of the regulated article.[33] A permit will be granted if APHIS determines that the conduct of the trial, under conditions specified by the applicant or required by the agency, will not pose a plant pest risk. Permits for environmental releases are generally processed within 120 days of receipt of a complete application.[34] That period may be extended if an EIS is required in addition to an EA. APHIS provides the state in which the release is planned with a copy of its initial review and a copy of the application.

2. Streamlining and Notification

By 1992, after having issued "over 300 permits for field tests and 1,000 permits for movement," APHIS reached the conclusion that "introductions of many regulated articles can be conducted with little or no plant pest or environmen-

---

29. Warren County v. North Carolina, 528 F. Supp. 276, 278, 12 ELR 20402, 20405 (E.D.N.C. 1981).

30. *See* http://www.aphis.usda.gov/biotech/pubs.html (last visited July 20, 2001).

31. 7 C.F.R. §340.1.

32. *See* SUBCOMMITTEE ON BASIC RESEARCH, COMMITTEE ON SCIENCE, U.S. HOUSE OF REPRESENTATIVES, SEEDS OF OPPORTUNITY: AN ASSESSMENT OF THE BENEFITS, SAFETY, AND OVERSIGHT OF PLANT GENOMICS AND AGRICULTURAL BIOTECHNOLOGY 106-B (Comm. Print 2000), *reprinted in* 19 BIOTECHNOLOGY L. REP. 449, 473 (2000) [hereinafter SEEDS OF OPPORTUNITY].

33. 7 C.F.R. §340.4.

34. *Id.* §340.4(b).

tal risk, provided that certain criteria and performance standards are met."[35] For that reason, APHIS amended Part 340 of its regulations to provide a simple "notification" process for regulated articles meeting specified criteria, including introductions of certain plant species (corn, cotton, potato, soybean, tobacco, and tomato) that meet specified requirements. Instead of having to submit a formal permit application, the plant breeder may field test a plant which meets the eligibility criteria by simply submitting a "notification" letter to APHIS and by meeting certain performance standards identified in the rule.[36]

The eligibility criteria require, among other things, that the genetic material be "stably integrated" in the plant genome, that the function of the genetic material is known and its expression does not result in plant disease, that it will not produce an infectious entity or be toxic to nontarget organisms, and that it has not been modified to contain certain genetic material from animal or human pathogens.[37] The performance standards include controls on shipment, storage, planting, identification, and conduct and termination of the field trial.[38] If the introduction is denied under the notification process, a permit application may still be submitted.

3. Petitioning for Nonregulated Status

This rule also provided for a petition process under which the USDA may declare certain plants to be no longer regulated articles. Anyone may challenge the determination of "regulated article" by filing a petition with APHIS for nonregulated status.[39] This often happens as testing proceeds and the applicant gathers information which demonstrates that the organism is not a plant pest risk. APHIS' assessment will consider data and information that demonstrate that, with the exception of the deliberately introduced trait, the genetically engineered line is the same as a nonengineered parental line with respect to a suite of agronomic traits.[40] "If this is true and there is sufficient familiarity[41] with the introduced trait, the recipient plant, and the environment, APHIS can determine with a high degree of confidence that the engineered plant is no more likely to be a plant pest than a traditionally bred plant."[42] Once a determination of nonregulated status is made, the new plant variety may be developed further through traditional breeding. It may be produced, marketed, distributed, and grown without any other special oversight on the part of APHIS. Nonregulated status permits unencumbered commercialization.

For example, APHIS has determined, based on data submitted by the Monsanto Company and Dekalb Genetics Corporation, that a type of corn that had been genetically engineered for tolerance to the herbicide glyphosate does not present a plant pest risk.[43] This involved a finding that the corn exhibited no plant pathogenic properties; that it was no more likely to become a weed than traditional corn; that it was unlikely to develop weediness potential in species with which it can interbreed; that it will not harm other organisms, including agriculturally beneficial organisms and endangered and threatened species; and that it should not cause damage to raw or processed agricultural commodities.[44] The effect of this determination was that the requirements relating to regulated articles under 7 C.F.R. Part 340 no longer applied to the testing, breeding, importation, production, or interstate movement of this particular line of corn or its progeny. An EA was prepared, pursuant to NEPA, to document the FONSI.

4. Risk Assessment

EAs conducted by APHIS are consistent with the biosafety review procedures contained in Annex 3 of the United Nations Environment Program Guidelines for Safety in Biotechnology. The steps that are followed include (1) identifying hazards, (2) assessing actual risks that may arise from a hazard, (3) determining how the risk can be managed and whether to proceed with the proposed action, and (4) comparing the risk with those posed by actions involving comparable organisms.

In conducting risk assessments, APHIS begins with consideration of the existing knowledge base and of the traditional procedures that are used in developing any new crop variety. This baseline enables APHIS to identify hazards and then determine whether the risk posed by a hazard is significantly different from those well-known risks that are identified established practice. This process, which is referred to as "familiarity," is described in case studies which have been prepared by an Interagency Working Group (IWG) established by the White House CEQ and the OSTP.[45] The concept of familiarity is based on the philosophy that the types of safety issues raised by genetically engineered plants are no different from those for traditional breeding when similar traits are being conferred, although the magnitude of a particular risk may differ. The extensive experience gained from traditional plant breeding provides useful information in establishing parallel risk associations for newly developed crops. For plants, familiarity takes account of knowledge and experience with:

- The particular crop, including its flowering/reproductive characteristics, ecological requirements, and past breeding experiences;
- The agricultural and surrounding environment of the trial site;
- The specific traits transferred to the plant;
- The results of previous research;
- The scale-up of lines of the plant crop varieties developed by more traditional techniques;
- The scale-up of other plant lines developed by the same technique;
- The presence of related and sexually compatible plants in the surrounding natural environment and knowledge of the potential for gene transfer between the crop plant and the relatives; and

35. 57 Fed. Reg. 53036 (Nov. 6, 1992).

36. 7 C.F.R. §340.3(b), (d).

37. *Id.* §340.3(b).

38. *Id.* §340.3(c).

39. *Id.* §340.5, .6.

40. *See Case Study No. II: Bt-Maize, supra* Chapter 1, note 57, at 10.

41. The concept of "familiarity" is discussed in the following section on Risk Assessment.

42. *Case Study No. II: Bt-Maize, supra* Chapter 1, note 57, at 10.

43. 62 Fed. Reg. 64350 (Dec. 5, 1997).

44. *Id.*

45. *See, e.g., Case Study No. II: Bt-Maize, supra* Chapter 1, note 57.

● Interactions among the crop plant, environment, and trait.[46]

Taking these factors into account, familiarity can range from very high to very low. APHIS indicates that, for genetically engineered crop plants commercialized to date in the United States, there has been a high degree of familiarity.[47]

The major hazards which have been identified by APHIS, and for which risks are assessed, are the following:

● Plant pathogenic potential of the transgenic plant, e.g., the ability of the transgenic crop to harm other plants;
● Potential to affect handling, processing, or storage of commodities containing the genetically engineered plant;
● Changes in cultivation that might accompany adoption of the transgenic variety;
● Potential harm to nontarget organisms;
● Changes in the potential of the genetically engineered crop plant to become a weed;
● Potential to affect weediness of sexually compatible plants; and
● Potential impacts on biodiversity.[48]

5. An Expansion of the Notification Process

By 1995, APHIS was prepared to expand the notification process developed in the 1992 rule to include most genetically engineered plants that are considered regulated articles, provided that the introduction met six eligibility criteria and is conducted in accordance with six applicable performance standards. A rule to that effect was proposed in 1995 and made final in 1997.[49] The range of species eligible for introduction under the notification process was thus expanded beyond those covered in the 1992 rule to include any plant species that is not listed as a noxious weed under 7 C.F.R. Part 360 of the regulations and, for releases into the environment, any regulated article that is not considered a weed in the area of the proposed release into the environment.[50]

With respect to interstate movement, APHIS amended its administrative procedures to eliminate a requirement that states provide concurrences for notifications of interstate movement prior to acknowledgment by APHIS of the notification. APHIS will continue to notify states of interstate movement of regulated articles and provide states with the opportunity to comment, but the concurrence of the receiving state is no longer requested. The PPA contains a preemption provision that bars states and political subdivisions from taking actions to regulate interstate commerce different from federal plant pest controls, absent a demonstration of special local circumstance.[51]

6. Extension of Previously Issued Determinations of Nonregulated Status

The 1997 final rule also amended the regulations relating to petitions for determination of nonregulated status by allowing the extension of a previously issued determination of nonregulated status to certain additional regulated articles that are closely related to an organism that was determined not to be a regulated article.[52] To qualify for such a determination, an applicant must show that the risk assessment that was developed for the antecedent organism is in fact adequate to address any potential plant pest risk issues for the regulated article. The burden is on the applicant to provide data, including data from field tests, to demonstrate this contention.[53]

7. Special Concerns Regarding Trees

In the 1997 rulemaking, APHIS noted the special concerns that were expressed by some commenters with respect to trees. Some believed that the expansion of eligibility requirements was too broad and that permitting procedures should remain in force for regulated articles that have wild relatives in the United States with which the plant can interbreed.[54] Concerns were expressed with respect to largely undomesticated species of forest trees. Special biological factors, such as the lifespan of the plant species in the field, were cited as being relevant to the application of performance standards to a particular field trial.

APHIS conceded that certain plant species would require more stringent confinement procedures to comply with the regulation's performance standards, but did not view that as an impediment to including trees under the notification procedures. APHIS noted that field trials of many species of trees can be safely performed over a period of several years under the notification procedures, based on the fact that trees do not become sexually mature for a considerable and well-established period of years.[55] Moreover, tree species can be effectively isolated from wild populations by the appropriate choice of test location or by the use of physical methods for confinement of pollen.[56]

Nevertheless, APHIS acknowledged that long-term vigilance was required. Field tests involving trees may be several years in duration and could involve unexpected exposures of nontarget organisms if continual adherence to performance standards is not maintained. Moreover, trees may reach sexual maturity considerably after the initial planting. Procedures used to ensure reproductive confinement during the first year of a field trail may not be adequate at a later time in the trial. For that reason, and to emphasize the level of continual vigilance that is required to ensure that all relevant biological factors are taken into account, APHIS required that all field trials under notification procedures that are to be greater than one year in duration must be renewed annually.[57] Thus, the final rule states that

---

46. *See* ORGANIZATION FOR ECONOMIC COOPERATION & DEVELOPMENT, FIELD RELEASES OF TRANSGENIC PLANTS, 1986-1992, AN ANALYSIS (1993).

47. *Case Study No. III: Herbicide-Tolerant Soybean, supra* Chapter 1, note 58, at 11.

48. *Id.* at 12.

49. 60 Fed. Reg. 43567 (Aug. 22, 1995); 62 Fed. Reg. 23945 (May 2, 1997); 7 C.F.R. §340.3(b), (c).

50. 7 C.F.R. §340.3(b)(1).

51. 7 U.S.C. §7756(b).

52. 7 C.F.R. §340.6(e).

53. 62 Fed. Reg. at 23952.

54. *Id.* at 23947.

55. *Id.*

56. *Id.*

57. *Id.*

APHIS will provide acknowledgment within 30 days of receipt that the environmental release is appropriate under notification. Such acknowledgment will apply to field testing for [one] year from the date of introduction, *and may be renewed annually by submission of an additional notification to APHIS.*[58]

Thus, trees that meet the six eligibility criteria reflected in 7 C.F.R. §340.3(b) and which are introduced pursuant to the six performance standards reflected in 7 C.F.R. §340.3(c) may be introduced under the APHIS notification process. The performance standards are designed to manage the introduced regulated article such that it or its offspring will not persist in the environment. The notification must be renewed annually. However, field test reports need only be provided within six months of the termination of the field test.[59] The notification must contain a certification that the regulated article will be introduced in accordance with the eligibility criteria and performance standards reflected in the rule. APHIS has provided guidance materials and sample notification letters at its website: http://www.aphis.usda.gov/biotech. As noted above, where introduction is denied under the notification process, breeders may still apply for a permit.

8. Case Study: Phytoremediation or Bioremediation Using Poplar Trees

One of the case studies developed by the CEQ/OSTP IWG addressed the development of a hybrid poplar tree that could represent a breakthrough in efforts to remove toxic chemicals from soil and water.[60] This hybrid poplar can be genetically engineered to detoxify the industrial chemical TCE at polluted sites throughout the nation. The poplar was chosen because it grows rapidly, it can grow in soils that have low levels of TCE, and it can be easily cloned by clipping twigs and rooting them to establish new and genetically identical plants.

The poplar has been gentically modified through insertion of a human cytochrome gene and is currently being tested using genes from other animals and plants. The genetically modified tree takes TCE from soil or water and expresses an enzyme that modifies the chemical into less toxic or nontoxic substances that are translocated to the stems and leaves. The desired chemical processes occur in roots, stems, and leaves. There is no need for the tree to flower. Thus, outcrossing with wild relatives can be controlled by pruning or by cutting trees down before they flower, or it can be controlled by techniques for inducing sterility. At this point, only laboratory tests have been performed; no field testing has been authorized.

The hydrid poplar qualified for introduction under the APHIS notification process. The applicant provided necessary information in a letter which was received at APHIS on October 22, 1999. The applicant certified that the engineered tree would be introduced pursuant to the six eligibility criteria and six performance standards prescribed in 7 C.F.R. §340.3. The "three major steps" which APHIS took in this case were described as "the standard ones." They were:

- Evaluate relevant information (both information submitted by the applicant and information gathered by APHIS from other primary and secondary sources);
- Notify and consult with regulatory officials in states where the applicant proposes to field test; and
- Reach a decision whether to acknowledge or deny notification.

On November 21, 1999, one month after receiving the letter of notification, the notification was acknowledged by APHIS. The notification will remain in force until August 1, 2003, and must be renewed if any factors are amended.

In terms of commercialization, APHIS cautions that "it is highly unlikely that trees (or any plant) intended for bioremediation would ever be granted deregulated status as has been done for glufosinate-tolerant soybeans and Bt maize."[61] If field testing is successful, and it is intended to plant these trees at various contaminated sites, then a permit will be necessary.

Field testing proceeds in two steps. The first is "proof of the concept." Trees that perform well in the greenhouse may not necessarily perform well in the field. Scientists generate hundreds of thousands of plants in the greenhouse in order to select the handful that will perform well in the field. This can take several years. The trees will be planted at uncontaminated sites, in containers with controlled concentrations of TCE. In the first five years, trees will be selected for metabolism of TCE and once a clone has been identified that detoxifies TCE, the "proof of concept" phase is ended. In the second phase, the number of trees would have to be increased, sites and site-specific environmental issues identified, and addressed through EAs and EISs. As noted above, APHIS is not planning to deregulate plants used in such an application. For a detailed description of bioremediation in the context of RCRA regulation, see Chapter 7.

9. The Record Under APHIS' Plant Protection Rules

A recent congressional report assessing the progress of agricultural biotechnology summarized APHIS' record to date under the Part 340 regulations:

Since 1987, APHIS has processed more than 5,000 permits and notifications for field testing at over 22,000 sites and nearly 50 petitions for deregulation. Of the 44 different types of plants modified using rDNA techniques, field testing has occurred for varieties altered for herbicide tolerance (28%), insect resistance (24%), product quality (19%), virus resistance (10%), agronomic properties (6%), fungal resistance (5%), and other properties, including bacterial resistance (8%). In no instance has any biotech plant approved for field testing by [the] USDA created an environmental hazard or exhibited any unpredictable or unusual behavior compared to similar crops modified using conventional breeding methods.[62]

---

58. 7 C.F.R. §340.3(e)(4) (emphasis added).

59. *Id.* §340.3(d)(4).

60. *See Case Study No. V: Bioremediation Using Poplar Trees, supra* Chapter 1, note 60.

61. *Id.* at 6.

62. SEEDS OF OPPORTUNITY, *supra* note 32, at 474.

G. Animals

1. Veterinary Biologics

As noted above, the VSTA applies only to biologics and microorganisms intended for use in the treatment of domestic animals.[63] It requires a license for the preparation of a virus, serum, toxin, or analogous product that will be sold, bartered, exchanged, or shipped in the United States.[64] It also requires a permit to import a virus, serum, toxin, or analogous product.[65] The VSTA specifically prohibits the preparation, sale, transport, or import of a "worthless, contaminated, dangerous, or harmful virus, serum, toxin, or analogous product intended for use in the treatment of domestic animals."[66]

The USDA has created a detailed regulatory scheme to implement the VSTA.[67] Every person who prepares biological products subject to the VSTA must hold a U.S. Veterinary Biologics Establishment License and at least one U.S. Veterinary Biological Product License.[68] The regulations define a "biological product" as

> all viruses, serums, toxins (excluding substances that are selectively toxic to microorganisms, e.g., antibiotics), or analogous products at any stage of production, shipment, distribution, or sale, which are intended for use in the treatment of animals and which act primarily through the direct stimulation, supplementation, enhancement, or modulation of the immune system or immune response.[69]

Biological products subject to VSTA are those intended for use in the treatment of "domestic animals," defined as "all animals, other than man, including poultry."[70]

To obtain a U.S. Veterinary Biologics Establishment License, the applicant must complete an application obtained from APHIS.[71] A separate application must be made for each establishment operated by the applicant, and a new application must be submitted when a change of ownership, operation, or location of an establishment is made.[72] The applicant for a U.S. Veterinary Biologics Establishment License must allow an inspection of the establishment prior to obtaining the establishment license.[73] APHIS conducts the inspection to determine whether the condition, equipment, and facilities of the establishment and the methods used to prepare biological products are in conformity with the VSTA's regulations governing licensed establishments.[74]

A person who applies for an establishment license must also apply for at least one product license; an establishment license will not be issued without a license authorizing the production of a biological product in that establishment.[75] Each application for a product license must include four copies of

an Outline of Production; three copies of test reports and research data sufficient to establish purity, safety, potency, and efficacy of the product; legends designating which facilities are to be used in the preparation of each fraction; and labels and all claims to be made on the labels and in advertising matter for the biological product.[76] Field testing of a biological product that has been expressed in a food animal would be conducted under 9 C.F.R. Part 103. These regulations currently apply to preparation and shipment of experimental biological products and the disposition of animals to which experimental biological products are administered.

Experimental products approved by APHIS and biological products produced under the direction of USDA are not required to have a U.S. Veterinary Biological Product License.[77] Also, products prepared by a veterinarian solely for administration to animals in the course of his or her licensed veterinarian practice and under a veterinarian-client-patient relationship are exempt from the licensing requirements of the VSTA.[78] Likewise, the establishment in which such a biological product is prepared is exempt from the VSTA's licensing requirements.[79]

APHIS may exempt certain persons from obtaining an establishment license and product license when the biological product being prepared by that person is solely for distribution within the state and is prepared pursuant to a license granted by such state.[80] The state must request the exemption, and APHIS must approve the state's licensing program and ensure that it prohibits the preparation, sale, barter, exchange, or shipment of worthless, contaminated, dangerous, or harmful biological products.[81]

Conditional product licenses are available to licensed establishments when necessary to meet an emergency condition, limited market, local situation, or other special circumstance.[82] One special circumstance eligible for a conditional product license is the production of a biological product solely for intrastate use under a state-operated program.[83]

A person who wishes to import a biological product into the United States must obtain a U.S. Veterinary Biological Product Permit from APHIS.[84] Three types of product permits are issued by APHIS: a permit for research and evaluation; a permit for distribution and sale; and a permit for transit shipment only.[85] A separate U.S. Veterinary Biological Product Permit is required for each shipment of a biological product to be imported.[86] Applications for a U.S. Veterinary Biological Product Permit are available from APHIS and require the applicant to specify the type of permit required, port of entry, estimated quantity, and anticipated date of importation.[87] Product permits may not be issued for biological products from countries known to have exotic diseases,

---

63. *See* 21 U.S.C. §§151-159.

64. *See id.* §§151, 154.

65. *See id.* §§152, 155.

66. *Id.* §§151, 152.

67. *See* 9 C.F.R. §§101-123.

68. *See id.* §102.

69. *Id.* §101.2.

70. *Id.*

71. *Id.* §102.3(a)(1).

72. *Id.* §102.3(a)(2), (6).

73. *Id.* §102.4.

74. *See id.*; *see generally id.* §§101-123.

75. *See id.* §102.2(b).

76. *Id.* §102.3(b)(2).

77. *Id.* §§102.1, 103, 106.

78. *Id.* §107.1.

79. *Id.*

80. *Id.* §107.2.

81. *Id.*

82. *See id.* §102.6.

83. *Id.*

84. *Id.* §104.

85. *Id.* §§104.2(a), 104.4- .6.

86. *Id.* §104.1(a).

87. *Id.* §104.3.

such as foot-and-mouth disease and rinderpest, if APHIS believes the products may endanger the livestock or poultry of the United States.[88] A product permit will not be issued until APHIS inspects the equipment and facilities of the producer, the applicant, or both.[89]

The regulations governing the VSTA set forth very detailed requirements for facility requirements[90]; sterilization and pasteurization at licensed establishments[91]; packaging and labeling of biological products[92]; standard requirements for working with bacterial vaccines and products, viral vaccines, and antibody products[93]; production requirements for biological products[94]; and animals at licensed establishments.[95] VSTA regulations also include provisions for suspending, revoking, or terminating biological licenses or permits.[96]

2. Regulation of Animal Pests

The regulations governing animal pests prohibit the importation into and the transport within the United States of organisms and vectors without a permit.[97] An "organism" is defined as "all cultures or collections of organisms or their derivatives, which may introduce or disseminate any contagious or infectious disease of animals (including poultry)."[98] A "vector" is defined as

> all animals (including poultry) such as mice, pigeons, guinea pigs, rats, ferrets, rabbits, chickens, dogs, and the like, which have been treated or inoculated with organisms, or which are diseased or infected with any contagious, infectious, or communicable disease of animals or poultry or which have been exposed to any such disease.[99]

However, no permit is required for the importation of organisms for which a U.S. Veterinary Biological Product Permit has been issued or for transportation of organisms produced at licensed establishments.[100]

3. The Veterinary Services Program Office

The APHIS Veterinary Services program office is divided into substantive program areas including the Center for Veterinary Biologics (CVB), the Center for Animal Health Monitoring, the Center for Epidemiology and Animal Health, the National Center for Import and Export, and the National Veterinary Services Laboratories.[101] The CVB implements the VSTA and its regulations to assure that pure, safe, potent, and effective veterinary biologics are available

for the diagnosis, prevention, and treatment of animal diseases.[102] For example, the licensing and policy development arm of the CVB is responsible for reviewing license applications for production facilities and biological products; reviewing applications for permits for importation of products; establishing licensing, testing, and permit requirements and procedures; and reviewing production method, labels, and supporting data involved in the licensing and permit process.[103]

The National Center for Import and Export regulates the importation of animal pests.[104] Permits to import animal pests are obtained from this center. The Center for Animal Health Monitoring has initiated the National Animal Health Monitoring System (NAHMS) to collect, analyze, and disseminate data on animal health, management, and productivity across the United States.[105]

4. Case Study: Farm Animals That Produce Animal Biologics

APHIS has identified two situations in which it would become involved in regulating health issues relating to transgenic animals.[106] The first is with respect to "animal or veterinary biological products" that are produced in transgenic animals as "biopharmaceuticals." APHIS anticipates that only a few such biopharmaceutical animals will be developed in the near future. The second, and perhaps more important situation, relates to regulation of "biological product" that confer disease resistance. The proposed organism/product would be a "biological product" that has been expressed in a farm animal to produce protection against a specific animal disease by means of an immune response.

Transgenic animals bearing such a product may be used in animal disease programs. Certain species of cattle may exhibit naturally occurring resistance to disease. While traditional selection for such resistance traits would take generations of breeding, transgenic animals exhibiting such traits can be produced in much shorter time periods. APHIS offers the examples of transgenic animals that have specific immunity against pathogenic strains of microorganisms that are not otherwise susceptible to antibiotics or transgenic animals that provide specific immunity against a disease such as bovine spongiform encephalopathy when no vaccine is available.[107]

A "biological product" that conferred protection against an animal disease based on specific immune response and that has been expressed in a food animal would be licensed under the VSTA. APHIS would evaluate the product for purity, safety, potency, and efficacy under the regulations reflected at 9 C.F.R. Parts 101-118. Part 103 governs field testing. The regulations governing animal pests, at 9 C.F.R. Part 122, ensure that farm animals and their progeny do not introduce or disseminate a communicable disease. For a "biolog-

---

88. *Id.* §104.2(b).

89. *Id.* §104.2(c).

90. *Id.* §108.

91. *Id.* §109.

92. *Id.* §112.

93. *Id.* §113.

94. *Id.* §114.

95. *Id.* §117.

96. *Id.* §105.

97. *Id.* §122.

98. *Id.* §122.1.

99. *Id.*

100. *See id.* §122.2.

101. *See* http://www.aphis.usda.gov/vs/vs_org.htm (last visited July 20, 2001).

---

102. *See* http://www.aphis.usda.gov/vs/cvb (last visited July 20, 2001).

103. *See* http://www.aphis.usda.gov/vs/cvb/LPD/index.htm (last visited July 20, 2001).

104. *See* http://www.aphis.usda.gov/NCIE (last visited July 20, 2001).

105. *See* http://www.aphis.usda.gov/vs/ceah/cahm/index.htm (last visited July 20, 2001).

106. *See Case Study No. IV: Farm Animal (Goat) That Produces Human Drugs, supra* Chapter 1, note 59.

107. *Id.* at 15.

ical product" that is expressed in a transgenic animal and that is not otherwise categorically excluded, an EA would be prepared for field testing and licensure. Because these animals would be confined to a pasture or barnyard, no significant adverse impact in comparison to their nontransgenic counterparts would be anticipated.

An applicant for a "biological product" license would be required to submit data or relevant references from scientific literature that the biological product is safe and efficacious for its intended use. Prior to issuance of a permit to field test a biological product derived from a live animal virus, APHIS would require preparation of an EA.

There is discussion within the agency as to the appropriateness of regulating, under the VSTA, the transgenic animal itself, in addition to the "biological product" that is expressed in such animal. The regulations do not describe procedures for field testing, licensure, or postlicense monitoring of the transgenic animal, even though the animal may be the source of the "biological product." APHIS is currently seeking legislative authority to fill this gap.

CHAPTER 4

I. The FDA

A. Statutory and Regulatory Authority

As stated in the FFDCA,[1] the mission of the FDA includes to "protect the public health by ensuring that [ ] foods are safe, wholesome, sanitary and properly labeled."[2] Generally, the FDA's responsibilities extend to all domestic and imported food, with certain exceptions, notably including meat and poultry, which are regulated by the FSIS of the USDA.

Most of the FDA's authority to regulate food derives from the FFDCA.[3] Chapter IV of the Act[4] contains the substantive provisions particular to food, but other parts of the statute are important to understanding how the FDA regulates foods. As discussed below, key provisions include those found in Chapter III,[5] which identifies prohibited acts and the FDA's enforcement authority, Chapter VII,[6] which spells out the FDA's inspection authority, and Chapter VIII,[7] which deals with imports and exports of FDA-regulated products.

Acting through authority delegated from the Secretary of Health and Human Services, the FDA has authority to issue regulations for enforcement of the FFDCA.[8] The FDA's substantive regulations regarding human food are found within Subchapter B of Title 21 of the *Code of Federal Regulations*,[9] for the most part, and the regulations regarding animal feeds are in Subchapter E.[10] Subchapter A of Title 21 contains regulations regarding procedure or of other, more general applicability.[11] Additionally, the FDA issues "guidance documents" that describe the agency's interpretation of, or policy on, a regulatory issue.[12] Although not binding on the agency (or the public), guidance documents "represent the agency's current thinking" on a given issue, and generally indicate the policy that the FDA will follow.[13]

B. FDA Regulation of Food

The FFDCA defines "food" to mean "(1) articles used for food or drink for man or other animals, (2) chewing gum, and (3) articles used for components of any such article."[14] Although quite broad and rather circular (in essence, "food means articles used for food"), the definition has not, for the most part, been the subject of much litigation. Within the FDA, responsibility for regulation of food rests with the Center for Food Safety and Applied Nutrition (CFSAN) and field staff in FDA offices around the country.

1. Post-Market Review: Adulteration and Misbranding

As a general rule, FDA approval is not required before a food may be marketed.[15] Rather, the availability of food in the U.S. market is regulated by means of prohibitions within the FFDCA against adulterating or misbranding food or taking certain actions, e.g., manufacturing, introducing into interstate commerce, with regard to food that is adulterated or misbranded.[16] Not surprisingly, the FFDCA spells out in some detail what constitutes adulteration and misbranding.

The statute identifies 20 or so conditions or situations that render a food adulterated.[17] Because, as discussed below, a genetic modification may fall within the definition of a "food additive," perhaps the most relevant provision is that which defines a food as adulterated if it bears or contains an unsafe food additive.[18] Other provisions include a food that:

- Bears or contains a poisonous or deleterious substance that may cause the food to be injurious to health[19];
- Bears or contains an unsafe pesticide chemical residue[20];
- Consists of any filthy, putrid, or decomposed substance, or is otherwise unfit for food[21]; or
- Has been prepared, packed, or held under unsanitary conditions such that it may have become con-

---

1. 21 U.S.C. §321 et seq.

2. FFDCA §903(b)(2)(A), 21 U.S.C. §393(b)(2)(A).

3. Other major acts providing the FDA authority to regulate food in ways not necessarily relevant to this discussion include the PHS, 42 U.S.C. §201 et seq., and the Fair Packaging and Labeling Act, 15 U.S.C. §§1451-1461.

4. FFDCA §§401-413, 21 U.S.C. §§341-350b.

5. *Id.* §§301-310, 21 U.S.C. §§331-337.

6. *Id.* §§701-756, 21 U.S.C. §§371-379v.

7. *Id.* §§801-803, 21 U.S.C. §§381-383.

8. *Id.* §701, 21 U.S.C. §371. As discussed further below, the FDA also has specific authority to take certain enforcement actions, both administratively and in court.

9. 21 C.F.R. pts. 100-190.

10. *Id.* pts. 500-589.

11. *Id.* pts. 1-99.

12. 21 C.F.R. §10.115(b)(1).

13. *Id.* §10.115(d)(3); *see also* Administrative Practices and Procedures; Good Guidance Practices; Final Rule, 65 Fed. Reg. 56468, 56471 (Sept. 19, 2000). FDA employees "may depart from guidance documents only with appropriate justification and supervisory concurrence." 21 C.F.R. §10.115(d)(3).

14. FFDCA §201(f), 21 U.S.C. §321(f).

15. Food additives, discussed below, are a notable exception.

16. FFDCA §301, 21 U.S.C. §331; *see* discussion of FDA enforcement below.

17. *Id.* §402, 21 U.S.C. §342.

18. *Id.* §402(a)(2)(C)(i), 21 U.S.C. §342(a)(2)(C)(i). As discussed below, a food additive is presumed unsafe unless there is a regulation establishing the conditions of its safe use. *Id.* §409, 21 U.S.C. §348.

19. If the substance is not added to the food, i.e., it is naturally occurring in the food, the food is not considered adulterated so long as the amount of the substance in the food "does not ordinarily render [the food] injurious to health." *Id.* §402(a)(1), 21 U.S.C. §342(a)(1). Where a substance is added to a food and is necessary for production or cannot be avoided, the FDA can set tolerances, and the food is adulterated only if the amount of added substance exceeds the tolerance. *Id.* §§402(a)(2)(A), 406, 21 U.S.C. §§342(a)(2)(A), 346.

20. *Id.* §402(a)(2)(B), 21 U.S.C. §342(a)(2)(B). The Act contains extensive provisions for establishing tolerances and granting exemptions. *Id.* §408, 21 U.S.C. §346a.

21. *Id.* §402(a)(3), 21 U.S.C. §342(a)(3).

taminated with filth or been rendered injurious to health.[22]

Similarly, although the Act lists a number of conditions that can render a food misbranded,[23] the provisions most likely to come into play with regard to genetically modified foods are those regarding false or misleading labeling,[24] and the need to describe the food on its label by a "common or usual name."[25] A product's "label" is the written, printed, or graphic material upon the immediate container,[26] and "labeling" includes not only the label, but also such material "accompanying" the product.[27] Material need not physically accompany the product in order to fall within the definition of "labeling"[28]; as a result, promotional materials are generally considered labeling.

2. Premarket Approval: Food Additives

As noted above, a food may be considered adulterated if it bears or contains an unsafe food additive.[29] The threshold issues, therefore, are defining what constitutes a "food additive" and determining whether it is safe. The FFDCA defines a "food additive" as

> any substance the intended use of which results or may reasonably be expected to result, directly or indirectly, in its becoming a component or otherwise affecting the characteristics of any food . . . , if such substance is not generally recognized, among experts qualified by scientific training and experience to evaluate its safety, as having been adequately shown . . . to be safe under the conditions of its intended use.[30]

Food additives include substances that added directly to food products, such as texturizers or flavoring agents, as well as what are known as "indirect additives," substances that are used on or in food or food contact surfaces or packaging materials and that may be expected to migrate to the food itself.[31] Just as the definition of "food" is somewhat tautological, i.e., a "food" is "an article used for food," it also can include a whole food when it is mixed with or used as a component of another food.[32] As a result, a wide range of foods can be considered to be food additives.[33]

If an article meets the statutory definition of "food additive," it is, as a matter of law, deemed to be unsafe unless (with certain exceptions) the FDA has issued a regulation establishing the conditions under which it may be safely used.[34] The FDA can issue such a regulation on its own initiative,[35] or in response to a food additive petition submitted to the agency.[36] Among other things, a food additive petition must include information regarding the chemical identity and composition of the food additive; its physical, chemical, and biological properties; and full reports of investigations made regarding the safety of the food additive.[37]

In the absence of "extraordinary circumstances," the FDA will publicly release much of the information submitted in a food additive petition, including (1) safety and functionality data and information; (2) study protocols; (3) reports of adverse reactions, product experiences, and consumer complaints; (4) a list of ingredients; and (5) analytical methods, including assays. In certain circumstances, some of this information may be protected from disclosure as trade secrets or confidential commercial information.[38]

A determination that a food additive is safe for the intended use reflects the FDA's determination that there is "a reasonable certainty in the minds of competent scientists that the substance is not harmful under the intended conditions of use."[39] Such a determination requires consideration of:

- The probable consumption of the substance and any substance formed in or on food because of its use;
- The cumulative effect of the substance in the diet, taking into account any chemically or pharmacologically related substance or substances in the diet; and
- Those safety factors experts generally recognize as appropriate.[40]

A regulation prescribing the conditions under which a food additive can be safely used can include specifications regarding:

- The specific foods or types of food in which the substance may be used;
- The maximum quantity of the substance that can be used;
- How the substance can be used; and
- Directions for use, or other labeling or packaging requirements.[41]

---

22. *Id.* §402(a)(4), 21 U.S.C. §342(a)(4).

23. *Id.* §403, 21 U.S.C. §343.

24. *Id.* §403(a)(1), 21 U.S.C. §343(a)(1).

25. *Id.* §403(i), 21 U.S.C. §343(i).

26. *Id.* §201(k), 21 U.S.C. §321(k).

27. *Id.* §201(m), 21 U.S.C. §321(m).

28. *See, e.g.,* Kordel v. United States, 335 U.S. 345 (1948). Although there is a distinction made between advertising and other promotional materials, the FDA has, in other contexts, asserted that advertising is a subset of labeling. *See, e.g.,* Warning Letter dated July 9, 1996, from Lillian J. Gill, CDRH Office of Compliance, to Valerie Castle, Positive Response Television, Inc.

29. FFDCA §402(a)(2)(C)(i), 21 U.S.C. §342(a)(2)(C)(i).

30. *Id.* §201(s), 21 U.S.C. §321(s); *see also* 21 C.F.R. §170.3(e).

31. 21 C.F.R. §170.3(e)(1).

32. *See, e.g.,* United States v. Two Plastic Drums, 984 F.2d 814, 817 (7th Cir. 1993) (citing National Nutritional Foods Ass'n v. Kennedy, 572 F.2d 377, 391 (2d Cir. 1978)).

33. As a practical matter, it is likely that most whole foods would be considered generally recognized as safe (GRAS) and, as discussed below, would therefore fall outside the definition of "food additive," even when used as a component.

34. FFDCA §409(a), 21 U.S.C. §348(a).

35. 21 C.F.R. §170.15.

36. FFDCA §409(b), 21 U.S.C. §348(b); 21 C.F.R. pt. 171.

37. FFDCA §409(b)(2), 21 U.S.C. §348(b)(2); 21 C.F.R. §171.1(c). A company planning to conduct experiments intended to demonstrate the safety of a food additive may have the FDA review the proposed experiments and opine on whether the agency believes they will yield data that are adequate to evaluate the product's safety. 21 C.F.R. §170.20(b).

38. 21 C.F.R. §171.1(h).

39. *Id.* §170.3(i).

40. *Id.* The regulatory standard also reflects recognition that it is not possible "to establish with complete certainty the absolute harmlessness of the use of any substance." *Id.*

41. *Id.* §171.100.

Food additives for which the FDA has issued regulations regarding their safe use are identified at 21 C.F.R. Parts 172-178.

3. Substances Generally Recognized as Safe (GRAS)

Certain substances that are "component[s] or otherwise affect[ ] the characteristics of" a food are nonetheless not food additives, and therefore not subject to premarket approval. The statutory definition of "food additive" excludes pesticide chemicals and pesticide chemical residues, color additives, new animal drugs, dietary supplements, or ingredients in dietary supplements, and "prior-sanctioned" ingredients, i.e., products that were specifically approved for use before the 1958 enactment of the Food Additive Amendments.[42] For most purposes, however, the most relevant exemption is for substances that are GRAS.[43]

A substance is GRAS if it is "generally recognized, among experts qualified by scientific training and experience to evaluate its safety, as having been adequately shown . . . to be safe under the conditions of its intended use."[44] Unless the substance was used in food before 1958, the basis for determining its safety must be "scientific procedures"; if used before 1958, a substance may alternatively be shown to be safe on the basis of "experience based on [the] common use [of the substance] in food."[45] The "scientific procedures" on which a product's GRAS status may be based include human, animal, analytical, or other scientific studies, both published and unpublished.[46] If a pre-1958 substance is to be considered GRAS on the basis of its "common use in food," there must be a substantial history of consumption of the substance as food by a significant number of consumers.[47]

The FDA has enumerated a list of substances that the agency considers to be GRAS for use in food.[48] As with regulations establishing the conditions of safe use for food additives, these determinations are either initiated by the FDA of its own accord or in response to the submission of a petition.[49] A manufacturer intending to use a food substance and hoping to avoid a regulation establishing conditions for safe use as a food additive may submit a petition seeking the FDA's affirmation that the ingredient is GRAS.[50] The petition must include, among other things, information about past use of the substance, methods for detecting the substance in food, and information to establish the safety and functionality of the substance, including published scientific literature and any adverse information or consumer complaints.[51] Further, the petition must be "a representative and balanced submission" that includes both favorable and unfavorable information regarding the safety and functionality of the substance.[52]

A GRAS determination on the basis of scientific procedures requires the same scientific evidence as is necessary for approval of a food additive petition, and typically is based on published studies, corroborated by unpublished studies, and other data and information.[53] The FDA has explained that one must show "a consensus of expert opinion regarding the safety of the use of the substance," and that, although "[u]nanimity among experts . . . is not required," a "severe conflict among experts . . . precludes a finding" that a product is GRAS.[54]

A conclusion that a substance is GRAS on the basis of its prior use in food obviously does not require the same quantity or quality of scientific procedures, and usually is based on generally available data and information.[55] A substance can be GRAS on the basis of its pre-1958 use outside the United States, although the FDA will likely look for greater documentation and corroboration of the ingredient's use.[56]

There is no requirement to have the FDA affirm the GRAS status of a food ingredient, however. In light of this, and the burdens of submitting a GRAS petition,[57] manufacturers often simply conduct their own review to gather information supporting the GRAS status of the product, and then begin using the product. The FDA believes many manufacturers are deterred from submitting GRAS affirmation petitions by the fact that the process is, for the petitioner and agency, a resource-intensive and relatively lengthy process.[58] To encourage manufacturers to more frequently submit information about their own GRAS determinations, the FDA in 1997, proposed a less burdensome scheme, under which manufacturers would merely notify the agency of their determinations of GRAS status, providing information as to the basis for their "GRAS exemption claim." The FDA would not conduct a detailed evaluation of the data relied on (which would not necessarily be submitted to the FDA, but would be available for the agency to review upon request), and accordingly would not affirm the GRAS status of an ingredient. Rather, the FDA would "evaluate whether the notice provides a sufficient basis for a GRAS determination and whether information in the notice or otherwise available to [the] FDA raises issues that lead the agency to question whether use of the substance is GRAS."[59] The FDA would respond to the notification in writing within 90 days, and would advise the submitter if the agency had identified any "problem" with the notice.[60]

---

42. FFDCA §201(s), 21 U.S.C. §321(s). Prior-sanctioned food ingredients are listed at 21 C.F.R. pt. 181.

43. FFDCA §201(s), 21 U.S.C. §321(s).

44. *Id.*

45. *Id.*

46. 21 C.F.R. §170.3(h).

47. *Id.* §170.3(f).

48. *Id.* pts. 182, 184, 186.

49. *Id.* §170.35.

50. *Id.* §170.35(c).

51. *Id.* §170.35(c)(1).

52. *Id.* §170.35(c)(1)(v).

53. *Id.* §170.30(b).

54. Substances Generally Recognized as Safe; Proposed Rule, 62 Fed. Reg. 18937, 18939 (Apr. 17, 1997) [hereinafter GRAS Notification Proposed Rule].

55. 21 C.F.R. §170.30(c)(1). Moreover, such a determination must be based solely on food use before 1958. *Id.*

56. *Id.* §170.30(c)(2).

57. A determination that a substance is GRAS requires the FDA to conclude both that the product is safe and that this safety is generally known and accepted. By contrast, approval of a food additive requires the FDA to reach a conclusion only as to an ingredient's safety. GRAS Notification Proposed Rule, *supra* note 54, at 18940 & n.1.

58. *Id.* at 18941.

59. *Id.*

60. *Id.*

When it proposed the GRAS notification program, the FDA encouraged manufacturers to avail themselves of it even before a final rule was adopted.[61] Although there still was no final rule by mid-2001, it appears that, as a practical matter, the notification program has replaced the GRAS affirmation petition process. By the end of 2000, the FDA reportedly had received several dozen GRAS notifications.[62]

C. Regulation of Bioengineered Food

In 1992, the FDA issued a policy statement regarding how the agency intended to regulate human foods and animals feeds derived from new plant varieties, including varieties developed using rDNA technology, which were referred to as "bioengineered foods."[63] In general, the FDA announced that bioengineered foods would be regulated no differently than foods developed through traditional plant breeding. As a class, bioengineered foods did not require special labeling nor were they subject to premarket approval. The FDA would look to the objective characteristics of the food and its intended use, not the method by which the food was developed.[64]

Generally, this meant that bioengineered foods would be subject to regulation for safety within the context of FFDCA provisions regarding adulteration and misbranding of food, and would be subject to premarket approval only if the genetic modification created a substance that fell within the definition of a food additive.[65] In that regard, however, the FDA noted that, "[i]n most cases, the substances expected to become components of food as a result of genetic modification of a plant will be the same as or substantially similar to substances commonly found in food, such as proteins, fats and oils, and carbohydrates."[66] For the most part, therefore, the FDA expected that the results of bioengineering would be GRAS.[67]

Nonetheless, the FDA did foresee certain potential issues related to bioengineering, although they could be addressed within the context of current provisions of the FFDCA. For example, if a bioengineered food contained a naturally occurring toxicant increased by the genetic modification, or an unexpected toxicant that first appeared in the food as a result of the genetic modification, the food might be considered adulterated as containing an added deleterious substance that "'may render' the food injurious to health."[68]

In the 1992 Planned Introductions, the FDA acknowledged the food industry's long-standing practice of consulting with the FDA in the early stages of developing food through new technologies. This practice, although not required, allowed the agency to identify and address issues regarding foods and food ingredients before they were marketed.[69] The FDA expressed its expectation that such consul-

tations would continue with regard to bioengineered foods.[70] In 1996, the FDA issued a guidance on procedures for those consultations.[71] A company that intends to commercialize a bioengineered food meets with the FDA at an "initial consultation" to identify and discuss possible issues regarding safety, nutritional, or other regulatory issues. A "final consultation" is held once the company believes it has developed the data and information necessary to address issues or concerns raised by the FDA.[72] The FDA believes that, through the end of the year 2000, all developers of bioengineered foods commercially marketed in the United States have consulted with the agency before marketing the food.[73]

Although the FDA's 1992 Planned Introductions has not been popular with some consumer groups and has spawned legislative efforts to change the statutory framework,[74] it has been upheld in court.[75] Nonetheless, the FDA is aware of continuing consumer concern, and in January 2001, issued two documents (discussed below) that, although based on the 1992 Planned Introductions, appear to be an attempt to go further in addressing consumers' concerns. The first document is a draft guidance to industry on issues that may arise with regard to labeling food as made with or without ingredients developed through biotechnology. The second is a proposed rule that would require developers of bioengineered foods to submit data and information to the FDA 120 days before commercial distribution of such foods, giving the FDA an opportunity to evaluate whether (1) the bioengineered food is as safe as comparable food, and (2) the proposed use complies with FFDCA requirements.

1. Draft Guidance on Labeling

In January 2001, the FDA issued a draft guidance for industry regarding labeling of bioengineered foods.[76] In the draft, the FDA reaffirms that special labeling is not required for such foods because there is "no basis for concluding that bioengineered foods differ from other foods in any meaningful or uniform way, or that, as a class, foods developed by the new techniques present any different or greater safety concern than foods developed by traditional plant breeding."[77]

Nonetheless, the draft guidance sets out several scenarios under which a bioengineered food might be mislabeled. For example, because a food must be labeled with a common or

61. Id.

62. Premarket Notice Concerning Bioengineered Foods; Proposed Rule, 66 Fed. Reg. 4706, 4717 n.12 (Jan. 18, 2001) [hereinafter Premarket Notice Proposed Rule].

63. Statement of Policy: Foods Derived From New Plant Varieties, 57 Fed. Reg. 22984 (May 29, 1992).

64. Id.

65. Id. at 22985.

66. Id.

67. Id. at 22990.

68. Id. (quoting FFDCA §402(a)(1), 21 U.S.C. §342(a)(1)).

69. Id. at 22991.

70. Id.

71. FDA, GUIDANCE ON CONSULTATION PROCEDURES: FOODS DERIVED FROM NEW PLANT VARIETIES (June 1996; revised Oct. 1997 to reflect organizational changes), available at http://www.cfsan.fda.gov/~/rd/consulpr.html (last visited July 20, 2001).

72. Id. §II.

73. Premarket Notice Proposed Rule, supra note 62; see also FDA, LIST OF COMPLETED CONSULTATIONS ON BIOENGINEERED FOODS, available at http://www.cfsan.fda.gov/~lrd/biocon.html (last visited July 20, 2001).

74. See, e.g., Genetically Engineered Food Right-to-Know Act, H.R. 3377, 106th Cong. (2000).

75. See Alliance for Bio-Integrity v. Shalala, 116 F. Supp. 2d 166 (D.D.C. 2000).

76. Draft Guidance for Industry: Voluntary Labeling Indicating Whether Foods Have or Have Not Been Developed Using Bioengineering; Availability, 66 Fed. Reg. 4839 (Jan. 18, 2001).

77. FDA, GUIDANCE FOR INDUSTRY: VOLUNTARY LABELING INDICATING WHETHER FOODS HAVE OR HAVE NOT BEEN DEVELOPED USING BIOENGINEERING 2 (2001) [hereinafter LABELING GUIDANCE].

usual name or an appropriately descriptive term,[78] the FDA notes that there may be instances in which a bioengineered food is "significantly different from" its traditional counterpart such that the common or usual name does not adequately describe the food, and the name must be changed to describe the difference.[79] As an example, the FDA has suggested that the term "high oleic acid soybean oil" would be required for a soybean oil that has been bioengineered to reduce the amount of saturated fat and, as a result, contains more oleic acid than traditional soybean oil.[80]

More generally, because a food can be misbranded if its labeling omits material information,[81] the FDA identifies certain circumstances in which labeling may require affirmative disclosures:

  ● If there is an issue regarding how a food is used or the consequences of its use;
  ● If the bioengineered food has a significantly different nutritional property; or
  ● If the bioengineered food contains an allergen that consumers would not expect to be in the food.[82]

The FDA understands that, notwithstanding the agency's conclusion that bioengineered foods do not require special labeling, manufacturers may want to respond to consumers' perceived interest in knowing whether a food product is the result of genetic modification. With that in mind, the draft guidance identifies (and in some cases, addresses) issues that are implicated by a decision to label a food as genetically modified or (the more likely scenario) to claim that it is not the result of genetic modification. The FDA's expressed goal is to help manufacturers avoid labeling that is false or misleading, either because of statements made or the omission of material information.[83]

With regard to foods that are bioengineered or that contain ingredients produced from bioengineered food, the FDA offers the following:

  ● A statement that the food or an ingredient is "genetically engineered" or "produced using biotechnology" is not necessary, but if used, is not likely to be misleading.
  ● A change in texture that makes a "significant difference" in the finished product that is noticeable to the consumer may need to be described on the label. If the difference would not be noticed by a consumer, however (a change made to facilitate processing, for example), it could actually be misleading to say that the food has been changed. In that instance, the FDA recommends that, if the change is identified, its purpose should be described to avoid misleading consumers, e.g., "These tomatoes were genetically engineered to improve texture for processing."
  ● It is permissible, but not necessary, to state that a food has been genetically altered to increase yield, but if such a statement is made, there must be sub-

stantiation of the stated difference.
  ● Care should be taken to make sure that statements about a bioengineered ingredient are understood to be about the ingredient, not the entire food.
  ● A statement that an ingredient has been nutritionally improved likely would be misleading if the food contains only a small amount of the ingredient, such that the overall nutritional quality of the food is not significantly improved.[84]

As to foods that are not the result of bioengineering, the FDA is concerned that terms such as "not genetically modified" or "GMO free" are in many instances not technically accurate, and may be misleading. Because genetic modification includes much of what is done in traditional plant breeding, not just bioengineering, a food that was not bioengineered may nonetheless be genetically modified. Similarly, because most foods do not contain organisms (seeds and yogurt are notable exceptions), a statement that a food is free of (genetically modified) organisms can be misleading, in the FDA's eyes.[85]

The FDA believes consumers understand a claim that a product is "free" of bioengineered material to mean that "zero" bioengineered material is present. Recognizing "the potential for adventitious presence of bioengineered material" and noting the absence of an agreed-upon threshold above which the terms should not be used, the FDA considers the term "free" to be possibly false or misleading. The agency suggests that manufacturers avoid the term, unless it is used in a context that makes clear that a "zero level" is not implied. As an alternative, the FDA suggests a statement that a food or its ingredients were "not developed using bioengineering."[86]

With regard to claims that a product is not the result of bioengineering, the FDA also suggests the following:

  ● A statement as to the absence of bioengineering is misleading if it implies that the food is superior to, e.g., safer or of higher quality, foods that are the result of bioengineering.
  ● A statement that an ingredient is not bioengineered may be misleading if the food contains another ingredient that is bioengineered.
  ● A statement that a food is not bioengineered may be misleading if no bioengineered varieties of that category of food are marketed.
  ● A statement that a food is not bioengineered should be substantiated. The FDA recognizes that although validated testing is the preferred method of substantiating such a claim, it is not always available or reliable. In such circumstances, manufacturers may be able to rely on careful documentation of the source of such foods, along with special handling to segregate bioengineered and nonbioengineered foods.
  ● Under regulations published by the USDA in December 2000, food identified as "organic" cannot be produced using biotechnology, and organic foods must be segregated from nonorganic foods.[87]

78. FFDCA §403(i), 21 U.S.C. §343(i).

79. LABELING GUIDANCE, supra note 77, at 4.

80. Id. at 8.

81. FFDCA §§201(n), 403(a)(1), 21 U.S.C. §§321(n), 343(a)(1).

82. LABELING GUIDANCE, supra note 77, at 4.

83. Id. at 6-7.

84. Id. at 7-10.

85. Id. at 11-12.

86. Id. at 12-13.

87. National Organic Program; Final Rule, 65 Fed. Reg. 80548 (Dec. 21, 2000).

In light of these regulations, the FDA concludes that food that meets the standards to be "certified organic" would also be able to be identified as not being produced using bioengineering.[88]

2. Proposed Rule on Premarket Notice

The same day it announced the availability of a draft guidance on labeling of bioengineered food, the FDA published a proposed rule that would require submission of data and information 120 days before placing on the market any plant-derived bioengineered food for humans or animals.[89] Even as it proposed these new obligations, the FDA reiterated its view, expressed in the 1992 *Planned Introductions*, that transferred genetic material can be presumed to be GRAS.[90] Nonetheless, pointing to ever-advancing technology, the agency identified several areas in which there may be regulatory issues, some of which are also raised in the labeling guidance. They include:

- Recognizing that rDNA technology now permits the introduction of genetic material from a wider range of sources than previously possible, there is a greater likelihood that a bioengineered food will contain substances that are not GRAS because they are significantly different from substances historically consumed as food, or present at a significantly higher level.
- There is the possibility of transferring a food allergen from one food into another food in which the allergen would not be expected, which could make the food misbranded, and perhaps adulterated, even with labeling disclosures.
- A bioengineered food could be different from its nonbioengineered counterparts in a way that is sufficiently significant to require a different common or usual name. As an example, the FDA points to the use of rDNA technology to introduce multiple genes to generate new metabolic pathways that are intended to lead to the synthesis of substances not normally present in the host plant.
- The risk of creating unintended changes to the characteristics of a food by introducing mutations into the plant's native genetic material raises potential adulteration or misbranding issues.
- Most of the previously reviewed genetic modifications have involved agronomic traits, i.e., characteristics of the plant, not of the food produced by the plant. The FDA is seeing more proposed modifications that are intended to modify the food itself, such as altered protein quality, increased carotenoid content, increased fruit solids, altered fiber quality, and increased fruit sweetness. Such changes are more likely than those in the past to raise regulatory issues.[91]

With the expressed goal of "enhanced agency awareness of all [bioengineered] foods intended for commercial distri-

bution,"[92] the FDA proposed that a premarket biotechnology notice (PBN) be required 120 days before commercial distribution of a plant-derived bioengineered food. The PBN could be submitted by any person who is responsible for the development, distribution, importation, or sale of the food, but the FDA expects seed developers and purveyors to be the reporting entity in most instances.[93] A PBN would be required for any bioengineered food unless:

- The food derives from a plant line that represents a transformation event that has been addressed in a previous PBN;
- The use or application of the food has been addressed in a previous notice to the FDA; and
- The FDA has issued a letter demonstrating that the agency has evaluated, and has no questions about, the use or application.[94]

Although EPA, not the FDA, has jurisdiction over pesticides and pesticide residues in food, a PBN would be required for a bioengineered food derived from a plant modified to contain a pesticidal substance. The FDA reasons that this is necessary for the agency to be able to meet its responsibilities for issues beyond those associated with the pesticide, such as unexpected or unintended compositional changes.[95]

As proposed by the FDA, the components of a PBN would include:

- A signed statement by the notifier that (1) the bioengineered food is as safe as comparable food, (2) the intended use complies with all applicable requirements, and (3) the PBN is a representative and balanced submission that includes favorable and unfavorable information pertinent to safety, nutritional, or other regulatory issues.[96]
- A report of the status of the food at other U.S. federal agencies, as well as whether the food is or has been the subject of review by any foreign government and, if so, a description of that review.[97]
- Data or information about the method of development, including characterization of the parent plant, construction of the vector used in the transformation of the parent plant, characterization of the inserted genetic material, and data or information related to the inheritance and genetic stability of the inserted material.[98]
- A discussion about any newly inserted genes that encode antibiotic resistance.[99]
- Data or information about substances introduced into, or modified in, the food, including their identify and function, the level of them in the food, di-

88. LABELING GUIDANCE, *supra* note 77, at 13-16.

89. Premarket Notice Proposed Rule, *supra* note 62.

90. *Id.* at 4709.

91. *Id.* at 4709-11.

92. *Id.* at 4712. The FDA notes that approximately 45% of U.S. plant-derived food is imported, and the percentage is increasing. *Id.* The proposed requirements would apply to bioengineered food manufactured in the United States, as well as foods intended for import into the United States. *Id.*

93. *Id.* at 4712, 4730 (proposed 21 C.F.R. §192.1(c)).

94. *Id.* at 4713, 4730 (proposed 21 C.F.R. §192.5).

95. *Id.* at 4713.

96. *Id.* at 4717-18, 4732 (proposed 21 C.F.R. §192.25(a)).

97. *Id.* at 4718-19, 4732 (proposed 21 C.F.R. §192.25(c)).

98. *Id.* at 4719, 4732-33 (proposed 21 C.F.R. §192.25(d)).

99. *Id.* at 4719, 4733 (proposed 21 C.F.R. §192.25(e)).

etary exposure to them, and the potential that an introduced protein will be an allergen.[100]

● Data or information about the bioengineered food, including an explanation of the basis for the conclusion that the bioengineered food is as safe as comparable foods and complies with all applicable requirements of the FFDCA.[101]

The FDA expects to have reviewed each PBN within 120 days, and to respond with a letter that either states that the agency has no questions regarding the submitter's view that the bioengineered food is as safe as comparable food and is otherwise lawful, or explains why the FDA has concluded that the PBN does not provide a basis for that view. The regulations would also provide for a 120-day extension of the review and response period. If the FDA either needs more time or concludes that the PBN does not support the requisite conclusion, the letter would state the agency's expectation that the food not be marketed.[102]

Because the rule would require premarket notification, not a requirement of approval, the marketing of a bioengineered food in the absence of the FDA's conclusion that the PBN is adequate would not be a violation of the FFDCA. In such a circumstance, however, it would be the FDA's intention to vigorously pursue the product as adulterated or misbranded.[103]

The FDA expects to be able to respond within 120 days because it anticipates that, before submitting a PBN, most companies will have been communicating with the agency in a presubmission consultation program that the proposed regulations would encourage, but not require. It is the agency's expectation that, by the time it submits a PBN, the company will be well aware of what information the FDA will need to come to the desired conclusion.[104]

Given that one of the goals of the PBN/presubmission consultation program is to increase "transparency" in the process of regulating bioengineered foods,[105] it is not surprising that the FDA expects to make publicly available much of the materials it obtains in a PBN submission and during the presubmission consultations.[106] The FDA believes that, in most cases, the data or information provided during a presubmission consultation or in a PBN would not be considered trade secrets or confidential commercial information.[107] The FDA also intends to make public the text of the agency's evaluation of each PBN, as well as the response letter.[108]

D. FDA Enforcement

Although the FDA typically enforces compliance with the FFDCA administratively, the agency also has authority to pursue civil and criminal remedies in court. Section 301 of the FFDCA enumerates acts that are prohibited; with regard to food, they include:

● Introducing or delivering for introduction into interstate commerce an adulterated or misbranded food;
● Adulterating or misbranding a food in interstate commerce;
● Receiving in interstate commerce an adulterated or misbranded food, and delivering or proffering delivery thereof;
● Refusing to permit the FDA to copy records of interstate shipment;
● Refusing to permit the FDA to inspect a warehouse, factory, or establishment in which food is manufactured, processed, packed, or held;
● Manufacturing an adulterated or misbranded food; or
● Doing any act with respect to a food that causes the food to be adulterated or misbranded, if the act is done while the food is held for sale after shipment in interstate commerce.[109]

The FDA often obtains information regarding violations through establishment inspections and record reviews. Interstate carriers and anyone who receives food in interstate commerce or holds articles of food received in interstate commerce must, upon written request, allow the FDA to review and copy records of movement in interstate commerce.[110] The FDA also has authority to enter and inspect a factory, warehouse, or establishment in which food is manufactured, processed, packed, or held.[111]

The FDA Form 483, the form for reporting inspectional observations that is presented to a company official at the close of an inspection, is often a means for the FDA to communicate about alleged violations. The agency also sends "warning letters," which are an informal but powerful way of informing a company of practices that it considers violative. When such informal methods seem inadequate, however, the agency has other avenues of redress. The FDA can file suit in federal court and obtain an injunction to restrain violations of FFDCA §301,[112] or for seizure, condemnation, and destruction of an adulterated or misbranded product.[113] Similarly, if a food offered for import into the United States appears to be (among other things) adulterated or misbranded, it may be detained and, unless the FDA agrees to means of bringing the product into compliance (which is not always an available option), the product will be refused admission and must be exported or destroyed.[114]

100. *Id.* at 4719-20, 4733 (proposed 21 C.F.R. §192.25(f)).
101. *Id.* at 4720-21, 4733 (proposed 21 C.F.R. §192.25(g)).
102. *Id.* at 4722-23, 4733 (proposed 21 C.F.R. §192.30).
103. *Id.* at 4722.
104. *Id.* at 4713-14, 4730-31 (proposed 21 C.F.R. §192.10). Even if a bioengineered plant is being developed for a non-food use, such as encoding pharmaceutical proteins or oral vaccines, the FDA encourages the developer to participate in the consultation program if there is the potential for the plant to inadvertently enter the food supply. *Id.* at 4714.
105. *Id.* at 4708.
106. *Id.* at 4714, 4731 (proposed 21 C.F.R. §192.10(c)-(d)), 4723-24, 4733-34 (proposed 21 C.F.R. §192.40).
107. *Id.* at 4714, 4723.
108. *Id.* at 4723-24, 4734 (proposed 21 C.F.R. §192.40(e)).

109. FFDCA §301(a)-(k), 21 U.S.C. §331(a)-(k).
110. *Id.* §703, 21 U.S.C. §373. Evidence obtained from a review conducted pursuant to a written request cannot be used in a criminal prosecution. *Id.*
111. *Id.* §704, 21 U.S.C. §374.
112. *Id.* §302, 21 U.S.C. §332. There are certain exceptions not relevant here.
113. *Id.* §304, 21 U.S.C. §334.
114. *Id.* §801, 21 U.S.C. §381.

With regard to drugs and medical devices, the FDA has also had some recent success obtaining civil judgments for sale of violative products under a theory of restitution or disgorgement.[115] Although this may not yet have been pursued with regard to a food product, it should be available to the agency under the same theory. Additionally, any violation of FFDCA §301 can be a criminal matter. A first violation is a misdemeanor, punishable with up to one year in prison and a $1,000 fine.[116] A violation committed with intent to defraud or mislead is a felony that can lead to a three-year prison term and a $10,000 fine, as is any second violation, i.e., after a first conviction.[117] It is well established that criminal liability extends to individual employees and officers.[118]

---

115. *See, e.g.,* United States v. Universal Mgmt. Servs., 191 F.3d 750, 760-64 (6th Cir. 1999).

116. FFDCA §303(a)(1), 21 U.S.C. §333(a)(1). There is an exception involving labeling or advertising for vitamins and minerals that is not relevant. *Id.* §303(d), 21 U.S.C. §333(d).

117. *Id.* §303(a)(2), 21 U.S.C. §333(a)(2).

118. *See, e.g.,* United States v. Park, 421 U.S. 658 (1975).

CHAPTER 5

I. EPA and FIFRA

A. Statutory Authorities

1. FIFRA

FIFRA regulates the manufacture, importation, sale, and use of pesticides anywhere in the United States. FIFRA is the primary federal statute for regulation of pesticides, including all antimicrobial products, all insecticides and insect repellents, all fungicides, herbicides, and vertebrate control agents, whether for agricultural, industrial, institutional or household use, and whether they consist of chemical or biological agents. In general, FIFRA is designed to provide premarket clearance of pesticide products and post-market surveillance of pesticides and pesticidal devices to ensure that they cause no unreasonable adverse effects on human health or the environment. EPA's regulations implementing FIFRA are codified at 40 C.F.R. Parts 150-189.

2. The FFDCA

The FFDCA[1] also affects the sale and use of pesticides by requiring that EPA establish a "tolerance" for pesticides used in connection with food or animal feed. A "tolerance" is the maximum level of a pesticide residue that may be present in food or animal feed. EPA will register a pesticide for use in connection with food or animal feed only if: (1) EPA has established a tolerance for the pesticide and, when the pesticide is used as directed, any residue from the pesticide falls within the tolerance; (2) EPA has granted an exemption from the tolerance requirement; or (3) the pesticide is GRAS.[2]

Both FIFRA and the FFDCA were significantly amended by the Food Quality Protection Act (FQPA), Public Law No.104-170, which was signed into law in August 1996. The FQPA requires that EPA consider a number of new factors in deciding whether to permit the marketing of a pesticide product, including the cumulative effect of pesticides.

B. The FIFRA Framework

Essentially, FIFRA requires that all pesticides sold or distributed in the United States must first be registered with EPA.[3] A "pesticide" is defined in FIFRA as any substance or mixture which is intended for preventing, destroying, repelling, or mitigating a pest or for use as a plant regulator, defoliant, or desiccant and any nitrogen stabilizer.[4] A "pest" is defined as any insect, rodent, nematode, fungus, weed, or any other form of terrestrial or aquatic plant or animal life or virus, bacteria, or other microorganism, except microorganisms on or in living man or other living animals.[5]

1. Intent Governs

It is not the nature of the substance but its intended use which determines whether a product is a pesticide.[6] In determining intent, EPA considers three factors. A person *intends* that a substance be used as a pesticide if:

- The person who sells or distributes the substance claims, states, or implies that the substance can or should be used as a pesticide or that it contains an active ingredient and that it can be used to manufacture a pesticide;
- The substance contains an active ingredient and has no significant commercially valuable use as sold other than use for a pesticidal purpose or to manufacture a pesticide; and/or
- The person who sells or distributes the substance has actual or constructive knowledge that the substance will be used or is intended for use as a pesticide.[7]

2. Active and Inert Ingredients

The term "pesticide" may refer only to an "active ingredient" which is used in the formulation of other products. An active ingredient is one that gives a product its pesticidal effect.[8] The term "pesticide" may also refer to a formulation that combines one or more "active ingredients" with one or more "inert ingredients." In conventional chemical pesticides, an inert ingredient (now referred to as "other ingredient") is not added for pesticidal effect, but gives the product other essential qualities, such as solubility, stability, spray capability, or fragrance. Most often, the term "pesticide" will refer to a combination of actives and inerts. Pesticides are regulated primarily on the basis of their active ingredients. For a formulated product, administrative burdens and registration data requirements are considerably reduced if the source of the active ingredient is already registered.

However, if an inert has never been used in a registered pesticide, EPA may require data sufficient to evaluate the risks associated with its use, including product chemistry, toxicology, environmental toxicity, and environmental fate data. Data on FIFRA inert ingredients is frequently generated under TSCA, since inert ingredients typically have multiple non-FIFRA uses as well.

A "manufacturing use" product is registered only for the purpose of formulating other products. An "end-use" product will typically contain both actives and inerts and bear labeling with specific instructions for using and applying

---

1. 21 U.S.C. §§301-397.

2. 40 C.F.R. §152.112.

3. 7 U.S.C. §136a(a), ELR Stat. FIFRA §3(a).

4. *Id.* §136(u), ELR Stat. FIFRA §2(u).

5. *Id.* §136(t), ELR Stat. FIFRA §2(t).

6. 40 C.F.R. §152.15.

7. *Id.*

8. *Id.* §152.3.

the product. Its labeling will not authorize use of the product, nor may it be used, to formulate other pesticide products. A pesticide registration will apply to a single pesticide product or formulation with a particular approved use, although EPA may approve several alternative formulations in a single registration. Generally, any change in the number, type, or percentages of ingredients, or any change in intended use of the product, will require a separate or amended registration.

3. The Registration Standard

EPA will register a pesticide if it determines, after consideration of any restrictions that may be placed on its use, that: (1) the pesticide is effective and warrants the proposed claims for it; (2) the labeling and other materials required to be submitted comply with FIFRA; and (3) the expected use of the pesticide will not generally cause "unreasonable adverse effects on the environment."[9] The term "unreasonable adverse effects on the environment" is defined in the Act as

> (1) any unreasonable risk to man or the environment, taking into account the economic, social, and environmental costs and benefits of the use of any pesticide, or (2) a human dietary risk from residues that result from a use of a pesticide in or on any food inconsistent with the standard under [§] 408 of the [FFDCA].[10]

The second criterion, relating to dietary risk from residues, was added in 1996 by the FQPA and applies to pesticides that may result in residues in or on food.

In general, a pesticide registration application must be accompanied by a Confidential Statement of Formula and by test data which demonstrates that the product will perform its intended function without unreasonable adverse effects on the environment. Test data is required to be generated consistent with EPA's "good laboratory practices," as specified in 40 C.F.R. Part 160.

4. Data Requirements and Data Compensation

EPA has prescribed in considerable detail the studies which must be conducted in support of registration and, in various sets of guidelines,[11] has identified the protocols for each study. Pesticide registrations will typically require product chemistry data and a set of six acute toxicity tests and may require considerably more in terms of chronic health effects, metabolism, mutagenicity, teratogenicity and reproductive effects, environmental fate, toxicity to birds, fish, plants and other organisms, residue chemistry and occupational and nonoccupational exposure, depending on the composition and use pattern.

Tables which detail the data requirements for particular uses and types of products are found at 40 C.F.R. Part 158. Some data are required for the active ingredient and some are required for the complete end-use formulation. Active ingredients are generally registered in anticipation of certain markets and uses and are tested accordingly. Data re-

quirements are most burdensome for a pesticide that contains a new active or that uses an active in a way (on a pest or site) that has not already been authorized. Part 158 includes tables that separately identify data requirements for biochemical pesticides, which are naturally occurring substances that control pests by nontoxic means, §158.690, and microbial pesticides, in which a microorganism is the active ingredient, §158.740, which are discussed below

As an alternative to generating and submitting data, FIFRA permits an applicant to cite to data that appears in public literature or that has previously been submitted to EPA by other registrants. Such use of data submitted by others is permitted only subject to the use compensation provisions of the Act.[12] If a new registrant wants to rely on data submitted in support of a registration containing an active ingredient first registered after 1978, EPA may not consider these data in support of the new registration for a period of 10 years after the initial registration unless the new registrant has written permission from the original data submitter.[13] This period may be extended for certain "minor use" registrations. Otherwise, for a period of 15 years after submission of data in support of a registration, EPA may consider such data to support a new registration, without the permission of the original data submitter, but only if the new registrant has certified to the Agency that he/she has made an offer to compensate the original data submitter.[14]

Some registrants may qualify for a "formulator's exemption" from certain data requirements. If an applicant does not manufacture the pesticide ingredients, but manufactures a pesticide product using registered pesticides manufactured by and purchased from other companies, that applicant will not be required to submit or cite to data pertaining to the purchased product and will be exempt from the related data compensation requirements.[15] This exemption applies only to data requirements relating to the purchased, registered material. Formulators must still submit data, e.g., a package of acute toxicity data, product chemistry data, for their own end-use product.

In addition, "me-too" applications for registration may qualify for expedited review under §3(c)(3)(B) of FIFRA. A "me-too" application is one for registration of a product that is "substantially similar" or identical to another EPA-registered product—not only in terms of active and inert ingredients, but also with respect to use patterns and use directions.[16]

5. Labels and Labeling

Pesticide labels and labeling must accurately communicate important precautions and instructions to the user so that each product is effective without causing unreasonable adverse effects to humans or the environment.[17] The term "la-

9. 7 U.S.C §136a(c)(5), ELR Stat. FIFRA §3(c)(5).

10. Id. §136(bb), ELR Stat. FIFRA §2(bb).

11. See U.S. EPA, Pesticide Assessments Guidelines (1999), available at http://www.epa.gov/pesticides/ (last modified Oct. 5, 2001) (these guidelines are in the process of being replaced by Harmonized Guidelines).

12. 7 U.S.C. §136a(c)(1)(F)(i)-(vi), ELR Stat. FIFRA §3(c)(1)(F)(i)-(vi).

13. Id. §136a(c)(1)(F)(i), ELR Stat. FIFRA §3(c)(1)(F)(i).

14. Id. §136a(c)(1)(F)(iii), ELR Stat. FIFRA §3(c)(1)(F)(iii).

15. Id. §136a(c)(2)(D), ELR Stat. FIFRA §3(c)(2)(D).

16. 40 C.F.R. §152.113(b).

17. EPA's requirements and policies governing pesticide labels and labeling are specified in the regulations at 40 C.F.R. §156.10, in Pesticide Regulation (P.R.) Notices, and in various decision documents related to specific chemicals, including Special Reviews, Registration Standards, and Reregistration Eligibility Decisions. To ensure

bel" means the written, printed, or graphic matter on, or attached to, the pesticide or device, or any of its containers or wrappers.[18] The term "labeling" includes all labels and all other written, printed, or graphic material which accompanies the product when sold or distributed, or to which reference is made on the product's label or in literature accompanying the product.[19] All pesticides must have EPA-approved labels that identify the active ingredients, describe the hazards that the pesticide poses, and provide directions on its proper use.[20] Copies of draft proposed labeling must accompany the registration application. Once approved, the label becomes a legally enforceable document. Moreover, any use of the pesticide that is inconsistent with the EPA-approved label is unlawful.[21]

A "misbranded" pesticide or device may not be sold, distributed, or offered for sale.[22] A pesticide or device is "misbranded" if its labeling "bears any statement, design, or graphic design relative thereto or to its ingredients which is false or misleading in any particular."[23] This includes both pesticidal and nonpesticidal claims. A product is misbranded if label information detracts from or obscures required label language, if the manufacturer cannot support any claims with test data, or if required information is omitted. To reduce the possibility that users will be misled, EPA generally forbids certain language, including the words "safe," "harmless," "not toxic to humans or pets," or "contains all natural ingredients."[24]

6. FIFRA-Authorized Exemptions—Section 25(b)

Section 25(b) of FIFRA authorizes EPA to exempt any pesticide from the requirements of FIFRA if: (1) EPA determines that the pesticide is adequately regulated by another federal agency, or (2) EPA determines that it is of a character not requiring FIFRA regulation, i.e., poses no unreasonable risk.[25] EPA has determined that two classes of substances are exempt because they are adequately regulated by another federal agency (40 C.F.R. §152.20):

- Certain biological control agents, except eucaryotic and procaryotic microorganisms and viruses[26]; and

---

consistency of interpretation among staff within the Agency, EPA has issued a *Label Review Manual*.

18. 7 U.S.C. §136(p)(1), ELR STAT. FIFRA §2(p)(1).

19. *Id.* §136(p)(2), ELR STAT. FIFRA §2(p)(2). In general, states may not impose any requirements for labeling or packaging that are different from those required under FIFRA. *Id.* §136v(b), ELR STAT. FIFRA §24(b). However, the definition of "labeling" has been narrowly interpreted in this regard so that additional statements or warnings are not within the definition of "labeling" (and, thus, not preempted) if they are posted at the point of sale or on affected property or if they consist of newspaper notification of pesticide use. *See, e.g.,* Chemical Specialties Mfrs. Ass'n v. Allenby, 958 F.2d 941, 22 ELR 20822 (9th Cir. 1990), *cert. denied*, 113 S. Ct. 80 (1992) (Proposition 65 warnings posted at point of sale).

20. 40 C.F.R. §156.10(a)(1).

21. 7 U.S.C. §136j(a)(2)(G), ELR STAT. FIFRA §12(a)(2)(G).

22. *Id.* §136j(a)(1)(E), ELR STAT. FIFRA §12(a)(1)(E).

23. *Id.* §136(q), ELR STAT. FIFRA §19(q).

24. 40 C.F.R. §156.10(a)(5).

25. 7 U.S.C. §136w(b), ELR STAT. FIFRA §25(b).

26. As discussed below, a "biological control agent" is "any living organism applied to or introduced into the environment that is intended

- Products that are offered solely for human use and which are regulated under the new drug provisions of the FFDCA or under the FDA's final monographs.

Section 152.25 of the regulations describes exemptions for pesticides which have been determined by EPA to be of a character not requiring FIFRA regulation. For example, if a material has been treated with a pesticide in order to protect the material itself against deterioration, and no claim is made of pest mitigation beyond the material, e.g., paints treated with antimicrobials for in-can preservation, the material is not a pesticide.[27] Materials that are advertised as being naturally pest-resistant, e.g., redwood, cypress, are not pesticides, as long as claims are not made for pest mitigation beyond the material itself.[28]

7. Pesticidal Devices

Registration is not required for a device. A device is any instrument or contrivance (other than a firearm) which uses physical or mechanical means to trap, destroy, repel, or mitigate any pest (other than microorganisms on or in living man or animals). Devices do not include equipment used in the application of pesticides, such as tamper-resistant bait boxes for rodenticides.[29] However, if an article incorporates a substance or a mixture of substances intended to prevent, destroy, repel, or mitigate any pest, it is a pesticide, not a device. Thus, an air filter which physically traps microorganisms is a device. An air filter which is effective against microorganisms because it contains or has been treated with a pesticide substance will be classified as a pesticide.

A device is not subject to the registration requirements of FIFRA. Devices are, however, subject to the labeling requirements of 7 U.S.C. §136(q)(1) and 40 C.F.R. Part 156 and devices are subject to the establishment registration and reporting requirements of 7 U.S.C. §136e and 40 C.F.R. Part 167.

8. The Registrant's Continuing Obligation

Even after registration, EPA may determine that additional data are needed to support continued registration of the pesticide and require all affected registrants to provide that additional data.[30] Moreover, §6(a)(2) of FIFRA imposes a continuing reporting obligation on registrants who obtain new information about their pesticides. That section requires that, "[i]f at any time after the registration of a pesticide the registrant has additional factual information regarding un-

---

to function as a pesticide against another organism declared to be a pest." 40 C.F.R. §152.3(i). The exemption for biological control agents does *not* apply to microorganisms. Eucaryotes (protozoa, algae, fungi), procaryotes (bacteria), and viruses are not included in the exemption. This essentially covers the entire field of microorganisms. Rather, the exemption covers "macroorganisms" used as biological control agents because these are adequately addressed by other federal agencies such as the USDA's APHIS and the DOI. *See* Statement of Policy, Plant Pesticides Subject to FIFRA and FFDCA, 59 Fed. Reg. 60496 (Nov. 23, 1994).

27. 40 C.F.R. §152.25(a).

28. *Id.* §152.25(f).

29. 7 U.S.C. §136(h), ELR STAT. FIFRA §2(h); 40 C.F.R. §152.500.

30. *Id.* §136a(c)(2)(B)(i), ELR STAT. FIFRA §3(c)(2)(B)(i).

reasonable adverse effects on the environment of the pesticide, the registrants shall submit such information to the Administrator."[31] Failure to do so is a violation of FIFRA, which can lead to significant penalties.[32] Thus, §6(a)(2) requires the reporting of information if that information is: (a) additional, (b) factual, and (c) relates to unreasonable adverse effects on the environment of the pesticide.[33]

9. Experimental Use Permits

Because persons intending to register a pesticide are frequently in the position of needing to gather data on (and thus needing to use) a pesticide that is not yet registered, or not registered for a proposed new use, FIFRA authorizes EPA to issue "experimental use permits" (EUPs). An EUP enables the registrant to test the pesticide and develop the data necessary to support the registration.[34] It is presumed that an EUP is not required when the experimental use is limited to laboratory or greenhouse testing or limited replicated field trials under certain specified acreage limitations and only when the purpose is to assess the pesticide's efficacy, toxicity, or other properties.[35] However, the regulations require notification to EPA of small-scale field testing involving intentional environmental introduction of certain microbial pesticides. Such prior notification is required for microbial pesticides whose pesticidal properties have been imparted or enhanced by the introduction of genetic material that has been deliberately modified or nonindigenous microbial pesticides that have not been acted upon by the USDA.[36]

C. Regulation of Pesticides That Are Derived From Natural Materials

1. Biopesticides

In 1994, the Biopesticides and Pollution Prevention Division was established within the OPP to facilitate the registration of "biopesticides" or "biological pesticides." These are pesticides that are derived from natural materials such a plants, animals, and microorganisms. Biopesticides tend to pose fewer risks than conventional pesticides. They tend to be effective in small quantities, to decompose quickly after use, and they generally affect only the target pest, reducing concerns that nontarget organisms will be adversely impacted. For these reasons, EPA generally requires less data to register a biopesticide than to register a conventional pesticide.

There are three categories of biopesticides. A "microbial pesticide" is one in which a microorganism, such as a fungus, virus, or bacterium, is the active ingredient.[37] There are fungi that can control cockroaches and bacteria that control plant diseases. The most widely know microbial pesticide is the bacterium Bt which acts by producing a protein that kills the larvae of certain insects.

A "biochemical pesticide" is a naturally occurring substance that controls pests by nontoxic mechanisms.[38] These include hormones, natural plant regulators, and insect pheromones. The latter interfere with the growth or mating of an insect. Because it can be difficult to determine whether a natural pesticide is controlling the pest by means of a nontoxic mode of action, EPA has established a committee to determine whether a pesticide is a biochemical pesticide.

Finally, "plant pesticides" or "plant-incorporated protectants" are pesticidal substances that plants produce from genetic material that is added to the plant. They also include the genetic material that is responsible for that pesticidal capability. Bt is also an example within this category. Scientists can take the gene for the Bt pesticidal protein and introduce it into a plant's own genetic material. Once that is done, the plant itself, instead of the Bt bacteria, will manufacture the substance that destroys the pest.

2. Plant Pesticides or Plant-Incorporated Protectants

Because the statutory definition of pesticide does not depend on the process by which the product is made, only the intent to use it as a pesticide, EPA has extended its FIFRA regulatory control to genetically engineered pesticides. In November 1994, EPA issued a set of five *Federal Register* proposals that together described the Agency's regulatory approach to plants which have been genetically modified with rDNA techniques to resist pests or disease.[39] Because these substances are "intended for preventing, destroying, repelling, or mitigating any pest," EPA's proposals indicated that the Agency would regulate them as "plant pesticides," which were defined in a proposed rule as "a pesticidal substance that is produced in a living plant and the genetic materials necessary for the production of the pesticidal substance, where the pesticidal substance is intended for use in the living plant."[40]

Two years after EPA's issuance of its proposed rule, Congress enacted the FQPA of 1996, which altered some aspects of the process for assessing food safety of pesticide chemical residues. EPA issued supplemental *Federal Register* notices addressing this aspect of its regulatory approach,[41] and made a final plant pesticides rule available for promulgation in the *Federal Register* in January 2001. Publication of this final rule in the *Federal Register* was delayed by a January 20, 2001 White House memorandum from the Bush Administration which imposed a temporary ban on new regulations. It finally appeared in the *Federal Register* on July 19, 2001.[42] Nevertheless, since 1995, EPA has used the basic approach reflected in these documents to register 11 plant pesticides.[43] This is discussed in greater detail below.

---

31. *Id.* §136d(a)(2), ELR Stat. FIFRA §6(a)(2).

32. *Id.* §136j(a)(2), ELR Stat. FIFRA §12(a)(2).

33. *Id.* §136a(a)(2), ELR Stat. FIFRA §3(a)(2).

34. *Id.* §136c, ELR Stat. FIFRA §5; 40 C.F.R. pt. 172.

35. 40 C.F.R. §172.3.

36. *Id.* §172.45; *see* 59 Fed. Reg. 45600 (Sept. 1, 1994).

37. 40 C.F.R. §158.65(b).

38. *Id.* §158.65(a).

39. 59 Fed. Reg. at 60496, 60519, 60535, 60542, 60545.

40. *Id.* at 60534.

41. *See* 66 Fed. Reg. 37772, 37777 (July 19, 2001).

42. 66 Fed. Reg. 37772 (July 19, 2001) [hereinafter Final PIP Rule].

43. 65 Fed. Reg. 48701, 48732 (Aug. 9, 2000).

3. Fitting Biological Control Agents Into the FIFRA Framework

In asserting jurisdiction over living organisms that are intended for use in preventing, repelling, destroying, or mitigating a pest it was necessary for EPA to make some distinctions. As noted above, §25(b) of FIFRA authorizes EPA to exempt any pesticide from the requirements of FIFRA if EPA determines that it is adequately regulated by another federal agency or if the pesticide is of a character not requiring federal regulation. This authority played a role in the development of EPA's approach to the products of biotechnology.

In 1982, EPA issued a rule in which it exempted from FIFRA regulation certain organisms which are used as biological control agents on grounds that these biological control agents are "adequately regulated by another Federal agency."[44] A "biological control agent" is defined as "any living organism applied to or introduced into the environment that is intended to function as a pesticide against another organism declared to be a pest."[45]

Ordinarily, when a living organism is intended for use in preventing, repelling, destroying, or mitigating a pest, or is intended for use as a plant regulator, defoliant or desiccant, it is considered to be a pesticide. Thus, EPA could not broadly exempt biological control agents because such living organisms "may have substantial potential for direct adverse effects on humans, or on the environment, through alteration of the ecosystems into which they are introduced."[46] EPA alone has mechanisms and authority for regulating all such organisms to prevent unreasonable adverse effects. However, in EPA's view, §25(b) narrowed the field in which the Agency needed to regulate biological control agents.

It was possible to exempt many biological control agents because other federal agencies exercised adequate regulatory control over these organisms. This was particularly the case for "macroorganisms." For example, the USDA regulates plants, plant pests, and articles capable of disseminating plant pests and diseases. At the same time, the DOI has regulatory authority over vertebrate life forms which may be injurious to humans or the environment.

In June 1982, EPA issued a final rule that employed §25(b)(1) ("adequately regulated by another Federal agency") to exempt from FIFRA regulation all living organisms with the exception of specified microorganisms, including bacteria, viruses, fungi, algae, and protozoa.[47] EPA noted that changes to the lists of exempt organisms could be made at a later date if future events demonstrate that certain biological control agents are not being adequately regulated by another agency.[48] In 1983, EPA issued testing guidelines for microbial pesticides or pesticides which have an active ingredient consisting of a microorganism. The following year, the Agency issued a rule which identified data requirements for registration of such pesticides, including those for genetically engineered microbial pesticides.[49]

While plants used as biological control agents were thus excluded from FIFRA regulation because they were adequately regulated by the USDA, substances that are extracted from plants and used as pesticides were not excluded.[50] As EPA later explained:

> [C]hrysanthemums produce pyrethrum, a substance that has insecticidal activity. The chrysanthemum plants that produce pyrethrum have been exempted from regulation when used as biological control agents (i.e., living chrysanthemums), but pyrethrum itself, as the pesticide substance, has not been exempted when extracted from chrysanthemums and applied to other plants as an insecticide.[51]

In 1994, EPA took a further step and clearly stated its policy for regulation of pesticidal substances that are produced in living plants but are *not* extracted from the plants.[52] These came to be known as "plant pesticides" or plant-incorporated protectants (PIPs).

4. Policy and Proposed Rule on Plant Pesticides

EPA's approach to §25(b)(1) exemptions was restated and expanded in 1994 when the Agency issued its policy statement on plant pesticides.[53] In that document, the Agency made clear that plants continue to be exempt from FIFRA regulation, but added that the pesticidal substances produced in plants required regulatory clarification. There are a number of substances that are produced in a plant that enable the plant to resist pest attack and disease. EPA noted that these can include substances that are considered a normal component of a plant as well as substances that would be new to a plant. Plants with greater resistance to pests and disease can be bred from progenitor plants that have high levels of resistance to the pest. Plants can also be modified to express toxins which confer pest resistance and which originate from invertebrates and microorganisms.

In its 1994 policy statement, EPA expressed its intent to regulate those plant pesticides which have the greatest potential for new environmental exposures and adverse effects on nontarget organisms and to exempt certain classes of plant pesticides based on their source and mechanism of action. The policy statement was accompanied by several other *Federal Register* notices, including a proposed rule to establish the scope of regulation of plant pesticides. As discussed below, that rule (the *Final PIP Rule*) was finalized in January 2001, and published on July 19, 2001. Among other things, that final rule changed the name of "plant pesticides" to PIPs.

5. Tolerances and the Applicability of Section 25(b)(2)

As noted above, §408 of the FFDCA provides that a pesticide residue on or in food is not safe unless (1) it is within tolerance limits which EPA has established for that use of

---

44. 47 Fed. Reg. 23928 (June 2, 1982) [hereinafter Biological Control Agent Final Rule].

45. 40 C.F.R. §152.3(i).

46. 46 Fed. Reg. 18322, 19323 (Mar. 24, 1981) (proposed rule).

47. Biological Control Agent Final Rule, *supra* note 44; 40 C.F.R. §152.20.

48. Biological Control Agent Final Rule, *supra* note 44; 46 Fed. Reg. at 18323.

49. 49 Fed. Reg. 42881 (Oct. 24, 1984).

50. *See* 59 Fed. Reg. at 60496, 60497.

51. *Id.*

52. 59 Fed. Reg. at 60496.

53. *Id.*

the chemical or (2) the residue is safe and exempt from the requirement of a tolerance because EPA has determined that "there is a reasonable certainty that no harm will result from aggregate exposure to the pesticide chemical residue, including all anticipated dietary exposures and all other exposures for which there is reliable information."[54]

The §408 safety standard embodied in the second clause of the last sentence was added in 1996 by the FQPA. It is measured by considering the aggregate risk from dietary exposure and other nonoccupational exposures, such as through drinking water or residential lawn uses. Section 408 also requires that EPA consider the harm that pesticide residues may cause to infants and children. EPA must consider whether tolerances are safe for children and assume, when appropriate, an additional safety factor to account for any uncertainties in the data.

As noted above,[55] §25(b)(2) of FIFRA authorizes EPA to exempt a pesticide from some or all of the requirements of FIFRA if it is of a character that is unnecessary to be subject to FIFRA. EPA interprets §25(b)(2) as authorizing an exemption for a pesticide or category of pesticides that (1) poses a low probability of risk to the environment and (2) that is not likely to cause unreasonable adverse effects on the environment even in the absence of any regulatory oversight under FIFRA.

The FFDCA §408 safety standard is relevant to such an exemption determination because it is used by EPA in evaluating whether a pesticide that is used in food meets these exemption criteria, at least with respect to human dietary risk. A pesticide which qualifies for an exemption from the requirement of a tolerance would be viewed by EPA as meeting both the first and second §25(b)(2) exemption criteria with respect to human dietary risk.[56] A pesticide which qualifies for an exemption from the requirement of a tolerance may also be viewed as meeting both exemption criteria with respect to human health risks arising from other nonoccupational routes of exposure. However, EPA is not authorized to exempt a pesticide based solely on consistency with the §408 standard. EPA must also evaluate the risks arising from occupational exposure, as well as environmental risks.[57]

Tolerances and exemptions from tolerance that were issued for plant pesticides prior to issuance by EPA of a *Final PIP Rule* are listed at 40 C.F.R. Part 180. In the near future, they will be relocated at 40 C.F.R. Part 174, Subpart W, which is part of the *Final PIP Rule* discussed below.

6. EPA's Approach to Plant Pesticides

In January 2001, after years of operating under a policy that was essentially laid out in 1994, EPA had a final "plant pesticides" rule ready for promulgation. As noted above, the change in administration caused the final rule to be delayed. It finally appeared in the *Federal Register* as of July 19, 2001. The rule embodies the policy and approach that EPA has taken to pesticidal substances produced and used in living plants as well as the genetic material necessary to produce the pesticidal substance.

In the final rule, EPA changed the name given to these regulated substances from "plant pesticides" to PIPs in response to comments expressing concern that "plant pesticide" had a negative connotation, suggesting to the public that they involve something lethal. Many of these substances actually enhance genetic mechanisms or merely make the crop plant undesirable to insects. For that reason, EPA substituted "protectants" for "pesticides." The change affects the name only, not the status of the pesticidal substance or the genetic material necessary to produce those substances. A PIP is defined as "a pesticidal substance that is intended to be produced and used in a living plant, or in the produce thereof, and the genetic material necessary for the production of such a pesticidal substance. It also contains any inert ingredient contained in the plant, or produce thereof."[58]

7. Why Are Plant Defense Substances Considered Pesticides?

A number of commenters on the rule questioned EPA's determination that what are essentially plant defense substances should be consider pesticides. To this EPA replied by citing to the definition of "pesticide," which includes any substance intended for preventing, destroying, repelling, or mitigating any pest. EPA stated that plant defense substances are clearly pesticides

> when humans *intend* to use them "for preventing, destroying, repelling, or mitigating any pest" regardless of how the pesticidal capabilities were introduced into the plant (e.g., whether by traditional breeding or through the techniques of modern biotechnology). . . . If the substances were isolated from the plant and sold as pesticides, no one would argue that they were pesticides.[59]

Moreover, the definition of pesticide in FIFRA §2(u) "is not, and never has been, limited to chemical pesticides."[60] EPA also rejected suggestions that PIPs be defined to include only substances that are introduced into plants from sources outside the plant kingdom.[61]

In addition, EPA stressed, in response to comments, that the genetic material necessary for the production of the pesticidal substance would continue to be part of the PIP definition.[62] This is also consistent with the FIFRA definition of pesticide. That genetic material is introduced into the plant with the intent to cause a pesticidal effect, that is, with the intent that the substance produced from the genetic template will ultimately result in a pesticidal effect. Moreover, including the genetic material maintains regulatory continuity important in comprehensively addressing potential risks during various stages of a plant's life cycle or in connection with plant parts, such as seed or pollen, where the pesticidal substance is not produced or is below the level of detection. It may also be more difficult to assay for the substance than it is for the genetic material.

On the question of "intent," EPA made clear that it did not base its determination that PIPs are pesticides on the belief

---

54. 21 U.S.C. §346a(a)(1), (c)(2).

55. 59 Fed. Reg. at 60519, 60521.

56. Final PIP Rule, *supra* note 42, at 37774.

57. *Id.*

58. *Id.* at 37778.

59. *Id.* at 37780 (emphasis added).

60. *Id.* at 37781.

61. *Id.* at 37782.

62. *Id.* at 37784.

that the *plant* intends to prevent, repel, or mitigate a pest.[63] EPA considers the actions of *humans* in selling, distributing, or using a substance. "To the extent that a human relies on a plant's existing pest control properties, the human demonstrates pesticidal intent; if he or she uses, or sells a plant knowing that it typically produces a pesticidal substance he or she 'intends' for it to be produced."[64]

For example, a company may advertise cotton seed that produces cotton plants expressing an insecticidal protein effective against lepidopteran pests or a certain variety of squash which resists fungal disease. A company may use a name for the product that includes the name of a substance commonly recognized as having pesticidal properties, thus implying pesticidal intent. A person who sells or distributes a product may also have "actual or constructive knowledge" that the product will be used for a pesticidal purpose. For example, the Bt delta-endotoxin is a well-known insecticidal protein with no other known function. Its introduction into a plant clearly shows pesticidal intent.[65] A substance in a plant evolving in the wild is not subject to FIFRA until a human intends the substance to be sold, distributed, or used to prevent, destroy, repel, or mitigate a pest.

The *Final PIP Rule*, which establishes a new Part 174 of 40 C.F.R., specifically for PIPs, makes clear that plants that are used as biological control agents will continue to be exempt from FIFRA regulation. PIPs, on the other hand, are subject to the requirements of FIFRA unless specifically exempted.

8. Exempt PIPs

The rule provides an exemption from FIFRA requirements for PIPs that are derived through conventional breeding from sexually compatible plants. The exemption now codified at 40 C.F.R. §174.25 states that a PIP is exempt if the following conditions are met:

- The genetic material that encodes the pesticidal substance or leads to the production of the pesticidal substance is from a plant that is sexually compatible with the recipient plant.
- The genetic material has never been derived from a source that is not sexually compatible with the recipient plant.

EPA determined that these PIPs presented a "low probability of risk" by considering (1) the large body of knowledge that exists on plants in sexually compatible populations derived through conventional breeding, (2) the low potential for novel exposures, (3) the low potential for quantitative changes in the levels of substances that might cause adverse effects, and (4) the low potential for outcrossing of the ability to produce these substances to wild and weedy relatives.[66] EPA determined that these PIPs are not likely to produce unreasonable adverse effects to the environment in the absence of oversight by considering the potential for dietary risk, occupational and nonoccupational risks, and environmental risks.[67]

9. Even Exempt PIPs Are Subject to Adverse Effects Reporting

This subcategory is exempt from all FIFRA requirements except adverse effect reporting requirements. Any person producing, for sale and distribution, an otherwise exempt PIP, who obtains any information regarding adverse effects of this otherwise exempt PIP on human health or the environment, must report that information to EPA within 30 days of possessing or knowing of the information.[68] EPA intends to issue specific guidance on this requirement for otherwise exempt PIPs in order to avoid confusion and unnecessary reporting. EPA recognized that unanticipated effects may occur in connection with otherwise exempt PIPs and offered the example of a celery variety expressing, for pesticidal purposes, high enough levels of psorlen, to cause dermatitis in humans. Such a celery variety apparently emerged from developmental programs once in the past 50 years.[69]

10. Inert Ingredients

New Subpart X of Part 174 lists the inert ingredients that may be used in PIPs that are exempt from FIFRA and FFDCA requirements. It states at §174.485 that an inert ingredient and residues of the inert ingredient are exempt if all of the following conditions are met:

- The genetic material that encodes the inert ingredient or leads to the production of the inert ingredient is derived from a plant sexually compatible with the recipient food plant.
- The genetic material has never been derived from a source that is not sexually compatible with the recipient food plant.
- The residues of the inert ingredient are not present in food from the plant at levels that are injurious or deleterious to human health.
- The *Final PIP Rule* defines "inert ingredient" as

any substance, such as a selectable marker, other than the active ingredient, where the substance is used to confirm or ensure the presence of the active ingredient, and includes the genetic material necessary for the production of the substance, provided the genetic material is intentionally introduced into a living plant in addition to the active ingredient.[70]

Selectable markers are genetic material introduced into the plant or plant cells at the same time as the genetic material that confers the pesticidal trait in order to distinguish and select plants or plant cells that have successfully incorporated the genetic material conferring the pesticidal trait from the vast majority of plants or plant cells that have not.

EPA notes that its long-standing regulatory definition of "inert ingredient" includes "any substance, other than the active ingredient, which is intentionally included in a pesticide product."[71] The definition captures all substances that are intentionally included in the product that are not active. The essential criterion is the intent of the producer to include

63. *Id.* at 37782.
64. *Id.*
65. *Id.*
66. *Id.* at 37799-802.
67. *Id.* at 37803.
68. Codified at 40 C.F.R. §174.71.
69. Final PIP Rule, *supra* note 42, at 37806.
70. *Id.* at 37815.
71. 40 C.F.R. §152.3(m).

the substance in the pesticide.[72] Because the requisite intent is present in the use of selectable markers in PIPs, the markers are considered inerts under EPA's traditional interpretation of the term.

11. EUPs for Plant Pesticides

Under §5 of FIFRA, a person who seeks to develop information necessary to register a pesticide that is unregistered, or to register a pesticide for an additional use, may apply to EPA for an EUP that authorizes testing of a pesticide outside the laboratory.[73] An EUP permits the registrant to gather data necessary for registration. If testing is to be done on a very limited scale, an EUP may not be required. An EUP may not be required if the purpose of the field test is to determine whether the substance has value as a pesticide or to determine its toxicity, as long as the person performing the test does not receive any pest control benefit and the test is conducted on less than 10 acres of land or a surface acre of water.[74] EPA has up to 120 days to review an application for an EUP.[75]

In its review of the EUP application, EPA may request additional information or impose restrictions or limitations on the testing. EPA may require that certain studies be conducted to determine whether use of the pesticide under the EUP will cause "unreasonable adverse effects on the environment."[76] The results of such studies must be reported to EPA before the pesticide can be registered. However, EPA will generally waive data requirements that are not necessary for evaluation of the hazards arising from use under the permit. If the application has "regional or national significance," the Agency will solicit public comments pursuant to 40 C.F.R. §172.11. If the experimental design involves the production of food for distribution in commerce, a tolerance or an exemption from tolerance may be necessary. This may be avoided by destroying the crop. A "crop destruct" requirement might be included in the EUP.

12. Issues Remaining

In issuing registrations for PIPs, EPA has followed its current labeling regulations, which are found at 40 C.F.R. Part 156. The Agency recognizes, however, that some types of labeling typically used for chemical pesticides may not be appropriate for PIPs. Currently, PIP informational material is provided to growers with bags of seed. The material indicates that the seed contains a registered PIP and conveys other information on the registration and the use of the PIP. Recognizing that the current regulations were written for chemical pesticides, EPA intends to propose labeling requirements specifically tailored to PIPs.

EPA also intends to establish data requirements that are specific to PIPs. In the 1994 policy statement, the Agency provided a general perspective on the information needed for registering PIPs. EPA will propose tests which it believes are more appropriate for PIPs and indicate the circumstances under which each study would be required. EPA has already begun this process with a series of public meetings of the FIFRA SAP.

13. The Potential for Development of Insect Resistance

One issue that has become particularly significant in connection with registration of plant pesticides is the development of resistance management plans as a condition of registration.[77] Many believe that increased use of Bt plant pesticides and of Bt itself in conventional spraying can accelerate the development of resistance to Bt. In order to minimize the potential for development of insect resistance, EPA may impose conditions on the registration, including limitations on the amount of the Bt product that can be planted in certain regions of the country, a requirement that each grower plant an appropriately sized refuge for non-Bt product, and a requirement that the registrant perform post-registration monitoring of field insect populations for all Bt crops in order to detect the development of resistance as early as possible.[78]

In February 1998, EPA asked the FIFRA SAP subpanel on Bt Plant Pesticide Resistance Management to make recommendations on insect resistance management. These recommendations became the basis for specific structured refuge requirements. For example, growers of Bt-maize must plant a refuge of non-Bt-maize within ¼ mile of their Bt-maize fields. The refuge must be equal to at least 20% of the acreage planted with Bt-maize and the plants in the refuge may be treated only with non-Bt insecticides. EPA has also established a condition on the registration that requires the registrant to enter a contract with the grower requiring that the grower plant the appropriate refuge. The registrant is obligated to take actions to ensure that the grower fulfills this aspect of the contract.[79] *Id.*

14. The StarLink™ Experience

When a genetically modified food crop has not received full approval for use in human food, it is important to ensure that the product does not find its way into food for human consumption. This was rather dramatically demonstrated by the experience of StarLink™ corn in 2000. Considerable upheaval on both the regulatory and marketing fronts resulted from the misdirection of StarLink™ corn, a biotechnology product that contains a version of the Bt insecticidal protein approved by EPA as a PIP. Corn containing the StarLink™ protein, Cry9C, was approved by EPA for use as animal feed but not for human consumption due to unresolved concerns about the potential for allergenicity. Despite segregation efforts, trace amounts of StarLink™ DNA appeared in taco shells, prompting large-scale recalls by Kraft Foods, Safeway, and ConAgra and a stop sale by StarLink™ producer Aventis. Traces of StarLink™ corn have also been found in corn shipments in the United States and overseas. At least one class action has been filed against Kraft alleging consumer fraud over the sale of StarLink™-containing foods.

---

72. Final PIP Rule, *supra* note 42, at 37791.

73. 40 C.F.R. pt. 172.

74. *Id.* §172.3.

75. 7 U.S.C. §136c(a), ELR Stat. FIFRA §5(a).

76. *Id.* §136c(d), ELR Stat. FIFRA §5(d).

---

77. *See, e.g.,* 62 Fed. Reg. 19115 (Apr. 18, 1997); 65 Fed. Reg. 54001 (Sept. 6, 2000).

78. *Case Study No. II: Bt-Maize, supra* Chapter 1, note 57, at 23-24.

79. *Id.*

While EPA had no evidence that food containing StarLink™ corn will cause any allergic reaction in people, and while the Agency believes that any potential risks are extremely low, in October 2000, EPA announced cancellation of the StarLink™ registration with the voluntary cooperation of Aventis. Thus, StarLink™ corn can no longer be planted for any agricultural purpose. EPA issued a preliminary assessment of StarLink™ corn in November 2000. The assessment does not draw final conclusions about the allergenicity of StarLink™ corn. In December 2000, the SAP found that there is a "medium likelihood" that StarLink™ protein is a potential allergen and that, given the low levels of StarLink™ in the U.S. diet, there is a "low probability" of allergenicity in the population exposed to the corn. The panel recommended that persons who claim to have experienced adverse effects from StarLink™ corn be studied as soon as possible, and the Centers for Disease Control (CDC) is conducting such a study.

D. Case Study: Bt-Maize—Refuges and Butterflies

One of the case studies provided by the OSTP examined maize or corn that was genetically altered to produce a protein throughout the corn plant that is toxic to certain insects. The Bt gene, which produces the toxin, was modified and added to the corn. The corn was developed to control various pest species that can cause serious problems for corn. These include the corn earthworm, the European corn borer, and the southwestern corn borer—insects that feed on corn and cause plant damage that results in decreased quantity and quality. The Bt-maize, which was developed by Monsanto, is referred to commercially as MON810. The substance produced through the genetic alteration is identified as d-endotoxin or the Cry1Ab protein. The grain harvested from MON810 is used in animal feed and processed into numerous food products for human consumption.

In approving MON810 for registration, EPA required details on the gene source (the organism), DNA and protein sequence data, details on the plasmid used in plant transformation, the method of transformation, the pesticidal substance encoded by the gene, expression levels under field conditions and where in the plant the Cry1Ab endotoxin accumulates, among other information. The Agency also required the applicant to explain the use pattern. It is important to know whether the crop will be used for human consumption, for animal feed, or merely for ornamental uses. MON810 is not used directly as human food, but processed products from the grain are used for human food products, as well as in paper components, adhesives, and pharmaceuticals. Most MON810 is used in animal feed.

Once the plant, the pesticidal substance, and the proposed uses have been identified, EPA identifies potential hazards to human health and the environment. The human health assessment includes an evaluation of the pesticidal substance in an oral assay, usually performed on rats or mice. Because these studies require large amounts of pure protein, it is sometimes necessary to use protein produced in a microbial system, such as e coli, as a substitute, as long as the applicant can demonstrate that the protein is identical to the substance produced in the plant. In the case of MON810, a protein produced in e coli was found to be equivalent to the plant product and was used

as the test substance. The dose level far exceeded possible human consumption and no toxicity was noted.

EPA also required a study on the digestion of the protein to determine the stability of the protein after ingestion. Cry1Ab was found to degrade in the gastric assay. Amino acid sequence data from the pesticidal substance are generally subjected to analysis by comparison to similarities to known allergens. Given the rapid degradation of the Cry1Ab protein in the gastric environment, the opportunity to act as an allergen is not provided.

The environmental assessment involves nontarget organism studies which include fish, aquatic invertebrates, earthworms beneficial insects, birds, and other species. The species chosen are representative of the organisms that are likely to be affected by a pesticide in a typical agricultural and environmental setting. A maximum hazard dose is used to detect toxicity based on the recommendations of an SAP. Other organisms may be chosen as needed. Endangered and threatened species are given special consideration. Bt-maize is generally nontoxic to all species, except certain lepidopteran insects.

EPA also analyzes the potential for development of insect resistance. EPA considered the existing and potential distribution of MON810, as well as other Bt plant pesticides. The Agency's analysis suggested that, without restrictions on MON810, there would be some potential for the development of insect resistance in pest species. With conditions on use of MON 810, this risk could be reduced to a biologically acceptable level.

EPA also evaluated the potential for outcrossing or hybridization of Bt-maize pollen with wild relatives of corn that are sexually compatible. It is necessary to determine whether there is a possibility of transfer of the pesticidal substance to other plant species. This is assessed based on the basic biology of the crop and the distribution of related species. EPA also considers, along with risks, the benefits of using the pesticide. One of the primary benefits of a plant pesticide is that it replaces pesticides that may pose greater risks in terms of groundwater contamination, dietary risks, and toxicity to nontarget organisms. Moreover, the hazard to farm workers and pesticide applicators is significantly reduced.

Based on the hazard identification, risk assessment, and risk-benefit analysis, EPA determined that the applications for MON810 met the statutory standards for issuing an experimental use permit, for registration, and for an exemption from a tolerance.[80]

The characteristics of Bt-maize led EPA to focus on two potential risks: (1) the development of insect resistance, and (2) the risk to nontarget insects. To minimize the potential for insect resistance, EPA imposed several conditions on the registration of MON810. These included limitations on the amount of MON810 that could be planted in certain regions of the country. These was also an important requirement that growers plant an appropriately sized refuge of non-Bt-maize. The registrant was also required to perform post-registration monitoring of field insect populations in order to detect the development of insect resistances as early as possible. Following the recommendation of the FIFRA SAP, as described in the preceding section, growers using

---

80. See 61 Fed. Reg. 40341, 40343 (Aug. 2, 1996).

MON810 must plant a refuge of non-Bt-maize within ¼ mile of their Bt-maize fields and the refuge must be equal to at least 20% of the acreage planted to Bt-maize, and the plants in the refuge may be treated only with non-Bt pesticides. In areas of the South, the refuge must be equal to 50% of the Bt-maize acreage and it must be placed within two miles of the Bt-maize field. The registrant must instruct growers to report any sudden increase in insect damage and pass this information on to EPA.

The potential impact on nonpest lepidopterian species, e.g., butterflies, was another area of concern. EPA considered potential toxicity to the Monarch Butterfly and related species and initially concluded that Bt-maize poses an extremely low risk. However, as a result of additional data, EPA has imposed certain data requirements on the registrant. To the extent that EPA identifies potential effects on nontarget insects, the Agency will require mitigation efforts to minimize the impacts.

E. Case Study: Herbicide-Tolerant Soybean—Updating a Tolerance

OSTM Case Study No. III examined a variety of soybean that had been genetically engineered by Aventis to be toler- ant to the herbicide glufosinate ammonium. A modified bacterium was added to the soybean which enables the plant to produce an enzyme that breaks down the herbicide before it can harm the soybean plant. The enzyme that is produced is known as phosphinothricin acetyl transferase (PAT).

When EPA considers a use for a herbicide on a herbicide-tolerant crop, it applies the same standard risk assessment methodologies to assess the environmental safety issues associated with the use of the herbicide as would be applied to any herbicide use prior to its registration. PAT enables the transgenic herbicide-tolerant soybeans to metabolize the herbicidally active moiety glufosinate ammonium into N-acetyl glufosinate which is not herbicidally active and is found only in the transgenic plant. The registrant of the herbicide was required to file a petition requesting an amendment to the provide new tolerances for residues of glufosinate ammonium and its metabolites.

Again, EPA does not regulate the soybean plants themselves, but rather regulates the use of the herbicide on those plants. In accordance with §408 of the FFDCA, information provided by the registrant of glufosinate allowed EPA to amend the label for the currently registered use to include the use of glufosinate on glufosinate-tolerant soybeans.

CHAPTER 6

I. EPA and TSCA

A. The Role of EPA Under TSCA

TSCA[1] provides EPA with statutory authority to regulate chemical substances which may present an unreasonable risk of injury to health or the environment during manufacture, processing, distribution in commerce, use, or disposal. EPA has, by rule, interpreted this authority to extend to intergeneric microorganisms.[2] Specific requirements contained in the *Microbial Products of Biotechnology* final rule apply to premarket review of such organisms, including research and development and test market exemptions. EPA has also asserted TSCA jurisdiction over multi-celled intergeneric plants and animals.[3]

This chapter will provide an overview of EPA's TSCA authorities, and their application to intergeneric organisms. The chapter will conclude with a review of the OSTP/CEQ case study on intergeneric biosensing bacteria.[4]

B. Principal Statutory Authorities of EPA Under TSCA

1. Definition of a "Chemical Substance"

A "chemical substance," for purposes of TSCA jurisdiction, is broadly defined to include "any organic or inorganic substance of a particular molecular identity, including–[(1)] any combination of such substances occurring in whole or in part as a result of a chemical reaction or occurring in nature and [(2)] any element or uncombined radical."[5]

A number of statutory exemptions exclude chemicals regulated by other agencies under other federal laws, including:

- Any pesticide when manufactured, processed, or distributed in commerce for use as a pesticide;
- Tobacco or any tobacco product;
- Any source material, special nuclear material, or byproduct material (as defined under the Atomic Energy Act of 1954 and its implementing regulations);
- Any article the sale of which is subject to a tax imposed by §4181 of the Internal Revenue Code; and
- Any food, food additive, drug, cosmetic, or device (as defined in the FFDCA) when manufac-

tured, processed, or distributed in commerce for use as a food, food additive, drug, cosmetic, or device.[6]

2. Primary Regulatory Provisions[7]

a. TSCA Inventory

TSCA §8(b) requires EPA to "compile, keep current, and publish a list of each chemical substance which is manufactured or processed in the United States."[8] This list was initially created through a reporting process established by EPA in the mid-1970s. It has been periodically updated. As new chemical substances or significant new uses of existing chemical substances are introduced into commerce, EPA notification and review is required to assure the new substances and new uses do not present unreasonable risks to man or the environment.

b. The Premanufacture and Significant New Use Notification Requirements

TSCA §5(a) prohibits the manufacture of a "new chemical substance" or the manufacture and processing of an existing chemical substance for a "significant new use" unless a premanufacture notice (PMN) or significant new use notice (SNUN) is submitted to EPA at least 90 days before the commencement of such manufacture or processing.[9] The PMN notification requires the manufacturer to file with EPA information on the chemical identity and structure of the new substance, categories of intended use, estimates of amounts to be manufactured or processed, anticipated byproducts, available toxicity data (both human and environmental) and exposure data. SNUN operate much like PMNs and require similar information but apply only to those new uses of existing chemicals which EPA has designated by rule.[10]

EPA reviews this material to determine whether the chemical presents an unreasonable risk. Following expiration of the 90-day review period, the manufacturer can generally proceed to market. If EPA needs additional time to review the PMN, or if it identifies a potential risk, it has several legal tools to use to extend the process. First, under TSCA §5(c), EPA can extend the review period for an additional 90 days. Second, under TSCA §5(e), EPA can issue a

---

1. 15 U.S.C. §§2601–2692, ELR Stat. TSCA §§2-412.

2. 40 C.F.R. pt. 725.

3. The provisions of the microbial commencement of activity notices (MCANs) rule and many of the supporting interpretative materials and information regarding EPA's implementation of the TSCA biotechnology program can be accessed at http://www.epa.gov/opptintr/biotech/index.html (last visited July 20, 2001).

4. EPA's TSCA biotechnology website provides a number of important source materials. *See* http://www.epa.gov/opptintr/biotech (last visited July 20, 2001). These include regulatory and guidance materials on the MCAN; a list of recent notifications; and EPA regional office contacts and links to other federal biotechnology websites.

5. 15 U.S.C. §2602(2)(A), ELR Stat. TSCA §3(2)(A).

6. *Id.* §2602(2)(B), ELR Stat. TSCA §3(2)(B).

7. This general discussion of the provisions of TSCA is intended only as background information on the statute necessary to understand the context of the TSCA biotechnology regulations discussed in the remainder of this chapter. For further detail, the reader is referred to TSCA Deskbook (Envtl. L. Inst. 1999).

8. 15 U.S.C. §2607(b), ELR Stat. TSCA §8(b).

9. *Id.* §2604(a), ELR Stat. §5(a). Whether use of an existing chemical on the inventory is a "significant new use" is a question of fact to be resolved through a rulemaking which considers projected volume of manufacturing and processing of the substance; the extent to which a use changes the type or form of exposure of human beings or the environment; the extent to which a use increases exposure; and the reasonably anticipated manner and methods of manufacturing processing, distribution in commerce and disposal. *Id.*

10. *See, e.g.,* 40 C.F.R. pt. 721.

proposed order prohibiting, or limiting the manufacture, processing, distribution, use, or disposal of the substance. The grounds for such an order include findings by the Agency that (1) existing information is insufficient to allow a reasoned evaluation of health and environmental effects, or (2) either the substance will or may present an unreasonable risk or there will or may be substantial human or environmental exposure. In practice, most TSCA §5(e) orders become consent orders if the manufacturer desires to proceed with the project.

TSCA §5(f) also authorizes the Agency to prohibit or restrict manufacture, distribution, processing, use, or disposal of the new substance. Unlike the TSCA §5(e) situation in which there is a data gap or uncertainty, which may be resolved favorably based on additional information. TSCA §5(f) is used where the Agency has determined that there is a reasonable basis to conclude that the substances does pose an unreasonable risk.

Certain activities are exempt from the PMN requirements. These include research and development activities, test marketing, certain polymers, and low-production volume chemicals. Research and development activities meeting defined statutory criteria are completely exempt; the other exemptions have limited notification requirements.

c. TSCA §4 Test Rules

Unlike FIFRA, TSCA does not require manufacturers and processors to develop specified human and environmental effects testing for submission as part of the PMN, but simply to summarize existing information. TSCA §4, however, does provide EPA with authority to require chemical manufacturers and processors to conduct health and environmental effects tests on specific chemical substances. The authority to issue such test rules is triggered by certain findings. These parallel the requirements described for the TSCA §5(e) consent orders described above. Test rules can be issued where (1) EPA finds that there may be an unreasonable risk of injury to health or the environment, or (2) there may be significant or substantial exposure to the substance and there is insufficient data available to make a reasonable decision as to risk.[11]

d. Regulation of Existing Chemicals

TSCA §6 authorizes EPA to restrict or ban the manufacture, processing, or distribution in commerce of chemical substances or mixtures upon a showing that the activity, or any combination thereof, "presents or will present an unreasonable risk of injury to health or the environment."[12] Regulations under this section range from labeling or warning through substance bans. The statute provides a number of specific requirements which EPA must satisfy before adopting a rule under this section, including selection of the least burdensome requirement.[13] Very few rules have been issued under this section, which has been interpreted by the courts as creating a difficult evidentiary burden for the Agency.[14]

TSCA §7 authorizes EPA to initiate proceedings in the district courts to prevent unreasonable risks associated with imminent hazards from chemical substances.[15] This is extraordinary relief, available where such risks cannot be addressed through TSCA §6 rules issued in a timely manner. EPA is authorized to seize such chemical substances, and/or seek any other appropriate relief.

e. Reporting and Recordkeeping Requirements

Finally, TSCA creates a series of recordkeeping and reporting obligations for manufacturers and producers. EPA has used this authority extensively to implement its various TSCA programs. TSCA §8(a) authorizes EPA to require any information deemed necessary.[16] TSCA §8(c) requires maintenance of records or significant adverse reactions to health and the environment. This includes records of consumer allegations of personal injury or harm to health, reports of occupational disease or injury and reports or complaints of injury to the environment. TSCA §8(d) requires submission of health and safety studies on chemical substances. TSCA §8(e) requires notification to EPA of any information which supports the conclusion that a chemical substance presents a substantial risk of injury to health or the environment.

f. Enforcement Provisions

In addition to the imminent hazard authority to take immediate action against existing chemical substances which are presenting imminent hazards, EPA has substantial authority to enforce all of the provisions of TSCA. TSCA §14 provides that it is unlawful for any person to:

- Fail or refuse to comply with any rule or order issued under TSCA or any of the foregoing substantive provisions;
- Use for commercial purposes a chemical substance or mixture which such person had reason to know was manufactured, processed or distributed in commerce in violation of TSCA §§5 or 6, or rules or orders issued under §§5 and 7;
- Fail or refuse to establish or maintain records, submit reports, notices or other information or permit access to or copying of required records, or;
- Fail or refuse to permit entry or inspection as required under §10.[17]

Substantial civil and criminal penalties are authorized for violations of the law. Civil penalties of $25,000 per day per violation are authorized to be imposed through administrative proceedings before the agency with judicial review in the U.S. Court of Appeals for the District of Columbia Circuit.[18] Criminal penalties of up to $25,000 per day and/or imprisonment for up to one year, are authorized where violations are committed knowingly or willfully.[19] Judicial interpretation of this phase in a variety of environmental laws has been broad.[20]

---

11. 15 U.S.C. §2603(a), ELR STAT. TSCA §4(a).

12. *Id.* §2605(a), ELR STAT. TSCA §6(a).

13. *Id.*

14. *See, e.g.*, Corrosion Proof Fittings v. EPA, 947 F.2d 1201, 22 ELR 20037 (5th Cir. 1991).

15. 15 U.S.C. §2606(a), ELR STAT. TSCA §7(a).

16. For examples of rules issued under this section, see 40 C.F.R. pt. 712.

17. 15 U.S.C. §2614, ELR STAT. TSCA §15.

18. *Id.* §2615(a), ELR STAT. TSCA §16(a).

19. *Id.* §2615(b), ELR STAT. TSCA §16(b).

20. It is well established under a variety of environmental laws that actual knowledge of the requirements of the statute or EPA implementing regulations is not required in order to satisfy the "knowingly" require-

C. The TSCA Jurisdictional Trigger for Genetically Modified Organisms

EPA has interpreted the definition of the term "chemical substance" to include new intergeneric microorganisms—that is, those microorganisms which are "formed by the deliberate combination of genetic material originally isolated from organisms of different taxonomic genera."[21] This definition distinguishes between naturally occurring organisms which are automatically listed on the TSCA inventory, and those microorganisms created through the use of modern biotechnology techniques. It is intended to ensure that risks associated with new or altered traits be evaluated prior to their release into the environment.

The requirements for new intergeneric substances parallel the PMN process for new chemicals but are sufficiently different that EPA has issued a separate rule providing the requirements for microbial commencement of activity notices (MCANs).[22] Examples of commercial uses of such microorganisms that would fall within EPA's jurisdiction under TSCA include specialty chemicals and enzyme production, bioremediation, biosensors of environmental contaminants, biofertilizers, ore mining, oil recovery, and biomass conversion. Intergeneric microorganisms which, due to their commercial function, are excluded from TSCA jurisdiction (such as microorganisms used in FFDCA drug or cosmetic products or FIFRA regulated pesticides) are not covered.

While EPA has announced that it is not currently asserting TSCA jurisdiction over multi-cell plants and animals it has taken the position that TSCA confers such jurisdiction on the agency and that it will be used in the future as needed.[23] EPA has recently reasserted this position in response to an inquiry from OSTP/CEQ in the case study development process.[24]

D. The MCAN Requirements

1. New Intergeneric Organisms—The Taxonomic Classification Test

A regulated microorganism for purposes of the MCAN rule is one which is classified in one of the following five kingdoms—Monera (or Procaryotae), Protista, Fungi, the Chlorophyta and the Rhodophyta of the Plantae, and a virus or virus-like particle.[25] In the preamble to the MCAN rule, EPA explains that its decision to define "new microorganisms" as those resulting from the deliberate combination of genetic material originally isolated from organisms classified in different genera was based on the following factors:

● The degree of human involvement;
● The significant likelihood of creating new combinations of traits; and
● The greater uncertainty regarding the effects of

such microorganisms on human health and the environment.[26]

In general, these relate to the traits of the modified organisms, such as survivability, host range, substrate utilization, competitiveness with other organisms, or protein or polysaccharide production.

Finding that such traits would more likely be of concern among distantly related organisms, the definition of "intergeneric organisms" applies to microorganisms which incorporate genetic material from another genus which is mobile. Thus, a microorganism regulated under TSCA

● Includes a microorganism which contains a mobile genetic element which was first identified in a microorganism in a genus different from the recipient microorganism; and
● Excludes a microorganism that contains introduced genetic material consisting of only well-characterized, non-coding regulatory regions from another genus.[27]

The theory is that this taxonomic classification is reasonable because while species within a genus may rather commonly trade genetic material, species in different genera do not. It is also a classification which is independent of the technology used to create the microorganism and thus consistent with the long-standing principles of the federal *Framework* that regulation should be keyed to the nature of the product itself, not to the process through which it was created.

2. Scope of the MCAN Rule and Provisions

The MCAN rule applies to use of an intergeneric microorganism for commercial purposes. As defined in the regulation, this means

[t]o import, produce, manufacture, or process with the purpose of obtaining an immediate or eventual commercial advantage . . . and includes, among other things, "manufacture" or "processing" *of any amount of a microorganism or microbial mixture.*[28]

The purpose of such activity can include commercial distribution, test marketing, product research and development, production as an intermediate, and even byproducts and impurities produced during the manufacture of other materials.

The particular requirements of the MCAN rule differ based on the type of commercial activity actually desired. The MCAN applies to the great majority of commercial activity. There is an exemption in the rule for certain well-defined and controlled activities. A TSCA experimental release approval (TERA) is otherwise required for field release experiments. Test market activities are also eligible

---

ment. *See, e.g.,* United States v. Hayes Int'l Corp., 786 F.2d 1499, 16 ELR 20717 (11th Cir. 1986). For further details, the reader is referred to ENVIRONMENTAL CRIMES DESKBOOK (Envtl. L. Inst. 1996).

21. 40 C.F.R. §725.1(a).

22. *Id.* pt. 725.

23. 59 Fed. Reg. 45527 (Sept. 1, 1994).

24. *Case Study No. VI: Bioremediation and Biosensing Using Bacteria, supra* Chapter 1, note 61, at 4 (U.S. EPA letter of Dec. 22, 2000).

25. This is the Whittaker classification system. *See* 62 Fed. Reg. 17913 (Apr. 11, 1997).

26. *Id.*

27. 40 C.F.R. §725.3. A "mobile genetic element" is defined as one that has the ability to move genetic material within and between organisms. Examples include all plasmids, viruses, transposons, insertion sequences, and other classes of elements with these general properties. A "noncoding regulatory region" is defined as a segment of introduced genetic material that (1) does not code for protein, peptide, or functional ribonucleic acid molecules and (2) solely controls the activity or other regions that code for protein or peptide molecules or act as recognition sites for the initiation of nucleic acid or protein synthesis. *Id.*

28. *Id.* (emphasis added).

for an expedited review, in the form of a test market exemption (TME).[29]

3. MCAN Requirements

An MCAN must be submitted at least 90 calendar days prior to manufacturing or importing a new microorganism or manufacturing, importing, or processing a microorganism for a significant new use.[30] There is no specific form to be used for this purpose but the regulation does specify in precise detail what information must be included and further detail is provided in EPA guidance.[31] This information includes:

- Submitter identification;
- Microorganism identity information, including description of the recipient microorganism and the new microorganism; genetic construction of the new microorganism; and phenotypic and ecological characteristics[32];
- Byproducts;
- Total production volume;
- Use information;
- Worker exposure and environmental release; and
- Health and environmental effects data, including test data on the new microorganism in the possession or control of the submitter; and other data concerning the health and environmental effects of the new microorganism that are known to or reasonably ascertainable by the submitter.[33]

EPA uses the 90-day review period to conduct its risk assessment review of the intergeneric microorganism to determine whether it can be introduced in commerce consistent with the mandate of TSCA, i.e., without unreasonable risk to man or the environment. As with the general TSCA provisions described earlier in the chapter, EPA may extend the 90-day period by agreement if it needs more time to complete the review or it may enter into a consent agreement with the MCAN submitter specifying conditions under which limited commercialization may occur pending the resolution of outstanding issues. EPA may also find that the MCAN presents an unreasonable risk and prohibit marketing. An example of the risk assessment process as described

in the OSTP/CEQ Case Study No. IV is provided for illustration purposes later in this chapter. In any case other than prohibition, the manufacturer is required to follow up with a notice of commencement of manufacture or import to EPA within 30 days.[34]

MCANs for a strain of rhizobuim meliloti (nitrogen fixing bacteria for soybeans) and several strains of various bacteria for enzyme production have been approved to date by EPA. Notifications under the rule have been averaging five to seven per year since finalization.[35]

E. MCAN Exemptions for Research and Development

A limited number of exemptions to the full MCAN process apply to research and development activities. These include

- A small outright exemption for certain activities conducted in accord with the NIH *Guidelines for Research Involving Recombinant DNA Molecules* which also meet certain other criteria;
- A qualified exemption for activities conducted inside a structure and certain activities with certain microorganisms outside a structure; and
- A TSCA experimental release permit for other activities.[36] The term "structure" for purposes of these provisions is defined as "a building or vessel which effectively surrounds and encloses the microorganism and includes features designed to restrict the microorganism from leaving."[37]

1. Scope

The requirements that relate to these research and development activities apply to everyone who is engaged in research and development for commercial purposes for immediate or eventual commercial advantage.[38] This means that the TSCA requirements apply to the following types of research:

- All research and development activities *funded in whole or in part by a commercial* entity (including direct contracts between the commercial entity and a university or researcher, conditional grants, joint venture arrangements and "any other situation"); and
- All research and development activities *not funded by a commercial entity where the researcher's intent is to obtain an immediate or eventual commercial advantage.* Indications of such an intent include research into a commercially viable improvement of a product already on the market, efforts by the researcher to secure commercial funding, and researcher or university efforts to patent a commercial application of its research.[39]

---

29. 40 C.F.R. §725.1(b), (c).

30. *Id.* §725.150(a). Currently there are no microorganism uses which have been designated by EPA through rulemaking as significant new uses.

31. OFFICE OF POLLUTION PREVENTION AND TOXICS, U.S. EPA, POINTS TO CONSIDER IN THE PREPARATION OF TSCA BIOTECHNOLOGY SUBMISSIONS FOR MICROORGANISMS (1997), *available at* http://www.epa.gov/opptintr/biotech (last visited July 20, 2001).

32. The degree of information requested for this element is very broad. It includes substantiation as to the taxonomic classification of the new organism, and a detailed description of the process of construction. With respect to activity of the new microorganism in the environment the regulations require a description of habitat, geographical distribution and source of the recipient microorganism; survival and dissemination under the relevant environmental conditions and methods for detecting the new organism in the environment; a description of anticipated biological interactions with multiple other organisms; and a description of anticipated involvement in biogeochemical or biological cycling processes.

33. 40 C.F.R. §725.155, .160.

34. *Id.* §725.190.

35. *See, e.g.,* http://www.epa.gov/opptintr/biotech/submain.htm (last visited July 20, 2001).

36. 40 C.F.R. pt. 725, subpt. E.

37. *Id.* §725.3.

38. *Id.* §725.205.

39. *See id.* §725.205(b).

2. NIH Guideline Exemption

This limited exemption excludes research which meets three conditions altogether. The activity must solely involve research and development; there is no intentional testing of an organism outside a structure; and the project involves a grant from another federal agency, a condition of which is compliance with the NIH *Guidelines*.[40]

3. Activities Conducted Within a Structure

This exemption establishes performance standards for research and development activities conducted inside a structure. Where these are met, MCAN is not required. The standard requires that:

- The microorganism is manufactured solely for research and development purposes;
- It is used under, by, or directly under the supervision of a technically qualified individual (an individual who because of education, training, or experience is capable of understanding the health and environmental risks associated with the organisms, is responsible for enforcing appropriate research methods and is responsible for safety assessments and clearances related to the materials);
- There is no intentional testing outside of the structure;
- Appropriate containment and/or inactivation controls are selected by the technically qualified person; approved by an authorized official of the institution conducting the test; and records are kept and changes as may be ordered by EPA; and
- All persons employed by the manufacturer or to whom the material is directly distributed are informed of any risks associated with the microorganism.[41]

Significant additional detail on the determination of risks, the notification process and methods, and recordkeeping requirements is specified in the regulations.[42] If the experiment is subject to Institutional Biosafety Committee review, the information submitted for review to the committee will satisfy TSCA recordkeeping requirements.[43]

4. Activities Conducted Outside a Structure

Virtually all of these activities require an experimental release approval, as described in the next section. There is a limited exemption for research and development in activities conducted outside a structure which involve certain intergeneric strains of *Bradyrhizobium japonicum* and *Rhizobium meliloti*. These nitrogen fixing bacteria for soybeans are well-characterized taxonomically and have been used in the environment for many years. The genetic modification included antibiotic resistance genes, introduced as markers to identify the strains. EPA determined that for purposes of small-scale field trials, the risk of transfer of resis-

tance markers to other microorganisms was low. The antibiotic resistance gene markers are integrated into the bacterial chromosome, and stable. The natural parents do not inhabit humans nor do the genetic modifications affect the ability to infect humans.[44]

Accordingly, no approval or field trials involving these organisms are required. A certification must be submitted to EPA prior to initiation of the activity. The certification must include identifying information on the manufacturer or importer, location, duration, and planned start date of the test. It must also certify compliance with the genetic structure requirements for the two organisms and limitation to no more than 10 terrestrial acres.[45]

5. The TERA

All other research and development releases of microorganisms require a TERA. An application for a TERA must be submitted at least 60 days in advance of the planned research and include the following information:

- Submitter identification and microorganism identity required for the MCAN;
- Phenotypic and ecological characteristics information as required for the MCAN as it would relate to the conditions of the proposed research and development activity;
- A detailed description of the proposed research and development activity including objectives and significance of the activity; number of microorganisms released; characteristics of the test site; target organisms; planned start date; and duration and evidence of state or local notification if required;
- Information on monitoring, confinement, mitigation, and emergency termination procedures; and
- All available health and environmental effects data.[46]

EPA has 60 days to review the TERA and may approve, disapprove, or approve with conditions. Once approved, the TERA is legally enforceable. Any deviation from the provisions of the approval subjects the submitter to enforcement action and civil and criminal penalties.[47] The regulations also provide that the TERA may be revoked or modified in the event that significant questions about risk arise. These may come from any source. EPA will notify the submitter in writing of these questions and provide a 10 day response period in which to provide argument or additional information. Thereafter, EPA will issue a decision as to whether the research can continue.

If EPA determines during the course of the research that there is an unreasonable risk of injury, it will notify the submitter in writing of additional safeguards which must be implemented or direct suspension of the research. EPA's instructions must be implemented within 48 hours.[48] If the

40. *Id.* §725.232.

41. *Id.* §725.234.

42. *Id.* §725.235.

43. *Id.* §725.235(c)(i)(A).

44. *See* 59 Fed. Reg. at 45544-46; *see, e.g.,* http://www.epa.gov/opptintr/biotech/1-3dec.html/bradyrhizobium japonicum (last visited July 20, 2001).

45. 40 C.F.R. §725.238, .239.

46. *Id.* §725.255, .260.

47. *Id.* §725.270.

48. *Id.* §725.288.

submitter determines that some change to the TERA is required to effectuate the research, he or she must notify EPA and receive approval for the change.[49]

F. The TME

The MCAN rule also provides limited exemptions for test marketing. These are essentially expedited reviews of MCAN information which are decided by EPA within 45 days of submission. A TME application is required, and it must provide sufficient information to EPA to permit a reasoned evaluation of the health and environmental effects of the planned test marketing activity. Thus, the submitter identification and microorganism identity information, phenotypic and ecological characteristics information, and all health and environmental effects data must be provided. In addition, the submitter must provide information on scope—how many people will be provided with the microorganism, maximum number of people exposed, and how the TME differs from full-scale commercialization.[50] Prenotice consultation with EPA is strongly recommended.[51]

G. General Exemptions for New Microorganisms (Tier I and Tier II Exemptions)

Some new but well-understood microorganisms are exempt from MCAN reporting altogether. The conditions to be met to qualify for the this exemption include the following:

- Use of a specified recipient microorganism (*Acetobacter aceti, Aspergillus niger, Aspergillus oryzae, Bacillus licheniformis, Bacillus subtillis, Clostridium acetobutylicum, Eschericia coli K-12, Penicillium roqueforti, Saccharomyces cerevisiae,* and *Saccharomyces uvarum*);
- Use of introduced genetic material meeting all of the following criteria: limited in size, well-characterized, poorly mobilizable, free of certain sequences (such as toxin-encoding sequences); and
- Use of a specified performance-based list of physical containment and control technologies (use of a structure designed and operated to contain the new microorganism; controlled access to the structure; written, published, and implemented safety and hygiene procedures; use of demonstrated and effective inactivation procedures, effective procedures to minimize viable microbial populations in aerosols and exhaust gases; and procedures to control dissemination of microorganisms through other routes and emergency cleanup procedures).[52]

Where all of these conditions can be met, a Tier I exemption applies. In order to establish eligibility for this exemption, the manufacturer or importer must submit to EPA a certification containing its identification information, identification of the recipient microorganism, and a certification of compliance with the conditions of the exemption.

A Tier II exemption is available for new microorganisms which meet the first two criteria but have some more complex or unusual physical containment or control technologies. Tier II exemptions must be specifically requested; a presubmission meeting with EPA is recommended; and EPA must review and approve Tier II requests.[53]

H. Administrative Procedures

The MCAN rule provides standard TSCA procedures for the review of MCANs, TERAs, TMEs, and other notifications.[54] These provide for publication in the *Federal Register* of notice of applications for an MCAN or exemption. The notice will include:

- The specific microorganism identity, or an acceptable generic name if the submitter claims confidentiality;
- The categories of use of the microorganism, or acceptable generic descriptors;
- A list of the health and environmental effects studies and information; and
- The submitters identity.[55]

Exemption decisions are also published in the *Federal Register.*

The regulations also contain procedures for asserting claims of confidentiality and requirements for assuring that where such claims are deemed valid, the opportunity for public participation is maintained.[56] Special rules apply to the development of generic names and uses.[57] Data from health and safety studies is presumptively not confidential unless such information relates to confidential processes used in manufacture or processing or is unrelated to the effects of a microorganism on health or the environment.[58] All claims of confidentiality must be substantiated; and copies of submissions provided for filing in the public docket with confidential business information excised.[59] Such materials are made available for public inspection in the TSCA Public Docket Office, 401 M St. SW, Rm. NE-B607, Washington DC 20024.

The administrative procedures provisions of the rules also require all notifications to be signed by a responsible officer of the submitter. For MCANs, the certification statement must state:

I certify that to the best of my knowledge and belief: The company named in this submission intends to manufacture, import, or process for a commercial purpose, other than in small quantities solely for research and development, the microorganism identified in this submission. All information provided in this submission is complete and truthful as of the date of submission. I am including

49. *Id.*

50. *Id.* §725.355.

51. *Id.* §725.350(a).

52. *Id.* §725.400–.426.

53. *Id.* §725.428–.470.

54. *Id.* pt. 725, subpt. B.

55. *Id.* §725.40.

56. *Id.* pt. 725, subpt. C.

57. *Id.* §725.85, .88.

58. *Id.* §725.92.

59. *Id.* §725.80.

with this submission all test data in my possession or control and a description of all other data known to or reasonably ascertainable by me as required by 40 CFR 725.160 or 725.260.

I. Case Study No. VI: Bioremediation and Biosensing Using Bacteria

The primary example from the OSTP/CEQ case studies on the application of the TSCA MCAN process to genetically modified bacteria is Case Study No. VI: Bioremediation and Biosensing Bacteria. This case study describes EPA's decision to allow field testing of a genetically engineered bacterium designed to detect and degrade hazardous chemical wastes. This case originated with submission of a PMN, as it occurred prior to EPA's 1997 finalization of the MCAN rules discussed in the previous section. However, the MCAN rules had been proposed at that time and the regulatory process essentially followed the MCAN model. EPA's risk assessment analysis of the information provided identified several issues on which additional data would be required prior to full-scale commercialization. The case resulted in a consent order entered on March 27, 1996 under TSCA §5(e), which approved a field test with conditions.

1. Pseudomonas Fluorescens Strain HK44

The new microorganism involved in this case study is the recombinant bacterium *Pseudomonas Fluorescens Strain HK44 (HK44)* jointly developed by the U.S. Department of Energy (DOE) and the University of Tennessee. It consists of the recipient strain *Pseudomonas Fluorescens Strain 18H* which contains a plasmid derived from three other sources, including a *photobacterium* and an *e. coli*.[60] *Pseudomonas* as a genus is known for its broad nutritional diversity and ability to use organic wastes as sources of carbon and energy. The introduced plasmid produces visible light when it encounters bioavailable polycyclic aromatic hyrdocarbons (PAHs).

PAHs consist of two or more benzene rings fused together with at least two common carbons. They are found in crude and refined oil petroleum products, particularly in certain fuel oils, coal tars, woodtreating chemicals, creosote, soot and refinery waste. PAHs are common contaminants found in soil at hazardous waste sites and a major concern due to their potential to cause adverse human and ecological effects.

Bioremediation of organic wastes such as PAHs has become a broadly accepted remediation technique in the United States and elsewhere. *HK44* was designed both to degrade PAHs and to detect them. Its light production genes can be either applied directly to the soil or placed in small photomultiplier probes. These produce light in amounts relative to the concentrations of PAH contaminants in polluted soil or groundwater.

Such biosensors offer a less expensive and more rapid way to monitor PAH concentrations in soils, sediments, and groundwater at hazardous waste sites, as compared with traditional chemical tools. This monitoring can identify what contaminants are on-site and at what concentrations, whether they are moving off-site and the degree of progress

in cleanup. They also may offer a means to identify with greater precision who much of the PAH is bioavailable for uptake by humans or animals.

2. EPA's Risk Assessment Review Under TSCA

The University of Tennessee filed a PMN for review of *HK44* with EPA in 1995, providing the information specified in EPA's *Points to Consider in the Preparation and Submission of TSCA Premanufacture Notices for Microorganisms*. EPA's Office of Pollution Prevention and Toxics conducted a full risk assessment for both the risks posed at the site of production (a fermentation site at the Oak Ridge National Laboratory (ORNL)) and at the site of release (the Y-12 field site). This included:

● Detailed analysis of potential human health and ecological hazards;
● Likely exposure scenarios; and
● Taxonomic and construct analyses.

Among the issues considered and analyzed were diseases associated with *Pseudomonas Fluorescens* and growth limiting temperature factors, the presence of the tetracycline resistance gene and its potential to spread to other taxa, possibly promoting antibiotic resistance and potential effects from PAH breakdown products in the soil. The complete use scenario was reviewed in detail, from production of the cells for use in fermentors, to loading into lysimeters for field testing to placement in the soil. Containment procedures were reviewed for all steps in the process. Exposure and engineering assessments were applied to identify risks at various stages of the process and appropriate mitigation measures.[61]

EPA concluded that the release of *HK44* at the ORNL Y-12 site did not pose an unreasonable risk so long as it was conducted under the provisions of a TSCA §5(e) consent order, which was issued on March 27, 1996. The consent order provided the following:

● The only release authorized was at the ORNL Y-12 test site;
● A pesticide applicator that minimized spray drift was required to be used for the introduction of *HK44*;
● Sanitization of soils and other contaminated samples, equipment, and instrumentation was required and a performance standard for such sanitization specified;
● Routine monitoring in the area was requested, particularly when aerosol generation was more likely; and
● Quarterly reports on the status of the experiment were required to be provided to EPA.

The consent order also identified three outstanding issues which would have to be resolved prior to any additional release or full-scale commercialization. These are:

● Frequency of transfer of tetracycline resistance to microbial pathogens—more data needs to be examined prior to commercialization to ensure

---

60. *Case Study No. VI: Bioremediation and Biosensing Using Bacteria, supra* Chapter 1, note 61, at app. 1.

61. *Id.* at 6-11 and app. 2.

that use of *HK44* does not contribute to antibiotic resistance;
● Potential for presence of persistent toxic metabolites; and
● Plant and animal pathogenicity concerns.

3. Role of Other Agencies

While this case study primarily focuses on EPA's primary role under TSCA, other agencies and other laws were involved in the process. The USDA examined *HK44* to evaluate whether it was or could become a plant pest for purposes of the PPA. The USDA concluded that it was not.[62] Most microorganisms being investigated for use in bioremediation are not plant pests.[63]

DOE also conducted a NEPA analysis of this release activity at its ORNL. DOE considered that, for its purposes, this field test qualified for a categorical exclusion from further NEPA review and consideration.[64] This finding is interesting and in many ways showcases the important regulatory gap-filling nature of TSCA. As is evident from the foregoing description, the TSCA review of the likely effects of *HK44* was substantial—a review described in the case study itself as "the functional equivalent of NEPA." The result of that review was approval with conditions of the test, but not commercialization. The difference between the TSCA review (substantial) and the review under a NEPA categorical exemption (none) demonstrates how significantly review of biotechnology applications could potentially differ under the existing federal *Framework*.

62. *Id.* at 7.

63. *Id.* at 6.

64. *Id.* at 11 (citing 10 C.F.R. §1021, subpt. D, app. B (small-scale research and development projects and small-scale pilot projects conducted (for generally less than two years) to verify a concept before demonstration actions, performed in an existing structure not requiring major modification)).

CHAPTER 7

I. EPA's Regulation of Bioremediation

A. The Role of EPA

EPA is responsible for regulating biotechnology directly through a number of laws that are discussed in other chapters of this deskbook.[1] This chapter discusses how EPA indirectly regulates the development of certain biotechnology activities through the combined authority of CERCLA (the "Superfund" legislation)[2] and RCRA.[3] Simply stated, EPA relies on CERCLA and RCRA to require the regulated community to properly manage, dispose, and clean up a wide variety of hazardous substances and wastes. As discussed below, CERCLA and RCRA were enacted over 20 years ago to give EPA the statutory authority to protect public health and the environment from improper waste management disposal and cleanup practices. As a direct result of EPA's implementation of its statutory authority in this area, the cost of proper waste management, disposal, and cleanup has grown steadily over the past two decades. In response to those rising costs, the regulated community has looked for cost-effective, environmental friendly alternatives to historic waste disposal practices such as landfilling and incineration. Bioremediation is a waste treatment process that has grown steadily in popularity. EPA regulates the use of bioremediation processes to clean up contamination caused by historic disposal of hazardous wastes and substances primarily under its CERCLA authority. Bioremediation processes that are used to treat, manage, and dispose currently produced hazardous wastes are regulated under RCRA.

B. Bioremediation Defined

The term "bioremediation" is not defined in either CERCLA or RCRA, but is commonly interpreted to mean a treatment process that uses naturally occurring microorganisms, e.g., yeast, fungi, or bacteria, to break down, or degrade, toxic substances into less toxic or nontoxic substances.[4] In one sense, bioremediation works in a manner similar to the human digestive system. Just like humans, microorganisms consume and digest organic substances to produce nutrients and energy. Organic materials are those that contain carbon and hydrogen. Some organic materials are toxic or hazardous to humans and the environment. From both cost and environmental protection perspectives, it is preferable to remove those toxic and hazardous materials from waste streams before they can enter the environment.

Bioremediation uses living microorganisms in a wide variety of applications designed for hazardous waste treatment and pollution prevention. These applications use microorganisms to identify and filter toxic and hazardous materials from manufacturing waste as part of the waste management process. Some more advanced systems using genetically modified microorganisms are being tested in waste treatment processes to remove materials that are difficult to degrade.[5]

Bioremediation can also be used to remove hazardous or toxic contaminants from environmental media after they have been disposed or otherwise released into the environment. For example, many common fuels and solvents are highly toxic to humans, plants, and animals when released in even small amounts in an uncontrolled manner to the environment. Cleaning up those fuels and solvents by removing them from the soil or groundwater by traditional pump and treat or incineration methods can be an expensive, lengthy, and potentially ineffective process. There are numerous microorganisms, however, that can "clean up" those contaminants by digesting them and breaking them down into harmless products like carbon dioxide and water. Once all the contaminants are degraded, the microorganism population is reduced naturally because their food source has been removed.[6] Dead microorganisms, or small populations in the absence of an available food source, pose no contamination risk. In some cases, the byproducts of the pollution fighting microorganisms are themselves useful. Methane, for example, can be derived from a form of bacteria that degrades sulfur liquor, a waste product of paper manufacturing.[7]

C. How Does Bioremediation Work?

Bioremediation can only take place when microorganisms are present, active, and healthy. Over the past two decades researchers have developed numerous techniques to create optimum environmental conditions to assist the growth of microorganisms and to increase the size and type of microbial populations.[8] Different microorganisms degrade different types of compounds and survive under different conditions. While discussion of those techniques is beyond the scope of this deskbook, they all rely on manipulating the type and quantity of microorganisms present, the site conditions, e.g., soil type, temperature, oxygen, and nutrient content, and the quantity and toxicity of contaminants to be digested. Essentially, the goal of all those techniques is to maximize the effectiveness of the specific microorganism's digestive process.

Bioremediation techniques fall into two broad categories: in situ or ex situ. In situ bioremediation treats the contami-

---

1. *See* Chapters 3, 5, and 6 *infra.*

2. 42 U.S.C. §§9601-9675, ELR STAT. CERCLA §§101-405.

3. *Id.* §§6901-6992k, ELR STAT. RCRA §§1001-11011.

4. BIOTECHNOLOGY INDUS. ORG., GUIDE TO BIOTECHNOLOGY (1999-2000), *available at* http://www.bio.org/issues.html (last visited July 31, 2001).

5. *See id.*

6. *Id.*

7. *See id. See also* OFFICE OF SOLID WASTE & EMERGENCY RESPONSE (OSWER), U.S. EPA, PROMOTION OF INNOVATIVE TECHNOLOGIES IN WASTE MANAGEMENT PROGRAMS (1996) (EPA 542-F-96-0012, OSWER Directive No. 9380.0-25) [hereinafter U.S. EPA, PROMOTION].

8. A compilation of hundreds of site-specific case studies can be found in U.S. EPA, ABSTRACTS OF REMEDIATION CASE STUDIES, MEMBER AGENCIES OF THE FEDERAL REMEDIATION TECHNOLOGIES ROUNDTABLE (2000) (EPA 542-R-00-006) [hereinafter U.S. EPA, ABSTRACTS].

nated material in the location in which it was found. Ex situ bioremediation processes require removing the contaminated material from its original locations before it can be treated.[9] Indigenous bioremediation occurs when the proper type of indigenous microorganisms necessary to treat a particular contaminant are present and their growth can be stimulated by modifying the site or waste stream conditions. Exogenous bioremediation occurs when the proper microorganisms are not present and other microorganisms are added to the site or waste stream.[10] To ensure the exogenous microorganisms thrive, the site or waste stream conditions must be adjusted to those that are preferred by the imported microorganism.

Bioremediation can take place under both aerobic and anaerobic conditions. In aerobic conditions, microorganisms use available atmospheric oxygen in order to function. With sufficient oxygen, microorganisms will convert many organic contaminants to carbon dioxide and water. Anaerobic conditions support biological activity in which no oxygen is present so the microorganisms break down chemical compounds in the soil to release the energy they need. Sometimes, during aerobic and anaerobic processes of breaking down the original contaminants, intermediate products that are less, equally, or more toxic than the original contaminants are created.[11]

D. Using Bioremediation Techniques to Reduce the Toxicity of Industrial Waste

Many industries are using bioremediation techniques to make their wastes streams less toxic or hazardous. The chemical, textiles, pharmaceutical, pulp and paper, food and feed, metal and minerals, and energy industries have all benefitted from cleaner, more energy-efficient production made possible by incorporating bioremediation techniques into their production processes.[12] Most of these improvements are due to a specific type of microorganism called biocatalysts, which are living organisms or their enzymes. Biocatalysts are more environmentally friendly than traditional chemical catalysts. Biocatalysts are more specific than chemical catalysts and produce fewer unwanted byproducts. They are water soluble and catalyze reactions most efficiently at relatively low temperatures, when compared to nonbiological catalysts. Biocatalysts also are self-propagating, so they are easier to produce and maintain.[13]

Biocatalysts offer many environmental advantages. Industrial scientists are actively working to expand the applicability of biocatalysts to industrial processes. Their activities are focused on improving the usefulness of existing biocatalysts, discovering or creating novel biocatalysts, and using genetically modified plants to provide both the biocatalytic machinery as well as the manufacturing facility for bioremediation activities.[14] Some examples of current

industrial uses of bioremediation techniques are briefly summarized below.[15]

1. Chemicals Industry

The environmental efficiency of the chemicals industry has been improved by the application of biocatalysis, the recycling of solvents and the biological treatment of wastewater. These innovations require less energy and produce more benign byproducts than traditional methods.

2. Pulp and Paper Industry

The pulp and paper industry extensively uses bioremediation techniques to reduce the level of chlorine used in manufacturing paper and paper products. For example, industrial enzymes are used extensively throughout manufacturing resulting in less-chlorinated products and byproducts. Additionally, pulp is manufactured through a process called biopulping which involves treating lignocellulosic materials with lignin-degrading fungi to manufacture the pulp. This results in a more benign waste stream.

3. Mining and Metals Industry

The mining and metals industry uses bioremediation techniques to leach valuable metals from ore and to treat wastewater resulting from the extraction process. Bioleaching uses bacteria, principally thiobacillus ferrooxidans and leptospirillum ferrooxidans and certain high-temperature bacteria, to leach metals of value—copper, zinc, and cobalt—from a sulfide mineral. The principal advantages of bioleaching are a shorter construction time for the extraction facility, and no noxious gases or toxic effluents are produced. The industry also uses metals bioremediation and recovery techniques in place of the traditional alkaline degreasing process that creates a large volume of wastewater containing heavy metals. The new technique using biologically created enzymes allows the extraction processes to occur at lower temperatures, with fewer waste byproducts. It also prolongs the life of degreasing and pickling baths, reduces water and acid consumption, and generates less waste which must be treated before disposal.

4. Energy Industry

Bioremediation techniques commonly used in the energy industry have improved the overall efficiency of many specific processes, particularly in the area of pollution control. Processes such as biodiesel (equivalent to petroleum distillates), bioethanol (fuels produced biologically from biomass), and biodesulphurisation (producing cleaner coal and petroleum, primarily through the removal of sulfur, have all benefitted by the application of various bioremediation techniques. The primary benefits have been a reduction in the type and quantity of environmental contaminants released during combustion and the generation of more benign byproducts.

9. AMERICAN ACAD. OF ENVTL. ENG'RS, BIOREMEDIATION (WASTECH Monograph Series 2000).

10. *Id.*

11. *Id.*

12. ORGANIZATION FOR ECON. COOPERATION & DEV., BIOTECHNOLOGY FOR CLEAN INDUSTRIAL PRODUCTS & PROCESSES (1998) [hereinafter CLEAN INDUSTRIAL PRODUCTS].

13. *Id.*

14. *Id. See also* GUIDE TO BIOTECHNOLOGY, *supra* note 4.

15. CLEAN INDUSTRIAL PRODUCTS, *supra* note 12.

E. Using Bioremediation Techniques to Perform Better Remedial Actions

In addition to reducing the quantity or concentration of toxic or hazardous substances in manufacturing waste streams, bioremediation techniques are being used to reduce the cost of cleaning up contaminants that have been released to the environment. At the same time, these bioremediation techniques are improving the efficiency and effectiveness of the cleanup actions. Bioremediation techniques have been used in thousands of instances where soil, surface water, or groundwater has been contaminated by toxic or hazardous pollutants, contaminants, and substances. EPA has long been a proponent of expanding the use of bioremediation techniques to clean up contaminated areas.[16] Some examples of bioremediation techniques being used to clean up contaminated areas are briefly described below.

1. In Situ Bioremediation of Soil

In situ techniques do not require excavation of the contaminated soils so may be less expensive, create less dust, and cause less release of contaminants than ex situ techniques. Also, it is possible to treat a large volume of soil at once. In situ techniques, however, may be slower than ex situ techniques, may be difficult to manage, and are most effective at sites with *permeable* (sandy or uncompacted) soil. The goal of aerobic in situ bioremediation is to supply oxygen and nutrients to the microorganisms in the soil. Aerobic in situ techniques can vary in the way they supply oxygen to the organisms that degrade the contaminants. Two such methods are bioventing and injection of hydrogen peroxide. Oxygen can be provided by pumping air into the soil above the water table (bioventing) or by delivering the oxygen in liquid form as hydrogen peroxide. In situ bioremediation may not work well in clays or in highly layered subsurface environments because oxygen cannot be evenly distributed throughout the treatment area. In situ remediation often requires years to reach cleanup goals, depending mainly on how biodegradable specific contaminants are. Less time may be required with easily degraded contaminants.[17]

2. Ex Situ Bioremediation of Soil

Ex situ techniques can be faster, easier to control, and used to treat a wider range of contaminants and soil types than in situ techniques. However, they require excavation and treatment of the contaminated soil before and, sometimes, after the actual bioremediation step. Examples of ex situ techniques include slurry-phase and solid-phase bioremediation. In slurry-phase bioremediation, contaminated soil is combined with water and other additives in a large tank called a bioreactor and mixed to keep the microorganisms in the soil in contact with the contaminants in the soil. Nutrients and oxygen are added. The conditions in the bioreactor are controlled to create the optimum environ-

ment for the microorganisms to degrade the contaminants. Upon completion of the treatment, the water is removed from the solids. If the solids still contain pollutants, they are further treated. Slurry-phase biological treatment can be a relatively rapid process compared to other biological treatment processes. The success of this process is highly dependent on the specific soil and chemical properties of the contaminated material. Slurry-phase technology is particularly useful where rapid cleanup is a high priority.[18]

Solid-phase bioremediation treats soils in above-ground treatment areas equipped with collection systems to prevent any contaminant from escaping the treatment. Moisture, heat, nutrients, or oxygen are controlled to enhance biodegradation. Solid-phase systems are relatively simple to operate and maintain, require a large amount of space, and cleanups require more time to complete than with slurry-phase processes. Solid-phase soil treatment processes include landfarming, soil biopiles, and composting.[19]

Landfarming is a relatively simple treatment method in which contaminated soils are excavated and spread on a pad with a built-in system to collect any leachate (contaminated liquids) that seeps out of the contaminant soaked soil. The soils are periodically turned over to mix air into the waste. Moisture and nutrients are controlled to enhance biodegradation. The length of time for biodegradation to occur will be longer if nutrients, oxygen, or temperature are not properly controlled. In some cases, reduction of contaminant concentrations actually may be attributed more to volatilization than biodegradation. When the process is conducted in enclosures controlling escaping volatile contaminants, volatilization losses are minimized.[20]

A soil biopile is a technique in which contaminated soil is piled in heaps several meters high over an air distribution system. Pulling air through the heap with a vacuum pump provides aeration. Moisture and nutrient levels are maintained at levels that maximize bioremediation. The soil heaps can be placed in enclosures. Volatile contaminants are easily controlled since they are usually part of the air stream being pulled through the pile.[21]

Composting is a technique in which biodegradable waste is mixed with a bulking agent such as straw, hay, or corncobs to make it easier to deliver the optimum levels of air and water to the microorganisms. Three common designs are static pile composting (compost is formed into piles and aerated with blowers or vacuum pumps), mechanically agitated in-vessel composting (compost is placed in a treatment vessel where it is mixed and aerated), and windrow composting (compost is placed in long piles known as windrows and periodically mixed by tractors or similar equipment).[22]

3. In Situ Bioremediation of Groundwater

In situ bioremediation of groundwater speeds the natural biodegradation processes that take place in the water-soaked underground region that lies below the water table. For sites at which both the soil and groundwater are con-

16. *See, e.g.,* U.S. EPA, PROMOTION, *supra* note 7; *see also* U.S. EPA, ABSTRACTS, *supra* note 8.

17. BIOREMEDIATION, *supra* note 9; *see also* U.S. EPA, HOW TO EVALUATE ALTERNATIVE CLEANUP TECHNOLOGIES FOR UNDERGROUND STORAGE TANK SITES: A GUIDE FOR CORRECTIVE ACTION PLAN REVIEWERS (1995) (EPA 510-B-94-003) [hereinafter U.S. EPA, GUIDE FOR CORRECTIVE ACTION].

18. U.S. EPA, ENGINEERING BULLETIN: SLURRY BIODEGRADATION (1990) (EPA 540-2-90-016) [hereinafter U.S. EPA, SLURRY BIODEGRADATION].

19. U.S. EPA, GUIDE FOR CORRECTIVE ACTION, *supra* note 17.

20. *Id.*

21. *Id.*

22. *Id.*

taminated, natural biodegradation is effective at treating both. Generally, an in situ groundwater bioremediation system consists of an extraction well to remove groundwater from the ground, an above-ground water treatment system where nutrients and an oxygen source may be added to the contaminated groundwater, and injection wells to return the "conditioned" groundwater to the subsurface where the microorganisms degrade the contaminants. One limitation of this technology is that differences in underground soil layering and density may cause reinjected conditioned groundwater to follow certain preferred flow paths. Consequently, the conditioned water may not reach some areas of contamination. Another frequently used method of in situ groundwater treatment is air sparging, which involves pumping air into the groundwater to help flush out contaminants. Air sparging is used in conjunction with soil vapor extraction.[23]

F. Introduction to CERCLA

CERCLA is a multifaceted program designed to respond to the harm, or potential harm, to human health and the environment that may be caused by hazardous substances. Each CERCLA site and related response action is unique. EPA has developed a formal process to evaluate each release of a hazardous substance and each site where hazardous substances are located. The process includes a series of assessments that allow the primary threats to human health and the environment to be identified, evaluated, and remedied. After carefully evaluating available remedial alternatives, EPA selects the best remedial alternative. The statutory goal of this process is to select the cleanup method that best protects human health and the environment, while complying with all applicable environmental laws, and provides a long-term, cost-effective solution. During the process of selecting the cleanup method, EPA indirectly regulates bioremediation by identifying and evaluating bioremediation techniques that can be used to clean up the site. The blueprint for all CERCLA response actions is set forth in the national contingency plan (NCP), which is codified in 40 C.F.R. Part 300. The NCP sets forth the procedures that EPA must follow when implementing the CERCLA program in situations where hazardous substances, pollutants, or contaminants have been released into the environment.

1. Discovery of Releases

In order for a site to be considered eligible for a CERCLA response, a release must be discovered and reported to the government. Release[24] can mean any spilling, leaking, pumping, pouring, emitting, emptying, discharging, injecting, escaping, leaching, dumping, or disposing into the environment. This broad definition includes the abandonment of barrels, leaks of hazardous substances from storage tanks, and spills of hazardous substances during transportation accidents. For the purpose of implementing NCP response procedures, release also means the threat of a release.[25]

Methods of site discovery, and the types of releases reported, are quite varied. Releases of hazardous substances may be discovered by various means, including:

- Mandatory CERCLA §103 notification;
- CERCLA §104(e) investigations;
- RCRA-required release notification;
- Inventory efforts or random observation by government agencies;
- Formal citizen petitions pursuant to 40 C.F.R. §300.420(b)(5);
- Review of state and federal records; and
- Informal community observation and notification.

2. The CERCLA Response Process

Response action is a general term that includes both removal and remedial action, including any related enforcement actions. Once a site is identified, EPA performs a preliminary assessment (PA) to determine if the site poses a potential hazard and whether a federal response is necessary.

The second stage in the CERCLA response process is the site inspection (SI), which involves an on-site investigation to ascertain the extent of a release or potential for release and any risks involved. The SI usually involves sample collection and may also include the installation of groundwater monitoring wells. During this phase, a hazard ranking system (HRS) score may be calculated to determine whether the site should be included on the national priorities list (NPL).[26] Only the most contaminated sites are placed on the NPL. Each NPL site must undergo a detailed assessment process set out in the NCP. The sites that need further attention but do not warrant placement on the NPL are addressed by the state or by the removal program, or by another EPA program, e.g., RCRA corrective action.

3. The HRS

Data gathered during the PA and the SI are used to develop a HRS score. The HRS is a methodology to evaluate relative risks to human health and the environment posed by uncontrolled hazardous waste sites, and is the mechanism by which EPA has listed over 95% of the sites currently on the NPL.[27] The HRS assesses four pathways of potential human exposure to contamination, i.e., groundwater, surface water, soil, and air, and calculates a score based on the results of each pathway evaluation.[28] For each pathway, the HRS assigns numerical values to factors that relate to or indicate risk based on conditions at the site. The score generated from each pathway evaluation is applied to a complex formula that produces a site-specific score between 0 and 100. Sites that have a score of 28.50 and above are eligible for the

---

23. *See* U.S. EPA, SLURRY BIODEGRADATION, *supra* note 18; *see also* U.S. EPA, A CITIZEN'S GUIDE TO SOIL VAPOR EXTRACTION AND AIR SPARGING (1996) (EPA 542-F-96-008).

24. CERCLA §101(22), 42 U.S.C. §9601(22), ELR STAT. CERCLA §101(22).

25. *Id.*

26. 40 C.F.R. pt. 300, app. B.

27. The HRS procedures are found in 40 C.F.R. pt. 300, app. A.

28. For more information on the revised HRS and the four pathways, see 55 Fed. Reg. 51532 (Dec. 14, 1990); U.S. EPA, HAZARD RANKING SYSTEM GUIDANCE MANUAL (2001) (OSWER Directive No. 9345.1-07); U.S. EPA, REVISION TO OSWER NPL POLICY "THE REVISED HAZARD RANKING SYSTEM: EVALUATING SITES AFTER WASTE REMOVALS" (1991) (OSWER Directive No. 9345.1-25); U.S. EPA, FACT SHEET, THE REVISED HAZARD RANKING SYSTEM: BACKGROUND INFORMATION (2000) (OSWER Directive No. 9320.7-03FS).

NPL. If the HRS score equals or exceeds 28.50, EPA will propose the site for inclusion on the NPL and, after appropriate public comment, will make a final decision on listing the site. All final NPL decisions are published in the *Federal Register.*

There are two additional mechanisms available for determining eligibility for inclusion on the NPL. First, each state may add a single site to the NPL by designating a site as its top priority, regardless of the HRS score.[29] Second, the Agency for Toxic Substances and Disease Registry (ATSDR) may add certain sites to the NPL. To be eligible for the NPL by the ATSDR, all three of the following conditions must be met: (1) the ATSDR must have issued a health advisory that recommends that humans avoid contact with a release; (2) EPA must determine that the release poses a significant threat to public health; and (3) EPA must determine that it will be more cost effective to use its long-term remedial authority rather than its removal authority to respond to the release.

4. Listing Policies

CERCLA restricts EPA's authority to respond to certain sites by expressly excluding some substances, e.g., petroleum, from the definition of hazardous substances.[30] In addition, EPA may as a matter of policy choose not to use CERCLA authority to act on a site. The rationale for this deferral is that the federal government can undertake or enforce cleanup under other laws, thus preserving CERCLA funds for sites not covered by those other laws. EPA has chosen not to use its CERCLA authority at hazardous waste sites regulated by RCRA corrective action. Instead, EPA requires cleanup of those sites under its RCRA authority. If EPA later determines that a deferred site is not being properly addressed under other laws or authorities, it may consider placing it on the NPL.

5. The Removal Process

Removal actions are short-term federal responses to prevent, minimize, or mitigate damage to the public or the environment at sites where hazardous substances, pollutants, or contaminants have been released or where there is a substantial threat of a release.[31] Removal actions may include, but are not limited to: repairs to a dike or impoundment wall, erecting a security fence, or transporting leaking drums to a RCRA treatment, storage, and disposal facility. A removal may be conducted during any step of the response process at an NPL site, and may even constitute complete cleanup of a site. Removal actions are often used to respond to emergencies and accidental releases during transport, or at operating facilities, as well as to uncontrolled releases at non-NPL sites. To make a clear distinction between short-term removal actions and long-term remedial actions, Congress placed limits on the time and money available to conduct a removal response. The spending limit is $2 million per re-

moval, and the removal must be completed in two months.[32] The spending and time limits may be extended only where continuation is required to prevent, limit, or mitigate an emergency which is an immediate risk to public health or the environment and it will not be acted upon by another party, or continuing the removal is consistent with a remedial action that will be taken at the site (applicable only to proposed and final NPL sites).[33]

6. Removal Action

If EPA determines that a removal action is appropriate, action begins as soon as possible. Not all removal actions will be equally urgent. For example, situations involving risk of fire or explosion, or contamination of a drinking water reservoir, may require more prompt and expeditious attention than certain drum removals or cleanups of surface impoundments. When a removal action takes place, EPA must consider other federal and state laws and regulations that provide relevant guidance for the response action.[34] These other laws and regulations are called applicable or relevant and appropriate requirements (ARARs). CERCLA requires that ARARs be met to the extent practicable, considering the urgency of the removal action. After the removal action is complete one of two events can occur. The site may be cleaned to the extent that no further response on the federal level is needed. In contrast, the site may be placed on the NPL so that EPA can continue with a long-term remedial action.

7. The Remedial Process

Remedial actions differ from removal actions in several ways. First, there are no set time or monetary limits placed on a remedial action as these activities are targeted for long-term, permanent response. Second, remedial actions involve more detailed planning and decisionmaking processes than removal actions and may only be conducted at sites on the NPL. Third, EPA directs remedial actions, with cleanup activities usually performed by remedial contractors.

8. Remedial Investigation/Feasibility Study (RI/FS)

After a site is added to the NPL, the task of selecting the most appropriate cleanup method begins. The RI/FS is a process of site and remedy evaluation that facilitates the selection of remedies that will most effectively eliminate, reduce, or control risks to human health and the environment.[35] The RI and FS are conducted concurrently. Each is discussed below. Conducting the RI/FS generally involves project scoping, data collection, risk assessment, treatability studies, analysis of alternatives, and identification of ARARs. By identifying and evaluating bioremediation techniques during this phase of a CERCLA response action, EPA indirectly regulates them. Moreover, as EPA attempts to identify the most appropriate remedy for a site during this phase of a CERCLA re-

29. CERCLA §105(a)(8)(B), 42 U.S.C. §9605(a)(8)(B), ELR STAT. CERCLA §105(a)(8)(B); *see also* 40 C.F.R. §300.425(c)(2).

30. CERCLA §101(14), 42 U.S.C. §9601(14), ELR STAT. CERCLA §101(14).

31. CERCLA §104(a)(2), (c)(1), 42 U.S.C. §9604(a)(2), (c)(1), ELR STAT. CERCLA §104(a)(2), (c)(1).

32. CERCLA §104(c)(1), 42 U.S.C. §9604(c)(1), ELR STAT. CERCLA §104(c)(1).

33. *See also* 40 C.F.R. §300.415(b)(5).

34. CERCLA §121(d), 42 U.S.C. §9621(d), ELR STAT. CERCLA §121(d).

35. 40 C.F.R. §300.430.

sponse action, EPA may promote the development of new and improved bioremediation techniques.

9. The RI

The purpose of the RI is to collect data necessary to adequately assess the risks to human health and the environment and to support the development, evaluation, and selection of appropriate response alternatives.[36] The RI may be performed in several stages in order to refine sampling efforts. It involves field investigations, treatability studies, a baseline risk assessment, and identification of ARARs. The field investigation enables the lead agency to characterize the nature of a threat posed by the hazardous substances and support the analysis and design of potential response actions. When necessary, bench-scale and pilot-scale studies are conducted to obtain enough data to select and implement a remedial action alternative. Bench-scale studies conducted during the RI phase are usually limited to treatability and materials testing activities to help identify, screen, and evaluate alternatives. Pilot-scale studies, which are larger, more expensive, and more time-consuming than bench-scale studies, are used to fine tune the selected treatment process and are usually conducted during the remedial design stage. The site-specific baseline risk assessment is needed to determine whether the contaminants of concern would pose a current or potential threat to human health and the environment if a remedial action were not undertaken. During the risk assessment, chemical-specific toxicity information, combined with quantitative and qualitative information relating to exposure, are compared to site conditions. These comparisons determine whether concentrations of contaminants at or near the site affect or may affect human health and the environment. The results of this baseline risk assessment will help establish acceptable exposure levels for use in developing remedial alternatives in the FS.

As with removal actions, ARARs must be identified in the remedial process as well. A major component of the RI/FS is the identification of ARARs. CERCLA specifies that on-site Superfund remedial actions shall attain other federal standards, requirements, criteria, limitations, or more stringent state requirements that are determined to be legally applicable, or relevant and appropriate to the specified circumstances at the site.[37] Examples of ARARs include:

- Ambient or chemical-specific requirements from the CWA or CAA;
- Performance, design, and other action-specific requirements such as RCRA closure regulations;
- RCRA land disposal restrictions; and
- Location requirements such as federal and state siting laws for hazardous waste facilities and the National Register of Historic Places.

On-site remedial activities must comply with substantive, but not administrative, requirements. Permitting is considered to be an administrative requirement. Thus, federal, state, and local permits are not required for on-site activities at fund-financed and CERCLA §106 remedial actions.[38] For example, compliance with RCRA landfill design and operating standards would be necessary for a Superfund action involving the management of hazardous waste, but a RCRA treatment, storage, and disposal permit would not be required.

10. The FS

The FS is conducted to develop and evaluate remedial alternatives. FS activities should be fully integrated with the RI. The FS can include an alternatives screening step to select a reasonable number of alternatives for detailed analysis. In developing and screening alternatives, EPA must establish remedial action objectives specifying contaminants of concern, potential exposure pathways, and remediation goals. The remediation goals establish the extent to which the site should be cleaned up in order to protect human health and the environment.[39] When considering the risk factors for known or suspected carcinogens, the remediation should achieve an upper-bound lifetime cancer risk level of between 10-4 and 10-6 for high-end receptors. This risk level indicates that between 1 in 10,000 to 1 in 1,000,000 people exposed to the site over a lifetime or a portion of a lifetime will be likely to contract cancer. For other types of toxicants, a safe exposure level should be established at the dose below which no adverse health effects have been observed in laboratory studies. Ecological threats should be addressed, particularly sensitive habitats and critical habitats of species protected under the ESA.

EPA identifies and evaluates potential suitable technologies, including innovative technologies and other bioremediation techniques. EPA must consider alternatives that reduce toxicity, mobility, or volume of contaminated material through treatment, including alternative treatment technologies or resource recovery technologies.[40] EPA then assembles a set of alternative remedial actions. There should be an initial screening of the remedial alternatives in accordance with the following criteria:

- Effectiveness: the degree to which an alternative reduces toxicity, mobility, or volume through treatment; minimizes risks and provides long-term protection; complies with ARARs; minimizes short-term impacts; and achieves protection quickly;
- Implementability: the technical feasibility and availability of the technologies each alternative would employ; and
- Cost: alternatives providing effectiveness and implementability similar to that of another alternative, but at a greater cost, may be eliminated.

Those alternatives that survive the preliminary analysis are evaluated through a detailed analysis process. The purpose of the detailed analysis is to objectively assess the alternatives with respect to nine criteria listed in 40 C.F.R. §300.430(e)(9)(iii), and to evaluate the advantages and dis-

---

36. *Id.* §300.430(d).

37. CERCLA §121(d), 42 U.S.C. §9621(d), ELR Stat. CERCLA §121(d).

38. 40 C.F.R. §300.400(e); CERCLA §121(e), 42 U.S.C. §9621(e), ELR Stat. CERCLA §121(e). *See also* 55 Fed. Reg. 8666, 8756 (Mar. 8, 1990).

39. 40 C.F.R. §300.430(e)(2)(i).

40. CERCLA §121, 42 U.S.C. §9621, ELR Stat. CERCLA §121.

advantages of each alternative relative to the criteria. CERCLA specifically provides that off-site transport and disposal or containment without treatment are the least favored alternatives.[41]

11. Remedy Selection

The selection of the remedial action for the site is a two-step process, requiring the development of a proposed plan and a record of decision (ROD). At this point, state agencies and the public are given the opportunity to participate in the remedy selection process. EPA prepares a plan that briefly describes the remedial alternatives that were analyzed, proposes a preferred remedial alternative, and summarizes the information used to make this decision.[42] The proposed plan is presented to the public, and revised in accordance with state and public comment, if necessary.

After evaluating all comments received on the proposed plan, EPA makes the final remedy selection decision. EPA documents the final decision in the ROD, which must be signed by the Regional Administrator. The ROD contains significant facts, analysis of facts, and site-specific policy determinations considered in the remedy selection process, and explains how the nine evaluation criteria were used to select the remedy.[43] The ROD is a major element of the administrative record and must be made available for public inspection. All legal challenges, appeals, and defenses rely on the ROD and the administrative record.[44]

12. Remedial Design/Remedial Action (RD/RA)

The RD is the engineering plan used to guide implementation of the selected remedy.[45] The RA is the physical implementation of the ROD and the RD. All RD/RA activities must conform to the remedy set forth in the ROD and other decision documents. If the RA differs significantly from the ROD, an explanation of significant differences (ESD) must be published, or the ROD must be amended.[46]

13. Operation and Maintenance (O&M)

At any site where the RA does not result in fully unrestricted use of the site, O&M measures will continue at the site to ensure effective implementation of the RA. O&M measures are initiated after the remedy is constructed and is determined to be operational and functional.[47] For fund-led sites, the state is responsible for funding long-term O&M activities and must enter into an agreement with EPA to that effect before RA begins. EPA will share O&M costs for the first

year. Federal funding of actions involving measures to restore groundwater may continue for up to 10 years after the remedy becomes operational and functional.[48]

14. Deleting Sites From the NPL

When no further response action is appropriate, sites can be deleted from the NPL in accordance with the procedures outlined in 40 C.F.R. §300.425(e). Prior to deleting a site, the state must be consulted, a notice of intent to delete must be published in the *Federal Register*, and public comments must be considered. In addition to deleting sites, EPA may move a site from the NPL to the "construction completion" category where remedial construction activities have been completed, but formal deletion is not yet appropriate.[49]

For several years, EPA's policy was to retain sites on the NPL until it completed a review five years after initiation of the RA. The five-year review, required by CERCLA §121(c), was intended to confirm that the RA completed was, and remains, protective of human health and the environment. In the mid-1990s, EPA separated the NPL deletion process and the five-year process, allowing sites to be deleted from the NPL as soon as the requirements specified in the ROD have been met.

G. RCRA Corrective Action

The RCRA corrective action program is designed to ensure the remediation of hazardous releases associated with RCRA-regulated facilities. EPA enforces the program principally through the statutory authorities established by the Hazardous and Solid Waste Amendments (HSWA) of 1984, which amended significantly the original RCRA program. There are minimal regulatory requirements at present, but EPA has issued a proposed rule that would establish a comprehensive regulatory framework for implementing the corrective action program.[50] Without an extensive regulatory program in place, EPA relies on the proposed rule and other guidance it has developed pursuant to statutory authorities to structure corrective action requirements in facility permits and orders.

The RCRA corrective action program is less mature than the CERCLA response action program. Although the RCRA corrective action program uses different terminology than the CERCLA response program, the programs operate in basically the same manner. In simple terms, each program is designed to: identify contamination that must be remediated; collect data describing the type and extent of the contamination; evaluate available remedial alternatives; select the best remedial alternative; and implement the selected remedy. EPA has chosen to operate the two programs similarly to ensure that the experience gained and the lessons learned in the CERCLA response program can be effectively used in the RCRA corrective action program.

1. RCRA Statutory Authority

Prior to HSWA, EPA's statutory authority to require remediation or corrective action measures at RCRA-regu-

---

41. CERCLA §121(b)(1), 42 U.S.C. §9621(b)(1), ELR STAT. CERCLA 121(b)(1).

42. 40 C.F.R. §300.430(f)(2).

43. The specific information required to be included in the ROD is listed in *id.* §300.430(f)(5).

44. RODs are publicly available from the National Technical Information Service (NTIS). ROD abstracts, searchable by state and city, are provided on EPA's Superfund home page, *available at* http://www.epa.gov/superfund (last visited July 31, 2001). A searchable RODs database containing the full text of each ROD is available through the Right-To-Know Computer Network or RTK-NET, *available at* http://rtk.net (last visited July 31, 2001).

45. 40 C.F.R. §300.430.

46. *Id.* §300.435(c)(2).

47. *Id.* §300.435(f)(2).

---

48. *Id.* §300.430(f)(3).

49. *See* 56 Fed. Reg. 5598 (Feb. 11, 1991).

50. *See* 55 Fed. Reg. 30798 (July 27, 1990).

lated facilities was limited to those situations in which there was an imminent and substantial hazard to human health or the environment.[51]

Specifically, EPA has the authority to seek legal relief in the appropriate U.S. district court or issue administrative corrective action orders for releases from any site where the handling, storage, treatment, transportation, or disposal of solid or hazardous waste may pose an imminent and substantial endangerment to human health or the environment. HSWA gave EPA substantial new statutory authority to develop a broader corrective action program. These provisions include:

- RCRA §3008(h)—authority to require corrective action at interim status facilities;
- RCRA §3004(u)—requires corrective action be addressed as a condition of a facility's Part B permit; and
- RCRA §3004(v)—authority to require corrective action for releases migrating beyond the facility boundary.

These corrective action authorities are implemented on a case-by-case basis in facility permits or orders issued by EPA.[52] EPA has not promulgated a comprehensive regulatory program describing the corrective action process. Currently, the corrective action process is defined by various policy and guidance documents. EPA, however, has promulgated regulations regarding the management of remediation wastes generated during corrective action.[53]

2. Releases at Permitted Facilities

RCRA requires corrective action for all releases of hazardous waste or constituents from any solid waste management unit (SWMU) at a facility seeking a permit, regardless of when the waste was placed in the unit.[54] An SWMU is any discernible unit at which solid wastes have been placed at any time, irrespective of whether the unit was intended for the management of solid or hazardous waste. This definition includes any area at a facility where solid wastes have been routinely and systematically released. EPA interprets this authority to apply to any facility seeking a permit, including operating permits, post-closure permits, and permits-by-rule, after November 8, 1984.[55] The cleanup must address releases to air, groundwater, surface water, and soil. Furthermore, facilities are required to maintain the permit until corrective action is completed. To ensure that cleanups are completed in a timely manner, EPA must include schedules of compliance and financial assurance for completing corrective action in a facility's permit when issued.[56]

To complement EPA's broad authority to direct RCRA cleanups of contamination on all contiguous property of a facility, HSWA added authority for EPA to require a facility owner/operator to clean up releases that have migrated be-

yond the facility boundary. Specifically, the facility owner/operator must institute corrective action wherever necessary to protect human health and the environment.[57] The exception to this requirement is when facility owner/operator demonstrates to the satisfaction of EPA that the facility owner/operator was unable to obtain the necessary permission from adjacent property holders to undertake such actions.[58] EPA has asserted that financial responsibility must be demonstrated for these off-site cleanup actions.

3. Interim Status Corrective Action

HSWA established EPA's authority to issue orders requiring cleanups at interim status facilities.[59] EPA may issue an administrative order or file a civil action whenever it determines on the basis of any information that there is or has been a release of hazardous waste into the environment from an interim status facility. This authority applies to facilities that are currently operating under interim status, that formerly operated under interim status, or that should have obtained interim status. It also applies to any release of hazardous waste or constituents from the facility.[60] In addition to requiring cleanup, EPA has the authority to revoke or suspend interim status. Finally, EPA may use its interim status authority to require corrective action beyond the facility boundary and to require proof of financial assurance for cleanup.

4. Existing Regulations

The RCRA corrective action program is implemented largely through statutory authorities and EPA guidance developed pursuant to those authorities. There are, however, some codified provisions that require corrective action for releases to groundwater from regulated units, e.g., landfills, surface impoundments.[61] Under these regulations, corrective action is the third step of a three-phase program for detecting, characterizing, and responding to releases to the uppermost aquifer from regulated units. In the corrective action phase, the owner/operator is required to remove or treat in place all contaminants present in concentrations above previously determined protection levels.[62] This type of corrective action applies only to regulated units as opposed to all SWMUs and follows a slightly different procedure because it involves significant groundwater monitoring.[63] RCRA's permitting regulations require anyone seeking a permit to identify, in the permit application, any SWMUs found at their facility and a plan for remediating any contamination associated with any SWMU.[64] EPA has promulgated regulations designed to mitigate the regulatory burden of handling remediation wastes generated during the corrective action process.[65]

51. RCRA §7003, 42 U.S.C. §6973, ELR Stat. RCRA §7003.

52. *See* 40 C.F.R. §§264.101, 270.1(c), .14(d).

53. *See id.* §264.552, .553.

54. RCRA §3004(u), 42 U.S.C. §6924(u), ELR Stat. RCRA §3004(u).

55. 50 Fed. Reg. 28702, 28715 (July 15, 1985).

56. RCRA §3004(u), 42 U.S.C. §6924(u), ELR Stat. RCRA §3004(u).

57. *Id.* §3004(v), 42 U.S.C. §6924(v), ELR Stat. RCRA §3004(v).

58. 40 C.F.R. §264.101(c).

59. RCRA §3008(h), 42 U.S.C. §6928(h), ELR Stat. RCRA §3008(h).

60. *Id.*

61. 40 C.F.R. pt. 264, subpt. F.

62. *Id.* §264.100.

63. *Id.* §264.101.

64. *Id.* §270.1(c), .14(d).

65. *Id.* §264.552, .553.

5. The Corrective Action Process

To better understand RCRA's corrective action program, it is important to know how a facility becomes subject to the corrective action process. A facility does not enter the program every time there is a spill of hazardous waste. There are primarily four ways a facility becomes subject to corrective action. The first, and most common, involves the identification of SWMUs during the permitting process. Second, a facility owner/operator may volunteer to perform corrective action. Third, EPA may issue an enforcement order, requiring a facility to implement corrective action. Fourth, during groundwater monitoring, if a facility owner/operator detects statistically significant evidence of increased contamination due to a release of hazardous waste or constituents from the facility.

6. Corrective Action Implementation

The *National RCRA Corrective Action Strategy* has governed EPA's implementation of the corrective action requirements.[66] The basic phases of the corrective action process are:

- A RCRA facility assessment (RFA) is conducted to determine whether there is sufficient evidence of a release to require the owner/operator to undertake additional steps to characterize the release. During an RFA, EPA typically compiles existing information on environmental conditions at a given facility and, as necessary, gathers additional facility-specific information on SWMUs and other areas of concern, releases, potential releases, release pathways, and receptors. After completion of the RFA, a schedule of compliance for the remaining steps will be developed, if necessary.
- A RCRA facility investigation (RFI) is conducted to characterize in detail the nature, extent and rate of migration of potentially significant releases identified in the RFA. The investigation may occur in stages to avoid unnecessary analysis.
- A corrective measures study (CMS) will be required in many cases to identify and evaluate potential remedial measures for facilities undergoing corrective action. Once a remedy has been selected, EPA will either modify the facility's permit or issue an order requiring the owner/operator to implement the remedy with EPA oversight.
- Corrective measures implementation (CMI) encompasses the design, construction, operation, and maintenance of the selected response action.
- Interim/stabilization measures are short-term RAs that can be conducted at any time to respond to immediate threats while long-term remedies are pursued. An RFI or a CMS is not required for these measures.

These procedures have been implemented on a case-by-case basis primarily for facilities going through the permit process.[67] In the absence of a detailed regulatory plan like the NCP, the details of the corrective action program have been governed by numerous guidance documents issued by EPA.[68] In general, the present program follows the format that is set forth in detail in the proposed rule described below.

7. The Proposed Corrective Action Regulations

In 1990, EPA proposed a new comprehensive regulatory framework for implementing corrective action requirements.[69] The rule would have amended the RCRA regulations to include a new Subpart S. In mid-1995, EPA responded to criticism of the proposal by reevaluating the corrective action program's "speed, efficiency, protectiveness and responsiveness, and environmental results," based on experience gleaned from implementation of the corrective action program.[70] On May 1, 1996, EPA published an advanced notice of proposed rulemaking (ANPR), which provided guidance on areas of the corrective action program not addressed by the 1990 proposal, and replaced the 1990 proposal as the primary corrective action implementation guidance.[71] By 1999, however, EPA had decided to withdraw most provisions of the 1990 Subpart S proposal. According to the EPA, it took this action because it believes that detailed regulations are not necessary to carry out the Agency's duties under RCRA §3004(u) and (v).[72]

EPA has developed five objectives for the corrective action program. First, EPA will create a consistent, holistic approach to cleanups. Second, EPA will establish protective, practical cleanup expectations. Third, voluntary cleanup will be encouraged (or, at least, regulatory disincentives will be removed) by shifting more of the responsibilities for achieving cleanup goals to the regulated community. Fourth, EPA will focus on opportunities to streamline and reduce costs of the cleanup process. Fifth, EPA will enhance opportunities for timely, meaningful public participation.

In accordance with the statutory mandate, EPA's corrective action guidance generally requires any facility seeking a permit under RCRA Subtitle C to implement corrective action "as necessary to protect human health and the environment." The guidance, however, does not apply to the following four types of RCRA permits: (1) permits for land treatment demonstrations; (2) emergency permits; (3) permits by rule for ocean disposal barges; and (4) research, development, and demonstration permits.[73] Permits will contain schedules of compliance where investigations or corrective action cannot be completed prior to issuance of the permit. In addition, owners/operators will be required to remedy releases that have migrated off-site.

The current guidance defines SWMU as:

> Any discernible unit at which solid wastes have been placed at any time, irrespective of whether the unit was in-

66. OSWER, U.S. EPA, NATIONAL RCRA CORRECTIVE ACTION STRATEGY (1985).

67. 61 Fed. Reg. 19431 (May 1, 1996).

68. OSWER, U.S. EPA, RCRA FACILITY ASSESSMENT GUIDANCE (1986); OSWER, U.S. EPA, RCRA FACILITY INVESTIGATION GUIDANCE (1989) [hereinafter U.S. EPA, RCRA FACILITY INVESTIGATION GUIDANCE]; OSWER, U.S. EPA, RCRA CORRECTIVE ACTION PLAN (1994) [hereinafter U.S. EPA, CORRECTIVE ACTION PLAN].

69. 55 Fed. Reg. at 30798.

70. 61 Fed. Reg. at 19431.

71. *Id.*

72. 64 Fed. Reg. 54604 (Oct. 7, 1999).

73. 61 Fed. Reg. at 19441.

tended for the management of solid or hazardous waste. Such units include any area at a facility at which solid wastes have been routinely and systematically released.[74]

8. Proposed Corrective Action Procedures

a. Preliminary Site Investigations

The corrective action process is structured around five elements: initial site assessment, site characterization, interim actions, evaluation of remedial alternatives, and implementation of the selected remedy. While EPA continues to encourage program implementers and facility owners/operators to focus on the desired result of a cleanup rather than a mechanistic cleanup process, these elements typically occur, to one degree or another, during most cleanups.[75] The initial site assessment, referred to as an RFA, serves as a screen to eliminate from consideration SWMUs, environmental media or entire facilities which present no evidence of a release posing a threat to human health or the environment or, alternatively, forms the basis for initiating full-scale site characterization.[76]

Site characterization, referred to as the RFI, is necessary to ascertain the nature and extent of contamination at a site and to gather information necessary to support selection and implementation of appropriate remedies. At this stage, the owner/operator typically develops a work plan for conducting the RFI, which becomes part of the schedule of compliance that is an integrated part of the permit.

The RFI itself will develop detailed information concerning the environmental characteristics of the facility, including such matters as hydrological and climatological conditions, soil characteristics, surface water and sediment quality, and air quality. EPA emphasizes that RIs should be tailored to the specific conditions and circumstances at the facility and focused on the units, releases, and exposure pathways of concern.

Eventually, the permittee would be required to submit a final report summarizing the RFI.[77] If it is determined that there have been no releases at the facility, no further action will be required. In the vast majority of cases, releases will be identified and the facility will move on to the next stage of the corrective action process.

b. Action Levels

A CMS will be required if the RFI shows that certain "action levels" have been exceeded.[78] These "action levels" are established on a site-specific basis for each environmental medium through which exposures may occur. EPA proposes to base them on existing standards, or to derive them from general criteria. For example, maximum contaminant levels (MCLs) establish contaminant-specific drinking water standards under the Safe Drinking Water Act which can be used as action levels for contaminated groundwater. If an MCL has not been established for the contaminant in question, EPA may establish an appropriate concentration level on a facility-specific basis or from standardized lists. Similarly, action levels for surface water will be numerical concentrations drawn from the state's water quality standards, but may also be derived by EPA according to the criteria set forth in the 1996 ANPR.[79]

Program implementers and facility owners/operators should ensure that action levels used at RCRA corrective action facilities reflect up-to-date toxicity information and that action level assumptions are consistent with the physical conditions and current or reasonably anticipated exposure assumptions at any given facility.[80]

c. A CMS

A CMS, which analyzes potential remedies for cleaning up releases from SWMUs, would vary in scope depending on the size of the facility and severity of the contamination. Each potential remedy will be evaluated based on site-specific conditions for performance, reliability, ease of implementation, and potential adverse impacts (such as safety concerns and the amount of residual contamination). The remedy's effectiveness, time required for implementation, estimated costs, and administrative or institutional requirements (such as state or local permits) will also be examined.[81]

d. Remedy Selection

On the basis of the CMS, EPA will select a remedy that: (1) is protective of human health and the environment; (2) achieves the "media cleanup standards" set by EPA for "releases" identified in the RFI; (3) controls the source of that release and any further releases to the "extent practicable"; and (4) properly manages wastes generated by remedial activity.[82] To assess whether a remedy complies with these standards, EPA considers the information developed during the CMS to evaluate the:

- Long-term reliability and effectiveness of the remedy, including the amount of wastes left at the site and the need for long-term management;
- Effectiveness of the remedy in reducing the toxicity, mobility or volume of the contaminants;
- Short-term effectiveness of the remedy, including the magnitude of reduction of existing risks, short-term risks to the community or workers, and the time until full protection is achieved;
- Ease of implementation, including potential technical or administrative problems and the availability of needed treatment, storage, or disposal

---

74. *Id.* at 19442.

75. *Id.* at 19443.

76. *Id.* The 1996 ANPR provides flexibility in the assessment process in two ways: first, by allowing facility owners/operators the option of conducting their own RFA, and second, by allowing a release assessment, following the RFA, to confirm or reduce uncertainty about areas of concern and potential releases identified during the initial site assessment "before full scale characterization, to focus subsequent investigations or eliminate certain units or areas from further consideration." *Id.*

77. U.S. EPA, CORRECTIVE ACTION PLAN, *supra* note 68.

78. 61 Fed. Reg. at 19446.

79. *Id.*

80. *Id.*

81. *Id.*

82. *Id.* at 19449.

services; and
● Cost.[83]

After evaluating each of the proposed remedies, EPA would select the remedy that best meets these standards and factors. EPA would also establish "media cleanup standards," which refers to broad cleanup objectives, and "media cleanup levels," which refers to site- and media-specific concentrations of hazardous constituents. The levels chosen will depend on site-specific factors, including current, as well as reasonably expected, uses of the media. As a starting point, however, cleanup standards for known or suspected carcinogens will be established at concentration levels representing an excess upperbound lifetime risk to an individual of between 1 x 10-4 and 1 x 10-6.[84] For other toxicants, the standard shall be the concentration to which a human may be exposed on a daily basis, without appreciable risk of deleterious effect during a lifetime.[85] EPA will establish specific compliance points where these standards must be met, as discussed below.

e. Remedy Implementation and Completion

To implement a corrective action remedy, the owner/operator is required to prepare a detailed RD (including plans, specifications, and schedules) which is incorporated into the permit's schedule of compliance.[86] Through the use of progress reports and on-site inspections, EPA oversees the remedy implementation. To complete a final remedy, the permittee must comply with media cleanup standards, address the source of contamination and remove all temporary structures required to conduct the selected remedy.[87]

Once the RD is implemented and the remedial goals achieved, the owner/operator submits to EPA a request that the corrective action compliance schedule be terminated.[88] This request must include a certification that the remedy was completed in accordance with the applicable rules and permit requirements. EPA must then determine (subject to public notice and comment) whether the remedy is complete. If EPA makes that determination, the compliance schedule is terminated.

f. Interim Measures

Over the last decade, EPA has increasingly emphasized the importance of interim actions and site stabilization in the corrective action program to address sites posing an immediate and ongoing threat to human health or the environment in advance of a final remedy. The threats which justify interim measures include: (1) exposure of populations to hazardous wastes; (2) contamination of drinking water supplies; (3) further degradation of the medium absent immediate response; (4) threat of release from drums or tanks; (5) potential migration of hazardous waste; or (6) risks of

fire or explosion. Interim measures do not replace a final remedy, but must be consistent with, and a necessary component of, any final remedy.[89]

g. Conditional Remedies

EPA could also impose a "conditional remedy" at a site to facilitate cleanup to levels appropriate for current uses of the medium.[90] Where final cleanup appears technically impracticable, a conditional remedy would primarily allow existing contamination to remain within the facility boundary. The permittee, however, must still: (1) achieve media cleanup levels for contamination beyond the facility boundaries; (2) control the source of contamination; and (3) give required financial assurances. As long as the risk of exposure remains insignificant and the permittee contains the contamination, then EPA will defer a final cleanup for the duration of the permit.

h. Corrective Action Management Units (CAMUs)

In certain situations, EPA allows somewhat relaxed management practices to facilitate cleanups and avoid unnecessary regulation. EPA may designate an area at a facility, used only for managing remediation wastes for implementing corrective action or cleanup requirements as a CAMU.[91] This designation allows hazardous wastes within the CAMU to be moved without being subject to the land disposal restrictions or minimum technology requirements.[92] One or more CAMUs may be designated at a facility, and uncontaminated areas may be included within a CAMU if EPA specifically finds that so doing will be more protective than managing such wastes at already contaminated areas.[93] "Remediation wastes" include all solid and hazardous wastes, and all media and debris which contain listed hazardous wastes managed for the purpose of implementing cleanup.[94] Remediation wastes specifically include wastes found within the facility boundary, i.e., all contiguous property under the control of the owner or operator, as well as wastes that have migrated beyond that boundary due to on-site releases. The definition excludes, however, new or as generated wastes. In other words, the wastes to be managed within the CAMU must result from implementing the corrective action rather than "new" or "as generated" wastes from active processes at the facility.[95]

In August 2000, EPA proposed amendments to the CAMU regulations in response to a settlement agreement between EPA and the Environmental Defense Fund. Under that settlement, EPA was to issue a final rule by October 8, 2001, that will "define the wastes eligible for management in CAMUs, establish minimum treatment requirements for

---

83. *Id.*; *see also* U.S. EPA, CORRECTIVE ACTION PLAN, *supra* note 68, at 54.

84. 61 Fed. Reg. at 19449-50.

85. 55 Fed. Reg. at 30878.

86. U.S. EPA, CORRECTIVE ACTION PLAN, *supra* note 68, at 59.

87. *Id.* at 71.

88. 61 Fed. Reg. at 19453.

89. *Id.* at 19446; *see also* U.S. EPA, RCRA FACILITY INVESTIGATION GUIDANCE, *supra* note 68.

90. U.S. EPA, MANAGING THE CORRECTIVE ACTION PROGRAM FOR ENVIRONMENTAL RESULTS: THE RCRA FACILITY STABILIZATION EFFORT (1991); 55 Fed. Reg. at 30879; 40 C.F.R. §264.525(f) (proposed).

91. 40 C.F.R. §260.10.

92. *Id.* §264.552.

93. *Id.*

94. *Id.* §260.10.

95. U.S. EPA, MANAGEMENT OF REMEDIATION WASTES UNDER RCRA (1998) (EPA 530-F-98-026).

such wastes, and set minimum technical standards for CAMUs."[96] The final rule may significantly change the current use of CAMUs.

9. The Philosophy of RCRA's Corrective Action Program

a. Relationship to CERCLA

RCRA's corrective action program is similar to CERCLA's response program set forth in the NCP. The RFA parallels CERCLA's PA/SI; the RFI parallels CERCLA's RI; the CMS parallels CERCLA's FS; the Remedy Selection parallels CERCLA's ROD; and the CMI parallels CERCLA's RD/RA. A primary objective of EPA's corrective action program is to achieve substantive consistency with the policies and procedures of the CERCLA program.[97] EPA views this consistency as desirable in order "to ensure that the regulated industry can gain no advantage by proceeding under one program rather than the other."[98] Within this overall objective, however, EPA recognizes that significantly more procedural flexibility is appropriate in dealing with SWMUs, particularly those present at active RCRA facilities. As noted in the preamble to the 1990 proposed rule, active RCRA sites differ from CERCLA sites in that they represent a controlled use situation where it will often be reasonable to require prompt cleanup to levels consistent with current use, but to defer final cleanup as long as the owner/operator remains under a RCRA permit.[99]

b. EPA's Management Philosophy

EPA's procedural flexibility is driven by the need to prioritize and rationalize the administrative response to a regulatory burden widely viewed as far outstripping that presented by CERCLA. There are more than 6,000 land disposal, incinerator, and treatment, and storage facilities in existence today which may need some amount of corrective action.[100] EPA estimates that the number of RCRA facilities that may ultimately need corrective action could be three times the number of sites currently on the NPL.[101] The sheer number of RCRA regulated facilities creates a significant problem for EPA, because the budget for developing regulations and guidance for RCRA corrective action is less than 15% of the amount budgeted for CERCLA.[102]

EPA has stated a management philosophy for RCRA's corrective action program which it believes will further its goals.[103] First, EPA's fundamental goal is to control or eliminate risks to human health and the environment and the corrective action process should, therefore, utilize risk-based decisionmaking. Second, program implementation should

focus on results, not mindless compliance with or fulfillment of a standardized process. Third, interim action and stabilization should be used to reduce risks and prevent exposures. Fourth, activities at corrective action facilities should be phased to focus on areas of the facility that represent the greatest risk to human health and/or the environment. Fifth, program implementation should provide for meaningful inclusion of all stakeholders. Sixth, corrective action obligations should be addressed using the most appropriate tool for any given facility. Seventh, states will be the primary implementers of the corrective action program and should therefore be fully involved in the development of corrective action implementation strategies, policy, guidance, and regulations.

Whether EPA will be able truly to implement this "philosophy" for RCRA's corrective action program and avoid the bureaucratic snarls that have plagued CERCLA's program remains an open question. However, EPA has taken steps to turn its policy into practice and achieve its cleanup goals by implementing the 1999 and 2001 Cleanup Reforms.

c. Cleanup Reforms

The RCRA Cleanup Reforms are a comprehensive effort to address the key impediments to cleanups, maximize program flexibility, and spur progress toward a set of ambitious national cleanup goals. The national cleanup goals focus on 1,712 RCRA facilities identified as warranting attention over the next several years because of the potential for unacceptable exposure to pollutants and/or for groundwater contamination. The goals, set by EPA under the Government Performance and Results Act (GPRA), are that by 2005, EPA will verify and document that 95% of these 1,712 RCRA facilities will have "current human exposures under control," and 70% of these facilities will have "migration of contaminated groundwater under control."[104]

The reforms are designed to achieve faster, more efficient cleanups at RCRA sites that have actual or potential contamination, by:

- Providing new results-oriented guidance with clear objectives;
- Fostering maximum use of program flexibility and practical approaches through training, outreach, and new uses of enforcement tools; and
- Enhancing community involvement including greater public access to information on cleanup progress.[105]

To achieve these goals, EPA has created two draft guidance documents[106] and announced plans for two additional guidance documents.[107]

In January 2001, EPA implemented a second set of administrative reforms to accelerate the cleanup of hazardous

96. 65 Fed. Reg. 51080, 51083 (Aug. 22, 2000).

97. 61 Fed. Reg. at 19441.

98. 55 Fed. Reg. at 30852.

99. *Id.* at 30803.

100. 65 Fed. Reg. at 51119.

101. 61 Fed. Reg. at 19440. *See also* U.S. EPA, THE NATION'S HAZARDOUS WASTE MANAGEMENT PROGRAM AT A CROSSROADS: THE RCRA IMPLEMENTATION STUDY (1990) [hereinafter U.S. EPA, CROSSROADS].

102. U.S. EPA, CROSSROADS, *supra* note 101, at 78.

103. 61 Fed. Reg. at 19435.

104. U.S. EPA, FACT SHEET, RCRA CLEANUP REFORMS: FASTER, FOCUSED, MORE FLEXIBLE CLEANUPS (1999) (EPA 530-F-99-018).

105. Corrective Action Completion and Results-Based Approaches to RCRA Corrective Action, 65 Fed. Reg. 15905 (Mar. 24, 2000).

106. U.S. EPA, INTERIM FINAL GUIDANCE FOR RCRA CORRECTIVE ACTION ENVIRONMENTAL INDICATORS (1999); U.S. EPA, DRAFT HANDBOOK OF GROUNDWATER POLICIES FOR RCRA CORRECTIVE ACTION (2000) (EPA 530-D-00-001).

107. 65 Fed. Reg. at 15906.

waste facilities regulated under RCRA.[108] While the 1999 reforms promoted faster, focused, and more flexible clean-ups, the 2001 reforms focus on innovative approaches, accelerating changes in culture, connecting communities to cleanup efforts, and capitalizing on redevelopment potential. The success of EPA's efforts to improve RCRA's corrective action program remains to be seen.

---

108. U.S. EPA, FACT SHEET, RCRA CLEANUP REFORMS, REFORMS II: FOSTERING CREATIVE SOLUTIONS (2001) (EPA 530-F-01-001).

CHAPTER 8

I. Liability and Litigation

Like any product involving substantial financial potential, genetically modified products (GMPs) will not escape litigation. In fact, GMPs may see more than their share of litigation, due to the increasing public and governmental concern and scrutiny over the safety of genetically manipulated products. The ability to predict the success of such litigation is considerably limited at present, however, by the novelty of the products and the litigation issues they raise, and by the lack of legal precedent on those issues.

Recognizing the limited basis from which to assess liability, this chapter nevertheless discusses a framework for considering and preparing for anticipated litigation generated by genetically modified (GM) crop, forestry, and animal-related products. We discuss the major arenas in which litigation can be anticipated; the theories likely to be asserted; and some strategic considerations for companies who wish to prepare for the lawsuits their products will face. The little current litigation that exists (apart from litigation over proprietary rights in GMPs, a subject beyond the scope of this deskbook) is in the areas of (1) GM food lawsuits arising out of the StarLink™ corn recall; and (2) environmental litigation involving government approvals of GMPs. Additional litigation, however, is likely because of the public notoriety and legal turmoil involving consumer products caused by the fallout from the StarLink™ corn situation and by growing opposition to GMPs by some groups.

Most companies involved with GM organisms are presently focused on the issues discussed in the remainder of this deskbook, particularly product development and the regulatory schemes. The litigation aspects, however, should not be ignored. As products make their way to market, litigation will undoubtedly follow and could prove as detrimental to a product's success as any scientific or regulatory hurdle.

A. GM Crop Product Litigation

1. The StarLink™ Recall and Subsequent Litigation

The highly publicized problems involving StarLink™ corn not only illustrate, but in some ways can be expected to generate, the kind of business and consumer litigation GMPs will likely face.

StarLink™ corn contains a GM protein, Cry9C, designed to kill the European corn borer, a natural insect predator. The corn's inventor, Aventis, obtained EPA regulatory approval under FIFRA to market the corn for use in animal feed,[1] but the approval for use in humans remained under regulatory review. The realities of the U.S. food distribution chain, however, were not conducive to keeping animal and human uses separate. In September 2000, an environmental group identified StarLink™ corn in a brand of taco shells.[2] Subsequent testing confirmed this and also found the protein in other corn-based products in the United States and elsewhere,[3] leading to a massive recall of those products.[4] Aventis has withdrawn StarLink™ from the market[5] and is presently dealing with the massive regulatory and distribution issues generated by these events. It is presently estimated that 430 million bushels of stored corn contain the StarLink™ protein.[6]

The maker of the taco shells, Kraft, and the producer of the corn flour used, Azteca Milling, have been sued in a consumer fraud class action lawsuit alleging that buyers of the affected taco shells were sold mislabeled and potentially dangerous goods.[7] The class action complaint alleges counts under the Illinois Consumer Fraud Act, the Uniform Deceptive Trade Practices Act, common-law fraud, negligence, and Uniform Commercial Code (U.C.C.) violations, primarily seeking a disgorgement of profits from sale of the shells. Kraft is a defendant because it sold the taco shells at issue, and Azteca is a defendant based on its alleged failure to segregate corn intended for human versus nonhuman consumption in the production of corn flour used in the shells. Interestingly, Aventis, the inventor and marketer of StarLink™ corn seed, is not a defendant in this lawsuit.

In a potentially more far-reaching class action lawsuit, a farmer has sued Aventis for economic damages from the loss of corn sales, even though he never grew StarLink™ corn.[8] The theory of this case is that StarLink™'s contamination of human corn supplies has wiped out the market for American corn in Europe and elsewhere, damaging even growers whose crops are not contaminated.

The companies involved in the StarLink™ situation have taken substantial steps to contain the repercussions of these events. Kraft almost immediately instituted a massive recall of the taco shells.[9] Aventis also cancelled the registration, recalled seed product from the market, and instituted a reimbursement system to cover the losses incurred by farmers and others.[10] The reimbursement program also extended to 17 state governments, with whom Aventis signed an agreement on January 23, 2001, to cover farmers' losses in those states.[11]

---

1. *See* 63 Fed. Reg. 43936 (Aug. 17, 1998); 65 Fed. Reg. 48701 (Aug. 9, 2000).

2. *See* Daily Env't Rep. (BNA), Sept. 19, 2000, at A-3.

3. *See Japanese Agriculture Ministry Confirms Presence of StarLink in Animal Feed Corn*, Daily Env't Rep. (BNA), Nov. 17, 2000, at A-7.

4. *See Biotech Corn Fuels a Recall*, WASH. POST, Sept. 23, 2000, at A1; *Kraft Recalls Taco Shells After Tests Reveal Presence of Unapproved Corn*, Daily Env't Rep. (BNA), Sept. 25, 2000, at A-9.

5. *See Aventis Halts Seed Sales of Genetically Engineered Corn*, WALL ST. J., Sept. 27, 2000, at A9.

6. *Biotech Grain Is in 430 Million Bushels of Corn, Firm Says*, WASH. POST, Mar. 18, 2001, at A8.

7. *See* Merri Place v. Kraft Foods, No. 00CH014114 (Cir. Ct. Cook County, Ill. filed Nov. 2, 2000).

8. Sutt v. Aventis, No. CL85480 (D. Iowa filed Feb. 5, 2001). *See Iowa Farmer Files Biotech Corn Class Action Suit Against Aventis*, LIABILITY & INS. WK., Feb. 12, 2001, at 8.

9. *See Kraft Recalls Taco Shells*, *supra* note 4.

10. *See* 66 Fed. Reg. 4825 (Jan. 18, 2001) (notice of registration cancellation).

11. *See Compensation Agreement Reached Between Aventis, State Representatives*, Daily Env't Rep. (BNA), Jan. 26, 2001, at A-4.

These efforts have probably served to limit the companies' liability but have not prevented the filing of class actions.

The most serious fallout from the StarLink™ matter, however, is the heightened public fear of GM consumer products that has arisen, rightly or wrongly, from StarLink™'s appearance in human products and the wide publicity surrounding these events. Other products labeled solely for animal use or otherwise intended for limited distribution should be considered high litigation-risk products, as it will be difficult to ensure complete segregation of those products. More importantly, even products labeled for human use could be pulled into litigation, driven either by the absence of labeling and disclosure of the GM basis of the product, or by cross-contamination of products that are supposedly GM-free, e.g., organic foods. The resulting market impacts could generate business-to-business lawsuits as companies seek indemnification and reimbursement for their losses.

2. Rejection, Segregation, and Labeling of Other GMPs

The StarLink™ situation has resulted in limited shipment rejections of product tested or suspected to contain the StarLink™ protein. More troubling is the rejection of other, or even *all* GM consumer products, by certain countries. For instance, several European countries, led by France, have refused to comply with European Union (EU) approvals of certain GM foods and seeds and will not allow either the importation or the production of GM consumer products—including any non-GM materials "contaminated" with approved GM material—within their borders.[12] Further, EU countries are moving toward segregation and labeling of all GMPs,[13] as well as requiring product traceability and recall ability throughout the food chain,[14] a practical nightmare for companies dealing with the production and distribution of these products. The USDA is also considering a segregation rule.[15] Reflecting the growing resistance to GMPs, a number of countries—including Egypt, Japan, and several EU Member states—have already announced that they do not intend to accept a new GM "roundup ready" wheat product developed by Monsanto that is not expected on the market for two to four years.[16] To alleviate these concerns over its new wheat product, Monsanto has agreed to a segregation plan under which the GM wheat will be grown and sold separately.[17]

Segregation and labeling, if accepted, may prove difficult to achieve completely.[18] The types of lawsuits likely to arise from the difficulties in obtaining complete segregation are discussed below.

3. Business Claims

If indeed GMPs begin to encounter difficulty in the marketplace, the impact of lost sales, recalls, etc., will likely generate a risk of lawsuits up and down the product chain. The StarLink™ situation, for example, has resulted in the rejection of shipments of corn and other grains to Europe and Japan, although there do not appear to be lawsuits from these rejections to date. Such lawsuits would likely focus on the contractual or tort causes of action aimed at responsibility for contamination of the food product, since StarLink™ corn is not supposed to be found in products for human consumption. These disputes may in large part be resolved short of lawsuits if the parties can identify the source of contamination and take business steps to eliminate what might otherwise be large-scale liability problems, e.g., Aventis' and Kraft's recall and claims-payment process.

If consumers reject GMPs that are *approved* for human consumption, however, the responsibility will be far less clear cut and the outcome of lawsuits more uncertain. Assume, for instance, that grocery chains—prompted by large-scale protests and media coverage—refuse to sell any baby food with GMP. There is arguably no obvious breach of contract or tort duty, yet hundreds or thousands of stores, distributors, product sellers, and growers could be hit by the financial ripples. Possible lawsuits could arise in the following two major areas:

a. Food Sale and Distribution Lawsuits

Lawsuits over product sales disruption could come from the end sellers who remove product from shelves; from the distributors whose warehouses are full of unsellable product; and from the farmers whose crops are no longer marketable. The legal theories of recovery in this setting could draw on the following:

- *Product liability theories* alleging design defect and strict liability for GM products that spread their characteristics to other products and thereby caused damage to those products;
- *Contractually derived theories* based on agreements between and among seed producers, seed distributors, growers, and food processers/sellers governing purity of the product, segregation of GM materials, and indemnification;
- *Third-party beneficiary theories* alleging that end users or sellers were the intended beneficiaries of contractual segregation or purity agreements;
- *Warranty and other U.C.C.-derived claims* alleging economic harm from products that did not perform as warranted; and
- *Business tort claims* such as tortious interference with contract or prospective relations, e.g., rejected shipments or sales, to the extent a direct contractual relationship cannot be established.

---

12. *See* Joe Kerwin, *Mandatory Segregation of GM Crops in U.S. Seen as Prerequisite to New EU Approvals*, available at http://www.biotech-info.net/mandatory_segregation.html (last visited Oct. 15, 2001); *Deal to Revise Laws on GMOs*, FIN. TIMES, Dec. 12, 2000, at 15.

13. *See, e.g.*, European Commission, Proposed Directive 2001/. . ./EC (PE-CONS 3664/00) on the deliberate release into the environment of GM organisms and repealing Council Directive 90/220/EEC; id. art. 4, ¶ 6 (requiring traceability and recall); art. 13, §2 (requiring labeling stating "this product contains genetically modified organisms" on all approved products). *See* ELR UPDATE, Aug. 6, 2001, *available at* http://www.eli.org (last visited July 31, 2001).

14. *See, e.g., Parliament Approves GM Rules That Could Clear Way for New Products*, Daily Env't Rep. (BNA), Feb. 16, 2001, at A-2.

15. *See USDA Considers Rule to Separate GM From Conventional Crops*, Daily Env't Rep. (BNA), Dec. 1, 2000, at A-8.

16. *Gene-Spliced Wheat Stirs Global Fears*, WASH. POST, Feb. 27, 2001, at A1.

17. *Id.* at A5.

18. *See Advisory Panel Says "Zero Tolerance" on Biotechnology Not Feasible*, Daily Env't Rep. (BNA), Dec. 4, 2000, at A-9.

Some of these theories would be of questionable viability, but the lawsuits would be heavily dependant on the facts and circumstances of each situation and the outcome is unpredictable.

b. Cross-Contamination Lawsuits

The nature of GM seed and crops creates a risk that GM seed, pollen, and product will make its way from authorized GM settings into non-GM settings. The introduction of GM seed or crop features from segregated GM fields into non-GM fields, for instance, will be difficult to prevent, as will the mixing of grain or other products once they are in the food and product chain. Even unrelated strains may be at risk if they can be easily cross-pollinated.[19]

Some of the legal theories discussed above are likely to come into play in a cross-pollination case, along with common-law claims based on trespass, nuisance, or conversion. One such lawsuit, against Monsanto, alleged cross-pollination through pollen drift of a non-GM farmer's canola crop.[20] Illustrating the complexity of these suits, Monsanto asserted this farmer had illegally obtained and planted Monsanto's patented seed, but the farmer cross-sued claiming that the Monsanto pollen was blown onto his property, contaminating his non-GM crops. The Canadian court recently ruled in Monsanto's favor, holding that the farmer did not have the right to plant cross-pollinated seed containing Monsanto's patented gene, even if the cross-pollination was accidental.[21]

Lawsuits over cross-pollination are even more likely if the crop, seed, or product affected is not permitted to contain GM elements. Under the few laws that currently exist, for instance, organic foods cannot contain GM material.[22] Thus, organic growers may seek compensation from nearby GM farmers or the originating seed company if their product is tested and found to contain GMP. Another immediate possibility is the rejection of grain shipments to Europe, where some countries are actively embargoing food containing any amount of GM material.

4. Consumer Lawsuits

Lawsuits alleging fraud in the failure to warn consumers of the GM content of foods could prove attractive under a number of state consumer protection statutes or common-law theories. As noted above, several such lawsuits have been filed in regard to the StarLink™ situation. Consumer fraud and unfair business practice statutes are often broadly worded to include any form of consumer transaction or business activity, and some permit individuals to sue on behalf of all citizens without a showing of causation, reliance, or injury.[23] These lawsuits are potentially amenable to class ac-

tions seeking, for instance, disgorgement of all profits from the affected product. GMP lawsuits could thus be brought by a single consumer claiming that all consumers have been defrauded by the product manufacturer/seller's misrepresentation as to the GM content of the product.

The defendants will have a ready defense in the approval of these products for human use, *and* the lack of any regulation requiring labeling of GM content. In addition, to date there is no persuasive science demonstrating that human-approved GMPs perform any differently or create any risks to consumers. State consumer protection statutes, however, do not depend necessarily on violations of law and may find fraud in the withholding of information designed to mislead the consumer.

5. Health Lawsuits

Health effects cases based on consumption of or exposure to GMPs are not necessarily as readily anticipated as consumer and business lawsuits, but some health litigation is likely to occur. One such health-related lawsuit has already been filed. That class action, *Finger v. Azteca Foods*,[24] alleges that the named plaintiff suffered an allergic reaction to StarLink™-contaminated corn tortillas.[25] The lawsuit blames Aventis, the holder of the intellectual property rights to StarLink™ corn, and Garst Seed, the distributor of StarLink™ corn seed, for failing to inform farmers about the need to maintain a buffer planting zone and to not sell the product for human consumption. The counts sound in consumer fraud, U.C.C. warranty and related claims, and negligence.

Personal injury damages in a case like this may be somewhat limited. The plaintiff in *Finger*, for instance, claims to have experienced a 24-hour episode of diarrhea, hives, and swelling with no apparent long-term effects. The FDA has received 48 complaints alleging allergic reactions to StarLink™, a dozen or so of which the FDA is treating seriously.[26] Some of these cases may involve anaphylactic shock, a life-threatening event.[27] Notwithstanding, most allergenic reactions, even if associated with GMPs, would probably not be sufficiently serious to generate large-scale health-related litigation. Nor are there currently any indications that GMPs are otherwise associated with health effects.[28]

---

sumer transactions); CAL. BUS. & PROF. CODE §17200 (West 2000); Committee on Children's Television v. General Foods Corp., 673 P.2d 660 (Cal. 1983) (unfair competition law does not require showing of injury, reliance, actual deception).

24. No. 01-CV-1181 (N.D. Ill. Feb. 21, 2001).

25. As to the actual risks posed by StarLink™ corn, see *SAP Finds Medium Likelihood That StarLink Corn Could Cause Allergies*, Daily Env't Rep. (BNA), Dec. 6, 2000, at A-7 (only a "low probability" of actual human allergenic reaction).

26. *Biotech Corn Is Test Case for Industry*, Wash. Post, Mar. 19, 2001, at A1.

27. *Id.*

28. *See* Press Release, European Commission, Facts on GMOs in the EU 5-6 (July 13, 2001) (EU research since 1986 into safety of GM crops and foods has shown no safety concerns); *Hearings on the Future of Food: Biotechnology and Consumer Confidence: Hearings Before the House Comm. on Health, Education, Labor, and Pensions*, 106th Cong. (2000) (statement of Joseph A. Levitt, Director, FDA Center for Food Safety and Applied Nutrition) ("[The] FDA is confident that the bioengineered plant foods on the U.S. market today are as safe as their conventionally bred counterparts.").

---

19. *See Protein Produced by StarLink Corn Found in Unrelated Strain*, Daily Env't Rep. (BNA), Nov. 24, 2000, at A-7.

20. *See* Marc Kaufman, *Farmer Liable for Growing Biotech Crops*, Wash. Post, Mar. 30, 2001, at A3.

21. *Id.*

22. *See* National Organic Program, 7 C.F.R. pt. 205; Oregon Organic Food Regulation Act, OR. REV. STAT. §§616.406-616.421 (2000); OR. ADMIN. R. 603-025-0220 (2000) (listing as "prohibited substance" any rDNA material); California Organic Foods Act, CAL. HEALTH & SAFETY CODE §§110810-110958 (West 2000).

23. *See, e.g.*, CAL. CIV. CODE §1750-56 (West 2000) (Consumer Legal Remedies Act proscribes numerous "unfair" acts in context of con-

Thus, as the *Finger* case demonstrates, health-based GMP litigation will likely be derivative of consumer fraud actions and not form an independent and significant ground of liability. The depth of antipathy toward GMPs among some groups, however, suggests that the risk of such allegations should not be minimized. The StarLink™ situation may yet lead to more serious lawsuits after the latency period for pregnancy, cancer, etc. has had time to run.

6. Strategic Considerations

Companies planning to develop and sell GM consumer products need to consider and address a number of critical regulatory, contractual, and scientific issues that could significantly affect any subsequent litigation. Some areas to consider include:

- *Contractual Provisions Regarding Segregation*: Because the allegations in consumer fraud cases are likely to focus on failure to segregate seed, crops or foods, and responsibility for commingling or contamination, these cases may well turn on the clarity of contractual obligations between or among the seed producer, distributor, and farmer.
- *Disclosures and Warnings:* The current and future consumer cases will focus on the nature and extent of alleged failures to warn about the presence of GM components of consumer products. Whether this theory can survive as to human-approved products, for which neither the FDA nor EPA has required any such warning, remains to be seen.
- *Contractual Assumptions of Liability:* As between and among commercial entities, the liability for rejected shipments, recalls, and unsellable product may turn on the provisions of sales and distribution contracts regarding commingling, segregation, risk of contamination, etc.
- *Quality of the Company's Science:* For health-related issues, the safety of these products will be challenged and probably determined based on the quality of the testing the company has conducted. For courtroom purposes, the quality of the company's science may depend on the documentation of that testing.
- *Regulatory Events:* Adverse regulatory action on a product is a likely precursor to litigation. GMPs have received a clean bill of health, for the most part, from U.S. regulators, but those products are very much at issue in Europe and of renewed interest in the United States because of the StarLink™ situation and pressure for labeling and other restrictions.

B. Environmental Litigation

GMPs have generated significant concern over possible environmental impacts. The regulatory aspects of EA are discussed above in Chapters 3-7. This section briefly focuses on litigation arising out of environmental allegations.

Environmental lawsuits likely will be a primary weapon of groups seeking to stop the regulatory approval of new GMPs. As an example, Greenpeace and 25 other groups sued EPA in 1997 alleging that EPA had violated NEPA, the APA, and the ESA in approving the use of Bt-maize genetically altered to contain an insecticide that repels insect pests.[29] Plaintiffs claimed that EPA had not sufficiently tested the corn's environmental and ecological effects. Plaintiffs dismissed their lawsuit in August 2000, citing the "complexity" of EPA's response to the administrative petition.[30] As Greenpeace's withdrawal of the Bt-maize suit demonstrates, the legal mechanisms for bringing environmental lawsuits involving GMPs are complex and somewhat limited. None of the current statutes that specifically address GMP registration and sale provide for private rights of action against regulated entities although in some instances they contain potent citizen suit provisions.

TSCA, for example, authorizes citizen suits to enforce compliance with listing of new chemical substances on the TSCA inventory, reporting obligations and other requirements of the statute.[31] EPA's broad assertion of jurisdiction over intergeneric organisms might provide a basis for such suits—the effect of which is to stop or delay commercialization. RCRA has a broader citizen suit provision authorizing suits for injunctive relief against any person contributing to the "past or present handling, storage, treatment, transportation or disposal of any solid or hazardous waste which may present an imminent and substantial endangerment to health or the environment."[32] NEPA, as described in Chapter 2, can also effectively stop projects with a federal funding or approval link which do not adequately consider environmental effects.

Possibly due to the limited applicability of current environmental laws, proposals exist that would make environmental liability a far more serious threat to GMPs. Both in Europe and the United States, the intentional introduction of GM seed or genetic material into the environment (for example, through the planting of research GM crops) is referred to as a "release."[33] To a U.S. environmental lawyer, familiar with the liability for "release" of hazardous substances under environmental statutes,[34] the use of this word illustrates that regulators view GM products as a potential environmental hazard. If the legitimate use of GM materials is thought of as an environmental "release," then liability may soon follow for unauthorized or unintended "releases" to nonapproved crops. The EU is considering a proposal to create CERCLA-like strict liability for any "releases" of genetic material to non-GMPs.

29. Greenpeace et al. v. Browner, No. 99-389(LFO) (D.D.C. Feb. 18, 1999).

30. *See Greenpeace Withdraws Biotech Case; Ecological, Legal Issues Persist in BT Review*, Daily Env't Rep. (BNA), Aug. 2, 2000, at 3.

31. 15 U.S.C. §2619(a), ELR Stat. TSCA §20(a).

32. 42 U.S.C. §6972(a)(1)(B), ELR Stat. RCRA §7002(a)(1)(B).

33. *See, e.g.,* 7 C.F.R. §340.1 (FDA regulation defining the use of a regulated GM article outside the constraints of physical confinement found in a laboratory, greenhouse, or fermenter as "release into the environment"); EU Directive 90/220/EEC, art. 2 (defining "deliberate release" as "any intentional introduction into the environment of a GM . . . without provisions for containment used to limit their contact with the general population and the environment").

34. 42 U.S.C. §§9601(22), 9604(a)(1), ELR Stat. CERCLA §§101(22), 104(a)(1).

federal register

Monday
December 31, 1984

Part II

Office of Science and Technology Policy

Proposal for a Coordinated Framework
for Regulation of Biotechnology; Notice

OFFICE OF SCIENCE AND TECHNOLOGY POLICY

Proposal for a Coordinated Framework for Regulation of Biotechnology

AGENCY: Executive Office of the President, Office of Science and Technology Policy.

ACTION: Notice for public comment.

SUMMARY: The purpose of this Federal Register notice is to provide a concise index of U.S. laws related to biotechnology, to clarify the policies of the major regulatory agencies that will be involved in reviewing research and products of biotechnology, to describe a scientific advisory mechanism for assessment of biotechnology issues, and to explain how the activities of the Federal agencies in biotechnology will be coordinated.

DATE: Comments must be received on or before April 1, 1985.

Public Participation: The Cabinet Council Working Group on Biotechnology through the Office of Science and Technology Policy, is seeking the advice of individuals, public interest groups, industry and academia on all aspects of this publication. The Working Group welcomes candid assessments of the process and the policy as well as questions raised regarding the scope of the proposal.

The intention of the Working Group is to republish this material in final form as soon as possible following the close of the comment period. This will assure that well understood regulatory policy and process are established in timely manner to enable a beneficial industry to proceed safely and efficiently.

Information submitted as comments to EPA on this notice may be claimed confidential by marking any part or all of that information as "Confidential Business Information." Information so marked will not be disclosed except in accordance with procedures set forth in 40 CFR Part 2. A sanitized copy of any material containing Confidential Business Information must be provided to EPA by the submitter for inclusion in the public record. Information not marked confidential may be disclosed publicly by EPA without prior notice.

ADDRESS: Comments specific to the EPA, USDA, or FDA policy statements should be addressed to:

EPA: Docket # OPTS 00049, Document Control Officer (TS–793), Office of Toxic Substances, Environmental Protection Agency, Room E–409, 401 M Street, SW., Washington, D.C. 20480

USDA: Docket # APHIS 00049, Ms. Karen Darling, Deputy Assistant Secretary, Marketing and Inspection Services, U.S. Department of Agriculture, Room 242–E, Administration Building, 12th and Independence Avenue, SW., Washington, D.C. 20250

FDA: Docket # 84N–0431, Dockets Management Branch, Food and Drug Administration (HFA–305), Room 4–62, 5600 Fishers Lane, Rockville, MD 20857

Any other comments should be provided to the following address: Dr. Bernadine Healy Bulkley, Deputy Director, Office of Science and Technology Policy, Executive Office of the President, NEOB—Room 5005, Washington, D.C. 20506.

Jerry D. Jennings,

Executive Director, Office of Science and Technology Policy.

December 21, 1984.

Table of Contents

Introduction

Only forty years ago, DNA was discovered to be the repository of genetic information. This discovery has been followed by an explosion in our understanding and ability to manipulate the gene as manifest by the new commercial biotechnology which has introduced a new and profound dimension into the field of classical genetics. Today, new techniques for manipulating genetic information offer exciting advances, as remarkable as the discovery of antibiotics or the computer chip.

While some techniques of biotechnology are not new—the use of yeast in baking and brewing began around 6000 B.C.—the most recently developed techniques are far more sophisticated. Modern biotechnology promises to benefit many fields of human endeavor by offering new services and a wide variety of products superior to those currently available because they will be more effective, convenient, safer, or more economical. Biotechnology already has successfully produced new drugs and improved existing drugs such as human insulin, interferons and vaccines. Exciting research is underway in agricultural applications to enhance plant and animal productivity to help feed the world's people. Within reach of commercial applicability are products to diagnose, prevent and treat animal diseases, to improve animal breeds and to improve specific plant characteristics. Microorganisms have also been developed in research laboratories to degrade pollutants, enhance oil recovery, convert biomass to energy, leach minerals, and concentrate metals. With this diversity of applications, biotechnology will alleviate many problems of disease and pollution and increase the supply of food, energy, and raw materials.

The United States is now the world leader in biotechnology. This leadership is derived from a strong science base, a vigorous entrepreneurial spirit and availability of venture capital. New uses of biotechnology have created intense domestic and international competition. Several other nations have elevated the development of biotechnology to a national priority. The tremendous potential of biotechnology to contribute to the nation's economy in the near term, and to fulfill society's needs and alleviate its problems in the longer term, makes it imperative that progress in biotechnology be encouraged.

While the potential benefits of biotechnology are widely acknowledged, legitimate concerns about safety have also been raised as additional products of biotechnology move from contained research laboratories into full contact with the public and the environment through commercial testing and applications in the environment. For example, concerns have been raised about the effect of genetic manipulations on the potential virulence of altered microorganisms, or the ability of new organisms to obtain a selective advantage. Certainly both the safety and effectiveness of new processes and products must be central issues in the design of new scientific developments or technological innovations. Accordingly, it is incumbent upon the government, the business community, and the public to take responsible and timely measures to insure that the public health and the environment are protected and that societal concerns are promptly addressed.

The Administration, recognizing its responsibility to confront the special concerns that surround modern biotechnology, formed an interagency working group under the White House Cabinet Council on Natural Resources and the Environment. The fundamental purpose of the Working Group is to insure that the regulatory process adequately considers health and environmental safety consequences of the products and processes of the new biotechnology as they move from the research laboratory to the marketplace. The Working Group recognizes the need for a coordinated and sensible regulatory review process that will minimize the uncertainties and inefficiencies that can stifle innovation and impair the competitiveness of U.S. industry. It recognizes that not only should approaches be consistent from agency to agency and within each agency from application to application, but also that regulatory decisions should be based upon the best available science.

The importance of addressing the emerging commercial aspects of biotechnology in a coordinated and timely fashion is captured in the recent report by the Congressional Office of Technology Assessment which warned: "Although the United States is currently the world leader in both basic science and commercial development of new biotechnology, continuation of the initial preeminence of American companies in the commercialization of new biotechnology is not assured." [1]

The Working Group recognizes that the manner in which regulations for biotechnology are implemented in the United States will have a direct impact on the competitiveness of U.S. producers in both domestic and world markets and the future development of basic science. Thus, the Working Group has endeavored to develop a coherent and sensible regulatory process, one based on the best available scientific facts and intended to minimize uncertainties, delays, overlaps, and inconsistencies. Attention will be paid also to international harmonization. The United States is seeking to promote scientific cooperation, mutual understanding of regulatory approaches and international agreement on a range of common technical problems such as the development of consistent test guidelines, laboratory practices and principles for assessing potential risks. The U.S. also is committed to reducing barriers to trade in biotechnology. U.S. regulatory agencies will provide similar treatment to domestic and foreign products with regard to their regulations and approval procedures. Barriers to trade of biotechnology products can only be avoided if the U.S. and other nations join together in working toward this goal. In achieving national consistency and international harmonization, regulatory decisions can be made in a socially responsible manner, protecting human health and the environment, allowing U.S. producers to remain competitive and, most importantly, assuring that everyone will reap the benefits of this exciting biological revolution.

Regulation of Biotechnology Processes and Products

In response to concerns of the scientific community in the early 1970s, the Federal Government sponsored a conference to explore the risks and benefits of recombinant DNA (rDNA) research. In 1974 the National Institutes of Health (NIH) chartered the Recombinant DNA Advisory Committee (RAC) to provide scientific advice and in 1976 developed the NIH Guidelines for Research Involving Recombinant DNA Molecules. It was reasoned that a cautious approach to this research was essential to assure safety while still fostering the advancement of this new technology. These guidelines have allowed research to flourish within appropriate constraints. Experience gained in rDNA laboratory research has mitigated many of the concerns about risk, thus allowing modification of the original guidelines and oversight mechanisms.

Almost a decade later as the pace of commercial application has accelerated, this new initiative was undertaken to review regulatory requirements and to articulate policy for biotechnology products. In April 1984. the Cabinet Council on Natural Resources and the Environment established an interagency working group to study and coordinate the government's regulatory policy for these products.[2] The group was asked to:

1. Review the regulatory requirements which have been applied to commercialized biotechnologies.

2. Identify existing laws and regulations that may be applicable to biotechnology.

3. Review the function of the NIH Recombinant DNA Advisory Committee and its role in biotechnology commercialization and safety regulation.

4. Clarify the regulatory path that a company with a new product would follow to meet Federal health and safety requirements.

5. Determine whether current regulatory requirements and Federal review are adequate for new products.

6. Develop specific recommendations for administrative or legislative actions to provide additional regulatory review if warranted, while maintaining flexibility to accommodate new developments.

7. Review court rulings regarding the granting of patents for biotechnology.

8. Review other Federal actions such as support of basic research and training, U.S. patents and trade laws, and other policy issues which affects commercialization and U.S. competitive position vis-a-vis international firms.

The results of the interagency effort to date are reflected in the publication of this notice for public review and comment. These include: (1) Regulatory matrix: a concise index of the current regulatory requirements that might be applicable to biotechnology; (2) Policy statements: a compilation of proposed statements of policy that describe how the U.S. Department of Agriculture, the Environmental Protection Agency and the Food and Drug Administration intend to apply their existing regulatory authorities to biotechnology products; (3) A Scientific Advisory Mechanism: a coordinated structure of scientific review to promote consistent risk assessment within statutory confines; and (4) Glossary: a glossary of terms used in the policy statements.

Given the evolving nature of biotechnology, the Working Group will continue to meet to review the ongoing process. If regulatory gaps emerge and the process is not responding to public concerns, the Working Group will make recommendations for either administrative reform or additional legislative authority.

1. Regulatory Matrix

The matrix outlines laws, regulations and guidelines that may be applicable to biotechnology products at some point in research, development, marketing, shipment, use, or disposal. To aid in understanding current requirements, the matrix has been divided into seven parts which have been cross-referenced when necessary:

I. Licensing and other premarketing requirements;

II Post-marketing requirements;

III. Export controls;

IV. Research and information gathering;

V. Patents;

---

[1] Commercial Biotechnology. "An International Analysis." Office of Technology Assessment. Pg. iii. 1984.

[2] The member agencies include: Departments of Interior, Justice, State, Agriculture, Commerce, Defense, Energy, Health and Human Services, and Labor; Environmental Protection Agency; Council on Environmental Quality; Council of Economic Advisors; Office of Management and Budget; Office of Policy Development; the National Science Foundation; Office of the U.S. Trade Representative; and the Office of Science and Technology Policy.

50858   Federal Register / Vol. 49, No. 252 / Monday, December 31, 1984 / Notices

VI. Air and water emissions standards; and

VII. Requirements for Federal agencies.

The matrix will be reviewed annually and updated as necessary.

2. Policy Statements

Individual "Statements of Proposed Policy" have been developed by the three regulatory agencies—FDA, USDA and EPA—that will be involved most extensively in oversight of research and industrial engaged in product development. These statements do not describe detailed regulatory requirements, but rather the general policy framework within which regulatory decisions will be made. They attempt to provide a clear understanding of how regulatory agencies will approach this evolving technology. At present the regulatory authorities that are in place appear to accommodate these new products.

The responsibilities of EPA, FDA and USDA are determined by statute (see the Matrix of Federal Authorities elsewhere in this notice), and are generally based upon key characteristics or uses of the end products. When new types of products are developed, such as will be the case with biotechnology, each agency must develop and apply certain rules for determining whether its statutes apply with possible modification of existing rules. For example, FDA must determine whether products containing genetically engineering microorganisms constitute food additives, drugs, or other products subject to FDA approval, EPA whether they are pesticides or industrial products, and USDA whether they are plant pests, animals biologicals, or other agricultural products subject to its authority. These decisions must be consistent with the statutory requirements of the laws each agency administers.

Regardless of the criteria used to determine whether a product is within the responsibility of a given agency, all three agencies will approach the review of biotechnology products and processes in similar ways. All conduct their assessments on a case-by-case basis,

employing internal staff, consultants, and expert advisory committees (described below). Each considers the ultimate safety of the product as a primary concern; other issues, such as efficacy, may also be considered. Also, each agency develops product review criteria and procedures which are consistent with its historical experience and scientific data bases developed from reviewing other products with similar uses.

EPA, FDA and USDA are committed to working together and with other members of the Cabinet Council Working Group to coordinate and improve the development of appropriate and useful scientific evaluation methods and administrative procedures for genetically engineered organisms and their products. All are striving for a balanced approach supported by sound science and incorporating the latest scientific and technological information. The statements of proposed policy which each has prepared and which are issued in this notice are viewed as among the first steps toward that goal.

3. Scientific Advisory Mechanism

The importance of the highest caliber scientific advice to the decision-making process for oversight of biotechnology is undisputed. NIH's experience with its RAC is an example of the value of using distinguished scientists to participate in the assessment of risk of new projects or proposals involving genetic manipulation. The experience of the RAC over the past ten years serves as a valuable model to the Working Group in structuring the proposed scientific review coordinating mechanism.

With the evolution of biotechnology and its increasing commercialization, the complexity and scope of scientific review broadens and the existing mechanisms for scientific review must be expanded. The Working Group proposes an adjunctive scientific advisory mechanism that will accommodate the needs of individual agencies and provide a central focus for scientific advice on biotechnology issues. It affords maximal opportunity to achieve scientific consensus and retains the flexibility in scientific policy guidance that has characterized the

existing NIH RAC. In addition, it can be implemented in a short time.

4. Glossary

The glossary included at the end of this notice is intended to provide definitions for terms appearing in the policy statements to assist the reader in reviewing the notice. The definitions are not to be considered legally binding on any Federal agency and may be revised as needed.

Interagency Coordination of Risk Management and Regulation in Biotechnology

In addition to coordination of scientific review, the Working Group recognizes the need for coordination of the regulatory activities of the federal government. An interagency committee is needed to foster timely and coordinated decision making via interagency communication on matters of regulation; discuss matters of jurisdiction among agencies; serve as a mechanism by which agencies can raise public and concerns; and consider generic approaches for translating risk industry assessment information into policy decisions.

The Cabinet Council Working Group also recognizes the need for this continuing coordinated mechanism also to address the broader issues within the regulatory process itself. Although at the present time existing statutes seem adequate to deal with the emerging processes and products of modern biotechnology, there are always potential problems and deficiencies in the regulatory apparatus in a fast moving field. We believe this interagency coordinating committee should monitor the changing scene of biotechnology and serve as a means of identifying potential gaps in regulation in a timely fashion, making appropriate recommendations for either administrative or legislative action.

For the time being the Cabinet Council Working Group can serve these needs. When its activities are concluded, an interagency coordinating committee for Biotechnology would, if still needed, be established to continue this effort.

BILLING CODE 4540-60-M

BIOTECHNOLOGY AUTHORITIES

AUTHORITY OR GUIDELINE	DESCRIPTION	AFFECTED PRODUCTS OR PROCESSES	AFFECTED AGENCIES	CROSS-REFERENCES	NOTES
I. LICENSING AND OTHER PREMARKETING REQUIREMENTS					
Food, Drug and Cosmetic (FD&C) Act (21 USC 301-392) Regulations: 21 CFR Parts 1, 71, 171, 314, 514, 571, 807	Premarketing approval required for: drugs — Sec. 505; medical devices — Sec. 515; food additives — Sec. 409; color additives — Sec. 706; animal drugs — Sec. 512	All human and animal drugs and human devices, food additives, animal feed additives, and color additives	HHS-FDA	Certain EPA statutes specifically exclude FD&C Act products. EPA sets tolerance levels for pesticide residues in the food chain, FDA provides human tolerance levels for animal drugs in food chain meat and poultry to the USDA-FSIS. Animal and human biologics are regulated under the Virus-Serum-Toxin Act (VST Act), a USDA statute, and the Public Health Service Act, respectively. FDA decisions are subject to National Environmental Policy Act (NEPA).	From the beginning of clinical research to premarketing approval takes for: human drugs: 7-10 years; animal drugs: 3-5 years; devices: 2-5 years; direct food additives: 5-7 years; indirect food additives: 3-5 years; color additives: 5-9 years. Important: FDA regulates biotechnology on a product-by-product basis. FDA will not be restructuring the process to regulate the products of biotechnology or the manufacturers of those products.
Public Health Service (PHS) Act Section 351(a) (42 USC 262) Regulations: 21 CFR 600-680	Licensing for marketing required for human biologics	Human biologics	HHS-FDA	USDA-APHIS licenses animal biologics produced by interstate manufacturers. FDA decisions are subject to NEPA.	The research use of investigational new drugs is regulated under the FD&C Act. From the beginning of clinical research to license takes approximately 2-8 years depending on the type of biologic, but 6-8 is more common.
"Points to consider in the characterization of cell lines used to produce biologicals"	FDA technical guidance for new product approval	Human drugs and biologics	HHS-FDA		
"Points to consider in the manufacture of Monoclonal Antibody Products for Human Use"	FDA technical guidance for new product approval	Human drugs and biologics	HHS-FDA		FDA reviews the adequacy of testing of all products on a case-by-case basis.

50860   Federal Register / Vol. 49, No. 252 / Monday, December 31, 1984 / Notices

AUTHORITY OR GUIDELINE	DESCRIPTION	AFFECTED PRODUCTS OR PROCESSES	AFFECTED AGENCIES	CROSS-REFERENCES	NOTES
"Points to consider in the production and testing of new drugs and biologicals produced by rDNA technology"	FDA technical guidance for new product approval	Human drugs and biologics	HHS-FDA		New Investigational New Drug (IND) and biological licenses and/or new drug approvals are required currently with rDNA technology even if the active substance is identical in molecular structure to a previously approved product.
PHS Act Section 353 (42 USC 263a) Regulations: 42 CFR 74	License required for clinical laboratories engaged in interstate commerce	Laboratory services	HHS-CDC HHS-Health Care Financing Admin.		To meet licensure requirements, laboratories must meet proficiency testing, quality control, and personnel standards.
Virus-Serum-Toxin Act (21 USC 151-158) Regulations: 9 CFR 101-117 and 122-123	License required for any virus, serum, toxin, or analogous product intended for use in treatment of domestic animals which are shipped interstate or imported. Regulations contain standards of efficacy, purity, safety and potency. They also contain labeling provisions.	9 CFR 101.2(w) defines "biological products" to mean "all viruses, serums, toxins, and analogous products of natural or synthetic origin, such as diagnostics, antitoxins, vaccines, live microorganisms, killed microorganisms and the antigenic or immunizing components of microorganisms intended for use in the diagnosis, treatment, or prevention of diseases of animals."	USDA-APHIS	USDA decisions are subject to NEPA. The definition of drugs in the FD&C Act includes biological products. The FD&C Act (21 USC 391) and its regulations exempt biological products regulated under the VST Act.	USDA's licensing policy for conventional or rDNA derived veterinary biologics is on a product-by-product basis, and requires that all license applicants for rDNA products comply with the NIH "Guidelines for Research Involving Recombinant DNA Molecules."
USDA's Licensing Policy for Biologicals Produced by rDNA	USDA technical guideline reviewing production and test considerations for evaluating rDNA product license applications.	Veterinary biologics and diagnostics	USDA-APHIS		Each veterinary biologic product is reviewed as a single entity. USDA evaluates each license application for conventional or rDNA biologics to ensure purity, potency, safety, and efficacy.
Veterinary Services Memorandum Number 800.68	USDA policy and procedures for new product license applicants	Veterinary biologics and diagnostics	USDA-APHIS		Technical guidelines used for licensing products developed through rDNA or hybridoma technology.

AUTHORITY OR GUIDELINE	DESCRIPTION	AFFECTED PRODUCTS OR PROCESSES	AFFECTED AGENCIES	CROSS-REFERENCES	NOTES
Memorandum of Understanding between USDA and FDA for Defining Jurisdiction of Animal Drugs. (See 47 FR 26458, June 18, 1982)	Agreement between APHIS and FDA regarding responsibility for regulating animal biologic products as biologics under the VST Act or as drugs under the FD&C Act.	Veterinary biologics or drugs	HHS-FDA USDA-APHIS		
Toxic Substances Control Act (TSCA) (5 USC 2601-2929)	TSCA applies to "chemical substances" defined as "any organic or inorganic substance of a particular molecular identity including...any combination of such substances ...occurring in nature..." TSCA requires premanufacture review of new chemical substances and authorizes regulation of new and existing substances.	Industrial chemicals produced by genetically engineered organisms or by-products (e.g., enzymes); organisms used in general industrial, commercial, and consumer applications, such as water pollution control, mineral leaching, drain cleaning, etc.; organisms used to make TSCA or Federal Insecticide, Fungicide and Rodenticide Act (FIFRA) chemicals	EPA, agencies that manufacture "chemical substances" for commercial purposes.	Drugs, biologics, foods, food additives, cosmetics, pesticides and tobacco products are excluded from TSCA review.	Provides broad range of authority over "chemical substances."
Section 5(a)(1)(A)	Requires submission of premanufacture notice (PMN) for "new chemical substances"	New products (including organisms) used for purposes listed above	EPA		Mandatory requirement; 90-day review, extendable for "good cause" to 180 days. EPA must make a finding of potential risk or exp~~re to regulate. R&D in small quantities (including small quantities of biotechnology R&D) are exempt from PMN. "Small quantities" as defined by rule would exempt most field testing.
Section 5(h)(3)	Exempts research and development activities from PMN requirements	Organisms and other substances used in the lab; products sold solely for R&D use (e.g., restriction enzymes)	EPA		
Section 5(a)(1)(B)	Authorizes EPA to require by rule reporting before "chemical substances" are used for "significant new uses"	TSCA chemicals proposed for new use	EPA		Discretionary. "Significant new uses" must be defined by rule. No regulations currently in place that affect biotechnology.

50862 Federal Register / Vol. 49, No. 252 / Monday, December 31, 1984 / Notices

AUTHORITY OR GUIDELINE	DESCRIPTION	AFFECTED PRODUCTS OR PROCESSES	AFFECTED AGENCIES	CROSS-REFERENCES	NOTES
Regulations: 40 CFR 720	PMN requirements	TSCA Chemicals	EPA, agencies that manufacture "new chemical substances" for commercial purposes.		Interprets mandatory statutory requirements.
Federal Insecticide, Fungicide and Rodenticide Act (FIFRA) (7 USC 136-136y)	Requires registration of pesticides before distribution or use (pesticide broadly defined as "any substance or mixture...intended for preventing, destroying, repelling or mitigating any pest, and ...intended for use as a plant regulant, defoliant, or desiccant.")	Biological pesticides (e.g., microorganisms or their chemical products). Includes INA bacteria.	EPA, USDA-FSIS, HHS-FDA	EPA sets tolerance levels for pesticide residue in the food chain which EPA and USDA-FSIS enforce.	Pesticides defined to include living organisms. EPA review period could vary from one to several years. Fourteen microbial pesticides (non-engineered) have been approved.
Section 3(c)(2)(A)	Authorizes EPA to publish "guidelines" specifying kinds of information needed for registration.				
Section 5	Authorizes EPA to issue experimental use permits for limited uses before registration.		EPA		120 day review period; can be extended.
Section 25(b)	Authorizes EPA to exempt a pesticide from registration.		EPA, USDA-APHIS	USDA has responsibility for higher plants and animals that are considered pesticides (40 CFR 162.5(c)(4)).	Higher plants and animals and certain pheromone attractants have been exempted.
Regulations: 40 CFR 158	Data requirements for pesticide registration including genetically modified microbial pesticides	Microbial pesticides	EPA	Section 3 of FIFRA	Includes data requirements for microbial pesticides. Testing requirements are tiered, with more complicated tests required where certain criteria are met. Additional requirements for genetically modified and other microbial pesticides determined on a case-by-case basis.

Federal Register / Vol. 49, No. 252 / Monday, December 31, 1984 / Notices   50863

AUTHORITY OR GUIDELINE	DESCRIPTION	AFFECTED PRODUCTS OR PROCESSES	AFFECTED AGENCIES	CROSS-REFERENCES	NOTES
40 CFR 162	Pesticide registration regulations	Microbial pesticides	EPA, USDA-APHIS, DOI	Section 3 of FIFRA; Biological control agents regulated by USDA, DOI, or other Federal agencies under express statutory authority not included.	Applies to viruses, bacteria, protozoa, fungi, etc., used as pesticides. Does not apply to higher plants and animals.
40 CFR 172	Experimental use permit regulations	Field-tested microbial pesticides	EPA	Section 5 of FIFRA	120 day review period which can be extended; for land uses, generally only need permit if test covers more than 10 acres, but EPA has authority to require permits for less than 10 acres under certain circumstances.
"Microbial Pesticides: Interim Policy on Small Scale Field Testing" (49 FR 40659 (1984))	EPA policy requiring notification prior to small scale field tests with certain microbial pesticides	Microbial pesticides containing nonindigenous or genetically altered microorganisms	EPA	Section 5 of FIFRA and 40 CFR 172	Applies to tests conducted on 10 or less acres of land or 1 or less acre of water (i.e., small scale field testing)
Guidelines: Pesticide (Subdivision M) Assessment Guidelines (October (1982))	Provides guidelines for developing data required under 40 CFR 158.	Microbial pesticides	EPA	FD&C Act Sections 406, 408, 409 FIFRA sets pesticide standards which are enforced by FDA and USDA.	
Reorganization Plan No. 3 of 1970, Section 2(4)(5 USCA App.)	Authorizes EPA to establish tolerances for pesticide residues in food chain	Pesticide products used so as to result in residues in food chain	EPA, HHS-FDA, USDA-FSIS		
Regulations; 40 CFR 162.7(a)(3)(v) and 162.18-4(a)(4)	Requires tolerances before registration	Pesticides to be registered for food or animal feed use	EPA, HHS-FDA, USDA-FSIS		
Guidelines: "Guidelines for Research Involving Recombinant DNA Molecules" (49 FR 46266 (1984))	Specifies practices for constructing and handling rDNA molecules and organisms and viruses containing rDNA molecules. Compliance is required for institutions that receive support for rDNA research from NIH.	All rDNA research conducted by institutions receiving NIH support as well as NIH itself.	All involved in rDNA research, primarily HHS and USDA, administered by HHS-NIH with the advice of the rDNA Advisory Committee (RAC)	Biotechnology R&D exempt from PMN requirement of TSCA.	Voluntary compliance for institutions that receive no NIH rDNA research funding.

BIOTECHNOLOGY DESKBOOK

Federal Register / Vol. 49, No. 252 / Monday. December 31, 1984 / Notices 50865

AUTHORITY OR GUIDELINE	DESCRIPTION	AFFECTED PRODUCTS OR PROCESSES	AFFECTED AGENCIES	CROSS-REFERENCES	NOTES
Regulations:					
29 CFR 1900-1910 Workplace Standards	Sets regulatory standards for specific workplace hazards	Primarily toxic chemicals	DOL-OSHA HHS-CDC-NIOSH	NIOSH recommends standards to OSHA	There is no general industry standard requiring compliance in the biotech area. A standard may be developed for each engineered area.
30 CFR 11 Workplace Respirator Standards	Sets a regulatory standard for respirators	Respirable toxins	HHS-CDC-NIOSH DOL-Mine Safety and Health Admin. (MSHA)	OSHA and MSHA require adherence to respirator standards	NIOSH has a regulatory role here.
29 CFR 1910.20 Access to Employee Exposure and Medical Records	Provides access to plant information on toxic substances and harmful physical agents and to medical monitoring data related to exposures	Toxic substances and physical and biological agents	DOL-OSHA HHS-CDC-NIOSH		
29 CFR 1910.1200 Hazard Communication	Requires manufacturers and importers to evaluate hazards of their products and communicate this information to employees through labels, material safety data sheets and training	Toxic substances	DOL-OSHA		Could include biological agents
TSCA Section 6	Authorizes EPA to regulate the manufacture, processing, distribution in commerce, use, and disposal of "chemical substances"	TSCA "chemical substances"	EPA, CPSC, OSHA, DOT		Discretionary authority can be exercised if EPA finds a substance "will present" an unreasonable r). Can be used to impose controls through all phases of manufacture, processing, use and disposal. Unlike PMN authority (Sec. 5(a)(1)(A)), Section 6 can be applied to R&D substances. No regulation affecting biotechnology in effect.

Federal Register / Vol. 49, No. 252 / Monday, December 31, 1984 / Notices   50865

AUTHORITY OR GUIDELINE	DESCRIPTION	AFFECTED PRODUCTS OR PROCESSES	AFFECTED AGENCIES	CROSS-REFERENCES	NOTES
Regulations:					
29 CFR 1900-1910 Workplace Standards	Sets regulatory standards for specific workplace hazards	Primarily toxic chemicals	DOL-OSHA HHS-CDC-NIOSH	NIOSH recommends standards to OSHA	There is no general industry standard requiring compliance in the biotech area. A standard may be developed for each engineered area.
30 CFR 11 Workplace Respirator Standards	Sets a regulatory standard for respirators	Respirable toxins	HHS-CDC-NIOSH DOL-Mine Safety and Health Admin. (MSHA)	OSHA and MSHA require adherence to respirator standards	NIOSH has a regulatory role here.
29 CFR 1910.20 Access to Employee Exposure and Medical Records	Provides access to plant information on toxic substances and harmful physical agents and to medical monitoring data related to exposures	Toxic substances and physical and biological agents	DOL-OSHA HHS-CDC-NIOSH		
29 CFR 1910.1200 Hazard Communication	Requires manufacturers and importers to evaluate hazards of their products and communicate this information to employees through labels, material safety data sheets and training	Toxic substances	DOL-OSHA		Could include biological agents
TSCA Section 6	Authorizes EPA to regulate the manufacture, processing, distribution in commerce, use, and disposal of "chemical substances"	TSCA "chemical substances"	EPA, CPSC, OSHA, DOT		Discretionary authority can be exercised if EPA finds a substance "will present" an unreasonable r. Can be used to impose controls through all phases of manufacture, processing, use and disposal. Unlike PMN authority (Sec. 5(e)(1)(A)), Section 6 can be applied to R&D substances. No regulation affecting biotechnology in effect.

59866 Federal Register / Vol. 49, No. 252 / Monday, December 31, 1984 / Notices

AUTHORITY OR GUIDELINE	DESCRIPTION	AFFECTED PRODUCTS OR PROCESSES	AFFECTED AGENCIES	CROSS-REFERENCES	NOTES
B. Drug Manufacturing Practices					
FD&C Act Section 501(a)-(e) (21 USC 351)	FDA establishes "current good manufacturing practices" (CGMPs) for drug products through regulation that are mandatory for manufacturers	Drugs, human biologics, and medicated feeds	HHS-FDA		Certain aspects are also applicable to premarketing manufacture.
Regulations: 21 CFR 210, 211, 225, 226					
C. Hazardous Waste					
Comprehensive Environmental Response, Compensation, and Liability Act (Superfund Act) (42 USC 9601-9657)					
Sections 102, 103	Requires reporting of releases of reportable quantities of hazardous substances	Substances identified as hazardous under Sections 101 or 102	EPA-Nat'l Response Center		"Hazardous substance" refers to (1) certain substances regulated under the Clean Water Act, Clean Air Act, TSCA, and Resource Conservation and Recovery Act, and (2) any other substances that may present substantial danger to public health, welfare, or the environment and are listed by EPA under Section 102 of Superfund Act. Some genetically engineered organisms or byproducts could meet the latter test; none now listed.
Section 104	Provides health assessment and specific public health activities at superfund sites	Substances identified as hazardous under Sections 101 or 102	HHS-Agency for Toxic Substances & Disease Registry (ATSDR)		
Section 105	Requires EPA to develop National Contingency Plan (NCP) for cleanup of hazardous substances; must specify methods for cleanup (e.g., use of biological materials).	products used to degrade hazardous substances.	EPA, other emergency response agencies (e.g., HHS-CDC, FEMA, DOT)		
Regulation: 40 CFR 300	National Contingency Plan	products used to degrade hazardous substances	EPA, other emergency agencies		Regulation identifies criteria for responding to releases and lists use of microorganisms for waste treatment.

Federal Register / Vol. 49, No. 252 / Monday, December 31, 1984 / Notices

AUTHORITY OR GUIDELINE	DESCRIPTION	AFFECTED PRODUCTS OR PROCESSES	AFFECTED AGENCIES	CROSS-REFERENCES	NOTES
Resource Conservation and Recovery Act (RCRA) (42 USC 6901-6987) Section 3001	Authorizes EPA to list and identify hazardous waste with assistance from ATSDR and the National Toxicology Program (NTP)	Waste identified as hazardous.	EPA, HHS-ATSDR, NTP		Discretionary authority to list waste as hazardous; no living organisms now listed. However, a biotechnology waste could be listed if concern warrants. If mixed with listed hazardous waste or if they exhibit hazardous waste characteristics, biological wastes could be regulated as hazardous waste.
Sections 3002-3004	Standards applicable to generators, transporters, and owners and operators of facilities that treat, store, and dispose of hazardous waste.	Solid waste identified as hazardous waste under RCRA.	EPA, DOT	DOT's authority under Hazardous Materials Transportation Act overlaps EPA's RCRA authority, but DOT and EPA have memorandum of agreement to divide responsibilities. (45 FR 51645 (1980))	
Section 3005	Requires permits for treatment, storage, disposal of hazardous waste.	Waste identified as hazardous.	EPA, DOT		
Sections 4005(a) and 1008	Prohibits "open dumping" of solid wastes	Solid waste	EPA		Biological products or byproducts would be subject to the prohibition when disposed.
Regulations: 40 CFR 260	Hazardous waste management system — general requirements		EPA		
40 CFR 261	Identification and listing of hazardous waste		EPA		
40 CFR 260-267	Standards for generators, transporters, and owners or operators of, facilities that treat, store, and dispose of hazardous waste.		EPA, DOT	DOT regulates transportation of hazardous "materials."	Would affect industries using biotechnology only to the extent they generated wastes identified as hazardous. No living organisms listed.

50868   Fedaral Register / Vol. 49, No. 252 / Monday, December 31, 1984 / Notices

AUTHORITY OR GUIDELINE	DESCRIPTION	AFFECTED PRODUCTS OR PROCESSES	AFFECTED AGENCIES	CROSS-REFERENCES	NOTES
40 CFR 270	Hazardous waste permit program		EPA		
Marine Protection, Research, and Sanctuaries Act (Ocean Dumping) (33 USC 1401-1445)					
Section 102, 103	Prohibits ocean dumping without a permit, authorizes EPA to issue permits for dumping all materials except dredged materials and materials specifically prohibited by statute.	Microbial products used in pollution control; waste and byproducts from manufacture, use, etc.	EPA, Corps of Engineers	Corps of Engineers authorized to issue permits for dredged material.	
Regulations: 40 CFR 227-228	Criteria for approving permits; prohibits dumping of wastes containing living organisms that would endanger health or the environment; exempts dredged material from that prohibition.		EPA, Corps of Engineers		
D. Other Containment and Transportation Requirements					
Federal Meat Inspection Act (21 USC 601 et seq.)	Regulates, through mandatory inspection, the slaughtering, preparation, labeling, marking, distribution of meat and meat food products to prevent "adulterated" or "misbranded" meat and meat food products from entering commerce.	Meat and meat food products (specifically cattle, sheep, swine, goat, horse, mule, or other equine). See definition in 9 CFR 301.2 (tt) and (vv)	USDA-FSIS	FDA sets residue tolerance levels for animal drugs in food-chain animals. FDA's regulatory authority is found in 21 CFR 556.	Both the Federal Meat Inspection Act and the Poultry and Poultry Products Inspection Act determine whether regulated articles contain any "biological residues" (see definitions in 9 CFR 301.2 (22) and 381.1 (7), and contain specific recordkeeping, buying, selling, and transportation requirements affecting foreign, interstate, and intrastate commerce.
Regulations: 9 CFR 301 et seq.					
Poultry and Poultry Products Inspection Act (21 USC 451 et seq.)	Regulates, through mandatory inspection, the slaughtering, preparation, distribution, disposition, marking, and labeling of poultry and poultry products to prevent "adulterated" or "misbranded" poultry and poultry products from entering commerce.	Poultry (specifically, any domesticated bird—chicken, turkey, ducks, geese, or guineas, whether live or dead) and poultry products. See definition in 9 CFR 381.1 (40) and (41).	USDA-FSIS		
Regulations: 9 CFR 381					

10

83

AUTHORITY OR GUIDELINE	DESCRIPTION	AFFECTED PRODUCTS OR PROCESSES	AFFECTED AGENCIES	CROSS-REFERENCES	NOTES
Hazardous Materials Transportation Act (49 USC 1801 et seq.) Regulations: 49 CFR 107, 171-177	Regulation of transportation of hazardous materials. Shippers must register with DOT. Authorizes halt of shipping immediately for "imminent hazard."	Etiologic agents	DOT-Ofc of Hazardous Materials Regulation	DOT consults with the ICC which is responsible for enforcement where it has authority. DOT has an agreement with EPA (RCRA) on duplicative authorities.	May regulate packing, labeling, and routing as well as the manufacture of packaging. Secretary may exempt shippers if they achieve a level of safety higher than the level of safety required or if no standard exists and public safety is maintained.
PHS Act Section 361 (42 USC 264) Regulations: 42 CFR 71-72	Authorizes regulation of introduction and control of communicable diseases, interstate transportation of etiologic agents and importation of etiologic agents and vectors.	Etiologic agents	HHS-CDC, FDA, NIH		The requirements of this regulation are in addition to and not in lieu of any other requirements of DOT, USDA, or EPA for importation or interstate transport.
Section 102, Organic Act of 1944, as amended, and the Act of April 6, 1937, as amended (7 USC 147a, 148, 148a-e. Regulations: 7 CFR 300-399	General authority to "carry out operations or measures to detect, erradicate, suppress, control, or to prevent or retard the spread of plant pests." Provides for inspection of plants and plant products offered for export.	"plant pests" are defined as: "any living stage of any insects, mites, nematodes, slugs, snails, protozoa, or other invertebrate animals, bacteria, fungi, other parasitic plants or reproductive parts thereof, viruses, or any organisms similar to or allied with any of the foregoing, or any infectious substances which can directly or indirectly injure or cause disease or damage in any plants or parts thereof, or any processed, manufactured or other products of plants."	USDA-APHIS	EPA also has authority over organisms that could act as plant pests.	Authority extends to cooperative action with States or political subdivisions, farmers associations and similar associations, individuals and governments of Western Hemisphere Countries.

50670   Federal Register / Vol. 49, No. 252 / Monday, December 31, 1984 / Notices

AUTHORITY OR GUIDELINE	DESCRIPTION	AFFECTED PRODUCTS OR PROCESSES	AFFECTED AGENCIES	CROSS-REFERENCES	NOTES
Federal Plant Pest Act, as amended (7 USC 150aa-jj) and Plant Quarantine Act, as amended (7 USC 151-164a, 166-167) Regulations: 7 CFR 300-399	General authority to regulate the importation into and the dissemination within the U.S. of plant pests, nursery stock, and other plants and plant products, and any product or article which may contain a plant pest at time of movement. Authority for USDA to import for scientific or experimental purposes any class of nursery stock, plants, fruits, vegetables, roots, bulbs, seeds, or other plant products for which importation may otherwise be forbidden.	"plant pests" are defined to be consistent with the definition of "plant pests" in Sec. 102 of the Organic Act.	USDA-APHIS		Authority to bring civil and criminal actions for violations of the Act or regulations promulgated thereunder. USDA may stop, and without a warrant, inspect, search, seize, examine, destroy or otherwise dispose of specified articles found to be moving or to have been moved in interstate commerce or to have been brought into the U.S. in violation of the Act or of a quarantine or order. In extraordinary emergency situations, USDA may stop intrastate activity as well.
"Animal Quarantine Laws" (21 USC 102-105; 21 USC 111; 21 USC 114a-114h; 21 USC 115-130; 21 USC 134-134h 21 USC 135-135b) Regulations: 9 CFR 1-199	In general, the animal quarantine laws regulate the importation, exportation, and interstate movement of certain animals to prevent the introduction or spread of communicable diseases of animals or of the contagion of any contagious, infectious, or communicable disease of animals or and live poultry.	21 USC 101-105 regulates cattle, sheep and other ruminants and all swine imported into or intended for export from the U.S. 21 USC 111 regulates that which could introduce or cause the dissemination in the U.S. of the contagion of any contagious, infectious, or communicable disease of animals and/or live poultry.	USDA-APHIS		

12

85

85

AUTHORITY OR GUIDELINE	DESCRIPTION	AFFECTED PRODUCTS OR PROCESSES	AFFECTED AGENCIES	CROSS-REFERENCES	NOTES
Federal Noxious Weed Act of 1974 (7 USC 2801-2813) Regulations: 7 CFR 360	Authority to issue permits to regulate the movement of noxious weeds into or through the U.S. Authority to regulate the sale, purchase, barter, exchange, advertisement, giving, or receiving of any noxious weed.	"Noxious weed" is defined as "any living stage (including but not limited to seeds and reproductive parts) of any parasitic or other plant of a kind or subdivision of a kind, which is of foreign origin, is new to or not widely prevalent in the U.S., and can directly or indirectly injure crops, other useful plants, livestock, or poultry or other interests of agriculture including irrigation or navigation or the fish and wildlife resources of the United States or the public health."	USDA-APHIS	No action may be taken to regulate interstate movement unless a State also takes a cooperative action to eradicate the noxious weed in its State.	Authority to seize, quarantine, treat, destroy or otherwise dispose of any product or article of any character whatsoever, which is moving into or through the U.S. or interstate and which is believed to be infested by any noxious weed, or contains any noxious weed, or which was infested or contained any noxious weed at the time of movement.
TSCA Section 13	Substance imported into the US must be in compliance with TSCA.	TSCA "chemical substances"	EPA, USDA-APHIS Treasury Dept.		Mandatory requirement.
Regulations: 40 CFR 707 19 CFR 12, 127	Section 13 import provisions; requires companies importing "chemical substances" to certify compliance with TSCA		EPA, USDA-APHIS Treasury Dept.	Federal Plant Pest Act, Federal Noxious Weed Act, "Exotic Organisms." Executive order 11987 also regulate imports	Rules were issued by Treasury Department and EPA.

50872   Federal Register / Vol. 49, No. 252 / Monday, December 31, 1984 / Notices

AUTHORITY OR GUIDELINE	DESCRIPTION	AFFECTED PRODUCTS OR PROCESSES	AFFECTED AGENCIES	CROSS-REFERENCES	NOTES
III. EXPORT CONTROLS Export Administration Act (§40 USC 2401, et seq.) Regulations: 15 CFR 368-399	Technical Data All non-public technical data exported to Eastern Bloc Countries, Libya, Cuba, N. Korea, Afghanistan, Kampuchea, and Vietnam requires a validated license.	Technical data related to all biotechnologies	Dept. of Commerce-Int'l Trade Admin. (DOC-ITA)		Statute provides discretionary authority to restrict technical data for three reasons: a) Foreign Policy b) National Security c) Short Supply Although authority to administer the EAA terminated, it was extended indefinitely by Executive Order 12370 of March 30, 1984.
	Commodities Listed products cannot be exported to any country except Canada without a validated license from the Department of Commerce.	Bacteria, fungi, protozoa, virus, human and animal vaccines, human and animal peptides and proteins, rDNA, nucleotides and side antibiotics and diagnostics, amino acids, vitamins, enzymes, pesticides, herbicides and seeds	DOC-ITA		Restrictions generally apply to Soviet Bloc countries and those countries with which we do not have diplomatic relations.
IV. RESEARCH AND INFORMATION GATHERING A. Research PHS Act Section 301 (42 USC 241)	Biomedical research authority, both intramural and extramural research	Basic and applied research related to foods, drugs, biologics, new surgical techniques, chemicals as carcinogens (NIEHS, NTP, NCTR), medical devices.	HHS-NIH, ADAMHA, CDC, FDA		HHS has many other research authorities for specific diseases, but Section 301 is sufficient to do biomedical research related to human health.
Organic Act of 1962 (7 USC 2201-2204)	Agricultural research authority, both intramural and extramural	Plants and animals	USDA-ARS		USDA also has many authorities for research, just as NIH, including: Domestic Animal, Dairy Industry, Arboretum, Forest and Rangeland, Cotton and Nutrition

Federal Register / Vol. 49. No. 252 / Monday, December 31, 1984 / Notices   50673

AUTHORITY OR GUIDELINE	DESCRIPTION	APPLIED PRODUCTS OR PROCESSES	APPLIED AGENCIES	CROSS-REFERENCES	NOTES
Organic Act of 1944 Section 101(d) (7 USC 430)	Authority to purchase and test samples of all tuberculin, serums, antitoxins, or analogous products, of foreign or domestic manufacture, which are sold in the U.S., for the detection, prevention, treatment or cure of diseases of domestic animals.		USDA-ARS		
TSCA, FIFRA, RCRA, Clean Water Act	Environmental research authority, both intramural and extramural	TSCA "chemical substances," pesticides, hazardous wastes, air and water pollutants	EPA		
B. Information Gathering					
Federal Seed Act (7 USC 1551-1611) Regulations: 7 CFR 201 et seq.	Requires specific recordkeeping on labeling, importation and interstate movement of seeds.	Agricultural and vegetable seeds	USDA-APHIS		The term "treated" means given an application of a substances or subjected to a process designed to reduce, control, or repel disease organisms, insects, or other pests which attack seeds or seedlings growing therefrom.
TSCA Section 4	Authorizes EPA to require manufacturers by rule to test specific "chemical substances"	TSCA "chemical substances"	EPA		Discretionary authority; could be used to require testing of specific products developed through genetic engineering (both organisms and chemicals produced by organisms); could be used to support activities of other agencies (e.g., OSHA, CPSC). No regulations affecting biotechnology now in effect.
TSCA Section 8(a)	Authorizes EPA to require manufacturers and processors to submit information on a product's identity, exposure, available health and safety data, etc.		EPA		Discretionary authority invoked by rule; can be used to support other agencies; small businesses generally exempt from reporting. No biotechnology rule now in effect.
TSCA Section 8(d)	Authorizes EPA to require submission of health and safety studies on products subject to TSCA.		EPA		Discretionary authority invoked by rule; no biotechnology rules now in effect.

15

59674   Federal Register / Vol. 49, No. 252 / Monday, December 31, 1984 / Notices

16

AUTHORITY OR GUIDELINE	DESCRIPTION	AFFECTED PRODUCTS OR PROCESSES	AFFECTED AGENCIES	CROSS-REFERENCES	NOTES
TSCA Section 8(e)	Requires submission of information on substantial risks from "chemical substances."	TSCA chemicals	EPA		Mandatory requirement if substance subject to TSCA and information shows substantial risk.
Guideline: 43 FR 11110 (1978)	Policy for submitting information under Sec. 8(e)	TSCA chemicals	EPA		Mandatory requirement if substance subject to TSCA.
FIFRA Section 6(a)(2)	Continuing obligation for registrants to supply data	All registered products	EPA		After registration, registrants must report additional information on unreasonable adverse effects of pesticide. The "interpretation" is undergoing revision currently.
Guideline: Interpretation of Requirements on Registrants by Section 6(a)(2), August 23, 1978 (43 FR 37611 and 44 FR 40716)					
FIFRA Section 3(c)(2)(B)	Authorizes EPA to request additional data in support of registration	All registered products	EPA		After registration, EPA may require additional data from registrants in order to maintain registrations.
V. PATENTS					
Patent and Trademark Laws (35 USC 1 et seq.)	Patent process	All products and devices	DOC-Patent and Trademark Office	Patent for new drugs issued well before FDA premarket approval. Important: Government research institutions can offer institutional Patent Agreements with universities for 5 to 8 years after market approval under PL 96-517.	
Regulations: 37 CFR					
Plant Variety Protection Act (7 USC 2321 et seq.)	Granting of patents for sexually reproduced varieties of plants.	New varieties of sexually reproduced plants	USDA-Agriculture Marketing Service (AMS)		
Regulations: 7 CFR 180					
Judicial Decisions:					
Diamond v. Chakrabarty, 447 US 303 (1980)	Supreme Court held that genetically engineered bacterium was patentable.			Court cited NIH guidelines in decision as addressing the problems of genetic engineering.	

Federal Register / Vol. 49, No. 252 / Monday, December 31, 1984 / Notices   50875

AUTHORITY OR GUIDELINE	DESCRIPTION	AFFECTED PRODUCTS OR PROCESSES	AFFECTED AGENCIES	CROSS-REFERENCES	NOTES
VI. AIR AND WATER EMISSIONS					
Clean Air Act (42 USC 7401-7642)	Requires emission standards to be set for hazardous air pollutants where there is no applicable ambient air quality standard.		EPA		Discretionary authority; no genetically engineered organisms now included, but could be set for biotechnology products if concern warranted.
Regulations: 40 CFR 61	Sets national emission standards for specific hazardous air pollutants		EPA		Regulations developed for drug manufacturers, pesticide manufacturers and hospital. (See 40 CFR 401-469, below.)
Clean Water Act (33 USC 1251-1376)	Pollutant discharges without National Pollutant Discharge Elimination System (NPDES) permit unlawful. Pollutant defined to include living organisms; requires EPA to establish effluent limitations for point sources.	Genetically engineered organisms or byproducts that are discharged into the waters of the U.S.	EPA, States	States establish water quality standards. States or EPA issue permits which incorporate technology-based limits and water quality-based limits.	
Regulations: 40 CFR 122, 125	NPDES permit program		EPA, States		Implemented by States and EPA. Source employing biotechnology will be required to adhere to permit restrictions.
40 CFR 120, 121	State water quality standards, State certification requirements		EPA, States		
40 CFR 401-469	Effluent guidelines and standards for categories of point sources		EPA, States		Specific biotechnology category not issued, but some categories could involve biotechnology products (e.g., part 439, pharmaceutical manufacturing; part 460, hospitals; and part 455, pesticides).
Safe Drinking Water Act (SDWA) (42 USC 300f et seq.)					
Section 300g-1	Authorizes promulgation of maximum containment levels for drinking water from public water systems.	Any physical, chemical, biological or radiological substances or matter in drinking water	EPA		No genetically engineered biological substances now included. Could be regulated if it presents a known or anticipated adverse effect on health.

50876   Federal Register / Vol. 49, No. 252 / Monday, December 31, 1984 / Notices

AUTHORITY OR GUIDELINE	DESCRIPTION	AFFECTED PRODUCTS OR PROCESSES	AFFECTED AGENCIES	CROSS-REFERENCES	NOTES
Section 300h-1	Requires state programs to regulate any injection of any substance into a well; provides for minimum regulatory standards for such programs in order to prevent underground injection that endangers drinking water.	Any substance injected into the subsurface through a well	EPA		See 40 CFR Parts 144, 145, and 146. If disposed of by deep well injection, subject to stringent requirements for Class I wells regarding well construction, operation, monitoring, and reporting; if not a deep well, then would be Class V, subject only to a general prohibition on endangerment to drinking water sources.
VII. REQUIREMENTS FOR FEDERAL AGENCIES					
National Environmental Policy Act (NEPA) Section 102(2)(C) (42 USC 4321-4361) Regulations: 40 CFR 1500-1508	Requires all agencies to prepare environmental impact statements on "major Federal actions significantly affecting the environment."		All Federal Agencies	Administered by Council on Environmental Quality.	Applies only to Federal actions (e.g., federally funded projects or premarket approval). Each agency develops its own guidelines or regulations under this Act. Procedural requirements generally held inapplicable to EPA actions.
Endangered Species Act of 1973, as amended, Section F (16 USC 1536) Regulations: 50 CFR 402	Require Federal agencies to insure that their activities or programs will not jeopardize the continued existence of a listed species.	All species of fish, wildlife and plants listed pursuant to the Endangered Species Act.	All Fed. agencies	Consultation required with the U.S. Dept. of the Interior or the National Marine Fisheries Service.	
Executive Order 11987 "Exotic Species"	Orders Executive Agencies (to extent permitted by law) to restrict the importation into the U.S., and introduction of exotic specimens into the natural ecosystems. Exempts from provisions of Executive Order 11987 the introduction or exportation of exotic species when USDA or USDI finds that the introduction or exportation will not have an "adverse effect on natural ecosystems."	"Exotic Species" is defined to mean all species of plants and animals not naturally occurring, either presently or historically, in any ecosystem of the U.S.	All Fed. agencies		Secretary of the Interior in consultation with Secretary of Agriculture is required to develop and implement by rule or regulation a system to standardize and simplify the requirements, procedures, and other activities appropriate for implementing the provisions of Executive Order 11987. No rule has been developed.

18

Federal Register / Vol. 49, No. 252 / Monday, December 31, 1984 / Notices   50877

19

AUTHORITY OR GUIDELINE	DESCRIPTION	AFFECTED PRODUCTS OR PROCESSES	AFFECTED AGENCIES	CROSS-REFERENCES	NOTES
Judicial Decisions: Foundation on Economic Trends v. Heckler, 14 ELR 20467 (D.D.C. 5/16/84)	Preliminary injunction prohibiting NIH approval of environmental release of organisms containing rDNA pending final judgment by the court regarding compliance with NEPA.	TNO-minus bacteria and all future submissions for NIH review.	HHS-NIH		Decision applies only to requests from institutions receiving NIH rDNA funding.

BILLING CODE 4680-60-C

Thursday
June 26, 1986

Part II

Office of Science and Technology Policy

Coordinated Framework for Regulation of
Biotechnology; Announcement of Policy
and Notice for Public Comment

23302   Federal Register / Vol. 51, No. 123 / Thursday, June 26, 1986 / Notices

OFFICE OF SCIENCE AND TECHNOLOGY POLICY

Coordinated Framework for Regulation of Biotechnology

AGENCY: Executive Office of the President, Office of Science and Technology Policy.

ACTION: Announcement of policy; notice for public comment.

SUMMARY: This Federal Register notice announces the policy of the federal agencies involved with the review of biotechnology research and products. As certain concepts are new to this policy, and will be the subject of rulemaking, the public is invited to comment on these aspects which are specifically identified herein.

DATE: Comments must be received on or before August 25, 1986.

Public Participation: The Domestic Policy Council Working Group on Biotechnology through the Office of Science and Technology Policy, is seeking advice on certain refinements published herein to the previously published proposed coordinated framework for regulation of biotechnology. These new aspects include the Biotechnology Science Coordinating Committee's (BSCC's) definitions for an "intergeneric organism (new organism)" and for "pathogen." These definitions are critical to the coordinated framework for the regulation of biotechnology because they establish the types of the organisms subject to certain kinds of review.

It is the intention of the Domestic Policy Council Working Group on Biotechnology, the Biotechnology Science Coordinating Committee (BSCC), the Department of Agriculture (USDA), the Environmental Protection Agency (EPA), the Food and Drug Administration (FDA), the National Institutes of Health (NIH), the National Science Foundation (NSF), and the Occupational Safety and Health Administration (OSHA) that the policies contained herein be effective immediately. In consideration of comments, modifications, if any, may be published either in a separate notice or as part of proposed rulemaking by the involved agencies.

Information submitted to an agency that is trade secret information or confidential business information should be clearly marked so that it can be accorded the protection provided to such by each respective agency.

ADDRESS: Comments specific to the BSCC definitions or overall comments to the Coordinated Framework for the Regulation of Biotechnology statements should be addressed to: BSCC; Docket #BSCC 0001, Office of Science and Technology Policy, Executive Office of the President, NEOB-Room 5005, Washington, DC 20506.

Comments relating to the policy statements of a particular agency should be sent directly to the agency contact identified at the beginning of the respective agency policy statement.

FOR FURTHER INFORMATION CONTACT: Dr. David T. Kingsbury, Assistant Director for Biological, Behavioral, and Social Sciences, National Science Foundation, 1800 G Street, N.W., Washington, D.C. 20550, (202-357-9854).

Jerry D. Jennings,

Executive Director, Office of Science and Technology Policy

June 18, 1986

Table of Contents

I Preamble
  A. Introduction
  B. The Coordinated Framework for the Regulation of Biotechnology
  C. Interagency Coordination Mechanisms
  D. BSCC Definitions
  E. International Aspects
II. Statements of Policy
  A. Food and Drug Administration
  B. Environmental Protection Agency
  C. U.S. Department of Agriculture
  D. Occupational Safety and Health Administration
  E. National Institutes of Health

A. Introduction

This notice describes the comprehensive federal regulatory policy for ensuring the safety of biotechnology research and products. Specifically addressed are agency policies that formed part of the previously proposed Coordinated Framework for the Regulation of Biotechnology, published in the **Federal Register** December 31, 1984 (49 FR 50856, hereinafter "the December 84 Notice"). These agency policies build upon experience with agricultural, pharmaceutical, and other commercial products developed by traditional genetic modification techniques.

Existing statutes provide a basic network of agency jurisdiction over both research and products: this network forms the basis of this coordinated framework and helps assure reasonable safeguards for the public. This framework is expected to evolve in accord with the experiences of the industry and the agencies, and, thus, modifications may need to be made through administrative or legislative actions.

The application of traditional genetic modification techniques is relied upon broadly for enhanced characteristics of food (e.g., hybrid corn, selective breeding), manufactured food (e.g., bread, cheese, yogurt), waste disposal (e.g., bacterial sewage treatment), medicine (e.g., vaccines, hormones), pesticides (e.g. *Bacillus thuringiensis*) and other uses. Federal agencies implement an array of laws which seek to ensure the safety of these products. A concise index of these U.S. laws was published in the **Federal Register** November 14, 1985 (50 FR 47174, hereinafter "the November 85 Notice"). These laws are product-specific because they regulate certain product uses, such as foods or pesticides. This approach provides the opportunity for similar products to be treated similarly by particular regulatory agencies.

Biotechnology also includes recently developed and newly emerging genetic manipulation technologies, such as recombinant DNA (rDNA), recombinant RNA (rRNA) and cell fusion, that are sometimes referred to as genetic engineering. While the recently developed methods are an extension of traditional manipulations that can produce similar or identical products, they enable more precise genetic modifications, and therefore hold the promise for exciting innovation and new areas of commercial opportunity.

Concerns were raised as to whether products resulting from the recently developed techniques would pose greater risks than those achieved through traditional manipulation techniques. For example, what might be the possible environmental consequences of the many anticipated agricultural and environmental applications that will take place outside the physical constraints of a contained facility? In particular, the environmental application of genetically engineered microorganisms may elicit concern because they are of microscopic size, and some may be able to reproduce, proliferate, and become established.

The underlying policy question was whether the regulatory framework that pertained to products developed by traditional genetic manipulation techniques was adequate for products obtained with the new techniques. A similar question arose regarding the sufficiency of the review process for research conducted for agricultural and environmental applications.

The Administration, recognizing its responsibility to confront these concerns, formed an interagency working group under the former White House Cabinet Council on Natural Resources and the Environment in the spring of 1984. The working group sought to achieve a balance between regulation adequate to ensure health and environmental safety while maintaining sufficient regulatory flexibility to avoid impeding the growth of an infant industry.

Upon examination of the existing laws available for the regulation of products developed by traditional genetic manipulation techniques, the working group concluded that, for the most part, these laws as currently implemented would address regulatory needs adequately. For certain microbial products, however, additional regulatory requirements, available under existing statutory authority, needed to be established.

The existing health and safety laws had the advantage that they could provide more immediate regulatory protection and certainty for the industry than possible with the implementation of new legislation. Moreover, there did not appear to be an alternative, unitary, statutory approach since the very broad spectrum of products obtained with genetic engineering cut across many product uses regulated by different agencies.

Because of the rapid growth in the scientific knowledge base, the working group felt strongly that the federal agencies needed to have an interagency mechanism for sharing scientific information related to biotechnology, particularly information on research and product applications submitted to the agencies.

The December 1984 Notice described the regulatory framework envisioned by the working group, and recognizing the evolutionary nature of its development, asked for comments. In summary, the Notice stated that the Food and Drug Administration (FDA) would regulate genetic engineering products no differently that those achieved through traditional techniques. The Environmental Protection Agency (EPA) described existing and proposed new policies for regulating pesticidal and nonpesticidal microorganisms. The Department of Agriculture (USDA) stated that under its different legislative authorities it could broadly regulate genetically engineered plants and animals, and plant and animal pathogens. The Notice also proposed an interagency science coordinating mechanism.

Many comments were received in response to the Notice. These contributed to the refinement of both the regulatory requirements and the interagency science coordination mechanism.

The interagency coordination mechanism, the Biotechnology Science Coordinating Committee (BSCC),

discussed in more detail in section C. of this Preamble, came into being while the agencies were still in process of refining their regulatory proposals. Consequently, the BSCC was able to play a helpful role in the formulation of two basic principles: (1) Agencies should seek to adopt consistent definitions of those genetically engineered organisms subject to review to the extent permitted by their respective statutory authorities; and, (2) agencies should utilize scientific reviews of comparable rigor.

The regulatory framework anticipates that future scientific developments will lead to further refinements. Experience with earlier basic scientific research has shown that as the science progressed and became better understood by the public; regulatory regimens could be modified to reflect more complete understanding of the potential risks involved. Similar evolution is anticipated in the regulation of commercial products as scientists and regulators learn to predict more precisely particular product use that require greater or lesser controls or even exemption from any federal review.

This framework has sought to distinguish between those organisms that require a certain level of federal review and those that do not. This follows a traditional approach to regulation. Within agriculture, for example, introductions of new plants, animals and microorganisms have long occurred routinely with only some of those that are not native or are pathogenic requiring regulatory approval. It should be noted that microorganisms play many essential and varied roles in agriculture and the environment and that for decades agricultrual scientists have endeavored to exploit their advantages through routine experimentation and introduction into the environment; and as a rule these agricultural and environmental introductions have taken place without harm to the environment.

B. The Coordinated Framework for the Regulation of Biotechnology

General Comments

This notice includes separate descriptions of the regulatory policies of FDA, EPA, OSHA and USDA and the research policies of the National institutes of Health (NIH), NSF, EPA and USDA. The agencies will seek to operate their programs in an integrated and coordinated fashion and together should cover the full range of plants, animals and microorganisms derived by the new genetic engineering techniques. To the extent possible, responsibility for a

product use will lie with a single agency. Where regulatory oversight or review for a particular product is to be performed by more than one agency, the policy establishes a lead agency, and consolidated or coordinated reviews. While this preamble seeks to convey an overview of the coordinated framework, it must be noted that the regulatory requirements are highly technical: reliance only on the simplified summary statements herein could be misleading and, thus, the agency policy statements must be consulted for specific details. In the event that questions arise regarding which federal agency has jurisdiction, an information contact is provided at the beginning of this notice.

While in part certain USDA and EPA requirements are new, the underlying regulatory regimens are not new. Members of the agricultural and industrial communities are familiar with the general requirements under these laws which include the Federal Plant Pest Act, The Plant Quarantine Act, the Toxic Substances Control Act (TSCA), and the Federal insecticide, Fungicide, and Rodenticide Act (FIFRA).

Because this comprehensive regulatory framework uses a mosaic of existing federal law, some of the statutory nomenclature for certain actions may seem inconsistent. Certain laws, such as USDA's Federal Plant Pest Act, require a "permit" before a microorganism pathogenic to plants may be transported or imported. Under other laws such as FIFRA, the agencies "license" or "approve" the use of particular products. TSCA requires a "premanufacturing notification (PMN)". There are also some variations among the agencies in the use of the phrase "genetic enginering." Regardless of the nomenclature, the public should be aware that the reviews conducted by each of the regulatory agencies are intended to be of comparable rigor. Agencies have agreed to have scientists from each other's staff participate in reviews. Each regulatory review will require that the safety, or safety and efficacy, of a particular agricultural or industrial product be satisfactorily demonstrated to the regulatory agency prior to commercialization.

The National Environmental Policy Act (NEPA) imposes procedural requirements on all federal agencies to prepare an analysis prior to making a decision to take any action that may significantly affect the environment. Depending on the characteristics of a proposal, an environmental assessment, or a broader environmental impact statement may need to be prepared in connection with the release of genetically manipulated organisms. EPA's actions under most of its environmental statutes have been considered to be the functional equivalent of NEPA compliance.

For the handling of microorganisms, agencies of the Department of Health and Human Services have established recommendations for the safe use of infectious agents. The CDC/NIH publication, *Biosafety in Microbiological and Biomedical Laboratories*, describes combinations of standard and special microbiological practices, safety equipment and facilities which are recommended for working with a variety of infectious agents in research laboratories, academic and industrial. The USDA also has issued guidance on other infectious agents.

The NIH has published guidelines for the contained use of DNA organisms in the *NIH Guidelines for Research Involving Recombinant DNA Molecules*, **Federal Register**, May 7, 1986 (51 FR 16958, NIH guidelines). The guidelines recommend physical containment at specific levels for different experiments, and exempt other experiments from containment requirements. However, they recommend Biosafety Level 1, the least stringent level of physical containment, for some "exempt" experiments. For large-scale exempt experiments, the NIH guidelines recommend "Biosafety Level 1-Large-Scale" although following review by the Institutional Biosafety Committee, "some latitude" in the application of these requirements is permitted.

The appropriate large-scale containment requirements for many low risk DNA derived industrial microorganisms will be no greater than those appropriate for the unmodified parental organisms. This concept is discussed further in the Organization for Economic Cooperation and Development (OECD) document, described in the International Aspects section below.

OSHA in its **Federal Register** Notice of April 12, 1984 (50 FR 14468) stated that its authority under the Occupational Safety and Health Act of 1970 (29 U.S.C. et seq.) provides an adequate and enforceable basis for protecting the safety and health of employees in the field of biotechnology and that no additional regulation is necessary. After consideration of comments in the April 1984 notice, OSHA is publishing this policy statement in final form without change.

Product Regulation

Agencies involved with regulating agriculture, foods, medical devices, drugs, biologics and pesticides have had extensive experience with products that involve living organisms in their manufacture and/or ultimate use including releases into the environment for these purposes. By the time a genetically engineered product is ready for commercialization, it will have undergone substantial review and testing during the research phase, and thus, information regarding its safety should be available. The manufacture by the newer technologies of food, the development of new drugs, medical devices, biologics for humans and animals, and pesticides, will be reviewed by FDA, USDA and EPA in essentially the same manner for safety and efficacy as products obtained by other techniques. The new products that will be brought to market will generally fit within these agencies' review and approval regimens.

The regulatory scheme for products is described in Chart I *Coordinated Framework—Marketing Approval of Biotechnology Products*.

CHART I.—COORDINATED FRAMEWORK—APPROVAL OF COMMERCIAL BIOTECHNOLOGY PRODUCTS

Subject	Responsible agency(ies)
Foods/Food Additives	FDA, FSIS.[1]
Human Drugs, Medical Devices and Biologics	FDA.
Animal Drugs	FDA.
Animal Biologics	APHIS.
Other Contained Uses	EPA.
Plants and Animals	APHIS,[*] FSIS[1], FDA.[2]
Pesticide Microorganisms Released in the Environment All	EPA.[*] APHIS.[3]
Other Uses (Microorganisms):	
Intergeneric Combination	EPA.[*] APHIS.[3]
Intrageneric Combination:	
Pathogenic Source Organism:	
1. Agricultural Use	APHIS.
2. Non-Agricultural use	EPA.[*4] APHIS.[3]
No Pathogenic Source Organisms	EPA Report.
Nonengineered Pathogens:	
1. Agricultural Use	APHIS.
2. Non-agricultural Use	EPA,[*] APHIS.[3]
Nonengineered Nonpathogens	EPA Report.

[*]Lead agency.
[1]FSIS, Food Safety and Inspection Service, under the Assistant Secretary of Agriculture for Marketing and Inspection Services is responsible for food use.
[2]FDA is involved when in relation to a food use.
[3]APHIS, Animal and Plant Health Inspection Service, is involved when the microorganism is plant pest, animal pathogen or regulated article requiring a permit.
[4]EPA requirements will only apply to environmental release under a "significant new use rule" that EPA intends to propose.

Jurisdiction over the varied biotechnology products is determined by their use, as has been the case for traditional products. The detailed description of the products and their review are found in the individual

agency policy statements contained in this **Federal Register** Notice. The following is a brief summary of jurisdiction as described in Chart I.

Foods, food additives, human drugs, biologics and devices, and animal drugs are reviewed or licensed by the FDA. Food products prepared from domestic livestock and poultry are under the jurisdiction of the USDA's Food Safety Inspection Service (FSIS).

Animal biologics are reviewed by the Animal and Plant Health Inspection Service, (APHIS). APHIS also reviews plants, seeds, animal biologics, plant pests, animal pathogens and "regulated articles", i.e., certain genetically engineered organisms containing genetic material from a plant pest. An APHIS permit is required prior to the shipment (movement) or release into the environment of regulated articles, or the shipment of a plant pest or animal pathogen.

"Other contained uses" refers to the closed system uses of those microorganisms, subject the TSCA, that are intergeneric combinations, i.e., deliberately formed microorganisms which contain genetic material from dissimilar source organisms. These are subject to EPA's PMN requirement. EPA is considering promulgating a rule to exempt certain classes of microorganisms from this requirement.

Microbial pesticides will be reviewed by EPA, with APHIS involvement in cases where the pesticide is also a plant pest, animal pathogen, or regulated article requiring a permit. (FDA may become involved in implementing pesticide tolerances for foods.)

"Other uses (microorganisms)" include uses involving release into the environment. For these, jurisdiction depends on the characteristics of the organism as well as its use. "Intergeneric combination"[*] microorganisms will be reported to EPA under PMN requirements, with APHIS involvement in cases where the microorganism is also a regulated article requiring a permit.

"Intrageneric combinations" are those microorganisms formed by genetic engineering other than intergeneric combinations. For these, when there is a pathogenic [1] source organism, and the microorganism is used for agricultural purposes, APHIS has jurisdiction. If the microorganism is used for nonagricultural purposes, then EPA has jurisdiction, with APHIS involvement in cases where the microorganism is also a

[1] "Intergeneric organisms (new organisms)" and "pathogen" are defined in section D. of the preamble.

regulated article requiring a permit. Intrageneric combinations with no pathogenic source organisms are under EPA jurisdiction although EPA will only require an informational report.

"Nonengineered pathogens" that are used for an agricultural use will fall under APHIS jurisdiction. Those that are for a nonagricultural use come under EPA jurisdiction, with APHIS involvement in cases where the microorganism is also a plant pest or animal pathogen requiring a permit. Nonengineered nonpathogenic microorganisms are under EPA jurisdiction which will require only an informational report.

Research

The coordinated framework for the regulation of biotechnology establishes requirements for the conduct of research.

Approximately ten years ago the NIH issued the NIH guidelines describing the manner in which research with organisms derived by rDNA techniques should be conducted. Since then the guidelines have been modified many times with gradual relaxation of these requirements. The guidelines prescribe the conditions under which institutions which receive NIH funds must conduct experiments. For a very small category of NIH funded experiments including environmental release, the guidelines require that the Director, NIH, approve each experiment on an individual basis. For each of these experiments, the RAC conducts a scientific review with an opportunity for public comment, and makes a recommendation to the NIH Director. As research experiments have expanded out of the biomedical area to environmental applications both agricultural and nonagricultural, other agencies have become involved, with shifting of responsibility for research approval to NSF (described in the November 85 Notice), USDA's S&E, and EPA. These other agencies' policies build, in part, on the NIH guidelines and NIH experience.

The S&E guidelines for agricultural research published separately for comment in this issue of the **Federal Register** have adopted the NIH guidelines with certain modifications including expansion of the scope to manipulation techniques other than rDNA; the table included with the S&E guidelines shows where particular elements of the NIH guidelines are used.

It should be noted that not all experiments involving the environmental release of genetically engineered organisms require prior federal approval. In plant applications there is a substantial body of research

indicating that such experiments are of low risk. For certain categories of microorganisms modified by traditional genetic modification techniques, there is also a substantial body of research indicating low risk for environmental experiments.

Chart II—*Coordinated Framework—Biotechnology Research Jurisdiction* shows which agency has responsibility for a particular experiment. If more than one agency has potential jurisdiction, one agency has been designated as the lead agency and it is marked with an asterisk on Chart II. The lead agency designation depends on which research agency is funding the research (e.g., NIH, S&E, or NSF) or which regulatory agency reviews specific purpose research (e.g. pesticides). In the chart and in this discussion, the authority refers to approval of the actual execution of experiments and not to their funding.

CHART II.—COORDINATED FRAMEWORK—BIOTECHNOLOGY RESEARCH JURISDICTION

Subject	Responsible agency(ies)
Contained Research. No Release in Environment:	
1. Federally Funded	Funding agency [1]
2. Non-Federally Funded	NIH or S&E voluntary review. APHIS [2]
Foods/Food Additives, Human Drugs, Medical Devices, Biologics, Animal Drugs:	
1. Federally Funded	FDA*, NIH guidelines & review
2. Non-Federally Funded	FDA*, NIH voluntary review
Plants, Animals and Animal Biologics	
1. Federally Funded	Funding agency [1,2] APHIS [2]
2. Non-Federally Funded	APHIS* S&E voluntary review
Pesticide Microorganisms Genetically Engineered:	
Intergeneric	EPA,* APHIS,[2] S&E voluntary review
Pathogenic Intrageneric	EPA,* APHIS,[2] S&E voluntary review
Intrageneric Nonpathogen	EPA,* S&E voluntary review
Nonengineered:	
Nonindigenous Pathogens	EPA,* APHIS
Indigenous Pathogens	EPA,*,[2] APHIS
Nonindigenous Nonpathogen	EPA *
Other Uses (Microorganisms) Released in the Environment:	
Genetically Engineered:	
Intergeneric Organisms:	
1. Federally Funded	Funding agency,*[1] APHIS,[2] EPA.*

CHART II.—COORDINATED FRAMEWORK—BIO-TECHNOLOGY RESEARCH JURISDICTION—Continued

Subject	Responsible agency(ies)
2. Commercially Funded	EPA, APHIS, S&E voluntary review.
Intrageneric Organisms:	
Pathogenic Source Organism:	
1. Federally Funded	Funding agency,*[1] APHIS,[2] EPA.[2]
2. Commercially Funding	APHIS,[2] EPA (* if nonagricul USE)
Intrageneric Combination.	
No Pathogenic Source Organisms	EPA Report
Nonengineered	EPA Report,* APHIS.[2]

* Lead Agency.
[1] Review and approval of research protocols conducted by NIH, S&E, or NSF
[2] APHIS issues permits for the importation and domestic shipment of certain plants and animals, plant pests and animal pathogens, and for the shipment or release in the environment of regulated articles.
[2] EPA jurisdiction for research on a plot greater than 10 acres
* EPA reviews federally funded environmental research only when it is for commercial purposes.

For contained federally funded research for biomedical and agricultural purposes, research approval will be granted by the funding agency. The NIH guidelines relate primarily to biomedical experiments and only to those using rDNA techniques. Research on foods/food additives, human drugs, medical devices and biologics will continue to rely on the NIH guidelines, with NIH approval required for certain experiments such as human gene therapy, and FDA permission for clinical trials.

Fashioned after the NIH guidelines, the S&E guidelines apply to agricultural research on plants, animals, and microorganisms and provide guidance for laboratory and field testing of organisms derived using rDNA manipulation and other technologies. Adherence to the appropriate set of guidelines is required for institutions receiving financial support from NIH, S&E, or NSF. These guidelines specify what type of review procedures are required for specific categories of experiments. Some experiments require individual approval by the respective agency providing institutional support. For those experiments that require agency approval, advisory committees at NIH, S&E and NSF, composed primarily of nongovernment scientists, may be asked to provide expert review. In addition, research on plants, animals, and animal biologics will come under APHIS permit requirements if a regulated article, plant pest, animal pathogen is involved. An APHIS permit

BIOTECHNOLOGY DESKBOOK

98

23306   Federal Register / Vol. 51, No. 123 / Thursday, June 26, 1986 / Notices

is required prior to the shipment (movement) or release of a regulated article, or the importation or shipment of a plant pest or regulated article used in any research experiment.

EPA has authority for all environmental research on microbial pesticides regardless of whether research is federally funded or not. EPA will regulate research under a two level review system based upon its evaluation of the potential risks posed by various types of microorganisms with lesser notification required for level I reporting and full review for level II.

For the "other uses" category from Chart II (research involving nonpesticide microorganisms released into the environment), jurisdiction for release may be under S&E, NSF, APHIS, or EPA depending primarily upon the source of the funding, but also upon the purpose of the research and the characteristics of the genetically engineered microorganism. Thus, federally funded research conducted for an agricultural use will require adherence to S&E guidelines and approval of certain experiments by S&E or NIH depending on which is the funding agency. EPA will review commercial research. APHIS's jurisdiction applies to issuing permits for regulated articles, plant pests, or animal pathogens. EPA will require an informational report for nonengineered microorganisms released into the environment, with APHIS involvement for the review of plant pests or animal pathogens.

There may be situations where one agency may choose to defer to, or ask advice from, another agency. If experiments requiring NIH, NSF or S&E review/approval are submitted for review to another agency, then NIH, NSF, or S&E may determine that such review serves the same purpose, and based upon that determination, notify the submitter that no NIH, NSF, or S&E review will take place, and the experiment may proceed upon approval from the other agency.

C. Interagency Coordination Mechanisms

The Domestic Policy Council Working Group on Biotechnology

The Domestic Policy Council Working Group on Biotechnology has been responsible for this coordinated framework for the regulation of biotechnology; it also considers policy matters related to agency jurisdiction, commercialization, and international biotechnology matters. The Working Group monitors developments in biotechnology and is ready to identify

problems and make appropriate recommendations for their solution. The Domestic Policy Council Working Group on Biotechnology is a continuation of a similar group established under the former Cabinet Council on Natural Resources and the Environment.

Although at the present time existing statutes seem adequate to deal with the emerging processes and products of modern biotechnology, there always can be potential problems and deficiencies in the regulatory apparatus in a fast moving field. The Working Group will be alert to the implications these changes will have on regulation, and in a timely fashion will make appropriate recommendations for administrative or legislative action.

The Biotechnology Science Coordinating Committee (BSCC)

The BSCC is responsible for coordination and consistency of scientific policy and scientific reviews. The BSCC, established October 31, 1985 as part of the Federal Coordinating Council for Science, Engineering and Technology (FCCSET), consists of senior policy officials of agencies involved in the oversight of biotechnology research and products. FCCSET is a statutory interagency coordinating mechanism managed by the Office of Science and Technology Policy, Executive Office of the President, with a mission to coordinate federal science activities among federal agencies. The November 85 Notice described the structure and activities of the BSCC.

One of the primary activities of the BSCC has been the development of definitions because a common scientific approach is essential to a coordinated federal regulatory framework. The underlying scientific issue, therefore, was defining those organisms subject to certain types of agency review.

The definitions are included in the following section of this preamble and have been incorporated, with modification, into the individual policy notices of the involved agencies. Explanatory material is also included in the agency policy statements. As mentioned elsewhere, the BSCC is seeking comments on these definitions.

Research to develop genetically modified organisms for environmental and agricultural applications (as for research on traditionally modified organisms) generally proceeds in a step-wise manner from highly contained facilities to progressively lesser degrees of containment as the investigator determines the safety and efficacy of experimental applications; these are conducted sequentially under controlled laboratory conditions, greenhouse

testing, small field trials, and full field trials. The BSCC recognizes the need for further work to define the nature and extent of physical and biological barriers that limit or manage environmental release of modified organisms during greenhouse testing and field research.

The BSCC is authorized to hold public meetings in order to discuss public concerns about scientific and other issues. Accordingly, the BSCC will hold its first public meeting shortly after publication of this notice for discussion of the scientific aspects of this notice and the receipt of comments from the public. The public meeting will be held in July 1986. Details regarding time and location will be separately announced in the Federal Register.

D. BSCC Definitions

Any proposal to regulate the research and products of genetic manipulation techniques quickly confronts the issue of what organisms should be considered appropriate for certain types of review. The BSCC formulated definitions are effective immediately but are open to comment; the text following the definition of "pathogen" contains details of the request for comments.

Organisms meeting two different sets of criteria are proposed. First are organisms formed by deliberate combination of genetic material from sources in different genera. It was recognized, however, that in certain precisely constructed "intergeneric organisms" the genetic material is not considered to pose an increased risk to human health or the environment; thus, such combinations are excluded from the definition. A detailed explanation of the scientific basis for these exclusions is found in the footnote after the definition of pathogen. The BSCC specifically requests comments on whether also to consider for exclusion those organisms that exchange DNA by known physiological processes, as explained in the text immediately following the definition of "intergeneric organism (new organism)."

The second definition is "pathogen." This includes microorganisms that belong to a pathogenic species or that contain genetic material from source organisms that are pathogenic. In certain precisely constructed modified organisms, the genetic material from a pathogenic donor is not considered to pose an increased risk to human health or the environment; and, therefore, such combinations are excluded from the definition.

The BSCC definitions of "intergeneric organism (new organism)" and "pathogen" describe the combinations genetic material that would cause a modified organism to come under review. This does not mean to suggest that the behavior of a genetically manipulated organism exempted from these definitions is wholly predictable (since any biological organism is never 100% predictable), but that the probability of any incremental hazard compared to the unmodified organism host is low. Also, this does not mean that any product manufacture or research experiment using an organism exempted from the definition should be conducted without adherence to proper manufacturing standards or research guidelines.

Given the statutory differences in the laws that they administer, the agencies adopted the principles underlying the definitions in ways consistent with their legislation. EPA, APHIS, and S&E are using the definitions to identify levels of review for microbial products within their jurisdiction. EPA, APHIS, FDA, S&E, and NSF are using the definitions as factors to consider in the review of products or experiments.

The BSCC is attempting to define what constitutes "release into the environment." The BSCC is establishing a working group on greenhouse containment and small field trials in order to develop scientific recommendations. The concept of "containment" has traditionally been used to describe physical conditions which severely limit release (for example, a contained laboratory fermentation facility). Containment can also be "biologic" because the ability of an organism to reproduce, exchange genetic information, or become established can be effectively limited biologically. Thus, the BSCC's exploration of the conditions that constitute release into the environment will consider circumstances of both physical and biological containment for particular organisms and the circumstances of their release. While the concept of physical containment may imply the high containment conditions found in certain laboratories and greenhouses, in agricultural practice many simpler effective barriers are routinely used; these include microplots for soil bacteria and fungi, paddocks for noninfective animals, and removing or covering the reproductive parts of plants and animals.

Release into the environment, for the time being, will have somewhat varying definitions for the regulatory and research review of the different agencies. There may be minor differences between agricultural and nonagricultural approaches and betweeen macro-and microorganisms.

Intergeneric Organism (New Organism)

Those organisms deliberately formed to contain an intergeneric combination of genetic material; excluded are organisms that have resulted from the addition of intergeneric materials that is well-characterized and contains only non-coding regulatory regions such as operators, promoters, origins of replication, terminators and ribosome binding regions.

"Well-characterized and contains only non-coding regulatory regions" means that the producer of the microorganism can document the following:

a. The exact nucleotide base sequence of the regulatory region and any inserted flanking nucleotides;

b. The regulatory region and any inserted flanking nucleotides do not code independently for a protein, peptide of functional RNA molecules;

c. The regulatory region solely controls the activity of other sequences that code for protein or peptide molecules or act as recognition sites for the initiation of nucleic acid or protein synthesis.

Pathogen

A pathogen is a virus or microorganism (including its viruses and plasmids, if any) that has the ability to cause disease in other living organisms (i.e., humans, animals, plants, microorganisms).

A microorganism (including viruses) will be subject to regulatory policies regarding pathogens if:

a. The microorganism belongs to a pathogenic species, according to sources identified by the agency, or from information known to the producer that the organism is a pathogen; excepted are organisms belonging to a strain used for laboratory research or commercial purposes and generally recognized as non-pathogenic according to sources identified by a federal agency, or information known to the producer and the appropriate federal agency (an example of a nonpathogenic strain of a species which contains pathogenic strains is *Escherichia coli* K–12; examples of nonpathogenic species are *Bacillus subtilis, Lactobacillus acidophilus,* and *Saccharomyces* species); or

b. The microorganism has been derived form a pathogen or has been deliberately engineered such that it contains genetic material from a pathogenic organism as defined in item a. above. Excepted are genetically engineered organisms developed by transferring a well-characterized, non-coding regulatory region from a pathogenic donor to a non-pathogenic recipient

"Well-characterized, non-coding regulatory region" means that the producer of the microorganism can document the following:

a. The exact nucleotide base sequence of the regulatory region and any inserted flanking nucleotides;

b. The regulatory region and any inserted flanking nucleotides do not code independently for a protein, peptide, or functional RNA molecules; and,

c. The regulatory region solely controls the activity of other sequences that code for protein or peptide moldecules or act as recognition sites for the initiation of nucleic acid or protein systhesis.

This definition excludes organisms such as competitors or colonizers of the same substrates, commensal or mutualistic microorganisms, or opportunistic pathogens.

The footnote contains the scientific basis for exempting non-coding regulatory regions from the definitions of intergeneric organisms and pathogen.[2]

[2] The BSCC has based the exemption of intergeneric transfers of regulatory regions on their lack of coding capacity for the production of proteins, peptides or functional RNA molecules. It has been recommended by other members of the scientific community that there should be additional exemptions such as ribosomal proteins, ribosomal RNAs and transfer RNAs. The BSCC has chosen to examine these suggestions in more detail during the next few months. At the present the BSCC has excluded:

1. Origins of replications;
2. Ribosome binding sites;
3. Promoters;
4. Operators; and,
5. Terminators

The basis for these exemptions is as follows. Each of these regulatory elements has no coding capacity for the production of any gene product and therefore does not promote the production of any new material. What these elements are responsible for is the initiation and modulation of nucleic acid synthesis at the specific region where they appear in the chromosome.

Bacterial genes are precisely regulated and this regulation is based on a series of regulatory elements. The principal regulatory unit is the *operon*. Operons are controlled primarily, but not exclusively, through the regulation of the rate of initiation of messenger RNA synthesis. This regulation is based on the interaction of two short nucleotide sequences in the DNA, the *promoter*, which is the site of RNA polymerase binding and the *operator*, which follows closely and acts as an off-on switch for the movement of the polymerase into the structural gene which follows. The function of the operator is to *bind* a cellular repressor protein which is synthesized in response to changing nutritional stimuli. *Terminator* regions are short nucleotide sequences which signal the termination of mRNA synthesis by the polymerase. They act as a signal for the dissociation of the polymerase from the DNA.

Replication of DNA in every biological system that has been examined is initiated at a specific site or group of sites in the chromosome. Those sites have broad specificity and a DNA molecule without the appropriate site will not be replicated. The sites which are critical to the initiation of replication are known as *origins of replication*. These regions are short nucleotide sequences which serve as initiation sites for specific enzyme action during the DNA replication process. For example, in order for mammalian DNA to replicate in bacteria, it must be associated with a bacterial origin of replication and vice versa.

Ribosome binding sites are short nucleotide segments at the beginning of messenger RNA molecules which signal the attachment of ribosomes for the initiation of protein synthesis. Functioning in this role they are not translated into the protein or peptide being processed.

The BSCC is requesting comments on these definitions during the period of sixty days following the date of this notice and specifically seeks comments addressing the following:

1. The suitability and applicability of these definitions to applications involving release into the environment, contained industrial large-scale applications, foods/food additives, drugs, medical devices, and other possible products.

2. Whether combinations of genetic material from organisms that exchange DNA by known physiological processes should be excluded from the definition of intergeneric organisms; i.e., should organisms be excluded which contain intergeneric combinations of certain specified rDNA molecules that consist entirely of DNA segments from different genera that exchange DNA by known physiological processes? As certain rDNA organisms are exempted under section III-D-4 of the NIH guidelines, the question was raised whether these organisms when used in the environment should be similarly exempted from federal product review. This exemption would not, however, exclude from review such "natural exchangers" that are also pathogens or plant pests. In the event that the exclusion of such different species that exchange DNA by known physiological processes is accepted as appropriate, a list of such species combinations that has been maintained and updated by the Office of Recombinant DNA Activities of the National Institutes of Health will be updated, in light of environmental use.

3. What are the most appropriate definitions of "release into the environment" for macro- and microorganisms.

E. International Aspects

The United States seeks to promote international scientific cooperation and understanding of scientific considerations in biotechnology on a range of technical matters. These activities add to scientific knowledge and ultimately contribute to protection of health and the environment.

The United States also seeks to reduce barriers to international trade. U.S. agencies apply the same regulation and approval procedures on domestic and foreign biotechnological products. We are seeking recognition among nations of the need to harmonize, to the maximum extent possible, national regulatory oversight activities concerning biotechnology. Barriers to trade in biotechnological products should be avoided as nations join

together in working toward this mutual goal.

The U.S. agencies that have published separate policy statements as part of this notice are committed to the policy described in this section on international harmonization and have incorporated by reference the language in this International Aspects section as part of their respective agency policy statements.

Organization for Economic Cooperation and Development (OECD)

The approach of the comprehensive framework contained in this notice takes into account, *inter alia*, the broad goals described by an Ad Hoc Group of Government Experts convened by OECD in their recent report entitled, *"Recombinant DNA Safety Considerations, Safety Considerations for Industrial, Agricultural and Environmental Applications of Organisms Derived by Recombinant DNA Techniques."* The United States is pleased to have had the opportunity for its experts to work with those of other governments in the preparation of this report. The report includes the following concepts:

Summary of Major Points

Recombinant DNA techniques have opened up new and promising possibilities in a wide range of applications and can be expected to bring considerable benefits to mankind. They contribute in several ways to the improvement of human health and the extent of this contribution is expected to increase significantly in the near future.

The vast majority of industrial rDNA large-scale applications will use organisms of intrinsically low risk which warrant only minimal containment, Good Industrial Large-Scale Practice (GILSP).

When it is necessary to use rDNA organisms of higher risk, additional criteria for risk assessment can be identified and furthermore, the technology of physical containment is well known to industry and has successfully been used to contain pathogenic organisms for years. Therefore, rDNA microorganisms of higher risks can also be handled safely under appropriate physical and/or biological containment.

Assessment of potential risks of organisms for environmental or agricultural applications is less developed than the assessment of potential risks for industrial applications. However, the means for assessing rDNA organisms can be approached by analogy with the existing data base gained from the extensive use of traditionally modified organisms in agriculture and the environment generally. With step-by-step assessment during the research and development process, the potential risk to the environment of the application of rDNA organisms should be minimized.

I. General Recommendations

1. Harmonization of approaches to rDNA technology can be facilitated by exchanging: Principles or guidelines for national regulations; developments in risk analysis; and practical experience in risk management. Therefore, information should be shared as freely as possible.

2. There is no scientific basis for specific legislation for the implementation of rDNA technology and applications. Member countries should examine their existing oversight and review mechanisms to ensure that adequate review and control may be applied while avoiding any undue burdens that may hamper technological developments in this field.

3. Any approach to implementing guidelines should not impede future developments in rDNA technology. International harmonization should recognize this need.

4. To facilitate data exchange and minimize trade barriers between countries, further developments such as testing methods, equipment design, and knowledge of microbial taxonomy should be considered by both national and international levels. Due account should be taken of ongoing work on standards within international organizations such as: World Health Organization; Commission of the European Communities; International Standards Organization; Food and Agricultural Organization; and, Microbial Strains Data Network.

5. Special efforts should be made to improve public understanding of various aspects of rDNA technology.

6. For rDNA applications in industry, agriculture and the environment, it will be important for OECD Member countries to watch the development of these techniques. For certain industrial applications and for environmental and agricultural applications of rDNA organisms, some countries may wish to have a notification scheme.

7. Recognizing the need for innovation, it is important to consider appropriate means to protect intellectual property and confidentiality interests while assuring safety.

II. Recommendations Specific for Industry

1. The large-scale industrial application of rDNA technology should wherever possible utilize microorganisms that are intrinsically of low risk. Such microorganisms can be handled under conditions of Good Industrial Large-Scale Practice (GILSP).

2. If, following assessment using the criteria outlined in the document, a rDNA microorganism cannot be handled merely by GILSP, measures of containment corresponding to the risk assessment should be used in addition to GILSP.

3. Further research to improve techniques for monitoring and controlling non-intentional release of rDNA organisms should be encouraged in large-scale industrial applications requiring physical containment.

III. Recommendations Specific for Environmental and Agricultural Applications

1. Considerable data on the environmental and human health effects of living organisms

exist and should be used to guide risk assessments.

2. It is important to evaluate rDNA modified organisms for potential risk, prior to applications in agricultural and the environment. However, the development of general international guidelines governing such applications is premature at this time. An independent review of potential risks should be conducted on a case-by-case basis prior to application. Case-by-case means an individual review of a proposal against assessment criteria which are relevant to the particular proposal; this is not intended to imply that every case will require review by a national or other authority since various classes of proposals may be excluded.

3. Development of organisms for agricultural or environmental applications should be conducted in a stepwise fashion, moving, where appropriate, from the laboratory to the growth chamber and greenhouse, to limited field testing and finally, to large-scale field testing.

4. Further research to improve the prediction, evaluation, and monitoring of the outcome of applications of rDNA organisms should be encouraged.

DEPARTMENT OF HEALTH AND HUMAN SERVICES

Food and Drug Administration

[Docket No. 84N-0431]

Statement of Policy for Regulating Biotechnology Products

AGENCY: Food and Drug Administration.

ACTION: Final policy statement for regulating biotechnology products.

SUMMARY: In the Federal Register of December 31, 1984 (43 FR 50878), the Food and Drug Administration (FDA) published a policy statement for regulating biotechnology products. The policy statement was part of a larger document that included an index of U.S. laws related to biotechnology, a description of the policies of the major regulatory agencies that are involved in reviewing the products of biotechnology, a description of a proposed scientific advisory mechanism for assessment of biotechnology issues, and an explanation of how the activities of the Federal agencies involving biotechnology will be coordinated. Of the comments FDA received on the policy statement, most favored the policy statement; some requested further clarification and guidance. The current action constitutes FDA's final policy statement which has been revised in response to the comments.

ADDRESS: Written comments should be submitted to the Dockets Management Branch (HFA-305), Food and Drug Administration, Room 4-62, 5600 Fishers Lane, Rockville, MD 20857.

FOR FURTHER INFORMATION CONTACT: Dr. Mary Ann Danello (HF-5), Food and Drug Administration, Room 14-90, 5600 Fishers Lane, Rockville, MD 20857, 301-443-4650.

SUPPLEMENTARY INFORMATION: FDA's policy statement of December 31, 1984 stated the FDA regulation must be based on the rational and scientific evaluation of products, and not on *a priori* assumptions about certain processes. Accordingly, FDA's administrative review of products, including those that employ specialized biotechnological techniques, is conducted in the light of the intended use of a product on a case-by-case basis. FDA believes the agency need not establish new administrative procedures to deal with generic concerns about biotechnology.

These views were supported by the majority of comments received in response to FDA's notice. Thirty-four comments were received, with 12 from manufacturers of regulated products, 16 from associations and universities, and 6 from individuals. A summary of the comments and the agency's response to them follow:

1. Many commenters urged the agency to publish additional "Points to Consider" documents to provide further guidance for biotechnology product applicants. These commenters specifically requested guidance in the area of animal drugs (especially protein drugs) and human foods and food additives.

FDA agrees that "Points to Consider" documents provide useful guidance, especially in areas involving new biotechnology, and will consider developing these documents where appropriate.

2. Related comments raised questions on FDA's general requirements for approving biotechnology products that are animal drugs, human foods, or food additives.

In response to these comments, FDA has amended the animal drug section ("General Requirements for Animal Food Additives and Drugs") to be more informative and has added a new section concerning its policies on human foods and food additives (see "General Requirements for Human Foods and Food Additives").

3. Many comments questioned the need for new or supplemental marketing applications for biotechnology products that are identical to products derived from conventional technology.

The agency has re-examined this issue and continues to believe that, as a general principle, new marketing applications will be required for most products manufactured using new biotechnology. For example, use of recombinant DNA (rDNA) technology has the potential to lead to new structural features in the product, result in product micro-heterogeneity, or introduce new contaminants (e.g., associated with new cell substrates), each of which may affect the safety, efficacy and stability of the product. Because of potential differences in the products resulting from use of recombinant DNA technology, the resulting products may be "new" products requiring separate approval under the applicable statutory provisions. However, each case will be examined separately to determine the appropriate information to be submitted. In some instances complete new applications may not be required. For example, the sponsor of a conventionally produced animal drug product who manufactures an identical or virtually identical product using biotechnology may be required to submit only a supplemental application. However, if the animal drug product manufactured using biotechnology differs significantly from the product manufactured by conventional processes, a complete original application would be required. The agency believes that each product must undergo adequate and appropriate testing and review to ensure that it is safe and effective regardless of the technology employed. Sponsors are urged to communicate with FDA to establish the scope of information required for products of biotechnology.

4. Many comments questioned the need for the proposed review mechanism by a Biotechnology Science Board (BSB). These comments stated that the additional layer of review would cause delays in the product approval process.

A notice published in the Federal Register of November 14, 1985 (50 FR 47174) discussed the establishment of the Biotechnology Science Coordinating Committee (BSCC) within the Federal Coordinating Council for Science, Engineering and Technology. That notice addressed various criticisms of the BSB. FDA believes that the new BSCC will facilitate sharing of biotechnology information among agencies and will not delay agency reviews of product applications.

In view of the foregoing, FDA's final policy statement for regulating biotechnology products reads as follows:

CASE STUDIES

I.   Introduction

On May 3, 2000, President Clinton directed the Council on Environmental Quality (CEQ) and the Office of Science and Technology Policy (OSTP) to "conduct a six month interagency assessment of Federal environmental regulations pertaining to agricultural biotechnology and, if appropriate, make recommendations to improve them." The assessment was undertaken as part of a larger set of policy measures intended to build consumer confidence and ensure that U.S. regulations keep pace with the latest scientific and product developments.

The President directed this assessment to further long-standing goals of public access to information and maintenance of strong, science-based regulation. The assessment was intended to focus on environmental regulations through the use of a set of case studies to describe in detail how specific products are being regulated or how they may potentially be regulated. The focus on environmental regulations was based on the premise that this aspect of biotechnology regulation is not well understood by the public and is the subject of considerable interest. The analysis was not intended to be comprehensive in scope, but rather to be based on a set of case studies that could illuminate current agency practices, identify strengths and potential areas for improvement.

In the intervening months, the assessment produced a set of working documents that provide rich detail and information on specific case studies for the public and for policymakers. However, due to time limitations, the interagency working group that was assembled to conduct the assessment was not able to conduct the analysis necessary to develop conclusions or recommendations. The selection of these particular case studies in no way indicates specific concern with previous regulatory findings. In fact, no significant negative environmental impacts have been associated with the use of any previously approved biotechnology product.

This introduction to these case studies provides additional background on the assessment, agricultural biotechnology, U.S. regulation of environmental aspects of biotechnology, and a request for public comment. As part of the generation of these case studies, agencies have been reviewing their own procedures and policies, and intend to continue to do so. Should an agency determine that major changes in policy or procedures are warranted, it would only do so through a notice and comment procedure to ensure full public participation.

II.   Scope and Organization of the Assessment

For the purposes of this assessment, agricultural biotechnology is defined as the use in the environment of any organism that has been genetically modified using recombinant DNA (rDNA) techniques. Environmental regulations include those that involve certain aspects of confinement as well as introduction into the environment under conditions with no or minimal physical confinement (e.g., field plantings, net pen aquaculture, and release of biological control agents).

CEQ and OSTP established an Interagency Working Group (IWG) to conduct the assessment. The IWG was composed of individuals from: the U.S. Department of Agriculture (USDA), including representatives from the Animal and Plant Health Inspection Service (APHIS), the Forest Service (FS), and the Food Safety Inspection Service (FSIS); the Environmental Protection Agency (EPA); the Department of Health and Human Services' Food and Drug Administration (FDA); the Department of the Interior (DOI); the Department of Commerce National Oceanic and Atmospheric Administration (NOAA), National Marine Fisheries Service (NMFS); the Office of Management and Budget (OMB); the Department of Justice (DOJ); and the Department of State (DOS). Reviews of the scientific information in the case studies were conducted by the Department of Health and Human Service National Institutes of Health (NIH), National Science Foundation (NSF), USDA Agricultural Research Service (ARS) and Cooperative State Research, Education and Extension Service (CSREES), and the DOI U.S. Geological Survey (USGS). Due to the inherent complexity associated with the regulation of such a diverse array of organisms and uses, the IWG selected a broad, but representative set of case studies for the assessment.

III.   Background on Agricultural Biotechnology

Products developed using biotechnology hold enormous promise for increasing agricultural production efficiencies and product quality as well as for improving environmental conditions and human well-being. For example, new crop varieties have been developed that are able to reduce, in many cases, chemical insecticide applications and allow for the utilization of more environmentally benign herbicides. Other applications of biotechnology control diseases that were otherwise impossible to control using more traditional means (e.g., control of some plant viruses). Future applications may boost the use of biofuels and produce inexpensive sources of vaccines and other pharmaceuticals. "Golden Rice" has been developed using biotechnology techniques to produce elevated levels of beta-carotene, the precursor to vitamin A. The production of beta-carotene enriched foods could have a major impact on reducing health problems associated with vitamin A deficiency (e.g., blindness and death) in the world's 800 million malnourished people. These are just a few examples of the potential of biotechnology products. However, the realization of all of these advances is dependent on a comprehensive and scientifically rigorous regulatory system that relies on risk assessment and not only ensures environmental and human health issues are adequately addressed, but are also done so in a way that is credible to the public.

For at least 10,000 years, humans have been selecting and cross-breeding plants, animals, and microorganisms to develop organisms with modified traits, such as disease resistance, herbicide tolerance, enhanced production of certain chemicals, and alterations

2

in growth and development. The concept of genetically modifying organisms is not new and oversight systems have been developed to identify and reduce any environmental risks that might be associated with their use, for example, in plant breeding. However, the recent application of rDNA technology, which vastly expands the potential to introduce new genetic material, required scientists, regulators, and the public to rethink the adequacy of these existing oversight mechanisms.

The National Academy of Sciences (NAS) found in 1987 and again in 2000 that:

- there is no evidence that unique hazards exist either in the use of rDNA techniques or in the movement of genes between unrelated organisms;

- the risks associated with the introduction of rDNA-engineered organisms are the same in kind as those associated with the introduction of unmodified organisms and organisms modified by other methods; and,

- assessment of the risks of introducing rDNA-engineered organisms into the environment should be based on the nature of the organisms and the environment into which it is introduced, not on the method by which it was produced.

These findings do not imply that products of biotechnology should not be evaluated for any potential hazards. For instance, the 2000 NAS report, Genetically Modified Pest-Protected Plants, states that toxicity, allergenicity, effects of gene flow, development of resistant pests and effects on non-target species are concerns for both conventional and transgenic pest-protected plants. Because both conventional (e.g., breeding) and rDNA methods have the potential to produce organisms of high or low risk, the NAS panel agreed that the *properties* of a genetically modified organism should be the focus of risk assessments, not the *process* by which it was produced. For example, genes that confer resistance to biotic (e.g., pests and diseases) and abiotic (e.g., metal toxicity and drought) stressors are utilized in both classical breeding and biotechnological approaches to crop improvement. The risks and benefits associated with these genes, regardless of the method of genetic modification, depends on the combination of the organism, the function of the new gene, and the environment into which the organism will be introduced. These organisms and products should be compared to their conventional counterparts. While there are no apparent unique environmental hazards associated with rDNA technology, the fact that a greater variety of genetic constructs now can be incorporated more quickly into organisms with different genetic backgrounds required regulatory agencies to develop specific regulations and guidance documents to provide appropriate risk-based oversight.

IV.   The Coordinated Framework for U.S. Regulation of Biotechnology

In response to concerns about how to best provide federal oversight for products of biotechnology, the Coordinated Framework for Regulation of Biotechnology Products

3

(Coordinated Framework) was adopted by federal agencies in 1986 (see 51 Fed. Reg. 23302 (June 26, 1986)). The Coordinated Framework is consistent with the judgment of the National Academy of Sciences that the potential risks associated with these organisms fall into the same general categories as those created by traditionally bred organisms. The Coordinated Framework provides a coordinated regulatory approach that is intended to ensure the safety of biotechnology research and products, using existing statutory authority and building upon agency experience with agricultural, pharmaceutical, and other products developed through traditional genetic modification techniques. The development of the Coordinated Framework anticipated that agencies might need to develop specific regulations or guidelines under existing statutory authority. The Framework also anticipated institutional evolution in accord with experience, including modifications made through administrative or legislative actions. Finally, the Coordinated Framework determined that interagency coordination mechanisms were necessary to ensure that policy and scientific questions would be addressed across agencies.

The regulatory approach articulated by the Coordinated Framework invokes many statutes and their implementing regulations and guidelines that potentially apply to products of biotechnology introduced into the environment. Some of these statutes apply only to specific types of products or activities and are administered by only one agency, while others apply across-the-board and thus pertain to all or virtually all agencies. With respect to the former, the principal agencies and statutes that regulate specific organisms are as follows:

- Animal and Plant Health Inspection Service (APHIS), in the U.S. Department of Agriculture:
  - **Animal Quarantine Laws (AQL)**, 21 U.S.C. 101-135.
  - **Plant Protection Act (PPA)**, 7 U.S.C. 7701-7772, which consolidated several previous statutes that APHIS used to regulate genetically engineered organisms, including the **Federal Plant Pest Act (FPPA)**, 7 U.S.C. 150aa-150jj, the **Plant Quarantine Act (PQA)**, 7 U.S.C. 151-164a, 166-167, and others. Because no regulations have yet been issued pursuant to the PPA, APHIS continues to regulate biotechnology products according to the regulations issued regarding the FPPA, PQA, etc.
  - **Virus, Serum, Toxin Act (VSTA)**, 21 U.S.C. 151-159.

- Environmental Protection Agency (EPA):
  - **Federal Food, Drug, and Cosmetic Act (FFDCA)**, 21 U.S.C. 321, 346a *et seq.*, as amended by the **Food Quality Protection Act (FQPA)**, Pub. Law 104-170 (1996).
  - **Federal Insecticide, Fungicide, and Rodenticide Act (FIFRA)**, 7 U.S.C. 136-136y, as amended by FQPA, *supra,*.
  - **Toxic Substances Control Act (TSCA)**, 15 U.S.C. 2601-2692.

- Food and Drug Administration (FDA), of the Department of Health and Human Services:
  - **FFDCA**, 21 U.S.C. 321-397
  - **Public Health Service Act (PHSA)**, 42 U.S.C. 262, 264.

- Food Safety Inspection Service (FSIS), of the U.S. Department of Agriculture:
  - **Federal Meat Inspection Act (FMIA)**, 21 U.S.C. 601-691.
  - **Poultry Products Inspection Act (PPIA)**, 21 U.S.C. 451-471.
  - **Egg Products Inspection Act (EPIA)**, 21 U.S.C. 1031-1056.

The statutes listed below are not currently used but might be potentially applicable to specific transgenic organisms:

- Department of the Interior:
  - **Lacey Act**, 16 U.S.C 3371 *et seq.* and 18 U.S.C. 42; and
  - **Non-Indigenous Aquatic Nuisance Prevention and Control Act**, 16 U.S.C. 4701 *et seq.*

- National Oceanic and Atmospheric Administration/National Marine Fisheries Service, the Department of Commerce
  - **Magnuson-Stevens Fishery Conservation and Management Act**, 16 U.S.C. 1801 *et seq.*
  - **Marine Mammal Protection Act**, 16 U.S.C. 1362 *et seq.*
  - **Coastal Zone Management Act**, 18 U.S.C. 1451 *et seq.*

As mentioned above, several statutes and guidelines exist that apply across-the-board to all agencies involved in regulating environmental uses of biotechnology products. For purposes of this report, the most significant of these are:

- **National Environmental Policy Act (NEPA)**, 42 U.S.C 4321-4375, overseen by the Council on Environmental Quality (CEQ), though EPA's regulatory activities are not subject to NEPA because they are considered to be the functional equivalent of NEPA;
- **Endangered Species Act (ESA)**, 16 U.S.C. 1531-1544, jointly administered by the Fish and Wildlife Service (FWS) in the Department of Interior and the National Marine Fisheries Service (NMFS) in the Department of Commerce;
- **Migratory Bird Treaty Act (MBTA)**, 16 U.S.C. 703-712;
- **Trade Secrets Act**, 18 U.S.C. 1905 (except when certain information is not statutorily exempt).
- The Occupational Safety and Health Administration laws apply to worker safety.
- National Institutes of Health's **Recombinant DNA Advisory Committee Guidelines** are used by federal agencies and others receiving federal funding to ensure the safety of laboratory research.

Most of the statutes and guidelines referred to above pertain to particular policy interests, and the applicability of each is determined by the presence of specific conditions. In some instances, interagency agreements or understandings also clarify regulatory roles and responsibilities. The actual regulatory coverage of a particular organism depends on a variety of factors, the most significant of which are:

- the stage of development (e.g., is it still in a contained laboratory setting or is it being field tested, or is it ready for commercial use in the United States);
- the uses (e.g., is it intended for bioremediation of pollution or for biocontrol of another organism, is it intended to be a human drug or an animal biologic, or might it eventually be used as food even though that is not its primary use);
- the type of possible hazards (e.g., does it have the potential to harm plants or contain new genetic material that might cause a plant to become a noxious weed, or does it have the potential to release pollutants into the atmosphere or bodies of water); and
- the type of organism (e.g., is it an animal, plant, or microorganism).

The following table lists common uses for which there is a statute that currently is used as the primary means of regulation:

Use	Statute	Agency
Food & food additives	FFDCA	FDA
Meat, poultry, egg products	FMIA, PPIA, EPIA	FSIS
Pesticide residues	FFDCA	EPA
Production of pharmaceuticals		
Human drugs	FFDCA	FDA
Human biologics	PHS Act, FFDCA	FDA
Animal drugs	FFDCA	FDA
Animal biologics	AQL, VSTA	APHIS
Production of pesticidal substances in plants	FIFRA	EPA
	PPA	APHIS
Production of herbicide tolerance in plants	PPA	APHIS
Herbicide usage on plants	FIFRA	EPA
Microbial pesticides	FIFRA	EPA
Microbial products other than pesticides	TSCA	EPA
Biocontrol of plants	PPA	APHIS
	FIFRA	EPA
Biocontrol of plant pests	PPA	APHIS
	FIFRA	EPA

As is inevitable with an emerging technology, not all aspects of biotechnology regulation were anticipated and addressed when the Coordinated Framework was issued. Therefore, regulatory policy is evolving, including through formal and informal understandings between agencies with respect to how a particular organism or set of organisms will be regulated. It is likely that more than one statute potentially applies to a particular organism or, in some cases, it may be unclear if any statute applies. In these cases, it may be necessary to consult the agencies to determine an appropriate regulatory oversight strategy.

V.   The National Environmental Policy Act

The National Environmental Policy Act (NEPA), 42 U.S.C. 4321 *et seq.*, establishes a consistent process by which federal agencies must consider the consequences of their proposed actions on the human environment prior to a decision. NEPA requires federal agencies to prepare a detailed "environmental impact statement" (EIS) for all major Federal actions significantly affecting the quality of the human environment. 42 U.S.C. 4332(2)(C). The Council on Environmental Quality (CEQ), an agency established by Congress in NEPA, has promulgated regulations that are applicable to federal agencies in their compliance with NEPA. See 40 C.F.R. 1500-1508. As well as specifying the process for preparation of an EIS, the CEQ regulations provide that federal agencies may prepare an environmental assessment (EA) to determine whether a proposed action is likely to have a significant impact on the environment, thus triggering the need to prepare an EIS. 40 C.F.R. 1501.3, 1501.4(e); 1508.9; 1508.13. CEQ regulations also provide that certain types of federal activities may be "categorically excluded" from NEPA review if the class of actions have no significant environmental effect, either individually or cumulatively, and there are no extraordinary circumstances in a given situation. 40 C.F.R. 1508.4. Public involvement and the participation of state, tribal and local governments is an important component of the NEPA process. Each federal department and agency is required to publish procedures, in consultation with CEQ, that identify how NEPA will be implemented for its typical actions. 40 C.F.R. 1507.3. EPA's decision making under statutes relevant to this assessment has been deemed to be "functionally equivalent" to the NEPA process.

VI.   Case Studies

The cases studies cover a range of biotechnology products, some of which government agencies have already approved for commercial production, others of which are currently under regulatory consideration, and still others which have not been presented for regulatory review. To the extent that the case studies address products that have already been reviewed by the government, the case studies are intended to be descriptive of the process the agency (or agencies) actually followed. Since an agency may have changed its past practices, such case studies should not be regarded as modifying any current policies or procedures. By the same token, to the extent that case studies address hypothetical future reviews, the case studies are intended to describe how current statutory authorities, policies, and procedures may be applied. Such case studies are not meant to articulate new policies or procedures, and therefore, they do not constitute binding rules on any regulated entity.

7

Based on criteria of representation of types of organisms, range of statutes used, and levels of public interest, the IWG decided to prepare the following six case studies and four shorter sidebars:

1. **Salmon:** The production of genetically engineered salmon in net pen aquaculture was selected as a case study because it is a near-term regulatory issue (a regulatory determination has not yet been made) and, with net pen aquaculture, there is a high probability for escape of fish into open waters. The principal statutes involved in this case study are FFDCA, ESA, and NEPA. The Lacey Act, the Non-Indigenous Aquatic Nuisance Prevention and Control Act, and the Section 10 provisions of the Rivers and Harbors Act are also discussed. The lead drafting agency for the case study was FDA. NMFS and DOI were also on the drafting team. The hypothetical goldfish sidebar is meant to explore the regulation of transgenic ornamental fish, which are not produced in net pens. The principal statutes discussed in this sidebar are the Lacey Act, TSCA, the ESA, and the Non-Indigenous Aquatic Nuisance Prevention and Control Act. DOI was the lead drafting agency.

2. **Bt-Maize:** Bt-maize was selected because it is grown widely in the United States and possible non-target effects of Bt pollen have been the subject of recent public and scientific debate. The food safety issues associated with the Bt Cry9C protein, which is found in StarLink corn, are not treated here, but are being addressed through extensive interagency collaboration and interaction with consumers, scientists, and industry. The principal statutes involved in this case study are FIFRA, FFDCA, FPPA, PQA, and PPA. The Migratory Bird Treaty Act and ESA are also discussed. EPA was the lead drafting agency. APHIS and DOI were also on the drafting team. The virus sidebar is included to describe how microbial pesticides, rather than Bt plant pesticides, are regulated. This sidebar briefly discusses FIFRA, FPPA, PQA, and NEPA. EPA was the lead drafting agency. APHIS and DOI were also on the drafting team.

3. **Herbicide-Tolerant Soybean:** A herbicide-tolerant soybean was selected because this type of genetically modified plant is grown widely in the United States and has the potential to alter significantly how herbicides are used to control agriculturally important weeds. The principal statutes involved in this case study are FPPA, PQA, PPA, FIFRA, FFDCA, FQPA, NEPA, and ESA. APHIS was the lead drafting agency for this case study. EPA and DOI were also on the drafting team. A hypothetical pharmaceutical-producing plant was included as a sidebar to describe the oversight of a plant with a different set of environmental exposure issues under some production conditions. The principal statutes discussed in this sidebar are the Virus-Serum-Toxin Act, Public Health Service Act, FFDCA, PPA, and NEPA. FDA was the lead drafting agency. APHIS was also on the drafting team.

4. **Animals Producing Human Drugs:** This hypothetical example was selected to describe the regulation of animals whose primary function is to produce pharmaceuticals. Depending on the confinement conditions, these animals potentially

present to the regulator a different set of environmental exposure issues. The principal statutes involved in the case study are the Public Health Service Act, FFDCA, and NEPA. FDA was the lead drafting agency. APHIS and FSIS were also on the drafting team. The animal biologics sidebar is included to describe how animal biologics, rather than human or animal drugs or human biologics, would be regulated. The principal statutes discussed in this sidebar include the Virus-Serum-Toxin Act, the Animal Quarantine Laws, TSCA, and the Animal Welfare Act. APHIS was the lead drafting agency. FDA and FSIS were also on the drafting team.

5. **Bioremediation Using Poplar Trees:** This case study, though not commercially developed, was selected to demonstrate the oversight of a perennial plant. Perennial plants present the regulator with a different set of environmental exposure issues compared to those of annuals like corn or soybean. The principal statutes involved in this case study are FPPA, PQA, PPA, and TSCA. FS was the lead drafting agency. APHIS, EPA, and DOI were also on the drafting team.

6. **Bioremediation and Biosensing Using Bacteria:** This case study was selected to describe the regulation of bacteria that are not plant pests or pesticides. The principal statute involved in this case study is TSCA. EPA was the lead drafting agency. DOI and APHIS were members of the drafting team.

VII.   Request for Comments

In order to further the assessment process, OSTP and CEQ believe it would be beneficial to have public input on federal regulation of environmental aspects of biotechnology informed by the case studies. Following public comments and other input, OSTP and CEQ will continue the IWG and assessment process, and recommend any appropriate steps to strengthen the science-based regulatory system. Public comments are requested by May 1, 2001.

Based on an initial review of the case studies, CEQ and OSTP request public comment in the following broad areas of overall federal regulation of environmental aspects of biotechnology:

- **Comprehensiveness and rigor of environmental assessment.**
- **Comprehensiveness and strength of statutory authority.**
- **Transparency of the environmental assessment and the decision making process.**
- **Public involvement.**
- **Interagency coordination.**
- **Confidential business information (CBI).**

VIII.   Address for Public Comments

Public comments are requested by May 1, 2001 and should be directed to:

Chair
Council on Environmental Quality

Director
Office of Science and Technology Policy

Executive Office of the President
17th and G Streets, NW
Washington, DC 20500
Attention: CEQ/OSTP Biotechnology Assessment

CASE STUDY No. I

GROWTH-ENHANCED SALMON

Overview

This case study concerns the potential aquaculture production or importation of Atlantic salmon (*Salmo salar* L.) genetically engineered to contain an additional fish growth hormone gene that is intended to make the Atlantic salmon grow faster and use feed more efficiently. In general, brood stocks of such fish would be raised in conventional inland hatcheries, where brood stock would be treated to produce 100% genetically female eggs. The eggs would then be treated to cause reproductive sterility (triploidy). The reproductively sterile, all-female offspring would be grown initially in hatcheries and then to maturity in ocean net pens, before being harvested for food. The ability of hatchery managers to ensure reproductive sterility is currently high but less than 100%. Therefore, escapes of fish from net pens may include some females that are capable of reproduction.

The case study is prospective in nature, and is generalized to encompass more than one type of genetic modification. The genetic engineering causes the salmon to contain a new animal drug, which is subject to regulation by the Food and Drug Administration (FDA). Other agencies, e.g., the National Marine Fisheries Service (NMFS), Fish and Wildlife Service (FWS), Army Corps of Engineers (ACE), and Environmental Protection Agency (EPA), would be involved in regulating the actual locations and facilities for use of the salmon in aquaculture in the U.S. During the development of this case study, Atlantic salmon population segments were listed in Maine were listed under the Endangered Species Act (ESA), 16 U.S.C. § § 1531-1544, as amended by the ESA Amendments of 1978, Pub.L. 95-632 (1978) and the ESA Amendments of 1982, Pub.L. 97-304 (1982), by the FWS and NMFS. Because this is one of a series of case studies aimed at elucidating the adequacy of federal environmental regulations pertaining to transgenic organisms, more detail is provided on the FDA regulatory process.

1. Description of proposed organism/product and its use (what, where, how much, and when)

Objectives of this case study

This case study focuses on environmental oversight of the potential production of transgenic Atlantic salmon in net pens or other ostensibly-contained conditions in or near the Atlantic or Pacific coastal waters of the United States, including tank rearing and hatchery operations associated with aquaculture production. The intent of the genetic modification is to produce a variety of salmon that grows faster and uses feed more efficiently. Transgenic Atlantic salmon that are currently being developed are contained in land-locked research facilities outside of the United States. To date, FDA is aware of no evidence that transgenic Atlantic salmon of any type have been used in commercial fish farming or have been marketed for human consumption in the U.S. There also has not been any complete application submitted to FDA for use of a transgenic fish.

This case study is not meant to apply to only one genetic construct or one variety of transgenic Atlantic salmon derived from that construct. The case study is aimed at illustrating the types of environmental safety considerations that would go into a U.S. government evaluation of a request for approval of a transgenic Atlantic salmon variety for use in aquaculture, and the government agencies and authorities involved. This case study is intended to give an overview of the federal oversight process, to point out any gaps, weaknesses, or ambiguities in that process, and to facilitate improvements in it. It is not intended to be an environmental risk assessment for transgenic Atlantic salmon in net pen aquaculture. It also does not encompass the types of environmental safety considerations that would go into a U.S. government evaluation of a request for approval of other possible uses of transgenic Atlantic salmon, for example of ocean ranching (release, return and re-capture strategies) or stocking in the open environment.

Because this is one of a series of case studies aimed at elucidating the adequacy of federal oversight of environmental risks posed by bioengineered organisms, this case study does not specifically examine food safety issues. Evaluation of food safety is, of course, an important component of the FDA approval process for transgenic food animals, such as the Atlantic salmon described in this case study.

Characteristics of the case study

Transgenic fish are fish that have been modified to contain copies of new genetic constructs introduced into their genome by modern genetic techniques (specifically, recombinant DNA techniques). The constructs consist of structural gene(s) (DNA sequences encoding a specific protein product) linked to regulatory sequence(s) (DNA sequences, e.g., a promoter, necessary for successful expression of the structural gene(s)) (Kapuscinski and Hallerman, 1991). This case study focuses on transgenic Atlantic salmon engineered to grow faster and use feed more efficiently. Such fish may be expected to contain at least one introduced structural gene for growth hormone and one introduced regulatory sequence for the control and expression of the introduced structural gene, thereby eliciting the phenotype of enhanced growth rate and feed efficiency.

The best known example of such a transgenic Atlantic salmon under investigation is the AquAdvantage variety being developed by Aqua Bounty. The AquAdvantage gene construct uses a Chinook salmon growth hormone gene and a promoter sequence derived from another fish, called an ocean pout (C.L. Hew, G.L. Fletcher and P.L. Davies, 1995; S.J. Du et al, 1992a, 1992b). The AquAdvantage construct has been inserted into Atlantic salmon of Canadian origin. However, many constructs are possible, including constructs that contain genetic codes for human growth hormone or the growth hormone found in other animals, for example bovine somatotropin, because many growth hormones are active in Atlantic salmon and other fish (R.H. Devlin, 1997).

If the modifications work as hoped, fish farmers would find the transgenic salmon more economical to rear for sale as food than other kinds of salmon. Each variety of transgenic salmon would be descended from one transgene integration event in a newly fertilized, undivided egg. The transgene would be inherited by the offspring of reproductively capable transgenic salmon. Back-crossing (i.e., repeated inbreeding and selection) would be performed to stabilize the genetic modification so that subsequent generations would retain the genetic construct and exhibit the same accelerated growth rate. The transgenic salmon would be raised as diploid animals (i.e., animals with two sets of chromosomes, one set from each of its two parents, and thus capable of sexual reproduction) in conventional inland salmon hatcheries to serve as broodstock (parents) of the fish that would ultimately be used in food production. It is expected that the fish to be used in food production would be sterile females raised in ocean net pens.

Approximately 1.5 million tons of wild and farmed salmon are harvested each year (United Nations Food and Agriculture Organization (FAO), 1996). The U.S. accounts for approximately 500,000 tons, of which 85-90% is wild caught salmon, principally Pacific salmon species (Productivity Commission, 1997). In recent years in the U.S., the wild catch has remained stable or decreased slightly, while the amount of farmed fish, predominantly Atlantic salmon, has increased. Norway, Chile and Scotland are the major producers of farmed Atlantic salmon, jointly accounting for over 80 per cent of world supply of Atlantic salmon. Canada is also a significant producer. In the U.S., farmed Atlantic salmon are produced in northern waters on both the East and West Coast.

Despite harvesting a significant amount of wild salmon and raising increasing amounts of farmed fish, the U.S. remains a large importer of salmon. In 1998, the U.S. imported most of its farmed salmon from Canada and Chile (Price Waterhouse Coopers, 1998). The total market value of imported, farmed salmon was approximately $512 million.

Because the U.S. is a major importer of farmed salmon, the developers of transgenic salmon generally want U.S. approval of these products for human food safety. This could either come in the form of an approved new animal drug application (which allows commercial use of the transgenic animal inside the U.S.), or an import tolerance for an unapproved new animal drug's residues in imported seafood (imported food products only, no U.S. commercial production allowed). Culture locations for transgenic salmon are likely to exist both within and outside the U.S., as well as in areas of shared coastal waters, such as the Bay of Fundy on the United States and Canadian borders. As for all Atlantic salmon, culture locations for transgenic Atlantic salmon are subject to approval by NMFS, FWS, ACE, and/or EPA. The EPA is reviewing the impacts to water quality associated with aquaculture. The outcome of that review may be specific standards on discharges.

How would the transgenic fish be used, including a brief description of management practices that would be associated with it?

Management systems used for production of transgenic Atlantic salmon are likely to be the same as, or a subset of, those currently in use for non-transgenic salmon. Typically, salmon are hatched in freshwater facilities. After 12–18 months the young salmon undergo smoltification (acclimation to salt water), after which they can survive in a marine environment. These fish are then called smolts and are transferred to sea farms where they are grown in sea cages, also referred to as net pens, located in estuaries, coastal inlets, and open ocean. Additionally, Atlantic salmon can be intensively reared in raceways and circular tanks, although the economic viability of such systems for food production has not been demonstrated. Heen, Monahan and Utter (1993) contains a good overview of Atlantic salmon management in aquaculture settings, including nutrition, net pen construction, disease management, and genetic and environmental issues.

The use of only sterile female salmon has been suggested as a means to minimize environmental impacts resulting from any escapes of transgenic salmon from net pens. Technology is available for producing all-female salmon (Bye and Lincoln, 1986). It involves masculinizing females with hormones to allow the reliable production of fertile eggs that produce all-female offspring. All-female eggs can be treated with temperature and pressure to yield triploid sterile offspring (offspring with three sets chromosomes and incapable of sexual reproduction). In contrast to the reliability of producing all-female offspring, the efficiency of the induction of triploidy varies from fish species to species and with the personnel conducting the work. Sponsors using this technology as a biocontainment mitigation would be expected to provide information as to the efficiency of their induction procedures and the measures they would use to maintain that efficiency. Triploid, all-female eggs, fry and fingerlings would then be sold or contracted out to fish farmers to grow out to market size for food, in net pens or other facilities.

Is there prior experience dealing with the same varieties not genetically engineered?

Wild Atlantic salmon have been harvested as food animals for millennia and farmed Atlantic salmon have been produced for many years. Captive Atlantic salmon have been used as broodstock and selective breeding programs, over many generations, have resulted in some limited improvements in growth rate, meat quality and disease resistance. Currently, net pen aquaculture of Atlantic salmon involves several generations of breeding for net pen conditions from a stock that often includes hybrids of European origin. These stocks have been preferred to natives because they are perceived to be more productive under the stresses of net pen aquaculture. Whether it is more protective of native salmon populations for humans to use stocks in aquaculture that are more or less genetically similar to co-existing wild populations is currently the topic of debate, and will be discussed under environmental risks.

Traditional breeding practices involved selecting individuals on the basis of the trait as measured in that individual or its offspring and breeding the best ones to each other. Now it is possible to use molecular markers that are highly correlated with the desired trait to select the best more quickly and with greater accuracy than growing them to adulthood and measuring them. Even so, the selected individuals need to be crossed to each other to the point where the gene or genes involved are stably inherited. With fish, the fastest and most precise way to make progress once the sequence of a desirable gene has been identified is to engineer it into an otherwise highly desirable stock. Once a particular combination succeeds, it can be multiplied through backcrossing and selection.

There is already a precedent for the production of Atlantic salmon in non-native environments, e.g. farmed (non-transgenic) Atlantic salmon operations in the Puget Sound and in the Pacific Ocean off the coast of Washington State, British Columbia, Canada, and Chile. The introduction of wild, reproducing populations of Atlantic salmon into the northwestern U.S. was attempted in the early part of the last century without success, and part of the rationale for using Atlantic salmon for aquaculture in that area was the failure of the species to establish there. Recently, there has been reported evidence of the first successful spawning of Atlantic salmon that escaped from net pen aquaculture in rivers in British Columbia (Rimmer, 1998; Volpe et al, 1999). However, U.S. and B.C. fisheries authorities still do not consider them "established", i.e., to be self-sustaining over the long term. Fleming et al. (2000) recently reported evidence of resource competition and competitive displacement of native salmon by farmed salmon intentionally released into a Norwegian river, although the reproductive success of the farmed fish was substantially lower than for native salmon.

While cultured Atlantic salmon might not have established themselves on the Pacific coast yet, the successful spawning of Atlantic salmon on the Pacific coast has raised concern that these fish may further jeopardize the continued existence of already fragile native Pacific salmonids through competition for food and occupation of underutilized habitat. Many of the Pacific salmon stocks have already been listed under the ESA.

Until the listing of Atlantic salmon under the ESA, the main federal regulation of net pen aquaculture associated with the production of Atlantic salmon has been through ACE permits issued for compliance with Section 10 of the Rivers and Harbors Act of 1899. Currently, applicants seeking permission to culture Atlantic salmon in state waters or waters of the US must obtain permits from both States (if in State waters) and the Federal Government (out to the edge of the Continental Shelf). Depending on the nature of the retention system, the State and Army Corps of Engineers will act as lead agencies in evaluating proposals and issuing appropriate water quality and structures permits.

The permit application must include a description of the purpose, proposed activities, location, character of the area and potential conflicting uses. The federal review process entails evaluations by the EPA, FWS and NMFS. Authority for involvement by the resource agencies is found in statutes such as the Fish and Wildlife Coordination Act (FWCA), ESA, Marine Mammal Protection Act (MMPA), 16 U.S.C. §§ 1361-1421, Clean Water Act (CWA), 33 U.S.C. §§ 1251-1387, and the National Environmental Policy Act (NEPA), 42 U.S.C. §§ 4321-4370e. Issuance of permits depends on a number of considerations usually defined as the "Public Interest Review" by the Corps of Engineers. The Public Interest Review normally includes issuance of a Public Notice regarding the proposed action. The Public Notice includes much of the information in the permit application as noted above.

Escape was not originally considered to be an important consequence of pen culturing Atlantic salmon. Initial information indicated that escapes would be minimal in number and the individuals not able to successfully compete with native stocks or form viable populations. When it was discovered that escapees could survive in the wild, some people believed that the fish would not successfully reproduce. It now appears that escaped fish can reproduce. NMFS is evaluating the consequences of escape and considering what measures might limit the ecological impact of escape. A risk management step being considered is to require the use of local, native strains as broodstock. Environmental impacts associated with unforeseen situations, such as escape, are normally covered by permit modification, suspension or revocation, when it is determined that such situations represent undesirable circumstances.

What are the projected locations and extent of production, use and disposal?

In the U.S., the principal locations for salmon culture are the northern waters of the East and West Coasts adjacent to similar fisheries in the coastal waters of Canada. Primary production is in the states of Washington and Maine where suitable habitat in the form of cold marine waters exists. In the U.S., net pen salmon production in 1997 was 33 million pounds, amounting to $75 million. These values have steadily increased since 1985 and are likely to continue to increase, based upon market demand (USDA, 1999). Atlantic salmon is a premium salmon product sold chilled, frozen or smoked.

Disposals resulting from the production, processing and consumption of salmon would be essentially the same for all salmon, transgenic or not. They would consist of disposals of waste material during production of feed and aquaculture of fish, during processing, and after consumption.

What types of adverse effects might be caused by the transgenic fish throughout its life cycle, and where might they occur?

Many of the potential adverse environmental effects that have been hypothesized for transgenic Atlantic salmon are similar to those associated with currently used farmed strains of Atlantic salmon. The potential for adverse effects is partly a function of the management systems employed for their production.

Adverse effects resulting from Atlantic salmon culture are associated with their exposure to the environment through the hatchery or the net pen and include:

1. Through escape:
   - Interbreeding with wild Atlantic salmon and gene introgression into wild salmon stocks;
   - Hybridization with brown trout (Atlantic salmon are more closely related to brown trout, a European species that has been stocked in North America, than to the various Pacific salmon species, which are close relatives of rainbow trout);

- Disturbance of habitat or displacement of wild stocks as a consequence of competition for resources, predation, or mis-matings.

2. Fouling of the hatchery effluent receiving waters and the seabed below net pens with fecal material and excess feed.
3. Spread of bacteria, viruses, and parasites such as Infectious Salmon Anemia and sea lice to wild salmon or other fauna.
4. Introduction of chemicals, e.g. those used in the treatment of fish diseases.

Currently, technologies to mitigate some of these effects, such as reducing the number of escaped fish, and increasing the effectiveness of sterility inducement, are under development. At the time of the environmental review of an application, the current status of the scientific information and technology would be assessed. Some or all of the above issues associated with the rearing and release or escape of non-engineered farm-raised Atlantic salmon, presumably would also apply to transgenic Atlantic salmon. Transgenic fishes may cause a greater or lesser magnitude of impact compared to fishes whose endogenous genes have been simply recombined through artificial selection, hybridization of closely related species, or ploidy manipulations, depending on several factors. These and similar issues are discussed in more detail in part 3, below.

What are the pathways for proliferation of those risks?

Proliferation of risk associated with gene introgression from transgenic and non-transgenic non-indigenous fish:

The amount of risk associated with gene introgression is a function of the scope of the release, the number of escaped animals and the number of potentially affected native species, the precise characteristics of the transgenic fish, and the interrelation of at least four population variables: reproductive potential of escaped individuals, frequency of introgression of the modified genes, fitness of the introgressed individuals, and potential demographic decline due to genetic load of introgressed genes.

The reproductive potential of escaped individuals is based on: (1) the survival rate and fertility of the individuals, and (2) environmental conditions affecting reproduction in the affected ecosystem, such as length of spawning season and available spawning habitat. The frequency with which introgressed genes will spread and increase within the population is related to gene flow. Several models are available to estimate this variable. Despite the prediction that introgressed individuals will exhibit lower fitness than non-introgressed individuals, not all genetic modifications will be maladaptive. Regarding the genetic load of introgressed genes, natural selection is expected to remove maladaptive genes from a population. However, depending on the severity of the maladaptation, the number of generations required for this process can be very large (USDA, 1995).

Risk of adverse events associated with introduction of triploid (both transgenic and non-transgenic) fish:

The sterility offered by inducing triploidy in some aquatic species reduces some concerns about a modified organism, and in many cases will mean that farming of a triploid transgenic species will likely pose less risk of environmental impact than similar farming of fertile non-transgenic species. Of course, to the extent that non-transgenic salmon are also made triploid prior to use for fish farming, they would obtain comparable benefits with regard to reduction in environmental, including genetic, risk. However, use of triploidy is not favored by fish farmers in currently-used Atlantic salmon stocks, as it is thought to reduce productivity and resistance to stress. Transgenic salmon, on the other hand, do not show reduced productivity when they are triploid. In addition, because of the likely enhanced productivity of the transgenic fish, small relative reductions in productivity may be more acceptable in transgenic fish than in non-transgenic fish.

However, the use of triploidy does not eliminate all environmental risk, and its ability to ensure environmental safety is complicated by three factors. First, the effectiveness of triploidy induction varies among species and the methods used. Second, although triploids are functionally sterile, the males may exhibit spawning behavior with fertile diploid females, leading to decreased reproductive success of the fertile diploid females. Third, in cases where large numbers of individuals are released, sufficient numbers of sterile triploids may survive and grow to pose heightened competition with diploid conspecifics (i.e., fish of the same species), perhaps including in some cases, predation on juvenile conspecifics (USDA, 1995).

Risk of adverse events associated with unexpected survival and persistence of escaped or intentionally released transgenic and non-native non-transgenic fish:

Despite familiarity with the unmodified Atlantic salmon, there remains some undefined degree of risk of adverse impacts associated with the unexpected survival and persistence of escaped or intentionally released transgenic <u>and</u> non-native (non-transgenic) fish. For example, experiences with releases of a different unmodified salmonid species, the pink salmon, suggest that genetically modified pink salmon could also survive, reproduce, and persist in a broader range of accessible ecosystems than would be expected from studies of their biology in their native range. In spite of assumptions that smolts and immature adults could not survive in fresh water, the Laurentian Great Lakes experienced population explosions of pink salmon two decades after 21,000 juveniles were flushed down the drain of a Lake Superior hatchery (United State Department of Agriculture (USDA), 1995)

What types of positive environmental impacts might occur because of this use?

If the fish can be shown to be sterile and remain that way throughout the culturing procedures, use of sterile triploid transgenic fish in conventional net pens could reduce the amount of gene introgression into wild stock that may currently be occurring as a result of escape by fertile, non-indigenous (imported) stocks that are presently being used for culture/breeding. Triploidy is available as an option for non-transgenic salmon, but there has been resistance to its acceptance by fish farmers because they are perceived to have depressed productivity, as described above. However, the use of sterile transgenic fish in aquaculture might stimulate interest in research and a re-evaluation of this technique for use with non-transgenic salmon, which would be a benefit.

Decreased harvest pressure on wild salmon fisheries could result from increased production of highly feed-efficient farmed transgenic varieties. Since, however, there is no current recreational or commercial harvest of Atlantic salmon, this effect would not have an impact on the environment of the east coast of the U.S. It might lead to reduced demand for sustainably managed wild populations in the Pacific Northwest and Alaska and potentially have economic impacts there. Similarly, reduced pressure for use of marginal net pen culture sites could result from increased productivity in more optimal sites. However, such reduced use of marginal sites is also a function of market saturation and other economic forces. It also remains to be seen whether transgenic fish will be accepted and used commercially so as to enable evaluation of the extent that such potential benefits may be realized.

Finally, the increased production potential with transgenic fish may allow the use of land-based contained facilities to become economically viable. If contained facilities were to be used, many of the environmental issues discussed above would not be relevant.

What is the rationale for using the transgenic fish, including its advantages vis-a-vis alternatives?

If the research goes as planned, the transgenic Atlantic salmon would exhibit an accelerated rate of growth related to the expression of the added growth hormone gene construct. The improvement may be dramatic, but is expected to vary among transgenic varieties. One variety being developed is purported to reach market-weight (3-4 kg) in about 18 months, versus 24-30 months for non-transgenic salmon. Because there would be less time required to reach market weight, there presumably would be less feed required for maintenance metabolism. Thus, the transgenic variety would be expected to use feed more efficiently. In other words, less feed would be required to produce a unit of salmon meat for human consumption, compared to non-transgenic varieties. Early indications are that despite the acceleration in the growth rate over the first 18 months, the transgenic Atlantic salmon do not appear to exceed the normal weight range of adult non-transgenic salmon, although this also may vary from one transgenic variety to another.

Economic benefits of such modifications would include increases in the number of culture cycles per time at a given location, and a reduction in the amount of resources (e.g., feed used, waste produced, and space required per pound of food for humans produced) required for rearing the fish over time. Higher feed efficiency would decrease the cost of feed per unit of food produced for humans (i.e., fish meat), resulting in decreased cost of the marketed product.

9

2.   Relevant regulatory agencies, regulatory authority and legal measures

Contained research

The National Institutes of Health (NIH) rDNA Guidelines (http://www4.od.nih.gov/oba/oct2000guide2.pdf) apply to research that is conducted at or sponsored by an institution that receives any support for recombinant DNA research from NIH, including research performed directly by NIH. NIH funding for recombinant DNA research at the institution at which the research is conducted is therefore the primary indicator as to whether a research project is covered by these guidelines.

The fundamental aspect of these guidelines is that they rate different kinds of rDNA research by the relative risks, and they determine the practices needed to safely contain the research at each stage (laboratories, and greenhouses for plants, arthropods and microorganisms, and animal rooms or securely fenced areas for animals) (Appendices P and Q, id.). Of key importance to the efficacy of these guidelines are the roles of the Institutional Biosafety Committee (IBC), the Biological Safety Officer, and the Plant, Plant Pathogen, or Plant Pest Containment Expert and the Animal Containment Expert (Section IV, ibid). Although the guidelines are voluntary for other federal agencies, the USDA Agricultural Research Service, for example, uses the IBC of the collaborating or nearby university in implementing the guidelines.

Compliance with these guidelines is monitored by a reporting process whereby any individual can present a claim of noncompliance to both the NIH/OBA and the relevant institution's IBC. If NIH or non NIH funded projects at a given institution are not in compliance, this can result in: 1) suspension, limitation or termination of NIH funds for recombinant DNA research at the institution, or 2) a requirement for prior NIH approval of any or all recombinant DNA projects at the institution. (Section I-D, ibid). If private individuals or organizations choose to use these guidelines and affiliate with an institution with an approved IBC, there are opportunities for protection of proprietary data as described in IV-D-5. To restate, the NIH guidelines are voluntary for those institutions, private organizations, and individuals that do not receive funds from NIH for recombinant DNA research. This includes other federal agencies.

Fish and Shellfish Research Performance Standards

With input from a wide range of aquatic science professionals, a U.S. Department of Agriculture-sanctioned working group developed the Performance Standards for Safely Conducting Research with Genetically Modified Fish and Shellfish as a tool for risk assessment and risk management. The Performance Standards were approved in 1995 by the Agricultural Biotechnology Research Advisory Committee of the USDA. These standards have been distributed widely as a two booklet set and are expected to guide evaluations of the performance and environmental safety of aquatic Genetically Modified Organisms (GMOs) in the United States and abroad. To facilitate use of the Performance Standards, a computer-based decision-support tool has been developed.

These are available on the web at http://www.nbiap.vt.edu, and select risk assessment and then Performance Standards for Fish and Shellfish.

These were established as voluntary standards. However, under Cooperative State Research Education and Extension Service (CSREES) (USDA) NEPA implementation, researchers can indicate they have utilized these standards or others. Most of the transgenic fish research funded through USDA is in contained indoor biosecure facilities. Auburn has the only pond system that has been approved by USDA for such work. These standards have been successful at raising the awareness for a variety of issues that must be considered when conducting this work.

USDA also developed an assessment of a research program, the Environmental Assessment and Finding of No Significant Impact relating to a USDA funded research program on transgenic carp (55 Fed. Reg.46661). These are believed to be the first federal NEPA documents to address environmental impacts of transgenic fish.

Authorities outside of contained facilities

Atlantic salmon farming is subject to a number of federal and state environmental controls that apply whether or not the fish being farmed are transgenic. Coastal zone management authorities in the states, the ACE, FWS, and the NMFS all are involved with site selection and permitting of net pens and hatcheries. EPA and the states enforce the CWA, regulating the potential harm that may be caused by fish wastes and disposal of new animal drugs used on fish. FDA evaluates the environmental impact of new [1]animal drugs used in fish farms, including new animal drugs contained in transgenic fish.

Several federal agencies manage the physical and social consequences of actions that encroach into public trust resources. The ACE is typically the lead Federal Agency for aquaculture projects in navigable waters of the U.S. The EPA becomes involved with discharges (National Pollution Discharge Elimination System (NPDES) permits) and has done so to varying degrees across the nation (their aquaculture management activities are now under internal review, as noted above). The U.S. Coast Guard is involved when aquaculture may affect navigation safety. For example, the Coast Guard will provide guidance on lighting or marking culture structures. The Minerals Management Service manages use of the seafloor. Requests for competing use of the seafloor/water column have not occurred but would require resolution. In the waters of the Gulf of Mexico, use of offshore petroleum production platforms is being pursued as the mooring system (the legs) for aquaculture activities. (In state waters there are counterpart elements of each of these agencies within the state government. Under the Coastal Zone Management Act (CZMA), 16 U.S.C. § § 1451-1465, States require that any federal action that can affect the State must show that the federal action is consistent with the State Coastal Zone Plan. The showing is termed a "Coastal Consistency." Additionally, EPA has the authority to delegate its water quality responsibilities to individual states. Forty-three states have

---

[1] ("New" with reference to animal drugs is a statutory term (21 U.S.C. § 321 (v)) that applies essentially to all animal drugs)

received EPA authority to manage the NPDES/SPDES waste discharge-permitting program.)

FWS and NMFS are routinely considered the "resource agencies" and are called upon to speak for and about fish and other aquatic resources in regulatory situations. For aquatic species, NMFS has primary purview in marine waters, and FWS in fresh water environments. These agencies are "consultants" to all federal agencies operating under a broad spectrum of federal legislation. The broadest intervention tool provided by federal legislation is the Fish & Wildlife Coordination Act. The ESA comes into play whenever listed species are suspected to occur within the impact area. The native Atlantic salmon population in Maine (see news release on the listing on the FWS website has been listed, jointly by FWS and NMFS as an endangered species under the ESA (listing of Distinct Population of Anadramous Atlantic salmon in the Gulf of Maine on November 17, 2000 (65 Fed. Reg. 69459). The last remaining wild stocks are co-managed by the FWS and the NMFS through the North Atlantic Salmon Conservation Organization (NASCO) established in 1984 under the Convention for the Conservation of Salmon in the North Atlantic Ocean. NASCO is an international body with the objective of contributing through consultation and cooperation to the conservation, restoration, enhancement and rational management of salmon stocks taking into account the best scientific information available. The Magnuson – Stevens Fishery Conservation and Management Act, as amended by the 1996 Sustainable Fisheries Act (Magnuson-Stevens Act), 16 U.S.C. § § 1801-1883, is invoked by NMFS when designated Essential Fish Habitat is present. Activities that might adversely affect those habitats must be assessed and measures taken to avoid, minimize, mitigate or compensate for such impacts. Failing that, the lead federal agency must explain why such measures will not be taken.

Most of the regulatory agencies noted above have integrated responsibilities, occasionally supplemented with Memoranda of Understanding or Agreement. They have responsibility for management and control of aquaculture to insure compatibility with wild fish management and their associated habitat. Prior experiences with environmental problems associated with aquaculture, coupled with pressures for environmental protection by various citizens groups, have heightened these agencies' concerns about, and requirements for, new uses of fish in aquaculture. The Department of Commerce (DOC) sees aquaculture as an important opportunity for the U.S. DOC recently issued an aquaculture policy (signed by Secretary Daley in 2000) that specifically targets aquaculture development, including support for new technologies and the domestication of additional species for aquaculture production in an environmentally sound manner. The Commerce goal is a $5 billion U.S. aquaculture industry by 2025 (a 5-fold increase from today).

There are a number of examples of guidance documents dealing with fish in aquaculture, including transgenic fish. NASCO, mentioned above, is the most applicable to this case study. It has published a thorough discussion of the genetic issues and potential solutions. NMFS and FWS are actively involved in the NASCO activities. The United Nation's FAO has developed a fisheries Code of Conduct (FAO, 1995). Article 9 of the document addresses aquaculture issues, including genetics. NMFS is using that document to facilitate development of a Code of Conduct for aquaculture activities in the U.S. Exclusive Economic Zone (those waters outside State waters and extending seaward 200 miles).

In most cases the applicant for an aquaculture site permit bears the responsibility of presenting evidence of environmental compatibility, limited risk and minimal conflict with other activities or uses of the proposed culturing site. NEPA applies to major federal actions, and the lead federal agency has the responsibility for preparing the NEPA analysis of significant environmental impacts, such as those that may be caused by granting a permit for an aquaculture site. However, the applicant routinely prepares much if not all the technical information for the Environmental Assessment (EA). This is done in cooperation with the lead federal agency.

APHIS coordinates state permit programs that control interstate movement of potentially diseased or parasitized fish and shellfish. See the APHIS website for a collection of state requirements (USDA, 2000). APHIS has not so far considered fish, fish eggs, and fish gametes to be "livestock" under the Animal Quarantine Laws, 21 U.S.C. §§ 101-135. If APHIS determined that the interstate movement of Atlantic salmon needed to be controlled more actively to prevent the spread of disease, it could change the status of this species to livestock under its regulations (9 CFR 49-99), and require health certification as applied to other livestock. In this event, these same authorities would be used to provide for health certification of live transgenic Atlantic salmon intended for import into or export from the United States.

In addition to other federal, state and local oversight that pertains in general to use of Atlantic salmon for fish farming, transgenic Atlantic salmon are subject to FDA oversight because they are considered to contain a "new animal drug."[2] The Federal Food, Drug, and Cosmetic Act (FFDCA), 21 U.S.C. §§ 371-379d, defines a "drug" to include "articles ... intended to affect the structure or any function of the body of man or other animals." 21 U.S.C. § 321(g). Because an introduced genetic construct will of necessity "affect the structure or . . . function" of transgenic animals, the genetic construct is a "drug." The genetic construct may also produce a protein that is a drug. Where the genetic material and the protein (when the protein is a drug) are not "generally recognized . . . as safe and effective for use under the conditions prescribed, recommended, or suggested in the labeling thereof", they are "new animal drugs." 21 U.S.C. § 321(v). ("New" is a statutory term (21 U.S.C. § 321(p)) that applies essentially to all animal drugs.)

Use of a new animal drug is considered "unsafe" under the FFDCA unless the FDA has approved an application for that particular use. 21 U.S.C. § 360b(a)(1). Thus, if the introduced genetic construct and, potentially, the protein it produces (the "articles") meet the definition of a new animal drug and were not approved by the FDA, they would be "unsafe" and subject to FDA enforcement action. The transgenic salmon's structure

---

[2] Fish modified to contain or produce a veterinary biologic would be subject to regulation by APHIS under the Virus-Serum-Toxin Act (VSTA), 21 U.S.C. §§ 151-159, rather than by FDA under the FFDCA. 21 U.S.C. § 902(c).

and function have been modified through insertion of the genetic construct into the genome of the salmon and the transgenic salmon therefore contains a new animal drug. In the transgenic salmon at issue, the growth hormone protein encoded by the inserted genetic construct also affects the structure and function of the salmon, and so also would be a new animal drug.

All subsequent generations of the salmon contain the inserted genetic construct and growth hormone protein, and therefore all contain a new animal drug. FDA approval of a new animal drug contained in transgenic fish would be specific to the use of the drug in the line(s) of salmon descended from the original transformation or microinjection event. Thus, FDA will evaluate the new animal drug and its intended use in the context of the fish line into which the drug has been engineered. Any conditions that FDA imposes on the new animal drug's use will apply to all fish derived from that original transgenic line.

A new animal drug enters the FDA regulatory process when the sponsor submits a Notice of Claimed Investigational Exemption (referred to as an investigational new animal drug, or INAD), before shipping the drug for clinical (effectiveness) tests in animals. 21 CFR 511.1(b)(4). Ordinarily, the agency is not permitted to disclose the existence of an INAD, unless the sponsor has publicly disclosed it. 21 CFR 514.12. For example, this case study notes that Aqua Bounty has filed an INAD for a transgenic Atlantic salmon because Aqua Bounty has previously disclosed this fact. The sponsor conducts research on the transgenic fish while the INAD is in effect. When completed, the research can become the basis of a new animal drug application (NADA). 21 U.S.C. § 360b(b)(1). FDA evaluates the NADA to determine whether the sponsor has demonstrated that the drug is safe and effective for its intended use. The burden of proving that the drug meets this standard is entirely on the sponsor.

Under the FFDCA, a new animal drug's safety is defined as having "reference to the health of man or animal." 21 U.S.C. § 321(u). The agency considers, as part of its safety assessment of the drug contained in a transgenic fish (or any other new animal drug), environmental effects that directly or indirectly affect the health of humans or animals as a result of FDA's allowing the new animal drug's "use." Only in the case of a potential adverse environmental effect that would not, directly or indirectly, pose a risk to the health of man or animals, for example an environmental impact that would detract from scenic beauty, would FDA not have authority to take such risk into account as part of its FFDCA safety assessment of a new animal drug.

Because granting an INAD and approving an NADA are federal actions under NEPA, the agency must comply with NEPA as it carries out these processes. INADs and NADAs require submission of a claim of categorical exclusion or an environmental assessment (EA). 21 C.F.R. 25.15, 21 C.F.R. 511.1(b)(10), 21 C.F.R. 514.1(b)(10). For transgenic fish, the EA will facilitate the environmental component of FDA's "safety" review under the FFDCA by providing information relevant to determining whether environmental consequences resulting from use of the new animal drug could adversely affect the health of humans or animals and possibly render the drug unsafe.

14

FDA conducts its environmental safety reviews for animal drug products under the broad umbrella of NEPA. NEPA provides a structure for environmental assessment that is well known as well as providing a mechanism for coordination with other Federal agencies. FDA relies on its authority under the FFDCA to require, where appropriate, environmental safety instructions on product labels, to enforce compliance with mitigations that are required as a condition of the product approval, and to refuse to approve or to withdraw approval of products that cause unexpected and unmitigatable environmental impacts that adversely affect, directly or indirectly, the health of humans or animals. Like all federal agencies, FDA must also comply with the ESA.

For example, in the pre-market environmental assessment of bovine somatotropin for dairy cows, FDA's Center for Veterinary Medicine (CVM) and the product sponsor considered among other things, the possibility that approval of the drug (1) might affect land-use patterns and water quality by affecting the types of feed ingredients grown for dairy cows, (2) might affect carbon dioxide emissions due to changed ration requirements and dairy populations, and (3) might present a used syringe disposal problem.

The first two areas did not prove to be significant. Because of concern about the risk to human health from used syringes, FDA required mitigation of the third area by an applicant-sponsored syringe collection system for customers. Had either of the first two issues proven to be significant, CVM was prepared to consider mitigations and/or refusal to approve the product because of the human and animal health impact of changes in water quality and carbon dioxide emissions. See Finding of No Significant and Environmental Assessment Impact for Sterile Sometribove Zinc Suspension for Use in Lactating Dairy Cows, NADA 140-872, May 7, 1993 (FDA, 1993), available on the CVM web site. This document also shows the scope and depth of studies that FDA required the applicants to conduct in order to assess potential environmental impacts. Such studies might be equivalent to the type of documents the sponsors of genetically engineered salmon will have to develop. The document is also an example of FDA reviews of the above information for quality and accuracy, and the agency's rationale for the decision of Finding of No Significant Impact in the case of bovine somatotropin.

For transgenic Atlantic salmon of the type being discussed in this case study, CVM plans to address the environmental assessment through the use of risk assessment approach, as described below in Section 3. This is an efficient approach, currently in use for preparing EAs for other new animal drug products. It is designed to identify likely hazards and acquire the information necessary to assess the level of risk and manage those that are significant, while at the same time reducing the burden on applicants. Unforeseen or low probability hazards are managed through post-approval monitoring by the applicant and FDA, including evaluation of new hazards that appear through that monitoring.

FDA expects the applicant to work with the scientific community to identify the reasonably anticipated hazards and either: (1) design a scientifically sound method for examining their likelihood and severity and design measures that will be taken to reduce the severity of a low probability event, or (2) design procedures that will avoid the hazard altogether. If an NADA for a transgenic Atlantic salmon is approved, the assessment, monitoring plans, and mitigations will be available for public review at the time of approval.

FDA intends to publish draft guidance on how the new animal drug provisions of the FFDCA pertain to transgenic animals, and on procedures by which companies developing transgenic animals can comply with those provisions. FDA also intends to hold workshops or public meetings to discuss scientific issues posed by particular kinds or uses of transgenic animals (such as transgenic salmon described in this case study) and at a later date to develop draft guidances on specific scientific issues raised by particular kinds or uses of transgenic animals.

One of the goals that NEPA is intended to achieve is a public airing of an agency's consideration of significant environmental impacts posed by a prospective agency action. 42 U.S.C. §4341. At the same time, the FFDCA and the Trade Secrets Act prohibit revealing any information that is acquired as part of the new animal drug approval process and that is entitled to protection as a trade secret. 21 U.S.C. § 331(j), 18 U.S.C. § 1905. CEQ's regulations state that an agency shall comply with NEPA to the fullest extent possible unless existing law applicable to the agency's operations expressly prohibits or makes compliance impossible. 40 C.F.R. 1500.6. Under FDA's current regulations, even if the existence of an INAD or an unapproved NADA has been publicly disclosed or acknowledged, no data or information contained in that INAD or NADA are available for public disclosure before an approval has been published in the Federal Register. 21 C.F.R. 514.11(d). Thus, the agency would be precluded from making a NEPA analysis public prior to approval of an NADA because the NEPA analysis is considered part of the INAD or NADA. The agency recognizes the difficulty this poses in ensuring a public process for evaluating possible environmental risks associated with any particular transgenic modification to a fish species and is considering what options it might have to address this situation.

In any case, FDA intends to publish for comment a draft guidance document describing its approach to conducting environmental assessments of the genetic construct contained in transgenic salmon, and will involve both the public and state and federal government entities in the process of developing this guidance. The draft guidance document will describe what issues sponsors should address in order to demonstrate that use of the drug contained in each transgenic salmon line is safe in the environment. The agency expects that the approach set out in the guidance will be relevant to all new animal drug applications involving transgenic salmon.

A number of federal statutes administered by agencies with the Department of the Interior (DOI) might be applied to regulate uses of genetically engineered fish if such fish are found to be harmful to natural ecological systems.

The Lacey Act, 18 U.S.C. § 42, prohibits importation into the United States or any United States territory or possession and the shipment between the continental United

States, the District of Columbia, Hawaii, the Commonwealth of Puerto Rico, and any possession of the United States of certain categories of wild animal species – including fish – determined to be "injurious to human beings, to the interests of agriculture, horticulture, forestry, or to wildlife or the wildlife resources of the United States." Wildlife and wildlife resources are defined broadly to include all wild animals and "all types of aquatic and land vegetation upon which such wildlife resources are dependent." Id. § 42(a)(1). Thus the Lacey Act may give the Secretary of the Interior the authority, which has been delegated to the U.S. Fish and Wildlife Service, to prohibit the importation and transportation of transgenic fish if they are found to be injurious to human-related interests or ecological systems of the United States. Regulations listing species of fish found to be injurious under the Lacey Act and therefore restricted are found at 50 C.F.R. 16.13; Salmon is not currently listed. In addition, no live fish, progeny, or fish eggs may be released into the wild without written permission from the appropriate wildlife conservation agency. Id. § 16.13(a)(1).

It is not clear at this time, however, whether Lacey Act prohibitions can be applied to transgenic fish. The statute applies to "species" of mammals, birds, fish, certain aquatic invertebrates, amphibians, reptiles, and the offspring and eggs of these animals. 18 U.S.C. § 42(a)(1). DOI is currently considering whether Congress intended transgenic forms of these species to be included under the scope of the Lacey Act.

A separate part of the Lacey Act, 16 U.S.C. § 3371 et seq., also has implications for the regulation of transgenic fish. This federal law, administered by both the Secretaries of the Interior and Commerce, makes it unlawful for any person to import, export, transport, sell, receive, acquire, or purchase (or attempt to commit any such act) in interstate or foreign commerce any fish taken, possessed, transported, or sold in violation of any federal, tribal, state, or foreign law. Id. § 3372(1), (2)(A), (4). Thus, while the statute does not substantively grant authority to regulate the importation, transportation, exportation, or possession of species such as transgenic salmon, violation of another federal, state, tribal, or foreign law governing these activities would become a violation of federal law and subject to civil and criminal penalties. See id. §§ 3373, 3374.

A third federal statute, jointly administered by the Secretaries of the Interior and Commerce, potentially affecting the use and dispersal of transgenic fish is the Endangered Species Act. The Endangered Species Act (ESA) requires importers of fish (other than nonlisted fish imported for the purpose of human or animal consumption or taken in U.S. waters or on the high seas for recreational purposes) to file declarations, and limits importation to designated ports. 16 U.S.C. § 1538(d), (f). Section 7 of the ESA requires any federal agency to insure that any action authorized, funded, or carried out by the agency not jeopardize the continued existence of any endangered or threatened species or adversely modify any critical habitat of such species. Id. § 1536(a)(2). Thus, each federal agency must consult with the U.S. Fish and Wildlife Service or the National Marine Fisheries Service, depending on the species, for any action that may affect a listed species. If the action is likely to adversely affect a listed species, the appropriate Service issues a Biological Opinion, which may authorize take that is incidental to the action or, if the federal action would otherwise jeopardize the continued existence of the species, offer alternatives to the federal action that will avoid such jeopardy. Id. § 1536(b). Any take of an endangered or threatened fish species unless otherwise authorized is unlawful under the statute. Id. § 1538. Thus, a federal agency will be held responsible for any take – unless authorized through an Incidental Take Statement issued by either the U.S. Fish and Wildlife Service or National Marine Fisheries Service – directly or indirectly caused by the authorization, funding, or other federal action associated with transgenic fish.

The Nonindigenous Aquatic Nuisance Prevention and Control Act, 16 U.S.C. § 4701 et seq., also has the potential to affect the introduction and dispersal of fish. Although the statute focuses primarily on the spread of nonindigenous species through ballast water releases, it also created a task force co-chaired by the Director of the U.S. Fish and Wildlife Service and the Undersecretary of Commerce for Oceans and Atmosphere to develop and implement a program to prevent the introduction and dispersal of aquatic nuisance species. The task force is to "establish and implement measures . . . to minimize the risk of introduction of aquatic nuisance species to waters of the United States." Id. § 4722(c). An aquatic nuisance species is defined broadly to mean "a nonindigenous species that threatens the diversity or abundance of native species or the ecological stability of infested waters, or commercial, agricultural, aquacultural, or recreational activities dependent of such waters," with nonindigenous species defined to include "any species or other viable biological material that enters an ecosystem beyond its historic range." Id. § 4702. Thus aquatic nuisance species can include any species that is not native to that region of the United States, and are not limited to foreign species. A transgenic fish, if found to meet the definition of aquatic nuisance species, could come under the scope of the act.

Finally, various federal land management statutes give federal agencies the authority to manage and regulate species occurring on or affecting federal lands. Authority for management actions comes from each agency's general management statute (including the National Park Service's Organic Act, 16 U.S.C. § 1 et seq.; the National Wildlife Refuge System Administration Act, 16 U.S.C. §§ 668dd, 668ee; and the Bureau of Land Management's Federal Land Policy and Management Act, 43 U.S.C. § 1701 et seq.), and the USDA Forest Service's Organic Act, as well as the Property Clause of the Constitution.

3.   Hazard identification and risk assessment

How are hazards/environmental safety issues associated with the transgenic fish identified?

FDA's CVM, in close cooperation with other federal, state, and tribal agencies with authorities relating to the transgenic animal in question, intends to utilize, in addition to its' considerable in-house expertise in aquaculture and environmental assessment, various sources to identify the environmental safety issues associated with investigational and commercial production of transgenic animals. CVM in-house expertise includes aquatic and microbial ecologists, veterinarians specializing in treating aquatic organisms, fish pathologists and aquaculturists. CVM also plans to use extensively scientific expertise available in other agencies, guidelines and performance standards, public meetings, discussions with affected industry groups, consultation and interaction with experts outside the government and the scientific literature. In particular, FDA gathers information from outside groups and interested individuals when developing guidance for industry.

There are several guidelines or performance standards that have been developed recently through expert working groups that provide information pertinent to identifying environmental safety issues associated with transgenic aquatic organisms (USDA, 1995; Wheelis, 1998). For example, as noted above, the Performance Standards for Safely Conducting Research with Genetically Modified Fish and Shellfish (1995) were developed by the USDA through Advisory Committee meetings and a workshop attended by various experts including experts on environmental safety, biotechnology and risk management from FDA.

FDA has utilized workshops and public meetings to hear stakeholders' concerns about critical issues. For example, FDA has held workshops on developing environmental risk assessment methods for xenobiotics used as new animal drugs and an extensive workshop on determining risk associated with antimicrobial resistance. As noted above, FDA is planning a similar workshop or public meeting for transgenic Atlantic salmon. The workshop will provide stakeholders, including consumers, academics, industry, and government representatives, with an opportunity to identify environmental safety issues as well as methods and criteria for testing, risk characterization, uncertainty evaluation and risk management.

FDA also intends to involve experts from other government agencies (federal, state and local) in its identification of hazards on a national, regional and local level. For example, NMFS has an extensive background in research and assessment of environmental consequences associated with aquaculture. Guidance on compatibility of native and exotic species (irrespective of whether they are transgenic) has been formulated and has been embraced by the U.S. and adjacent nations. This background enables NMFS to offer to be a co-sponsor and participate with FDA in any approach to stakeholders for input on the environmental aspects of the use of transgenic salmon.

The environmental impacts of net pen aquaculture itself, without the use of transgenics, is currently controversial (see Naylor et al. 2000 and rejoinder). Impacts of any aquaculture activities on the management of wild stocks of salmon, be they Atlantic salmon on the east coast or native Pacific salmonids on the west coast, need to be considered. Technologies are developing to address these concerns with increased sensitivity to the environment (e.g., containment, sterility, different sources of fish feed ingredients). FDA and others would have to assess the status of these technologies in order to determine whether they could contribute to an improved environmental impact profile prior to their application to transgenic salmon culture.

There is also a growing body of literature that specifically addresses environmental concerns associated with transgenic aquatic organisms. For example,

Hindar, 1993, Kapuscinski and Hallerman, 1991, and Tiedje et al, 1989, provide extensive reviews of potential environmental and evolutionary adverse impacts associated with transgenic aquatic organisms. The National Academy of Sciences is expected to revisit this issue in 2001.

One goal of extensive cooperation at the federal, state and tribal levels is to ensure that all government entities with authorities for protecting natural resources are able to exercise their respective legal roles at the earliest possible time.

FDA will work with its federal partners in preparing draft and, after taking into account public comment, final guidance that will set out which environmental issues sponsors need to address for individual proposed products. As with all other products reviewed under its new animal drug authority, FDA is requiring data collection as part of its review of individual varieties of transgenic Atlantic salmon. The data collection should contribute to further identifying and quantifying potential adverse impacts, which in the case of a transgenic fish would principally be effects on the health of fish and other animals in the aquatic environment. The information becomes the basis for a NEPA environmental assessment of each transgenic variety and for an assessment of the safety of the new animal drugs contained in each transgenic variety.

NMFS and FWS rely primarily on in-house expertise to identify environmental safety issues, and would do so for transgenic fish. In-house expertise includes fisheries biologists, geneticists, and ecologists. ACE coordinated with the resource agencies to utilize this expertise. It is also possible that for cases as controversial and publicly sensitive as that for transgenic fish, public meetings would be warranted to identify the possible safety issues.

How are environmental safety/risks assessed for the transgenic fish?

FDA/CVM, in consultation with its federal partners, intends to apply accepted ecological risk assessment methodology for assessing the safety of transgenic Atlantic salmon. For example, the Guidelines for Ecological Risk Assessment (EPA, 1998) that were developed as part of the Risk Assessment Forum, sponsored by the EPA, may be a useful tool for the risk assessment of transgenic salmon. CVM participated in the development of this guideline as a member of the Forum and on the peer review committee. The methodology basically consists of 1) identifying possible adverse events (assessment endpoints) associated with transgenic salmon to be considered in the risk assessment, 2) determining which exposures and effects are probable, and 3) characterizing the risk associated with each adverse event that may occur as a result of the introduction of the transgenic fish. Uncertainty analysis would also be included.

Appropriate testing and information collection would occur as part of the methodology. The methodology is iterative in that if new adverse events are identified, those events must be incorporated into the environmental assessment. Additionally the methodology is flexible enough to allow incorporation of quantitative performance data as they accumulate. Once the risk of the adverse events has been characterized, a determination can be made about conducting further testing or implementing risk management. Depending upon the adverse event, including its magnitude, uncertainties, and available risk management methods, the risk assessment may include both qualitative and quantitative determinations of risk.

How are relevant issues considered by the regulatory agency (e.g., biological factors, pathways for proliferation of risk, etc.)?

CVM intends to utilize a risk assessment process for considering possible adverse events that are identified in association with the development and commercial use of transgenic Atlantic salmon. For example, information and ideas might be obtained from a variety of sources including workshops, other experts (government, industry and academia) and the scientific literature to define potential adverse events. The relevant adverse events might be included in a conceptual model in which the studies necessary for assessing the risk associated with each adverse event would be identified. The environmental risk assessment then could enter an analysis stage, where data and information would be collected to analyze exposures and effects. This process is scientific and methodical.

After sufficient data have been collected, CVM would conduct a risk characterization. During its risk characterization, CVM would estimate the ecological risk for each adverse event, determine the overall degree of confidence in each risk estimate, cite evidence supporting the risk estimates, and provide an interpretation of the adversity of ecological effects. A good risk characterization should express results clearly, articulate major assumptions and uncertainties, identify reasonable alternative interpretations, and separate scientific conclusions from policy judgments. (Suter, 1993).

What types of risk are considered by the regulatory agency (provide definition for risk if appropriate)?

FDA intends to publish draft guidance on the kinds of information sponsors should provide to address environmental safety issues as part of a new animal drug application for the new animal drug contained in transgenic fish. FDA is providing the following discussion to illustrate an approach to review of risk associated with transgenic fish. It is derived from Hindar (1993) and Kapuscinski and Hallerman (1991).

In general, there are two themes for assessing adverse events from escaped transgenic fish that should be considered. They are (1) full spectrum of biological effects caused by the escapees on native populations whether or not the escapees spawn successfully, and (2) the reproductive success of the escaped fish.

As observed by Kapuscinski and Hallerman (1991), a gene can be completely characterized with regard to its DNA sequence; however, the primary feature of transgenic individuals that will likely determine the types of ecological questions needing attention is characterization of the nature and magnitude of specific phenotypic changes elicited by expression of the transgenes. Based on these changes, the evolutionary and

21

ecological factors that should be addressed include: (1) the fitness of transgenic individuals; (2) natural interactions of the unmodified species with other organisms and the related consequences of possible differences exhibited by transgenic conspecifics; (3) the natural role of the unmodified species in ecosystem processes; (4) the related consequences of possible differences exhibited by transgenic individuals; and (5) the scale and frequency of introductions into an aquatic ecosystem since these will influence the likelihood of establishment, amount of genetic diversity, amount of genetic material available for recombination, genetic adaptation, and degree of ecological risk. Phenotypic changes in one or more categories may modify life history patterns or spatial or temporal habitat distributions of transgenic fish compared to non-transgenic conspecifics. Transgenic individuals may have surprising ecological impacts associated with their degree of fitness, interaction with other organisms, role in ecosystem processes or potential for dispersal and persistence.

Among the specific phenotypic changes that ordinarily should be examined are:

1.   Metabolic rates that influence nutrient and energy flow and other organisms. For example, growth hormone has been shown to modify the metabolic rate of salmonids.

2.   Range of tolerance values for physical factors, such as, temperature, pH, salinity, dissolved oxygen, or turbidity effects. These effects could be pleiotropic. Growth hormone plays a role in osmoregulation.

3.   Behavior changes that effect reproduction, feeding, territorial defense, migration, or other life history features that could change population dynamics, interactions with other species or genetic stocks, and possibly could lead to destabilization of the aquatic community. In some cases, the phenotypic effect and adaptive significance of particular single genes are well known but influences of polygenes, pleiotropic gene interactions and the environment may also be involved. This might lead to examining the effects of growth hormone under different environmental conditions.

4.   Changes in resource or substrate use could have direct impact on nutritional requirements of the transgenic. Indirect effects on food webs such as added growth hormone increasing size at a given age that may lead to increases in the size of their selected prey. There may also be alterations in appetite and feed conversion.

5.   Resistance to population regulating factors including disease, parasitism, or predation may have population effects.

If crossbreeding occurs, then the hybrids produced by crosses of transgenic and wild fish will include some that are heterozygous for the transgenic trait. The strength of natural selection for (or against) a new trait will depend on the expression of the trait in heterozygotes relative to homozygotes. It should be noted that when immigration rates into natural populations are very high, inflowing genes, irrespective of the strength of the selection might swamp the recipient populations.

It is also noted that transgenic fish in aquaculture production will usually have gone through one bottleneck more than traditionally bred fish (Kapuscinski and Hallerman, 1991). This bottleneck results from inbreeding when homozygous lines are produced from established transgenic individuals, something not always done with conventional fish breeding. Escapes of fertile transgenics can therefore lead to an even more rapid loss of genetic variation in the recipient native populations than escape of other cultured strains of the same species, other factors being equal. Transgenics could cause significant changes in the natural populations' genetic structure and lead to loss of genetic adaptation to local environmental conditions. It has also been noted that only a few fertile individuals can cause changes in the genetic structure of the wild type (Hindar, 1993; Muir and Howard, 1999). Recognition of these potential adverse events have led to consideration of various risk management methods (e.g., physical containment, sterility, etc.) that would prevent release and subsequent significant gene introgression from transgenic fish.

Lastly, the potential for the product of the genetic modification to have an impact on the environment should be included in the risk assessment. For example, if the product is additional growth hormone, the assessment should address whether the growth hormone is available to predators of the transgenic fish, whether it is metabolized or excreted and released into the environment and whether the excreted product may have effects on non-target organisms via bioaccumulation or biomagnification.

Escapes of salmon from currently designed net pen facilities are common and range from minor incidents where a few fish escape to massive escapes. Escapes may be due to operational errors, catastrophic failure of the containment systems during heavy weather events, or damage sustained from ships or large predators such as sea lions. As an example, about 4,500 farm-reared non-transgenic Atlantic salmon recently escaped into Johnstone Strait off the northeast coast of Vancouver Island from a boat transporting them to a processing plant because one of the screens in the cargo hold was not secured properly. Although salmon farm operators are attempting to prevent escapes by upgrading containment systems, installing predator deterrent devices, and taking other actions, it still must be assumed that escapes will occur.

As understanding of fish population genetics and ecology has improved, the environmental and management concerns associated with non-natives or non-local stocks breeding with and competing with native fish species, or local fish populations, have been increasingly recognized and scientific understanding further developed. Efforts need to be made to incorporate consideration of all relevant environmental issues into decisions both on fish stocking and net pen aquaculture.

Currently many states stock non-native or non-local hatchery fish, which obviously may cause some of the same concerns as net pen aquaculture in terms of breeding or competing with native populations. For example, environmental introduction and establishment of Atlantic salmon into the upper Great Lakes has been attempted. Though they were once native to Lake Ontario, after more than 100 years of trying, agencies of the governments of Canada and the United States have yet to establish these ocean-going salmon in the fresh waters of any of the Great Lakes. Every year since 1993, the State of Michigan has planted two non-native strains of Atlantic salmon in Lakes Michigan and Huron. One of these strains, "Gullspang" Atlantic salmon, comes from the freshwater lakes of Sweden, where they have been landlocked since the Ice Ages. Michigan and Wisconsin have at times experimented with a strain of Atlantic salmon that spawns in the rivers of Quebec province, and Minnesota continues to stock this species (Wheelis et al, 1998; a Michigan website details these and other releases: http://www.dnr.state.mi.us).

Experience gained from releases and escapes of non-transgenic fish is useful, not only for helping develop new approaches to environmental oversight of fish in general, but also in predicting the consequences of escaped transgenic fish. As noted, salmonids and other fish have been both intentionally and accidentally introduced into non-native habitats. In many cases the fish have not become established. In other cases, the introduced species have become established and have even displaced native species. To date, farmed Atlantic salmon has not been proven to successfully establish in new habitats in North America, although this is currently a subject of intense study and debate. Introductions of living non-native organisms are considered to be a major cause for the loss of global biodiversity. It has been reported that introductions of non-native organisms have significantly contributed to extinctions of North American fish species during the past century (Hindar 1993, Kapuscinski and Hallerman 1991). The Invasive Species Council established pursuant to Executive Order 13112 (1999) is considering management strategies to minimize harmful introductions of non-native species.

Are possible future changes in social and ecological conditions (e.g., climate) under which the transgenic fish will be used taken into account?

As part of environmental risk assessments, agencies may consider possible future changes in social and ecological conditions, taking into account how reliably such future changes can be predicted. At present, the agencies do not consider such predictions to be reliable enough to warrant their use.

Are possible environmental risks in other countries considered?

In accordance with Executive Order 12114, "Environmental Effects Abroad of Major Federal Actions," FDA considers environmental effects abroad including environmental risks in other countries and on the global commons as part of the NEPA analysis. 21 CFR 25.60.

Atlantic salmon culture operations in both the northeast and northwest U.S. are virtually contiguous with culture operations in Canada. In view of the shared resource and shared market for food derived from farmed Atlantic salmon, coordination of the review and any conditions of approval will be important, in the event that either country becomes ready to approve net pen culture of transgenic Atlantic salmon varieties. FDA regularly contacts the various Canadian authorities under a variety of disclosure agreements to ensure a coordinated review of this and other animal drug products for salmon to be used in shared border waters.

How are uncertainties taken into account?

Sources of uncertainty include variability, uncertainty about a quantity's true value, and data gaps. An additional source includes human error, such as mistakes in handling the fish, unclear communication, improper manipulation of data and errors in data and information collection.

In general, uncertainty is addressed by empirical data that reduce the uncertainty, in combination with various conservative assumptions, such as safety factors, that compensate for the unknown. The greater the uncertainty, the greater the value or number of the safety factors applied to each uncertainty. For each case, there may be a level of uncertainty reached that cannot be compensated for by safety factors, in which case the contemplated action could not be approved because it would not be regarded as safe.

FDA has used a variety of methods for analyzing and describing uncertainty. The methods range from simple to complex. In the simplest form, professional judgment is used in estimating the degree of uncertainty. Uncertainty has also been analyzed utilizing classical statistical methods (e.g., confidence limits, percentiles). FDA also uses models. In the recent antibiotic resistance risk assessment, Monte Carlo analysis was used. Other mathematical methods (e.g., fuzzy mathematics, Bayesian methodologies) could also be used for evaluating uncertainty in our ecological risk assessment of transgenic fish. As with other U.S. regulatory agencies, FDA is in a transition toward using more quantitative risk assessment models to analyze uncertainty (EPA, 1998; Suter, 1993).

Once uncertainties have been characterized, either additional data are collected to reevaluate the risk of an adverse event or the uncertainty is considered in risk management. Additionally, at some point in the assessment, it may be decided that safety factors should be applied to data to characterize the potential for an adverse event to occur. Safety factors are often applied to handle uncertainty when there is a lack of knowledge, or the additional data collection will not help in increasing the confidence of a decision. If additional data are to be collected, then risk assessment returns to the data collection and analysis phase. If additional data are not collected, then the uncertainties, including any safety factors, are considered in the risk management. Within risk management, there is a range of possibilities for handling uncertainties. The range would depend on the degree of the uncertainty and the magnitude of the possible adverse event. Management methods could range from limiting the use of the product, to imposing certain conditions, e.g., confinement or numerical limitations, to not approving the new animal drug product because the agency cannot determine the drug is "safe."

Like all U.S. federal agencies, NMFS uses a precautionary approach to deal with uncertainty in decision-making. NMFS follows the approach described in FAO fisheries documents on the "precautionary principle."

What is the standard that the regulatory agency uses for determining safety and what is the baseline for comparison?

Under the FFDCA, the environmental safety of a new animal drug is determined through a risk analysis. Environmental safety is to be demonstrated by "adequate tests by all methods reasonably applicable to show whether or not such drug is safe for use under the conditions prescribed, recommended, or suggested in the proposed labeling.." 21 U.S.C. § 360b(d)(2). A determination of whether the new animal drug in a transgenic fish is "safe" includes an evaluation of the direct and indirect environmental effects on the health of fish and other animals in the aquatic environment. In addition, there must be reasonable certainty of no harm from the fish to humans who consume it.

Do regulatory agencies consult on issues of mutual interest and, if so, how?

Yes. FDA consults with EPA through the NEPA process or with FWS, NMFS or Forest Service on issues where expertise in the area is needed. FDA may also consult with local or state environmental and regulatory experts on local environmental issues. Additionally, under some laws, such as the ESA or the Migratory Bird Treaties Act, FDA must consult with NMFS or FWS on issues where they have direct legislative jurisdiction. For example, if it is apparent that transgenic salmon likely would interact and impact other aquatic species, including other Atlantic salmon, that have been declared endangered or threatened, consultation with NMFS and/or FWS would be required.

The FWS, NMFS and the states manage numerous fish stocks under the Atlantic Coastal Cooperative Fisheries Act. The FWS has actively worked with the New England Fishery Management Council to determine and designate essential fish habitat for Atlantic salmon. The FWS is actively involved with NMFS and the State of Maine in management of the resource and its habitat.

The environmental agencies routinely meet and coordinate regulatory activities. Programs such as the Joint Processing Programs brings them together to discuss the issues surrounding issuance of permits pending before the ACE. This coordination would be expected for aquaculturing any species in the waters of the U.S.

Are there any significant factors that agencies don't consider / have authority to consider?

EPA, FWS and NMFS have authority to consider a wide spectrum of environmental factors when reviewing a plan to grow salmon in areas where managed fish species occur. NMFS manages more than 900 fish stocks through 40 active Fisheries Management Plans, as authorized by the Magnuson-Stevens Act. Under the essential fish habitat provision of that act, NMFS has the authority to review any activities that might negatively impact habitat. For example, the impact of salmon farms on plant or benthic communities that are part of specific fish habitats are covered by these provisions of the

Magnuson-Stevens Act, and would have to be taken into account in reviewing any plan to grow salmon in areas where managed fish species occur.

The essential fish habitat (EFH) Consultation process is coordinated among the lead federal agency, the applicant and NMFS. The consultation requires that the designated EFH be identified, its functions noted and the impacts, means of neutralizing or compensating those impacts identified and an EFH compatible course of action described (resource recommendations). The intent of all NMFS involvement in the regulatory processes is to ensure that all aspects of a proposed aquaculture activity provide adequate environmental protection.

The EFH Consultation process is not a stand-alone activity, but is incorporated into the overall regulatory process for reviewing aquaculture plans. If the Endangered Species Act (ESA) is invoked, the consultation process can be led by either the EFH or ESA procedures.

FDA likewise has authority to take into account a wide spectrum of environmental factors in its oversight of transgenic fish. Under NEPA, FDA must evaluate the full scope of environmental impacts defined under NEPA that might be associated with a major federal action and communicate and coordinate with other agencies that might be affected by the action. The FFDCA provides FDA with authority to take actions based on environmental impacts that the agency determines are likely to directly or indirectly affect the health of humans or animals. FDA anticipates that most potential adverse environmental effects from use of transgenic fish would likely have at least indirect adverse effects on fish or other animals in the food web. For example, if a new animal drug adversely affects a plant population that is a significant food source for an aquatic animal population to an extent that would adversely affect the health of that population, the use of the new animal drug would have an indirect impact on the aquatic animal by adversely affecting its food source.

4.   **Information and data (what, why and how is data and information collected and generated)**

CVM is currently regulating transgenic fish as containing a new animal drug. CVM approves a new animal drug application (NADA) when it finds that the new animal drug is safe and effective for its intended use(s). The safety determination encompasses safety to the target animal, to humans if it is a food-producing animal, and to humans and other animals in the environment. Thus, in the case of a transgenic fish, the safety of the drug would include safety to the transgenic fish (including safety of eating the transgenic fish) as well as safety to fish and other animals in the environment that may be affected by the use of the new animal drug contained in the transgenic fish. The safety determination would also include the safety to animals of feed containing components of the transgenic fish.

In addition, as part of the demonstration of safety, CVM requires information demonstrating that the new animal drug can be manufactured in a consistent form (which, in the case of a transgenic animal means that the genetic modification is stable and consistently expressed in the variety of transgenic animal).

The data to satisfy requirements for approval are collected from effectiveness, target animal safety, food safety, environmental safety, and manufacturing chemistry and stability studies. All data for these studies with the exception of effectiveness trials are subject to Good Laboratory Practices (GLP) standards codified under 21 CFR 58. The effectiveness trials currently are conducted under regulations (21 CFR 511) and guidance documents addressing good target animal study practices. Some of the food safety aspects of regulation are touched upon below, even though this assessment does not address food safety, to clarify relationships among these FDA authorities and those relating to other aspects of transgenic animals.

The review process for a new animal drug normally starts with a sponsor filing an INAD with CVM and, if desired, requesting authorization to slaughter and render research animals treated with the investigational drug. CVM grants an authorization to slaughter or to render investigational animals only after determining that such animals are safe for use as food or feed. New animal drugs that do not have an established INAD or an approved NADA, or are not used in accordance with the extra-label provisions of Section 512(a)(5) of the FFDCA are in violation of the FFDCA, and FDA can take or recommend enforcement action against the product, the distributor and/or the sponsor. The only exception to this is basic laboratory research: 21 CFR 511.1(a) allows new animal drug research to be conducted without an INAD as long as the animals are used solely for laboratory research, including that the animals may not be used for any food or feed purpose.

In particular, sponsors would need to establish INADs when they have a commercially viable product that they intend to eventually market to the public, when the transgenic animals are non-laboratory semi-domesticated animals that pose containment issues (such as the fish to be grown in ocean net pens), or when the animals are to be disposed of through slaughter or rendering for human food or animal feed. In some cases, sponsors may want to establish an INAD earlier in the process, because some studies in the very early stages of development are needed for product approval.

Investigations with new animal drugs are controlled under 21 CFR Part 511. The goal of investigations of a transgenic salmon intended for food use would be to gather data for an application that can be approved under 21 U.S.C. § 360 b(b)(1) as implemented by 21 CFR Part 514. The technical sections for an NADA are developed during the investigational period. All data relevant to the application must be included, whether it is considered pivotal or not by the applicant, regardless of whether it is supportive of the approval. FDA provides close oversight of the testing being conducted, the integrity of the data collected and the interpretation of results. In addition to in-house scientific experts, the agency uses contracts, advisory committees, and experts from other Federal agencies to obtain specialized expertise where needed.

The sponsor generally provides to the agency for review a proposed plan of how it intends to address all the requirements of obtaining approval of an NADA. Also, the sponsor must provide all known published documentation on the product under consideration. Some of this published documentation may be able to be used to satisfy some requirements of an NADA. Studies conducted by or behalf of the sponsor are normally needed to complete the NADA. When new studies are needed to satisfy requirements for an NADA, the sponsor is encouraged to provide study protocols for review and comment by FDA. Once concurrence is reached, a protocol provides the basis for how the study is to be conducted. All studies can be conducted by the sponsor or can be contracted out to qualified research facilities capable of conducting research under applicable regulations and statutes.

Clinical effectiveness trials are generally conducted under conditions that are representative of commercial "real life" situations. These effectiveness trials also usually provide the agency with further information about safety and conditions of use that cannot be obtained from more controlled experimental trials. In the case of transgenic salmon, conducting clinical effectiveness trials presents a particular environmental problem, because of the risk of fish escaping, in that biocontainment should be agreed upon in advance, at least for the limited trial sites. Because the results of these studies are to be used as proof of safety or effectiveness for an NADA approval, sponsors generally seek FDA agreement on study protocols in advance. An environmental problem created as a result of a clinical trial could be evidence that the product would not be safe under commercial use and could be used as grounds to refuse to approve the product.

Data collected for studies conducted under the INAD are subject to three different types of bioresearch monitoring inspections: sponsor/monitor, GLP and clinical investigator. Effectiveness studies are routinely inspected as deemed necessary by CVM personnel. Inspections are generally data audits of specific trials and are conducted by FDA field investigators who may be assisted by CVM personnel.

A sponsor generally conducts testing of a new animal drug in its final form. Changes to a product formulation occur for many reasons and are allowed as long as proper testing is done to ensure that the modified formulation is equivalent to that used in prior testing. For transgenic fish, this means that testing will generally need to be conducted on the transgenic variety, as it will be marketed in commerce, as opposed to earlier crosses and backcrosses. After a sponsor has completed testing, it submits the generated information to the agency for review. This usually entails a variety of reports, statistical analyses and copies of source data records.

FDA has authority to conduct inspections and to review records. Thus, if a reviewer suspects data integrity problems in submitted documents, he or she can request that inspections be conducted to assess the validity of the data. If the data from studies are determined to be invalid, these studies are excluded from any further consideration in the submission. When significant questions regarding data integrity are raised, FDA ordinarily will place an application under its application integrity policy, thereby deferring substantive scientific review pending a validity assessment. Such an action could delay product approval or, if data integrity problems are confirmed, could lead to a product never being approved or to the withdrawal of a product approval.

The environmental safety review component of new animal drug applications for transgenic animals, including transgenic Atlantic salmon, follows the NEPA format in terms of scoping, development of alternatives, consideration of cumulative effects, related social and economic impacts. This facilitates organizing and coordinating the review among the several agencies that regulate environmental resources that might be affected by an approval, and so goes beyond just those areas that are directly under FDA/CVM authority.

5.   Mitigation and management considerations: approvals and conditions on research, development, production, distribution, marketing, use and disposal

There is a comprehensive permitting program for non-transgenic aquaculture. Permits are required for the placement of culturing facilities in or use of waters of the U.S. The regulatory program is lead by the ACE, using two principal pieces of federal legislation: Section 10 of the Rivers and Harbors Act (structures) and Sections 401 and 404 of the CWA (fill). EPA, FWS, Department of Commerce, National Oceanic and Atmospheric Administration, NMFS and their State government counterparts are the principal parties in the program. Associated with their federal mandates, the involved State(s) provide regulatory overview through the Coastal Consistency clause of the Coastal Zone Management Act.

EPA is currently evaluating the need for requiring NPDES permits for culturing facilities and is developing guidelines and standards for all U.S. aquaculture facilities that are expected to be in place in 2004. If such permits are adopted, state agencies would ordinarily be responsible for issuing and monitoring compliance with conditions set in permits.

Disposal of materials resulting from processing is already treated as a point source discharge by EPA and is regulated under the provisions of the CWA. NPDES permits authorizing discharges from such facilities are required. The types of disposals from these facilities may include discharges of processing wastes, process disinfectants, sanitary wastewater and other wastewaters, including domestic wastewater, cooling water, boiler water, freshwater pressure relief water, refrigeration condensate, water used to transfer seafood to a facility, and live tank water. Additionally, processing facilities are required to collect and route all seafood processing wastes and wastewater to a treatment system consisting of 1 mm screens or equivalent technology. All seafood solid wastes are collected and transported to the by-product recovery facility or are recovered through an in-house fish powder plant. By-products from the salmon industry are typically processed into animal feed ingredients, including fish food (EPA, 1995).

Disposals following consumption of food derived from transgenic salmon are typically the same as other restaurant and household disposal and usually consist of disposal in domestic wastewater, treatment in municipal or private (septic) wastewater treatment facilities, or collection for disposal as solid wastes in landfills.

NMFS' role in aquaculture is multifaceted. It assesses environmental impact and compatibility, designs and test protocols, and monitors the effects of culturing of aquatic species. NMFS is obligated to identify situations where the risk to the environment of introduction or culturing is unacceptable, and to make recommendations to the ACE as to whether a request for an aquaculture permit should be granted. NMFS has a research and regulatory program through which it gains the expertise necessary to justify recommendations regarding a proposed activity. Monitoring and routine evaluations of aquaculture operations are components of each successful permit request. Environmental monitoring is usually required of the operating company, and the data verified through site visits by NMFS. Suspension or revocation of a permit, or financial penalties, are all available where a party does not comply with its permit. In all cases, the burden of proof of environmental compatibility resides with the proponent/applicant.

NMFS and FWS have had considerable experience with the Atlantic salmon industry. The net-pen industry with which NMFS is most familiar has a routine, significant escape of salmon from their facilities. Escapes can occur *inter alia* through equipment failure, during fish handling and transport operations, through large predator intrusion into facilities, and as a result of storms. Current technologies and procedures in the industry cannot ensure that escapes will not occur. NMFS considers the escape problem as one related to operational practices. It is related, also, to the evolving nature of the culturing technology and human error. Information on the consequences of escape is being collected and NMFS is revisiting permits and the associated assumptions of impact. The regulatory tools available for insuring permit compliance or modification are found in the ACE regulations, Permit Conditions, the ESA, Magnuson – Stevens Act and Fish & Wildlife Coordination Act. Escapement is difficult to address due to the diversity of causes.

Some information exists on the behavior of salmon that escape from aquaculture facilities that indicates that they have a tendency to stay near the area of escape, probably because of a food dependency. This behavior allows the recovery of a substantial number of post-escape fish by employing seine nets or hook and line fishing.

NMFS and FWS also have considerable knowledge of reproductive sterilization techniques that might be used to mitigate interbreeding of escapees with wild stocks. To date, none of these techniques has been shown to be 100% effective, and analysis of all fish to ensure sterility of individuals may not be economically or practically viable. The present Atlantic salmon farming practices do not include a requirement that only sterile fish be cultured. A request for growing transgenic Atlantic salmon individuals may. There is a reasonably successful program in place already that is overseen by the FWS to assure triploidy in grass carp. It is possible that something similar can be developed for Atlantic salmon.

NMFS and FWS have land-based facilities that are being used to study non-transgenic Atlantic and Pacific salmon behavior and could be used as a first approach to evaluating the behavior of transgenic salmon in quasi-natural environments. Such work, however, would be costly and time consuming, and would require interpretation of results against completely natural situations.

The Gulf of Maine distinct population segment of Atlantic salmon has been listed as endangered under the ESA. NMFS and FWS have been working with the State of Maine to address the potential impacts of escapees of domestic farmed origin, including those of European origin. These potential impacts include genetic introgression, ecological competition (food, space, mates), and disease transmission. Possible measures to reduce and/or eliminate this potential impact include a phase-out of European stocks, upgraded containment systems, marking of all fish reared in net pens, and a monitoring program to document any escapes that do occur.

Various mitigation measures or management controls that will prevent or reduce the potential for adverse environmental impacts to occur can be considered during the pre-market review of transgenic Atlantic salmon under the new animal drug provisions of the FFDCA. These mitigations would have to be considered in the context of the environments where the transgenic salmon would be reared, the management procedures that would be followed, their feasibility, and the probability that properly used mitigation measures would be effective. Such measures can therefore be different for various research sites and for varying production sites, according to the environmental context and rearing systems employed.

Ensuring environmental safety is a reason why FDA might place restrictions on product development, production, transportation, distribution, and marketing for transgenic salmon as part of the new animal drug approval process. These mitigations could include physical or biocontainment performance requirements, predator exclusion design, or outright prohibition from use in certain locations. Also, because under the FFDCA food containing unapproved new animal drugs is considered adulterated and therefore may not be sold, food products derived from the transgenic variety may not be sold, imported, taste tested or test marketed without express prior approval from FDA of the new animal drug contained in the transgenic fish. Approval from FDA includes consideration of not just the genetic construct, but also the effects due to its insertion and expression.

6.   Monitoring and consideration of new information

NMFS has the legal authority and an infrastructure to prescribe and evaluate monitoring of aquatic organisms held in aquaculture facilities in navigable waters of the US. These authorities are found in the legislation empowering NMFS to address ESA, EFH and the environmental consequences of authorizing culturing activities in waters of the U.S. NMFS adds such monitoring requirements to the permit requirements issued by ACE pursuant to the Rivers and Harbors Act when circumstances warrant. Because aquaculture activities represent such a wide diversity of technologies and species and the information pool varies in adequacy, the conditions of permit issuance vary from case to case and species to species. Generally, NMFS has seen a reduction in the level of monitoring required of culturists. Often, the monitoring has revealed less than expected or a lack of adverse impacts associated with culturing practices. Typical monitoring and reporting requirements can include escapes, inventory tracking, stock tagging and environmental monitoring related to water quality and changes to the benthic environment in the area of the facility. In cases where facilities are in state waters, NMFS can transfer monitoring and reporting authorities to the state.

FDA has legal authority and existing programs to prescribe and evaluate monitoring requirements for marketed products. These requirements can be imposed on the transgenic fish sponsors as a part of approval under the new animal drug approval process. See 21 U.S.C. § 360b(l) and implementing regulations under 21 CFR 510.300. FDA requires regular product experience reporting, maintains an adverse event reporting system that obligates product sponsors to quickly report specified adverse events that might be associated with approved products, and also encourages reporting of adverse events (including adverse environmental events) by veterinarians, other government agencies and consumers into the same system. FDA follows up with inspections of product sponsors to ensure that product complaints are being addressed, that appropriate records are kept, and that labeling, promotional material, and adverse event reports received by the sponsor are being submitted to FDA on a regular basis.

If post approval-monitoring programs for environmental effects are necessary, they are ideally designed prior to product approval. However, if, subsequent to approval, FDA finds that a product cannot be safely used without a monitoring program, FDA can initiate steps to withdraw the approval unless the sponsor implements a monitoring program. FDA can utilize experts in other Federal agencies, special government employees, including experts from academia or industry and Advisory Committees and workshops to design such programs for classes of products and for specific products.

When new information is received through these monitoring programs (or is provided to FDA by other agencies or is otherwise obtained by FDA), FDA has legal authority to take a range of actions based on that information, including additional or modified information or record collection requirements, label changes, or withdrawal of approval. 21 U.S.C. §§ 360b(e), (l). Other agencies may be involved in the monitoring, either in design or use of the results for considerations under, for example, the Endangered Species Act or other resource management statutes. As the agencies involved may vary according to the species under consideration, the FDA has had to decide which agencies were likely to be interested and make contacts on a product-by-product basis.

7.   Enforcement and compliance

NMFS has an enforcement office with shore-side and on-the-water presence. The U.S. Coast Guard has co-responsibility for enforcing fishing regulations, and for this purpose aquaculture has been defined as a fishing activity under the Magnuson-Stevens

Fisheries Conservation and Management Act. The resources of NFMS and the U.S. Coast Guard for fisheries and aquaculture enforcement are probably not adequate, especially if substantial new aquaculture activity occurs that requires additional enforcement intervention.

NMFS may seek revocation of ACE permits when unexpected or excessive adverse environmental impacts are identified. With the authorities provided under the ESA and Marine Mammal Protection Act and to some degree, the Magnuson – Stevens Act, NMFS has separate authorities that allow it to force cessation of unacceptable culturing activities.

The FWS has a law enforcement division that enforces Lacey Act violations and for the case of ASMFC activities also helps enforce FMPS. We anticipate a role for FWS law enforcement in enforcement of activities related to the Atlantic salmon listing.

FDA could initiate a compliance action under the FFDCA if an NADA approval for use of a genetic construct in salmon, another fish, or any other animal were to include measures aimed at mitigating environmental impacts that affect the health of man or animals, and the sponsor failed to take these mitigation measures. Under the FFDCA, if the use of a new animal drug does not conform to its approved application, it is considered "unsafe." 21 U.S.C. § 360b(a)(1)(B). Thus, if environmental mitigation measures are part of the approved application and the sponsor fails to take these measures, the use of the new animal drug would not conform to its approved application and it would be unsafe. Unsafe new animal drugs are considered adulterated drugs under the FFDCA. 21 U.S.C. § 351.

The FFDCA prohibits interstate commerce in adulterated drugs. 21 U.S.C. § 331. Violation of this provision could result in an *in rem* seizure of the violative drugs and injunction proceedings against or criminal prosecution of those responsible for distributing such drugs. 21 U.S.C. §§ 332-334.

FDA can require sponsors to keep records that are pertinent to the safety of the new animal drug and that were not previously submitted to FDA, including new studies that become available after the new animal drug approval, and to periodically submit such records to FDA. 21 CFR 510.300(a)(1), 510.300(b)(4)(1), 21 U.S.C. § 360b(l), 331(e). FDA has the authority to inspect and copy such records. 21 U.S.C. § 360b(l)(2). If new studies showing that a particular new animal drug contained in a variety of transgenic salmon causes environmental harm become available after the approval of that variety under an NADA, the sponsor would be obligated to bring the studies to FDA's attention. If the sponsor failed to do so, FDA could withdraw approval of the NADA for the new animal drug contained in the transgenic salmon, 21 U.S.C. § 360b(e)(2)(A), and/or seek penalties against the sponsor. 21 U.S.C. § 333.

Under the FFDCA, if a sponsor submits false data, FDA can withdraw approval of the NADA. 21 U.S.C. § 360b(e)(1)(E). Prosecution is also possible.

8.   Public involvement and transparency

For aquaculture projects in Federal waters, a public notice of permit application is required. The notice is released by the Army Corps of Engineers. It is possible that the permit application would contain confidential commercial or trade secret information, and if so, the information would be redacted. There is less uniformity among states for notice of applications to the public. The Public Notice is used to inform the general public and adjacent property owners of the application and includes a work description. The comments stimulated by the notice are included in the record and are usually addressed in the Statement of Findings created for the acceptability determination of a proposed action. Should there be compelling issues raised by the public, the Corps of Engineers can request additional information about the proposed action, hold public hearings on the matter, modify the project design or deny the permit request. Typically, project modification is the avenue most frequently used by the regulated community.

As mentioned previously, FDA intends to hold one or more open public meetings or workshops to discuss environmental risk assessment and risk management questions posed by transgenic fish and shellfish, including Atlantic salmon. In addition, FDA is considering using an advisory committee to address any unresolved or controversial scientific questions, particularly regarding environmental issues, prior to completing its evaluation of the first NADA for a transgenic fish. Therefore, the agency believes that it will be able to provide public dialogue on the scientific foundation for making a decision on approval or limitations of such applications.

At the time of publication in the Federal Register of a notice of approval of NADA, FDA makes available through a Public Docket and increasingly as time goes on via its website, an extensive Freedom of Information summary and NEPA documentation required for the approval of the application (although information that still qualifies as trade secret information would not be disclosed). At this point, a member of the public could submit a Citizen Petition that requests withdrawal of approval of the application. For example, such a petition could point out information that should have been submitted in the application that was relevant to the approval or provide an alternative interpretation of data used in the decision. At any time after the approval, new information that has a bearing on the approval of the NADA can be brought to the agency by anyone in the form of a Citizen Petition. FDA considers the information submitted, replies to the Petition, and takes appropriate action based on its reply that could include withdrawal of approval of the NADA, following applicable procedures.

As noted earlier, FDA is not permitted to disclose the filing of an INAD or NADA, absent sponsor agreement, unless the sponsor has publicly disclosed it. 21 CFR 514.12 and 21 CFR 514.11. For example, the filing of the INAD for a transgenic Atlantic salmon has previously been disclosed, but FDA is not permitted to discuss whether or not INADs have been filed for other transgenic fish. FDA is considering whether there may be mechanisms by which it could make public its NEPA analyses of products for which there is considerable public interest and controversy over environmental issues (such as transgenic fish) and invite public comment prior to making the decision.

FDA recognizes that there are special situations (such as those described in this case study) in which it would be preferable to allow greater public access to information. In these situations, FDA encourages the sponsor to release relevant information addressing public concerns. For issues relating to a class of products, CVM uses public workshops to clarify issues that must be evaluated and the means to address them. It also utilizes the CVM advisory committee (a committee subject to the Federal Advisory Committee Act (FACA)), in public meetings where possible, to identify and advise the agency about these issues. In some cases, CVM uses other advisory committees (also subject to FACA) from elsewhere in FDA, consensus conferences in the National Institutes of Health, or requests expert reviews by the Institute of Medicine and the National Academy of Sciences. CVM also discusses issues relating to safety and effectiveness of classes of products and individual products in various international fora, including the International Conference on Harmonization of Technical Requirements for Registration of Veterinary Medicinal Products (VICH) and the Codex Alimentarius Commission. In general, these meetings and/or the reports of their deliberations are open to the public.

REFERENCES

Bye, V. and R. Lincoln. 1986. Commercial methods for the control of sexual maturation in rainbow trout (*Salmo gairdneri* R.). Aquaculture 57: 299-309.

CFR. 2001. Code of Federal Regulations. Title 21. Volume 1, Parts 1 to 99.

Devlin, R. H. 1997. Chapter 19. Transgenic Salmonids in: L.M. Houdebine, ed. Transgenic Animals: Generation and Use. pp: 105-117. Harwood Academic Publishers, Amsterdam ISBN 90-5702-069-6.

Du, S.J., et al. 1992. Growth enhancement in transgenic Atlantic salmon by the use of an "all fish" chimeric growth hormone gene construct. BioTechnology 10: 176-181.

Du, S.J., et al. 1992b. Development of an all-fish gene cassette for gene transfer in aquaculture. Molecul. Marine Biol. and Biotechnology 1:290-300.

Endangered Species Act of 1973 (as amended through December 1996)

FAO. 1996. World review of fisheries and aquaculture. Food and Agricultural Organization of the United Nations. ftp://ftp.fao.org/FI/document/sofia/1996/soreviee.pdf

FDA. 1993. Finding of No Significant and Environmental Assessment Impact for Sterile Sometribove Zinc Suspension for Use in Lactating Dairy Cows, NADA 140-872, May 7, 1993. Docket Number 93-27876, FDA Dockets Management Branch.

FFDCA. 1998. Federal Food, Drug and Cosmetic Act As Amended February 1998

Fleming, I.A., K. Hindar, I.B. Mjolnerod, B. Jonsson, T. Balstad and A. Lamberg. 2000. Lifetime success and interactions of farm salmon invading a native population. Proc. R. Soc. Lond. B, 267, 1517-1523.

Heen, K., R.L. Monahan and F. Utter. 1993. <u>Salmon Aquaculture.</u> Fishing News Books, A Division of Blackwell Scientific Publications Ltd., Oxford, UK. ISBN 0-85238-204-9. 278 pages.

Hew, C.L., G.L. Fletcher and P.L. Davies. 1995. Transgenic salmon: tailoring the genome for food production. J Fish Biol. 47 (Supplement A), 1-19.

Hindar, K. 1993. Genetically engineered fish and their possible environmental impact. Norsk Institutt for Naturforskning Oppdragsmelding 215: 1-48.

Kapuscinski A.R. and E. M. Hallerman. 1991. Implications of introduction of transgenic fish into natural ecosystems. Fisheries and Oceans 48(Suppl 1): 99-107.

Muir, William M. and Richard D. Howard. Possible ecological risks of transgenic organism release when transgenes affect mating success: sexual selection and the Trojan gene hypothesis. Proc. Nat. Acad. Sci. 96:13853-13856.

Price Waterhouse Coopers. 1998. Salmon farming Overview: 1998. Presentation to the BC Salmon Farmers Association, Annual Meeting, May 20, 1999. Vancouver, BC. http://www.salmonfarmers.org/network/PDF%20Files/David Egan/index.htm

Productivity Commission. 1997. Australian Atlantic Salmon: Effects of Import Competition (7 January 1997). MELBOURNE, Australia, VIC. http://www.indcom.gov.au/research/irrs/salmon/chap2.pdf.

Rimmer, D.W. 1998, Atlantic Salmon (Salmo salar) in Tsitika River,1998. Ministry of Environment, Lands and Parks, Fisheries Section 2080A Labieux Road, Nanaimo, B.C., V9T 6J9. December.

Suter, G. W. 1993. Ecological Risk Assessment. Lewis Publishers. Boca Raton, FL pp. 27-33, 41-47, 391-401.

Tiedje, J. M., et al. 1989. The planned introduction of genetically engineered organisms: ecological considerations and recommendations. Ecology 70: 298-315.

U.S.C. United States Code Title 21,

USDA. 2000. U.S. State and Territory Animal Import Regulations for Aquatic Species. http://www.aphis.usda.gov/guidance/regulations/animal/state/aquatic/

USDA. 1995. Performance Standards for Safely Conducting Research with Genetically Modified Fish and Shellfish. U.S. Department of Agriculture, Agriculture Biotechnology Research Advisory Committee, Working Group on Aquatic Biotechnology and Environmental Safety. http://www.nbiap.vt.edu/perfstands/ psmain.html.

U.S. EPA. 1995. Compilation of Air Pollutant Emission Factors, AP-42, Fifth Edition, CHAPTER 9, Food and Agricultural Industries. Environmental Protection Agency, Office of Air Quality Planning and Standards, Clearinghouse for Inventories and Emissions Factors. http://www.epa.gov/ttn/chief/ap42c9.html

U.S. EPA. 1998. Guidelines for Ecological Risk Assessment. Risk Assessment Forum, Washington, DC. EPA/630/R-95/002F.

Rimmer, D.W. 1998, Atlantic Salmon (Salmo salar) in Tsitika River,1998. Ministry of Environment, Lands and Parks, Fisheries Section 2080A Labieux Road, Nanaimo, B.C., V9T 6J9. December.

Wheelis, M., et al. 1998. Manual for Assessing Ecological and Human Health Effects of Genetically Engineered Organisms. Part One: Introductory Materials and Supporting Text for Flowcharts. Scientists' Working Group on Biosafety. The Edmonds Institute. Edmonds, Washington, USA. http://www.edmonds-institute.org/manual.html.

SIDEBAR No. I.A

ORNAMENTAL FISH (GOLDFISH*)*

Overview

This case study concerns the possible introduction of genes into goldfish to increase tolerance to freezing temperatures, thus allowing the fish to survive in colder water. The genes, which come from other fishes, encode production so-called antifreeze proteins that prevent the growth of ice crystals in the serum of the fish. The U.S. government is not aware of any plans to develop such fish for commercialization and such development may not be permitted in some states. Nonetheless, this sidebar illustrates some of the regulatory and environmental issues that could arise were such fish to be developed and commercialized for use as bait.

1.   Description of proposed organism and its use

The goldfish (*Carassius auratus*), native to China, portions of southeast Asia, central Asia, and far eastern Europe, was introduced into the United States more than 300 years ago, making it the first introduced exotic fish in North America (Berg 1949). Today, it is one of the most popular aquarium and ornamental pond fishes throughout the world. More recently in the United States, it has been raised commercially for the fish-bait and fish-food industries. The "generalist" life history characteristics of goldfish, including its omnivorous feeding habit and ability to persist across a wide range of temperatures in various freshwater lotic (i.e., actively moving water) and lentic (i.e., still water) habitats, have allowed this species to establish wild populations in nearly every state and province of North America. Goldfish are believed to have been introduced to new bodies of water via intentional and unintentional release by aquaculturists, ornamental fish hobbyists, fishermen, and individuals desiring to free their pet fish.

Goldfish are widely regarded as a nuisance species, competing with native fish for food and habitat. This exotic species is considered to be detrimental to the fisheries industry in several states (e.g., Garling et al. 1995) and may be responsible for the extirpation of native fish species, including several listed under the Endangered Species Act (ESA), such as the Pahrump poolfish (*Empetrichthys latos latos*; Deacon et al. 1964) and the White River spinedace (*Lepidomeda albivallis*; U.S. Fish and Wildlife Service 1994).

What are the anticipated characteristics of the genetically engineered organism?

Teleost fishes (i.e., bony fishes), as well as some other plants and animals, have evolved a mechanism to reduce the freezing point of their bodily fluids without appreciably changing their osmolarity or their the ability to move as a result of osmosis (Davies, et al. 1999, Fletcher et al. 1999). Antifreeze proteins (AFPs) serve as antifreeze agents by specifically adhering to the surface of ice crystals as they form, thereby preventing their growth. This contrasts with the action of most solutes (e.g., electrolytes) that prevent freezing by colligative mechanisms (i.e., quantity of molecules). Because of the unique aspects of their tertiary structures, these proteins are up to 500 times more effective at lowering the freezing temperature than any other known solute molecule. Several distinct classes of AFPs, distinguished by their molecular structure, have been isolated from fish, insect, and plant sources (Cheng 1998, Davies and Hew 1990). To date, however, those from fish sources are perhaps best known and have been more thoroughly characterized than those from other species. Antifreeze glycoproteins (AFGPs) have been found in Antarctic *Notothenioidei* teleosts and northern cods. So-called type I AFPs are found in righteye flounder (Pleuronectidae) and in shorthorn sculpin (*Myoxocephalus scorpius*); type II AFPs are found in sea ravens, smelts, and herring; and type III AFPs are found in ocean pout and wolffishes (Davies and Hew 1990, Davies et al. 1999, Fletcher et al. 1988). Recently, a new kind of fish antifreeze, designated Type IV, was isolated from the longhorn sculpin (*Myoxocephalus octodecimspinosus)* (Deng et al. 1997, Deng and Laursen 1998, Zhao et al. 1998). The evolution of these AFPs and their genes has been reviewed (Cheng 1998, Davies et al. 1993).

Several commercial applications for AFPs have been identified and are currently being pursued (Wallace et al. 1993). These include the following:

    _   cold protection of mammalian cells, tissues, and organs;
    _   enhanced tumor cell destruction during cryosurgery;
    _   longer shelf life for and better quality of frozen foods;
    _   protection of fish and plants against cold and freezing temperatures;
    _   improved growth characteristics in transgenic fish by using AFP gene promoters.

The first three applications of AFPs listed above utilize purified AFP from natural sources or recombinant expression systems while the last two are implemented by gene transfer to the target organism. Genes encoding AFPs have been transferred into Atlantic salmon (Du et al. 1992, Hew et al. 1999, Hew et al. 1992), goldfish (Wang et al. 1995), and tilapia.

In research conducted outside of the United States, a gene from flounder (*Pleuronectes americanus*) that encodes AFPs has been transferred to goldfish, affording transgenic individuals higher survival rates at cold temperatures compared to non-transgenic goldfish (Wang et al. 1995). No other phenotypic traits unique to the transgenic form of goldfish have been described in the literature. However, relatively little research has been conducted on AFPs and goldfish.

AFP genes have been transferred into fish to provide freeze protection during aquaculture production. Although first attempts did not provide the level of protection desired, new constructs consisting of more effective AFPs with stronger promoter and enhancer elements are underway.

How would the genetically engineered organism be used, including brief description of management practices that would be associated with it?

Commercialization of transgenic goldfish containing the AFP gene has not been approved in the United States, hence its intended use is not completely known at this early stage of research and development. Current biotechnology research using goldfish is not extensive in either the United States or overseas, although at least one laboratory is examining the insertion of AFP genes into goldfish oocytes (i.e., eggs before maturation) (Wang et al. 1995).

Two scenarios are likely based upon current commercial propagation of non-transgenic goldfish: (a) ornamental (aquarium and fish garden) fish, and (b) bait-fish industries. The latter use, in particular, offers a major advantage to both aquaculturists who raise the fish, and to anglers who use the fish as bait. Transgenic goldfish containing the AFP gene are likely to persist and mature under a broader range of water temperatures, allowing aquaculturists greater flexibility in the conditions under which the fish are propagated. Likewise, goldfish genetically engineered to include the AFP protein may be more active in colder waters than non-transgenic individuals, thereby enhancing the attractiveness of transgenic goldfish as a baitfish.

The actual utility of transgenics in the baitfish industry from a socioeconomic standpoint is open to debate. Some experienced with the industry consider that the use of transgenic goldfish for baitfish is not likely at all. They feel that most baitfish producers are well aware of the environmental and public concerns around transgenics and would not even consider production of transgenic fish. Many states already outlaw the use of goldfish for bait. To these individuals, it seems unlikely that the industry would invest in research, development and FDA approval for bait that would be illegal to sell in most states.

Nevertheless, if transgenic fish were to be used in the industry, management systems used for production of transgenic goldfish would likely be similar to those currently in use for non-transgenic goldfish. The goldfish is one of three major baitfish propagated in the United States, with most raised in southern states. Goldfish raised for the bait fish industry are propagated one of two ways: (a) spawning indoors in tanks, with eggs transferred from fiber spawning mats to other indoor tanks or to outdoor ponds; or (b) spawning outdoors on fiber spawning mats placed along the edges of ponds, with eggs transferred to other ponds for incubation and growth of fry. Goldfish can be harvested from ponds throughout the year with large seines, held for a short while to separate viable from unhealthy fish, then shipped via livehaul truck or plastic lined shipping boxes to bait shops (Arkansas Cooperative Extension Service). Goldfish are used as forage in the fish propagation and aquaculture industry and as live bait for sportfishing (e.g., for largemouth bass, *Micropterus salmoides*).

Is there prior experience dealing with the same varieties not genetically engineered?

Goldfish have been artificially propagated for more than 300 years in the United States, and much longer than that in other parts of the world. More than 100 varieties of *Carassius auratus* have been developed through traditional breeding technologies, and many of these are widely sold and discussed via hobbyist groups throughout the ornamental fish industry. In addition, the baitfish industry generates more than $1 billion in annual revenue in the United States, with much of these profits generated by goldfish propagation.

What are the projected locations and extent of production, use and disposal?

The aquarium fish industry operates in all fifty states, with most participants being associated with relatively small operations (pet stores, fish hobbyists, etc.). Goldfish aquaculture associated with the fish bait industry, in contrast, is concentrated in southern states from Georgia to Arkansas.

Intentional and unintentional release of non-native aquarium and bait fish have led to severe environmental problems in the United States, including serving as a primary cause in the population declines of several native fish species. Nearly 150 exotic fish species from the aquarium industry have been found in the wild in the United States (Cohen 2000). Dozens of additional species used as baitfish have established populations outside of their native ranges in the United States. Several species of escaped aquarium and baitfish have been implicated in the listing of threatened and endangered species under the ESA (Lassuy 1995). For example, released aquarium fish have been identified as a chief cause for the threatened and endangered status of the Moapa dace (*Moapa coriacea*), desert pupfish (*Cyprinodon macularius*), White River spinedace (*Lepidomeda albivallis*), and Railroad Valley springfish (*Crenichthys baileyi*).

What types of adverse environmental effects might result from the genetically *engineered organism?*

The adverse environmental effects that have been hypothesized or observed for non-transgenic goldfish introduced into the United States are likely to be similar to those exhibited by transgenic goldfish released into the environment. That is, goldfish have been documented to: exhibit competitive advantages over native fishes, including endangered species (Moyle 1976); hybridize with related species, such as the common carp (*Cyprinus carpio*; Trautman 1981); and alter aquatic vegetation and water conditions (Richardson et al. 1995).

An example of the first of these is that transgenic goldfish with the AFP gene are likely to maintain a competitive advantage over some native species if notable, periodic temperature decreases represent a demographically limiting factor for fish populations in those geographic areas. In many areas of the United States, water temperature is a limiting factor for fish distribution. These conditions can be lethal to many fishes including goldfish, and mortalities from "superchill" are frequently reported for species such as the Atlantic salmon (Maclean et al. 1995, Martinez et al. 1996). Goldfish eggs injected with AFP genes produced offspring that were significantly more tolerant of low temperatures than controls (Wang et al. 1995). The "acquired" ability to withstand those types of "ecological crunches" may afford transgenic goldfish a competitive (demographic) advantage over other species (see also below).

Potential adverse effects that might result from the intentional or unintentional release of transgenic goldfish can outlined as follows.

Proliferation of the Transgene

The transgene may move to a related species via hybridization (e.g., goldfish-carp hybrids) or to wild populations by introgression.

Behavior and Life History Modification

Because all transgenes (by design) modify some characteristic of the target organism, transgenic organisms are expected to outperform their non-transgenic counterparts during at least some life history stage under some ecological conditions. One example of how this might result in unforeseen consequences is addressed in the so-called "Trojan gene hypothesis" (Muir and Howard 1999). Many animals (including Atlantic salmon) exhibit mate selection based on male body size. Transgenic males exhibiting larger than average adult body size, as a result of a growth hormone transgene for example, may have a mating advantage over their wild counterparts. Thus, the frequency of the transgene may increase rapidly in the wild population. However, it is generally assumed that the biological load imposed by a transgene will eventually result in a net disadvantage to the genetically modified animal thus keeping the transgene in check. For example, in transgenic medaka, Oryzias latipes, transgenic young exhibited lower fitness than the non-transgenic young. Under certain conditions, the introgression of the transgene into the wild population would cause the ultimate collapse of both the wild and transgenic populations.

Range Expansion and Increase of Invasiveness

Some transgenes such as those coding for the production of AFP may well allow escaped animals to occupy colder climes than their current range. Further, these fish may be able to remain active during cold weather while native species are dormant, thereby depleting both habitat and forage. Goldfish, for example, are already widespread and considered a nuisance in many areas. Freeze-resistant animals could potentially overwhelm many aquatic habitats. The propensity of goldfish to hybridize with carp could allow the migration of this trait into that species, thereby exacerbating the problem.

What are the pathways for proliferation of those risks?

Proliferation of risk associated with gene introgression from transgenic __and__ non-indigenous (currently used, non-transgenic) fish:

The amount of risk associated with gene introgression is a function of the scope of the release, the number of escaped animals, the number of potentially affected native species, and the interrelation of at least four population variables: reproductive potential of escaped individuals, frequency of introgression of the modified genes, fitness of the introgressed individuals, and potential demographic decline due to the genetic load of introgressed genes.

The reproductive potential of escaped individuals is based on: (1) the survival rate and fertility of the individuals, and (2) environmental conditions affecting reproduction in the affected ecosystem, such as length of spawning season and available spawning habitat. The frequency with which introgressed genes will spread and increase within the population is related to gene flow. Several models are available to estimate this process. Despite the prediction that introgressed individuals will exhibit lower fitness than non-introgressed individuals, not all new genetic modifications will be maladaptive. Regarding the genetic load of introgressed genes, natural selection is expected to remove maladaptive genes from a population; however, depending on the severity of the maladaptation, the number of generations required for this process can be very large, and an introgressed population may crash before the process is completed.

Proliferation of risk associated with introduction of triploid fish:

The sterility offered by inducing triploidy in some aquatic species reduces concerns about a modified organism escaping and mating with other fish. In many cases, this will mean that aquaculture of a triploid (three sets of chromosomes in contrast to the typically occurring diploid) transgenic species will likely pose less environmental risk than similar aquaculture of fertile non-transgenic species. However, the use of triploidy does not eliminate all environmental risks and its ability to ensure environmental safety is complicated by three factors. First, the effectiveness of triploidy induction varies among species and the methods used. Second, although triploids are functionally sterile, the males may exhibit spawning behavior with fertile diploid females, leading to decreased reproductive success of the fertile diploid females. Third, in cases where large numbers of individuals are released, sufficient numbers of sterile triploids may survive and grow for an indeterminate number of years beyond the normal life span to pose heightened competition with diploid conspecifics or other species.

Proliferation of risk associated with unexpected survival and persistence of escaped or intentionally released transgenic and non-native (non-transgenic) fish:

Despite familiarity with the unmodified organism, there remains some amount of risk associated with the unexpected survival and persistence of escaped or intentionally released transgenic and non-native (non-transgenic) fish. Once colonized or persistent in new habitats, there may be resulting impacts in native population ecosystems not adapted to the presence of the species. This may also lead to the possible loss of some species.

What types of positive environmental impacts might occur because of this use?

No significant positive environmental effects are envisioned through use of transgenic goldfish containing an AFP gene.

What is the rationale for using the genetically engineered organism, including its advantages vis-a-vis alternatives?

The expected advantage of inserting an AFP gene into goldfish is development of a more cold-tolerant brood stock of aquarium and baitfish. Cold tolerance would be desirable in backyard garden ponds in colder climates because it would reduce winter mortality.

2.   Relevant regulatory agencies, regulatory authority and legal measures

The regulatory process for genetically engineered goldfish would be similar to that described in the growth-enhanced Salmon case study (No. I) from the FDA and some of the Department of Interior statutes. Since there would not be net pens and goldfish are not marine, NMFS and ACE would not be involved.

EPA also has authority under the Toxic Substances Control Act to regulate animals, including genetically engineered animals, when they are used for a purpose not excluded under section 3 of the Act. Further information on TSCA regulations and biotechnology products can be found in this report in the Bioremediation and Biosensing using Bacteria case study and the EPA website.

REFERENCES

Berg, L. S. 1949a. Freshwater fishes of the U.S.S.R. and adjacent countries. Vol. 2. Academy of Sciences of the U.S.S.R. Zoological Institute. Guide to the fauna of the U.S.S.R. 29. 1964 translation by Israel program for scientific translations. 496 pp.

Cheng, C. H. 1998. Evolution of the diverse antifreeze proteins. Curr. Opin. Genet Dev. 8:715-20.

Cohen, A.N. 2000. Nonindigenous organisms in the aquarium industry that have been released into U.S. waters. [www.mcbi.org/caulerpa/invaders.html]

Courtenay, W. R. Jr., and D. A. Hensley. 1980. Special problems associated with monitoring exotic species. Pages 281-307 in C. H. Hocutt and J. R. Stauffer Jr., editors. Biological monitoring of fish. Lexington Books. Lexington, Mass.

Davies, P. L. F., G. L.; Hew, C. L. 1999. Pages 61-80 *In* K. B. Storey (ed.), Environmental Stress and Gene Regulation. Bios Scientific Publishers Ltd, Oxford, UK.

Davies, P. L., and C. L. Hew 1990. Biochemistry of fish antifreeze proteins. Faseb. J. 4:2460-8.

Davies, P. L. E., K. V.; Fletcher, G. L. 1993., p. 279-291. *In* T. P. H. Mommsen, P. W., (ed.), Fish Biochemistry and Molecular Biology, vol. 2. Elsevier, New York, NY.

Deacon, J. E., C. Hubbs, and B. J. Zahuranec. 1964. Some effects of introduced fishes on the native fish fauna of southern Nevada. Copeia 1964(2):384-388.

Deng, G., D. W. Andrews, and R. A. Laursen 1997. Amino acid sequence of a new type of antifreeze protein, from the longhorn sculpin *Myoxocephalus octodecimspinosis* FEBS Lett. 402:17-20.

Deng, G., and R. A. Laursen 1998. Isolation and characterization of an antifreeze protein from the longhorn sculpin, *Myoxocephalus octodecimspinosis*. Biochem. Biophys. Acta. 1388:305-14.

Du, S. J., Z. Y. Gong, G. L. Fletcher, M. A. Shears, M. J. King, D. R. Idler, and C. L. Hew 1992. Growth enhancement in transgenic Atlantic salmon by the use of an "all fish" chimeric growth hormone gene construct. Biotechnology (N Y). 10:176-81.

Fletcher, G. L. G., S. V.; Davies, P. L.; Gong, Z. Ewart, K. V.; Hew, C. L. 1988., p. 239-265. *In* H. O. P. Pörtner, R. C., (ed.), Cold Ocean Physiology. University Press, Cambridge, UK

Garling, D., S. Dann, T. Edsall. T. Grischke, S. Miller, and L. Ramseyer. 1995. Status and potential of Michigan natural resources. Michigan State University Extension Ag Experiment Station Special Reports, No. 74. Michigan Agricultural Experiment Station, East Lansing, Michigan.

Hew, C., R. Poon, F. Xiong, S. Gauthier, M. Shears, M. King, P. Davies, and G. Fletcher 1999. Liver-specific and seasonal expression of transgenic Atlantic salmon harboring the winter flounder antifreeze protein gene. Transgenic Res. 8:405-14.

Hew, C. L., P. L. Davies, and G. Fletcher 1992. Antifreeze protein gene transfer in Atlantic salmon. Mol. Mar. Biol. Biotechnol. 1:309-17.

Howells, R.G. 1992. Guide to identification of harmful and potentially harmful fishes, shellfishes and aquatic plants prohibited in Texas. Texas Parks and Wildlife Department Special Publication, Austin, Texas. 182 pages.

Jonsson, E., J. I. Johnsson, and B. T. Bjornsson 1996. Growth hormone increases predation exposure of rainbow trout. Proc. R. Soc. Lond., B Biol. Sci. 263:647-51.

Lassuy, D.R. 1995. Introduced species as a factor in extinction and endangerment of native fish species.

Maclean, N., D. W. Williams, and F. L. Lavender. 1995. Molecular biology in fish, fisheries and aquaculture. An international symposium. Fisheries Society of the British Isles, Plymouth, UK.

Martinez, R., M. P. Estrada, J. Berlanga, I. Guillen, O. Hernandez, E. Cabrera, R. Pimentel, R. Morales, F. Herrera, A. Morales, J. C. Pina, Z. Abad, V. Sanchez, P. Melamed, R. Lleonart, and J. de la Fuente 1996. Growth enhancement in transgenic tilapia by ectopic expression of tilapia growth hormone. Mol. Mar. Biol. Biotechnol. 5:62-70.

Moyle, P. B. 1976b. Fish introduction in California: history and impact on native fishes. Biological Conservation 9:101-118.

Muir, W. M., and R. D. Howard 1999. Possible ecological risks of transgenic organism release when transgenes affect mating success: sexual selection and the Trojan gene hypothesis. Proc. Natl. Acad. Sci. USA. 96:13853-6.

Richardson, M. J., F. G. Whoriskey, and L. H. Roy. 1995. Turbidity generation and biologica impacts of an exotic fish *Carassius auratus*, introduced into shallow seasonally anoxic ponds. Journal of Fish Biology 47:576-585.
Trautman, M. B. 1981. The fishes of Ohio. Ohio State University Press, Columbus, OH.

U.S. Fish and Wildlife Service. 1994. White River spinedace, *Lepidomeda albivallis*, recovery plan. U.S. Fish and Wildlife Service, Portland, Oregon. 45 pages.

Wang, R.X., P.J. Zhang, Z. Gong, and C.L. Hew. 1995. Molecular Marine Biology and Biotechnology 4:20-26.

Zhang, P. J., M. Hayat, C. Joyce, L. I. Gonzalez-Villasenor, C. M. Lin, R. A. Dunham, T. T. Chen, and D. A. Powers 1990. Gene transfer, expression and inheritance of pRSV-rainbow trout-GH cDNA in the common carp, *Cyprinus carpio* (Linnaeus). Mol. Reprod. Dev. 25:3-13.

Zhao, Z., G. Deng, Q. Lui, and R. A. Laursen. 1998. Cloning and sequencing of cDNA encoding the LS-12 antifreeze protein in the longhorn sculpin, *Myoxocephalus octodecimspinosis*. Biochem. Biophys. Acta. 1382:177-80.

CASE STUDY No. II

Bt-MAIZE

Overview

This case study examines maize (corn) that was genetically engineered to produce a protein that is toxic to certain insects. A gene from the bacterium *Bacillus thuringiensis* (Bt), which produces the toxin, was modified and added to the corn. Promoters (genetic material that initiates transcription of the gene) and terminators (genetic material which stops transcription of the gene) were also added, from a virus and another bacterium, respectively, which are known plant pathogens. The Bt-maize considered in this case study is referred to as MON810.

MON810 was subject to regulation primarily by Environmental Protection Agency (EPA) under the Federal Insecticide, Fungicide and Rodenticide Act (FIFRA), 7 U.S.C. §§ 136-136y, Federal Food, Drug and Cosmetic Act, (FFDCA), 21 U.S.C. §§371-379d, and by the Animal and Plant Health Inspection Service (APHIS) under the Federal Plant Pest Act (FPPA), 7 U.S.C. §§ 150aa-150jj, and the Plant Quarantine Act (PQA), 7 U.S.C. §§ 151-164a, 166-167, as amended. EPA issued an Experimental Use Permit for field testing MON810; and it later registered MON810 for commercial sale and use subject to a time limit and specified conditions (which subsequently have been strengthened) and exempted the pesticidal portion from the requirement of having a residue limit (tolerance) in food. APHIS authorized field testing of MON810 and subsequently granted it non-regulated status, i.e., APHIS determined that MON810 is not subject to APHIS' regulatory oversight based on current knowledge. APHIS conducted an Environmental Assessment under National Environmental Policy Act (NEPA), 42 U.S.C. §§ 4321-4370e, on the basis of which it issued a finding of no significant impact on the environment (FONSI) and also concluded that there were no issues under the Endangered Species Act (ESA), 16 U.S.C. §§ 1531-1544.

1.   Description of Proposed Organism and Its

Maize or corn, *Zea mays* ssp. *mays*, is a member of the Poaceae (grass family) and is grown for forage, silage, but most notably for its grain, which is borne in ears (or cobs). *Zea mays* is a wind-pollinated, monoecious, annual species with imperfect flowers. This means that spatially separate tassels (male flowers) and silks (female flowers) are found on the same plant, a feature that limits inbreeding. A large variety of types are known to exist (*e.g.*, dent, field, flint, flour, pop, sweet) and have been selected for specific seed characteristics through standard breeding techniques (Hitchcock, 1971). Maize cultivars and landraces are known to be diploid (2n = 20), that is they contain a set of 10 paired chromosomes which contain the DNA or genetic material, and are interfertile to a large degree. However, some evidence for genetic incompatibility exists within the species (*e.g.*, popcorn x dent crosses; Mexican maize landraces x Chalco teosinte). *Zea mays* has been domesticated for its current use by selection of key agronomic characters, such as non-shattering rachis (ear), grain yield and resistance to pests (Kiesselbach, 1949). The origin of corn is thought to be in Mexico or Central America, based largely on archaeological evidence of early cob-like maize in indigenous cultures approximately 7200 years ago. These issues are considered when examining the potential for outcrossing / pollination between a crop and its wild relatives.

The Monsanto Company has developed a genetically modified line of field corn (also referred to as "maize") that produces a protein throughout the corn plant that is toxic to certain insect species. The resulting plant line is identified commercially as "MON810," and the crop is one of several transgenic corn varieties generally referred to as Bt-corn or Bt-maize. The substance produced through the genetic alteration is identified as d-endotoxin or the Cry1Ab protein.

MON 810 was developed by co-transforming corn with two vectors, one carrying a synthetic *cry1Ab* gene and the second bearing the two herbicide resistance genes (*EPSPS* and *gox*). The genetic alteration that produced MON810 incorporated a truncated form of the syntheticform *cry1Ab* gene from the bacterium, *Bacillus thuringiensis* subsp. *kurstaki*, into a Hi-II type corn line (see details below). *B. thuringiensis* subsp. *kurstaki* is a common soil bacterium that has been isolated worldwide. The modified *cry1Ab* gene maintained its ability to produce the δ-endotoxin in plant tissues at levels that are toxic to certain lepidopteran insects. The *cry1Ab* gene is expressed from an enhanced 35S promoter (E35S) derived from cauliflower mosaic virus, a known plant pest, and is joined to the nopaline synthase 3' transcription terminator, NOS 3', derived from *Agrobacterium tumefaciens*, a plant pathogenic bacterium. These genetic elements (promoter, gene, termination sequence) are all necessary for proper expression of the introduced trait (*i.e.*, Bt protein) in the maize plant.

The corn line that was the recipient of the added genes is a derivative of the A188 and B73 inbred lines of corn. These are publicly available inbred lines developed by the University of Minnesota and Iowa State University, respectively. Designated "Hi-II", the recipient material is approximately 50:50 of the two lines (Armstrong et al, 1991). The material was developed to have a higher regeneration potential (from the combination of genes from A188 and B73) along with acceptable commercial performance in hybrids (from B73).

These genes were introduced into corn line MON810 via microprojectile bombardment transformation, wherein microscopic beads of gold are coated with DNA and physically forced into maize cells such that the DNA can integrate with the maize DNA / chromosomes in the nucleus. The two plasmid vectors were introduced by microprojectile bombardment into cultured plant cells. This is a well-characterized procedure that has been used for over a decade for introducing various genes into plant genomes. Southern blot analysis and Mendelian genetics

2

data demonstrate that the introduced gene is stably integrated into the corn genome and stably inherited. Glyphosate-tolerant transformed cells were selected, then cultured in tissue culture medium for regeneration of whole plants.

No marker genes (*i.e.*, *npt II, C4 EPSPS*) are expressed in the subsequent generations of corn plants / progeny from this transformation. Through traditional breeding practices, the marker genes (*i.e.*, antibiotic and herbicide resistance) have been segregated out of the final commercial hybrid (*i.e.*, MON810) and are no longer present in the genome or DNA of the plant as demonstrated by molecular analyses.

Southern analysis indicated one integrated DNA segment which included a truncated copy of the cry1A(b) gene, inserted without rearrangement. The corn line has been crossed into several diverse corn genotypes for 4 generations and the protection against ECB has been maintained. MON810 was derived from the third generation of backcrossing and therefore the single insert appears to be stably inherited.

MON810 Bt-maize was developed for control of various insect pest species that cause serious pest problems in corn: corn earworm (CEW), European corn borer (ECB) and Southwestern corn borer (SWCB). Monsanto's petition to APHIS only claimed that MON810 was developed for control of ECB. These insect species feed on corn causing plant damage that ultimately results in decreased quality and quantity of yields. During field testing of plants of corn line MON810, ECB infestations were significantly reduced as compared to non-transgenic control plants.

Monsanto markets MON810 Bt-maize throughout the corn growing areas of the United States that include the primary Corn Belt of the Midwest, Great Plains and significant acreage in the southern states, including areas that also raise cotton. The grain harvested from MON810 is used in animal feed and processed into numerous food products for human consumption and non-food uses. The harvested product is used both in domestic foods and feed products and is exported to numerous foreign countries. Most corn is stored and marketed as a bulk commodity, and this practice means that, absent special handling procedures, transgenic corn would normally be mixed with conventionally bred types of corn.

2.   Relevant Regulatory Agencies, Regulatory Authority and Legal Measures

Two federal agencies, EPA's Office of Pesticide Programs (OPP) and USDA's Animal and Plant Health Inspection Service (APHIS), share the primary responsibility for regulating Bt-maize, and other "plant-pesticides." Whenever claims are made for reducing damage caused by pests, the product becomes a "pesticide" subject to EPA oversight. EPA registers and regulates pesticides, including the plant-pesticides, genetically engineered plants and products (GEOPs) that contain a gene for controlling a pest, such as an insect, or plant disease organism (FIFRA

2(u)). EPA's review includes an assessment of the potential impacts on human health, as well as impacts on non-target wildlife and the broader environment. It is well established that, because FIFRA is the functional equivalent of NEPA, EPA is not required to prepare an Environmental Assessment ("EA"), an Environmental Impact Statement ("EIS"), or a Programmatic EIS ("PEIS") when registering pesticides pursuant to the procedures established in FIFRA. Environmental Defense Fund v. EPA, 489 F.2d 1247, 1256-57 (D.C. Cir. 1973).

If there are residues of a plant-pesticide in or on food or feed, EPA would also be involved in establishing maximum limits (tolerances) for the amount of residues of such pesticide in food. USDA / APHIS analyzes genetically engineered organisms for potential impact on agriculture, as well as for impacts on the broader environment. APHIS regulates organisms; products that are not viable are not covered under APHIS regulations 7 CFR part 340. APHIS regulates the introduction (importation, interstate movement, or release into the environment) of certain genetically engineered organisms and products under authority granted by the Plant Protection Act (PPA), 7 U.S.C. §§ 7701-7772.

In addition, the U.S. Department of the Interior (DOI) and the Food and Drug Administration (FDA) have consultative and regulatory roles. DOI has a consultation role under the Endangered Species Act and Migratory Bird Treaty Act. FDA evaluates information provided by developers during a consultation process to ensure that human and animal food safety issues or other regulatory issues (*e.g.*, labeling) are resolved prior to commercial distribution.

Statutory authority

EPA

EPA administers two statutes that contain authority to regulate Bt-maize and other plant-pesticides: FIFRA and the FFDCA. The Food Quality Protection Act (FQPA), that amended both FIFRA and FFDCA, was enacted shortly after MON810 was conditionally registered. In addition, the ESA and the federal Migratory Bird Treaty Act (MBTA), 16 U.S.C. §§ 703-712, apply to EPA. EPA fulfills its obligations in these respects in consultation with the DOI. EPA's Field and External Affairs Division serves as a contact point or informal or formal consultations with DOI where listed species are considered as possibly affected. Consultations were not considered necessary in the case of MON810.

1. Federal Insecticide, Fungicide and Rodenticide Act (FIFRA)

FIFRA defines a "pesticide" as "any substance or mixture of substances intended for preventing, destroying, repelling, or mitigating any pest . . . ." (FIFRA 2(u)). Unless it is exempted or falls within certain minor exceptions, under FIFRA, a pesticide may be sold or distributed in commerce only if EPA has issued either an experimental use permit or a registration for the product (7 U.S.C. § 136). Plants themselves are exempted from FIFRA oversight (40 CFR 152.20). In general, EPA may approve the sale and distribution of a pesticide only if the Agency determines that use of the product will not cause "unreasonable adverse effects on the environment." FIFRA defines "unreasonable adverse effects on the environment" to mean (1) any unreasonable risk to man or the environment, taking into account the economic, social, and environmental costs and benefits of the use of a pesticide, or (2) in the case of a pesticide that requires approval under FFDCA, a human dietary risk from residues from a use which causes a pesticide residue in food that is not "safe." (FIFRA 2(bb)) The latter portion of the standard is a "risk-only" standard, while the first part of the FIFRA standard involves balancing risk and benefits. The proponent of the pesticide use bears the burden of showing that the pesticide meets the applicable statutory standards. The statute authorizes EPA to establish requirements for information that an applicant must satisfy in order for the Agency to consider its request to sell or distribute the pesticide.

Under FIFRA, EPA may establish requirements concerning the composition, packaging, and labeling of a pesticide. In particular, the labeling of a pesticide may specify the manner in which the pesticide is allowed to be used. FIFRA prohibits the use of a pesticide in a manner inconsistent with its labeling. Once a product is registered, FIFRA requires the registrant to report to EPA any information concerning the unreasonable adverse effects of the pesticide on the environment (FIFRA 6(a)(2)). FIFRA also authorizes EPA to issue "data call-in notices," which require the registrants of a pesticide to develop and submit any additional information the Agency needs to evaluate the pesticide to determine whether the registration may remain in effect. For MON810 Bt-maize, a time-limited registration was enacted to provide for a reassessment of the conditions of registration after five years.

Because the development of plant-pesticides represented a novel approach to pest control and a new technology, a provision for re-evaluation of the active ingredients was included at the time of registration. This provides for the reassessment of the status of certain Bt-crops (*i.e.*, corn and cotton) and to determine if further data will be required to ensure that an adequate risk assessment can be performed. Any outstanding data requirements would have to be fulfilled in order to support the renewal of the existing registrations. The currently registered Bt-corn crops all have registrations expiring in September, 2001.

2. Federal Food, Drug, and Cosmetic Act (FFDCA) The FFDCA makes unlawful the sale and distribution in interstate commerce of adulterated food. Food is defined broadly, and includes both food for humans and animals. Food is "adulterated" if it contains the residue of a "pesticide chemical" for which EPA has not established either a "tolerance" or an exemption from the requirement of a tolerance. (Almost all "pesticides" are "pesticide chemicals".)

The FFDCA authorizes EPA to establish a tolerance for a pesticide if the "residue in or on food is safe." Similarly, EPA may establish an exemption from the requirement of a tolerance if the Administrator determines that the exemption is "safe." In 1996, the Food Quality Protection Act amended the FFDCA to define "safe" to mean that "the Administrator has determined that there is a reasonable certainty that no harm will result from aggregate exposure to the pesticide chemical residue, including all anticipated dietary exposures and all other exposures for which there is reliable information."[1] Any person may petition the EPA to establish a tolerance or an exemption from the requirement of a tolerance for a pesticide and its residues in food; the law authorizes EPA to require information in support of the petition to show that the tolerance or exemption would be safe.

Implementing regulations

EPA has defined a "plant-pesticide" as "a pesticidal substance produced in a living plant and the genetic material necessary for the production of the substance, where the substance is intended for use in the living plant."[2] In other words, EPA regulates the pesticidal substance - the pesticidal substance produced in a living plant and the nucleic acid sequence (DNA) or genetic material necessary for directing synthesis of such a substance - but not the plant itself.

Experimental use permits. EPA=s regulation of the pre-registration sale or distribution of a pesticide occurs primarily through its experimental use permit (EUP) process. The Agency will typically allow small scale field tests (less than 10 acres of land or 1 acre of water, per pest being examined) following notification of the EPA that a GEOP is being evaluated in a field situation and some methods of confinement are being instituted. If a larger field test is planned, then an EUP is required. The Agency approves testing only for the purpose of gathering data to support an application for registration, and only for an area sufficient to collect reliable information. Typically, EPA does not approve field testing of GEOPs for more than 5000 acres.

In addition, if the experimental design involves the production of food for distribution in interstate commerce, a tolerance, temporary tolerance or exemption must be established. A person may avoid the need for a tolerance by destroying the crop treated with the unregistered pesticide; a "crop-destruct" requirement would then be included in the EUP.

Granting an EUP is contingent on satisfactory data to support a risk assessment and a finding that the proposed experimental use will not result in unreasonable adverse effects on the environment. The data required to support a request for an EUP are detailed in 40 CFR Part 158

---

[1]EPA initially registered and established tolerances for MON810 before the FQPA amendments. But, because the MON810 registration expires in 2001, EPA will be reevaluating both the registration and the tolerance exemption under the new statutory standard created by FQPA, as the Agency decides whether to renew its approvals.

and as discussed under Section 3, EPA's Hazard Identification, Risk Assessment and Regulatory Review of Bt-Maize. Site visits to the experimental plots can and have been performed, resulting in plot destruction in one instance for failure to follow the conditions established in the EUP (this example did not involve Bt-maize).

Registration. Like an EUP, a person must apply for registration of a pesticide. An application for registration typically requires substantially more data than an EUP. The data requirements depend on the type of product for which registration is sought. See 40 CFR Part 158. EPA regulations describe labeling and packaging requirements for pesticide products. See 40 CFR Parts 156 and 157. On a case-by-case basis, EPA may impose additional requirements or conditions on registration for individual products. For example, EPA may issue a "seed increase registration" which allows a registrant to plant a GEOP for the purpose of producing seed for propagation and future sale. The genetically altered seeds, however, could not be sold until a new "full-scale" registration was approved. If the identical *cry* gene (as in MON810) encoding the insecticidal protein was transformed into another crop species, a new registration or an amendment to the existing registration would likely would be required for sale and distribution of this plant-pesticide.

Tolerances. The tolerance process starts with the submission of a petition to establish a tolerance or an exemption from the requirement of a tolerance. The petitioner must provide toxicity data related to human health comparable to that to support a registration. Environmental and non-target effects are not considered within a food tolerance petition. When EPA receives a petition, the Agency publishes in the Federal Register a notice of receipt of the petition, together with a summary of the petition's contents. Following review of the petition and any comments from the public, EPA may publish a final rule establishing the tolerance or exemption, provided that the available information demonstrates that the action would comply with the statutory standard. Once the pesticidal substance is assessed for its toxicity to man, a determination is made to provide a tolerance limit for pesticide residues or to exempt the pesticidal substance from the requirement. Any exemption from the requirement of a tolerance is tied to the levels of pesticidal substance (*e.g.*, Cry protein) expressed and accumulated within the plant as compared to the levels of test substance utilized in the toxicity studies. That is, if the levels of active ingredient or pesticidal substance accumulate above the level tested in the toxicity studies, then the tolerance exemption would not be supported by the data and such studies would have to be repeated with increased levels to maintain the food tolerance (*i.e.*, distribution of the crop into the food supply).

USDA/APHIS

The USDA's Animal and Plant Health Inspection Service (APHIS) has the authority to regulate the importation, interstate movement, and release into the environment of plant pests and other articles to prevent direct or indirect injury, disease, or damage to plants or plant products. APHIS regulates genetically engineered organisms under authority granted by the Plant Protection Act (PPA), (7 U.S.C. §§ 7701-7772) which states "it is the responsibility of the Secretary to facilitate exports, imports, and interstate commerce in agricultural products and other commodities that pose a risk of harboring plant pests or noxious weeds in ways that will reduce, to the extent practical, as determined by the Secretary, the risk of disseminating plant pests or noxious weeds." A genetically engineered organism is deemed a "regulated article" if either the donor organism, recipient organism, vector or vector agent used in engineering the organism belongs to one of the taxa listed in 7 CFR Part 340.2 of the regulations, or if it is not identified taxonomically. That is to say, the development of genetically engineered plants using biological vectors or regulatory sequences derived from plant pathogenic sources serves as a regulatory trigger, initiating an evaluation process to assure that there is not a plant pest risk. Importantly, products of genetic engineering may still be regulated by APHIS, even if not developed using a plant pest, if there is a reason to believe that the product itself might pose a plant pest risk. Field testing is typically used to demonstrate that genetically engineered crops exhibit the expected biological properties and to demonstrate that, although they may be derived using components from plant pests, they do not possess plant pest characteristics.

The PPA, effective as of June 22, 2000, replaces the Federal Plant Pest Act (FPPA) and Plant Quarantine Act (PQA) as APHIS's regulatory authority for genetically engineered organisms. The present case study focuses on regulatory authority and activities at the time of de-regulation of MON 810, i.e., authority granted by the FPPA and PQA. APHIS is presently analyzing whether there are changes in authorities or potential for change based on the new PPA.

Movement, importation, and field testing (introduction). Prior to the introduction of a regulated article, a person is required under '§340.1 of the regulations to either (1) notify APHIS in accordance with 7 CFR 340.3 or (2) obtain a permit in accordance with 7 CFR 340.4. Prior to April 1993, the only regulatory option for the planned introduction of transgenic plants covered by APHIS regulations was the permit. Regulations stipulate that once a complete permit request has been submitted, APHIS has 120 days in which to reach a decision whether to issue or deny a permit.

The early 1990's were marked by a rapid increase in the number of field trials in the United States of transgenic plants and plant-associated microbes, and there was an associated rise in permit requests, as these organisms were subject to APHIS regulatory authority to control articles that posed a plant pest risk. After the first six years of evaluating permits and considering the results of field trials under permit, experience demonstrated that criteria and performance standards could be defined for certain field tests that do not present novel plant pest risks. This gave rise to a new option, the notification, effective in April of 1993. Transgenic plants which raised certain safety issues, for example pharmaceutical-producing plants, plants transformed with genes of unknown function, or plants expressing sequences from human or animal viruses, were not eligible for the new option. The notification option originally covered six major crops, including corn, and was modified in May of 1997 to cover nearly all plants. The notification option represents a simpler, streamlined application and review process for importation, interstate movement and field testing. Notifications are logged into the USDA database, reviewed by one of the scientific staff for qualification, completeness (see section 4 for Data Requirements) , and then a recommendation is sent to the appropriate State department of agriculture for review. If the State concurs with an APHIS recommendation of approval, an acknowledgment is then issued to the applicant. The regulations stipulate that the entire process will take no longer than 30 days from receipt of the notification.

The notification option (7 CFR 340.3) requires that the introduction meet specified eligibility criteria and performance standards. The eligibility criteria impose limitations on the types of genetic modification that qualify for notification, and the performance standards impose limitations on how the introduction may be conducted. These performance standards, compliance with which is subject to APHIS inspection, help to assure confinement of the regulated articles (see sections 5 and 7). Confinement is of central importance in APHIS's approach to the regulation of field testing. Confinement ensures that any environmental impact will be negligible because the article will not move beyond the field site and will not persist at the site beyond the intended duration of the test. All crop plants and most plants that are not listed as noxious weeds, as described in regulations at 7 CFR 360 under the Federal Noxious Weed Act at 7 U.S.C. § 2809, can be field tested under notification. Nearly 99 per cent of all field tests, importations, and interstate movements of engineered plants are performed under this system. The three major steps APHIS takes in this process are to: (1) evaluate relevant information (both that submitted by the permit applicant and that gathered by APHIS from other sources); (2) notify and consult with regulatory officials in States where the applicant proposes to field test; and (3) reach a decision as to whether to acknowledge or deny the notification.

In the particular case of corn, performance standards were established that would maintain physical isolation of the plants and seeds.

Petition for determination of non-regulated status. As testing of one of these regulated articles proceeds, an applicant gathers information typically to establish for him/herself that the product has the new intended property, and also gathers information to demonstrate that the organism is not a plant pest risk. Evidence for safety relies in part on data that demonstrate that the engineered plant is biologically equivalent to a corresponding non-engineered line, with the exception of the intended new trait(s). When enough information is gathered, the applicant may petition APHIS for what is called a Determination of Non-regulated Status.

When APHIS gets a petition, the receipt of the application is announced in the Federal Register and copies are made available to the public (see Section 8, Public Involvement and Transparency). The announcement marks the start of a 60-day public comment period on the petition, after which any comments are considered in the final determination and Environmental

Assessment (EA). The EA is conducted pursuant to the National Environmental Policy Act (NEPA). Since mid-1999, in addition to the 60-day comment period on the petition itself, notice of the availability of an EA is also published and public comments are solicited and accepted on the EA for a 30-day period. During the remaining 180 days, consultations are made as necessary with other agencies having expertise, the determination document is prepared, and the completed decision documents are subject to legal review.

In general, the petitioner has to supply data and supporting information to indicate that the product does not present a plant pest risk at any time during the 180-day assessment process. The APHIS assessment relies on data and other information that demonstrate that, with the exception of the deliberately introduced trait, the genetically engineered line appears to be the same as a non-engineered parental line with respect to a suite of agronomic traits. If this is true, and if there is sufficient familiarity with the introduced trait, the recipient plant, and the environment, APHIS can determine with a high degree of confidence that the engineered plant is no more likely to be a plant pest than a traditionally bred plant. Likewise, issues and risks that are not science-based, such as consumer acceptance and marketability of genetically engineered products, are not a part of the APHIS analysis.

Once a Determination of Non-regulated Status is issued, the new variety may be developed further through traditional breeding, produced, marketed, distributed, and grown without any other special oversight on the part of APHIS. However, before some plants can be used commercially, additional reviews may be necessary by the Environmental Protection Agency and the Food and Drug Administration. For example, the consultation process between FDA and Monsanto for MON 810 maize was not completed until 1997, and so the product was not used as food or feed before that date.before

Consideration by APHIS of a broad range of environmental issues is mandated under NEPA, which addresses the general decision making process for all government actions. In considering the broad range of possible impacts under NEPA, APHIS expertise overlaps with that of other federal agencies, namely with EPA for a host of environmental concerns such as non-target effects, and worker exposure, and with the National Institutes of Health and FDA for potential negative impacts on animals and humans.

The Bt-corn line MON 810, due to the presence of sequences derived from plant pests listed in 7 CFR Part 340.2, clearly meets the definition of a regulated article and is subject to APHIS regulation. All seven field test releases were conducted after APHIS approval from 1992 through 1996 when Monsanto filed a petition for non-regulated status on January 17, 1996. Following a review of the petition, a deficiency letter was sent to Monsanto to obtain additional information and clarification. Such letters are routine and are sent in response to virtually every petition, reflecting the thoroughness of the APHIS review. Upon receipt of the additional information, the petition was announced in the Federal Register and made available for public reading and comments (see section on "Transparency and Public Involvement"). A determination of non-regulated status under 7 CFR 340 was granted for MON 810 on March 15, 1996. APHIS decision documents are available at http://www.aphis.usda.gov/biotech.

In the case of MON810, Monsanto submitted a petition in January 1996 asking APHIS to extend to MON 810 the same determination of non-regulated status that APHIS had granted August 22, 1995, to a very similar maize line, MON80100 (APHIS Petition 95-093-01P). In fact, MON 810 had been one of several lines included in petition 95-093-01P, but Monsanto withdrew MON 810 from consideration until it could be more thoroughly characterized. By 1996, the new petition provided the more thorough characterization and documentation of MON810 and another line, MON809, to support the conclusion that these lines posed no plant pest risk and should no longer be considered regulated articles. After careful review of all available data, APHIS published an announcement in the Federal Register on March 15, 1996, stating that "the APHIS determination of non-regulated status of August 22, 1995, applies as well to Monsanto's two new transformed corn lines, MON 809 and Mon 810." Both of the decision documents are available from APHIS (USDA, 1996).

In 1997, APHIS amended its regulations to provide a more formal procedure for developers to seek an extension of a previous determination of non-regulated status (7 CFR 340 Part 340.6). APHIS has also provided a complementary Users' Guide for Extensions at the agency web site (http://www.aphis.usda.gov/biotech/gaddbeg.htm). Under the current system, in place since 1999, APHIS publishes in the Federal Register a notice that it has received a petition for an extension for a determination of non-regulated status. APHIS conducts its analysis and prepares an Environmental Assessment that is then made available to the public for comment during a 30-day period. The agency then considers any comments received from the public before making its final decision and announcing the decision in the Federal Register.

FDA

FDA considers, based on Agency scientist's' evaluation of available information, whether any unresolved issues exist regarding a food derived from a new plant variety that would result in legal action by the Agency if the product were introduced into commerce. Examples of unresolved issues may include, but are not limited to, significantly increased levels of plant toxicants or anti-nutrients, reduction of important nutrients, new allergens, or the presence in the food of an unapproved food additive.

DOI

The Department of Interior (DOI) administers the provisions of the federal MBTA and the ESA, with the Fish and Wildlife Service (FWS) being the sole administering Agency for the MBTA and shared authority for the ESA between DOI/FWS and the National Marine Fisheries

Service (NMFS) at the Department of Commerce (DOC). Under the ESA, any 'take' of a listed species is prohibited unless otherwise exempt or authorized. As appropriate, EPA will contact DOI /FWS or DOC to initiate a consultation through its Field and External Affairs Division when an EPA action may affect a listed species. These consultations involve only the resource agency (FWS or NMFS) and the action Agency or Agencies.

The MBTA prohibits 'take' of migratory birds. However, what qualifies as 'take' varies between the two statutes. Under the ESA, for example, 'take' includes harassment of any species listed as threatened or endangered. Any action that rises to the level of 'take' under the respective statute could be subject to a governmental action or a suit brought by a private citizen. The provisions of ESA and MBTA apply to both genetically engineered species and non-engineered species equally. In the case of MON 810, a determination that no biological impact or affect to listed species would result from registration of this plant-pesticide was made following the Agency's risk assessment. Therefore, no formal consultation was required between EPA and DOI.

Interagency Coordination

Under the Coordinated Framework for the Regulation of Biotechnology published in 1986, EPA and USDA have the major regulatory responsibilities for genetically modified plants with pesticidal properties. EPA's role is to protect human health (both dietary and worker exposure) and the environment. Related to environmental effects for products such as MON810, EPA conducts analyses on ecological effects to non-target species, environmental fate, threatened and endangered species, and insect resistance management. APHIS' authority overlaps considerably with that of other federal agencies, namely EPA, for a host of environmental concerns such as non-target effects. In addition, APHIS is to ensure that the product will not be a threat to agriculture. FDA's role is to protect the food supply and as such shares regulatory responsibility with EPA under the Federal Food, Drug, and Cosmetic Act. Under the FFFDCA, EPA is authorized to establish, modify, or revoke tolerances for pesticide chemical residues on food. Thus, EPA is responsible for establishing maximum allowable residues of the Bt protein produced by the Bt maize that may be present in edible corn. In addition, the Department of the Interior is responsible for potential effects to fish and wildlife and their responsibility overlaps with EPA for ESA and MBTA. Of course, the provisions of NEPA must be followed by the DOI, while EPA / OPP's review of environmental impact is considered as functionally equivalent as that expected from NEPA oversight (although EPA maintains a record keeping and review of implementation function under NEPA guidelines).

Agencies consult with each other as warranted to properly review a new genetically engineered organism. There are currently no regularly scheduled meetings to review submissions that might be made to each Agency, but rather they are dealt with on a case-by-case basis. In many instances the registrants of plant-pesticides have previously been through a review process with the USDA-APHIS biotechnology group, and although the focus of the risk assessment differs between agencies, there is significant overlap in some areas. Dialogue is initiated in those areas of mutual interest, especially in the consideration of non-target impacts, so that both groups benefit from the combined expertise. More recently, an effort is underway to hold scheduled conference calls between the EPA and APHIS when submissions regarding the same regulated article or plant-pesticide are made to both agencies. The timing and frequency of these conferences will be determined by the rate of the review process and the novel aspects of the plant-pesticide at hand. Currently, there is an Herbicide Tolerance Working Group with both EPA and APHIS members and a BT working group is about to begin cooperation. Issues of confidential business information and proper clearance under the statutory guidelines, however, may prohibit free exchange of data or review materials in some instances.

Additionally, scientists from EPA and APHIS regularly attend any relevant SAP (Science Advisory Panel) meetings and scientific workshops, which provide for exchange of ideas and information in areas of mutual interest. The NC-205 (North Central States Committee) meetings are another example of joint efforts wherein the Agencies meet informally to discuss regulatory matters.

USDA/APHIS, FDA, DOI and EPA

1. Endangered Species Act (ESA) and Migratory Bird Treaty Act (MBTA)

The Endangered Species Act (ESA), jointly administered by the Secretaries of the Interior and Commerce, could also affect the use and dispersal of plant-pesticides. The Endangered Species Act requires importers of plants to file declarations, and limits importation to designated ports. 16 U.S.C. §§ 1538(d), (f). Section 7 of the ESA requires any federal Agency to ensure that any action authorized, funded, or carried out by the Agency not jeopardize the continued existence of any endangered or threatened species or adversely modify any critical habitat of such species. Id., at § 1536(a)(2). Thus, each federal Agency must consult with the U.S. Fish and Wildlife Service or the National Marine Fisheries Service, depending on the species, for any action that "may affect" a listed species. If the action is likely to adversely affect a listed species, the appropriate Service issues a Biological Opinion, which may authorize 'take' of fish or wildlife species that is incidental to the action or, if the federal action would otherwise jeopardize the continued existence of the species, offers alternatives to the federal action that will avoid such jeopardy. Id., at § 1536(b). Any take of an endangered or threatened fish or wildlife species unless otherwise authorized is unlawful under the statute. Id., at sec.1538.§ 1538. If the action is likely to adversely affect a listed plant, the situation is somewhat different. Section 9 prohibitions on take do not apply to plants, see id., at § 1538(a)(2), but cautions can be provided in the Biological Opinion on prohibitions against removal or disturbance of plants. Thus, a federal Agency will be held responsible for prohibited acts affecting both wildlife and plants that result from authorization, funding, or other federal action associated with a GEOP.

A Biological Opinion from the Department of Interior Fish and Wildlife Service was issued on December 18, 1986, concerning possible effects of foliar spray of B. t. subsp. kurstaki on threatened and endangered species. Based on difference in exposure routes between foliar spray and expression in plants, APHIS believes that the Biological Opinion is inapplicable, and that re-initiation of consultation is not necessary. The majority of endangered lepidopterans have very restrictive habitat ranges; and their larvae typically feed on specific host plants, none of which include corn or its sexually compatible relatives. An examination of county distribution of endangered lepidopterans shows that, for the most part, they do not occur in agricultural settings where corn is grown.

Additionally, the federal MBTA also requires that any federal action that might impact migratory avian species be minimized or excluded so as not to harm populations.

Voluntary Standards

For most crop plants there are breeders' organizations and seed certifying agencies, some of which are state, regional or national in scope. Compliance with the guidelines proposed by these organizations is necessary if a breeder wants to sell seed as being officially certified. Their oversight, however, is voluntary in the sense that it is not necessary to obtain their certification in order to produce or sell seed. Companies buying crops for processing into foodstuffs may mandate in their contracts that only certified or foundation seed of a particular variety be planted for their use; however, these are not covered by any statute or regulation. Additionally, very little certified maize seed is grown in the U.S. for processing. Most of what is grown as 'certified' is meant for export. In no instance is the scrutiny accorded GE (genetically engineered) crops approached by non-GE voluntary oversight in terms of safety assessment (*i.e.*, toxicity or environmental impact). All crop varieties, regardless of the genetic techniques used to produce them, receive a great deal of review and analysis to meet the demands of producers and consumers.

When the commercial line of a plant species is developed through classical breeding without subsequent transformation (*i.e.*, is non-GE), state seed foundations and crop councils prescribe distances between breeders' lots or fields to ensure a degree of purity from pollen spread / cross hybridization. Guidelines for seed certification are defined by the Association of Official Seed Certifying Agencies (AOSCA) and they are followed by member organizations or agencies. There are also parameters to ensure that the amount of weed seed inadvertently carried with the maize seed is minimal. The percent germination of seed lots is also tested. The details of distances between seeds and the definitions of plant types, etc., may vary state to state. AOSCA defines the number of generations of backcrossing required in generation of a hybrid and what

14

constitutes an inbred line.

Commercial companies follow these guidelines to ensure that their seed is competitive in the marketplace and of general high quality. In some instances this may include outside testing by a state seed foundation or other university associated program to establish seed quality and genetic purity / varietal identity. Presence of disease organisms is also examined in some crops or certain regional situations where a known pathogen is problematic.

A. EPA.3.   Hazard Identification, Risk Assessment, and Regulatory Review of Bt-Maize

EPA

FIFRA requires EPA to consider all relevant factors in reviewing and approving a plant-pesticide for registration. This includes a risk / benefit analysis and any safety assessment to preclude unreasonable adverse effects.

EPA regulatory authority only covers the actions occurring within the borders of the United States and its possessions and territories. If a potential problem existed at the border with another country due to proximity of the GEOP, the Agency could exclude distribution of that plant-pesticide in a defined area (as has been done with other plant-pesticides for reasons of outcrossing to wild relatives). FIFRA § 2(bb) mandates that EPA ensure a reasonable certainty of no harm to man and the environment. This includes the potential for environmental impact to non-target species, such as those wild or feral relatives of crops. If a plant-pesticide were known to result in adverse effects in another country, it is possible that this matter could be considered under a risk / benefit analysis performed in accordance with FIFRA.

EPA's focus in considering these issues is on the statutory determination of unreasonable adverse effects the Agency must make with respect to pesticides, rather than on the engineered plant itself. In particular, these plant-related issues may potentially impact use patterns of pesticides, which are of relevance to the Agency.

1. EPA's hazard identification and risk assessment of Bt-maize.

Product characterization requirements for MON810 included details of the gene source (what organism), DNA and protein sequence data, details of the plasmid (DNA) used in plant transformation (annotated map), method of transformation, the pesticidal substance encoded by the gene, expression levels under field conditions and where in the plant the Cry1Ab endotoxin accumulates, glycosylation of the pesticidal protein (presence / absence and similarity of sugar residues on proteins produced in microbial and plant forms), serological relatedness of plant and microbial forms of Cry1Ab (Western blot and Enzyme Linked ImmunoSorbent Assay), and

15

bioassayed against larvae of the corn ear worm or the European corn borer.

The Agency also required the applicant to explain the use pattern (*i.e.*, will the crop be used for human consumption, animal feed only, ornamental uses, etc.). MON810 is used as a traditional field corn *i.e.*, the whole grain is not directly used by humans for food, although processed products from the grain are used both for human food products, and for non-food items, *e.g.*, wallboard and paper components, adhesives, pharmaceuticals. The majority of harvested MON 810 maize will be used as an animal feed. in human dietary, *e.g.*, starches, fructose, alcohol and non-food items, *e.g.*, wallboard and paper components, adhesives, pharmaceuticals, ethanol fuel additive. The majority of harvested MON810 maize will be used as an animal feed.

Once the product (*i.e.*, the plant and associated pesticidal substance) and its proposed uses are adequately identified by the registration applicant, EPA evaluates the potential hazards of plant-pesticides in two broad areas: human health and environmental effects. Risks to humans and animals via the dietary route (*e.g.*, as food and feed) and to non-target organisms through exposure via water, wind, soil and direct consumption of the GEOP are all considered within the risk assessment. If other routes of potential exposure exist, such as dermal absorption, these risks are also addressed.

Human health. The human health assessment includes the evaluation of the pesticidal substance in an oral toxicity assay, typically performed on rats or mice. This is a maximum hazard dose assay in which the laboratory test animals are dosed with purified pesticidal substance (all proteins to date) at the rate of 4000 to 5000 mg/kg body weight. Animals are then observed for any clinical manifestations, decreases in body weight gain, and mortality. After a 14 day observation period, animals are sacrificed and a gross necropsy performed to ascertain if there were any major changes in organ size or evidence of pathology.

Because these human health studies require large amounts of pure protein, it is sometimes necessary to use protein produced in a microbial system, such as *E. coli* or *B. thuringiensis*, as the test substance. In such cases, the applicant is required to demonstrate that the protein is identical to the substance produced in the plant. Assays to verify this may include the sequence of the genes used in plant and microbial systems as well as the protein sequence and any glycosylation sites that may be present on the processed protein. This was done with MON810 Bt-maize, and the microbially (in *Escherichia coli*) produced protein was found to be equivalent to the plant product and was, therefore, allowed as a test substance (EPA / BPPD, 1995). Moreover, no toxicity was noted. In these toxicity studies, the dose level of endotoxin administered to the test animals far exceeded the possible human consumption levels via the diet or exposure in the environment through soil and water. Having this leeway one can expect that the level of human exposure to Cry1Ab from MON810 will fall far below any potential effect level.

EPA also requires a study on the digestion of the protein in a simulated gastric assay, to determine the stability of the protein after ingestion. Proteins and digested fragments are analyzed on a polyacrylamide gel to separate them and characterize molecular mass. Proteins that are resistant to digestion are considered as potentially more allergenic or toxic as they may remain intact for longer periods in the stomach and intestines where they could be absorbed. This does not imply that any protein which remains intact after passage through the stomach is an allergen or a toxin, it only means that those proteins which do exhibit these properties generally remain intact, or largely so, following gastric passage. Cry1Ab endotoxin was found to degrade in the gastric assay.

Amino acid sequence data from the pesticidal substance are also subjected to analysis by comparison of similarities to known allergens using a database of protein sequences and a program that will highlight any sequence homology of 8 amino acids or longer. This is considered the minimum length of amino acids that may constitute an allergen. At the time MON810 was registered this database and search capability did not exist. Given the rapid degradation of the Cry1Ab protein in the gastric environment, the opportunity to be absorbed and act as an allergen is not afforded.

Environmental assessment. Non-target organism studies include the toxicity characterization for:

- fish (catfish or trout),
- aquatic invertebrates (Daphnia),
- earthworms,
- Collembola (springtails),
- beneficial insects (green lacewing, ladybird beetle, honey bee, parasitic wasp),
- birds (Bobwhite quail or Mallard duck) and
- any other species considered as being exposed or at risk from the pesticidal substance.

The species chosen for testing are representative of the main groups of organisms likely to be affected by a pesticide in a typical agricultural and environmental scenario. In addition, these species are readily available for testing and allow for valid comparisons between studies, even when performed by different testing laboratories. Other organisms are chosen as needed to conduct any further toxicity or pathogenicity testing based upon the evidence of any specific risk to that group of organisms or if the proposed use pattern of the pesticide indicates that a species or group of organisms not represented in the standard toxicity tests may be exposed during use of the pesticide. A maximum hazard dose is used to detect toxicity based upon the recommendations of a scientific advisory panel during formulation of the testing guidelines. Endangered or threatened species are given special consideration, and EPA may require testing with related, abundant species to assess possible non-target effects. Scientists within EPA review the proposed application sites of the plant-pesticide and the potential for exposure to any endangered species to produce a risk assessment. Consultations with the Fish and Wildlife Service of DOI are also carried out wherein questions arise. With MON810 there were no concerns for harm to endangered species based on the areas planted with Bt-corn and the containment of the pesticidal substance within the plant.

Studies of non-target species are typically designed as single dose, maximum hazard toxicity assessments, and animals are observed for varying time frames depending on the species (14 to 30 days typically). Toxicity studies with the organisms listed above are carried out on dried whole-plant tissues (*e.g.*, grain) as opposed to purified endotoxin, although there are some exceptions to this. Grain and Cry1Ab endotoxin had no observed effect in the studies outlined above. With proteins as potential toxicants, short-term toxicity assessments are considered as satisfactory in assessing the potential for long term effects through consumption since they are generally degraded rapidly within the digestive system. Similarly, proteins are not usually considered as mutagens or teratogens the way that some other organic molecules might be. Tests to measure these possible effects are in the guidelines (40 CFR) for biochemicals and traditional chemical pesticides.

No adverse effects were observed on larval honey bees at a maximum hazard dose of 20 ppm *B.t.k.* HD-1 protein. An LC_{50} was not possible to calculate since this was a single dose test. Therefore, the no observable effect level (NOEL) is greater than 20 ppm. There were no statistically significant differences among the various treatment and control groups due to the sizable mortality that occurred in all treatments of adult honeybees. *B.t.k.* HD-1 protein at 20 ppm resulted in a mean mortality of 16.2%. Because mortality was observed at the single dose tested, a NOEL could not be determined from this study, but it was less than 20 ppm. It was determined that 20 ppm is significantly higher than exposure conditions in the environment.

No adverse effects were observed at a maximum hazard dose of 20 ppm *B.t.k.* HD-1 protein to *Brachymeria intermedia*, an insect parasitic wasp. Since this is a single dose study, an LC_{50} cannot be calculated. The NOEL is greater than 20ppm. With green lacewing bioassays, there were no adverse effects observed at a maximum hazard dose of 16.7 ppm *B.t.k.* HD-1 protein after 7 days. The NOEL is, therefore, greater than 16.7 ppm. Similarly, there were no adverse effects observed in lady beetle bioassays at a maximum hazard dose of 20 ppm *B.t.k.* HD-1 protein. The NOEL is greater than 20 ppm.

Oral toxicity (feeding) studies with Northern Bobwhite Quail indicated no treatment related mortality or differences in food consumption, body weight or behavior occurred in birds fed 50,000 or 100,000 ppm transgenic corn meal derived from Monsanto's MON801 corn line (which contains Cry1Ab protein) relative to birds fed corn meal made from parental corn lines which did not express Bt toxin. Although this study utilized Monsanto's MON801 Bt corn for testing, the test material was considered sufficiently similar to the MON810 corn grain to bridge the data because of the similarity in Cry1Ab levels.

The 14-Day LC_{50} value for earthworms exposed to Cry1Ab insecticidal protein derived from *E. coli* in an artificial soil substrate was determined to be greater than 200 mg/kg (ppm), which was the single concentration tested. There were no statistically significant effects at the single dose tested. Therefore, the NOEL is greater than 200 ppm. Although this study was graded supplemental, Bt toxins expressed in the corn plant are not expected to generate a toxic effect in the earthworm; therefore, no additional follow-up of this study was required.

Impacts on non-target soil organisms are of interest because of the residual *B.t.k.* protein that exists in the corn plant at physiological maturity and the potential for incorporation into the soil. In the study submitted by Monsanto on the toxicological effect on two species of Collembola (*Folsomia candida* and *Xenylla grisea*), *B.t.k.* leaf tissue containing Cry1Ab insecticidal protein had an LD_{50} over a 28 day exposure period that was > 50 % of the diet formulation by weight. The NOEL for mortality was 50 % of the diet. The estimated concentration of Cry1Ab in the lyophilized tissue was 50.6 µg/g dry weight.

The study "Evaluation of the European Corn Borer Resistant Corn Line MON801 as a Feed Ingredient for Catfish" was reviewed to determine potential impacts on channel catfish from Monsanto's MON810 corn lines. Feed per fish, feed conversion ratios, final weight, percentage weight gain and survival were not significantly different between fish fed the control MON 800 diet when compared to those fed the diet containing transgenic corn from the test line MON801. Body composition data exhibited no significant differences in percentage moisture, fat, or ash, with a higher protein content in the test fish on a dry weight basis. This difference in protein content disappears when one expresses the results on a wet weight basis. Data in this study are consistent with historical controls for catfish grown at the Delta Research and Extension Center. Although this study utilized Monsanto's MON801 Bt corn for testing, the test material was considered sufficiently similar to the MON810 corn grain to bridge the results for the data requirement since the levels of Cry1Ab in the MON801 grain tested were similar to MON810 levels.

After a 48-hour exposure of aquatic invertebrates to corn pollen containing the Bt Cry1Ab toxin (100 mg/L), no mortality was seen to *Daphnia magna*, a sensitive aquatic invertebrate. The data suggest that at the expected environmental concentration, no effects are expected on aquatic invertebrates.

The Agency also examines the environmental fate of the endotoxin. At the time of registration of MON810, the fate of Cry1Ab toxin in the soil from plant residues was considered to be essentially the same as other proteins added to the soil ecosystem, namely that they would be degraded by physical, chemical and biological processes associated with soil. With the measured lack of toxicity to soil invertebrates and other non-target organisms (as noted above), the presence of the δ-endotoxin in the soil profile is not considered to adversely impact the soil microflora and microfauna. *B.t.k.* Cry1Ab protein bioactivity, added to the soil as a component of Bt-maize tissue, decreased with an estimated 50 % degradation in 1.6 days and an estimated DT_{90} of 15 days. The bioactivity of purified Cry1Ab protein in soil decreased 50 % within 8.3 days and an estimated DT_{90} of 32.5 days (Sims and Holden, 1996). Subsequent laboratory studies simulating field conditions measured the rate of degradation of the endotoxin in soil and in the plant tissue, without soil present. In the Workshop on Ecological Monitoring of Genetically Modified Crops (Stotzky, 2000), it was reported that no differences were observed in terms of soil microbes (bacteria, fungi, protozoa, nematodes) and enzymes when comparisons were made between soil from Bt crops versus conventional crops. The same degree of Cry protein persistence was observed in soils treated with microbial Bt applications as with Bt from modified crops.

EPA also analyzes the potential for the development of insect resistance. The development of resistance to Cry1Ab endotoxin within the insect pest populations (CEW, ECB, SWCB) is another way adverse effects could occur. Larval resistance could potentially occur by selection of genotypes that are resistant to the toxin, whether these genotypes already exist in the population or develop through evolutionary forces, such as genetic drift, mutation or gene flow. For an insect species that feeds on maize, natural selection of insects on Bt cultivars of maize would tend to increase the frequency of resistant insects within the population. As these genotypes increased within the insect populations, greater crop damage would occur and lead to an increasing need for alternative control measures (*e.g.*, other Bt endotoxins, biological and chemical controls). The cross resistance of ECB to different forms of Bt endotoxins is not well understood (Denolf *et al.*, 1993; U.S. EPA, 1998; Bolin *et al.*, 1999).

In general, the more widely Bt plant-pesticides are used, the greater the possibility for the development of insect resistance to the endotoxin. Thus, for MON810, EPA considered the existing and potential distribution of the MON810, as well as other Bt plant-pesticides. The Agency's analysis suggested that, without restrictions on MON810, there was some potential for the development of resistance in the pest species, but with conditions on the use of MON810, the risk could be minimized to a biologically acceptable level. That is, the impact of the MON810 plants when deployed as indicated in the registration documents, would not significantly hasten the potential development of resistance in the target pest species to Cry1Ab.

EPA also evaluates the potential for outcrossing or hybridization of Bt-maize pollen with wild relatives of maize that are sexually compatible. In other words, is there a possibility of transfer of the pesticidal substance to other plant species that might result in an entirely new exposure scenario? The potential for transfer of the pesticidal gene to wild relatives is assessed based upon the basic biology of the crop plant and the distribution of related species. Since the only relatives of maize that exist in the United States or its territories and have the potential to cross hybridize are in special plantings, herbaria and research plots, this is not considered a problem (U.S. EPA/BPPD, 2000A). Of course, Bt-maize can cross with other maize hybrids (*i.e.*, sweet corn, popcorn, field corn), but these are harvested and do not persist in the environment where chance escapes or volunteer plants occur.[3] Plants that may develop from scattered seed are not aggressive or competitive and are dealt with by cultivation or herbicides used for weed management.

The potential for outcrossing to traditional cultivars of maize from MON810 or other registered plant-pesticides is not currently reviewed within the guidelines (40 CFR). Since the mammalian toxicity and environmental evaluations have indicated that the plant-pesticidal substance (*i.e.*, δ-endotoxin) is not a threat to man or the environment, there is not a risk associated with MON810 pollen fertilizing traditional maize. Traditional culture methods and breeding (*i.e.*, seed production) have resulted in cross-pollination between open pollinated varieties, hybrids and inbred lines for centuries with no known ill effects. This has similarly transferred genes for disease and insect resistance between varieties in the past.

EPA does not attempt to evaluate the possible future changes in social and ecological conditions (*e.g.*, climate) nor the marketability of the grain produced. Predictability of climatic change is difficult at best. The GEOP is evaluated under different conditions (*e.g.*, temperatures, drought stress) to examine expression of the pesticidal gene as the local environment changes. The limit dose testing performed for the assessment of toxicity is at a level that exceeds the amounts of pesticidal substance present in the plant under any foreseeable conditions. The longevity of a cultivar and associated resistance genes is considered finite at the time of deployment and by the time any significant climatic or social changes alter the ability to grow certain crops or tastes for specific foods, it is likely this GEOP (MON810) will no longer be of utility (*i.e.*, will be replaced by other plant-pesticides). The EPA regulatory process does not end with registration, but continues and has the ability to modify the registration at a later date as

---

[3]With other genetically modified crops that EPA has reviewed for registration where the potential for outcrossing exists (*i.e.*, sexually compatible relatives are present in the U.S. or its territories), these plant-pesticides have been precluded from distribution in those areas where wild relatives occur. For example, Bt-cotton is restricted from planting in Hawaii by EPA due to the presence of a wild relative of upland cotton (Stewart, 1991; U.S. EPA/BPPD, 2000B). If it became known that a sexually compatible relative of maize had established itself within U.S. borders, then it would be necessary to consider whether regulatory measures to prevent outcrossing are appropriate or necessary in those areas as a means of preventing outcrossing.

warranted.

The focus of EPA's analysis of plant-pesticides is prescribed by FIFRA and FFDCA based upon the presence of a pesticidal substance and the gene(s) necessary to produce it being present in the plant.

Finally, EPA takes into account any other relevant information. In the case of MON810, EPA considered the long history of the use of Cry1Ab in microbial sprays. This experience showed that the endotoxin has virtually no toxicity to mammalian and other non-target species, based upon studies reviewed by EPA and a review of the relevant literature.

2. EPA's Consideration of the Risks and Benefits of Bt-maize.

As noted above, FIFRA's standard for registration decisions involves an assessment of risks and benefits of using a pesticide. One of the primary benefits of a plant-pesticide is the replacement of pesticides that may pose greater risks, *e.g.*, groundwater contamination, toxicity to non-target organisms, or dietary risks to infants and children. To date, however, decisions to register plant-pesticides have relied primarily on their lack of toxicity to all organisms tested, except target pests. Nonetheless, EPA has also considered possible benefits that might result from use of MON810. Planting of MON810 likely will reduce the use of other insecticides and thereby will avoid the types of risks those insecticides might have had, if applied to the same acreage as MON810.

Targeting the δ-endotoxin to the point of feeding of pest insects should minimize the impact of pesticides on non-target organisms and minimize ground water contamination, as may occur with use of some conventional chemical pesticides. Since many of the previously deployed insecticides were broad-spectrum in their activities, the potential for impacts on the beneficial insect populations was significant. Populations of beneficial insects should increase over time as more GEOs are planted and fewer toxic (*i.e.*, broad spectrum) pesticides are used. Even though Bt expressing maize is an effective control method for the target pests, many species of the beneficial insect community associated with a maize field do not prey upon or parasitize the target insects. Those that do, typically rely on several hosts or prey insects to sustain their populations throughout the season. Since some insecticides have effects on non-insect organisms (*e.g.*, earthworms, nematodes), the reduction or elimination of these pesticides will help to nurture these populations as long as cultural practices of soil management are adequate.

Additionally, the hazard to farm workers, pesticide applicators and the public in general is reduced when a plant-expressed pesticide takes the place of a more toxic chemical spray alternative. Residues on food are also less a concern with MON810, since the δ-endotoxin is known to be non-toxic to humans and other mammals. Fuel costs for transporting, packaging in containers, disposal and application are also not expended when using GEOPs as compared to conventional chemical pesticides or microbial sprays. Spray drift is often problematic with chemical applications, but this is not an issue with plant-pesticides / GEOPs.

3. History of EPA's regulatory review of Bt-maize.

Based on the hazard identification, risk assessment, and risk-benefit analysis described above, EPA determined that the applications for MON810 met the statutory standards for issuing an experimental use permit, registration, and an exemption from the requirement of a tolerance (40 CFR 180.1173; 61 FR 40343, Aug 2, 1996). Because MON810 and other similar Bt-maize products involve a new technology about which there is some uncertainty, EPA issued time limited registrations. At the time of registration, the details of insect resistance management plans were under development and a time line for reassessment was determined. Currently, all Bt-maize registrations will expire in 2001; MON810 registration expires on September 30, 2001. EPA is presently re-evaluating all registered Bt-GEOPS and will determine if continued registration is warranted and if all food tolerance exemptions will be continued without change.

As noted above, Bt-maize is generally non-toxic to all species, except certain lepidopteran insects. These characteristics led EPA to focus primarily on two types of potential risks: 1) the development of insect resistance; and 2) the risk to non-target insects. These risk scenarios require proper monitoring of insect resistance, implementation of resistance management plans, and examination of potential non-target influence on insects inhabiting the area of Bt-maize planting to prevent or mitigate adverse effects. That is, if an adverse event should be observed, the potential hazard could be mitigated by halting further seed sales, altering the distribution of a specific pesticidal substance (region of growth of crop) or other remedial measures. Failure by the registrant to monitor or analyze the data gathered from such assessments would be a potential avenue for proliferation of these risks by allowing resistance to develop unchecked. Growers are required by contract to implement a refuge plan for insect resistance management and their compliance is monitored by the registrant. The registrants of Bt-maize plant-pesticides, the Biotechnology Industry Organization and the National Corn Growers Association have formed a consortium (Agricultural Biotechnology Stewardship Technical Committee) to closely coordinate the sampling and bioassay of insect populations for resistance to Bt δ-endotoxins in cooperation with university and USDA/ARS scientists.

Insect resistance. To minimize the potential for the development of insect resistance, EPA imposed several different conditions on the registration of MON810: 1) limitations on the amount of MON810 that could be planted in certain regions of the country; 2) a requirement that each grower plant an appropriately sized refuge of non-Bt maize (based on recommendations from the USDA NC-205 [http://biotech-info.net/NC_205.html] research committee on ecology and management of European corn borer and other stalk-boring Lepidoptera working group on insect resistance management and sanctioned by EPA); and 3) a requirement that the registrant perform post-registration monitoring of field insect populations for all Bt-crops in order to detect the development of resistance as early as possible.

Because EPA had previously approved a Bt cotton plant-pesticide, at the time of the initial registration of MON810, the Agency's greatest concerns about insect resistance centered on the southern part of the United States. Bt-cotton was targeted against some of the same insect pest species as MON810, and was already widely planted in the South. To constrain the overall use of Bt-based products in this region of the country, the Agency limited use/planting of MON810 in the South to 100,000 acres. Since the cotton acreage in the south was significantly greater than the maize acreage and the pests which crossover move from maize to cotton (and have different developmental ontogenies within the two crops), maize acreage was initially restricted. This restriction did not apply to other parts of the country and later was relaxed to allow for more planting in the South after February 1999, based on EPA's conclusion that insect resistance could be managed by adopting a requirement for non-Bt refuges.

In February 1998, EPA requested that the FIFRA Scientific Advisory Panel (SAP) subpanel on Bt plant-pesticide resistance management review existing IRM strategies for Bt crops (SAP, 1998). Following the recommendations of this SAP subpanel, EPA began to mandate specific structured refuge options for new Bt corn registrations (those products registered prior to that time were still expected to implement voluntary refuge options). The specific structured refuge requirements were based on the technical recommendations of the February 1998 FIFRA SAP subpanel and USDA NC-205 research committee on ecology and management of European corn borer and other stalk-boring Lepidoptera. The NC-205 regional research committee, consisting of USDA/ARS and university scientists published IRM recommendations in 1997 and 1998. In 1998, NC-205 recommended at least a 20-30% untreated (not treated for the target pests) refuge or 40% treated (not treated with microbial Bt products, but other insecticides acceptable) refuge planted within close proximity. That is, the refuge should be planted within the same half section (section = 640 acres) wherein the Bt maize is planted.

Following registration of MON810 Bt-maize, a proposed draft refuge management plan was mandated by the Agency for submission by 8/98. The final structured refuge management plan was required to be in place by 1/99. These initial insect resistance management plans were proposed voluntarily by the registrant and agreed upon by the Agency in the early stages of Bt-maize registrations (*i.e.*, 1995-1997). Insect resistance management plans were mandated after 1/31/00 and required establishment of a refuge[4] Currently, growers using MON810 must plant a

---

[4] EPA has established a condition on the registration of MON810 that requires Monsanto to enter into a contract with every grower who uses MON810. The contract must require the grower to plant an appropriate refuge. The condition on the registration also obligates Monsanto to take actions to assure that growers fulfill this aspect of the contract. A pattern of contract violations by growers would lead EPA to reconsider whether, without further restrictions on the

'refuge' of a non-Bt maize within 1/4 mile of their Bt-maize fields. The refuge must be equal to at least 20 % of the acreage planted to Bt-maize, and the plants in the refuge may be treated only with non-Bt insecticides. In areas of the South where cotton is grown in significant acreage, EPA requires growers to plant a refuge equal to 50% of the Bt-maize acreage, and it must be placed within 2 mile of the Bt-maize field. This is largely due to issues of cross resistance when insects feeding on maize are known to cross over to feed on cotton and experience selection for resistance to a similar Cry endotoxin protein in Bt-cotton.

Insect resistance management plans for MON810 also require Monsanto to monitor field insect populations for development of resistance and reporting to the Agency any adverse events. Further, the registration of MON810 requires Monsanto to instruct growers to report any sudden increase in insect damage to the Bt-maize crop, and the company is mandated both to examine such reports thoroughly and to pass such reports on to EPA[5]

Finally, to discourage overuse that might contribute to the emergence of insect resistance, the seed bags must also contain a statement indicating that this seed is for use in controlling specific pests, such as the ECB.

Impacts on non-target insects. The potential for toxicity to non-target organisms is another area where adverse effects could occur. In particular, one area EPA considered was potential impact on non-pest lepidopteran species (*e.g.*, butterflies) to determine if they might be adversely impacted. No threat to listed (threatened or endangered) species was found for MON810 following an analysis by EPA risk assessors. EPA considered the potential toxicity of Bt-maize to Monarch butterflies and related species. EPA concluded that Bt-maize poses an extremely low risk (Sims, 1995). This conclusion rested on an expectation that there would be relatively few milkweed plants (Monarch food source) near or in maize fields and on an expectation that the amounts of MON810 pollen which might land on adjacent milkweed plants would be below toxic levels. Since the demonstration by Losey *et al.* (1999) that Bt-maize pollen can be toxic to monarch larvae when present in significant amounts, a wealth of field and lab

---

registration, the use of MON810 may lead to the emergence of insect resistance.

[5] If resistance to Cry1Ab were noted in a particular region, the Agency would need to decide whether further regulatory action would be appropriate. EPA would be able to choose among a range of measures to address the potential risk, including: requiring changes in refuge size and spray/treatment options; restricting sales of MON810 in an area; limiting distribution of Cry1Ab in other crops; or cancellation of the plant-pesticide registration.

data has been collected (Hansen and Obrycki, 2000; Herms *et al.*, 1997; Pilcher *et al.*, 1997; Pimentel and Raven, 2000; Wraight *et al.*, 2000). To date, these further studies have confirmed EPA's earlier finding that the risk to monarch butterflies from Bt-maize pollen is extremely low. In addition, Monarch larvae have been shown to avoid pollen in amounts that would be required to deliver a detrimental dose of Cry1Ab (Losey *et al.*, 1999). Finally, the aerodynamics of corn pollen are such that deposition of pollen grains in concentrations sufficient to harm other lepidopterans beyond 1 m from the field edge is highly unlikely as determined from field studies.

Following registration of MON810, academic researchers conducted a laboratory study in which larval Monarch butterflies (*i.e.* caterpillars) were fed Bt-maize pollen combined with milkweed, the Monarch's food source. The study showed that the endotoxin in this form and dose level was toxic to the Monarch caterpillar (Losey *et al.*, 1999). In order to evaluate more fully the potential risk to Monarch butterflies, EPA imposed the following requirements for data on the registrant:

- determination of the land mass involved with growth of milkweed plants and inhabited by Monarch butterflies;
- distribution of milkweed plants near maize fields;
- species of milkweed actually fed upon by Monarchs;
- effect of herbicides used in maize on milkweed;
- toxicity of Cry1Ab to Monarch larvae;
- lethality of pollen from MON810 plants to Monarch larvae;
- palatability of maize pollen to Monarch larvae; and
- various information on the natural history of Monarch butterflies.

At the time of this writing, EPA is in the process of reviewing this information to assess the potential risks and the need for possible mitigation measures. Milkweed issues are addressed because milkweeds are the host plants for monarch larvae, so their distribution relative to corn agriculture represents an important component for evaluating the potential for effects of *Bt* corn on monarchs. Milkweeds are considered a weed in corn agriculture, and are therefore subject to control measures by cultural practices (*e.g.*, tillage, cultivation, herbicides). In areas where weed control is practiced this may result in much higher milkweed densities in non-corn areas, such as pastures, roadsides, and fallow fields. The larvae of approximately 90% of the monarch butterflies passing through the corn belt will feed on the 7 most common milkweed species found in that area (Monarch Watch, 2000).

Roughly 50% of the monarchs in the US may pass through the corn belt each year (Wassenaar and Hobson, 1998). Recent estimates (MBRS, 1999; USDA, 2000) are that approximately 1.5 million square miles represent the summer monarch breeding area, with 10.5 % of this area comprised of corn fields. In the corn belt, 16.4 % of the potential summer monarch breeding range is estimated to comprise corn fields. More recent estimates are in the 10 % range (USDA, 2000).

Based on data from the 1997 U.S. Census of Agriculture, the total area under corn cultivation in states that have been identified as breeding areas for the monarch butterfly is approximately 105,174 square miles. This represents 18 percent of the 570,045 square miles of crop, pasture, and range land associated with monarch breeding sites. If hazard to monarchs is limited to milkweed at the field edge, the analysis indicates that a 1-m field edge margin typically represents a 1 % increment of the planted field area. The field edge habitat estimate may have minor significance in light of new information collected in the summer of 2000. The new studies show that milkweed grows-well between corn rows and that monarch larvae were seen on these plants during the peak breeding period (Marcotty, 2000). This would indicate that monarch larva exposure to *Bt* pollen would take place in *Bt* corn fields in geographical locations where there is an overlap of pollen shed and monarch breeding. Here one needs to factor in the preliminary data showing that there is no pollen shed and monarch breeding overlap in most of the corn belt, except in the northern range. And in assessing hazard in the northern corn belt, one needs to look at the findings that MON810 corn pollen at levels found in the fields showed no detrimental effect on monarch development.

It is the larval stages of monarchs, not the adults, that are potentially affected by Bt corn pollen because it is the larvae that may ingest *Bt* corn pollen. The Cry proteins incorporated into Bt corn need to be ingested to exert their toxicity; *Bt* corn products do not represent contact toxins. Pollen from these events are unlikely to be found in densities that may affect non-target lepidopterans, even on milkweeds within a corn field. Additionally, modeling work on the overlap of pollen shed timing with the presence of monarchs indicates that, for most of the corn belt, except for the northern range, the monarch larvae are not present during pollen shed. Biological activity of Bt corn pollen against sensitive lepidopteran larvae is significantly reduced within approximately one week, or less in wind and rain, after pollen shed.

For MON810 no effects on larval survival were observed at pollen concentrations up to 1,445 pollen grains/sq. cm of leaf surface, although slight-to-moderate effects on larval weight were seen. No effects on larval weight were observed at 1,100 grains/sq. cm. 90% of the pollen distribution on milkweed leaves in corn fields is below 500 grains/sq. cm. Other studies show mean pollen deposition in fields as low as 60 to 150 grains/sq. cm. Several Bt and non-Bt corn field studies showed no differences in monarch larval survival. In general the field data show that larval survival increases with closeness to corn fields. In sweet corn treated with conventional spray pesticides a 90-100% larval mortality was seen within one hour of pesticide application. MON810 has only trace levels (<90 ng/g dry wt.) of Cry1Ab protein in pollen. [The above data were collected during the 2000 growing season were presented at the USDA Monarch Data Review Workshop, November 16-17, 2000, Chicago, IL.]

To the extent EPA identifies any potential effects on non-target insects, especially beneficial or non-pest insects, the Agency will require mitigation efforts to minimize exposure to the endotoxin. In the case where pollen expresses the endotoxin protein and pollen falls in sufficiently heavy amounts on the host plants fed upon by non-target insects, a potential for harm to non-target insects might exist. This hazard, where it exists, could be alleviated by a change in the promoter sequences that drive expression of the endotoxin in pollen. Also, the planting of sufficient border rows of non-Bt maize to halt drift and deposition of Bt-pollen onto host plants (*e.g.*, milkweed) outside of the maize field would mitigate exposure of non-target insects to the endotoxin in that area. As mentioned above, this is not a problem with MON810 due to the low level of expression of Cry1Ab in the pollen and its low toxicity to monarch larvae.

USDA/APHIS

In many respects, the main elements of hazard identification are embodied in the statutory authorities of USDA, EPA, and FDA that were summarized when the Coordinated Framework for the Regulation of Biotechnology was published in 1986. These legal authorities address risks that may be associated with organisms that harm plants (plant pests), pesticides which may be toxic to humans or other nontarget organisms, and foods and feeds that are adulterated, improperly labeled, or have significantly altered nutritional qualities.

To perform risk assessments, APHIS has recognized that it is necessary to identify and focus on specific hazards that are potential components of risk based on the particular organism in question and its use. Here, the organisms in question are crop plants intended for use in agriculture, or to be eaten as food, or used to make ingredients in food. To identify these hazards, it is necessary to start with a good understanding of the existing traditional knowledge base and of the procedures that are routinely carried out in the course of developing any new crop variety that is released for commercial use. This knowledge serves as a baseline to decide whether the risk posed by a specific hazard is significantly changed in potential magnitude from any well-known one that is part of established practice. It also enables the hazard identification.

The use of knowledge and experience gained from traditional breeding as a basis for establishing parallel risk associations for newly developed crops is referred to as familiarity. The concept of familiarity is based on the philosophy that the types of safety issues raised by genetically engineered plants are no different from those for traditional breeding when similar traits are being conferred, though the magnitude of any particular risk may differ (NRC, 1989, NRC 2000). Thus, the extensive record provided by experience with traditional plant breeding provides useful information for evaluation of genetically engineered crops with similar alterations and, as with traditionally bred crops, such alterations are likely to pose few ecological problems. (Tiedje et al., 1989). Familiarity is not a risk/safety assessment in itself (NRC, 1989). However, the concept facilitates risk/safety assessments, because to be familiar, means having enough information to be able to make a judgment of safety or risk (NRC, 1989). Familiarity can also be used to indicate appropriate management practices including whether standard agricultural practices are adequate or whether other management practices are needed to manage the risk (Organization for Economic Cooperation and Development (OECD), 1993). As familiarity depends also on the knowledge about the environment and its interaction with introduced organisms, the risk/safety assessment in one country may not be applicable in another country. However, as field tests are performed in different locations, information will accumulate about the organisms involved and their interactions with other organisms in these varied environments.

Familiarity comes from the knowledge and experience available for conducting a risk/safety analysis prior to large-scale introduction of any new plant line or crop cultivar in a particular environment. For plants, for example, familiarity takes account of, but need not be restricted to, knowledge and experience with:

- the crop plant, including its flowering/reproductive characteristics, ecological requirements, and past breeding experiences; the agricultural and surrounding environment of the trial site;
- specific trait(s) transferred to the plant line(s);
- results from previous basic research including greenhouse/glasshouse and small-scale field research with the new plant line or with other plant lines having the same trait;
- the scale-up of lines of the plant crop varieties developed by more traditional techniques of plant breeding;
- the scale-up of other plant lines developed by the same technique
- the presence of related (and sexually compatible) plants in the surrounding natural environment, and knowledge of the potential for gene transfer between crop plant and the relative; and
- interactions between/among the crop plant, environment and trait. (OECD, 1993)

With respect to the above factors, familiarity can range from very high to very low. For genetically engineered crop plants commercialized to date in the U.S., there has been a high degree of familiarity. This is certainly the case for corn. The degree of familiarity is important to the assessment, and could affect the type of data required to perform the assessment.

APHIS environmental assessments are consistent with Annex 3 of the United Nations Environment Program (UNEP) Guidelines for Safety in Biotechnology, which lays out the broad steps in biosafety review. These can be paraphrased as (1) identifying hazards; (2) assessing actual risks that may arise from the identified hazard; (3) determining how identified risks can be managed and whether to proceed with proposed action; (4) comparing the assessed risks with those posed by actions with comparable organisms. These steps are relevant to both APHIS's authority to regulate under the Plant Protection Act and to its obligations under NEPA. The APHIS assessments are based on the principle that the environmental risks that may be posed by a certain use of a particular organism will depend on: the properties of the organism, the way the organism is to be used (including whether the organism is to be used under containment or in the context of an environmental release), and safeguards that are built into experimental design or conditions of use.

APHIS has worked closely with member countries of the OECD, and in other fora, to bring about international consensus on the safe development, testing, and use of genetically modified plants and microorganisms. In 1986, OECD published its first safety considerations for genetically engineered organisms (OECD, 1986). These included the issues (relevant to human health, the environment and agriculture) that might be considered in a risk/safety assessment. These issues were re-iterated in a recent report on harmonization of regulatory oversight in biotechnology published in 2000 (OECD, 2000). OECD has also published several consensus documents that are useful in risk assessments.

In specific terms, the following represent the major hazards that have been identified by APHIS and for which risks are assessed:

- Plant pathogenic potential of the transgenic plant (i.e., either symptomology in the transgenic crop plant or the ability of the transgenic crop to harm other plants)
- Potential to affect handling, processing, or storage of commodities containing the genetically engineered plant.
- Changes in cultivation that might accompany adoption of the transgenic variety
- Potential to harm nontarget organisms
- Changes in the potential of the genetically engineered crop plant to become a weed
- Potential to affect "weediness" of sexually compatible plants
- Potential impacts on biodiversity

Based on the data provided by Monsanto, available information about the crop (corn), and the engineered genes, APHIS assessed the risks of introduction of MON 810. The assessment can be summarized as follows:

- Plant pathogenic potential of the transgenic plant - Though the transgenic plant contains certain sequences from plant pathogens, specifically, the promoter and terminator sequence from 35S CaMV and the *nos* terminator from *Agrobacterium tumefaciens,* APHIS concluded that these did not pose a significant risk of imparting plant pathogenicity. All of the sequences are well -characterized regulatory sequences that are not transcribed or translated to protein and all have a history of safe use in transformed plants. Evaluation of data from field tests did not identify plant pathogenic effects due to the introduced sequences.

- Potential to cause harm to commodities - Because the harvested products are the same for the MON 810 corn as for traditional varieties with respect to the required methods for handling, processing, and storage, APHIS did not identify a risk to raw or processed commodities.

- Changes in cultivation that might accompany adoption of the transgenic variety - Due to the very nature of the product, use of the MON 810 could be accompanied by a shift in insecticide usage patterns, depending on the prevalence of the target insect species and other crop insect pests which are not sensitive to the Cry1Ab protein. As noted above, EPA has the authority under FIFRA to regulate the pesticidal use of this Cry protein and other pesticides used in the cultivation of crops.

- Potential to harm nontarget organisms - APHIS considered the mode of action of the delta-endotoxin Cry1Ab, the documented low toxicity of EPA-registered microbial formulations, and field observations of MON810 that revealed no negative effects on nontarget organisms and on endangered species.

- Potential of the crop plant to become a weed - Central to the conclusion that MON 810 maize is not likely to become a weed is the significant evidence that maize does not possess weedy tendencies, nor is it listed in standard texts or references as a weed. The introduced characteristic of resistance to some lepidopteran species is not expected to add any characteristics of weediness to MON 810. In the highly unlikely event that there was a need to control MON 810 as a weed, a wide range of options are available.

- Potential to affect "weediness" of sexually compatible plants - In general, wild relatives of corn do not grow in the United States, except in some isolated plantings. Cultivated corn and wild diploid and tetraploid members of *Zea* can be crossed to produce fertile offspring. Nonetheless, in the wild, introgressive hybridization does not occur because of differences in flowering time, geographic separation, block inheritance, developmental morphology, seed dissemination, and dormancy.

- Potential impacts on biodiversity - APHIS concluded that MON 810 maize does not pose a threat to biodiversity based on: 1) It will not become a weed and does not significantly hybridize with related species, 2) The high specificity of the Cry protein and its lack of toxicity to humans, other mammals, and threatened and endangered species will result in an insignificant threat to nontarget species. 3) APHIS can envision no threat to biodiversity for MON 810 that does not apply to traditionally bred maize.

APHIS applied the foregoing principles of hazard identification and risk assessment in the course of authorizations for field testing and the later determination as to the regulated status of MON 810 maize. MON 810 was field tested from 1992-1996 under seven separate APHIS authorizations which specified biological confinement of viable plant material. Prior to the revision of the regulations in 1993 to include a notification procedure for APHIS authorizations, field tests were conducted under APHIS permits.

In 1995, Monsanto originally included line MON 810 among other BT-maize lines in a petition submitted to APHIS for a determination of non-regulated status (APHIS# 95-093-01p). Monsanto later amended their petition to drop MON 810 from the petition, because MON 810 was not sufficiently characterized to meet APHIS standards. The other BT-maize line (MON80100) of this petition went on to be granted non-regulated status from APHIS in 1995. In 1996, Monsanto submitted a petition (APHIS # 96-017-01p) requesting an extension of nonregulated status granted in Petition 95-093-01p to lines MON809 and MON810, which are very similar to the antecedent organism (MON80100) granted non-regulated status under petition 95-93-01p.

In 1997, APHIS amended its regulations to provide a formal mechanism for addressing extensions of previous determinations. APHIS conducted its assessment of MON810 in the same manner as the antecedent organism, MON801. APHIS reached a determination of non-regulated status for MON810, and the agency adopted the previous environmental assessment through reference to-95-093-01p, because the organisms were so similar (the EA for 95-093-01 is available at (http://www.aphis.usda.gov/biotech/pubs.html). APHIS concluded that extending the determination of non-regulated status to MON 810 would likewise pose no significant impact on the environment.

Announcement of the APHIS review of MON 810 under NEPA and APHIS' conclusion of FONSI was published in the Federal Register and made available for public reading and comments (see section on "Transparency and Public Involvement" for additional discussion)(the FONSI and determination documents can also be found at http://www.aphis.usda.gov/biotech/pubs.html.

Coordination of USDA, EPA and Other Federal Agencies

As indicated above, some overlap exists in the scope of the risk assessments conducted by APHIS and EPA with respect to determining the potential of a GEOP to impact the agricultural environment including issues of outcrossing, weediness and plant pathogenicity. Many of the registrants that submit a data package to EPA for consideration of an EUP or Section 3 registration have already submitted a data package to APHIS for their risk assessment. While the specific evaluations or tests requested from the company differ with respect to what they are trying to accomplish, enough relevance and common ground exists such that both Agencies may benefit from sharing of risk assessments and related information.

When areas of regulatory overlap indicate a need for EPA or APHIS to consult with the other Agency, this is most often accomplished by a simple telephone call or e-mail communication. More recently, an effort is underway to hold scheduled conference calls between the two groups when submissions regarding the same regulated article or plant-pesticide are made to both agencies. The timing and frequency of these conferences will be determined by the rate of the review process and the novel aspects of the plant-pesticide at hand.

The improved coordination being discussed is likely to include periodic meetings between the agencies. Specific coordination measures that are likely to be implemented include the following. APHIS will provide EPA a copy of its draft Environmental Assessment (EA) prior to its publication to discuss impact of plant-incorporated pesticide on nontarget organisms, threatened and endangered species, and issue associated with gene flow. EPA will provide list of the currently registered pesticides used to control the target pest.

APHIS and EPA have worked closely with member countries of the OECD, and in other fora, to bring about international consensus on the safe development, testing, and use of genetically modified plants and microorganisms. In 1986, OECD published its first safety considerations for genetically engineered organisms (OECD, 1986). These included the issues (relevant to human health, the environment and agriculture) that might be considered in a risk/safety assessment.

4.   Information and Data (What and How is Data and Information Collected and Generated)

EPA

FIFRA and FFDCA give EPA the authority to require whatever studies are necessary to complete a risk assessment of a pesticide. EPA regulations (40 CFR Part 158) detail the standard data requirements for plant-pesticides. Applicants may request waivers for required studies if they deem such studies unnecessary for a risk assessment. Guidelines (885 series) determine the protocols that may be used for most of the required toxicity tests. Any significant variations from the protocol proposed by an applicant normally require independent validation of the novel test method. Additionally, primary literature (peer-reviewed) is a key source of new developments that may influence the type of data requested from registrants and if EPA will accept waivers for certain studies. After reviewing any waiver requests, Agency scientists determine on a case-by-case basis what studies will be required for a specific GEOP.

Generally EPA-required data for product characterization and toxicity tests are generated directly by the applicant or through the use of a commercial laboratory that specializes in performing chemistry / toxicity studies. Fate data, field expression data and product characterization studies are also generally performed by the applicant. Toxicity and non-target studies are usually done by an outside contract lab that has experience in toxicology and the application of EPA guideline requirements. If the guideline requirements are not met (*i.e.*, the study was not performed using accepted procedures), then an additional study may be required. In the case of MON810, an additional study on the aquatic invertebrate, *Daphnia magna*, was required to assess the toxicity of Cry1Ab to this organism because the original maize line submitted for review (MON801) showed a decrease in Cry1Ab expression due to inbreeding effects. The new line proposed, MON810, expressed Cry1Ab in pollen, potentially increasing the exposure of organisms like *Daphnia* to the endotoxin.. MON810 and MON801 were each transformed with the same plasmid construct (PV-ZMCT01). The MON810 progeny express a slightly truncated version of Cry1Ab compared to MON801, but the active site is still retained. The MON810 progeny do not express in detectable levels the marker gene products found in MON801 progeny. On 5/29/96, BPPD registered *Bacillus thuringiensis* delta-endotoxin as produced by the *cry1Ab* gene and the genetic material necessary for its production (PV-ZMCT01) in corn. Although this new active ingredient is not limited to a particular corn line, the registration was originally limited to corn line MON801.

On 7/16/96, BPPD amended this registration to allow plantings of corn line MON810. However; additional studies of quail, catfish, and *Daphnia* were required for the full commercial registration of MON810. These studies were listed as data gaps because although some of the data in the nontarget organism database supporting the registration were generated using *E. coli* produced Bt protein, the test substance for the quail and catfish studies already reviewed was MON801 seed.

All submitted studies are reviewed by Agency scientists. Outside scientific experts may be contacted for the purpose of verifying scientific background information as needed. On particularly critical scientific issues, EPA may consult with its FIFRA SAP (a Federal Advisory Committee Act-chartered group of independent experts in scientific issues related to pesticides). The SAP's advice may concern broad issues, *e.g.* modifying existing guidelines or creating new ones, or may concern a specific pending regulatory action.

Appropriate scientific and regulatory expertise exists within APHIS, EPA and FDA to review all submissions for scientific accuracy and interpretation EPA evaluates data for scientific soundness based on experience with the types of studies and the anticipated results. EPA scientists (4 reviewing product chemistry and health effects data, 7 reviewing environmental effects and insect resistance management data) have the right to question any data that appear to be erroneous, falsified or otherwise questionable in nature. This may take the form of a request for clarification or another study with modifications.

Penalties for falsification of data can range from a monetary fine to imprisonment and combinations thereof. An extensive auditing program exists within EPA's Office of Enforcement and Compliance Assurance to ensure that laboratories are capable of carrying out the prescribed studies and that their equipment is in satisfactory working order. These audits can be carried out on a random basis or targeted to a specific laboratory if there is reason to believe that data have been falsified or in any manner misrepresented.

34

USDA-APHIS

APHIS requires different types of data depending on the particular regulatory process at hand. The particulars are described below for notifications and permits for importation, interstate movement, or field testing, and for the petition for determination of non-regulated status.

Movement, importation, and field testing (introduction). Permits are required for importation, interstate movement and field testing for articles, which do not qualify for notification; these include microorganisms, arthropods, pharmaceutical-producing plants, and insect viruses. In the permit the applicant lists:

- the regulated article or product,
- donor organism,
- recipient organism,
- vector or vector agent,
- date of the importation, movement or release,
- quantity of the regulated article, and,
- the port of importation or site of release.

In addition, detailed information is required as applicable on:

- the anticipated or actual expression of the altered genetic material in the regulated article and how it differs from a non-modified parent organism,
- the molecular biology of the system,
- the country or locality where the donor, recipient, and vector were collected and produced,
- the experimental design at the release site,
- the facilities at the destination,
- the measures to insure containment, and,
- the final disposition.

This data is required so that a decision can be made to conclude that the transgenic plant is adequately characterized, that no transgenic plant material will persist in the environment, and that any unintentional or unanticipated effects, if any, can be restricted to the confined field site and be managed in such a way that there are no environmental risks after the confined field release is terminated. All field test approvals require that a field data report be filed after the experiment is complete. In the case of importation and movement, the information allows for a decision which can conclude that the transgenic plants are adequately characterized and not considered to pose a plant pest risk, and/or can be considered to be contained in the receiving facility ensuring no dissemination into the environment, and thereby, posing no plant pest risk.

Under notification, much of the same information is required as for permits, but the format is more rigid and is streamlined such that the information is more easily catalogued and assessed by APHIS and thus allowing for a more rapid review process. The applicant must state that his article meets the eligibility requirements and that any actions taken will meet certain performance standards mandated in the regulations and described in the notification user's guides. It should be understood that the primary emphasis for field releases under both notification and permit is containment and that the constraints imposed should effectively eliminate the potential for significant impact to the environment.

Petitions for determination of non-regulated status. The most comprehensive data packages received by APHIS for scientific review are the Petitions for Determination of Non-regulated Status. The petition process allows for removal of a transgenic plant from regulatory obligation. De-regulation may be a practical requirement for commercialization of common agronomic crops, which are to be grown on a large scale, but may not be for certain specialized applications, for example, commercialization of pharmaceutical-producing plants. In order to make the determination on a petition, APHIS uses specified information and data supplied by the applicant to make risk assessments relative to the hazards listed previously.

The assessments rely on answers to a number of specific questions that are included as Appendix C. Information requirements may vary with plant species, the specific types of modifications, and end use. The information criteria listed in Appendix C are currently being developed mainly for crop plants with the exception of trees and aquatic plants. They represent a compilation of a range of issues that have been considered in past decisions depending on the specific case. Reviews are still conducted on a case-by-case basis that allows for reviewing additional or fewer criteria. These assessments are conducted by APHIS scientists.

5. **Mitigation and Management Considerations: Approvals and conditions on Research, Development, Production, Distribution, Marketing, Use and Disposal**

EPA

This case study has already discussed many different types of conditions that may be imposed on an experimental use permit or registration of a plant-pesticide. It has also described the conditions that were imposed with reference to MON810. In addition, for non-commercial field release (*i.e.*, > 10 acres, but plants not to enter the food supply; fields monitored for volunteer plants), containment of the test site can be mandated to preclude movement of the GEOP into the wild. As discussed in the review of APHIS' program below, this can be achieved in a variety of ways, with both physical and biological barriers.

USDA-APHIS

Interstate movement, importation, and field testing (introduction). APHIS regulations require that measures must be taken to minimize dissemination of the engineered organism into the environment during movement and while in the receiving facility (laboratory, growth chamber, or greenhouse) as specified in 7 CFR 340. The risk mitigation measures include: (1) adequate identification, packaging and segregation measures to prevent or minimize mixing, spillage and dissemination of viable transgenic plant material, including the flow of fertile transgenic pollen to sexually compatible plants during transit and in the receiving facility; (2) when applicable, methods to minimize the flow of fertile transgenic pollen to other sexually compatible plants within the contained facility or to such plants on the outside; (3) devitalization/disposal of transgenic plant material by suitable means, when no longer in use or authorized. Means of devitalization/disposal could include, but are not limited to, dry heat, steam heat, crushing, deep burial and/or chemical treatment.

For field tests, measures must be taken to confine the transgenic plants to the field site during the defined period of the release and to prevent the transgenic plants or their progeny from persisting in the environment in subsequent growing seasons either within or outside of the site of the confined release. Both the reproductive isolation measures and post harvest land use restrictions should be based on the reproductive biology and seed dormancy characteristics of the species, surrounding land use, proximity of sexually compatible plants and presence of pollinators. Additional mitigation measures may be necessary based on the nature of the introduced trait(s).

During the growing season, measures must be taken to achieve reproductive isolation from plants of the same species and other sexually compatible species that are not part of the confined release, whether they are cultivated, weedy or wild species. Depending on the plant species, this can be achieved by the use of one or a combination of the following: isolation distance, pollen or pollination-proof caging, netting or bagging of plants prior to flowering, guard rows/ border rows of plants to attract pollinators or trap transgenic pollen, flower removal prior to pollination, use of male sterile lines, use of plant growth regulators to block reproductive development, different flowering time, and/or termination of the confined field release prior to flowering. Generally, isolation distances that are used to ensure purity of certified seed (such as breeder seed or foundation classes of certified seed) may be adapted successfully to prevent or minimize outcrossing of transgenic pollen to sexually compatible plants that could produce viable progeny capable of persisting outside the confined field release site. When isolation distances are used, these zones are also monitored for the presence of the same species, related species and for proximity of fields of the same species.

Post-harvest land use restrictions may be necessary for a certain number of years following harvest of the transgenic plant material to allow monitoring, removal and destruction of volunteers. Generally, for maize, this would involved monitoring for volunteers either immediately after harvest in warm climates where conditions favorable for germination can be maintained, or in the next growing season in colder climates. Generally, the post-harvest periods used to ensure purity of certified seed may be adapted successfully. For certain plant species, and for certain specific cases, post-harvest land use restrictions may also be necessary for the perimeter of the confined field site itself to monitor for volunteers resulting from potential dissemination of seed, e.g., during mechanical harvesting operations.

Other risk mitigation activities for field tests include: (1) Adequate identification, packaging and segregation measures to prevent seed mixing, spillage and dispersal into the environment during transit; (2) Adequate cleaning of seeding and transplanting machinery at the confined field site prior to removal to another location to prevent dissemination of viable transgenic plant material into the environment; (3) Devitalization/destruction of surplus seed or seedlings, and any viable transgenic plant material remaining after transplantation or after harvesting at the confined field site by suitable means which could include, but are not limited to, dry heat, steam heat, crushing, deep burial, discing into the soil, burning, treatment with appropriately labeled herbicides and/or chemicals (harvested transgenic seed and/or plant material from the confined field site may only be retained in an approved facility if requested at the time of the submission and authorized by the regulatory authority, and should be clearly identified, securely transported, and stored separately from other seed/or plant material to avoid mixing); (4) A contingency plan for destruction of viable transgenic plant material in case of accidental release. The plan should include site marking and monitoring to ensure destruction of viable material and immediate notification of regulatory authorities.

Even in the granting of a notification, APHIS still retains the option of requiring additional information from an applicant about the conduct of the trial if there is concern that in the particular instance a performance standards may be difficult to meet or if new information or data becomes available. No such requirement was necessary in the case of MON 810 maize.

Petitions for Determination of Non-Regulated Status. Once an article has been granted non-regulated status APHIS has no authority to impose conditions on research, production, distribution, marketing, use, or disposal other than phytosanitary restrictions that may be applicable. However, if new information indicates that a de-regulated article is causing harm as a plant pest, APHIS can revoke non-regulated status and again regulate under its authority as previously described.

6.   Monitoring and Consideration of new Information

EPA

As discussed above, EPA has considerable ongoing authority to regulate the post-registration use of a plant-pesticide. This authority includes: 1) issuance of data call-in notices to obtain additional information from registrants needed to evaluate the safety of a pesticide (see section 3. A. 1., above) and 2) assuring compliance with conditions imposed on the plant-pesticide's registration.

As a condition on the registration of MON810, EPA required Monsanto to develop and implement plans for monitoring insect resistance management. A key element of the monitoring plans for MON810 is the observation of ECB, CEW and SWCB for evidence of the buildup of resistance. The registrant must educate growers through a formal program to recognize and report any lack of efficacy in MON810 and unusual damage to plants from the target insects. Any adverse incident reports received by the registrant must be filed with Agency. The registrant must also conduct grower surveys to assess the degree of compliance with refuge implementation and any related monitoring issues. Because the Agency does not have the capacity to undertake the implementation of the monitoring plan, the registrant must supply the necessary infrastructure to ensure that the monitoring for resistance, grower education and refuge requirements are enforced.

EPA, however, performed and will continue to take an active oversight role in both the development and implementation of the monitoring plans, as well as in assuring that there is compliance with other requirements. The monitoring plans were developed by the registrant using a process that included input from Agency scientists, university researchers and guidance from the SAB / SAP. Once developed, the Agency required the registrant to submit detailed regional monitoring plans for review and approval.

The Agency has also requested data on compliance from registrants and has the legal authority to further investigate any issues associated with conditions of registration. Typically, EPA reviews the data submitted to assess the degree of monitoring performed and the potential need for further alterations to address specific concerns. The Agency has the authority to inspect and evaluate monitoring and other conditions of registration if it deems this necessary. Some degree of compliance is assured through a comparison of USDA-NASS data (http://www.usda.gov/nass/pubs/histdata.htm) with the information submitted by the registrant.

USDA-APHIS

Interstate movement, importation, and field testing (introduction). APHIS personnel and appropriate state officials may inspect a site or facility where regulated articles are proposed to be released into the environment or contained after their interstate movement or importation. Failure to allow the inspection of the premises prior to the issuance of a permit or notification shall be grounds for the denial of the permit (7 CFR 340.4 (d) 7). APHIS has qualified inspectors in every State and Territory to perform inspections and take remedial action if necessary.

APHIS regulations (7 CFR 340.4(f) 10) require applicants to notify the agency within the time periods and manner specified below, in the event of the following occurrences: (1) orally notified immediately upon discovery and notify in writing within 24 hours in the event of any accidental or unauthorized release of the regulated article; (2) in writing as soon as possible but not later than within 5 working days if the regulated article or associated host organism is found to have characteristics substantially different from those listed in the application, or suffers any unusual occurrence (excessive mortality or morbidity, or unanticipated effect on non-target organisms). APHIS was not notified of any such occurrences with MON 810 maize.

A final data report is required regardless of whether a field test is authorized under notification or permit. The regulations require that these reports include: methods of observation, resulting data, and analysis regarding all deleterious effects on plants, nontarget organisms, and the environment (specific instructions to applicants can be found on http://www.aphis.usda.gov/biotech/notgen.html under section B). APHIS coordinates the approval processes with the states, and federal regulations require that access to facilities, field test sites and pertinent records be allowed by officials from APHIS and the states. APHIS site inspections help to ensure the compliance with the mandated performance standards. Violations can result in fines or termination of the field test.

Petitions for Determination of Non-Regulated Status. Once an article has been granted non-regulated status, APHIS has no authority to require monitoring, perform site inspections, or require data reporting. If it were founded later to pose a plant pest risk, however, it could return to regulated status and the authorities to conduct these activities would then be available.

7.   **Enforcement and Compliance**

EPA

FIFRA and FFDCA generally provide the authority to enforce all provisions regarding regulation of pesticides and presence of pesticide residues on food products. As noted above, EPA relies on an assessment by the registrant to determine compliance. Grower surveys have been conducted by some university scientists as well, to estimate the degree of compliance with insect resistance management requirements. As part of the Agricultural Biotechnology Stewardship Technical Committee and the NC-205 research committee, scientists sample insect populations for development of resistance. The registrant is required to report any adverse events, such as the development of insect resistance or the sudden increase in pest related crop damage, to the EPA under the FIFRA § 6(a)2 reporting requirement provision.

EPA can take regulatory action to impose penalties (fines) or to restrict or prohibit the sale and distribution of any registered product (*i.e.*, cancellation of the product), if it necessary to prevent unreasonable adverse effects on the environment, or necessary to prevent threatened violations of the FIFRA. This could include, for example, seizure of pesticide-product (*i.e.*, seeds) or the assessment of civil and/or criminal penalties. FIFRA Sections 6, 8 and 9 provide statutory authority for the Agency to inspect the producing establishment, inspect books and records, and, although rarely needed, to cancel or suspend registration.

USDA-APHIS

APHIS has qualified personnel in every State that can inspect field sites for compliance to the performance standards for all field testing. In addition, to APHIS field inspectors, officials of the State Department of Agriculture can inspect sites. Also, members of the headquarters staff will continue on a case-by-case basis to inspect sites that potentially raise unique containment issues with respect to engineered organisms.

USDA-APHIS reviews the experimental design protocols for field tests to ensure that performance standards are met. Failure to comply with performance standards under notification or permit conditions can result in the owner being ordered to take remedial action (7 U.S.C. § 7714(b)(1)) if necessary to prevent the spread of plant pests (7 CFR 340.4 d 7). If the owner fails to take such action, the Department can take the action and recover the cost of the action from the owner (7 U.S.C. § 7714(b)(2)). The owner can also be assessed a criminal or civil penalty for failing to comply with the regulations (7 U.S.C. § 7734). For example, some remedial actions might involve removing the plants by burning , spraying herbicide, hoeing or discing. No failure to comply was detected with MON 810 maize field tests.

Interstate movement, importation, and field testing (introduction). Failure of applicants to submit complete and accurate information for all introductions may result in a fine of not more than $10,000 or imprisonment for not more than 5 years or both (18 U.S.C. § 1001).

Failure to comply with performance standards under notifications or permit conditions can result in compliance infractions. From 1995 through 2000, APHIS recorded a total of 63 such compliance infractions. After an infraction has been identified, APHIS decides on the appropriate course of action. In some cases, such as minor infractions where the applicant identifies the infraction, notifies APHIS immediately, and takes prompt and appropriate remedial action, an formal written APHIS response may not be necessary. In other cases, written warnings are issued. For the most serious of infractions, an investigation is conducted by APHIS Investigations and Enforcement Services Staff that usually results in applicants being fined. If necessary, to protect the environment or public health, the transgenic organisms can be subjected to the application of remedial measures (including disposal) if determined by the Administrator to be necessary to prevent the spread of plant pests (7 CFR 340.4 d 7). These remedial actions include removing the plants by burning, spraying herbicide, hoeing or discing. No infractions were identified in the case of MON 810.

41

Petitions for determination of non-regulated status. Every applicant must sign the following statement when submitting a petition for non-regulated status:

"The undersigned certifies, that to the best knowledge and belief of the undersigned, this petition includes all information and views on which to base a determination, and that it includes relevant data and information known to the petitioner which are unfavorable to the petition."

APHIS knows of no peer reviewed or anecdotal evidence that suggests that any plant that has been deregulated is a plant pest or has behaved in a manner significantly different with respect to its plant pest characteristics than a similar cultivar developed by traditional plant breeding. As explained above, APHIS has no authority to require monitoring *per se* after granting non-regulated status, however, if data becomes available that an organism granted non-regulated status does pose a plant pest risk, a deregulated organism could again be deemed a "regulated article" and could be subjected to the application of remedial measures (including disposal) if determined by the Administrator to be necessary to prevent the spread of plant pest (7 CFR 340.4 d 7).

8. Public Involvement and Transparency

EPA

EPA publishes Federal Register Notices announcing the receipt of applications for an Experimental Use Permit (EUP) and for registration, and invites public comment on the proposed action. For MON810, no comments were received from the public. In addition, Federal Register notices announcing approval of EUPs and registration of pesticides containing new active ingredients are also published. EPA also publishes Federal Register Notices announcing the notice of receipt of a request for a food tolerance or exemption and provides opportunity for public comment on the petition. Although not required by statute, EPA also holds meetings with groups and individuals interested in particular pending regulatory actions. During the course of registration of MON810, for example, several groups (*e.g.*, corn growers associations, biotechnology industry groups, environmental groups) visited EPA to discuss issues and concerns relative to this GEOP.

Additionally, the Agency has held workshops on GEOPs within which concerned citizens, non-governmental scientists and other researchers were provided the opportunity to discuss and add to the process. Open Scientific Advisory Panel (SAP) meetings have been held on various topics including insect resistance management, toxicity, allergenicity, non-target organism effects and other aspects associated with plant-pesticides (GEOPs). During these Panel meetings, the public is invited to make public statements and engage the panel in discussion of specific topics. The degree of public input varies with the topic of the meeting. Typically each presenter is allowed to make an oral presentation and subsequent interchange with the Panel occurs if the Panel raises questions. Written statements are also received and included in the docket. EPA considers all comments in making its regulatory decisions.

All studies submitted to the Agency that are not considered as confidential business information (CBI) and all submissions to the SAP are made available through the public docket. The docket number and contact information is published in the Federal Register Notice announcing the registration or tolerance associated with a pesticide. For an SAP meeting, a docket is similarly established for receipt of comments. Information on upcoming and recently held SAP meetings can be found on the EPA website listed below. Portions of the product chemistry section associated with the genetic sequence of introduced genes and the details of the transformation methodology are often restricted as CBI. This can vary based upon what is requested by the registrant and what EPA deems appropriate. Results of toxicity studies are not classified as CBI. EPA works with all stakeholders as part of an open and transparent regulatory process.

The Agency website (http://www.epa.gov/oppbppd1/biopesticides/) and published materials (*e.g.*, booklets, proceedings of workshops, pamphlets) help disseminate information related to GEOPs. Both APHIS and EPA websites provide a list and links to regulations and provides an explanation of the process. Regulatory decisions and the outcome of EPA's toxicology reviews are posted for public review. The website also provides for contact directly with Agency scientists and regulators to address issues of concern. Additionally, scientists may publish articles in trade and peer-reviewed journals, monographs and books that outline Agency position on topics related to regulation of GEOPs.

Finally, EPA maintains a public docket that contains a large number of documents available for inspection and copying, including scientific reviews on safety issues and Reregistration Eligibility Decisions (REDs) on individual plant-pesticides. The Freedom of Information Act (FOIA) also provides for the request of any document submitted to support a pesticide registration as long as it does not contain confidential business information.

USDA-APHIS

APHIS has involved and informed the public on a broad range of Agency biotechnology activities through an array of mechanisms. The public has been involved in establishing the criteria for the regulatory and environmental assessment framework and subsequent amendments as the Agency gained experience and adapted to the developments in the technology. The public has been informed through written regulations (the first government biotechnology regulations), guidance documents, and through both formal notice in the Federal Register and informal information systems such as home pages on the Internet. Two advisory committees have had a significant role in providing a public source of advice from stakeholders to the Agency, the Agriculture Biotechnology Advisory Committee, and the Agricultural Biotechnology Advisory

Committee.

When the APHIS biotechnology regulations (7 CFR 340) were first established in 1987, there were a number of public meetings involving a broad spectrum of interested individuals and groups to discuss the types of data necessary to make informed decisions for safe field testing of genetically engineered organisms. Those discussions included the scope, breadth, and specific environmental concerns that should be considered in environmental analysis under NEPA.

APHIS continues to hold public meetings as needed to inform and involved the public. Meetings have included topics such as program efficiency, timeliness of review, clarity of regulations and guidance documents, applicant satisfaction, paperwork reduction, and identification of scientific or environmental considerations for future reviews by APHIS. All APHIS-sponsored meetings, such as our regular customer service meetings, are announced on the Internet and in the Federal Register and are open to the public. No public meetings were held specifically for review of MON 810. From time to time, APHIS also holds more focused public meetings on specific issues of scientific interest, such as the meeting in 1999 on the ecological effects of pest resistance genes in managed ecosystems. Comments at these meetings are considered in evaluating the need for regulation changes, changes in review procedures or criteria, and for the scope of consideration of environmental issues in NEPA documents.

The APHIS biotechnology home page, http:\\www.aphis.usda.gov\biotech, was one of the first government home pages to be established. It has been one of the primary sources of information globally on biotechnology regulation and a source of information on actual developments in the technology. The Internet has been used by APHIS as a mechanism to compliment and augment other more traditional information and transparency processes such as Federal Register notices, NEPA documents, and public meetings. The home page contains copies of the regulations; guidance documents; lists of notifications, permits, and determinations of non regulated status; recent environmental assessments; and numerous links to other sources of information on biotechnology.

Interstate movement, importation, and field testing (introduction). Every permit and notification for the introduction of a genetically engineered organism is announced on the APHIS Internet home page (http://www.aphis.usda.gov/batik/status.html) the day after it have been received. The information listed includes: the name of organism, the State where the introduction will take place, and whether the proposed action has been authorized. Every application is sent to the State regulatory official where the introduction will take place and the State must concur with APHIS before any action can take place. The public can also comment on the permits and notifications either by contacting APHIS directly or by contacting the State official if the field test is in their state. Contacts for State Departments of Agriculture can be found on the APHIS website at (http://www.aphis.usda.gov/biotech/lt_sta.html). Additional information on each application is available by searching the APHIS on-line database (http://www.nbiap.vt.edu/cfdocs/fieldtests1.cfm), a service provided by Virginia Tech's Information Systems for Biotechnology (ISB) web server.

APHIS prepares EAs for field tests in accordance with its NEPA implementing regulations (7 CFR 372) and accepts written comments received following announcement of the EA in the Federal Register. APHIS distributes copies of EAs via mail or electronically.

Petitions for determination of nonregulated status. Every petition submission is announced on the APHIS Internet home page (http://www.aphis.usda.gov/petday.html) the day after it has been received. After petitions have been reviewed by APHIS scientists and have been deemed complete, USDA announces the receipt of the petition in the Federal Register and the public has 60 days to submit comments. All petitions are available for reading at the Reading Room at the South Building of the USDA Headquarters in Washington, DC and when requested, APHIS provides the public with free copies of all petitions. Subsequently, when a draft environmental assessment is completed, APHIS announces in the Federal Register that the EA is available (electronically or a hard copy) and the public has 30 days to submit comments. APHIS considers all public comments in its decision-making. APHIS announces in the Federal Register when it has reached a Finding of No Significant Impact (FONSI) for the EA that the engineered organisms do not meet the definition of regulated articles. The FONSI, analysis of public comments (if any), the EA, and the determination of nonregulated status are all available electronically at the APHIS home page or in hard copy. Copies of APHIS decision documents are available at the APHIS web site (http://www.aphis.usda.gov/biotech/pubs.html).

As the biotechnology regulations have matured over the years, so have procedures implementing NEPA for decisions subject to those regulations. Initially, environmental assessments were completed before the decision on the issuance of every permit for release to the environment (field test) and notice of availability was published in the Federal Register for each one. After a few years, notice of availability for environmental assessments was published first monthly and then quarterly, as the number of requests for copies of individual environmental assessments decreased and as web-based information became the preferred mode for receiving that information.

In 1995 APHIS established NEPA implementing regulations in 7 CFR 372 that established criteria for the level of documentation for Agency action including biotechnology decisions. The implementing regulations set the following environmental assessment triggers for biotechnology:

> "(b)(4) Approvals and issuance of permits for proposals involving genetically engineered or nonindigenous species, except for actions that are categorically exclude, as provided in paragraph (c) of this section (7 CFR 372.5)."

The relevant categorical exclusion reads as follows:

> "(c) (ii) Permitting, or acknowledgment of notifications for, confined field releases of genetically engineered organisms and products. . ."

except for

> "(d) (4) When a confined field release of a genetically engineered organism or product involves new species or organisms, or novel modifications that raise new issues."

As a matter of policy, APHIS also completes an environmental assessment before making a decision of non-regulated status in response to an applicant's petition. Since 1999, notice of availability of draft environmental assessments for determinations for non-regulated status are published in the Federal Register and provide for a 30-day comment period. Comments are considered before completion of findings of impact.

A fairly large volume of environmental assessments and technical decision documents are made available to the public. These are made available in paper copy or electronically at the preference of the recipient.

APHIS will complete an EIS when an EA does not support a finding of no significant impact. To date, environmental assessments to support biotechnology decisions have resulted in findings of no significant impact. EIS documents would also be available for public comment.

Notifications do not have environmental assessment prepared in accordance with APHIS NEPA implementation regulations (7 CFR 372). The rationale is that these are not exposed to the environment due to the performance standards that ensure confinement (see bentgrass sidebar for example of performance standards). Due to the changes in the regulations regarding notification in 1993 and 1997, species currently under notification may have had EAs prepared in the past, when the same species were required to apply for a permit that may have required an EA.

REFERENCES

Bolin, P., W.D. Hutchison, and D.A. Andow, 1999, Long-term selection for resistance to *Bacillus thuringiensis* Cry1Ac endotoxin in a Minnesota population of European corn borer (Lepidoptera: Crambidae). Journal of Economic Entomology 92:1021-1030.

Denolf, P., S. Jansens, M. Perferoen, D. Degheele, and J. Van Rie. 1993. Two different *Bacillus thuringiensis* delta-endotoxin receptors in the midgut brush border membrane of the European corn borer, *Ostrinia nubilalis*. Applied and Environmental Microbiology 59:1828-1837.

Hansen, L.C. and J.J. Obrycki. 2000. Field deposition of Bt transgenic corn pollen: lethal effects on the monarch butterfly. Oecologia (Published online; http://link.springer.de/link/service/journals/00442/index.htm)

Herms, C., McCullough, D., Bauer, L., Haack, R., Miller, D., and N. DuBois. 1997. Susceptibility of the endangered Karner Blue butterfly (Lepidoptera: Lyaenidae) to *Bacillus thuringiensis* var. *kurstaki* used for Gypsy moth suppression in Michigan. Great Lakes Entomologist. 30: 125-141.

Hitchcock, A.S. (revisions by Agnes Chase) 1971. Zea L., *In*, Manual of the Grasses of the United States (Miscellaneous Publication 200, U.S. Department of Agriculture), 2nd Edition, pp. 794-795, Dover, NY, NY. (ISBN 0-486-22718-9).

Kiesselbach, T.A. 1949. The structure and reproduction of corn. Nebraska Agricultural Experiment Station Bulletin 161: 1-96.

Losey, J., L. Raynor, and M. Carter. 1999. Transgenic pollen harms monarch larvae. Nature 399:214.

Marcotty, J. 2000. Monarch butterfly caught up in corn battle. Minneapolis-St. Paul Star Tribune. August 28, 2000

MBRS, 1999. Monarch Butterfly Research Symposium, 2 Nov 1999, Chicago, IL Agricultural Biotechnology Stewardship Working Group.

Monarch Watch. 2000. http://www.monarchwatch.org

Monsanto Company. 1996. Petition for Determination of Nonregulated Status: Additional Yieldgard Corn (*Zea mays* L.) Lines with the *cryIA(b)* Gene from *Bacillus thuringiensis* subsp. *kurstaki*. (submitted January 17, 1996, to the United States Department of Agriculture, Petition Number 96-017-01p) and available from USDA-APHIS, Unit 147, 4700 River Road, Riverdale, MD 20737

NRC (National Research Council) 2000. Genetically Modified Pest-Protected Plants: Science and Regulation. Washington, D.C. National Academy Press.

NRC (National Research Council) 1989. Field Testing of Genetically Modified Organisms: Framework for Decision. Washington, D.C. National Academy Press.

OECD 1986. Recombinant DNA Safety considerations. OECD, Paris. Available electronically at http://www.oecd.org/ehs/public.htm

OECD 1993. Field Releases of Transgenic Plants, 1986-1992, an analysis. OECD, Paris. Available electronically at http://www.oecd.org/ehs/public.htm

OECD 2000. Report of the Working Group on Harmonization of Regulatory Oversight in Biotechnology.

OSTP (Office of Science and Technology Policy). 1986. Coordinated Framework for the Regulation of Biotechnology: Announcement of Policy and Notice for Public Comment. Fed. Reg. 51, 23302-23393.

Pilcher, C.D., M.E. Rice, J.J. Obrycki and L.C. Lewis. 1997. Field and Laboratory Evaluations of *Bacillus thuringiensis* Corn on Secondary lepidopteran pests (*Lepidoptera: Noctuidae*), J. Econ. Entomol. 90 (2): 669-678.

Pimentel, D.S. and P. H. Raven. 2000. Commentary. Bt Corn Pollen Impacts on Nontarget Lepidoptera: Assessment of effects in Nature. July 18,2000. Proc. Natl. Acad. Sci. USA, Vol. 97, Issue 15, 8198-8199.

SAP, 1998, Final Report on Bt Plant-Pesticides and Insect Resistance Management, Meeting held Feb. 9 and 10, 1998. http://www.epa.gov/scipoly/sap/1998/february/finalfeb.pdf
Sims S.R 1995. *Bacillus thuringiensis* var. *kurstaki* (CryIA(c)) protein expressed in transgenic cotton: effects on beneficial and other non-target insects. Southwestern Entomologist 20(4): 493-500

Sims S.R 1995. *Bacillus thuringiensis* var. *kurstaki* (CryIA(c)) protein expressed in transgenic cotton: effects on beneficial and other non-target insects. Southwestern Entomologist 20(4): 493-500

Sims S.R. and L.R. Holden (1996) Insect bioassay for determining soil degradation of *Bacillus thuringiensis* subsp. *kurstaki* Cry1Ab protein in corn tissue. Environ. Entomol. 25 (3), 659-664

Stewart, J.M., 1991. Gene transfer between contiguous cultivated cotton and between cultivated cotton and wild relatives: report to Monsanto Company (1991) in: Serdy, Information submitted to the United States Environmental Protection Agency, Office of Pesticide Programs, Registration Division, in support of an application for an experimental use permit to ship and use a pesticide for experimental purposes only. EPA DP Barcode #: 171306 (1991).

Stotzky, G. 2000, Workshop on Ecological Monitoring of Genetically Modified Crops, National Research Council, Washington, DC, July 13 and 14, 2000.

Tiedje, J.M., Colwell, R.K., Grossman, Y.L., Hodson, R.E., Lenski, R.E., Mack, R.N., Regal, P.J. 1989. The Planned Introduction of Genetically Engineered Organisms: Ecological Considerations and Recommendations. Ecology 70:298-315.

USDA (United States Department of Agriculture) 1995. Environmental Assessment and Determination of Non-Regulated Status - Petition Number 95-093-01p (line MON80100 of BT corn; the antecedent organism for the extension of nonregulated status granted to MON810). Available electronically at "http://www.aphis.usda.gov/biotech/pubs.html" or write to USDA-APHIS, Unit 147, 4700 River Road, Riverdale, MD 20737.

USDA, 2000. Monarch Workshop, Kansas City, MO. 24 - 25 February 2000.

U.S. EPA / BPPD, 1995, U.S. Environmental Protection Agency, Office of Pesticide Programs, Biopesticides and Pollution Prevention Division, Memorandum from Kough, J. to Mendelsohn, M., Review of Product Characterization and Mammalian Toxicology Data Submitted by Monsanto Corporation for Corn Expressing Cry IA(b) δ-endotoxin (Oct. 4, 1995).

U.S. EPA / BPPD, 1998, U.S. Environmental Protection Agency, Office of Pesticide Programs, Biopesticides and Pollution Prevention Division, White Paper on *Bacillus thuringiensis* Plant-pesticide Resistance Management, pp. 36-37 (EPA 739-S-98-001).
U.S. EPA / BPPD, 2000A, U.S. Environmental Protection Agency, Office of Pesticide Programs, Biopesticides and Pollution Prevention Division, Memorandum from Wozniak, C.A. to M. Mendelsohn, *Tripsacum* and *Zea* species present in the United States and its territories: the potential for hybridization with *Zea mays* (February 16, 2000).

U.S. EPA / BPPD, 2000B, U.S. Environmental Protection Agency, Office of Pesticide Programs, Biopesticides and Pollution Prevention Division, Memorandum from Wozniak, C.A. to M. Mendelsohn, *Gossypium* species Present in the United States and its Territories: the Potential for Hybridization with related species (April 26, 2000).

Wassenaar, L.I. and K. A. Hobson. 1998. Natal origins of migratory monarch butterflies at wintering colonies in Mexico: New isotopic evidence, Proc. Natl. Acad. Sci., USA 95: 15436-15439.

Wraight, C. L., Zangerl, A. R., Carroll, M. J. & Berenbaum, M. R. (2000).Absence of toxicity of *Bacillus thuringiensis* pollen to black swallowtails under field conditions. Proc. Natl. Acad. Sci. USA 97, 7700-7703

Appendix A - **BIBLIOGRAPHY OF SUBMITTED STUDIES - EPA**

See http://www.epa.gov/oppbppd1/biopesticides/news/news-bt-crops-sap-oct.htm
EPA's Biopesticide Registration Action Document for Bt crops is available on the web site and
details the studies submitted in support of MON810 Bt-maize.

Study Title	MRID #
Molecular Characterization of Insect Protected Corn Line MON 80100: Lab Project Number: MSL 13924. Unpublished study prepared by Monsanto Co. 100 p.	43533201
Compositional Comparison of *Bacillus thuringiensis* subsp. *Kurstaki* HD-1 Protein Produced in European Corn Borer Resistant Corn and the Commercial Microbial Product, DIPEL: Lab Project Number: 94-01-39-12: MSL 13876. Unpublished study prepared by Monsanto Co. 35 p.	43533203
Molecular Characterization of Insect Protected Corn Line MON 810: Lab Project Number: MSL 14204. Unpublished study prepared by Monsanto Co. 61 p.	43665501
Assessment of the Equivalence of the *Bacillus thuringiensis* subsp. *kurstaki* HD-1 Protein Produced in *Escherichia coli* and European Corn Borer Resistant Corn: Lab Project Number: 94-01-39-09: MSL 13879. Unpublished study prepared by Monsanto Co. 94 p.	43533204
Acute Oral Toxicity Study of *Btk* HD-1 Tryptic Core Protein in Albino Mice: Lab Project Numbers: 92069: 11985:ML92069. Unpublished study prepared by Monsanto Co. 264 p.	43468001

Assessment of the In vitro Digestive Fate of *Bacillus thuringiensis* subsp. *kurstaki* HD-1 Protein: Lab Project Number: 93-01-39-04. Unpublished study prepared by Monsanto Co. 44 p.	43439201
Stability of the CryIA(b) Insecticidal Protein of *Bacillus thuringiensis* var. *kurstaki* (B.t.k. HD-1) in Sucrose and Honey Solutions Under Non-refrigerated Temperature Conditions: Lab Project Numbers: IRC-91-ANA-11: MSL 13375:13375.	43468002

Unpublished study prepared by Monsanto Co. 32 p.	
Evaluation of the Dietary Effects of Purified B.t.k. Endotoxin Proteins on Honey Bee Larvae: Lab Project Number: IRC-91-ANA-13. Unpublished study prepared by Monsanto Co. 51 p.	43439202
Molecular Characterization of Insect Protected Corn Line MON 810: Lab Project Number: MSL 14204. Unpublished study prepared by Monsanto Co. 61 p.	43665501
Evaluation of Insect Protected Corn Lines in 1994 U. S. Field Test Locations: Lab Project Number: 94-01-39-01: 14065: 14179. Unpublished study prepared by Monsanto Co. 147 p.	43665502
Activated Btk HD-1 Protein: A Dietary Toxicity Study With Green Lacewing Larvae: Lab Project Numbers: WL-92-155: 139-3388. Unpublished study prepared by Monsanto Co.; and Wildlife Int'l, Ltd. 21 p.	43468003
Activated Btk HD-1 Protein: A Dietary Toxicity Study With Ladybird Beetles: Lab Project Numbers: WL-92-156: 139-321. Unpublished study prepared by Monsanto Co.; and Wildlife Int'l, Ltd. 23 p.	43468005
Activated Btk HD-1 Protein: A Dietary Toxicity Study With Parasitic Hymenoptera (*Brachymeria intermedia*): Lab Project Numbers: WL-92-157: 139-320. Unpublished study prepared by Monsanto Co.; and Wildlife Int'l, Ltd. 24 p.	43468004
Evaluation of the Dietary Effects of Purified B.t.k. Endotoxin Proteins on Honey Bee Adults: Lab Project Number: IRC-91-ANA-12. Unpublished study prepared by Monsanto Co. 70 p.	43439203

A Dietary Toxicity Study with MON80187 Meal in the Northern Bobwhite: Lab Project Number: WL 94-150: 139-387. Unpublished study prepared by Wildlife International Ltd. 32 p.	43533205
Corn Pollen Containing the CryIA(b) Protein: A 48-Hour Static-Renewal Acute Toxicity Test with the Cladoceran (*Daphnia magna*): Final Report: Lab Project Number: WL-96-322: 139A-201: 95-152E2. Unpublished study prepared by Wildlife	44271502

International Ltd. 23 p.	
Evaluation of the European Corn Borer Resistant Corn Line MON801 as a Feed Ingredient for Catfish: Lab Project Number: 94-01-39-16: 14066:95-459-720. Unpublished study prepared by Mississippi State University Delta Research and Extension Center. 39 p.	43887901
Effect of the *Bacillus thuringiensis* Insecticidal Proteins CryIA(b), CryIA(c), CryIIA, and CryIIIA on *Folsomia candida* and *Xenylla grisea* (Insecta: Collembola): Lab Project Number: 93-081E1. Unpublished study prepared by Monsanto Co. 22 p.	43941601
Chronic Exposure of *Folsomia candida* to Corn Tissue Expressing CryIA(B) Protein: Lab Project Number: 7140-97-0030-AC-001: XX-97-064: 95-152E2. Unpublished study prepared by Ricerca, Inc. 91 p.	44271501
CryIA(b) Insecticidal Protein: An Acute Toxicity Study with the Earthworm in an Artificial Soil Substrate: Final Report: Lab Project Number: 139-417: WL-95-281. Unpublished study prepared by Wildlife International Ltd. 25 p.	43887902

Appendix B - Pesticide Fact Sheet - EPA

See http://www.epa.gov/oppbppd1/biopesticides/factsheets/fs006430t.htm
for a fact sheet detailing the product chemistry, health effects and environmental risk
assessments, and regulatory history of MON810 maize.

APPENDIX C - Plant Phenotypic and Environmental Interactions- USDA-APHIS

1.   Phenotypic expression
Phenotypic expression of the transgenic plant relative to its nearest nontransgenic counterpart and/or to a range of cultivated types. Observed changes may warrant further in-depth studies. Applicants may provide valid scientific rationale to demonstrate that certain information requirements are unnecessary or impossible to provide.

1.1.   How does the transgenic plant compare to its non-transgenic counterpart with respect to the following reproductive and survival biological characteristics?
      a.   Growth habit - changes in basic morphology
      b.   Life-span - annual, biennial, perennial
      c.   Vegetative biomass / vigor
      d.   Overwintering capacity
      e.   Flowering period / Days to first flowering
      f.   Days to maturity
      g.   Seed production - number of seeds produced per plant and a description of the various environmental conditions, to evaluate number of seeds produced in favorable and in variable environments.
      h.   Continuous seed production -Length of time (days) of seed production
      I.   Seed dormancy
      j.   Seedling emergence -proportion of seeds planted that emerge as seedlings under field conditions and a description of the various environmental conditions, to evaluate emergence in more variable environments, especially those outside the

         managed ecosystems
      k.   Seedling survival to reproduction
      l.   Outcross frequency within species (e.g. 0-1, 2-20, 21-100%)
      m.   Cross pollination vectors -change in pollinator species
      n.   Pollen viability - proportion viable and length of survival
      o.   Fertility or infertility - male or female
      p.   Self-compatibility or -incompatibility
      q.   Asexual reproduction, i.e. vegetative reproduction
      r.   Dispersal ability, i.e., seed shattering, digestibility, or palatability to birds or mammals

1.2.   How does the transgenic plant compare to its counterpart with respect to the following stress adaptations (specifically note which stresses were observed)?
      a.   Biotic stress factors: includes pathogens, competitors, symbionts, and herbivores
      b.   Abiotic stress factors: includes atmosphere (i.e., ozone, NOx), soil nutrients, temperature, and moisture

c.   Pesticides

1.3.   Does the transgenic plant differ in nutritional composition from its nontransgenic counterparts (e.g., protein, lipids, etc.)?

1.4.   Does the transgenic plant differ from its counterparts in levels of known naturally expressed toxicants?

2.   Potential nontarget effects

2.1.   Is the introduced gene product a novel part of the diet of humans, animals, or insects?

2.2.   Does the introduced DNA directly or indirectly lead to the expression of a toxin or other product that is known to affect metabolism, growth, development, or reproduction of animals, plants, or microbes?

2.3.   Is there a potential effect (toxic or nontoxic) to organisms that may be associated with the crop, including insect, avian, aquatic, or mammalian species, and organisms that are beneficial (pollinators, predators, parasites, biological control organisms, soil microbes), from both endogenous [naturally expressed] or non-endogenous [transgenic] compounds? APHIS considers routes of exposure to all plant parts that express the gene, i.e., direct feeding or other exposure to the plant or plant part, dispersed plant parts, or organisms that have fed on the plant.

2.3.1. In what parts of the plant is the gene product expressed and at what levels?

2.3.2. Has typical pollinator and other insect activity (i.e. feeding) been observed on the transgenic plant?

2.4.   Is there potential for adverse human health effects, e.g., exposure to toxins, irritants, and allergens? APHIS considers estimated level and most likely route of human exposure to the gene products, breakdown products and by-product.

2.5.   Does the transgenic plant differ from the nontransgenic plant in residual effects on soil microflora and microfauna?

2.6.   Will the introduced trait directly or indirectly result in altered physiological or behavioral characteristics of animals (e.g., pheromones, hormones, or attractants; altered seed morphology; altered growth habit)?

3.   Growing the Transgenic Plant - Interactions of the transgenic plant in the environment (Agricultural ecosystems)

3.1   Description of the growing area

3.1.1.   Is the transgenic plant intended to be grown in all of the U.S.? If in a specific region of the country, please provide.

3.1.2.   What is the projected total area being grown?

3.1.3.   Will the transgenic plant be grown outside of the normal geographic areas for the species?

3.1.3.1 If yes, identify and describe the new geographical area(s) in which the transgenic plant can be grown.

3.1.4.   Will the transgenic plant be grown outside of the usual managed ecosystems for the species?

3.1.4.1 If yes, identify and describe the new ecosystems in which the transgenic plant can be grown.

3.1.4.2 Will the introduced trait allow the plant to be grown or survive in a new habitat where it could impact nontarget organisms including populations of plants with which it can interbreed?

3.2.   Description of cultural practices

3.2.1.   Will the cultural practices (land preparation, fertilizer usage, weed and pest control, harvest, post-harvest protocols, etc.) involved in growing the transgenic plant vary from those traditionally used?

3.2.1.1 If yes, describe the change in cultural practices. Provide information showing the effect of these changes on sustainability, pesticide use, frequency of tillage, soil erosion and consequential changes in energy and soil conservation.

3.2.2.   Will volunteer plants of the transgenic plant necessitate altered cultural practices for succeeding crops?

3.2.2.1 If yes, describe alternative practices to control volunteers?

3.2.3.   Are any specific deployment strategies recommended for this transgenic plant?

3.2.3.1 Insect Resistance Management - Has an insect resistance management (IRM) strategy been submitted to EPA or is this product under an existing IRM with EPA?

3.2.3.2 Herbicide Resistance Management - Describe any strategies that will be needed to delay the development of resistant weeds.

3.3.   If it is anticipated that the transgenic plant will be grown only under contract/controlled conditions (e.g. Pharmaceuticals, biologics), describe:
  _   any control and mitigation procedures;
  _   post-harvest procedures, including procedures for disposal of remaining plant matter.

4.   Introgression - Potential Environmental Effects Resulting from Introgression

4.1.   Will the crop be grown in proximity to species with which it can interbreed?

4.2.   Does the introduced trait increase the likelihood of introgression between the crop and species with which it can interbreed?

4.3.   Where there is potential for gene flow from the transgenic plant into related species, detail the consequences of novel gene introgression into those species and resulting expression. Interactions identified for the transgenic plant should be considered, as appropriate, for these species.

4.3.2.   Is the compatible wild relative considered a weed and/or is it invasive?

4.3.3.   Does the introduced trait increase reproductive fitness or confer a selective advantage on the wild relative?

4.3.3.1 Is the potential for the trait to increase reproductive fitness or confer a selective advantage different than the potential for this to occur from a similar trait, if there is one, in a traditionally bred line of the same crop?

4.3.3.2 Is the introduced trait similar to a trait found currently in natural populations of the compatible wild relatives?

4.3.4.   Does the introduced trait have a significant impact on the establishment and spread of populations of wild relatives?

<u>SIDEBAR No. II.A</u>

BIOCONTROL USING A VIRUS (AcMNPV)

Overview

This sidebar examines a baculovirus that affects gypsy moths and which has been genetically modified to express scorpion toxin. The transgenic virus kills tobacco budworm and corn earworm, which are plant pests, more quickly than the unmodified virus. This GEO is still in small-scale field test stage.

1.   Proposed Organism and Use

Granuloviruses (GVs) and nucleopolyhedroviruses (NPVs) belong to a family of insect viruses called baculoviruses. Baculoviruses infect insects, such as moths and beetles, and certain closely related species. Most of the research on GVs and NPVs has involved viral species that infect insect larvae that harm plants; all of the baculovirus species approved as of February 2000 for use in pesticide products act against moth larvae. Baculoviruses are relatively specific regarding their target insects. For example, the gypsy moth NPV seems capable of infecting only gypsy moth larvae and other Lymantriids.

GVs and NPVs have a more complicated structure than most viruses. Most known viruses exist as individual viral particles, with each particle consisting of viral nucleic acid surrounded by a protein shell. By contrast, GVs and NPVs are complex viruses, protected by a protein overcoat. For NPVs, there are usually one or more enveloped virus particles or virions embedded in a proteinaceous matrix, called polyhedrin. GVs, by contrast, have one enveloped virus particle or virion embedded in a protein matrix called granulin. For both kinds of insect viruses, the protein overcoat and everything within it is called an "occlusion body." It keeps the virus particles occluded, or separate, from the outside environment. Because the occlusion bodies are the actual structural units that infect larvae, EPA has registered the occlusion bodies of individual viruses as the pesticide active ingredient.

These insect viruses become active only after susceptible larvae ingest the occlusion bodies. In the larval gut, the protein overcoat quickly disintegrates, and the viral particles proceed to infect digestive cells. Within a few days, the larvae become unable to digest food, and they weaken and die.

Tests show that the GV and NPVs that EPA has registered as pesticide active ingredients specifically infect only certain species of moth larvae. The viruses do not harm other organisms, including plants, beneficial insects, other wildlife, or the environment. These viruses occur naturally in their insect hosts.

The nuclear polyhedrosis virus (AcMNPV) of Autographa californica has been genetically modified to express the toxin of the scorpion, Leiurus quinquestriatus hebraeus. This multiple embedded wild type nuclear polyhedrosis virus (AcMNPV) has the ability to infect Trichoplusia ni, Heliothis virescens, Helicoverpa zea, and, to a lesser extent, Spodoptera exigua and S. frugiperda. The addition of the insect-specific scorpion toxin to the viral genome provides for a rapid mortality among infected insects, but does not alter the host range of the virus significantly (AcMNPV/LqhIT2), if at all.

In total, six submissions have been received for field testing of genetically modified baculoviruses from May 1995 through August of 1998. Four of these utilized the AcMNPV with additions of insect-specific toxin genes: three from two different scorpions and one from a mite. Two others are based upon modified Helicoverpa zea single-embedded nuclear polyhedrosis virus (HzSNPV) each using an insect-specific scorpion toxin from one of two scorpion species. Since the issues are very similar between the various baculovirus constructs, only the AcMNPV/LqhIT2 biopesticide will be discussed herein.

The AcMNPV/LqhIT2 would be sprayed onto leaf surfaces and thereby consumed by leaf feeding insects, such as the tobacco budworm / corn earworm (Heliothis virescens / Helicoverpa zea). The virus does not replicate to the same degree as wild type AcMNPV and, therefore, is somewhat limited in its spread. Since the mortality observed for wild type and modified AcMNPV/LqhIT2 was similar in the H. zea system, it is concluded that the genetic modification (i.e., addition of the scorpion toxin gene) does not alter the basic pathogenicity or host range of the AcMNPV.

The modified virus (GEO) will be applied to tobacco, cotton, cabbage, broccoli, and a few other vegetables for control of foliar feeding insects (e.g., corn earworm, cabbage looper). AcMNPV occlusion bodies are produced by mass infection of susceptible insects in the laboratory and harvest of the cadavers after a prescribed time. Insect cadavers contain large numbers of infective occlusion bodies, which contain individual viral particles in a membrane bound matrix. Homogenization and formulation of these particles is needed to prepare a workable biopesticide. When applied to vegetable and other crops, the particles reside on the external plant surfaces and are consumed by feeding insects. Once ingested, the particles will find their way into the cells of susceptible individuals. There they take over the host cell machinery and produce more infective virions within the occlusion body matrix. This may take several days and the inclusion of the insect-specific scorpion toxin to the viral genome speeds up the time to death for the infected insects. This, of course, results in less feeding damage to the crop as even infected insects will continue to feed.

Since the virus is not particularly stable on the plant surface, especially when exposed to sunlight and temperature extremes, and the transfer of virus from deceased host to a new living host is minimized compared to wild type virus, the AcMNPV/LqhIT2 will not persist very well in the environment. The host range of AcMNPV/LqhIT2 could conceivably include other insects than the target pest. Although the host range is known to be broader than some other NPV, the insects coming into contact with this biopesticide are likely to be pests as well, given the application site scenario. The AcMNPV/LqhIT2 is modified to provide a quicker death to the target insect, but does not show indications that the host range is enhanced or broadened. Field test and laboratory evaluations were conducted and reviewed, indicating that the host range is the same as wild type viruses already present in the environment. These baculoviruses are known from the literature to be specific to lepidopteran insects.

If the AcMNPV/LqhIT2 was able to proliferate and outcompete wild type NPV, it is conceivable that persistence of this biopesticide could alter the mortality of the subset of lepidopteran insects known to be susceptible. This is not likely to occur however, since the behavioral changes in infected larvae (with AcMNPV/LqhIT2) are known to be contrary to that contributing to a sustained epizootic. Larvae infected with AcMNPV/LqhIT2 form small, hard cadavers after being paralyzed by the insect-specific scorpion toxin and fall to the ground. In contrast, wild type NPV infected larvae liquefy and spread their viral load onto the leaf surface after death.

Given the specificity of AcMNPV/LqhIT2 and the target pests proposed, a general reduction in use of more broad-spectrum, chemical insecticides should ensue. This could encourage the proliferation of beneficial insect predators. Additionally, some of these pests do considerable damage even after being infected with wild type NPV or other entomopathogens, while the time to death following infection with the modified NPV reduces this window. The reduction in use of less specific (i.e., more toxic) control agents is a plus and the more rapid kill of the target pests results in less damage (i.e., better yield). For some crops (e.g., cabbage), the cosmetic appearance of the harvested product is key to marketability. By having the AcMNPV/LqhIT2 result in a faster kill, the overall marketable harvest may be drastically increased.

2.   Relevant Regulatory Agencies, Regulatory Authority and Legal Measures

Two federal agencies, EPA's Office of Pesticide Programs and USDA's Animal and Plant Health Inspection Service (APHIS), share the primary responsibility for regulating microbial pesticides. Whenever claims are made for reducing damage caused by pests, the product is a "pesticide" subject to EPA oversight. EPA registers and regulates pesticides, including genetically engineered organisms (GEOs) intended to be used to control a pest, such as an insect, or plant disease organism. EPA's review includes an assessment of the potential impacts on human health, as well as impacts on non-target wildlife and the broader environment. If there are residues of a microbial pesticide in or on food or feed, EPA must establish either a tolerance or a tolerance exemption for the food or feed bearing those residues to move in interstate commerce (i.e., be sold). USDA analyzes GEOs for potential impact on agriculture, as well as for impacts on the broader environment.

In addition, the U.S. Department of the Interior and the Food and Drug Administration (FDA) have consultative and regulatory roles. FDA acts to review any GEOs that may cause an alteration in the nutritional state of a food or otherwise contribute to a food safety issue.

The following discussion focuses on those aspects of the regulatory regime most relevant to this sidebar. More details may be found in the accompanying case study (Bt-Maize).

Statutory authority

EPA

EPA administers two statutes which contain authority to regulate AcMNPV/LqhIT2 and other microbial pesticides: the Federal Insecticide, Fungicide and Rodenticide Act (FIFRA), 7 U.S.C. 136-136y, and section 408 of the Federal Food, Drug, and Cosmetic Act (FFDCA), 21 U.S.C. 371-379d. Section 408 of the FFDCA was amended by the Food Quality Protection Act (FQPA), Pub. Law 104-170 (1996), after AcMNPV/LqhIT2 was approved for a small-scale field test. In addition, the Endangered Species Act (ESA) and the federal Migratory Bird Treaty Act (MBTA) impose obligations on EPA, which the Agency discharges in consultation with the Department of the Interior.[6] Conducting these small-scale field tests in agricultural areas is not expected to expose any endangered or threatened species to this biopesticide. No listed species are known to feed on the crops being evaluated. A narrow host range for this baculovirus also minimizes the possibility a listed species might be harmed by exposure to AcMNPV/LqhIT2. Based on these provisions, no formal consultation with the DOI was required.

The FFDCA authorizes EPA to establish a tolerance for a pesticide if the "residue in or on food is safe." Similarly, EPA may establish an exemption from the requirement of a tolerance if the Administrator determines that the exemption is "safe." AcMNPV/LqhIT2 was approved for field testing on a "crop-destruct" basis, hence, no tolerance was required.

Implementing regulations

---

[6] Courts have determined that EPA's risk assessment process is functionally equivalent to the NEPA process and therefore EPA is not required to conduct an EA or EIS as aprt of its registration process.

At least 90 days prior to conducting any small scale test of a genetically modified microbial pesticide, other than those described at 40 C.F.R. 172.45(d), a Notification must be submitted to the EPA in which the details of the genetic modification, proposed application methods and sites, and any potential toxicity or non-target organism effects are delineated. 40 C.F.R. 172, subpart C. Measures must also be outlined in the Notification submission which indicate the methods of containment and monitoring used to ensure the GEO does not become established in the ecosystem. 40 C.F.R. 172.48. The data required to support a request for a Notification are detailed in 40 C.F.R. Part 172.48. If the proposed field test is to be greater than 10 acres of treated land per pest evaluated, or greater than 1 acre for aquatic uses, then an experimental use permit is necessary. 40 C.F.R. 172.3.

Both of the genetically modified NPV biopesticides that have been considered by the Agency were processed through a Notification procedure for small-scale field tests. Neither NPV has been approved for an EUP or registered.

EPA's regulation of the pre-registration sale or distribution of a pesticide occurs primarily through its experimental use permit process. The agency approves testing only for the purpose of gathering data to support an application for registration, and only for an area sufficient to collect reliable information. Typically, EPA does not approve field testing of GEOs for more than 5000 acres.

In addition, if the experimental design involves the production of food for distribution in interstate commerce, a tolerance or temporary exemption is necessary to allow the food to be moved in commerce. A person may avoid the need for a tolerance by destroying the crop treated with the unregistered pesticide; a "crop-destruct" provision would then be imposed on the EUP. See 40 C.F.R. 172.4(b)(2).

Granting of an EUP is contingent on satisfactory data to support a risk assessment and a finding that the proposed experimental use will not result in unreasonable adverse effects on the environment. The data required to support a request for an EUP are detailed in 40 CFR Part 158. Site visits to the experimental plots can and have been performed, resulting in plot destruction in one instance for failure to follow the conditions established in the EUP.

USDA-APHIS

The USDA's Animal and Plant Health Inspection Service (APHIS) has the authority to regulate plant pests and other articles, including insect viruses, to prevent direct or indirect injury, disease, or damage to plants, plant products, and crops. Under authority granted by the Plant Protection Act, 7 U.S.C. 7701-7772, APHIS regulates the introduction (importation, interstate movement, or release into the environment) of certain genetically engineered organisms and products. A genetically engineered organism is deemed a regulated article if either the donor organism, recipient organism, vector or vector agent used in engineering the organism belongs to one of the taxa listed in §340.2 of the regulations and is also a plant pest; if it is unclassified; or, if APHIS has reason to believe that the genetically engineered organism presents a plant pest risk (7 CFR Part 340).

The National Environmental Policy Act (NEPA), 42 U.S.C. 4321-4375, applies to the APHIS review process and mandates consideration by APHIS of a broad range of environmental issues. In fulfilling its NEPA responsibilities, APHIS prepares an Environmental Assessment (EA) in which APHIS determines whether it has adequate information to conclude its proposed regulatory action will have no significant impact on the environment. If APHIS can make a "finding of no significant impact" (FONSI), NEPA requires no further analysis. If APHIS cannot make a FONSI, APHIS must prepare a draft environmental impact statement (EIS) and make it available for interagency and public comment.

As with other genetically engineered products, particularly insect viruses, USDA examines whether application of AcMNPV/LqhIT2 poses a direct or indirect plant pest risk to agriculture or the environment under its regulatory authority. AcMNPV/LqhIT2 was determined not to pose a plant pest risk, and therefore not regulated by APHIS. Thus further regulatory activities, including the environmental review, were deferred to EPA.

3.   Hazard Identification, Risk Assessment and Regulatory Review of Product

FIFRA allows EPA to consider all relevant factor in reviewing and approving a pesticide for registration. This includes a risk / benefit analysis of the potential environmental and occupational impacts, and an assessment of all potential human health impacts. EPA may only register a pesticide if it finds that, when used in accordance with widespread and commonly recognized practice, the pesticide will not generally cause unreasonable adverse effects on the environment. FIFRA sections 2(bb) & 3(c)(5).

1. EPA's Hazard Identification and Risk Assessment of AcMNPV/LqhIT2

Product characterization requirements for AcMNPV/LqhIT2 included details of the gene source (what organism), DNA and amino acid sequence data, details of the vector used in transformation (annotated map), method of transformation, the pesticidal substance encoded by the gene, expression levels under field conditions wherein the insect-specific toxin is expressed in susceptible insects, glycosylation of the pesticidal protein where appropriate (presence/absence and similarity between microbial and invertebrate forms), and bioassays against larvae of the corn ear worm or the cabbage looper.

The Agency also required the applicant to explain the use pattern (i.e., will the crop be used for human consumption, animal feed only, ornamental uses, etc.). AcMNPV/LqhIT2 is used for control of leaf feeding insects in various vegetable crops and tobacco.

Once the agency has understood the product and its proposed uses, EPA evaluates the potential hazards of microbial pesticides in two broad areas: human health and environmental effects. Risks to humans and animals via the dietary route, and to non-target organisms via water, wind, soil and direct consumption of the GEO are all considered within the risk assessment. If other routes of potential exposure exist, such as dermal absorption, these risks are also addressed.

Human health

No toxicity was noted in mammalian toxicity evaluations with the insect-specific scorpion toxin. In these toxicity studies, the dose level of toxin administered to the test animals far exceeded the possible human consumption levels via the diet or exposure in the environment through soil and water. Having this leeway one can expect that the level of human exposure to scorpion toxin from AcMNPV/LqhIT2 will fall far below any potential effect level.

Environmental assessment

Non-target organism studies include the toxicity characterization for: fish (catfish or trout), aquatic invertebrates (Daphnia), earthworms, Collembola (springtails), beneficial insects (green lacewing, ladybird beetle, honey bee, parasitic wasp), birds (Bobwhite quail or Mallard duck), and any other species considered as being exposed or at risk from the pesticidal substance.

Endangered or threatened species are given special consideration, and EPA may require testing with related, abundant species to assess possible non-target effects. Studies of non-target species are typically designed as single dose, maximum hazard toxicity assessments, and animals are observed for varying time frames depending on the species (14 to 30 days typically).

EPA does not attempt to evaluate the possible future changes in social and ecological conditions (e.g., climate). Predictability of climatic change is difficult at best. The limit dose testing performed for the assessment of toxicity is at a level that exceeds the amounts of pesticidal substance present on the plant surface under any foreseeable conditions. The EPA regulatory process does not end with registration, but continues and has the ability to modify the registration at a later date as warranted.

Finally, EPA takes into account any other relevant information. In the case of AcMNPV/LqhIT2, EPA considered the history of the use of baculoviruses as a microbial biopesticide and the wealth of literature regarding host range and mode of activity of these agents. This experience showed that the NPVs have a limited host range and the insect-specific toxin has virtually no toxicity to mammalian and other non-target species. Any effect on other species vis-a-vis the insect-specific scorpion toxin would require infection of that species' cells as a prerequisite. Hence, the introduction of the toxin to the non-target organisms would be precluded.

2. EPA's Consideration of the Risks and Benefits of AcMNPV/LqhIT2

As noted above, FIFRA's standard for registration decisions involves an assessment of risks and benefits of using a pesticide. One of the primary benefits of a biopesticide is the replacement of pesticides that may pose greater risks, e.g., groundwater contamination, toxicity to non-target organisms, or dietary risks to infants and children. To date, however, decisions to approve NPVs have relied primarily on their lack of toxicity to all organisms tested, except target pests. Nonetheless, EPA has also considered possible benefits that might result from use of AcMNPV/LqhIT2. Application of AcMNPV/LqhIT2 will likely reduce the use of other insecticides and thereby will avoid the types of risks those insecticides might have had, if applied to the same acreage as AcMNPV/LqhIT2.

Targeting the insect-specific toxin to the point of feeding of pest insects should minimize the impact of pesticides on non-target organisms and minimize ground water contamination, as may occur with use of some chemical pesticides. Because many of the previously deployed insecticides were broad-spectrum in their activities, the potential for impacts on the beneficial insect populations was significant. Populations of beneficial insects should increase over time as more GEOs with host specificity are used and fewer broad-spectrum pesticides are applied. Since some insecticides have effects on non-insect organisms (e.g., earthworms, nematodes), the reduction or elimination of these pesticides will help to nurture these populations as long as cultural practices of soil management are adequate.

Additionally, the exposure of farm workers, pesticide applicators and the public in general is reduced when a biological pesticide takes the place of a chemical spray alternative. Residues on food are also less a concern with AcMNPV/LqhIT2, because the insect toxin is known to be non-toxic to humans and other mammals. Spray drift is often problematic with chemical applications, but this is not a significant issue with target specific NPVs.

3. History of EPA's Regulatory Review of AcMNPV/LqhIT2.

Based on the hazard identification, risk assessment, and risk-benefit analysis described above, EPA determined that the notifications submitted for AcMNPV/LqhIT2 met the statutory standards for issuing approval for a small-scale field test. Because AcMNPV/LqhIT2 and other similar modified NPV involve a new technology about which there is some uncertainty, EPA issued the permission with some restrictions: all crops treated must be destroyed; field tests must not be conducted in areas of endangered species habitat; and each field test must include a non-recombinant NPV control inoculation to ensure a source of competing baculovirus and thereby reduce the persistence of AcMNPV/LqhIT2.

As noted above, AcMNPV/LqhIT2 is generally non-toxic to all species, except certain insects. These characteristics led EPA to focus primarily on two types of potential risks: (1) the persistence of AcMNPV/LqhIT2 in the environment, and (2) the risk to non-target insects. These risk scenarios require proper monitoring of proliferation of the AcMNPV/LqhIT2 based biopesticide, and examination of potential non-target influence on insects inhabiting the area of application to prevent or mitigate adverse effects. That is, if an adverse event should be observed, the potential hazard could be mitigated by halting further applications, altering the distribution of this biopesticide geographically or other remedial measures. Failure to monitor or analyze the data gathered from such assessments would be a potential avenue for proliferation of these risks.

4. Information and Data

FIFRA and FFDCA give EPA the authority to require whatever studies are necessary to complete a risk assessment of a pesticide. EPA regulations (40 CFR Part 158) detail the standard data requirements for plant-pesticides. Applicants may request waivers for required studies if they deem such studies unnecessary for a risk assessment. Guidelines (885 series) determine the protocols that may be used for most of the required toxicity tests. Any significant variations from the protocol proposed by an applicant normally require independent validation of the novel test method. Additionally, primary literature (peer-reviewed) is a key source of new developments that may influence the type of data requested from registrants and if EPA will accept waivers for certain studies. After reviewing any waiver requests, agency scientists determine on a case-by-case basis whether studies will be waived, or additional studies will be required for a specific GEO.

Generally EPA-required data for product characterization and toxicity tests are generated directly by the applicant or through the use of a commercial laboratory that specializes in performing chemistry / toxicity studies. Fate data, field expression data and product characterization studies are also generally performed by the applicant. Toxicity and non-target studies are usually done by an outside contract lab that has experience in toxicology and the application of EPA guideline requirements.

All submitted studies are reviewed by Agency scientists. Outside scientific experts may be contacted for the purpose of verifying scientific background information as needed. On particularly critical scientific issues, EPA may consult with its FIFRA Science Advisory panel (SAP), a Federal Advisory Committee Act-chartered group of independent experts in scientific issues related to pesticides. The SAP's advice may concern broad issues, e.g. modifying existing guidelines or creating new ones, or may concern a specific pending regulatory action.

Appropriate scientific and regulatory expertise exists within APHIS, EPA and FDA to review all submissions for scientific accuracy and interpretation. EPA evaluates data for scientific soundness based on experience with the types of studies and the anticipated results. Agency scientists have the right to question any data that appear to be erroneous, falsified or otherwise questionable in nature. This may take the form of a request for clarification or another study with modifications.

Penalties for falsification of data can range from a monetary fine to imprisonment and combinations thereof. An extensive auditing program exists within EPA's Office of Enforcement and Compliance Assurance to ensure that laboratories are capable of carrying out the prescribed studies and that their equipment is in satisfactory working order. These audits can be carried out on a random basis or targeted to a specific laboratory if there is reason to believe that data have been falsified or in any manner misrepresented.

5.   Mitigation And Management Considerations: Approvals And Conditions On Research, Development, Production, Distribution, Marketing, Use And Disposal

This paper has already discussed many different types of conditions that may be imposed on an experimental use permit or registration of a microbial pesticide. In addition, for non-commercial field release, containment of the test site can be mandated to preclude movement of the GEO into the wild. This can be achieved in a variety of ways, with both physical and biological barriers.

6. Monitoring And Consideration Of New Information

As discussed above, EPA has considerable ongoing authority to regulate the post-registration use of a microbial pesticide. This authority includes: (1) issuance of data call-in notices to obtain additional information from registrants needed to evaluate the safety of a pesticide (see section 3. A. 1., above) and (2) assuring compliance with conditions imposed on the pesticide's approval for field testing.

As a condition on the approval for field testing of AcMNPV/LqhIT2, EPA required DuPont to develop and implement plans for monitoring persistence of AcMNPV/LqhIT2. A key element of the monitoring plans for AcMNPV/LqhIT2 is the observation of environmental persistence. The registrant must ensure the safe application to the area of the target insects while precluding any exposure to endangered species or other susceptible non-target organisms. Any adverse incident reports must be filed with Agency.

EPA, however, performed and will continue to take an active oversight role in both the development and implementation of the monitoring plans, as well as in assuring that there is compliance with other requirements. The monitoring plans were developed by the registrant using a process that included input from Agency scientists.

7.   Enforcement and Compliance

FIFRA and FFDCA generally provide the authority to enforce all provisions regarding regulation of pesticides and presence of pesticide residues on food products. As noted above, FDA is responsible for enforcing EPA's tolerance requirements. With respect to FIFRA compliance, as noted in the preceding paragraph, EPA relies on the independent assessment by researchers and the registrant to determine compliance.

EPA can take regulatory action to impose penalties or to restrict or prohibit the sale and distribution of any approved pesticidal product, including AcMNPV/LqhIT2, if it necessary to prevent unreasonable adverse effects on the environment, or necessary to prevent threatened violations of the FIFRA. This could include, for example, seizure of pesticide-product (i.e., formulated NPV) or the assessment of civil and/or criminal penalties. FIFRA sections 13 & 14. FIFRA sections 8 and 9 provide statutory authority for the Agency to inspect the producing establishment, inspect books and records. In addition, if a pesticide does not comply with the provisions of FIFRA, or as a result of widespread misuse, EPA may cancel a pesticide registration. FIFRA section 6(b). EPA may also cancel or suspend a pesticide if necessary to prevent unreasonable adverse effects on the environment. FIFRA sections 6(b)-(c).

8. Public Involvement and Transparency

In addition to the general description in the accompanying case study (Bt-maize), open Scientific Advisory Panel (SAP) meetings have been held on various topics including insect resistance management, toxicity, non-target organism effects and other aspects associated with GEOs. During these panel meetings, the public is invited to make public statements and engage the panel in discussion of specific topics.

The Agency website (http://www.epa.gov/oppbppd1/biopesticides/) and published materials (e.g., booklets, proceedings of workshops, pamphlets) help disseminate information related to GEOs. Both APHIS and EPA websites provide a list and links to agency regulations and provides an explanation of the process. Regulatory decisions and the outcome of EPA's toxicology reviews are posted for public review. The website also provides for contact directly with Agency scientists and regulators to address issues of concern. Additionally, scientists may publish articles in trade and peer-reviewed journals, monographs and books which outline Agency position on topics related to regulation of GEOs.

Finally, EPA maintains a public docket, which contains a large number of documents available for inspection and copying, including scientific reviews on safety issues and Reregistration Eligibility Decisions (REDs) on individual plant-pesticides. The Freedom of Information Act (FOIA) also provides for the request of any document submitted to support a pesticide registration as long as it does not contain confidential business information. Comments were received following publication of Federal Register Notices describing genetically engineered baculoviruses. Comments were concerned with persistence of the virus in the environment and methods used for containment of field tests. The Agency responded by imposing stricter containment provisions on the field tests. Studies described above also indicate that the host range of the modified virus is not extended and the replication of biopesticide is decreased relative to wild type forms. Hence, the opportunity for persistence through a sustained infection cycle is lessened. Given the rapid death of AcMNPV/LqhIT2 hosts as compared to wild type AcMNPV and the production of fewer new virus particles per cadaver, greater exposure of other organisms to the modified NPV are not expected.

Brief Overview of Regulation of Genetically Modified Arthropods

Genetic engineering of arthropods that may be released into the environment might include: engineering for more effective biocontrol (which may invoke FIFRA), and engineering of disease vectors (such as mosquitoes) in disease control for human or animal health. The effectiveness of the above in meeting the desired goals when they are in the environment depends on understanding of the complex interactions between the arthropods, their hosts, other organisms and the environment. Future uses might include production of chemicals or pharmaceuticals in insects and genetic engineering of pet arthropods.

APHIS authorities over arthropods

APHIS has established regulations (7 CFR 340) under the Federal Plant Pest Act and the Plant Quarantine Act to provide oversight for genetically engineered (transgenic) arthropods that are plant pests or that can impact plant pests. These regulations cover plant pests, vectors of plant diseases, and biocontrol agents. Various APHIS procedures are in place to process permit applications for importation, interstate movement, and release into the environment.

APHIS has overall statutory authority (21 U.S.C. 111) and general regulatory authority (9 CFR 122) to take whatever measures deemed necessary to prevent the introduction and/or dissemination of contagious/infectious/communicable diseases of animals (21 U.S.C. 134), and to restrict the importation and movement of organisms and vectors of those diseases (51 FR 23341).

At the moment, however, APHIS statutes and regulations do not specifically address the issue of Agency oversight for genetically engineered vectors of animal diseases. APHIS presently is considering whether there is a need for specific regulations in this area, and may eventually develop new regulations by publishing an Advance Notice of Proposed Rulemaking and a subsequent Proposed Final Rule and a Final Rule.

Further information on permits issued and an environmental assessment for a field trial of a genetically engineered mite can be found on the APHIS website: "http://www.aphis.usda.gov/biotech/arthropod/".

EPA Authority

Under TSCA, EPA has jurisdiction with respect to the manufacture of new and existing chemicals for commercial purposes. Production of new chemicals by use of arthropods is required to be notified to EPA. The arthropods themselves may also be regulated by EPA if they qualify as chemical substances under TSCA.

CASE STUDY No. III

HERBICIDE-TOLERANT SOYBEAN

Overview

This case study examines the approved product glufosinate-tolerant soybeans. This variety of soybean was genetically engineered by AgrEvo (now Aventis) to be tolerant to the herbicide glufosinate ammonium (herein referred to as glufosinate), a chemical already in agricultural use. A modified bacterium gene was added to the soybean so that the plant produces an enzyme that breaks down the herbicide before it can harm the soybean plant. Genetic material from other sources was inserted to control the expression of the enzyme. As with many other genetically engineered products, glufosinate tolerant soybeans are regulated by various regulatory agencies as described in the "Coordinated Framework for Regulation of Biotechnology" (Office of Science and Technology Policy (OSTP), 1986).

The United States Department of Agriculture (USDA) assessed whether the growing of glufosinate-tolerant soybeans poses a direct or indirect plant pest risk to agriculture or the environment under its regulatory authority. The United States Environmental Protection Agency (EPA), being responsible for regulation of all pesticides, assessed the new use of glufosinate on soybeans and established the maximum residue levels ("tolerances") that were safe for human consumption. The safety and labeling of such soybeans for use as food or animal feed is regulated by the Food and Drug Administration (FDA). FDA enforces pesticide tolerances set by EPA. In addition, EPA has the authority under TSCA to address the potential for the development of herbicide-resistant relatives, or to otherwise regulate unreasonable risks to human health or the environment presented by herbicide tolerant plants.

1. Description of Proposed Organism and Its Use

Glufosinate-tolerant soybeans, comprised of multiple lines described in a petition submitted by AgrEvo (AgrEvo, 1996), have been genetically engineered to tolerate the herbicidal compound by producing phosphinothricin acetyl transferase (PAT), an enzyme that detoxifies the herbicide. The synthetic *pat* gene that was added was a modified version of the native *pat* gene from the soil bacterium *Streptomyces viridochromogenes*. Genetic lines described in the petition fell into two groups representing two different transformation vectors used to produce them. One group contained a promoter sequence designated as P-35S from cauliflower mosaic virus and a terminator sequence designated as T-*nos* from the plant pathogenic bacterium *Agrobacterium tumefaciens*. The other lines contained both promoters (P-35S) and terminators (T-35S) derived from cauliflower mosaic virus. Each group also contained other sequences from varying sources that were not expressed in plants.

Soybeans were grown on over 72 million acres in the U.S. during 1999 and represent one of the most important crops in the U.S. for both export and internal consumption. The most important production area is the Midwest, but production also takes place in the southern Mississippi River valley, the southern coastal plains, and elsewhere along the eastern seaboard. Traditionally, pre-emergence herbicides have been the major tool used for weed control in conventional soybean production, in which entire fields are treated prior to or at planting before crops and weeds have emerged. Recently, due in part to the advent of effective post emergence herbicides, there has been a shift toward no-till production. No-till production systems involve planting crops into the stubble of previously-grown crops without plowing the soil, providing the advantages of decreased fuel use and less soil compaction due to reduced travel of heavy machinery through the fields, reduced soil erosion, and soil moisture conservation. Glufosinate-tolerant soybeans facilitates post emergence weed control which is critical to no-till agriculture. Under this production system, weeds can be more efficiently managed by applying herbicide when and where the weeds occur after planting, in contrast to a conventional soybean production system in which herbicides are applied as preventative measure prior to planting. The glufosinate herbicide is effective against a broad range of monocot and dicot plant species, and has low residual activity, low soil leaching and low toxicity to nontarget organisms.

It is anticipated that glufosinate tolerant soybeans might be grown in virtually all important soybean-growing areas of the U.S. The harvested product is used in a variety of domestic foods and feed products and is exported to numerous foreign countries. Most soybeans have been stored and marketed as bulk commodities such that transgenic soybeans are mixed with conventionally bred types.

2.   Relevant Regulatory Agencies, Regulatory Authority and Legal Measures

USDA/APHIS

The USDA's Animal and Plant Health Inspection Service (APHIS) has the authority to regulate the importation, interstate movement, and release into the environment of plant pests and other articles to prevent direct or indirect injury, disease, or damage to plants or plant products. APHIS regulates genetically engineered organisms under authority granted by the Plant Protection Act (PPA), (7 U.S.C. §§ 7701-7772) which states "it is the responsibility of the Secretary to facilitate exports, imports, and interstate commerce in agricultural products and other commodities that pose a risk of harboring plant pests or noxious weeds in ways that will reduce, to the extent practical, as determined by the Secretary, the risk of disseminating plant pests or noxious weeds." A genetically engineered organism is deemed a "regulated article" if either the donor organism, recipient organism, vector or vector agent used in engineering the organism belongs to one of the taxa listed in 7 CFR Part 340.2 of the regulations, or if it is not identified taxonomically. That is to say, the development of genetically engineered plants using biological vectors or regulatory sequences derived from plant pathogenic sources serves as a regulatory trigger, initiating an evaluation process to assure that there is not a plant pest risk.

Importantly, products of genetic engineering may still be regulated by APHIS, even if not developed using a plant pest, if there is a reason to believe that the product itself might pose a plant pest risk. Field testing is typically used to demonstrate that genetically engineered crops exhibit the expected biological properties and to demonstrate that, although they may be derived using components from plant pests, they do not possess plant pest characteristics.

The PPA, effective as of June 22, 2000, replaces the Federal Plant Pest Act (FPPA) and Plant Quarantine Act (PQA) as APHIS's regulatory authority for genetically engineered organisms. The present case study focuses on regulatory authority and activities at the time of de-regulation of the glufosinate tolerant soybean, i.e., authority granted by the FPPA and PQA. APHIS is presently analyzing whether there are changes in authorities or potential for change based on the new PPA.

Movement, importation, and field testing (introduction). Prior to the introduction of a regulated article, a person is required under §340.1 of the regulations to either (1) notify APHIS in accordance with 7 CFR 340.3 or (2) obtain a permit in accordance with 7 CFR 340.4. Prior to April 1993, the only regulatory option for the planned introduction of transgenic plants covered by APHIS regulations was the permit. Regulations stipulate that once a complete permit request has been submitted, APHIS has 120 days in which to reach a decision whether to issue or deny a permit.

The early 1990's were marked by a rapid increase in the number of field trials in the United States of transgenic plants and plant-associated microbes, and there was an associated rise in permit requests, as these organisms were subject to APHIS regulatory authority to control articles that posed a plant pest risk. After the first six years of evaluating permits and considering the results of field trials under permit, experience demonstrated that criteria and performance standards could be defined for certain field tests that do not present novel plant pest risks. This gave rise to a new option, the notification, effective in April of 1993. Transgenic plants which raised certain safety issues, for example pharmaceutical-producing plants, plants transformed with genes of unknown function, or plants expressing sequences from human or animal viruses, were not eligible for the new option. The notification option originally covered six major crops, including soybeans, and was modified in May of 1997 to cover nearly all plants. The notification option represents a simpler, streamlined application and review process for importation, interstate movement and field testing. Notifications are logged into the USDA database, reviewed by one of the scientific staff for qualification, completeness (see section 4 for Data Requirements), and then a recommendation is sent to the appropriate State department of agriculture for review. If the State concurs with an APHIS recommendation of approval, an acknowledgment is then issued to the applicant. The regulations stipulate that the entire process will take no longer than 30 days from receipt of the notification.

The notification option (7 CFR 340.3) requires that the introduction meet specified eligibility criteria and performance standards. The eligibility criteria impose limitations on the types of genetic modification that qualify for notification, and the performance standards impose limitations on how the introduction may be conducted. These performance standards, compliance with which is subject to APHIS inspection, help to assure confinement of the regulated articles (see sections 5 and 7). Confinement is of central importance in APHIS's approach to the regulation of field testing. Confinement ensures that any environmental impact will be negligible because the article will not move beyond the field site and will not persist at the site beyond the intended duration of the test. All crop plants and most plants that are not listed as noxious weeds, as described in regulations at 7 CFR 360 under the Federal Noxious Weed Act at 7 U.S.C. § 2809, can be field tested under notification. Nearly 99 per cent of all field tests, importations, and interstate movements of engineered plants are performed under this system. The three major steps APHIS takes in this process are to: (1) evaluate relevant information (both that submitted by the permit applicant and that gathered by APHIS from other sources); (2) notify and consult with regulatory officials in States where the applicant proposes to field test; and (3) reach a decision as to whether to acknowledge or deny the notification.

In the particular case of soybean, performance standards were established that would maintain physical isolation of the plants and seeds.

Petition for determination of non-regulated status. As testing of one of these regulated articles proceeds, an applicant gathers information typically to establish for him/herself that the product has the new intended property, and also gathers information to demonstrate that the organism is not a plant pest risk. Evidence for safety relies in part on data that demonstrate that the engineered plant is biologically equivalent to a corresponding non-engineered line, with the exception of the intended new trait(s). When enough information is gathered, the applicant may petition APHIS for what is called a Determination of Non-regulated Status.

When APHIS gets a petition, the receipt of the application is announced in the Federal Register and copies are made available to the public (see Section 8, Public Involvement and Transparency). In 1996, when the glufosinate soybean petition was received and evaluated, the announcement marked the start of a 60-day public comment period on the petition and comments were then considered in the final determination and Environmental Assessment (EA). The EA was prepared pursuant to the National Environmental Policy Act (NEPA), 42 U.S.C. §§ 4321-4335. Since mid-1999, in addition to the 60-day comment period on the petition itself, notice of the availability of an environmental assessment (EA) is also published and public comments are solicited and accepted on the EA for a 30-day period. During the remaining 180 days, consultations are made as necessary with other agencies having expertise, the determination document is prepared, and the completed decision documents are subjected to legal review.

In general, the petitioner has to supply data and supporting information to indicate that the product does not present a plant pest risk at any time during the 180-day assessment process. The APHIS assessment relies on data and other information that demonstrates that, with the exception of the deliberately introduced trait, the genetically engineered line appears to be the same as a non-engineered parental line with respect to a suite of agronomic traits. If this is true, and if there is sufficient familiarity with the introduced trait, the recipient plant, and the environment, APHIS can determine with a high degree of confidence that the engineered plant is no more likely to be a plant pest than a traditionally bred plant. Issues and risks which are not science-based, such as consumer acceptance and marketability of genetically engineered products, are not a part of the APHIS analysis. Once a Determination of Non-regulated Status is issued, the new variety may be developed further through traditional breeding, produced, marketed, distributed, and grown without any other special oversight on the part of APHIS, however, before some plants can be used commercially, additional reviews may be necessary by the EPA and FDA. For example, the consultation process between FDA and AgrEvo for glufosinate tolerant soybeans was not completed until 1998, and so the product was not used for food or feed before that date.

Consideration by APHIS of a broad range of environmental issues is mandated under NEPA, which addresses the general decision making process for all government actions. In considering the broad range of possible impacts under NEPA, APHIS expertise overlaps with that of other federal agencies, namely with EPA for a host of environmental concerns such as nontarget effects, and worker exposure, and with NIH and FDA for potential negative impacts on animals and humans.

Glufosinate tolerant soybean, due to the presence of sequences derived from plant pests listed in 7 CFR Part 340.2, clearly meets the definition of a regulated article and is subject to APHIS regulation. All releases were conducted after APHIS approval in the form of 8 permits and 24 notifications issued from 1992 through 1996 when AgrEvo filed a petition for non-regulated status on March 8 of 1996. Following a review of the petition, a deficiency letter was sent to obtain additional information and clarification. Such letters are routine and are sent in response to virtually every petition, reflecting the thoroughness of the APHIS review. Upon receipt of the additional information the petition was announced in the Federal Register and made available for public reading and comments (see section on "Transparency and Public Involvement"). Eight comments were received from universities, extension centers, and a seed company. All supported the petition. A determination to deregulate under 7 CFR 340 and an environmental assessment to fulfill the NEPA obligation were prepared and the glufosinate tolerant lines were deregulated on August 16, 1996. Both of the decision documents are available at http://www.aphis.usda.gov/biotech (USDA, 1996).

EPA

Under Federal law, the EPA is responsible for regulating all pesticides, and setting the maximum levels ("tolerances") of pesticide chemical residues allowed in or on food and animal feed. In the case of glufosinate-tolerant soybean, EPA does not regulate the soybean plants themselves, but rather regulates the use of the herbicide on those plants. EPA's authority, and the limits to that authority, are contained in two core statutes, the Federal Insecticide, Fungicide, and Rodenticide Act (FIFRA), 7 U.S.C. §§ 136-136y, and the Federal Food, Drug, and Cosmetic Act (FFDCA), Section 408. In 1996, both statutes were amended by the Food Quality Protection Act (FQPA), Pub.L.104-170 (1996).

With minor exceptions, FIFRA requires that before anyone can sell or distribute a pesticide in the United States, they must obtain a registration, or license, from EPA. When making a registration decision, including those pertaining to the herbicides used on herbicide-tolerant crops, EPA must find that the pesticide, when used according to label directions, will not cause unreasonable adverse effects to human health or the environment. The registration of glusofinate on soybeans is considered to be a new use because heretofore the herbicide had not been used on soybeans. Registration decisions are based primarily on EPA's evaluation of the test data provided by applicants. FIFRA also requires a periodic reassessment of registrations to ensure they are meeting current scientific and regulatory standards, including with respect to the generation of data. FIFRA § 4.

Data requirements for pesticide registration are specified in the Code of Federal Regulations (40 CFR Part 158). Various types of data are required to assess the hazards and exposures for new chemicals prior to registration. Once a chemical is registered (which was the case here), there can be new data required to ascertain the additional exposure and ensure that the pesticide continues to meet the safety standard, i.e., that it "will not cause unreasonable adverse effects on the environment." In addition, a tolerance or a tolerance exemption may be required for the pesticide chemical residues resulting from this new use. Alternatively, the tolerance may be modified to change the existing tolerance level. What are usually required for herbicide-tolerant crops are data from field use on the herbicide-tolerant crop to provide an assurance about expected residues and any questions related to new metabolites or other products resulting from the activity of the newly introduced enzyme. EPA may also require other data relevant to determining whether the pesticide meets the safety standard. Specific reports submitted by the registrant in support of registration of the new use and a tolerance on herbicide-tolerant soybeans are cited in Appendix A.

EPA has established other requirements, such as the Good Laboratory Practice Standards, to ensure the quality and integrity of pesticide data. Depending on the type of pesticide, EPA's Office of Pesticide Programs can require more than 100 different tests. Testing is needed to determine whether a pesticide has the potential to cause adverse effects to humans, wildlife, fish, and plants, including endangered species. In addition to allowing the use of new pesticides, the Agency's Registration Program includes many activities related to the ongoing registration of existing pesticides. This may include, for example, label changes in where and how pesticides are used in order to reduce risks or in response to requests by registrants. These approved labels have the force of law, and any use, which is not in accordance with the label directions and precautions, may be subject to civil and/or criminal penalties.

Section 408 of the FFDCA, 21 U.S.C. § 346a, governs, among other things, the establishment of pesticide tolerances for food and feed products and gives the EPA authority to establish tolerances or exemptions from the requirement for a tolerance for pesticide chemical residues. A tolerance is the maximum level of pesticide chemical residues allowed in or on human food and animal feed.

The FFDCA makes unlawful the sale and distribution in interstate commerce of adulterated food. Food is defined broadly, and includes both food for humans and animals. Food is "adulterated" if it contains the residue of a "pesticide chemical" for which EPA has not established either a "tolerance" or an exemption from the requirement of a tolerance. (Almost all "pesticides" are "pesticide chemicals.")

The FFDCA authorizes EPA to establish a tolerance for a pesticide if the "residue in or on food is safe." Similarly, EPA may establish an exemption from the requirement of a tolerance if the Administrator determines that the exemption is "safe."

The Food Quality Protection Act (FQPA), signed into law on August 3, 1996, amended both FIFRA and FFDCA. The new FFDCA section 408 safety standard requires EPA to ensure that there is "a reasonable certainty that no harm will result from aggregate exposure to the pesticide chemical residue, including all anticipated dietary exposures and all other exposures for which there is reliable information." 21 U.S.C. § 346a(b)(2)(A)(ii). The new safety standard is measured by considering the aggregate risk from dietary exposure and other non-occupational sources of exposure, such as drinking water and residential lawn uses. In addition, to improve protection for all consumers, particularly the young, when setting new, or reassessing existing tolerances under the new standard, EPA must now focus explicitly on exposures and risks to infants and children. Decisions must consider whether tolerances are safe for children assuming, when appropriate, an additional safety factor to account for uncertainty in data. Any person may petition the EPA to establish a tolerance or an exemption from the requirement of a tolerance for a pesticide and its residues in food; the law authorizes EPA to require information in support of the petition to show that the tolerance or exemption would be safe.

In accordance with FIFRA and section 408 of the FFDCA, as amended by the FQPA, the information provided by the registrant (of glufosinate) allowed the EPA to amend the label for the currently registered use to include the use of glufosinate for use on glufosinate-tolerant soybeans in Spring of 1997. Since EPA is concerned with the risks associated with the uses of the herbicide, EPA does not necessarily reevaluate its analysis of the risks when a new herbicide-tolerant soybean variety with the same genetic transformation event, different events, or different constructs is created.

EPA also has authority under the Toxic Substances Control Act to regulate plants, including genetically engineered plants, when they are used for a purpose not excluded under section 3 of the Act. EPA's authority under TSCA extends from the research and development phase, through commercial manufacture, use, and disposal. For example, EPA has authority to require pre-market notification and Agency review of a new chemical substances, as well as existing chemical substances whose uses EPA has determined (by rule) to be a significant new use. EPA is also authorized to regulate an existing chemical substances under TSCA section 4 (data generation), sections 6 and 7 (impose restrictions to prevent unreasonable risks of injury to human health or the environment), and section 8 (information collection). Further information on TSCA regulations and biotechnology products can be found in this report in the Bioremediation and Biosensing using Bacteria case study and the EPA website.

Implementing regulations

Experimental use permits. EPA's regulation of the pre-registration sale or distribution of a pesticide occurs primarily through its experimental use permit (EUP) process. EPA does not typically require an EUP if a field test is less than 10 acres. The agency approves testing only for the purpose of gathering data to support an application for registration, and only for an area sufficient to collect reliable information. Typically, EPA does not approve field testing for more than 5,000 acres.

In addition, if the experimental design involves the production of food for distribution in commerce, a tolerance, temporary tolerance, or exemption must be established. A person may avoid the need for a tolerance by destroying the crop treated with the unregistered pesticide; a "crop-destruct" provision would then be imposed on the EUP. Granting of an EUP is contingent on satisfactory data to support a risk assessment and a finding that the proposed experimental use will not result in unreasonable adverse effects on the environment. The data required to support a request for an EUP are detailed in 40 CFR Part 158. Specific reports submitted by the registrant in support of the EUP and temporary tolerance on herbicide-tolerant soybeans are cited in Appendix B.

Registration. An application for registration typically requires substantially more data than an EUP. The data requirements depend on the type of product for which registration is sought. See 40 CFR Part 158. EPA regulations describe labeling and packaging requirements for pesticide products. See 40 CFR Parts 156 and 157. On a case-by-case basis, EPA may impose additional requirements or conditions on registrations for individual products. For example, EPA may issue a "seed increase registration" for an herbicide that allows a registrant to apply the herbicide to the GEOP breeding stock for the purpose of producing seed for propagation and future sale. The genetically altered seeds, however, could not be sold pursuant to the terms and conditions of the "seed increase registration" until a full-scale registration was approved for the use of the herbicide on the crop for which the seed was produced. Specific reports submitted by the registrant in support of registration of the new use and tolerance of herbicide-tolerant soybeans are cited in Appendix A.

Tolerances. The tolerance process starts with the submission of a petition to establish a tolerance or an exemption from the requirement of a tolerance. The petitioner must provide data to support the tolerance. When EPA receives a petition, the agency publishes in the Federal Register a notice of receipt of the petition, together with a summary of the petition's contents. 21 U.S.C. § 346a(d)(3). For the notice of receipt for the glufosinate residues on soybeans, see 60 Fed. Reg. 54689. In order to set a new tolerance, the Agency also reevaluates all existing tolerances for a chemical. Following review of the petition and any comments from the public (no comments were received in response to this filing), EPA may publish a final rule establishing the tolerance or exemption, provided that the available information demonstrates that the action would comply with the statutory standard. The final rule announcing the new soybean tolerances for glufosinate was published in the Federal Register on February 5, 1997 (62 Fed. Reg. 5333 – 5338.

All Federal Agencies

The Endangered Species Act (ESA), as amended, jointly administered by the Secretaries of the Interior and Commerce, could also affect the use and dispersal of transgenic plants.

The ESA requires importers of plants to file declarations, and limits importation to designated ports. Id. §§ 1538(d), (f). Section 7 of the ESA requires any federal agency to ensure that any action authorized, funded, or carried out by the agency not jeopardize the continued existence of any endangered or threatened species or adversely modify any critical habitat of such species. Id. § 1536(a)(2). Thus, each federal agency must consult with the U.S. Fish and Wildlife Service or the National Marine Fisheries Service, depending on the species, for any action that "may affect" a listed species. If the action is likely to adversely affect a listed species, the appropriate Service issues a Biological Opinion, which may authorize take of fish or wildlife species that is incidental to the action or, if the federal action would otherwise jeopardize the continued existence of the species, offers alternatives to the federal action that will avoid such jeopardy. Id. § 1536(b). Any take of an endangered or threatened fish or wildlife species unless otherwise authorized is unlawful under the statute. Id. § 1538. If the action is likely to adversely affect a listed plant, the situation is somewhat different. Section 9 prohibitions on take do not apply to plants, see *id.* at § 1538(a)(2), but cautions can be provided in the Biological Opinion on prohibitions against removal or disturbance of plants. Thus, a federal agency will be held responsible for prohibited acts affecting both wildlife and plants that result from authorization, funding, or other federal action associated with a genetically engineered organism or product (GEOP).

Additionally, the Federal Migratory Bird Treaty Act (MBTA), administered by the Department of the Interior, also requires that any federal action that might impact migratory avian species be minimized or excluded so as not to harm populations.

3.   Hazard Identification and Risk

USDA

In many respects, the main elements of hazard identification are embodied in the statutory authorities of USDA, EPA, and FDA that were summarized when the Coordinated Framework for the Regulation of Biotechnology was published by the Office of Science and Technology Policy in 1986 (OSTP, 1986). These legal authorities address risks that may be associated with organisms that harm plants (plant pests), pesticides which may be toxic to humans or other nontarget organisms, and foods and feeds that are adulterated, improperly labeled, or have significantly altered nutritional qualities. As described in Section 2, USDA now derives authority from the Plant Protection Act, enacted in 2000, but the elements of hazard identification remain essentially unchanged.

To perform risk assessments, APHIS has recognized that it is necessary to identify and focus on specific hazards that are potential components of risk based on the particular organism in question and its use. Here, the organisms in question are crop plants intended for use in agriculture, or to be eaten as food, or used to make ingredients in food. To identify these hazards, it is necessary to start with a good understanding of the existing traditional knowledge base and of the procedures that are routinely carried out in the course of developing any new crop variety that is released for commercial use. This knowledge serves as a baseline to decide whether the risk posed by a specific hazard is significantly changed in potential magnitude from any well-known one that is part of established practice. It also enables the hazard identification.

The use of knowledge and experience gained from traditional breeding as a basis for establishing parallel risk associations for newly developed crops is referred to as familiarity. The concept of familiarity is based on the philosophy that the types of safety issues raised by genetically engineered plants are no different from those for traditional breeding when similar traits are being conferred, though the magnitude of any particular risk may differ (NRC, 1989, NRC 2000). Thus, the extensive record provided by experience with traditional plant breeding provides useful information for evaluation of genetically engineered crops with similar alterations and, as with traditionally bred crops, such alterations are likely to pose few ecological problems. (Tiedje et al., 1989). Familiarity is not a risk/safety assessment in itself (NRC, 1989). However, the concept facilitates risk/safety assessments, because to be familiar, means having enough information to be able to make a judgment of safety or risk (U.S. NRC, 1989). Familiarity can also be used to indicate appropriate management practices including whether standard agricultural practices are adequate or whether other management practices are needed to manage the risk (OECD, 1993). As familiarity depends also on the knowledge about the environment and its interaction with introduced organisms, the risk/safety assessment in one country may not be applicable in another country. However, as field tests are performed in different locations, information will accumulate about the organisms involved and their interactions with other organisms in these varied environments.

Familiarity comes from the knowledge and experience available for conducting a risk/safety analysis prior to large -scale introduction of any new plant line or crop cultivar in a particular environment. For plants, for example, familiarity takes account of, but need not be restricted to, knowledge and experience with:

- the crop plant, including its flowering/reproductive characteristics, ecological requirements, and past breeding experiences;
- the agricultural and surrounding environment of the trial site;
- specific trait(s) transferred to the plant line(s);
- results from previous basic research including greenhouse/glasshouse and small-scale

field research with the new plant line or with other plant lines having the same trait;

- the scale-up of lines of the plant crop varieties developed by more traditional techniques of plant breeding;
- the scale-up of other plant lines developed by the same technique;
- the presence of related (and sexually compatible) plants in the surrounding natural environment, and knowledge of the potential for gene transfer between crop plant and the relative; and
- interactions between/among the crop plant, environment and trait. (Organization for Economic Cooperation and Development (OECD), 1993)

With respect to the above factors, familiarity can range from very high to very low. For genetically engineered crop plants commercialized to date in the U.S., there has been a high degree of familiarity. This is certainly the case for soybeans. The degree of familiarity is important to the assessment, and could affect the type of data required to perform the assessment.

APHIS environmental assessments are consistent with Annex 3 of the United Nations Environment Program (UNEP) Guidelines for Safety in Biotechnology, which lays out the broad steps in biosafety review. These can be paraphrased as (1) identifying hazards; (2) assessing actual risks that may arise from the identified hazard; (3) determining how identified risks can be managed and whether to proceed with proposed action; (4) comparing the assessed risks with those posed by actions with comparable organisms. These steps are relevant to both APHIS's authority to regulate under the Plant Protection Act and to its obligations under NEPA. The APHIS assessments are based on the principle that the environmental risks that may be posed by a certain use of a particular organism will depend on: the properties of the organism, the way the organism is to be used (including whether the organism is to be used under confinement or in the context of an environmental release), and safeguards that are built into experimental design or conditions of use.

APHIS has worked closely with member countries of the OECD, and in other fora, to bring about international consensus on the safe development, testing, and use of genetically modified plants and microorganisms. In 1986, OECD published its first safety considerations for genetically engineered organisms (OECD, 1986). These included the issues (relevant to human health, the environment and agriculture) that might be considered in a risk/safety assessment. These issues were re-iterated in a recent report on harmonization of regulatory oversight in biotechnology published in 2000 (OECD, 2000). OECD has also published several [1]consensus documents that are useful in risk assessments.

---

[1]Relevant to this case study, OECD has published a consensus document specifically on the genes responsible for glufosinate (syn.=phosphinothricin) tolerance and their enzyme products in plants (OECD, 1999), but this report was not available at the time glufosinate tolerant soybeans were de-regulated.

In specific terms, the following represent the major hazards that have been identified by APHIS and for which risks are assessed:

- Plant pathogenic potential of the transgenic plant (i.e., either symptomology in the transgenic
- crop plant or the ability of the transgenic crop to harm other plants)
- Potential to affect handling, processing, or storage of commodities containing the genetically engineered plant.
- Changes in cultivation that might accompany adoption of the transgenic variety
- Potential to harm nontarget organisms
- Changes in the potential of the genetically engineered crop plant to become a weed
- Potential to affect "weediness" of sexually compatible plants
- Potential impacts on biodiversity

Based on the data provided by AgrEvo, available information about the crop (soybean), and the engineered genes, APHIS assessed the risks of introduction of glufosinate tolerant soybeans. The assessment can be summarized as follows:

— Plant pathogenic potential of the transgenic plant - Though the transgenic plant contains certain sequences from plant pathogens, specifically, the promoter and terminator sequence from 35S CaMV and the *nos* terminator from *Agrobacterium tumefaciens,* APHIS concluded that these did not pose a significant risk of imparting plant pathogenicity. All of the sequences are well-characterized regulatory sequences that are not transcribed or translated to protein and all have a history of safe use in transformed plants. Evaluation of data from field tests did not identify plant pathogenic effects due to the introduced sequences.

— Potential to cause harm to commodities - Because the harvested products are the same for the glufosinate tolerant varieties as for traditional varieties with respect to the required methods for handling, processing, and storage, APHIS did not identify a risk to raw or processed commodities.

— Changes in cultivation that might accompany adoption of the transgenic variety - Due to the nature of the product, use of transgenic soybeans will likely be accompanied by a shift in herbicide usage patterns. Traditionally, soybean weeds have been managed on a field-wide basis as a preventative strategy, but the availability of an effective broad-spectrum post-emergence weed control option encourages farmers to treat weeds when and where they emerge on an "as needed" basis. The advent of effective post-emergence herbicides has also facilitated a move toward no-till production systems in soybeans and glufosinate tolerant soybeans are likely to be cultivated in this way. APHIS does not find any negative impacts associated with these changes in cultivation.

— Potential to harm nontarget organisms - APHIS considered the mode of action of the PAT enzyme, the lack of any known toxicity associated with the enzyme, as well as data

12

supplied by the company that showed that the protein shares no homology with proteins known to be toxic, that the protein has no characteristics of a toxin or allergen, and field observations from numerous sites revealing no negative effects on insects, birds, and other species. Because information developed by the company and the scientific literature show no toxicity, no specific monitoring protocol could be developed. In this case, APHIS depended on adverse effects reports noted by the company for this information. Based on the scientific literature and the information from the company described above, APHIS concluded that glufosinate tolerant soybeans pose an insignificant threat to nontarget organisms, including endangered species.

–   Potential of the crop plant to become a weed - Central to the conclusion that soybean is not likely to become a weed is the substantial evidence that soybean does not possess weedy tendencies, based on it having not established populations outside of agriculture despite years of wide-spread cultivation, and that fact that it is not listed in standard texts or references as a weed. The introduced characteristic of glufosinate tolerance is not expected to add any characteristics of weediness to soybean. In the highly unlikely event that there was a need to control soybean as a weed, for example volunteer soybeans in fields that were converted to another crop, chemical options other than glufosinate are available.

–   Potential to affect "weediness" of sexually compatible plants - There are no wild relatives of soybean nor any other plants sexually compatible with soybean in the continental United States, though some occur in U.S. territories in the South Pacific. In addition, there are significant barriers to outcrossing. Soybeans are nearly exclusively self-pollinating. Hybrid crosses between cultivated soybean (*Glycine max*) and other members of the subgenus *Glycine* as are found in the Pacific territories, have been achieved only through seed culture. These hybrids are generally sterile with further offspring only being obtained with extreme difficulty.

–   Potential impacts on biodiversity - APHIS concluded that glufosinate tolerant soybeans do not pose a threat to biodiversity based on: 1) soybeans will not become a weed and do not significantly hybridize with related species; 2) the high specificity and lack of toxicity of the PAT enzyme result in an insignificant threat to nontarget species; 3) APHIS can envision no threat to biodiversity for glufosinate tolerant soybeans that will not apply to traditionally bred soybeans.

EPA

In evaluating a pesticide registration application, EPA examines the ingredients of the pesticide; the particular site or crop on which it is to be used; the amount, frequency, and timing of its use; and storage and disposal practices. The Agency also assesses a wide variety of potential human health and environmental effects associated with use of the pesticide. The registrant (typically the manufacturer of the pesticide) must provide data from specific, required studies (tests) conducted according to EPA guidelines. These tests are needed to allow the Agency to determine whether a pesticide has the potential to cause adverse effects on humans, wildlife, fish, invertebrates, and plants, including endangered species and other non-target organisms, as well as possible contamination of surface water or groundwater from leaching, runoff, and spray drift.

As the Agency considers a use for an herbicide on an herbicide-tolerant crop, it applies the same standard risk assessment methodologies to assess the environmental safety issues associated with the use of the herbicide, as would be applied to any herbicide use prior to its registration. For chemical pesticides, the Agency relies on the data generated under Good Laboratory Practices (see 40 CFR Part 160) to assess hazard and exposure. Glufosinate-ammonium was first registered by the EPA in 1993 as a non-selective, water soluble herbicide for application as a foliar spray for the control of emerged annual and perennial grasses and broadleaf weeds. Its original end-use products included home owner uses for weed control around trees, shrubs, fences, walks, patios, driveways, sidewalks, in flower beds, and to spot kill weeds in lawns. Another product (Ignite 1SC) targeted light industrial non-food uses such as trimming and edging of landscape areas, recreation and public areas, nursery uses such as field grown and container stock weed control, and non-food use around farmsteads.

EPA's review of the environmental studies concluded that glufosinate-ammonium was practically nontoxic to birds and aquatic species. Laboratory studies indicated that the chemical was mobile and persistent, which resulted in a groundwater advisory statement on the product label that contained the light industrial non-food uses.

Avian studies using the technical grade product (i.e., a product that is solely or primarily intended to be used for the manufacture of pesticide end-use products) indicated that the avian acute oral LD50s were greater than 2000mg/kg (mallard and bobwhite) and the dietary LC50s of 5000 ppm for both mallard duck and bobwhite quail indicated that glufosinate-ammonium is practically nontoxic to birds. The avian reproductive NOEL value for both mallard and bobwhite appears to be greater than 400 ppm based on statistical analysis.

Aquatic studies using the technical grade product indicate that the fish LC50s for both rainbow trout and pumpkinseed were greater than 320 ppm, indicating that glufosinate-ammonium is practically nontoxic to both warm water and cold water fish species. The LC50 for *Daphnia magna* was 667 ppm that indicates that glufosinate-ammonium is practically nontoxic to aquatic invertebrates.

Toxicity studies using the formulated product (i.e., an end-use pesticide product, here Ignite) indicate that the LC50s ranged from 26.7 ppm for rainbow trout to 65 ppm for bluegill sunfish; Ignite can be classified as being slightly toxic to fish. The LC50s for *Daphnia magna* ranged from 15.0 to 79.5 ppm indicating that Ignite is slightly toxic to aquatic invertebrates. The available honeybee toxicity data for Ignite (LC50 greater than 100 ug/bee for the 20% active ingredient product; LC50 = 345.5 ug/bee for the 95.3% active ingredient product) indicate that this chemical is practically nontoxic to bees.

A summary of the environmental fate characteristics for glufosinate-ammonium indicates a hydrolysis half-life greater than 300 days at pH 5, 7, and 9; an aerobic soil metabolism half-life greater than 120 days (sandy loam soil); an aerobic aquatic metabolism half-life greater than 64 days; high mobility; photodegradation in soil declined to 87.5% of applied during 45 hours irradiation; photodegradation in water showing no degradation at pH 5, 7, and 9; anaerobic soil metabolism of 45 to 60 days; terrestrial field dissipation less than 3 to 4 days (loamy sand); and no accumulation in fish (bluegill).

Laboratory studies indicated that glufosinate-ammonium and its degradates were mobile and persistent. Thus, the potential for groundwater contamination did exist. However, the use of the homeowner products for spot treatments on turf was not expected to present a risk for groundwater contamination. A groundwater advisory statement was required for the Ignite label with light industrial non-food uses that read as follows: "Glufosinate-ammonium and its degradates have those properties normally associated with pesticides that have been detected in ground water. Use of this product in areas with coarse soils and high water tables may result in ground water contamination."

Additional data were required of the registrant in order to register glufosinate-ammonium on soybeans. These data were needed to assess the likelihood and magnitude of glufosinate residues in the soybeans. The registrant had to provide the EPA with an in-depth metabolism study for the herbicide-tolerant crop. The nature of the residues and the magnitudes of the components of the residues were determined. The residue of concern for dietary exposure considerations is defined as those components (parent compound and/or metabolites/degradants) for which there is a significant toxicological concern. The residue of concern for enforcement purposes is defined as the parent and/or possibly one or more metabolites, depending on the relative magnitude of the residue components, the toxicological concerns for the components, and the capabilities of proposed enforcement analytical methods. The process is essentially identical for herbicide-tolerant and traditional crops. Additionally, a full complement of field trials in the principle growing regions was required with the herbicide-tolerant crop variety to ascertain the magnitude of the residue under actual growing conditions. Again, the metabolism/residue requirements for herbicide-tolerant and traditional crops are generally the same.

For glufosinate-ammonium, tolerances on several traditional commodities such as almonds, grapes, and tree nuts (40 CFR 180.473(a)(1)) have been established for residues of glufosinate-ammonium and its metabolite, 3-methylphosphinico-propionic acid. For the glufosinate-tolerant soybeans, there was also the possibility that new metabolites or other products that could result from the presence of the new enzyme function. The transgenic herbicide-tolerant soybeans contain a gene for an enzyme (phosphiothrion-acetyl-transferase) that enables the plant to metabolize the herbicidally active moiety of glufosinate-ammonium into N-acetyl glufosinate (2-acetamido-4-methylphosphinico-butanoic acid), which is not herbicidally active. This metabolite is found only in the transgenic plants, and this information was obtained from metabolism studies conducted on the transgenic crop. The metabolite N-acetyl glufosinate was added to the residue definition for crops for which herbicide-tolerant versions have been developed (40 CFR 180.473(a)(2)), and an enforcement analytical method was required for this metabolite.

The enforcement method for the genetically unaltered (traditional) crops determines glufosinate-ammonium and 3-methyophosphinico propionic acid by a GC/FPD method after extraction, anion-exchange chromatography, and derivitization with trimethylorthoacetate. The method inadvertently includes N-acetyl glufosinate in the measured residue by converting it and the parent to the same derivative. The inclusion is of no consequence, since the metabolite is not expected to occur in crops lacking the acetyl transferase enzyme. A modified method was developed to determine each of the compounds of interest in transgenic crops. Both field trial data and processing study data were required for the transgenic soybeans.

In the Federal Register of October 25, 1995 (60 FR 54689) (FRL-4982-4), EPA issued a notice pursuant to section 408(d) of FFDCA, 21 U.S.C. § 346a (d), announcing the filing of a pesticide tolerance petition by AgrEvo USA Co. The petition requested that 40 CFR 180.473 be amended by adding tolerances for residues of glufosinate-ammonium and its metabolites 2-acetamido-4-methylphosphinico-butanoic acid and 3-methylphosphinico-propionic acid, in or on the following raw agricultural commodities (RACs): corn, field, grain at 0.2 part per million (ppm); corn, field, forage at 4.0 ppm; corn, field, silage at 3.5 ppm; corn, field, fodder at 5.5 ppm; soybean seed at 2.0 ppm; and soybean hulls at 6.0 ppm. In the Federal Register of July 31, 1996 (61 FR 39964)(FRL-5384-7), EPA issued a notice of an amendment to the petition. The tolerances requested were changed to residues of glufosinate-ammonium and its metabolites, 2-acetamido-4-methylphosphinico-butanoic acid and 3-methylphosphico-propionic acid expressed as glufosinate free acid equivalents, in or on the following RACs: corn, field, grain, at 0.2 ppm; corn, field, forage, at 4.0 ppm; corn, field, fodder, at 6.0 ppm; soybeans, at 2.0 ppm; aspirated grain fractions, at 25.0 ppm; eggs, at 0.05 ppm; poultry, meat at 0.05 ppm; poultry, fat at 0.05 ppm; and poultry, meat by-products (mbyp) at 0.10 ppm. The revised petition also requested that a maximum residue level be established for the same residues in or on the processed commodity under section 701 of FFDCA: soybean hulls at 5.0 ppm.

In the Federal Register of November 18, 1996 (61 FR 58684) (FRL-5572-7), EPA issued a third Notice of Filing to amend the petition to bring the petition in conformity with FQPA (Pub. L. 104-170). The notice contained a summary of the petition prepared by the petitioner and this summary contained conclusions and arguments to support its conclusion that the petition complied with section 408 of the FFDCA, as amended by FQPA. In this instance the petitioner proposed to amend 40 CFR 180.473 by establishing tolerances for residues of glufosinate ammonium in or on the following RACs: corn, field, grain, at 0.2 ppm; corn, field, forage, at 4.0 ppm; corn, field, fodder, at 6.0 ppm; soybeans, at 2.0 ppm; soybean hulls, at 5.0 ppm; aspirated grain fractions, at 25.0 ppm; eggs, at 0.05 ppm; poultry, meat at 0.05 ppm; poultry, fat at 0.05

ppm; and poultry, mbyp at 0.10 ppm. The residues of glufosinate-ammonium were defined as butanoic acid, 2-amino-4-(hydroxymethylphosphinyl)-, monoammonium salt and its metabolites: 2-acetamido-4-methylphosphinico-butanoic acid and 3-methylphosphinico-propionic acid expressed as glufosinate free acid equivalents.

There were no comments or requests for referral to an advisory committee received in response to the notices of filing. The Notice of Filings were incorrectly stated for eggs and the poultry commodities because the residue chemistry data showed only the parent chemical and one metabolite, 3-methylphosphinico-propionic acid. The subject regulation was therefore amended accordingly. The data submitted in the petition and other relevant material have been evaluated and time-limited tolerances established for residues of the herbicides glufosinate ammonium (butanoic acid, 2-amino-4-(hydroxymethylphosphinyl)-, monoammonium salt) and its metabolites: 2-acetamino-4-methylphosphinico-butanoic acid and 3-methylphosphinico-propionic acid, in or on various raw agricultural commodities (RACs), derived from transgenic field corn and transgenic soybeans. The final rule announcing the new soybean tolerances for glufosinate-ammonium was published in the Federal Register on February 5, 1997 (Volume 62, Number 24, pp. 5333 - 5338).

An important aspect of EPA's risk assessment methodology is the use of monitoring as a condition of use to provide information for further assessment and refinement as the crop and herbicide are used. This is described further in section 6, below.

FDA

As for all plant foods, FDA is the federal agency responsible for overseeing the safety and appropriate labeling of glufosinate tolerant soybeans, apart from the safety issues presented by pesticide chemicals and metabolites. FDA has a voluntary consultation process through which companies resolve any safety or other regulatory issues prior to marketing foods from bioengineered plants. FDA considers, based on agency scientists' evaluation of submitted information, whether any unresolved issues exist regarding a food derived from a new plant variety that would necessitate legal action by the agency if the product were introduced into commerce. Examples of unresolved issues may include, but are not limited to, significantly increased levels of plant toxicants or anti-nutrients, reduction of important nutrients, new allergens, or the presence in the food of an unapproved food additive. FDA has just published a proposed rule, that, if finalized, will require companies to notify FDA at least 120 days in advance of marketing a bioengineered plant food and provide FDA with data and information to demonstrate that the food is as safe as its conventional counterparts.

Interagency Coordination

At the time of the soybean case study, interagency coordination between APHIS and EPA was based on individual contacts between agency scientists conducting reviews. Both agencies felt the need to improve their coordination, especially on the review of herbicide tolerant crops.

Since January 2000, the USDA and EPA have been identifying procedures that will improve coordination between the two agencies in their reviews of herbicide-tolerant crops and their respective herbicides. Currently, the APHIS reviews of the GEO and EPA reviews of the herbicide are done without any formalized joint reviews or sharing of information.

The improved coordination being discussed is likely to include an ad hoc interagency work group that will establish a protocol for exchanging completed scientific reviews between the agencies, whereby potential gaps and differences could be identified more readily and more expertise could be systematically brought to bear in these analyses. This would also speed the reviews in some instances by providing insight and perspective to agencies trying to answer very similar questions.

Specific coordination measures that are likely to be implemented include the following. APHIS will provide EPA a copy of APHIS petitions for non-regulated status for herbicide-tolerant crops. After APHIS drafts its Environmental Assessment (EA), APHIS will consult with EPA, especially as to any discussions of available herbicides for a given crop and their practical utility, i.e., efficacy on key weed pests. To this end, EPA will supply APHIS with current lists of herbicides registered for use on the crop in question, and any readily available information as to their efficacy. APHIS would also supply the work group with copies of extensions to existing petitions. This would keep the work group informed of any new transformation events in a crop that encode the same herbicide-tolerant phenotype from the same company.

APHIS will ask each petitioner of herbicide-tolerant crops to submit a voluntary stewardship plan for the management of pesticide resistance and potentially weedy volunteer crops in their herbicide-tolerant crops. Since APHIS receives petitions from registrants of herbicide-tolerant crops far in advance of EPA's receiving an application for registration of the herbicide on that crop, APHIS will consult with EPA as to the viability of the stewardship plans while preparing the APHIS EA. Having the two agencies concur on a stewardship plan early on in the registration process will ensure that the concerns of both agencies are addressed, and that these concerns are discussed in the EA along with the details of the plan and its implementation. The opportunity for the public to comment on both the petition and EA ensures transparency in the joint review process.

APHIS will, on an annual basis, keep EPA and the work group informed of what is in the registration pipeline by supplying a list of the herbicide-tolerant plants that are field tested each year. This advance notification system could alert the EPA to potential high-risk uses that might be of concern from an environmental or human health perspective.

4.   Information and Data

USDA

APHIS requires different types of data depending on the particular regulatory process at hand. The particulars are described below for notifications and permits for importation, interstate movement, or field testing, and for the petition for determination of non-regulated status.

Movement, importation, and field testing (introduction). Permits are required for importation, interstate movement and field testing for articles which do not qualify for notification; these include microorganisms, arthropods, pharmaceutical-producing plants, and insect viruses. In the permit, the applicant lists:

- the regulated article or product,
- donor organism,
- recipient organism,
- vector or vector agent,
- date of the importation, movement or release,
- quantity of the regulated article, and
- the port of importation or site of release.

In addition, detailed information is required as applicable on:

- the anticipated or actual expression of the altered genetic material in the regulated article and how it differs from a non-modified parent organism,
- the molecular biology of the system,
- the country or locality where the donor, recipient, and vector were collected and produced,
- the experimental design at the release site,
- the facilities at the destination,
- the measures to ensure confinement, and
- the final disposition.

This data is required so that a decision can be made to conclude that the transgenic plant is adequately characterized, that no transgenic plant material will persist in the environment, and that any unintentional or unanticipated effects, if any, can be restricted to the confined field site and be managed in such a way that there are no environmental risks after the confined field release is terminated. All field test approvals require that a field data report be filed after the experiment is complete. In the case of importation and movement, the information allows for a decision which can conclude that the transgenic plants are adequately characterized and not considered to pose a plant pest risk, and/or can be considered to be contained in the receiving facility ensuring no dissemination into the environment, and thereby, posing no plant pest risk.

Under notification, much of the same information is required as for permits, but the format is more rigid and is streamlined such that the information is more easily catalogued and assessed by APHIS and thus allowing for a more rapid review process. The applicant must state that his article meets the eligibility requirements and that any actions taken will meet certain performance standards mandated in the regulations and described in the notification user's guides. It should be understood that the primary emphasis for field releases under both notification and permit is confinement and that the constraints imposed should effectively eliminate the potential for significant impact to the environment.

Petitions for determination of non-regulated status. The most comprehensive data packages received by APHIS for scientific review are the Petitions for Determination of Non-regulated Status. The petition process allows for removal of a transgenic plant from regulatory obligation. De-regulation may be a practical requirement for commercialization of common agronomic crops that are to be grown on a large scale, but may not be for certain specialized applications, for example, commercialization of pharmaceutical-producing plants. In order to make the determination on a petition, APHIS uses specified information and data supplied by the applicant to make risk assessments relative to the hazards listed previously.

The assessments rely on answers to a number of specific questions that are included as Appendix C. Information requirements may vary with plant species, the specific types of modifications, and end use. The information criteria listed in Appendix C are currently being developed mainly for crop plants with the exception of trees and aquatic plants. They represent a compilation of a range of issues that have been considered in past decisions depending on the specific case. Reviews are still conducted on a case-by-case basis that allows for reviewing additional or fewer criteria. These assessments are conducted by APHIS scientists.

EPA

FIFRA and section 408 of the FFDCA give EPA the authority to require studies necessary to determine whether a pesticide and its residues meet the statutory standards contained in each of the statutes. EPA regulations (40 CFR Part 158) detail the standard data requirements for pesticides. Appendix A contains a list of reports that were submitted to the EPA in support of the registration of glufosinate-ammonium on glufosinate-tolerant soybeans, and for the establishment of a tolerance. Applicants may request waivers for required studies if they believe such studies unnecessary for a risk assessment. Guidelines determine the protocols that should be used for most of the required toxicity tests. Any significant variations from the protocol proposed by an applicant normally require independent validation of the novel test method. Additionally, primary literature (peer-reviewed) is a key source of new developments that may influence the type of data requested from registrants and whether EPA will accept waivers for certain studies. After reviewing any waiver requests, agency scientists determine, on a case-by-case basis, what studies will be required for a specific herbicide registration on a herbicide-tolerant crop.

Generally, EPA-required data for product characterization and toxicity tests are generated directly by the applicant or through the use of a commercial laboratory that specializes in performing chemistry / toxicity studies. Fate data (i.e., where the chemical eventually is found in the environment), field expression data, and product characterization studies are also generally performed by the applicant. Non-target studies are usually done by an outside contract lab that has experience in toxicology and the application of EPA guideline requirements.

All submitted studies are reviewed by agency scientists. Outside scientific experts may be contacted for the purpose of verifying scientific background information as needed. On particularly critical scientific issues, EPA may consult with its FIFRA Science Advisory Panel (SAP), a Federal Advisory Committee Act-chartered group of independent experts in scientific issues related to pesticides. The SAP's advice may concern broad issues, e.g., modifying existing guidelines or creating new ones, or may concern a specific pending regulatory action. No SAP reviews have been required as of the date of this writing for issues related to herbicide-tolerant crops.

Appropriate scientific and regulatory expertise exists within APHIS, EPA and FDA to review all submissions for scientific accuracy and interpretation.[2] EPA evaluates data for scientific soundness based on experience with the types of studies and the anticipated results. Agency scientists have the right to question any data that appear to be erroneous, falsified or otherwise questionable in nature. This may take the form of a request for clarification or another study with modifications.

Penalties for falsification of data can range from a monetary fine to imprisonment and combinations thereof. An extensive auditing program exists within EPA's Office of Enforcement and Compliance Assurance to ensure that laboratories are capable of carrying out the prescribed studies and that their equipment is in satisfactory working order. These audits can be carried out on a random basis or targeted to a specific laboratory if there is reason to believe that data have been falsified or in any manner misrepresented.

There are some areas in need of additional baseline research. At the top of this list would be field studies to assess the potential for the development of weed resistance. Weed resistance to herbicides could result from high selection pressure from the excessive use of a single herbicide mode of action. The agency is concerned that the development of weed resistance could result in farmers using higher application rates, additional applications of herbicides, or having to use additional, and potentially less environmentally benign herbicides to control their weeds.

Additionally, the agency would like to learn more about the environmental effects of gene transfer to other plants, the benefits of herbicide usage on herbicide-tolerant crops to growers and consumers, and would like to obtain improved usage data reporting for herbicide-tolerant crops and pesticides used in herbicide-tolerant crops.

---

[2]Current resources are adequate to evaluate GEOs submitted for review. EPA, however, expects the number and complexity of submissions to increase, and it is clear that future budget appropriations may need to be increased to ensure continued adequate staffing.

5.   Mitigation and Management Considerations: Approvals and Conditions on Research, Production Distribution, Marketing, Use and Disposal.

USDA

Interstate movement, importation, and field testing (introduction). APHIS regulations require that measures must be taken to minimize dissemination of the engineered organism into the environment during movement and while in the receiving facility (laboratory, growth chamber, or greenhouse) as specified in 7 CFR 340. The risk mitigation measures include: (1) adequate identification, packaging and segregation measures to prevent or minimize mixing, spillage and dissemination of viable transgenic plant material, including the flow of fertile transgenic pollen to sexually compatible plants during transit and in the receiving facility; (2) when applicable, methods to minimize the flow of fertile transgenic pollen to other sexually compatible plants within the contained facility or to such plants on the outside; (3) devitalization/disposal of transgenic plant material by suitable means, when no longer in use or authorized. Means of devitalization/disposal could include, but are not limited to, dry heat, steam heat, crushing, deep burial and/or chemical treatment.

For field tests, measures must be taken to confine the transgenic plants to the field site during the defined period of the release and to prevent the transgenic plants or their progeny from persisting in the environment in subsequent growing seasons either within or outside of the site of the confined release. Both the reproductive isolation measures and post harvest land use restrictions should be based on the reproductive biology and seed dormancy characteristics of the species, surrounding land use, proximity of sexually compatible plants and presence of pollinators. Additional mitigation measures may be necessary based on the nature of the introduced trait(s).

During the growing season, measures must be taken to achieve reproductive isolation from plants of the same species and other sexually compatible species that are not part of the confined release, whether they are cultivated, weedy or wild species. Depending on the plant species, this can be achieved by the use of one or a combination of the following: isolation distance, pollen or pollination-proof caging, netting or bagging of plants prior to flowering, guard rows/ border rows of plants to attract pollinators or trap transgenic pollen, flower removal prior to pollination, use of male sterile lines, use of plant growth regulators to block reproductive development, different flowering time, and/or termination of the confined field release prior to flowering. Generally, isolation distances that are used to ensure purity of certified seed (such as breeder seed or foundation classes of certified seed) may be adapted successfully to prevent or minimize outcrossing of transgenic pollen to sexually compatible plants that could produce viable progeny capable of persisting outside the confined field release site. When isolation distances are used, these zones are also monitored for the presence of the same species, related species and for proximity of fields of the same species.

Post-harvest land use restrictions may be necessary for a certain number of years following harvest of the transgenic plant material to allow monitoring, removal and destruction of volunteers. Generally, for soybeans, this would involve monitoring for volunteers either immediately after harvest in warm climates where conditions favorable for germination can be maintained, or in the next growing season in colder climates. Generally, the post-harvest periods used to ensure purity of certified seed may be adapted successfully. For certain plant species, and for certain specific cases, post-harvest land use restrictions may also be necessary for the perimeter of the confined field site itself to monitor for volunteers resulting from potential dissemination of seed, e.g., during mechanical harvesting operations.

Other risk mitigation activities for field tests include: (1) adequate identification, packaging and segregation measures to prevent seed mixing, spillage and dispersal into the environment during transit; (2) adequate cleaning of seeding and transplanting machinery at the confined field site prior to removal to another location to prevent dissemination of viable transgenic plant material into the environment; (3) devitalization/destruction of surplus seed or seedlings, and any viable transgenic plant material remaining after transplantation or after harvesting at the confined field site by suitable means which could include, but are not limited to, dry heat, steam heat, crushing, deep burial, discing into the soil, burning, treatment with appropriately labeled herbicides and/or chemicals (harvested transgenic seed and/or plant material from the confined field site may only be retained in an approved facility if requested at the time of the submission and authorized by the regulatory authority, and should be clearly identified, securely transported, and stored separately from other seed/or plant material to avoid mixing); (4) a contingency plan for destruction of viable transgenic plant material in case of accidental release. The plan should include site marking and monitoring to ensure destruction of viable material and immediate notification of regulatory authorities.

Even in the granting of a notification, APHIS still retains the option of requiring additional information from an applicant about the conduct of the trial if there is concern that in the particular instance a performance standards may be difficult to meet or if new information or data becomes available. No such requirement was necessary in the case of the glufosinate tolerant soybeans.

Petitions for Determination of Non-Regulated Status. Once an article has been granted non-regulated status APHIS has no authority to impose conditions on research, production, distribution, marketing, use, or disposal other than phytosanitary restrictions that may be applicable. However, if new information indicates that a de-regulated article is causing harm as a plant pest, APHIS can revoke non-regulated status and again regulate under its authority as previously described.

EPA

Using the information gathered for a risk assessment, EPA decides whether to approve a pesticide chemical and/or use, as proposed, under FIFRA or whether additional protective

23

measures are necessary to eliminate unreasonable risks and unsafe dietary exposures. For example, the Agency may prohibit a pesticide from being used on certain crops because of environmental risks that would be associated with that cropping system. Buffer zones around the cropped land might be required to protect vulnerable surface or ground water sources. Application rates and the number of applications could be altered to ensure protection of the environment from risks from the use of the pesticide.

If, after considering all appropriate risk reduction measures, the pesticide still does not meet FIFRA's safety standard, the Agency will not allow either 1) any uses of the proposed chemical, or 2) specific high-risk uses of the chemical.

6.   Monitoring and Consideration of New Information

USDA

Interstate movement, importation, and field testing (introduction). APHIS personnel and appropriate state officials may inspect a site or facility where regulated articles are proposed to be released into the environment or contained after their interstate movement or importation. Failure to allow the inspection of the premises prior to the issuance of a permit or notification shall be grounds for the denial of the permit (7 CFR 340.4 (d) 7). APHIS has qualified inspectors in every State and Territory to perform inspections and take remedial action if necessary.

APHIS regulations (7 CFR 340.4(f) (10) require applicants to notify the agency within the time periods and manner specified below, in the event of the following occurrences: (1) orally notified immediately upon discovery and notify in writing within 24 hours in the event of any accidental or unauthorized release of the regulated article; (2) in writing as soon as possible but not later than within 5 working days if the regulated article or associated host organism is found to have characteristics substantially different from those listed in the application, or suffers any unusual occurrence (excessive mortality or morbidity, or unanticipated effect on non-target organisms). APHIS was not notified of any such occurrences with the glufosinate tolerant soybeans.

A final data report is required regardless of whether a field test is authorized under notification or permit. The regulations require that these reports include: methods of observation, resulting data, and analysis regarding all deleterious effects on plants, nontarget organisms, and the environment (specific instructions to applicants can be found on **http://www.aphis.usda.gov/biotech/notgen.html** under section B). APHIS coordinates the approval processes with the states, and federal regulations require that access to facilities, field test sites and pertinent records be allowed by officials from APHIS and the states. APHIS site inspections help to ensure the compliance with the mandated performance standards. Violations can result in fines or termination of the field test.

Petitions for Determination of Non-Regulated Status. Once an article has been granted non-regulated status, APHIS has no authority to require monitoring, perform site inspections, or require data reporting. If it were found later to pose a plant pest risk, however, it could return to regulated status and the authorities to conduct these activities would then be available.

EPA

As discussed above, EPA has considerable authority to regulate the post-registration use of a pesticide. EPA has the legal authority, technical capacity, and resources to prescribe monitoring requirements for the use of the herbicide on herbicide-tolerant crops should risk concerns warrant it. This authority includes: 1) issuance of data call-in notices to obtain additional information from registrants needed to evaluate the safety of a pesticide, and 2) assuring compliance with conditions imposed on the pesticide's registration. The EPA has required, as conditions of herbicide registration on herbicide-tolerant crops, that the registrant report annually on 1) changes in herbicide usage on the crop, and 2) on whether any adverse changes in agronomic practices accompany the use of the herbicide on the herbicide-tolerant crop. This additional reporting resulted, in part, from public concerns that herbicide-tolerant crops would foster farmers' reliance on herbicides, and that these registrations might adversely affect the use of no-till or other conservation tillage practices.

Data reported to EPA show that herbicide-tolerant crops often require lower application rates or fewer herbicide applications. In many cases, herbicide-tolerant crops also allow farmers to use more benign herbicides instead of more harmful ones, and allow farmers to use them prescriptively as post-emergent herbicides instead of making prophylactic applications before the crops and weeds emerge. The herbicides registered thus far for use with herbicide-tolerant crops have also proven to be highly compatible with conservation tillage practices. The Agency is currently assessing the quality of the usage information provided by the registrants, and is considering providing guidance on more robust collecting and reporting. If herbicide usage on herbicide-tolerant crops results in an increase in environmental risks, risk mitigation can be required.

EPA has authority to obtain additional data about a pesticide post-registration. Section 6(a)(2) of FIFRA (which contains an adverse effects reporting requirement) requires registrants to inform the agency of "additional factual information regarding unreasonable adverse effects on the environment of the pesticide" (see 40 CFR Part 159 for specific reporting requirements). Section 3(c)(2)(B) of FIFRA allows EPA to require submission of additional data where necessary. In addition, to reflect the current science, FIFRA proides for a periodic review of all pesticides under section 3(g) and/or 4.

7.   Enforcement and Compliance

USDA

Interstate movement, importation, and field testing (introduction). Failure of applicants to submit complete and accurate information for all introductions may result in a fine of not more than $10,000 or imprisonment for not more than 5 years or both (18 U.S.C. § 1001 APHIS has qualified personnel in every State that can inspect field sites for compliance to the performance standards for all field testing. In addition, headquarters staff has inspected (in 2000), and will in the future inspect, field sites that raise new confinement issues, as decided on a case-by-case basis. Failure to comply with performance standards under notification or permit conditions can result in compliance infractions and the applicant can be ordered to take remedial action (7 U.S.C. § §7714(b)(1)) if necessary to prevent the spread of plant pests (7 CFR 340.4 d 7). From 1995 through 2000, APHIS recorded a total of 63 compliance infractions. After an infraction has been identified, APHIS decides on the appropriate course of action. In some cases, such as minor infractions where the applicant identifies the infraction, notifies APHIS immediately, and takes prompt and appropriate remedial action, an formal written APHIS response may not be necessary. In other cases, written warnings are issued. For the most serious of infractions, an investigation is conducted by APHIS Investigations and Enforcement Services Staff that usually results in applicants being fined. The applicant can also be assessed a criminal or civil penalty for failing to comply with the regulations (7 U.S.C. § 7734). If necessary, to protect the environment or public health, the transgenic organisms can be subjected to the application of remedial measures (including disposal) if determined by the Administrator (7 CFR 340.4 d 7). If the owner fails to take such action, the Department can take the action and recover the cost of the action from the owner (7 U.S.C. §7714(b)(2)). These remedial actions include removing the plants by burning, spraying herbicide, hoeing or discing. No infractions were identified in the case of the glufosinate-tolerant soybean.

Petitions for determination of non-regulated status. Every applicant must sign the following statement when submitting a petition for non-regulated status:

> The undersigned certifies, that to the best knowledge and belief of the undersigned, this petition includes all information and views on which to base a determination, and that it includes relevant data and information known to the petitioner which are unfavorable to the petition".

APHIS knows of no peer reviewed or anecdotal evidence that suggests that any plant that has been deregulated is a plant pest or has behaved in a manner significantly different with respect to its plant pest characteristics than a similar cultivar developed by traditional plant breeding. As explained above, APHIS has no authority to require monitoring *per se* after granting non-regulated status, however, if data becomes available that an organism granted non-regulated status does pose a plant pest risk, a deregulated organism could again be deemed a "regulated article" and could be subjected to the application of remedial measures (including disposal) if determined by the Administrator to be necessary to prevent the spread of plant pest (7 CFR 340.4 d 7).

EPA

FIFRA generally provides the authority to enforce all provisions regarding regulation of pesticides. EPA can take regulatory action to impose penalties or to restrict or prohibit the sale and distribution of any registered product, if necessary, to prevent unreasonable adverse effects on the environment, or necessary to prevent threatened violations of the FIFRA. This could include, for example, seizure of pesticide product or the assessment of civil and/or criminal penalties. FIFRA Sections 6, 8 and 9 provide statutory authority for the Agency to inspect the producing establishment, inspect books and records, and, although rarely needed, to cancel or suspend registration.

The EPA's Toxics and Pesticides Enforcement Division (TPED) within the Office of Enforcement and Compliance Assurance (OECA) is responsible for case development, policy and enforcement issues for the FIFRA. Although FIFRA Section 26 provides states with the primary enforcement responsibility for pesticide use violations, TPED enforces FIFRA violations other than use violations and proposes penalties for such violations. Congress, in FIFRA, describes the various unlawful acts that may be committed in connection with the sale and distribution of pesticide products. For example, it is unlawful for persons to sell or distribute an unregistered, misbranded, or adulterated pesticide, as well as a pesticide whose claims made for it substantially differ from claims made for it in connection with its registration under Section 3. Moreover, it is unlawful to use any pesticide in a manner inconsistent with its labeling. EPA's enforcement response may include the issuance of a civil administrative complaint, a stop sale use and removal order, or the imposition of criminal sanctions. When proposing a penalty the Agency must consider the violator's size of business, the effect the penalty will have on the violator's ability to continue in business, and the gravity of the violation.

EPA receives its legal authority to enforce FIFRA through the following sections of the Act:

FIFRA Section 6(a)(2) Adverse Effects Reporting

TPED sends referrals to the appropriate regional office for review and potential case development. TPED may develop and issue the case if the matter is nationally significant. There have been no adverse effects reported regarding glufosinate.

FIFRA Section 7 Registration of Pesticide Producer Establishments

The Section 7 database is managed by the Office of Compliance within OECA. The regional offices take the majority of the enforcement actions for Section 7 violations.

FIFRA Section 17 Import/Export Notification

TPED is presently involved in efforts to strengthen the enforcement program and provide guidance to the regional offices.

Worker Protection Standard

TPED sends referrals to the appropriate regional office for review and potential case development. TPED may develop and issue the case if the matter is nationally significant.

8.   Public Involvement and Transparency

USDA

APHIS has involved and informed the public on a broad range of agency biotechnology activities through an array of mechanisms. The public has been involved in establishing the criteria for the regulatory and environmental assessment framework and subsequent amendments as the agency gained experience and adapted to the developments in the technology. The public has been informed through written regulations (the first government biotechnology regulations), guidance documents, and through both formal notice in the Federal Register and informal information systems such as home pages on the Internet. Stakeholders to the agency, such as the Agriculture Biotechnology Advisory Committee have played a significant role in providing a public source of advice to the agency.

When the APHIS biotechnology regulations (7 CFR 340) were first established in 1987, there were a number of public meetings involving a broad spectrum of interested individuals and groups to discuss the types of data necessary to make informed decisions for safe field testing of genetically engineered organisms. Those discussions included the scope, breadth, and specific environmental concerns that should be considered in environmental analysis under NEPA.

APHIS continues to hold public meetings as needed to inform and involved the public. Meetings have included topics such as program efficiency, timeliness of review, clarity of regulations and guidance documents, applicant satisfaction, paperwork reduction, and identification of scientific or environmental considerations for future reviews by APHIS.   All APHIS-sponsored meetings, such as our regular customer service meetings, are announced on the internet and in the Federal Register and are open to the public. No public meetings were held specifically for review of glufosinate tolerant soybeans.   From time to time, APHIS also holds more focused public meetings on specific issues of scientific interest, such as the meeting in 1999 on the ecological effects of pest resistance genes in managed ecosystems. Comments at these meetings are considered in evaluating the need for regulation changes, changes in review procedures or criteria, and for the scope of consideration of environmental issues in NEPA documents.

The APHIS biotechnology home page, http:\\www.aphis.usda.gov\biotech, was one of the first government home pages to be established. It has been one of the primary sources of information globally on biotechnology regulation and a source of information on actual developments in the technology. The Internet has been used by APHIS as a mechanism to compliment and augment other more traditional information and transparency processes such as Federal Register notices, NEPA documents, and public meetings. The home page contains copies of the regulations; guidance documents; lists of notifications, permits, and determinations of non-regulated status; recent environmental assessments; and numerous links to other sources of information on biotechnology.

Interstate movement, importation, and field testing (introduction). Every permit and notification for the introduction of a genetically engineered organism is announced on the APHIS Internet home page (http://www.aphis.usda.gov/batik/status.html) the day after it had been received. The information listed includes: the name of organism, the State where the introduction will take place, and whether the proposed action has been authorized. Every application is sent to the State regulatory official where the introduction will take place and the State must concur with APHIS before any action can take place. The public can also comment on the permits and notifications either by contacting APHIS directly or by contacting the State official if the field test is in their state. Contacts for State Departments of Agriculture can be found on the APHIS website at (**http://www.aphis.usda.gov/biotech/lt_sta.html**). Additional information on each application is available by searching the APHIS on-line database (http://www.nbiap.vt.edu/cfdocs/fieldtests1.cfm), a service provided by Virginia Tech's Information Systems for Biotechnology (ISB) web server.

If an environmental assessment is prepared for a specific field test performed under permit (not done for notifications) in accordance with APHIS' NEPA implementation regulations (7 CFR 372), a Federal Register notice will announce a 30-day public comment period on the EA. Copies of the EAs and Finding of No Significant Impact (FONSI) will be distributed via mail or electronically.

Petitions for determination of non-regulated status. Every petition submission is announced on the APHIS Internet home page (http://www.aphis.usda.gov/batik/status.html) the day after it has been received. After petitions have been reviewed by APHIS scientists and have been deemed complete, USDA announces the receipt of the petition in the Federal Register and the public has 60 days to submit comments. All petitions are available for reading at the Reading Room at the South Building of the USDA Headquarters in Washington, DC and when requested, APHIS provides the public with free copies of all petitions. Subsequently, when a draft environmental assessment is completed, APHIS announces in the Federal Register that the EA is available (electronically or a hard copy) and the public has 30 days to submit comments. APHIS considers all public comments in its decision-making. APHIS announces in the Federal Register when it has reached a FONSI for the EA that the engineered organisms do not meet the definition of regulated articles. The FONSI, analysis of public comments (if any), the EA, and the determination of non-regulated status are all available electronically at the APHIS home page or in hard copy. Copies of APHIS decision documents are available at APHIS web site "http://www.aphis.usda.gov/biotech/pubs.html".

As the biotechnology regulations have matured over the years, so have procedures implementing NEPA for decisions subject to those regulations. Initially, environmental assessments were completed before the decision on the issuance of every permit for release to the environment (field test) and notice of availability was published in the Federal Register for each one. After a few years, notice of availability for environmental assessments was published first monthly and then quarterly, as the number of requests for copies of individual environmental assessments decreased and as web-based information became the preferred mode for receiving that information.

In 1995 APHIS established NEPA implementing regulations in 7 CFR 372 that established criteria for the level of documentation for agency action including biotechnology decisions. The implementing regulations set the following environmental assessment triggers for biotechnology:

> "(b)(4) Approvals and issuance of permits for proposals involving genetically engineered or nonindigenous species, except for actions that are categorically exclude, as provided in paragraph (c) of this section (7 CFR 372.5)."

The relevant categorical exclusion reads as follows:

> "(c) (ii) Permitting, or acknowledgment of notifications for, confined field releases of genetically engineered organisms and products. . ."

except for

> "(d) (4) When a confined field release of a genetically engineered organism or product involves new species or organisms, or novel modifications that raise new issues."

As a matter of policy, APHIS also completes an environmental assessment before making a decision of non-regulated status in response to an applicants petition. Since 1999, notice of availability of draft environmental assessments for determinations for non-regulated status are published in the Federal Register for 30 days comment. Comments are considered before completion of findings of impact.

A fairly large volume of environmental assessments and technical decision documents are made available to the public. These are made available in paper copy or electronically at the preference of the recipient.

APHIS will complete an EIS when an EA does not support a finding of no significant impact. To date, environmental assessments to support biotechnology decisions have resulted in findings of no significant impact. EIS documents would also be available for public comment.

Notifications do not have environmental assessment prepared in accordance with APHIS' NEPA implementation regulations (7 CFR 372). The rationale is that these are not exposed to the environment due to the performance standards that ensure confinement Due to the changes in the regulations regarding notification in 1993 and 1997, species currently under notification may have had EAs prepared in the past, when the same species were required to apply for a permit that may have required an EA.

EPA

EPA publishes Federal Register notices announcing the receipt of applications for an Experimental Use Permit (EUP) where the EUP is of regional or national significance, and for registration of a new active ingredient or a new use pattern; and EPA invites public comment on the proposed action. In addition, Federal Register notices announcing approval of EUPs and registration of pesticides containing new active ingredients are also published. 40 CFR 172.11(c); 40 CFR 152.102. EPA also publishes Federal Register Notices announcing the notice of receipt of a request for a food tolerance or exemption, and provides opportunity for filing public comment. Within 60 days after a final rule granting a tolerance or exemption is issued, any person may file objections to the petition. The Federal Register Notice for the final rule announcing the food tolerances for glufosinate ammonium on soybeans can be found on the EPA web site at http://www.epa.gov/fedrgstr/EPA-PEST/1997/February/Day-05/p2838.htm. Although not required by statute, EPA also may hold meetings with groups and individuals interested in particular pending regulatory actions, either at its own initiative or at the request of others.

The EPA makes many individual decisions in its regulation of pesticides, including herbicides, e.g., in its registration, reregistration, and special review programs. The Office of Pesticide Programs (OPP) uses a variety of tools to guide these decisions and inform its many stakeholders. Various advisory committees have been established under the Federal Advisory Committee Act (FACA), including the Pesticide Program Dialogue Committee (PPDC). This Committee provides a forum for a diverse group of stakeholders to provide feedback to the Pesticide Program on various pesticide regulatory, policy and program implementation issues. Membership to the Committee includes environmental and public interest groups, pesticide manufacturers and trade associations, user and commodity groups, public health and academic institutions, Federal and State agencies, and the general public. OPP develops regulations, policy documents, guidelines and analyses covering scientific, legal, and international matters. Proposed regulations are published for notice and comment in the Federal Register (FR) and are publicized on the Agency's web site as well as oftentimes in the press. OPP makes policy, guidance and other documents available through a variety of mechanisms as well, such as the Government Printing Office (GPO), direct mailings, and increasingly, through electronic dissemination. When final, regulations are incorporated in the Code of Federal Regulations (CFR) that is available to the public.

The agency also employs a Scientific Advisory Panel (SAP) that provides scientific advice on pesticides and pesticide related issues as to their impact on health and the environment. The role of the SAP has been expanded to that of a peer review body for current scientific issues that may influence the direction of OPP's regulatory decisions. Open meetings of the SAP are held on an average of six times per year. The agenda items for the meetings are chosen by OPP

Division Directors at the beginning of the fiscal year, although emergency meetings may be called if the need arises, such as in the case of a proposed pesticide cancellation. Specific actions that OPP is required to present to the SAP include proposed and final regulations (which also require review by the Secretary of Agriculture), operating guidelines utilized by EPA personnel, and notices of intent to cancel or change a pesticide registration or classification undertaken under the procedures of FIFRA 6(b). The agency does not typically go to the SAP for routine registration decisions on new chemical uses.

Finally, EPA maintains a public docket that contains a large number of documents available for inspection and copying, including scientific reviews on safety issues and Reregistration Eligibility Decisions (REDs) on individual pesticides. Because glusofinate was registered relatively recently, it has not yet been subject to registration review.

No public comments were received in response to the Federal Register notices regarding the applications for an EUP or registration for the use of glufosinate on soybeans (which was also the notification for the tolerance). When the registrant petitioned the agency in request of tolerances for glufosinate-ammonium on soybeans, a docket number was cited in the Federal Register Notice, (PP-5F4578/R-2277) but no public comments were received. The Freedom of Information Act (FOIA) also provides for the request of documents submitted to support a pesticide registration as long as they do not contain confidential business information.

The Agency and OPP have also increasingly undertaken a variety of other communication and outreach efforts to ensure that the public has the information it needs to make responsible decisions about pesticides and to promote public health and environmental protection goals. To achieve this goal, OPP issues announcements and publications, provides information by telephone and electronic networks, responds to written and verbal inquiries, maintains a public docket, holds public meetings, and presents speeches and Congressional testimony.

REFERENCES

AgrEvo USA. 1996. Petition for Determination of Nonregulated Status for Glufosinate Resistant Soybean Transformation Events (submitted to the United States Department of Agriculture, Petition Number 96-068-01p) and available from USDA-APHIS, Unit 147, 4700 River Road, Riverdale, MD 20737

NRC (National Research Council) 2000. Genetically Modified Pest-Protected Plants: Science and Regulation. Washington, D.C. National Academy Press.

NRC (National Research Council) 1989. Field Testing of Genetically Modified Organisms: Framework for Decision. Washington, D.C. National Academy Press.

OECD 1986. Recombinant DNA Safety considerations. OECD, Paris. Available electronically at http://www.oecd.org/ehs/public.htm

OECD 1993. Field Releases of Transgenic Plants, 1986-1992, an analysis. OECD, Paris. Available electronically at http://www.oecd.org/ehs/public.htm

OECD 1999. Series on Harmonization of Regulatory Oversight in Biotechnology No. 11, Consensus Document on General Information Concerning the Genes and Their Enzymes that Confer Tolerance to Phosphinothricin Herbicide. Available electronically at http://www.oecd.org/ehs/public.htm

OECD 2000. Report of the Working Group on Harmonization of Regulatory Oversight in Biotechnology.

OSTP (Office of Science and Technology Policy). 1986. Coordinated Framework for the Regulation of Biotechnology: Announcement of Policy and Notice for Public Comment. Fed. Reg. 51, 23302-23393.

Tiedje, J.M., Colwell, R.K., Grossman, Y.L., Hodson, R.E., Lenski, R.E., Mack, R.N., Regal, P.J. 1989. The Planned Introduction of Genetically Engineered Organisms: Ecological Considerations and Recommendations. Ecology 70, 298-315.

USDA (United States Department of Agriculture) 1996. Environmental Assessment and Determination of Non-Regulated Status - Petition Number 96-068-01p (glufosinate tolerant soybean). Available electronically at "http://www.aphis.usda.gov/biotech/pubs.html" or write to USDA-APHIS, Unit 147, 4700 River Road, Riverdale, MD 20737.

APPENDIX A

BIBLIOGRAPHY OF SUBMITTED STUDIES

<u>**Product:**</u>	Liberty™ Herbicide
<u>**EPA Pesticide Petition Number:**</u> 5F4578	
<u>**EPA File Symbol:**</u>	45639-ROO
<u>**Purpose of Submission:**</u>	Data in Support of Application for Registration of Liberty™ Herbicide and Petition for Tolerance of Glufosinate-Ammonium on Corn and Soybean
<u>**Date of Submission:**</u>	August 15, 1995

Volume Number	Study Title	Submitter Document Number	EPA Guidelines Reference Number	EPA Data Requirement	EPA MRID Number (Assigned by EPA on 9/6/95)
Reasonable Grounds in Support of the Petition and Safety Evaluation					
1 of 36	Use of Glufosinate-Ammonium on Glufosinate-Ammonium Resistant Corn and Soybean: Reasonable Grounds in Support of the Petition and Safety Evaluation	N/A	N/A	N/A	43778401
Product Chemistry Data Requirements					
2 of 36	Discussion of the Product Identity, Disclosure of Ingredients, Beginning Materials and Manufacturing Process, Formation of Impurities, and Certification of Ingredient Limits for Liberty™ Herbicide	A54483	61-1, 61-2, 61-3 and 62-2	Chemical Identity, Begin. Mat. & Mfg. Proc; Disc. of Impurities, Cert. of Limits	43766901

3 of 36	The Validation of Analytical Method Used to Determine Glufosinate-Ammonium in Liberty™ Herbicide (Formulation Code: Hoe 039866 OH SL 18 A5)	A54469	62-3	Analytical Method	43766902
4 of 36	The Determination of the Color of Liberty™ Herbicide (Formulation Code: Hoe 039866 OH SL 18 A5)	A54467	63-2	Color	43766903
5 of 36	The Determination of the Physical State of Liberty™ Herbicide (Formulation Code: Hoe 039866 OH SL 18 A5)	A54475	63-3	Physical State	43766904
6 of 36	The Determination of the Density of Liberty™ Herbicide (Formulation Code: Hoe 039866 OH SL 18 A5)	A54465	63-7	Density	43766905
7 of 36	The Determination of the pH of Liberty™ Herbicide (Formulation Code: Hoe 039866 OH SL 18 A5)	A54474	63-12	pH	43766906
8 of 36	The Determination of Oxidizing/Reducing Action of Liberty™ Herbicide (Formulation Code: Hoe 039866 OH SL 18 A5)	A54473	63-14	Oxidizing/Reducing Action	43766907
9 of 36	The Determination of the Flammability of Liberty™ Herbicide (Formulation Code: Hoe 039866 OH SL 18 A5)	A54471	63-15	Flammability	43766908
10 of 36	The Determination of the Explodability of Liberty ™ Herbicide (Formulation Code: Hoe 039866 OH SL 18 A5)	A54464	63-16	Explodability	43766909
11 of 36	The Determination of the Viscosity of Liberty™ Herbicide (Formulation Code: Hoe 039866 OH SL 18 A5)	A54470	63-18	Viscosity	43766910
12 of 36	The Determination of the Miscibility of Liberty™ Herbicide (Formulation Code: Hoe 039866 OH SL 18A5)	A54472	63-19	Miscibility	43766911

13 of 36	The Determination of the Corrosion Characteristics of Liberty™ Herbicide (Formulation Code: Hoe 039866 0H SL 18 A5)	A54466	63-20	Corrosion Characteristics	43766912
Toxicology Data Requirements *(EPA DP Bar Code D219070 Assigned 9/8/95)*					
14 of 36	Hoe 039866-^{14}C: Metabolism in Male and Female Rats Following Single Oral Administration of Test Substance at a Dose Level of 2 mg/kg Body Weight	A49981	85-1	General Metabolism	43766913
15 of 36	Hoe 039866-^{14}C, Glufosinate-Ammonium: Metabolism in Male and Female Rats Following Single Oral Administration of Test Substance at a Dose Level of 500 mg/kg Body Weight	A54334	85-1	General Metabolism	43766914
16 of 36	Hoe 039866-^{14}C: Sampling of Blood, Excrements, Organs and Tissues for Metabolism Studies in Male and Female Rats Following Single Oral Administration of Approximately 500 mg/kg Body Weight	A54450	85-1	General Metabolism	43778402
Environmental Fate Date Requirements *(EPA DP Bar Code D219073 Assigned 9/8/95)*					
17 of 36	Terrestrial Field Dissipation of Ignite® Herbicide Applied to Transgenic Corn	A54505	164-1	Terrestrial Field Dissipation	43766915
18 of 36	Terrestrial Field Dissipation of Ignite® Herbicide Applied to Transgenic Soybean	A54506	164-1	Terrestrial Field Dissipation	43766916
Residue Chemistry Data Requirements *(EPA DP Bar Code D219069 Assigned 9/8/95)*					
19 of 36	Uptake Of ^{14}C- Glufosinate-Ammonium Residues in Soil by Rotational Crops Under Confined Conditions	A54272	165-1	Confined Rotational Crop	43766917
20 of 36	Metabolism of (^{14}C)-Glufosinate in a Lactating Goat	A54158	171-4(b)	Nature of Residue - Livestock	43766918
21 of 36	Metabolism of (^{14}C)-Glufosinate in Laying Hens	A54159	171-4(b)	Nature of Residue - Livestock	43766919

22 of 36	Testing of Hoe-099730 Through FDA Multiresidue Protocols A Through G	A54502	171-4©	Residue Analytical Method - Plant	43766920
23 of 36	Magnitude of Glufosinate-Ammonium Residues in the Tissues and Milk of Dairy Cows Dosed with Glufosinate-Ammonium and Hoe-099730 At 1,3 and 10 Times the Estimated Maximum Daily Intake, for 28 Consecutive Days, USA, 1994	A54503	171-4(j)	Magnitude of the Residue - Meat, Milk and Eggs	43766921
24 of 36	Magnitude of Glufosinate-Ammonium Residues in the Tissues And Eggs of Chickens Dosed With Glufosinate-Ammonium and Hoe-099730 At 1,3 And 10 Times the Estimated Maximum Daily Intake, for 28 Consecutive Days, USA, 1994	A54485	171-4(j)	Magnitude of the Residue - Meat, Milk and Eggs	43766922
25 of 36	Magnitude of the Residue Of Glufosinate-Ammonium in or on Transgenic Field Corn Following Two Applications of Ignite® Herbicide	A54160	171-4(k)	Magnitude of the Residue - Crop Field Trials	43766923
26 of 36	Magnitude of the Residue of Glufosinate-Ammonium in or on Transgenic Soybeans Following Two Applications of Ignite® Herbicide	A54156	171-4(k)	Magnitude of the Residue - Crop Field Trials	43766924
27 of 36	Magnitude of Glufosinate-Ammonium Residues in or on Soybean Hay and Seed Resulting from Application of Ignite® Once at Third Node or Twice At Three Growth Stage Combinations, USA, 1994	A54108	171-4(k)	Magnitude of the Residue - Crop Field Trials	43766925
28 of 36	Magnitude of the Residue of Glufosinate-Ammonium in or on Transgenic Field Corn Processed Commodities Following Two Applications of Ignite® Herbicide	A54284	171-4(l)	Magnitude of the Residue - Processed Food	43766926

29 of 36	Magnitude of the Residue of Glufosinate-Ammonium in or on Transgenic Soybean Processed Commodities Following Two Applications of Ignite® Herbicide	A54283	171-4(l)	Magnitude of the Residue - Processed Food	43766927
PAT Protein Safety Studies					
30 of 36	L-Phosphinothricin N-Acetyltransferase Biochemical Characterization	A50188	N/A	N/A	43766928
31 of 36	L -Phosphinothricin N-Acetyltransferase Inactivation by Pig and Cattle Gastric Juice	A51230	N/A	N/A	43766929
32 of 36	Fate Of Introduced DNA in Gut: Degradation Of Phosphinothricin Acetyl Transferase Gene from Transgenic Rape HCN 92 (*Brassica Napus*) in Stomach Fluids From Pig, Chicken and Cow	A51613	N/A	N/A	43766930
33 of 36	Expression of the Phosphinothricin Acetyltransferase in Glufosinate Resistant T14 and T25 corn	A53356	N/A	N/A	43766931
34 of 36	Comparison of the Phosphinothricin Acetyltransferase Enzyme Expressed in *Escherichia coli*, Corn (T14 and T25) and Canola (HCN-92)	A53391	N/A	N/A	43766932
35 of 36	Digestion of the Phosphinothricin Acetyltransferase Enzyme in Human Gastric Fluid (Simulated)	A53425	N/A	N/A	43778403

36 of 36	Comparison of the Synthetic PAT Gene and the PAT Protein with Other Known Nuclotide and Protein Sequences	A53504	N/A	N/A	43766933

APPENDIX B

BIBLIOGRAPHY OF SUBMITTED STUDIES

<u>Products:</u>   Liberty™ Herbicide

<u>Temporary Tolerance Petition No:</u>   5G4466

<u>EPA EUP Number:</u>   45639-EUP-56

<u>Purpose of Submission:</u>   Application for Experimental Use Permit
                                     For Liberty™ Herbicide and Petition For
                                     Temporary Tolerance of Glufosinate-
                                     Ammonium on Corn and Soybean

<u>Date of Submission:</u>   January 18, 1995

1 of 12	Use Of Glufosinate-Ammonium on Glufosinate-Ammonium Resistant Crops:Toxicology Overview and Risk Assessment	N/A	N/A	N/A	43515601
2 of 12	^{14}C-Glufosinate-Ammonium: Nature of the Residue in Field Corn	Pan-Ag Study Number 93260; Sponsor Project Number 93-0025	171-4(a)	Nature of the Residue - Plants	43515602
3 of 12	Metabolism of [^{14}C]-Glufosinate Ammonium in Soybeans,Treated Under Normal Field Conditions	500BK Report A53607	171-4(a)	Nature of the Residue - Plants	43515603
4 of 12	Method Validation - Determination of Residue Levels of Glufosinate-Ammonium and Metabolites in Various Field Corn and Soybean Matrices	Xenos Number XEN 93-19A Sponsor Project Number 93-027	171-4(c)	Residue Analytical Method - Plant	43515604
5 of 12	Independent Laboratory Confirmation of the Analytical Method AE-24 (Draft) - Revision 4A for Glufosinate-Ammonium Residues in or on Crops, USA, 1994	BK-94R-05	171-4(c)	Residue Analytical Method - Plant & PRN # 88-5	43524601

6 of 12	Determination of Possible Analytical Interference From Other Pesticides During the Analysis of Crops for Residues of Glufosinate-Ammonium	Pan-Ag Study Number 94428 Sponsor Project Number BK-94R-07	171-4(c)	Residue Analytical Method - Plant	43515605
7 of 12	**Part 1 of 3:** Magnitude of the Residue of Ignite Herbicide in Transgenetic Field Corn Following Application of Ignite Herbicide	Pan-Ag Study Number 93224 Sponsor Project No. HRAVC 93-0006	171-4(k)	Magnitude of the Residue - Cropfield Trials	43515606
8 of 12	**Part 2 of 3:** Magnitude of the Residue of Ignite Herbicide in Transgenetic Field Corn Following Application of Ignite Herbicide	Pan-Ag Study Number 93224 Sponsor Project No. HRAVC 93-0006	171-4(k)	Magnitude of the Residue - Cropfield Trials	
9 of 12	**Part 3 of 3:** Magnitude of the Residue of Ignite Herbicide in Transgenetic Field Corn Following Application of Ignite Herbicide	Pan-Ag Study Number 93224 Sponsor Project No. HRAVC 93-0006	171-4(k)	Magnitude of the Residue - Cropfield Trials	
10 of 12	Magnitude of the Residue in Transgenetic Soybeans Following Application of Ignite Herbicide	Pan-Ag Study Number 93225 Sponsor Project No. HRAVC 93-0007	171-4(k)	Magnitude of the Residue - Cropfield Trials	43515607
11 of 12	Magnitude of the Residue of Ignite Herbicide in Transgenetic Field Corn RAC and Corresponding Processed Commodities Following Application of Ignite Herbicide	Pan-Ag Study Number 93230 Sponsor Project No. HRAVC 93-0006	171-4(l)	Magnitude of the Residue - Processed Commodities	43515608

| 12 of 12 | Magnitude of the Residue in Transgenetic Soybean Processed Commodities Following Application of Ignite Herbicide | Pan-Ag Study Number 93231 Sponsor Project No. HRAVC 93-0007 | 171-4(I) | Magnitude of the Residue - Processed Commodities | 43515609 |

APPENDIX C

1.   Phenotypic expression

Phenotypic expression of the transgenic plant relative to its nearest nontransgenic counterpart and/or to a range of cultivated types. Observed changes may warrant further in-depth studies. Applicants may provide valid scientific rationale to demonstrate that certain information requirements are unnecessary or impossible to provide.

1.1.   How does the transgenic plant compare to its non-transgenic counterpart with respect to the following   reproductive and survival biological characteristics?
  a.   Growth habit - changes in basic morphology
  b.   Life-span - annual, biennial, perennial
  c.   Vegetative biomass / vigor
  d.   Overwintering capacity
  e.   Flowering period / Days to first flowering
  f.   Days to maturity
  g.   Seed production - number of seeds produced per plant and a description of the various environmental conditions, to evaluate number of seeds produced in favorable and in variable environments.
  h.   Continuous seed production -Length of time (days) of seed production
  i.   Seed dormancy
  j.   Seedling emergence -proportion of seeds planted that emerge as seedlings under field conditions and a description of the various environmental conditions, to evaluate emergence in more variable environments, especially those outside the managed ecosystems
  k.   Seedling survival to reproduction
  l.   Outcross frequency within species (e.g. 0-1, 2-20, 21-100%)
  m.   Cross pollination vectors -change in pollinator species
  n.   Pollen viability - proportion viable and length of survival
  o.   Fertility or infertility - male or female
  p.   Self-compatibility or -incompatibility
  q.   Asexual reproduction, i.e. vegetative reproduction
  r.   Dispersal ability, i.e., seed shattering, digestibility, or palatability to birds or mammals

1.2.   How does the transgenic plant compare to its counterpart with respect to the following stress adaptations (specifically note which stresses were observed)?
  a.   Biotic stress factors: includes pathogens, competitors, symbionts, and herbivores
  b.   Abiotic stress factors: includes atmosphere (i.e., ozone, NOx), soil nutrients, temperature, and moisture
  c.   Pesticides

1.3.   Does the transgenic plant differ in nutritional composition from its nontransgenic counterparts (e.g., protein, lipids, etc.)?

1.4.   Does the transgenic plant differ from its counterparts in levels of known naturally expressed toxicants?

2.   Potential nontarget effects

2.1.   Is the introduced gene product a novel part of the diet of humans, animals, or insects?

2.2.   Does the introduced DNA directly or indirectly lead to the expression of a toxin or other product that is known to affect metabolism, growth, development, or reproduction of animals, plants, or microbes?

2.3.   Is there a potential effect (toxic or nontoxic) to organisms that may be associated with the crop, including insect, avian, aquatic, or mammalian species, and organisms that are beneficial (pollinators, predators, parasites, biological control organisms, soil microbes), from both endogenous [naturally expressed] or non-endogenous [transgenic] compounds? APHIS considers routes of exposure to all plant parts that express the gene, i.e., direct feeding or other exposure to the plant or plant part, dispersed plant parts, or organisms that have fed on the plant.

2.3.1.   In what parts of the plant is the gene product expressed and at what levels?

2.3.2.   Has typical pollinator and other insect activity (i.e. feeding) been observed on the transgenic plant?

2.4.   Is there potential for adverse human health effects, e.g., exposure to toxins, irritants, and allergens? APHIS considers estimated level and most likely route of human exposure to the gene products, breakdown products and by-product.

2.5.   Does the transgenic plant differ from the nontransgenic plant in residual effects on soil microflora and microfauna?

2.6.   Will the introduced trait directly or indirectly result in altered physiological or behavioral characteristics of animals (e.g., pheromones, hormones, or attractants; altered seed morphology; altered growth habit)?

3.   Growing the Transgenic Plant - Interactions of the transgenic plant in the environment   (Agricultural ecosystems)

3.1   Description of the growing area

3.1.1. Is the transgenic plant intended to be grown in all of the U.S.? If in a specific region of the country, please provide.

3.1.2. What is the projected total area being grown?

3.1.3. Will the transgenic plant be grown outside of the normal geographic areas for the species?

3.1.3.1 If yes, identify and describe the new geographical area(s) in which the transgenic plant can be grown.

3.1.4. Will the transgenic plant be grown outside of the usual managed ecosystems for the species?

3.1.4.1 If yes, identify and describe the new ecosystems in which the transgenic plant can be grown.

3.1.4.2 Will the introduced trait allow the plant to be grown or survive in a new habitat where it could impact nontarget organisms including populations of plants with which it can interbreed?

3.2.   Description of cultural practices

3.2.1. Will the cultural practices (land preparation, fertilizer usage, weed and pest control, harvest, post-harvest protocols, etc.) involved in growing the transgenic plant vary from those traditionally used?

3.2.1.1 If yes, describe the change in cultural practices. Provide information showing the effect of these changes on sustainability, pesticide use, frequency of tillage, soil erosion and consequential changes in energy and soil conservation.

3.2.2. Will volunteer plants of the transgenic plant necessitate altered cultural practices for succeeding crops?

3.2.2.1 If yes, describe alternative practices to control volunteers?

3.2.3. Are any specific deployment strategies recommended for this transgenic plant?

3.2.3.1 Insect Resistance Management - Has an insect resistance management (IRM) strategy been submitted to EPA or is this product under an existing IRM with EPA?

the development of resistant weeds.

3.3.   If it is anticipated that the transgenic plant will be grown only under contract/controlled conditions (e.g. Pharmaceuticals, biologics), describe:
- any control and mitigation procedures;
- post-harvest procedures, including procedures for disposal of remaining plant matter.

4.   Introgression - Potential Environmental Effects Resulting from Introgression

4.1.   Will the crop be grown in proximity to species with which it can interbreed?

4.2.   Does the introduced trait increase the likelihood of introgression between the crop and species with which it can interbreed?

4.3.   Where there is potential for gene flow from the transgenic plant into related species, detail   the consequences of novel gene introgression into those species and resulting expression. Interactions identified for the transgenic plant should be considered, as appropriate, for these species.

4.3.2.   Is the compatible wild relative considered a weed and/or is it invasive?

4.3.3.   Does the introduced trait increase reproductive fitness or confer a selective advantage on the wild relative?

4.3.3.1 Is the potential for the trait to increase reproductive fitness or confer a selective advantage different than the potential for this to occur from a similar trait, if there is one, in a traditionally bred line of the same crop?

4.3.3.2 Is the introduced trait similar to a trait found currently in natural populations of the compatible wild relatives?

4.3.4.   Does the introduced trait have a significant impact on the establishment and spread of populations of wild relatives?

SIDEBAR No. III.A

PHARMACEUTICAL-PRODUCING PLANT

Overview

This sidebar examines the proposed use of genetically engineered plants and plant viruses to produce protein biologics for use in human or animal therapy, referred to in the sidebar as "human biologics" and "veterinary biologics," respectively. Human biologics are regulated by the Food and Drug Administration (FDA), while veterinary biologics are regulated by the Center for Veterinary Biologics (CVB) of the Animal and Plant Health Inspection Service (APHIS) of the United States Department of Agriculture (USDA). The plants that are engineered to produce the biologic, or infected with a virus engineered to produce the biologic, are regulated by Plant Protection and Quarantine Staff (PPQ) of APHIS. If they produce a human biologic, they are also regulated in part by FDA as part of its oversight of production of the biologic. FDA is responsible for ensuring that the plant is grown and maintained in a manner that will enable consistent production of a safe, pure, and potent biologic. If plants are engineered to produce a veterinary biologic, the plants are likewise also regulated in part by APHIS CVB as part of its oversight of production of the veterinary biologic.

The principal example used in the sidebar is that of a tobacco mosaic tobamovirus (TMV) engineered to cause tobacco plants to produce thrombopoetin, a hematologic growth factor that stimulates the production of platelets by bone marrow. The thrombopoetin would be extracted from the tobacco plants and purified for use in treating human cancer patients who have received chemotherapy. The sidebar also notes some issues posed by food crops engineered to produce pharmaceuticals or other non-food material, such as the need to ensure that such products do not inadvertently enter the food supply. Because no products from pharmaceutical-producing plant systems have completed the federal regulatory process, the sidebar cannot be as detailed or definitive as it otherwise might be.

1. Description of proposed organism/product and its use

TMV is a small RNA virus (that is, its genome is ribonucleic acid (RNA), rather than DNA). It causes a severe disease in tobacco world-wide. TMV occurs naturally only in solanaceous plants (Gibbs 1986). Tobamoviruses, (the class of viruses to which TMV belongs) reach high quantities in infected plants. They are easily transmitted by mechanical inoculation, but not by insects or other common agents. Most tobamoviruses are not transmitted via the embryo (true seed transmission), but the virus often contaminates the external mucilage, testa, and sometimes the endosperm of tobacco plants. Surface virus particles can infect tobacco seedlings during transplanting, but not if the seeds are undisturbed (Broadbent 1965). Tobamoviruses cause a wide variety of symptoms from mild yellowing to necrosis depending on virus strain and the host plant. Tobamoviruses are controlled by a number of methods, including the use of resistant or tolerant cultivars, elimination of sources of inoculum such as weeds and infected debris, decontamination of infested equipment, and the use of mild strains of the virus to cross protect against virulent strains of the virus.

TMV RNA codes for at least four proteins, all of which are required for efficient viral multiplication. To engineer the virus to produce thrombopoetin, scientists modified a strain of TMV known as U1. They replaced most of the U1 coat protein (except for its promoter) with the coat protein from the most distantly related tobamovirus. The thrombopoetin gene was inserted next to the remaining U1 coat protein promoter. (see appendix A for details). One of the advantages of this construction is that the fusion gene is not stably maintained by the virus. Experiments have shown that after passing through four or five generations of tobacco plants, the replicating virus will no longer contain the thrombopoetin gene, thereby minimizing any long-term environmental risk that persistence of such engineered viruses might pose.

The manufacturing schema includes mechanically inoculating tobacco plants with the engineered TMV in ten-acre fields. After viral infection, thrombopoetin is produced in the infected plant cells. It generally is harvested from the intracellular spaces in the leaves about a month after inoculation, prior to flowering. Pharmaceutical-producing tobacco plants are routinely deflowered to allow vegetative growth to continue, and to put more of the plant's energy into leaf (and therefore pharmaceutical) production. The tobacco is to be grown and harvested by contract farmers and the processing of the plant material will ultimately be covered by an approved Biologics License Application. Any unharvested tobacco plants, and the solid material remaining after extraction of the harvested plants, will be plowed into the field on which the plants were grown. Other wastes will be sent to the local wastewater treatment facility after deactivation with chlorine bleach, in accordance with 9 CFR 114.15.

The process of infecting the tobacco plants and growing the infected plants is under the jurisdiction of FDA from the point of view of ensuring the safety, purity and potency of the biological product to be licensed, and under the jurisdiction of USDA from the point of view of controlling any plant pest risks posed by the virus and infected plants.

Pharmaceutical Producing Plants

While this sidebar addresses a TMV in a plant, using plants themselves to produce pharmaceuticals is increasingly of interest, and confined field trials of such plants are currently ongoing. Researchers and companies are interested in using crop plants to produce pharmaceuticals for a number of reasons. The need for very large quantities of biologics, projected to be 500 to 1000 kilograms per year for some human biologics, is growing rapidly. Production costs may be lower than with traditional fermentation technology, both because of reduced energy costs and reduced cost of raw materials. The energy-expensive process of cleaning and sterilization of large fermentors is not necessary and the need for large volumes of purified culture medium is eliminated. In addition, the use of crop plants removes the potential for contamination of the biologic with animal viruses that potentially can be pathogenic to humans. An inherent risk with biologics produced in animals or animal cells is that the animals or animal cells will become infected with a pathogenic virus that may then contaminate the product. This risk is avoided by producing the biologic in plants, because there are no known plant viruses that can infect people.

However, using crop plants to produce pharmaceuticals does pose potential risks that conventional manufacturing establishments do not. Most obviously, the kinds of potential effects on the environment are quite different when pharmaceutical-producing plants are grown in the outdoors than when pharmaceuticals are produced in indoor fermentation establishments. In addition, when pharmaceuticals are produced in crop plants that are ordinarily used for human food or animal feed (e.g., corn), there is a need to ensure that the "pharm plants" are strictly segregated so that they cannot inadvertently end up in food or feed and their pollen cannot pollinate varieties of the crops that are intended for food or feed.

Procedures are necessary to ensure adequate control (including of gene flow) of food plants whose genome has been engineered to produce pharmaceuticals or other non-food products. These procedures would include control of gene flow during field growth, and segregation of seeds, plants, and plant products prior to planting and after harvest. As mentioned in Section 3, the agencies are reviewing what procedures will be necessary, and whether appropriate regulations and adequate authority exist, to ensure adequate segregation of such bioengineered non-food-use varieties of food crop species, both on the farm and when harvested and distributed for processing. Recent experience with StarLink corn has shown the difficulties in mitigating and managing the effects of lack of appropriate segregation. If a food plant produced an industrial chemical instead of a pharmaceutical, these concerns would be similar, but the chemical would be regulated under TSCA by EPA.

For pharmaceutical plants that do not meet the definition of regulated article, APHIS authorities under the PPA are based on the "reason to believe" clause.

Relevant regulatory agencies:

APHIS

The introduction (importation, interstate movement, or release into the environment) of certain genetically engineered organisms and products are regulated by APHIS under 7 CFR Part 340, promulgated pursuant to authority granted by the Plant Protection Act (PPA) (Title IV, Pub. L. 106-224, 114 Stat. 438, 7 U.S.C. §§ 7701-7772). Use of biologic products in animals is regulated by the USDA under the Virus-Serum-Toxin Act (VSTA), 21 U.S.C. §§ 151-159.

Because TMV is classified as a regulated article under 7 CFR 340.2, anyone wishing to import it, transport it across state lines, or release it into the environment must apply for and be issued a permit from APHIS prior to engaging in these activities. The permitting process provides federal regulatory oversight by APHIS over not only the release of the agent into the field, but also the disposal of potentially contaminated waste material. All of the controls outlined in the analogous APHIS section of the glufosinate-ammonium (GA) tolerant soybean case study apply to this product, too. It is noteworthy, however, that APHIS' regulations (7 CFR 340.3(b)4(iii)) clearly state that plants that encode products intended for pharmaceutical use do not qualify for simple notification under 7 CFR 340.3 and therefore are required to apply to APHIS for a permit for interstate transport and field testing.

Thus, before initiating field trials of the TMV in tobacco plants, a sponsor would need to go through the APHIS permitting process described in the accompanying glufosinate-ammonium tolerant soybean case study. Similarly, before initiating field trials of a food crop, such as corn, that is itself engineered to produce a pharmaceutical or other non-food material, a sponsor would need to go through the same APHIS permitting process.

To clarify what pharmaceutical means, APHIS has provided the following guidance. If commercialization of the pharmaceutical produced in plants will require approval from FDA's CBER (human biologic), CDER (human drug), CVM (animal drug), or USDA's CVB (animal biologic), then the engineered plant is intended for pharmaceutical intent. The term "commercialization" with plant-derived biologic means that the biologic is approved by FDA or CVB for its intended use. It does not mean that the plants or plant viruses could be grown in the U.S. without APHIS authorization. APHIS cannot currently envision plant-derived biologics that would be granted a determination of nonregulated status, nor could they qualify for release under notification procedures (7 CFR 340.3). APHIS believes that the plant-derived biologics will always be grown under APHIS permit and concurrently regulated by either FDA or CVB.

FDA

The production of bioengineered plant-derived biologics or drugs, intended for diagnostic, preventive, or therapeutic use in humans is regulated by the FDA under authority of the Public Health Service Act (PHS Act), 42 U.S.C. §§ 201 et seq. and the Federal Food, Drug, and Cosmetic Act (FFDCA), 21 U.S.C. §§ 301 et seq.

Individuals or organizations wishing to perform clinical testing of a biologic product in humans must submit an Investigational New Drug application (IND) to the Center for Biologics Evaluation and Research (CBER) of the FDA for prior review. If, after completing clinical trials to demonstrate that the biologic is safe and effective, the sponsor wishes to market the biologic for human therapy, the sponsor must submit a Biologics License Application (BLA) to CBER for review and approval.

FDA oversight of the thrombopoetin, and of the engineered TMV and TMV-infected tobacco plants (and similarly, FDA oversight of a human biologic derived from a bioengineered plant), would begin at the time the sponsor submitted an Investigational New Drug (IND) application. This typically would occur near the time the sponsor was ready to begin clinical trials with the plant-derived biologic. Under the PHS Act and FFDCA, FDA regulatory authority encompasses environmental issues that pertain to human health.

In addition, under the National Environmental Policy Act of 1969 (NEPA), 42 U.S.C. §§ 4321 et. seq., FDA would be responsible for identifying and evaluating any potential environmental impacts related to FDA's action on the IND or biologics license application. (The Center for Veterinary Biologics of APHIS has the same responsibility under NEPA when reviewing a license application for a veterinary biologic such as an animal vaccine.) The FDA will review the environmental assessment or the request for a categorical exclusion submitted in the IND and BLA in accordance with the Council on Environmental Quality (CEQ) regulations implementing NEPA (40 CFR Parts 1500-1508) and FDA's regulations (21 CFR Part 25) that implement CEQ's regulations.

Although INDs are ordinarily categorically excluded, given the nature of the environmental issues potentially posed by pharmaceutical-producing bioengineered expression systems, it is likely FDA would consider that such products represent an "extraordinary circumstance" and would therefore not receive a categorical exclusion. If, after FDA reviews the environmental assessment submitted to it, FDA determines that an environmental impact statement is necessary, this will be prepared in accordance with the CEQ and FDA requirements implementing NEPA. It is envisioned that should an environmental impact statement be needed, it would likely be jointly prepared by FDA and APHIS, and potentially by other interested or affected agencies as well.

Because such pharmaceutical-producing plants or plant-virus systems will always be grown under APHIS permit, and because permits enabling field trials will always be obtained prior to submission of an IND to FDA for human clinical trials of the plant-derived biologic, APHIS will have the responsibility to identify and evaluate the environmental effects potentially posed by such plants and plant-virus systems, and FDA's NEPA analysis will take into account APHIS' environmental reviews.

APHIS PPQ provides confidential copies of all importation, interstate movement, and field testing permits for plant-derived biologics to FDA or APHIS CVB. Also, since 1999 FDA and USDA have been cooperating on preparing a document entitled, "Guidance for Industry: Draft Guidance on Plant-Derived Biologics for Use in Human and Animals". As part of the information-gathering for preparing this guidance document, the Agencies held a joint scientific meeting and public hearing in April 2000 in Ames, Iowa (transcripts of the meeting and public hearing are available at: http://www.fda.gov/cber/minutes/plnt1040500.pdf and http://www.fda.gov/cber/minutes/plnt2040600.pdf.)

3.   Hazard identification and environmental evaluation

In order to evaluate whether there are any significant impacts to the environment posed by the recombinant TMV, APHIS requires that various laboratory and field studies be conducted, and the results submitted in the APHIS permit application. These studies include evaluations of the ability of the virus to spread from infected plants to other plants in the vicinity. Spread of the virus is tested in plants in direct contact and plants at a distance.

APHIS is aware of no evidence that plant viral genes can be transferred to the genomes of microorganisms, plants, or animals (Amabile-Cuevas and Chicurel 1993). However, genes can be transferred from TMV to other closely related tobamoviruses, e.g. tomato mosaic tobamoviruses (ToMV), via recombination. Fortunately, ToMV (the closest related plant virus) is unlikely to be present in tobacco fields (Gooding 1986). Additionally, those viruses likely to infect tobacco plants via insect vectors such as aphids (e.g., potyviruses) are unlikely to recombine with TMV (Falk and Bruening 1994). To further minimize the chances of viral gene transfer, and also because infection of the experimental plants with other plant viruses would jeopardize data collection, APHIS requires applicants to make every effort to exclude other plant viruses from infecting the experimental plants.

Any unanticipated effects on non-target organisms must be reported to APHIS within five working days. However, the potential for adverse effects of the TMV-based pharmaceutical production system on non-target beneficial or threatened and endangered species is believed to be minimal. Probably because of the production of nicotine, few organisms feed on tobacco plants. The only organisms that are routinely associated with tobacco plants are its pests, tobacco budworm, tobacco hornworm, and tobacco aphid. There are no birds or mammals that eat tobacco, so no effects on these species are expected. Similarly, earthworm populations decline in tobacco fields, probably because of nicotine production by tobacco plants. In addition, because these plants generally will be deflowered or harvested before flowering occurs, bees and any other potential pollinators generally will not visit these plants, and therefore, generally will not be affected.

Generally speaking, the potential risk to threatened or endangered species will be evaluated on a case-by-case basis, taking into account the pharmaceutical product, the host-plant and expression system, the location and size of the field, the time period of growth, harvest, and clean-up, and the potentially effected species. Such information is generally included in the environmental assessment component of the sponsor's permit application to USDA and will be reviewed by APHIS. APHIS does not anticipate a risk from the TMV- tobacco plant system to any threatened or endangered species, because it has not identified a direct or indirect effect of the field release of the engineered TMV on any wild plant or animal species.

For expression systems that utilize germ-line transformed plants for production of biologic products, pollen and seed-production are of greater concern than in the TMV system. For these expression systems, the sponsor must comply with APHIS permit requirements to avoid pollination of nearby agricultural crops or wild relatives. This may include de-flowering, the use of sterile male plants, or other measures. In situations where the biologic-producing plant (or a plant engineered to produce other non-food-use products, like plastics or industrial enzymes) is from a species that is also used for food or feed (for example, corn or other cereal grains), APHIS and FDA are considering what mechanisms will be needed to ensure that the pharmaceutical-producing plant, and grain or other products of the plant, are kept completely segregated from food/feed-use varieties of the crop (both in the field and when harvested and distributed for processing), and that such segregation is effectively monitored This is a new area, and may require new legislation or new regulations.

4.   Information and data

APHIS

APHIS requires data and information on the host plant, the genes that have been introduced into the plant, and the interaction of the engineered plant and the environment. This process is described in greater detail in the Herbicide-tolerant Soybean case study (No. III).

FDA

To satisfy the requirements of the FFDCA and PHS Act, sponsors will have to provide to FDA data and information about the plant or plant-virus system necessary to demonstrate that the biologic produced by the plant system will consistently be safe, pure and potent.

In addition, FDA generally requires an applicant to prepare an environmental assessment to enable the agency to determine whether the system will have a significant impact on the environment. (see 21 CFR 25.40 (b)). The FDA is ultimately responsible for the scope and content of environmental assessments and may supplement the information provided by the applicant in environmental documents when warranted. The reliability of sponsor-generated data is assessed during review of the licensing application and upon inspection of the manufacturing site. As noted in section 2, FDA intends to base its environmental assessment upon the environmental assessment made by APHIS as part of its evaluation of permit applications for such plant systems, and thus FDA would likely request a sponsor to submit a copy of the APHIS permit and the environmental documentation for an environmental assessment.

5. Mitigation and management

Under the APHIS permitting process, the distribution of the recombinant virus can be controlled by the sponsor in a number of ways. The following is a list of mechanisms that have been used in field tests of TMV-infected tobacco plants. The permittee is responsible to ensure that these conditions are complied with:

1) No plants in the Solanaceae family are grown near the field site. The closest commercial tobacco production site would likely be used to grow TMV-resistant cultivars because they are readily available and effectively control this disease. A strip of fallow ground would be maintained around the field of tobacco that is to be infected with the TMV and the Solanaceous weeds that are hosts for TMV (horsenettle, black nightshade and ground cherry) would be controlled on site by either herbicide application or roguing.

2) A non-host species (e.g., corn) is grown in the arable land adjacent to this strip of fallow ground to act as a barrier to the spread of the virus to other fields.

3) Inoculation of the tobacco plants with the virus is performed by hand-held spray applicators to control the distribution of the virus.

4) Plants are de-flowered to eliminate seeds that would produce 'volunteer' plants that could act as hosts for the virus in the following year.

5) Harvest of the tobacco is performed with a crosscut mower and the plant material is collected in covered containers for transport to the purification facility.

6) All farm implements that come in contact with infected plants will be washed thoroughly with soap and then will be cleaned with 1% sodium hypochlorite solution (Gooding 1986).

7) Because TMV persists in soil only when infected tissue is present (Gooding 1986), the field site will be redisked at least twice after final harvest to facilitate natural decay of plant material. Additionally, any solid waste plant material resulting from the extraction and purification process is also plowed into the field. The following year a non-host species is grown in the field to allow additional time for remaining TMV to biodegrade. This crop of non-host species is not harvested for use as food or feed, but is again plowed into the field. In the next year, the field again may be used for any purpose.

8) Potentially infectious liquid waste from the purification process is inactivated in accordance with USDA regulation (9 CFR 114.15) and sent to the local waste water treatment facility.

9) Evidence submitted by the applicant and other published data (reviewed by Mushegian and Shepherd 1995) show that the engineered virus either reverts to wildtype virus or is not competitive in mixed infections with wildtype TMV.

10) The gene inserted into the virus has never been shown to be involved in plant pathogenicity and its expression within the plant would not broaden the host range of the TMV.

11) If the engineered virus did escape and infect another susceptible plant, the engineered virus would be at a competitive disadvantage to endemic tobamovirus of that host.

12) Although TMV is a problem in tobacco growing regions in US, it is not routinely a problem in tomato fields. ToMV out competes TMV in mixed infection in tomatoes. Therefore,

TMV is eliminated during mixed infections.

These containment conditions have been used in previous tests of engineered TMV and have proved adequate to contain the virus.

6.   Monitoring

Under permits, APHIS will require monitoring programs to test for residual virus in surrounding fields on which recombinant TMV has been previously used. The results from monitoring activities can be reviewed by APHIS during site inspections and as part of the review of applications for permit renewal.   If the sponsor were found to be out of compliance, their permit may be cancelled or not renewed and it could trigger an enforcement action. If monitoring led to the detection of adverse effects, APHIS would review them to determine what appropriate mitigating actions might be required.

7.   Enforcement

The penalties imposed by the USDA as outlined in the Herbicide-tolerant Soybean case study (No. III) would apply to this sidebar as well. FDA has authority to take actions to enforce requirements instituted to ensure the safety, purity, or potency of a human biologic produced from a bioengineered plant. FDA also has authority to take actions against adulterated and misbranded foods, such as would likely be the case if a food product contained a pharmaceutical (e.g., if corn from a corn plant engineered to produce a pharmaceutical inadvertently entered the food supply).

8.   Public involvement

APHIS permits for interstate transport and field studies can be viewed on the USDA/APHIS website as described in the soybean case study.

Public involvement in FDA actions will be in accordance with 21 CFR Part 25, subpart E. Prior to approval of a biologics license application for a plant-derived biologic, FDA would consider convening an advisory committee of outside experts to review the environmental concerns and provide additional guidance as necessary. Advisory committee meetings are generally open to the public, although on occasion they may have closed segments to deal with confidential commercial information.   At this time, the existence of an IND is considered confidential and therefore information in an IND, including NEPA documentation, would not be releasable to the public. NEPA information and other non-confidential safety-related information would be releasable once a BLA had been licensed or denied.

REFERENCES

Amabile-Cuevas, C., Chicurel, M. 1993. Horizontal gene transfer. American Scientist 81:332-341.

Broadbent, L. H. 1965. The epidemiology of tomato mosaic. X. Seed-transmission of TMV. Annuals of Applied Biology 56:177-205.

Falk, B. W., Bruening, G. 1994. Will transgenic crops generate new viruses and new diseases. Science 263:1395-1996.

Gibbs, A. 1986. Tobamovirus classification. In: The Plant Viruses, vol. 2. M. H. V. van Regenmortel and H. Fraenkel-Conrat (cds.). pp.168-180. Plenum Press, New York.

Gooding, G. V. 1986. Tobacco mosaic virus: Epidemiology and control. pp. 133-152.

Mushegian, A. R., Shepherd, R. J. 1995. Genetic elements of plant viruses as tools for genetic engineering. Microbiological Reviews 59:548-578.

Appendix 1: Engineering of Tobacco mosaic virus. Dotted lines represent ribonuleotides.

1. Genome of TMV. The □up□ represents the promoter sequence for the coat protein from the TMV U1 strain.

> 5' end----RNA polymerase/helicase---movement protein----^{UP}-coat protein--3' end

2. Exchange of coat protein from the common strain for coat protein and its promoter from the orchid strain (labeled □op□ and highlighted in bold). Notice the promoter for U1 strain is still present.

> 5' end----RNA polymerase/helicase---movement protein----^{up}-^{OP}-coat protein--3' end

3. The gene sequence of thromopoetin is inserted in the genome between the two promoters. The orchid strain was selected because the sequence of its coat protein promoter is the most divergent (different) from the tobacco strain while still being able to encapsidate TMV viral RNA. When the promoters have high degree of homology, the inserted gene is rapidly deleted via homologous recombination between the identical promoter sequences. With the sequence difference between orchid and tobacco coat protein promoters, the engineered virus loses the insert protein at a lower frequency than when they have identical sequences.

5' end---RNA polymerase/helicase---movement protein----^{up}*thromopeotin*-^{OP}-coat protein--3' end

4. Eventually the thromopeotin gene is deleted. The resulting virus is very similar to the initial virus described above in number 1 expect the coat protein is now from the orchid strain not tobacco strain that has identical biological properties.

5' end---RNA polymerase/helicase---movement protein----^{up}-coat protein--3' end

CASE STUDY No. IV

FARM ANIMAL (GOAT) THAT PRODUCES HUMAN DRUGS

Overview

This case study examines in a general way the proposed use of genetically engineered animals to produce protein biologics for use in human therapy, referred to herein as "human biologics[1]," "human proteins," or "transgenic proteins," including the disposition of those animals. The case study uses the example of a goat engineered to express a human protein in its milk. The protein is then extracted and purified for therapeutic use in humans. While there are products under review, because no such product has completed the Food and Drug Administration (FDA) regulatory process, this case study is relatively general.

1. Description of proposed organism/product and its use

Genetically engineered (transgenic) farm animals are currently being developed through the use of recombinant DNA methods for production of therapeutic proteins for human medical uses. For example, exogenous DNA encoding a human protein may be inserted into an animal genome in such a way as to allow the expression of the heterologous protein in the milk of the transgenic animal. Once secreted into the milk, these recombinant proteins can be efficiently purified from milk and manufactured into biological products that are used therapeutically to treat disease in human beings. Transgenic animals modified to produce proteins for extraction, purification, and therapeutic use are referred to in this case study as "biopharm animals".

Production of medically useful human proteins in the milk of biopharm animals has the potential for providing an efficient and convenient method for generating large quantities of biologically active proteins and for thereby reducing the cost of pharmaceutical manufacturing. Currently, several blood clotting factors and enzymes for replacement therapy in metabolic diseases are being manufactured using this technology and are in early stages of development and testing. It is anticipated that other biological products, including therapeutic, blood and vaccine products for human use will be considered for production in biopharm animals. Several species of animals including goats, sheep, cows and rabbits are being developed for transgenic production of biologically active proteins. Research and development of this technology is currently being performed at specialized research farms and facilities in several sites in the U.S. and Europe.

---

[1] The term "human biologic" refers to a biologic intended for treating people. Human biologics generally are derived from biological sources and include substances such as blood, vaccines, and biologically active proteins. The term "human protein" is used in this case study to refer to a protein produced in humans, or the same protein produced in an animal through genetic engineering. The term "transgenic protein" refers to a protein produced from a gene introduced into the animal by genetic engineering. In this case study, the terms are used interchangeably, because the transgenic protein to be used as a biologic is a human protein.

Biopharm animals are initially generated in the laboratory by introducing well-characterized, sequenced recombinant DNA either into gametes (i.e., a mature reproductive cell --haploid set of chromosomes-- capable of fusing with a similar cell of opposite sex to yield a zygote) or early embryonic stages. Once the DNA is stably integrated into the animal genome, it can be transmitted to subsequent generations through breeding. The genetic construct is engineered so that the transgenic DNA is present in all cells in the animal but the encoded protein is expressed at high levels only in the milk.

Transgenic animal production of biologics begins with the generation and maintenance of animals producing recombinant proteins in the milk. This occurs on specialized dairy farms that are well-controlled facilities that provide both animal husbandry and milk collection services. These dairy facilities are designed to utilize state-of-the-art milking practices and equipment for single-product-dedicated milking. Milk containing the human protein is collected from lactating animals, pooled after initial testing and then frozen. The frozen milk is shipped to other manufacturing facilities where the human protein/biologic is extracted, purified and characterized. The final product is further tested and formulated for clinical use. Because of the yield advantage of biopharm production, it is anticipated that in most cases, at least for the kinds of products currently under development, relatively small farms with small herds could produce sufficient amounts of product to satisfy all medical need.

Companies have strong economic incentives to ensure that their animals, which are very expensive to develop, do not escape and interbreed with other animal stock. Biopharm animals producing milk are held in dedicated and separated pens and paddocks enclosed in areas with double fence-lines to facilitate isolation of animals from contact with other livestock, predators and pests, and to prevent escape of the animals. General management practices for these specialized farms include: relative isolation from other livestock on land without a history of infectious disease affecting livestock; use of breeding stock that are free of infectious disease; construction of high quality facilities that serve as a barrier to disease introduction from local feral and domestic livestock; maintenance of high standards of animal husbandry and veterinary care; careful monitoring of the health of animals and personnel; disease prevention programs; tracking of all animals and farm resources; and adhering strictly to written standard operating procedures (SOPs). In addition, the facilities are designed to prohibit entry by unauthorized personnel or equipment.

Disposal of ex-producer animals may require specialized facilities for burial or cremation. Environmental issues posed by burial or cremation would in general be associated with the amount of biomass of animal to be disposed of, rather than specific to the fact that the animals were transgenic. As discussed in Section 2 below, should developers propose to dispose of research animals or ex-producer animals by slaughtering or rendering them for food or feed, they would need prior approval from FDA, and to get such approval would have to demonstrate to FDA that meat from such animals would be safe for food or feed. In addition, developers would need Food Safety Inspection Service (FSIS) approval for slaughter of the animals for food. FDA is considering developing draft guidance to address various issues pertaining to FDA regulation of transgenic animals, including the kinds of information necessary to get approval for food or feed use. This draft guidance will have formal public input before becoming final. FDA and FSIS also intend to engage in public discussion on public policy issues pertaining to the potential disposal of biopharm animals through slaughter or rendering for food or animal feed use.

Sanitary waste generated from farms growing biopharm animals is handled the same way as waste generated from any animal production facility in which animal drugs are used. Farms housing biopharm animals follow federal, state, community and Tribal rules pertaining to agricultural waste. Waste is directed to local septic tanks and subsurface septic fields and is not released into public sewage.

Advantages of transgenic animal production of human pharmaceuticals

The use of transgenic animals to produce therapeutic proteins can have potential economic advantages that also provide indirect benefits to the environment, such as reduced energy and other manufacturing inputs, as compared to traditional protein production methods that use large scale bioreactors in conventional large-scale production plant facilities.

Transgenic animal production of therapeutic proteins offers several potential technical advantages compared to production in bacteria such as E. coli, in fungi, and in cell tissue culture. Production in E. coli is very efficient but limited to simple, non-glycosylated proteins, which makes this approach unusable for many human biologics. Although the cost of production in E. coli is low, the usefulness of the final protein product may be limited due to the lack of proper folding and post-translational processing.

Systems that use fungi such as yeast or filamentous fungi are efficient in production of some secreted proteins, but glycosylation patterns are non-mammalian. Non-mammalian glycosylation can reduce the efficacy of the resulting biologic by affecting the pharmacokinetics and immunogenicity of the protein. In general, proteins produced in transgenic animals are usually complete and have the same, or very similar, folding and processing characteristics as native protein.

Cell tissue culture provides the standard method for producing complex glycosylated proteins that are properly folded with useful post-translational processing. However, low yields and associated high cost of production are limiting factors for the number of proteins that can be developed. Because of the high yield of protein per animal, transgenic animals potentially can provide a cost-competitive means for large-scale production of therapeutic complex proteins. Several factors, including high milk yield, high recombinant protein content, short gestation period and short time-to-maturation make goats particularly well suited for biopharmaceutical development and scale-up for commercial production.

2. Relevant regulatory agencies, regulatory authority and legal measures

Transgenic animals that produce human biologics are regulated under both the Public Health Service Act (PHS Act) and the Federal Food, Drug, and Cosmetic Act (FFDCA). As discussed below, such animals contain both a new[2] animal drug and a human biologic, and in most cases would be regulated by both the Center for Veterinary Medicine (CVM) and Center for Biologics Evaluation and Research (CBER) of FDA. Sponsors are also subject to Environmental Protection Agency (EPA), state, local and tribal requirements regarding disposal of wastes. In addition, under FSIS regulations, livestock and poultry used for research must receive FSIS approval prior to slaughter for human food.

The agency intends to issue draft guidance to address various issues pertaining to FDA regulation of transgenic animals. It is currently envisioned that the first of these documents will explain how the PHS Act and FFDCA apply to transgenic animals, help developers understand their obligations under the relevant provisions of those laws, and clarify the respective roles of CVM and CBER in regulating the animal drug and human biologic components of transgenic animals. Other guidances will be developed as the technology matures. Scientific and open public meetings on the use of transgenic animals to produce pharmaceuticals may also provide subjects for further guidance documents.

The PHS Act states that a biological product "means a virus, therapeutic serum, toxin, antitoxin, vaccine, blood, blood component or derivative, allergenic product, or analogous product . . . applicable to the . . . treatment of a disease or condition of human beings." 42 USC 262(i). Thus, the transgenic protein extracted from a biopharm animal and intended to be used for the "treatment of a disease or condition of human beings" would be regulated as a biological product under the PHS Act. It also would meet the definition of a drug, as would the gene encoding the transgenic protein.

The FFDCA defines a "drug" to include "articles . . . intended to affect the structure or any function of the body of man or other animals." 21 USC 321(g). Because an introduced genetic construct encoding a human biologic would of necessity "affect the structure or . . . function" of a biopharm animal, the genetic construct meets the definition of a "drug." Because in general the genetic construct would not be "generally recognized . . . as safe and effective for use under the conditions prescribed, recommended, or suggested in the labeling thereof," it would meet the definition of a "new animal drug." 21 USC 321(v). This means that the gene construct in the biopharm animal is both a new animal drug and part of the process for the production of a human biologic. FDA, therefore, has the authority to regulate a transgenic animal engineered to produce a human biologic under two distinct but complementary regulatory schemes.

---

[2] ("New" with reference to animal drugs is a statutory term (21 U.S.C. 321(v)) that applies essentially to all animal drugs.)

Under the FFDCA new animal drug approval scheme, use of a new animal drug is considered "unsafe" unless the FDA has approved an application for that particular use. 21 USC 360b. A sponsor can conduct research on an unapproved new animal drug under an exemption for an investigational new animal drug (INAD). 21 U.S.C. 360b(j). 21 CFR 511.1. A sponsor can conduct new animal drug research without an INAD as long as the animals are used solely for laboratory research, and also not to be used for any food or feed purpose. The sponsor conducts research on the biopharm animal while the INAD is in effect. When completed, the research can become the basis of a new animal drug application (NADA). 21 U.S.C. 360b(b)(1).

FDA evaluates the NADA to determine whether the sponsor has demonstrated that the new animal drug is safe and effective for its intended use. The burden of proving that the drug meets this standard is entirely on the sponsor. The determination of whether a new animal drug is "safe" includes an evaluation of the new animal drug's environmental effects on the health of humans and animals. For new animal drugs intended to be used in food animals, FDA has to determine whether food products (e.g., meat, milk, eggs) from animals treated with the new animal drug are safe for human consumption. While the INAD is in effect, were a sponsor to propose to slaughter or render a transgenic animal for human food or animal feed, the sponsor would first have to obtain FDA authorization to do so. 21 CFR 511.1(b)(5). FDA would inform FSIS of its decision. Under 9 CFR 309.17 and 381.75, a sponsor would also have to get FSIS authorization to slaughter a transgenic research animal for human food.

Under the PHS Act, in order for a manufacturer to ship a biological product in interstate commerce, the manufacturer needs an approved Biologics License Application (BLA) for that product. 42 USC 262(a)(1). FDA will approve a BLA on the basis of a demonstration that the product is safe, pure, and potent and that the facility and animals in which it is manufactured meets standards designed to ensure its continued safety, purity, and potency. 42 USC 262(a)(2)(B). For a human biologic, the "safety" determination includes an evaluation of the biologic's potential environmental effects on human health.

FDA usually begins to regulate a human biological product under the FFDCA at the time that the sponsor is preparing to initiate human clinical trials of the product. This regulation includes licensure under the PHS Act and continues through the monitoring of post-marketing compliance with applicable requirements. Initially, the sponsor will either submit an Investigational New Drug application (IND) or request a pre-IND meeting to discuss the product and its clinical development. To initiate a clinical study, a sponsor must have an IND in effect. 21 USC 355(i); 21 CFR Part 312. The IND regulations are designed to protect human subjects in clinical trials and thus set forth requirements for sponsors and investigators concerning, among other things, reporting, record keeping and informed consent.

At the IND stage, considerable information about the product and its mode of manufacture are required to assess its suitability for clinical trials. Much of this data, including specific information about the transgene, its stability, the animal husbandry

5

used to maintain the animals and their ultimate disposition are useful in determining whether a potential for an adverse environmental impact exists.

Because FDA will evaluate information about the introduced genetic construct as part of its evaluation of the biological product under the IND, and in most cases will also evaluate the genetic construct under an INAD, FDA will coordinate these submissions to avoid duplication. As stated above, the agency is considering developing guidance to clarify the circumstances in which it will expect a sponsor to submit information under an INAD and the circumstances in which it will expect a sponsor to submit information under an IND.

When a manufacturer wants to move past the investigational stage, it must get a BLA. As part of the BLA, the manufacturer must submit detailed information concerning manufacturing methods and processes. 21 CFR 601.2(a). These manufacturing methods would include development, use, maintenance, and eventual disposition of the biopharm animal. The Guidance for Industry for the Submission of Chemistry, Manufacturing, and Controls Information for a Therapeutic Recombinant DNA-Derived Product or a Monoclonal Antibody Product for In Vivo Use (1996, http://www.fda.gov/cber/gdlns/cmcdna.pdf) outlines the information that should be submitted in a BLA that includes manufacture using a transgenic animal. Applicants submit the specifics of development, care, maintenance and disposal of the animals in the BLA. This information is even more detailed than that provided in the IND.

FDA would also inspect the manufacturing facilities, including farms, laboratories, and storage areas used for the maintenance of the transgenic animals. The inspections also cover quality control and quality assurance records involving the husbandry of the animals. The standard operating procedures covering all aspects of the husbandry of the transgenic animals will be inspected, as well as those covering personnel training, access to the facility and incident reporting. Those SOPs that are considered to be particularly significant may also be required to be submitted as part of the license application. FDA considers all of this information in its final evaluation of the product.

Once the product is licensed, the applicant is required to report any significant changes to the information contained in the BLA. 21 CFR 601.12. This would include any changes to the construct or the biopharm animal itself, as well as changes to the final product. Depending upon the type of change, the applicant may have to obtain approval from FDA prior to implementing the change. As long as the license is in effect, there will also be routine inspections by FDA to ensure that current good manufacturing practices (GMPs) are being followed and that all required reports have been made appropriately.

FDA intends to coordinate requirements, and avoid duplications, in any situations where sponsors of biopharm animals need both an NADA and a BLA, and expects to address this issue in guidance. In broad strokes, the agency expects that the process would work as follows, recognizing that details would change with circumstances.

In general, during the research stage of development of a transgenic biopharm animal producing a human biologic, a sponsor would have to file an INAD with CVM. In particular, INADs would be needed for non-laboratory feral animals that pose containment issues (such as fish in net pens (see Case Study No. I)), and for any animals that a sponsor would *propose* to dispose of through slaughter or rendering for human food or animal feed. CVM would inform FSIS of its decision regarding disposition.

Once the sponsor was ready to conduct human clinical trials with the extracted purified biologic, sponsors would submit an IND to CBER. If the clinical studies and other information showed that the product was safe, pure, and potent CBER would issue a BLA for the human biologic under the PHS Act. If the license holder wanted the animal to be slaughtered or rendered for food or feed at the end of its productive life, he or she would need FDA approval, likely in the form of an NADA filed under the FFDCA. In such cases, to avoid unnecessary duplication, CVM and CBER would cooperate in the reviews of the animal drug (the inserted genetic construct) and the human biologic (the protein), and their possible effect on safety of the animal for food or feed. CVM would inform FSIS of its decision regarding disposition.

Because permitting an INAD or IND to go into effect and approving a new animal drug or BLA are federal actions under the National Environmental Policy Act (NEPA), the INAD, IND, BLA and NADA processes must comply with NEPA. These processes require preparation of an environmental assessment (EA), or the existence of a categorical exclusion from the requirement to submit an EA. 21 CFR 25.15, 21 CFR 511.1(b)(10), 21 CFR 601.2(c)(2).

In addition, as noted above, the FFDCA gives FDA authority to consider the environmental effects of a new animal drug on the health of humans and other animals, and the FFDCA and PHS Act give FDA authority to consider the environmental effects of a human biologic on human health. In both instances, FDA considers both direct and indirect effects.

FDA will examine the potential for environmental impacts in an EA and, if necessary, require mitigations for any potential impacts that would adversely affect human or animal health. Additionally, there may be applicable environmental requirements with respect to runoff from animal production facilities and land receiving animal waste under the Clean Water Act and other statutes. Waste generated from the processing of milk into biologics would also be regulated by the EPA in the same way that it regulates other pharmaceutical manufacturing facilities.

Farms housing biopharm animals are subject to all federal, state, local and Tribal laws pertaining to agricultural waste. These laws include rules defined by state environmental protection departments, Tribal governments, the USDA, and Natural Resources Conservation Service (NRCS). In addition, sponsors have internal Institutional Animal Care and Use Committees composed of professionals with varied backgrounds such as scientists, physicians, veterinarians, and ethicists, with some members from outside institutions and the community. These committees oversee and approve research protocols, herd maintenance and herd health programs. This helps to ensure that the facilities operate in accordance with all environmental and animal welfare regulations and guidelines.

3. Hazard identification and risk assessment

General

Because transgenic animals are contained and carefully monitored, it is unlikely that animals would escape into the environment. In the event that animals escape, passage of the DNA in an inheritable form could only occur by breeding (e.g., goats with other goats). If such breeding occurred, the transgene could be passed to offspring and be expressed in the milk of lactating females.

Potential environmental effects of transgenic animals and their products

Potential adverse effects on the environment by domesticated biopharm animals such as goats generally would include those associated with non-transgenic varieties of such animals. Any additional potential adverse environmental effects would depend on the nature of the modification. There is little likelihood that the kinds of modifications discussed in this case study would cause domesticated biopharm animals to pose additional environmental risks beyond that of unintentionally passing the modification to conventional counterpart animals through mating. The transgene itself is an isolated segment of DNA. It would be no more likely to be taken up and incorporated into the genome of other organisms than any other piece of DNA of the animal, and so would have no different direct or indirect impact on the environment.

The human protein secreted into the milk by itself poses limited toxic risk to the environment. If the milk is accidentally spilled, the transgenic protein would be rapidly degraded along with other milk proteins. In general, transgenic proteins in these systems are expressed primarily in the milk of the animal and are not present in significant amounts in meat, stool, urine or other secretions. If sponsors were to intend to dispose of such animals through slaughter or rendering, then protein expression and potential biological effects would need to be evaluated in tissues to be used as food or feed.

FDA has used several resources to identify the hazards and environmental safety issues associated with biopharm animals. FDA staff includes scientists with expertise in animal husbandry, infectious disease, molecular biology, environmental science, food safety, and gene expression. Many FDA scientists continue to do laboratory research in these areas and to publish in scientific journals. FDA staff has training and expertise allowing identification and assessment of potential environmental hazards associated with the use of transgenic animal systems for production of therapeutic proteins. In addition, FDA scientists consult with outside experts, attend scientific conferences and public meetings, and stay apprised of recent developments in the scientific literature. FDA has published several guidances, such as the guidance mentioned above on the manufacture and testing of therapeutic products in transgenic animals, that have been recently developed through expert working groups that provide information pertinent to identifying the hazards and environmental safety issues associated with transgenic animals.

FDA representatives have attended and given presentations at workshops and public meetings to obtain stakeholders concerns associated with critical issues, including the environmental impact of transgenic animal use. For example, FDA representatives consulted with Health Canada at the 1998 Consultation on Regulating Livestock Animals and Fish Derived from Biotechnology. This consultation involved intensive efforts to identify hazards and environmental safety issues associated with transgenic animals as well as test methods, risk characterization criteria and risk management recommendations. As needed, FDA also involves experts in other government agencies in its identification of hazards and safety issues on a national and local level. Advisory committees and ad hoc committees might also be used to address relevant questions in a public forum, as they have been in other instances

FDA staff consider a wide variety of issues in their scientific reviews, including: animal health, diseases susceptibility, zoonotic potential, animal welfare, animal husbandry, impact on domestic and wildlife populations, ability to survive in a farm environment, monitoring, and disease screening capabilities. Transgenic animals may have differing environmental effects depending on their fitness, interaction with other organisms, role in ecosystem or potential for persistence. In addition, FDA consults the Guideline for Ecological Risk Assessment (1998), that was developed by the Environmental Protection Agency, in order to assess environmental safety and risks associated with transgenic animals. In the process, FDA appraises the need for appropriate testing and information collection. Once the risks have been characterized, any necessary risk management is considered and included to determine whether risks can be minimized or eliminated.

4. Information and data

FSIS has published several policy documents regarding slaughter of transgenic research animals. FSIS explained its responsibility regarding safety, wholesomeness, and proper labeling of meat and poultry food products derived for animals subjected to the techniques of biotechnology in: Federal Register, Vol. 51, No. 123, Thursday, June 26, 1986 - "Final Policy Statement for Research and Regulation of Biotechnology Processes and Products." FSIS further elaborated its policies in two additional documents. Federal Register, Vol. 56, No. 249, Friday, December 27, 1991 - "Livestock and Poultry Connected with Biotechnology Research." and Federal Register, Vol. 59, No. 52, Thursday, March 17, 1994 - "Update on Livestock and Poultry Connected With Biotechnology Research."

FDA has published documents that describe the kinds of information and data generally needed to support applications. Guidance for manufacturing and testing is provided in Points to Consider in the Production and Testing of New Drugs and Biologics Produced by Recombinant DNA technology (1985), and in a guidance for the

Manufacture and Testing of Therapeutic Products for Human Use Derived from
Transgenic Animals (1995) http://www.fda.gov/cber/ptc/ptc_tga.txt. Guidance for
investigations under INADs are provided in Guidance for Industry Submitting a Notice of
Claimed Investigational Exemption (1/99)
http://www.fda.gov/cvm/guidance/guidance.html.

These guidance documents outline information to be collected, recorded and
submitted by the sponsor in the IND and INAD applications. This includes
characterization of the transgene construct and expression system, characterization and
analysis of the transgenic founder animal and method of gene introduction. Other
important information includes genetic stability and location of gene expression and
information on the generation and selection of the production herd, including animal
history, genealogy, and breeding techniques.

The guidance documents describe maintenance of animals, including monitoring
the health of the animals, feeding, housing facilities, and disposal of animals. They also
address information on product characterization, including methods of product recovery
and definitions of product lots. Products are analyzed for adventitious and potentially
infectious endogenous agents, which may arise from the host animal or tissue. Pathogen
testing in the animals and milk products are described and protocols and data for
elimination are presented. The product is analyzed for biochemical identity, purity, and
potency. Lot release testing is described and data provided along with preclinical safety
evaluation. All this information is submitted in the IND and is reviewed by product
specialists, environmental scientists, veterinarians, biochemists, physicians trained in
clinical trial design and other scientific and regulatory experts.

Data on different aspects of animal and product development are generated by the
sponsor and then submitted in the IND or INAD, subsequent amendments, and BLA and
NADA submissions. FDA staff review these data and if necessary consult with advisory
committees when specific issues arise regarding the safety and efficacy of the product.
Recommendations from internal review are transmitted back to the sponsor for
clarification and response. The agency may inspect manufacturing facilities and take
appropriate actions as necessary. The agency has the legal authority, technical capacity
and resources to assess whether the sponsor is following specified regulations and
procedures for manufacturing and using these products.

5. Mitigation and management considerations: approvals and conditions on research, development, production, distribution, marketing, use and disposal

Management practices designed to mitigate environmental risk include raising,
identifying, and maintaining transgenic animals in specialized facilities that minimize
contact of the transgenic herd with people, other animals, insects, and infectious agents.
These facilities include physical and biocontainment capabilities.

In addition to FDA requirements pertaining to research and marketing of
transgenic animals, sponsors are subject to requirements and oversight by Institutional
Biosafety Committees and Animal Care and Use Committees (described above), and

generally are covered by the NIH Guidelines for Recombinant DNA Technology. These guidelines are mandatory for government funded research, and also are generally followed by industry.

The transition from research and development to production and distribution of a therapeutic product is covered by the IND, INAD, BLA and NADA. FDA has the legal authority under the FFDCA and PHS Act to prevent studies from proceeding under an IND and to prevent further use of a product if it determines that appropriate conditions for product manufacture and clinical development are lacking. FDA maintains the appropriate legal, regulatory, and scientific expertise to identify and respond to environmental threats that affect health posed by transgenic animals by placing conditions on the development, production, distribution, marketing, use and disposal of transgenic animals. Under certain circumstances, EPA or FSIS may also have oversight authority of appropriate disposal of transgenic animals.

6. Monitoring and consideration of new information

FDA has the legal authority, technical capacity and resources to establish monitoring requirements for marketed drug or biologic products and such products under investigation. With input from local, state and federal environmental agencies, sponsors develop and implement individual programs to monitor for environmental effects during development of the product. The monitoring of the manufacturing facilities and farms is performed primarily by the sponsor and investigators, and they submit the data they collect to the agency for review. FDA staff performs inspections of the research and manufacturing facilities, the primary data, and the clinical sites. FDA can utilize outside experts within the federal government and non-government experts on advisory committees for input into these programs depending on the specific product.

7. Enforcement and compliance

Certain SOPs on various aspects of manufacturing are required to be in place before FDA will authorize the start of clinical trials. If FDA finds a critical SOP to be inadequate, FDA has authority to stop the clinical trial until the SOP is fixed. SOPs that are believed to be particularly critical to the purity, potency or safety of the product may be included in the BLA. If a license-holder violates such an SOP, FDA has the authority to suspend or revoke the license, and impose civil and criminal penalties. If a license-holder wishes to change one of these critical SOPs for a licensed product, he or she usually must first obtain FDA approval for the change. Such approval is not required if the SOP is not specifically included in the BLA or if FDA has determined that changes to that SOP have a minimal potential for adverse impact (21 CFR 601.12).

If a sponsor establishes, in an IND, SOPs for managing environmental risks to human health during the investigational phase of product development, or in a BLA for licensure of the product, the sponsor is required to follow those procedures for continued IND authorization or licensure. If the sponsor fails to follow its written SOPs for mitigation or monitoring of the environmental risk to health prior to or during development of the product, the IND can be put on clinical hold. This means that no additional activity could occur under the IND until the FDA is satisfied that the safety issues have been addressed. If the agency were to discover that previously agreed-upon procedures were not being followed prior to licensure of the product, FDA has the authority to withhold approval of the license until the problems were resolved. This would mean that the sponsor could not market the biological product. If the sponsor were found to have failed to comply with environmental safety procedures after licensure, it would be subject to suspension or revocation of its license. 21 CFR 601.5, 601.6. FDA has authority to impose civil or criminal sanctions for this behavior.

A sponsor of a biological product under an IND is required to submit an annual report to FDA. 21 CFR 312.33. Such annual reports have to include information on steps the sponsor has taken to comply with any proposed mitigation or monitoring activities included in the IND. Inspections of the sponsor's facility may occur at any time during the development and marketing of products under an IND or BLA. Prior to BLA approval, an inspection of the manufacturing facility, which would include the animal area, would be performed to ensure that all procedures or facility features described in the BLA were in effect.

If the sponsor makes minor changes in its safety procedures (including environmental safety), it must report them in an annual report. 21 CFR 601.12(d). A sponsor may not make major changes (as described in 21 CFR 601.12(b)) in its safety procedures without receiving prior approval from FDA. Manufacturing plant inspections are scheduled every two years after licensure. However, FDA will inspect more frequently if there is cause to do so.

8. Public involvement and transparency

Public involvement in the development of a specific human biologic, whether through the use of transgenic animals or via more conventional manufacturing methods, is somewhat limited. Generally speaking, the agency has not disclosed information about specific licensure or approval applications, including the fact that a license or approval has been applied for, until after a decision has been made, and has not disclosed the existence of an IND or INAD unless the sponsor has publicly disclosed it, because FDA has considered this information to be confidential commercial information. In addition, SOPs generally constitute confidential commercial information. This limits the amount of public information and input possible for products prior to approval. The agency is considering whether there may be mechanisms by which it could make public its NEPA analyses, or components of its NEPA analyses, of products for which there is considerable public interest, and invite public comment prior to approval.

The agency does hold public workshops and advisory committee meetings to address scientific issues relevant to specific biological products. Notices of these events are published in the Federal Register and on the FDA web site. Public comment is encouraged at these on proposed regulations and guidances before enactment. In addition FDA informs the public using press releases on the approval of products and with letters to industry on a variety of product safety issues. In addition, as mentioned previously, FDA and FSIS intend to encourage public discussion of public policy implications of disposal of biopharm animals through slaughter or rendering.

Currently, at the time of approval of a BLA and at the time of publication in the Federal Register of a notice of approval of an NADA, certain information in the application is available for public disclosure. This information can include safety and effectiveness data, study protocols, and environmental documents. In some cases, FDA makes such information available via its website. At this point, a member of the public could submit a Citizen Petition that requests withdrawal of approval of the application. At any time after the approval, new information that has a bearing on the approval of the NADA or BLA can be brought to the agency by anyone in the form of a Citizen Petition. FDA considers the information submitted, replies to the Petition, and takes appropriate action based on its reply that could include withdrawal of approval of the NADA or BLA, following applicable procedures.

SIDEBAR No. IV.A

FARM ANIMAL THAT PRODUCES ANIMAL BIOLOGICS

Overview

The Animal and Plant Health Inspection Service (APHIS) is involved in regulating health issues relating to transgenic animals in two situations. First, APHIS has authority to regulate "animal or veterinary biological products" that are produced in transgenic animals as biopharmaceuticals. APHIS anticipates that a small number of such biopharmaceutical animals will be developed in the near future.

Second, APHIS would regulate "biological products" that confer disease resistance, as when a "biological product" confers specific immunity when expressed in the blood the transgenic animal. Expression of immune proteins (antigens, antibodies, or other immune proteins) in nonbiopharm food animals are near physiological levels and otherwise are commonly present in animal blood and tissue. By contrast, expression levels of such proteins in the milk of biopharm animals would be considerably higher. Veterinary biological products confer immunity through a specific immune response. Certain cytokines are "veterinary biologics" when they are involved in the stimulation of a specific immune response.

There is currently considerable discussion within the agency as to the appropriateness of regulating under the Virus Serum Toxin Act (VSTA, 21 U.S.C 151-159, as amended by the Food Security Act of 1985) the transgenic "animal" itself as opposed to the "biological product" that is expressed in such animal. APHIS has current authority to regulate the purity, safety, potency, and efficacy of the "biological product" that confers specific immunity under the VSTA and regulations. These regulations, however, do not specify procedures for the field testing, licensure, or postlicense monitoring of the transgenic "animal" even though the animal may be the source of the "biological product" addressed under the regulations. APHIS believes that this regulatory gap should be addressed under new authorities that allow regulation of the "animal". APHIS is currently seeking new authorities under its Animal Health Protection Act that would largely help fill this gap in APHIS authorities. Reference to transgenic "animal" in the following discussion addresses the "animal" that expresses the "biological product" to confer specific immunity. The following discussion focusses on "biological products" expressed in transgenic food animals that confer specific immunity.

1. Description of the proposed organism/product and its use.

The proposed article would be a "biological product" that had been expressed in a farm animal to produce protection against a specific disease by means of an immune response. Transgenic animals bearing such "biological products" may be used in APHIS animal disease control programs, by farmers, veterinarians, or for export to foreign nations. Protection against specific disease would be expected to provide economic benefit and preclude the introduction or dissemination of animal disease. The use of such animals would be expected to have trade benefits for the United States and other nations that utilized such animals.

Certain species of cattle may exhibit naturally occurring resistance to disease. Traditional selection for such resistance traits requires several generations of breeding and as many or more years of time. Transgenic animals exhibiting similar traits would be produced in shorter time periods for use on farms and in breeding operations.

No adverse effects on the environment are anticipated through the introduction of an animal expressing a "biological product" that confers immunity against specific disease. To the contrary, the "biological product" conferring immunity against specific disease would be expected to offer a positive benefit on the human environment through reduced economic loss, carcass disposal, and dissemination of disease.

The rationale for developing transgenic animals with a "biological product" conferring immunity against specific disease is to improve the health and well being of animals in addition to preventing economic loss due to animal disease. Transgenic animals may be developed, for example, with specific immunity against pathogenic strains of microorganisms that are not otherwise susceptible to known antibiotics. In addition, transgenic animals may provide specific immunity against disease, such as bovine spongiform encephalopathy (BSE), when no vaccine is available. A "biological product" such as an antibody that is targeted against specific prion proteins to prevent communicable disease would fall under the definition of a veterinary "biological product".

Constitutive expression of an immunoglobulin transgene in a farm animal species as a model to confer protection against specific disease was reported nearly 10 years ago (Lo, D. et al, Eur. J. Immunol. 21:1001-1006 (1991)).

2. Relevant Regulatory Agencies

A "biological product" that conferred protection against an animal disease based on a specific immune response and that had been expressed in a food animal would be licensed under the Virus-Serum-Toxin Act. APHIS would evaluate the product based on purity, safety, potency, and efficacy under the VSTA and regulations (9 CFR 101-118). Field testing of the experimental "biological product" that had been expressed in a food animal would be conducted under 9 CFR part 103. APHIS would review the genetic insert as part of the licensing process.

The Animal Quarantine Laws (AQL, 21 U.S.C. 101-135) and regulations under 9 CFR 122 ensure that farm animals and their progeny do not introduce or disseminate communicable disease. These statutes and regulations are administered by APHIS and would be applicable to transgenic farm animals. Because a "biological product" may be a component of an infectious agent, APHIS has to ensure that the animal bearing the "biological product" does not pose a risk of infectious disease.

As for any animal exposed to communicable disease, a transgenic animal infected with a live virus may be deemed a "vector" and may be issued a permit (hereinafter "permitted") for interstate movement. Alternatively, cells that are infected with genetic material derived from other organisms may be deemed "organisms" regulated under 9 CFR 122. Interstate movement would be prohibited under 9 CFR 122 for an organism or vector that had not been permitted or that contained a live "biological product", organism, or vector that posed a risk of introduction or dissemination of a contagious disease. In addition, the importation of animals would be permitted under 9 CFR 122 based on animal disease risk.

In the case of transgenic food animals, slaughter would be overseen by the Food Safety and Inspection Service (FSIS) under 21 U.S.C. 601 et seq. and regulations under 9 CFR 309.17 and 381.75. An MOU exists between APHIS and FSIS regarding the presence of a "biological product" in a food animal.

For a "biological product" that is expressed in a transgenic animal and that is not otherwise categorically excluded APHIS' regulations implementing the National Environmental Policy Act (7 CFR part 1b and 372), an environmental assessment would be prepared for field testing and licensure of the "biological product". Since transgenic farm animals other than fish or birds would normally be kept in the pasture or confined to the barnyard, no significant adverse impact on the human environment over their nontransgenic counterparts would be anticipated. For example, transgenic barnyard animals produced with a gene for growth hormone are not known to be significantly larger than their nontransgenic counterparts. Except for transgenic animals expressing animal biologics in their milk, most, if not all, of the transgenic farm animals expressing "biological products" licensed by APHIS would be for food production and therefore would be subject to slaughter approval by the Food Safety and Inspection Service.

Applications would be received by APHIS for the field testing, interstate movement, and licensure (for commercialization) of the "biological product" expressed in the transgenic farm animal. In addition, APHIS is currently implementing a national animal identification program under the AQL to facilitate APHIS's disease control and eradication programs. Such an animal identification program extended to transgenic animals would aid in the identification of genetically modified farm animals for such regulatory activities as interstate movement, import and export permits, animal health certification, disease control and surveillance, identification of biopharmaceutical animals, and slaughter approval.

Currently, the Virus-Serum-Toxin Act and regulations under 9 CFR 101-118 apply to recombinant and nonrecombinant animal biologics (vaccines, bacterins or bacterial antigens, allergens, antibodies, antitoxins, toxoids, antigenic components of live organisms, and diagnostic components for animal disease). The definition of a "veterinary biological product" would include a DNA-recombinant product that, when expressed in the transgenic farm animal, would render the animal resistant to disease.

The Animal Welfare Act (21 U.S.C. 2131-2159) and regulations (9 CFR 112) would also apply to transgenic food animals derived from experimental research. The care and housing of such animals would be considered, as would the affliction, if any, of pain and distress in the production of the transgenic animal.

3. Hazard Identification.

Under the Virus-Serum-Toxin Act and regulations, an applicant for a "biological product" license must demonstrate purity, safety, potency, and efficacy of the product prior to licensure. The applicant must demonstrate, based on appropriate tests, that the product is safe and efficacious for its intended use. The agency has extensive experience in the field testing and licensure of live recombinant animal vaccines, including live virus gene-deleted marker vaccines (Category II product under the 1986 Coordinated Framework for Biotechnology; see 51 Fed. Reg. 23339, 1986) and their companion diagnostic kits and live viral-vectored animal vaccines (Category III product under the 1986 Coordinated Framework).

Safety of "biological products" pertains to freedom from properties causing undue systemic reactions when used as recommended by the manufacturer (9 CFR 101.5(d)). The standard here is based on host animal response to administration of the "biological product".

In the case of live recombinant viral vectors, characteristics of safety and transmission must be examined before questions and concerns dealing with safety to humans, animals, and the environment can be answered and before such products can be considered for licensing (51 Fed. Reg. 23339, 1986). The licensing process would be intended to ensure that such live viral vector were no longer capable of transmissible disease.

Genomic DNA may also be transfected directly into a variety of mammalian cells. Alternatively, in such cases, the stable transfected cells could be considered as Master Seed (51 Fed. Reg. 23340, 1986). Tests to characterize the product may be required to demonstrate consistent gene expression (51 Fed. Reg. 23341, 1986).

Primary cells and cell lines used for production of Master Seed or vaccines must be tested in accordance with 9 CFR 113.51 and 113.52 for freedom from extraneous agents and characterized to establish genetic stability. Tumorigenicity and oncogenicity tests must also be conducted on cell lines if direct or indirect evidence indicates that the cell may induce malignancies in the species for which the product is intended (49 Fed Reg. 50899, 1984).

Efficacy of "biological products" pertains to the ability of the "biological product" to effect the result for which it is offered when used as recommended by the manufacturer (9 CFR 101.5(g)). The standard is based on comparable products prepared under a Standard Requirement for that class of product. It is anticipated that an analogous Standard Requirement would be prepared for "biological products" that are expressed in the transgenic animal.

APHIS Animal Health Programs regulates the health of livestock animals. The National Center for Import and Export approves the international movement of animals and animal products based on disease risk. APHIS endorses the health certificates issued for such international movement and performs risk assessments in response to requests to regionalize areas of the world for freedom from animal disease.

APHIS National Animal Health programs is also involved in control of major diseases of farm animals including pseudorabies, brucellosis, bovine tuberculosis, and scrapie.

APHIS National Veterinary Services Laboratory prepares reagents and performs diagnostic testing related to animal disease. Plum Island Foreign Animal Disease Laboratory conducts tests and research for animal diseases exotic to the United States.

Consultations continue between APHIS, the FDA, and FSIS regarding issues of food safety.

The agency is represented on the Office Internationale des Epizooties (OIE, the principal international organization for world animal health) International Animal Health Code Standards Commission and Diagnostic Test and Vaccines Standards Committee. The agency is thus involved in international harmonization of standards for animal health and biologics.

APHIS experience would be directly applicable to the regulation of transgenic farm animals. This experience includes the licensure of recombinant live virus animal vaccines and vaccines for fish, environmental risk assessment and approval of recombinant vaccines for field testing and commercialization, control of diseases of farm animals and poultry, animal health certification and risk assessment for international movement of animals and animal products including fish based on disease risk.

4. Information and data.

The applicant for a "biological products" license would be required to submit data or relevant references from the scientific literature that the "biological product" is safe and efficacious for its intended use, e.g., to prevent specific disease.

Data obtained from host animal challenge studies would be required by APHIS to demonstrate that the "biological product" is efficacious for its intended use, i.e., that it protects against infection by a specific microorganism or protects against specific disease. Safety studies in the host animal would be required to demonstrate that the "biological product" poses no danger to the host animal or its progeny.

Prior to the issuance of a permit to field test a "biological product" derived from a live animal virus, APHIS would require an environmental assessment prepared under the National Environmental Policy Act (42 U.S.C. 4321-4335) and Council on Environmental Quality regulations (40 CFR 1500-1508) and guidelines (46 Fed. Reg. 18206, March 23, 1981).

5. Mitigation and management considerations

APHIS would require a permit under 9 CFR 122 for the interstate movement or importation of DNA-recombinant product expressed in a transgenic food animal based on disease risk. APHIS would issue a permit for the interstate movement or importation of such products expressed in animals.

If APHIS finds that such transgenic animal were affected with or had been exposed to an infectious disease, APHIS would prohibit the interstate movement or importation of such animal, as it would with a nontransgenic animal. APHIS may issue an order that such affected or exposed animal be moved directly to a slaughter facility or disposed of in a manner acceptable to APHIS. (9 CFR parts 50-99, and 122).

APHIS would issue a permit for the field testing of an experimental "biological product" that had been expressed in a transgenic animal (9 CFR 122) or licensure of a "biological product" expressed in such animal under 9 CFR 101-118.

A license may be revoked upon a finding that the "biological product" poses a danger to domestic animals (9 CFR 105).

6. Monitoring

APHIS veterinary biologics field operations would license production establishments and monitor postlicensing issues related to "biological products" expressed in transgenic animals. During the licensing process, APHIS Animal Health programs would be consulted regarding incorporation of transgenic animals into disease control programs. APHIS would ensure that transgenic animals bearing a licensed "biological product" did not pose a risk of disease transmission.

Veterinary Services would endorse animal health certificates for the export of transgenic animals expressing "biological products" licensed by APHIS. State Animal Health authorities may also be involved in monitoring the animal health status of transgenic animals.

7. Enforcement and compliance

APHIS Animal Health Statutes and regulations provide, among other enforcement authorities, for inspection of biologics facilities for compliance with APHIS regulations, detention and condemnation of worthless "biological products", civil and criminal penalties, revocation of permits or licenses for violations of the VSTA and regulations, and disposal orders for contaminated animals and animal products under the AQL.

Public Involvement and Transparency

APHIS regulations pertaining to transgenic organisms are subject to Notice and Comment rulemaking including public notification and comment during the rulemaking process. APHIS has held public meetings related to biotechnology policy for recombinant vaccines prior to policy implementation or rulemaking. Draft environmental assessments are subject to public comment prior to preparation of a final environmental assessment under NEPA (7 CFR 1b and 372). Unless otherwise exempted, environmental assessments with opportunity for public comment are prepared prior to field testing or licensure of a recombinant veterinary "biological product".

APHIS intends to issue guidelines with opportunity for public comment regarding its policy related to transgenic farm animals.

CASE STUDY No. V

BIOREMEDIATION USING POPLAR TREES

Overview

This case study examines a hybrid poplar that has been genetically engineered to detoxify a widespread industrial toxic chemical, trichloroethelene (TCE). The poplar, which was originally modified through the insertion of a human cytochrome gene, is still being tested in the laboratory using genes from other animals and plants, and has not yet been tested in the field. The federal agencies that will be involved in regulating the poplar will be the Animal and Plant Health Inspection Service (APHIS) and the Environmental Protection Agency (EPA).

1. Description of proposed organism/product and its use (what, where, how much and when)

Introduction

Scientists have been searching for inexpensive and safe ways to remove toxic chemicals from the soil and water on polluted sites. One approach being considered is the use of plants, including those that are genetically engineered. In a recent publication (Doty et al., 2000), scientists have shown that plants engineered with a gene from a mammal degrade the toxic chemical trichloroethylene (TCE). TCE is an environmental contaminant found throughout the industrialized world. It was commonly used as a metal degreasing agent and a dry cleaning solvent. Forty percent of all Superfund sites are contaminated with TCE. It is an EPA priority pollutant and a suspected human carcinogen. It is now known that exposure can result in central nervous system depression, hepatotoxicity, and nephrotoxicity (Costa, 1980, cited from Doty et al., 2000).

One plant species that has been engineered to detoxify TCE is a hybrid poplar, which is the subject of this case study. Poplar has been chosen because the nonengineered tree can grow in soils with low levels of TCE (Newman et al, 1997), it grows rapidly, and it can be vegetatively propagated (i.e., twigs can be clipped from the tree and rooted to establish additional, genetically identical plants). The latter two are key attributes if bioremediation is to succeed. In this case of phytoremediation (bioremediation using plants), a tree takes up a chemical from the soil or water and expresses an enzyme that modifies the chemical into less toxic or nontoxic substances that are translocated to the stems and leaves. There is no functional requirement for these plants to flower, since the desired chemical processes occur in the roots, stems and leaves. Therefore, outcrossing with wild relatives can be controlled in the field testing stage through cutting down the trees before they flower, or through other techniques of inducing sterility, without decreasing the effectiveness of bioremediation.

The organism in this case study is a hybrid between two cottonwood species, black cottonwood (*Populus trichocharpa*) and eastern cottonwood (*Populus deltoides*), both native to the U.S. Because these hybrids belong to the genus *Populus*, which includes poplars, aspen and cottonwoods, they tend to be generically known as "hybrid poplars," and will be referred to as such for the rest of the case study. They are monoecious (spatially separate male and female reproductive features occur on each plant), wind-pollinated woody plants. Further information on the two cottonwood species and their hybrids can be found in the United States Department of

Agriculture Forest Service's Agriculture Handbook 654 <u>Silvics of North America</u> at the following website: " http://willow.ncfes.umn.edu/silvics_manual/volume_2/ ".

Because it is relatively easy to vegetatively propagate poplars and their hybrids, clones1 (genetically identical cuttings taken originally from one individual) are generally used in experimentation and field production. Two such clones, 184-402 and H11-11, were used in the APHIS notification that is the basis for this case study. These clones were genetically engineered using a mammalian cytochrome gene to improve degradation of the compound TCE (Doty et al., 2000). The human cytochrome gene used, P450 2E1, has been intensively studied and the gene product oxidizes a range of compounds including TCE, ethylene dibromide (EDB), carbon tetrachloride, benzene, and styrene, chloroform and others. Details of the original construct are the same as in Doty et al., (2000), except that a different promoter (35s promoter from the cauliflower mosaic virus) was used. Due to the fact that the developers are currently experimenting with other cytochromes, this case study will not focus on the specifics of the original mammalian cytochrome construct. Nevertheless, if a real environmental assessment were to be developed by APHIS or EPA for such an organism, the specific information on the construct would be essential to adequately assess the risks.

To date, no genetically engineered poplars have been field tested that detoxify TCE, although this is planned as soon as laboratory and greenhouse testing satisfies bioremediation goals of the developers. Unlike glufosinate-tolerant soybeans and Bt maize (described in other case studies), based on current understanding of this organism, APHIS believes that there are certain purposes, such as plants for bioremediation, in this case, or plants the produce pharmaceuticals, for which the plants will not be subject to deregulation. Plants for bioremediation will not be sold to the public. Trees grown at Superfund sites will require regulatory oversight by Federal, State and Tribal agencies whenever and wherever they are grown to ensure that workers and the environment are protected.

Is there prior experience dealing with the same varieties not genetically engineered?

Long, well-documented experience exists with regard to growing *Populus* species and hybrids for fiber and biomass production, and for riparian restoration. For eastern cottonwood in particular, growth of clonal plantations generated via rooted or unrooted cuttings has been conducted for decades, and management practices for these plantations are well developed (Zsuffa 1976, Cooper 1990). Hybrid cottonwoods *(Populus trichocarpa x P. deltoides)* have already been demonstrated to oxidize TCE to produce CO2 and other metabolites (Strand et al. 1995, Newman et al. 1997, Newman et al. 1999).

What are the projected location and extent of production, use and disposal?

There are thousands of contaminated sites in the U.S. and abroad. Industrial sites and air force bases commonly have TCE contamination, and often there is free TCE existing in the aquifer. It is possible that if a clone or clones were developed that could grow in different environments, they could be widely used on these kinds of sites. On a typical site, stems would

---

1 The term clone can be used to describe a transformation event, or a vegetatively propagated plant. In this case study, the term is used to mean a vegetatively propagated poplar. Whether the plant is genetically engineered or not should be clear from the context.

probably be harvested on short (5-7 year) rotations to preclude flowering, and the trees would continue to be cut down and allowed to resprout (coppiced) until TCE had been reduced to targeted levels.

Depending on the metabolites remaining in stem tissue, it is possible that the trees might be used for paper. It was hypothesized that the chemical reactions in pulping would break down any organochlorine compounds remaining in the tree. This was found to be the case in experiments by Newman and Gordon in the summer of 2000 (Gordon, personal communication). If this paper were to be produced and used, the Occupational Health and Safety Administration (OSHA) would regulate the safety of the manufacturing process. EPA would regulate air and water emissions.

What types of adverse effects might occur by the GEOP throughout its life cycle, and where might they occur?

Risks fall into four categories: (1) health and ecological risks from the products of the TCE breakdown process on the sites being remediated; (2) risk of escape of transgenes into the native eastern or black cottonwood populations, or other reproductively compatible *Populus* species; (3) risks of the transgenic trees themselves becoming weeds or otherwise invasive; and (4) health and ecological risks from materials and products derived from the trees. As stated above, characterizing the entire genetic construct would be essential in estimating risks.

With regard to health risks, trees and other engineered plants have the potential to release small amounts of TCE's into the air through transpiration. The levels of TCE transpired to air by non-engineered poplar plants are within the 4% to 7% range, as judged from field studies (Newman et al., 1997). This area of research is currently developing and undergoing continuing discussion via scientific workshops and publications. The actual amount of TCE transpired will vary depending on such factors as the analysis technique employed, availability of water, ambient air temperatures, and age of the trees. The half-life of TCE once in the air, and in the presence of sunlight, has been estimated to be approximately 9 hours. Metabolites in trees and resulting products are currently under study. The studies that have been performed to date with TCE and with the remediation of TCE by hybrid poplar indicate that the compound is completely destroyed within the poplar trees (Gordon, personal communication). There are very small quantities of intermediate metabolites--perhaps 1% of the original material is found as metabolites--but these are eventually also metabolized into CO_2 and chlorine ions (Newman et al., 1999). Nevertheless, organisms that encounter metabolites in trees or tree parts might be affected. Studies with insects have indicated that feeding herbaceous insects with residue of poplars treated with TCE has no effect on the growth rate or fecundity of the insects (Sorbet, 1998). Further research may be needed to study the effects on non-target species prior to field use of these trees.

The breakdown products of TCE degradation in hybrid poplar are chloride in the soil and trichloroethanol and conjugates, and di- and tri-chloroacetic acid in the plant tissue, which are ultimately broken down within the plant into CO_2 and chlorine. It is expected that chloride in the soil would not be a concern, as it is not harmful to soil flora or water quality at the concentrations that would occur (Newman, personal communication).

Both eastern and black cottonwoods are perennial, undomesticated plants. Thus, not only would transgenic plants persist for several years, they also could have wild relatives within pollination distance. Therefore, precautions will need to be taken to prevent escape of the transgenes to the wild population by either seeds or pollen. Greenhouse studies indicate that the phytoextraction processes will be performed very effectively by juvenile trees. Thus, stems can be cut and disposed of before the trees reach flowering and fruiting age. Since hybrid poplars can propagate itself vegetatively, using the practice of coppicing, the trees could be cut and allowed to resprout for several cycles, if necessary, without them ever reaching flowering age.

There are a number of methods currently under investigation in which the possible spread of genetically engineered material could be avoided without needing to cut down the trees before they flower. One method is the use of triploids where seeds or pollen would be approximately 99+% sterile, but not absolutely sterile, and research is ongoing on this and other mechanisms (Meilan, 1997). These sterility mechanisms would have to be tested in field trials over the relevant period of time (from the initiation of flowering age until when they would be cut down) in order to ensure that they would be effective prior to any operational use in trees for bioremediation.

Gene flow to related native species could have a variety of different impacts, depending on the gene involved. Due to the long-lived nature of trees, their importance as hosts to a variety of vertebrates and invertebrates, their well-developed capacity for pollen and seed dispersal and ability to colonize disturbed habitats, there are many environmental issues that related specifically to forest trees. Indeed, there is also a concern as to the integrity of native gene pools. It should be observed however, that some species of forest trees have been selected for two or three generations for timber or pulp production or disease resistance through traditional breeding. These activities have heretofore met with relatively little concern as to their impact on native gene pools. Nevertheless, the changes possible by genetic engineering can be different in kind and degree than traditional breeding, or marker assisted traditional breeding, due to the fact that genes can be transferred from other species, and it is not simply a matter of increasing the frequency of a gene already existing within a species or population. In addition, such traits as enhanced TCE degradation may lead to phenotypes that might be less fit in a forest environment, and the outcome is not clear without long term tests in a variety of environments. On the other hand, traits that have been the subject of traditional breeding efforts, such as height and diameter growth and disease resistance, are selection criteria that are generally known to contribute to long-term health and survival of trees in forest environments. Compared to crops, forestry production systems generally require more time on the landscape (10-100) years, and due to the long period of investments, forest landowners can afford less intervention with, for example, pesticides and fertilizers. Because of these long time periods, and the inherent risk of these long-term investments, foresters tend to be conservative with changes in plant material and practices, and tend to prefer proven robust and adapted genetic material.

Some have argued that forest gene pools are already "contaminated" due to the introduction of sympatric species from other parts of North America, Asia, and Europe. Like traditional breeding, however, these are *Populus* genes adapted to a *Populus* genetic background.

Dr. Steven Strauss, a prominent molecular geneticist, believes that there would be strong resistance of wild poplar stands to significant introgression from plantations for a variety of reasons (Ecological effects of pest resistance genes in managed ecosystems, available at http://www.isb.vt.edu/cfdocs/proceedings.cfm). The experimental evidence for these concepts should be readily available if appropriate experiments were conducted. Other tree population geneticists have measured gene flow from a wide variety of wind-pollinated tree species and have generally found it to be substantial (e.g., Friedman and Adams, 1985).

While some individuals consider cottonwoods to be capable of growing where they are not planted in some environments, there is no reason to believe that the mammalian or other cytochrome gene would make them more so. On the other hand, there is no *a priori* reason to consider that they would not be, because the behavior of mammalian cytochrome genes in plants has not been characterized for these kinds of environments. Nevertheless, this could be tested experimentally prior to release into the environment during the confined field testing phase.

What are the pathways for proliferation of those risks?

If any TCEs remain, or if there are any remaining metabolites that pose risks, these could be passed on through dissemination of trees and their parts, including roots, leaves, stem material, seeds and pollen. These could be disseminated by wind, water, and terrestrial and aquatic animals that feed on or transfer material. For example, a bird might take a piece of branch or "cotton" surrounding the seed for its nest. Remaining TCE or TCE metabolites could also be disseminated through the use of trees and tree parts as firewood or in other products.

Another pathway for risk of proliferation is through gene flow from the transgenic trees to other sexually compatible species, whether native, ornamental or commercially grown. This could happen if trees are not carefully monitored for flowering or if they are not cut down before they flower, or if other sterility mechanisms are not effective. Once pollen or seeds are dispersed, the potential arises for the transgenes to enter the wild population. Also, because these trees have the ability to resprout, stumps and root systems would have to be killed when the task of remediation was finished. Depending on future land uses, this could be accomplished through stump treatments with herbicides, or by removing stumps and large roots with equipment. The latter is currently common practice in management of hybrid poplars for paper.

What types of positive environmental impacts might occur because of this use?

Hybrid poplars engineered to break down contaminants in soil and water would ultimately enable the ecological structure and function of contaminated sites to be restored, at least with respect to the contaminant that is removed by the poplars. Where necessary or desirable, these areas would be able to return to agriculture, forestry, residential or industrial uses. In addition, while the remediation process is occurring, the root systems of the transgenic trees will help to hold the soil in place and prevent erosion, thereby stabilizing the disturbed ecosystem. Trees also provide humus and microclimatic changes that can, compared to other kinds of plants, provide an environment more hospitable to a wide variety of other organisms.

What is the rationale for using the GEOP, including its advantages vis-à-vis alternatives?

TCE is one of the most widespread contaminants in the environment of the U.S. (Doty et al., 2000). TCE is stable in groundwater and can persist for decades as dense nonaqueous-phase liquids. Difficulty in pinpointing the location of these pools of TCE can greatly hinder attempts at remediation. The fact that TCE is a suspected carcinogen (Newman et al. 1997, Gordon et al., 1997) has lent urgency to cleanup efforts. The principal methods for remediation of groundwater

5

contaminated with TCE are pumping water from the aquifer and stripping the TCE by aeration or by charcoal absorption. These procedures can take years or decades and can be very expensive (Newman et al., 1999). Other techniques use bacteria to degrade TCE, sometimes through co-metabolism (which requires the use of inducers such as toluene or phenol, which themselves pose health and environmental risks, for degradation to occur) and sometimes, albeit more slowly, directly. Another option is monitored natural attenuation.

Hybrid poplars were chosen for a variety of reasons. Poplar has a wide geographical distribution and can be grown from southern Alaska into Central America, and therefore could, if successfully developed, serve to remediate diverse sites. It is not likely that one poplar clone would be environmentally adapted to such a diverse area, but if successful in one clone, the transformation could be applied to other poplar clones adapted to different environments. Members of the species can be easily crossed sexually. Propagation by cuttings is simple, yielding clones of a given individual, and poplars can be grown axenically (i.e., without bacteria or molds) in culture. Therefore it is relatively easy and inexpensive to propagate a genetically desirable individual, at least compared to other trees. Poplars have an enormous water absorption capacity from their roots' surface that can approach 300,000 km/ha (Gordon et al. 1997). Trees are able to take up water from both soil and shallow aquifers, potentially remediating both. There are also procedures for purifying deep-lying ground water by pumping it up to the surface and using it to irrigate level stands of poplar trees, so that the number of sites that can be remediated using poplars is greatly expanded. Finally, poplars can be used to provide beneficial products such as wood and paper, and can help restore entire impacted ecosystems, while providing the specific environmental service of remediating toxic chemicals.

Poplars are capable of breaking down TCEs without genetic engineering. The addition of a cytochrome gene would enable faster metabolism of TCE, thereby decreasing the amount of time until sites are restored, and thus the time organisms are exposed to TCE. The investigators at University of Washington found as much as a 600-fold enhancement in TCE metabolism in tobacco using the mammalian cytochrome (Doty et al., 2000). As of summer 2000, when this case study was written, the investigators found only a 4-fold increase in metabolism of TCE in transgenic poplars compared to non-transgenic poplars in greenhouse experiments. Due to public concerns with genetically engineered organisms, the investigators have chosen to use rabbit or plant cytochrome genes instead of human genes, and also to experiment in the greenhouse until they achieve a much more significant improvement compared to transgenic poplars in the greenhouse before conducting field testing.(Gordon and Newman, personal communication).

2.   Relevant regulatory agencies, regulatory authority and legal measures

The overall APHIS process for authorizing introductions of transgenic organisms is described in the regulatory section more fully in the Herbicide-Tolerant Soybean case study. Under authority granted by the Federal Plant Pest Act (FPPA), 7 U.S.C. §§ 150aa-150jj as amended, and the Plant Quarantine Act (PQA), 7 U.S.C. §§ 151-164a, §§ 166-167 as amended, APHIS regulates the introduction (i.e., importation, interstate movement, or release into the environment) of certain genetically engineered organisms and products. APHIS believes that is highly unlikely that trees (or any plant) intended for bioremediation would ever be granted deregulated status as has been done for glufosinate-tolerant soybeans and Bt maize (as described in the case studies about those organisms). Thus, a permit would still be required from APHIS for actual bioremediation applications.

The FPPA and PQA, together with several other statutes, were consolidated in August 2000 in the Plant Protection Act (PPA), 7 U.S.C. §§ 7701-7772. The regulations issued pursuant to FPPA and PQA will continue in effect until APHIS issues new regulations under the PPA.

The hybrid poplar qualifies for introduction under APHIS' notification process. The applicant provided the kind of information in the letter in Appendix 1, including certifying that the engineered tree will be introduced in accordance with the eligibility criteria and the performance standards set forth in 7 CFR 340.3. The three major steps APHIS took in this case are the standard ones: (1) evaluate relevant information (both that submitted by the permit applicant and that gathered by APHIS from other primary and secondary sources); (2) notify and consult with regulatory officials in States where the applicant proposes to field test; and (3) reach a decision as to whether to acknowledge or deny the notification. Additional information on USDA regulations pertaining to plants can be found at the USDA web site, http://www.aphis.usda.gov/bbep/bp/. The letter was received on 10/22/99, and on 11/21/99 a notification was acknowledged. The notification will remain in force until 8/01/03. Another notification would be required if any factors are amended. As described above, because the trees did not exhibit the desired levels of TCE metabolism in the greenhouse, field testing has not been initiated. If the field testing were successful, and it was desired to plant these trees for bioremediation on various contaminated sites, then a permit would be necessary. Permits are described further in the Herbicide Tolerant Soybean case study.

EPA

EPA has established regulations under section 5 of the Toxic Substances Control Act, applicable to intergeneric microorganisms for uses such as the clean-up of wastes. (40 C.F.R. Part 725). While EPA has not issued similar regulations for transgenic plants, EPA's authority under TSCA section 5 is also applicable to transgenic plants. Section 5 of TSCA establishes requirements for EPA review of new chemicals and significant new uses f existing chemicals. Although EPA's regulations are currently focused on microbial products and on the requirements of TSCA section 5 (see Bioremediation and Biosensing Using Bacteria Case Study), the breadth of EPA's jurisdiction under TSCA is much broader. EPA has publicly asserted jurisdiction over other living organisms, such as certain plants intended for the clean-up of wastes. In the preamble of the proposed rule establishing Part 725, EPA expressly stated that it was reserving authority under TSCA to screen transgenic plants and animals, as needed to protect the environment and human health. (59 Fed. Reg. 45526, 45527 (September 1, 1994)). The preamble to the proposed rule states:

> Plants and animals could also be chemicals substances under TSCA. Nevertheless, as a matter of policy, EPA has limited this rulemaking to microorganisms, e.g., microalgae of the plant kingdom.....Traditional chemicals extracted from a plant or animal may also be subject to TSCA, as are other chemical substances. EPA is reserving authority under TSCA to screen transgenic plants and animals in the future as needed.(59 Fed. Reg. at 45527).

In addition, EPA's authority under TSCA is not restricted to the requirements of section 5. EPA is also authorized to regulate "existing" chemical substances under TSCA section 4 (data generation), sections 6 and 7 (impose restrictions to prevent unreasonable risks of injury to human health or the environment), and section 8 (information collection). Further information on TSCA regulations and biotechnology products can be found in this report in the Bioremediation and Biosensing using Bacteria case study and the EPA website http://www.epa.gov/opptintr/batik.

The introduction of TCE-remediating trees to waste sites on a commercial scale will likely require regulatory coordination with other legal mandates. For example, on a Superfund site, there is generally an EPA Remedial Project Manager (RPM) in charge of the selection of which remedy, or remediation technology, to clean up a site. The RPM has nine criteria, as laid out under Superfund laws, used to direct the remedy selection process. One of the criteria to consider is the extent to which the remedy provides overall protection of human health and the environment. For more on the Superfund risk assessment process, see Rock and Sayre (1999). The information in the TSCA risk assessment and consent order could be passed on for consideration by RPMs. Similar coordination with site managers could occur for non-Superfund sites, where RCRA and/or State or Tribal considerations dominate site decisions.

Interagency Coordination

In 1998, APHIS and EPA's TSCA Biotechnology Program held a series of meetings to evaluate the status of regulation of plants that might currently have issues related to or were in the pipeline for use in bioremediation. The agencies concluded that the current process adequately addressed the issues that were identified and assessed. This meeting and discussion focused on field testing and disposal.

3.   Hazard Identification and Risk Assessment

APHIS

Field testing of these plants can be divided into two phases. The first is "proof of concept" and the second is successful bioremediation of contaminated soils. For example, before field tests are begun, scientists perform preliminary experiments in greenhouses or growth chambers to determine if the plant detoxifies the TCE. However, decades of experience have shown that only a few percent of plants that perform well in greenhouse tests will perform well in the field. Therefore, scientists generate hundreds or thousands of plants in the greenhouse to test in the field to identify and select the handful that perform as intended. This selection process takes several years. With respect to hybrid poplars, the plants are likely to be planted for testing at sites that are not contaminated with TCE, in specially designed containers with controlled concentrations of TCE (designed with the help of the State Department of Ecology for Washington State). In the first five years before flowering, trees can be selected for both good growth and metabolism of TCE. When a clone has been identified that detoxifies TCE and has acceptable growth characteristics, the proof of concept phase is over.

Before bioremediation can begin on a large scale, the number of trees would have to be increased. This would be accomplished by taking cuttings from the selected clones and vegetatively propagating them, taking cuttings from those cuttings when they are large enough and so on. This could take several years. During this time, APHIS envisions that coordination between other Agencies (EPA, INT, NIH, FS and others as appropriate), States, and Tribal governments, as appropriate, would take place. At this time, sites would be identified and site-specific environmental issues identified and addressed through site specific Environmental

Assessments (EAs) or Environmental Impact Statements (EISs) or other relevant EPA decision processes.

The assessment criteria that needed to be, and were, met for this notification are:

1. The introduced genetic material is "stably integrated" in the plant genome.

2. The function of the introduced genetic material is known and its expression in the regulated article does not result in plant disease.

3. The introduced genetic material does not: (i) cause the production of an infectious entity, (ii) encode substances that are known or likely to be toxic to nontarget organisms known or likely to feed or live on the plant species, or (iii) encode products intended for pharmaceutical use.

4. To ensure the introduced genetic sequences do not pose a significant risk of the creation of any new plant virus, they must be: (i) noncoding regulatory sequences of known function, or (ii) sense or antisense genetic constructs derived from viral genes from plant viruses that are prevalent and endemic in the area where the introduction will occur and that infect plants of the same host species.

5. The plant has not been modified to contain the following genetic material from animal or human pathogens: (i) any nucleic acid sequence derived from an animal or human virus, or (ii) coding sequences whose products are known or likely causal agents of disease in animals or humans.

APHIS decided that the above conditions were met for this notification. In addition, confinement would be ensured by following the protocols previously derived for other genetically engineered poplars. These are described in Section 5.

If these trees were to be used operationally for bioremediation in the future, APHIS would coordinate the development of t an environmental assessment with the other regulatory agencies consistent with NEPA implementing regulations of all Agencies. To reiterate, APHIS is not planning to deregulate plants used for this application. For an example of an APHIS EA for a poplar, see those for the permits numbered 9303902r, 8910903r and 9503101r on the APHIS website.

3.   **Information and data (what, why and how is data and information collected and generated)**

At any time, APHIS may request from applicants any additional information necessary to ensure that the performance standards are being met. This can include information on containment and potential impacts on nontarget organisms.

For a discussion of how EPA approaches information in the context of applying TSCA to mircroorganisms, see the Bioremediation and Biosensing Using Bacteria Case Study.

4.   **Mitigation and management considerations: approvals and conditions on research,**

development, production, distribution, marketing, use and disposal

The APHIS document on confinement considerations for *Populus* species can be found at http://www.aphis.usda.gov/bbep/bp/sec6j.html. In transgenic poplars, genes can easily escape by windborne pollen and seed, or by vegetative means. Because of this, and the wide distribution of sexually compatible species within the U.S., steps must be taken to prevent gene flow and persistence of plants in the environment by these methods in order to perform field trials under notification. A wide range of poplar nursery practices for pollination, fertilization, and cloning have been developed over decades. After trees reach reproductive maturity, some means to either prevent flowering, remove flowers, or prohibit pollen shedding must be made to preclude gene escape to other sexually compatible poplars in the general area. Some means must also be taken to prevent seed set or to restrict shedding of the seeds. Finally, steps must be taken to prevent movement of vegetative parts out of the site, and to destroy any vegetative parts, both above ground and below ground, which may remain after the test is complete. For example, transgenic poplars could be cut down and the vegetative material killed by a broad spectrum herbicide prior to flowering. The remaining stumps and root systems could be treated with an appropriate herbicide. The dead tree stumps could be removed from the test site and along with any plant stems, roots, and suckers removed from the site for analysis, these could be killed by high temperature treatment (autoclaving, oven baking, or incineration). Following removal of transgenic plant material, the test site could be treated with an appropriate herbicide and cultivated to control any volunteers prior to flowering in subsequent seasons.

Use of transgenic poplars beyond the field testing stage is likely to require additional information about the behavior of the new varieties and their interactions with wild and/or weedy relatives. For certain experiments designed to investigate these parameters, it may be appropriate to perform field trials under permit.

In addition, once field tests occurred on sites with TCEs, specific mitigation considerations would be developed at each site in accordance with CERCLA, RCRA or TSCA. An approach to disposal within the context of TSCA and bacteria can be found in Bioremediation and Biosensing Using Bacteria Case Study.

5.   Monitoring and consideration of new information

Monitoring of the field tests under APHIS would be expected to be similar to other tree field tests. Monitoring is authorized under the Plant Protection Act for obtaining information on plant pest risks. Since APHIS would not deregulate trees used in bioremediation, it would still be possible to change the performance standards of the permit as new information was acquired on the basis of plant pest risk.

6.   Enforcement and compliance

APHIS has qualified personnel in every State that can inspect field sites for compliance to the performance standards for all field testing. In addition, headquarters staff will be inspecting plant derived biologics applicants on a yearly basis and will inspect field tests performed under notification on a case-by-case basis.

USDA ensures that the conditions described in the notification, e.g., not flowering or isolation strips, would be maintained by reviewing the design protocol to ensure that it will meet performance standards, and inspections by both USDA and State Department of Agriculture officials on site. Failure to comply with performance standards under notification or permit conditions can result in the owner being ordered to take remedial action (7 U.S.C. § 7714(b)(1)) if necessary to prevent the spread of plant pests (7 CFR 340.4 d 7). If the owner fails to take such action, the Department can take the action and recover the cost of the action from the owner (7 U.S.C. § 7714(b)(2)). The owner can also be assessed a criminal or civil penalty for failing to comply with the regulations (7 U.S.C. § 7734). For example, some remedial actions might involve removing the plants by burning, spraying herbicide, hoeing or discing. Since these trees have not yet been outplanted, either under confinement under notification, nor under permitting, there has been no opportunity to observe compliance.

If the trees were used for bioremediation (compared to field tests under notification) the same kind of audit procedure would ensure that conditions of the permit were met (7 USC §§ 7714, 7734).

In terms of TSCA, if issues related to TSCA were seen, then monitoring and termination procedures would be put into place. See Bioremediation and Biosensing Using Bacteria Case Study for further information.

7.   **Public involvement and transparency**

A description of the overall APHIS approach to public involvement is described further in the Herbicide Tolerant Soybean Case Study. This involves posting all notifications and permits on the website. Comments are received from the public on them. Also, people may ask for information on permits and notifications from their State Departments of Agriculture, and if the material is not confidential business information, the State can make that available and also take comments from the public. In this case, the information is not confidential, so these two methods can be used to give input on the decision.

Notifications do not have an environmental assessment prepared in accordance with APHIS' NEPA implementation regulations (7 CFR 372). The rationale is that these are not exposed to the environment due to the performance standards that ensure confinement (see the Ornamental Plant (Bentgrass) sidebar for example of performance standards). Due to the changes in the regulations regarding notification in 1993 and 1997, species currently under notification may have had EAs prepared in the past, when a permit was required for that species, and the permit required an EA. For this reason there are EAs for other genetically engineered poplars (engineered for traits other than bioremediation) available on the APHIS website (9303902r, 8910903r and 9503101r).

If an application for deregulation were submitted, the standard process would be as described in the Herbicide-tolerant Soybean case study. However, as noted above, APHIS believes that this application will not be deregulated. During the permitting process, which would occur prior to operational use, the application for the permit would be made public and comments received on it. APHIS would then prepare an environmental assessment (if the biotechnology staff determine that there are significant new issues compared to previous poplar EAs) under NEPA and then either the Agency would issue a FONSI (finding of no significant impact) or an EIA would be developed. Since 1999, APHIS has been making its draft EAs available for a 30 day comment period, so that would occur for any permitting of a poplar for

11

bioremediation To the extent that the Comprehensive Emergency Response, Compensation, and Liability Act (CERCLA), 42 U.S.C. §§ 9601-9675, would be involved in the field sites for bioremediation, the criteria for the decision on the cleanup technique includes community acceptance determined by the result of obtaining public notice and comment (EPA Rules of Thumb, EPA 540-R-97-013).

REFERENCES

Cooper, D.T. 1990. Populus deltoides, Eastern cottonwood. In Silvics of North America, Vol 2. Hardwoods (R.M. Burns and B.H. Honkala, Eds.). USDA Forest Service Agriculture Handbook 654, Washington, DC. pp. 530-537.

Costa, A.K., I.D. Katz and K. M.Ivanetich. 1980. Biochemical Pharmacology 29:433-439. Cited from Doty et al., 2000.

Dix, M.E., N.B. Klopfenstein, J.-W. Zhang, S.W. Workman and M.-S. Kim. 1997. Potential use of Populus for phytoremediation of environmental pollution in riparian zones. In Micropropagation, Genetic Engineering, and Molecular Biology of Populus (N.B. Klopfenstein, Y.W. Chun, M.-S. Kim, and M.R. Ahuja, Eds.). USDA Forest Service Gen. Tech. Rep. RM GTR-297, Fort Collins, CO. pp. 206-211.

Doty, S.L., T.Q. Shang, A. M. Wilson, J. Tangen, A. D. Westergreen, L.A. Newman, S. E. Strand and M. Q. Gordon. 2000. Enhanced metabolism of halogenated hydrocarbons in transgenic plants containing mammalian cytochrome P450 2E1. Proc Natl. Acad. Sci. U S A 2000 Jun 6; 97(12):6287-91.

Friedman, S.T. and W.T. Adams. 1985. Estimation of gene flow into two seed orchards of loblolly pine (Pinus taeda L.). Theor. and Appl. Genet. 69:609-615

Gordon, M., N. Choe, J. Duffy, G. Ekuan, P. Heilman, I. Muiznieks, L. Newman, M. Ruszaj, B. B. Shurtleff, S. Strand, and J. Wilmoth. 1997. Phytoremediation of Trichloroethylene with hybrid poplars. In: American Chemical Society Symposium Series 664, E. L. Kruger, T. A. Anderson, and J. R. Coats, eds. pp 177-185.

Meilan, R., and S.H. Strauss. 1997. Poplar Genetically Engineered for Reproductive Sterility and Accelerated Flowering. In: Micropropagation, genetics engineering, and molecular biology of Populus. (Klopfenstein, N. B.; Chun, Y.W.; Kim, M.S.; Ahuja, M.R., eds.) U.S. Department of Agriculture, Forest Service Gen.Tech. Rep. RM-GTR-297. Fort Collins, CO. pp. 212-219.

Newman, L, S. Strand, J. Duffy, G. Ekuan, M. Raszaj, B. Shurtleff, J. Wilmoth, P. Heilman, M. Gordon. 1997. Uptake and biotransformation of trichloroethylene by hybrid poplars. Environmental Science and Technology. 31: 1062-1067.

Newman, Lee A., Xiaoping Wang, I. A. Muiznieks, G. Ekuan, M.Ruszaj, R. Cortellucci, D. Domroes, G. Karscig, T. Newman, R. S. Crampton, R.A. Hashmonay, M. G. Yost, P. E. Heilman, J.Duffy, M. P. Gordon, and S. E. Strand. 1999. Remediation of trichloroethylene in an artificial aquifer with trees: a controlled field study. Environmental Science & Technology, Vol 33(13): 2257-2265.

Rock, S. and P. Sayre. 1999. Phytoremediation of Hazardous Wastes: Potential Regulatory Acceptability. Environmental Regulation and Permitting, John Wiley & Sons, Inc., Vol 8(3): 33-42

Sorbet, Martha. 1998. Impact of contaminated litter from a TCE phytoremediation project and major metabolites of TCE on terrestrial isopods and aquatic amphipods. Thesis, Clemson University, SC

Strand, S.E., L. Newman, M. Ruszaj, J. Wilmoth, B. Shurtleff, M. Brandt, N. Choe, G. Ekuan, J. Duffy, J.W. Massman, P.E. Heilman and M.P. Gordon. 1995. Phytoremediation of trichloroethylene from polluted aquifers using poplars. In Proceedings of the International Poplar Symposium: Populus Biology and its Implications for Management and Conservation, August 20 25, 1995, Seattle, WA. p. 88.

Zsuffa, L. 1976. Vegetative propagation of cottonwood by rooted cuttings. In Proceedings of the Symposium on Eastern Cottonwood and Related Species (B.A. Thielges and S.B. Land, Jr., Eds.), September 28 - October 2, 1976, Greenville, MS. pp. 99-108.

Appendix 1.   Sample Release Notification Letter

USDA, APHIS, PPQ   (submit on letterhead)
Biotechnology Evaluations
Unit 133
Riverdale Park, MD 20737
E-mail: biotech@usda.gov
FAX 301-73410

1. Reference Number: (leave blank for APHIS' use)

2. Applicant Reference Number:

3. Applicant/Responsible party:
Ma's Potatoes, Inc.   Dr. Ida Solanum
1992 Tuberosum Dr.   (315) 789-1011
Tatertown, NY 12345   fax   (315) 789-1213

4. Duration of Introduction:
Release: February 21–September 1, 1994

5. Recipient: Potato, Solanum tuberosum cultivar Russet Burbank

6. Regulated Article:

a) designation of transformed line: VR67
   category: VR
   phenotype: PVY resistant
   construct: pCP123
   genotype:
        promoter: enhanced 35S 5' from cauliflower mosaic virus (CaMV)
        gene: anti-sense coat protein from PVY, strain O
        enhancer: alcohol dehydrogenase (adh) intron 1 from Zea mays
        terminator: nopaline synthase (nos) 3' from Agrobacterium tumefaciens T-DNA
                 selectable marker:
        promoter: 35S 5' from CaMV
        gene: phosphinothricin acetyltransferase (bar) from Streptomyces hygroscopicus
        terminator: nos 3' from A. tumefaciens T-DNA

b) designation of transformed line: VR19
   category: VR
   phenotype: PVY resistant   construct: pCP456
   genotype:
        promoter: 35S 5' from CaMV
        gene: coat protein from PVY, strain O
        terminator: nos 3' from A. tumefaciens T-DNA

14

selectable marker:
promoter: 35S 5' from CaMV
gene: β-glucuronidase (uidA) from E. coli
terminator: 35S 3' from CaMV
promoter: 35S 5' from CaMV
gene: neomycin phosphotransferase (nptII) from E. coli Tn5
terminator: 35S 3' from CaMV

c) designation of transformed line: VR327
    category: VR
    phenotype: PVY resistant
    construct: pCP123 and pCP456
    genotype: (see descriptions above)

7. Mode of Transformation: disarmed A. tumefaciens for line VR67; electroporation for line VR19; microprojectile bombardment for line VR327

8. Introduction:

Release:
    NUMBER OF STATES/TERRITORIES AND SITES: ID(1), ME(1), WI(1)
    Russ Burbank's Farm, Bingham County, ID, 1.5 acres;
    Pa's Potato Farm, Hancock County, ME, 1 acre; and
    Potato Research Farm, Oneida County, WI, 1 acre

9. Certification: I certify that the regulated article will be introduced in accordance with the eligibility criteria and the performance standards set forth in 7 CFR 340.3. The above information is true to the best of our knowledge. If there are any changes, we will contact APHIS.

    Signature _____   Date
    Name Typed

CASE STUDY No. VI

BIOREMEDIATION AND BIOSENSING USING BACTERIA

Overview

This case study examines the federal regulatory process with respect to a bacterium that was genetically modified to detect the presence of, and degrade, hazardous wastes derived from petroleum. Genes from several other organisms were introduced into the transgenic bacterium. The primary regulatory statute involved is the Toxic Substances Control Act (TSCA), 15 U.S.C. §§ 2601-2692, administered by the United States Environmental Protection Agency (EPA).

1.   Proposed Organism and Use

This case study examines the decision to allow the field testing of a genetically engineered bacterium designed to detect and degrade hazardous chemical wastes. These wastes, derived from crude or refined petroleum products, are found in many hazardous waste sites, and present a serious public health risk. The recombinant bacterium, with genes introduced from several other organisms, was developed by the Department of Energy (DOE) and the University of Tennessee. The genus *Pseudomonas,* on which the recombinant bacterium is based, is known for its broad nutritional versatility. This versatility enables pseudomonads to use many naturally-occurring and synthetic wastes as sources of carbon and energy, thus reducing organic wastes to less toxic metabolites (Silver, et al., 1990). This genus was, therefore, a logical candidate to enhance for biodegradative and biosensor applications.

The recombinant bacterium *Pseudomonas fluorescens Strain HK44* was released in 1996 for the detection and biodegradation of polycyclic aromatic hydrocarbons (PAHs) in soil. This small-scale field test represented the first environmental release of a recombinant microorganism for bioremediation in the U.S. *Pseudomonas fluorescens Strain HK44*, containing the recombinant plasmid pUTK21, was released to large partially enclosed containers referred to as lysimeters. These lysimeters are located at the Department of Energy's (DOE's) Y-12 site at the Oak Ridge National Laboratories near Oak Ridge, Tennessee.

Pseudomonas fluorescens Strain HK44 was intended to both degrade PAHs, and to serve as a biosensor which produces visible light in the presence of bioavailable PAHs. PAHs are found in crude and refined petroleum oil products, and consist of two or more benzene rings fused together with at least two common carbons. PAHs are present in higher concentrations in heavier petroleum hydrocarbon blends and particularly in certain fuel oils, coal tars, wood-treating chemicals, creosote, soot, and refinery wastes. These compounds have limited water solubility, and adhere strongly to subsurface materials. PAHs are a concern due to their potential to cause adverse human and ecological effects, and are present in the soils and sediments of many hazardous waste sites across the U.S. Substances containing PAHs are recognized, for example, as skin carcinogens in humans and animals. Biosensors such as HK44 offer a less expensive and more rapid way to monitor PAH concentrations in soils, sediments, and groundwater at hazardous waste sites, as opposed to traditional chemical detection methodologies. Such monitoring is useful to assess initial concentrations of contaminants, determine contaminant movements off-site, and assess the progress of clean-up activities associated with a site. Further, biosensors may provide a way to assess what fraction of PAHs at a site are actually bioavailable for uptake by humans or wildlife.

Bioremediation of organic wastes such as PAHs and other contaminants has become a broadly accepted remediation technology in the U.S. and elsewhere: the technology can often be applied in a cost-effective manner, and it employs naturally-occurring bacteria and other microorganisms which often utilize organic wastes as carbon sources for growth. In addition to bioremediation, the use of genetically engineered microorganisms as alternative means of detecting hazardous wastes is the subject of research at present. Bacteria such as HK44 may offer a way to detect wastes in a less expensive way than by chemical means (gas chromatography, mass spectroscopy, electrophoresis, etc.) (Rogers and Gerlach, 1999). Strain HK44 cells which produce light (due to introduced light-producing genes) can be either applied directly to the soil, or placed in small photomultiplier probes; the organisms then produce light in amounts relative to the concentrations of contaminants in polluted soil or groundwater.

Strain HK44 was identified by EPA as a *P. fluorescens* Biovar II, and was fully characterized in terms of the taxonomy of the recipient bacterium and its introduced DNA on plasmid pUTK21. The recipient strain, and the donor strain for the plasmid pKA1 on which the recombinant plasmid pUTK21 is based, were both identified as members of the species *P. fluorescens*. Additional DNA used in constructing HK44 came from the bacteria *Photobacterium fischeri* and *Escherichia coli*. Details on the construction of HK44, identity of taxa and DNA used, and explanation of how HK44 functions as a PAH degrader and biosensor, can be found in **Appendix 1**.

2.   Relevant Regulatory Agencies, Regulatory Authority, and Legal measures

Pre-release approval for Strain HK44 was obtained under the Toxic Substances Control Act (TSCA) authority of the U.S. Environmental Protection Agency (EPA), after submission to EPA of a Pre-Manufacture Notification (PMN). The PMN was prepared by the University of Tennessee and contained the bulk of the safety information reviewed. This information was also considered by the U.S. Department of Agriculture Animal and Plant Health Inspection Service (USDA/APHIS) as part of its review under the Plant Pest Act, by DOE safety coordinators involved with the field test, and by DOE under the National Environmental Policy Act (NEPA), 42 U.S.C. §§ 4321-4370e. The initial release of 10^{14} cells and subsequent survival of Strain HK44 were monitored over a two-year period by Oak Ridge National Laboratory (ORNL) and University of Tennessee under an EPA Consent Order issued under TSCA. A summary of the risk assessment for the release of Strain HK44 can be found in Sayre (1997), while the results of the field test can be found primarily in Ripp, et al. (2000). Details of these processes are described below.

TSCA applies to microorganisms for uses not specifically excluded by Section 3 of the statute (e.g., pesticides which are covered under the Federal Insecticide, Fungicide, and Rodenticide Act (FIFRA), 7 U.S.C. §§ 136-136y; and drugs addressed under the Federal Food, Drug, and Cosmetics Act (FFDCA), 21 U.S.C. 301 et seq.) Under Section 5 of TSCA (15 U.S.C.

§ 2604), EPA conducts premanufacture reviews of "new" microorganisms, as well as traditional chemicals, which are manufactured or imported into the U.S. Such reviews apply to "intergeneric" microorganisms, irrespective of the process by which they were created. The TSCA Section 5 authority extends broadly to a number of different types of microorganisms. According to the TSCA regulations, "*microorganism* means an organism classified, using the five-kingdom classification system of Whittaker in the kingdoms of Monera (or Procaryotae), Protista, Fungi, and the Chlorophyta and the Rhodophyta of the Plantae, and a virus or virus-like particle."(40 CFR725.3). If there is reason to believe a microorganism might be a plant pest, APHIS also has authority to review the applications.[1]

EPA has defined intergeneric microorganisms as those microorganisms resulting from the deliberate combination of genetic material originally isolated from organisms classified in different genera: for example, a *Pseudomonas sp.* bacterium, with DNA from an *Escherichia sp.* bacterium, would be considered intergeneric (40 CFR 725.3). Examples of commercial uses of microorganisms subject to TSCA include specialty chemical and enzyme production, bioremediation, biosensors of environmental contaminants, biofertilizers, ore mining, oil recovery, and biomass conversion.

The Office of Pollution Prevention and Toxics (OPPT) issued final TSCA biotechnology regulations in 1997 that describe both the various biotechnology submissions, and exemptions (62 Fed. Reg. 17, 190 (April 11, 1997)). These regulations created a reporting vehicle specifically designed for microorganisms: the Microbial Commercial Activity Notice (MCAN) (40 CFR 725.3 and 725, Subpart D). Persons intending to use intergeneric microorganisms for commercial purposes in the U.S. must submit an MCAN to EPA at least 90 days before such use. EPA has 90 days to review the submission in order to determine whether action is necessary to protect human health or the environment. The rules also address intergeneric microorganisms used in research and development (R&D) for commercial purposes and create a vehicle for reporting on testing of new microorganisms in the environment -- the TSCA Experimental Release Application or TERA (40 CFR 725.3 and 725, Subpart E). A TERA must be submitted to EPA at least 60 days prior to initiating such field trials. The TERA is designed, in recognition of the needs of researchers, to provide a high measure of flexibility and a shorter review period (60 days).

In addition to these types of submissions under TSCA, certain intergeneric microorganisms are exempt from the requirement to submit an MCAN if the manufacturer meets criteria defining eligible microorganisms, introduced DNA, and containment practices. This exemption is most applicable to the manufacture of specialty and commodity chemicals, particularly industrial enzymes. Intergeneric microorganisms used for R&D in contained structures are exempt from EPA reporting requirements, if researchers maintain records demonstrating eligibility. Researchers are exempt from this record-keeping requirement when

---

1 Some examples of transgenic fungi for which APHIS has prepared environmental assessments include: *Cephalosporium gramineum* (APHIS number 96-127-02r), a pathogen of wheat, which was engineered with a marker gene to gain a better understanding of the biology of the fungus and the mechanism of its infection process, and *Fusarium moniliforme*(98-355-01), genetically engineered to not produce fumonisin toxins and to be resistant to the antibiotic hygromycin B.

the researcher or institution is in mandatory compliance with the National Institutes of Health (NIH) "Guidelines for Research Involving Recombinant DNA Molecules" (59 FR 34496, July 5, 1994). Those researchers voluntarily following the NIH Guidelines can, by documenting their use of the NIH Guidelines, satisfy EPA's requirements for testing in contained structures. Alternatively, researchers can take the exemption by documenting that they meet eligibility criteria identified by EPA, including oversight of the research by a technically qualified individual, and containment and inactivation of microorganisms used. Certain intergeneric microorganisms in R&D field testing are also exempt due to prior experience with their release. For example, testing on ten acres or less involving *Bradyrhizobium japonicum* and *Rhizobium meliloti* is exempt when the criteria specified by these rules are met. These criteria address the inclusion of only specific introduced genetic material (that which is poorly mobilizable), and specify restrictions on exposure to the rhizobia during field testing.

When considering intergeneric microorganisms under Section 5 of TSCA and the implementing regulations at 40 CFR Part 725, EPA reviews the microorganisms for their potential to cause unreasonable risks to human health and the environment (15 U.S.C. § 2604(a)). TSCA does not expressly define unreasonable risk"; however it does provide a list of factors in section 6 to consider when making that determination (15 U.S.C. § 2605(c)(i), see also § 2604(b)(4)(A)(ii)). These factors make it clear that during its review, EPA is required to consider both the extent to which risks would be avoided by regulation and the burden imposed by that regulation. If EPA identifies any unreasonable risks, it is required to take action to prevent the unreasonable risks before the microorganism can be manufactured or imported either for research and development, or on a commercial scale (15 U.S.C. § 2604(f), see also 40 CFR Part 725). With a few exceptions established in the regulations, this would include situations prior to a release to the environment. The TSCA review is considered the functional equivalent of a NEPA review because it encompasses all foreseeable hazards/risks, whether to human health or the environment.

This case study focuses on the premarket approval process for an intergeneric bacterium proposed for use in bioremediation and biosensing under Section 5 of TSCA and its accompanying regulations. However it should be noted that other microorganisms- intergeneric and naturally occurring- can be addressed under other sections of TSCA if there exists a need and these products are already in commerce. If a microorganism subject to TSCA is not intergeneric (e.g., intrageneric or naturally occurring), and concerns are raised regarding its safety through TSCA § 8(e) notifications, TSCA FYI notifications, or other means, EPA has authority to address these issues under Sections 4, 5, 6, 7, and 8 of TSCA (15 U.S.C. §§ 2603-2607). EPA has also publicly asserted jurisdiction over other living organisms, such as certain plants intended for the cleanup of wastes. When EPA proposed the rule for intergeneric microorganisms, it said, "EPA is reserving the authority under TSCA to screen transgenic plants and animals in the future as needed" (EPA, 1994a). This was confirmed in a letter to participants in the current regulatory assessment from EPA dated December 22, 2000.

EPA regulations at 40 CFR 725.3 define microorganisms to include organisms in the kingdoms Monera, Protista, and Fungi, the Chlorophyta and the Rhodophyta of the Plantae, and viruses and virus-like particles. Genetically engineered, or naturally occurring, microorganisms from all these kingdoms (including fungi and algae) would be regulated under these regulations if the organism were intergeneric, or if EPA had, by rule, designated their use to be a Asignificant new use." Moreover, if necessary, EPA could rely on its authority under TSCA sections 4, 6, 7, or 8 to regulate such organisms, either genetically engineered or naturally occurring. Research and development for commercial purposes are those activities that are funded directly, in whole or in part, by a commercial entity regardless of who is actually conducting the research; or which will obtain for the researcher an immediate or eventual commercial advantage.

EPA did not finalize its TSCA Part 725 biotechnology regulations until 1997 (EPA, 1997). Therefore, the 1995 OPPT review of Strain HK44 did not follow these regulations. However, the substantive nature of the OPPT review process was available in the 1994 proposed TSCA biotechnology rule (EPA, 1994a), and the TSCA portion of the Office of Science and Technolgy Policy (OSTP) "Coordinated Framework for the Regulation of Biotechnology; Announcement of Policy and Notice for Public Comment" (51 Fed. Reg. 23313-23338.). EPA had also provided guidance on preparation and submission of premanufacture notices for microorganisms under TSCA in its "Points to Consider" document (EPA, 1984). Finally, EPA had available its longstanding procedure for reviewing premanufacture notifications under 40 CFR Part 720 to guide its consideration of Strain HK44. Therefore, the risk assessment and review done on Strain HK44 under TSCA in 1995 was equivalent to what would have been done under the 1997 final TSCA regulations.

Under Section 5 of TSCA, EPA had 90 days in which to review the PMN submission for Strain HK44. If the 90 days passed without action by EPA, the submitter would have been free to manufacture or import Strain HK44 without controls. However, the review period can be extended under TSCA section 5(c) for good cause; it may also be suspended voluntarily by the mutual consent of EPA and the PMN submitter. During the review period, EPA may take action under TSCA section 5(e) or 5(f) to prohibit or limit the production, processing, distributing in commerce, use, and disposal of new chemical substances that raise health or environmental concerns.

For Strain HK44, most of the information EPA reviewed to make its regulatory decision was supplied by the submitter, who had been guided by the EPA "Points to Consider" document. The specific details of the Strain HK44 safety review are discussed below. In addition to consideration of the potential risks of the organism, the potential benefits of its use were also factored into the regulatory decision. EPA concluded that there was sufficient uncertainty about the risks of the field test that regulatory controls were appropriate at the Y-12 site, and that there were outstanding issues which needed to be addressed before HK44 was marketed commercially. The mechanism EPA used to impose controls was a consent order under section 5(e) of TSCA, as described below.

In summary, EPA regulates intergeneric microorganisms under TSCA for any uses not excluded under Section 3 of the Act. EPA's role during this review is to identify and prevent any unreasonable risk of injury to health and the environment from manufacture, processing, use or disposal of the microorganism. EPA works with other agencies, as appropriate, in its review of these intergeneric microorganisms to ensure that all relevant issues are considered. For example, EPA will review an intergeneric microorganism used as a pesticide intermediate under

TSCA, while it will review the pesticide itself under FIFRA. EPA will also refer manufacturers of intergeneric microorganisms to other agencies when review is appropriate under multiple statutes. In addition, EPA may defer regulatory oversight altogether, when the requirements of TSCA section 9 are met. EPA's regulation of intergeneric microorganisms extends from research and development for commercial purposes to commercial manufacture and use.

A review of microorganisms is conducted under USDA/APHIS regulations, in addition to that done under TSCA, if the microorganism (in this case *Pseudomonas fluorescens*) is regarded as a possible plant pest. The USDA review was integrated into the TSCA risk assessment for Strain HK44. As a general matter, most microorganisms being investigated for use in bioremediation are not plant pests. USDA/APHIS has regulations and a procedure for determining if a microorganism is regulated. APHIS regulations (7 CFR 340.2) lists groups of microorganisms which are or contain plant pests. Any organism belonging to any taxa contained within any listed genera or taxa is only considered to be a plant pest if the organism "can directly or indirectly injure, or cause disease, or damage in any plants or parts thereof, or any processed, manufactured, or other products of plants." A particular unlisted species within a listed genus would be deemed a plant pest for purposes of 7 CFR 340.2, if the scientific literature refers to the organism as a cause of direct or indirect injury, disease, or damage to any plants, plant parts or products of plants. If there is any question concerning the plant pest status of an organism belonging to any listed genera or taxa, the person proposing to introduce the organism in question should consult with APHIS to determine if the organism is subject to regulation. If APHIS determines that the microorganism is a plant pest or has the potential to be a plant pest, the organism introduction (importation, interstate movement, and field release) would be regulated as described in the herbicide tolerant soybean case study.

3.   **Hazard Identification, Risk Assessment, and Regulatory Review of Product**

Overview of Risk Assessment Process under TSCA

The information submitted to EPA by University of Tennessee in conjunction with the Department of Energy was that specified in the EPA's "Points to Consider in the Preparation and Submission of TSCA Premanufacture Notices (PMNs) for Microorganisms" (EPA, 1994). An updated version of TSCA "Points to Consider" is available at www.epa.gov/opptintr/biotech. Using this information, the EPA's Office of Pollution Prevention and Toxics conducted a full risk assessment under TSCA based on the PMN submission, and additional information received from the submitters at EPA's request prior to the field test. This information is publicly available in the EPA Docket in Washington, D.C., and a summary of the risk assessment is also in the literature (Sayre, 1997).

The risk assessment process used to evaluate the proposed ORNL field test included detailed analyses of potential human health and ecological hazards, likely exposure scenarios, and taxonomic and construct analyses. The risk assessment addressed the risks posed at the sites of production (fermentation site at ORNL), and use (the Y-12 field site) of the HK44 microorganism. These conclusions are in the EPA's risk assessment (Broder, 1995) which provided the basis for the TSCA 5(e) Consent Order, and approval for the field test itself. The full range of scientific assessments used to reach a conclusion on risks during the EPA review of the proposed field test, and the justifications for statements and issues noted in the Consent Order, are listed in Appendix 2. In addition to these reviews used for the risk assessment, an economic analysis was done to determine the cost of complying with TSCA and the product's benefits. The following sections under item 3 summarize the findings of the EPA risk assessment, and the regulatory conclusions reached.

Organism Characteristics

The identification of major microbial taxa and introduced DNA form a fundamental basis for assessing the potential hazards posed by a new microorganism, as well as for determining aspects of genetic stability and transfer of DNA associated with Strain HK44. The taxonomy of the recipient bacterium and identification of the introduced DNA used in constructing Strain HK44 have already been described in section 1 of this case study and its associated appendix (Appendix 1).

Review of Health and Ecological effects of Strain HK44 due to its Placement in the Pseudomonas fluorescens Biovar II Taxon

The health and ecological impacts of *P. fluorescens* have been reviewed in separate reports by Syracuse Research Corporation for EPA (1995) and by McClung (1995), respectively. Pathogenicity and toxicity information on the species *P. fluorescens* (Ballows, et al., 1991) indicates that clinical cases have been documented for this species include emphysema, urinary tract infections, postoperative infection, pelvic inflammatory disease and fatal transfusion reactions due to contaminated blood. Palleroni (1984) notes that *P. fluorescens* is not prevalent in clinical laboratories and hospitals; its ability to grow at refrigerator temperatures can lead to contamination of clinical samples, but it may not be able to grow at body temperature. *P. fluorescens* is a complex species with some members being innocuous or beneficial, and other being potentially harmful. For example, although some strains of *P. fluorescens* have beneficial effects in that they inhibit the growth of some microbial plant pathogens, some strains within *P. fluorescens* Biovar II also causes soft rot of onions (Wright and Hale, 1992), alfalfa (Turner and Van Alfen, 1983), broccoli (Canaday et al., 1991), lettuce (Miller, 1980), and other plants. Further, some strains can cause blight of cucumbers (Ohta, et. al., 1976), and have been associated with opportunistic pathogenicity in fish which are under stressed conditions (Bullock, 1964). A letter from USDA to Dr. Gary Sayler at University of Tennessee (USDA, 1996) placed the parental strains of Strain HK44 into the *Pseudomonadaceae RNA Group I Biotype D* and concluded that Strain HK44 is not a plant pathogen. Therefore, the strain was not considered a regulated article as set forth in 7 CFR Part 340. Further details from USDA supporting this conclusion, and the letter sent to USDA by Dr. Gary Sayler with information used by USDA to make its conclusions, were not available.

Environmental and human health pathogenicity were addressed in part by data requested by EPA: growth curve information (Sayler, 1995c) showed that Strain HK44 does not increase in numbers at 37°C, so it was considered to be unlikely to grow at mammalian body temperatures. This finding indicated that it was unlikely that HK44 posed any human health or other mammalian toxicity/pathogenicity issues.

Review of Health and Ecological Effects of Strain HK44 due the introduced pUTK21 DNA, and the role of Gene Transfer

A concern with the introduced DNA was identified in the EPA health and ecological reviews (SRA, 1995; and McClung, 1995) is the presence of the tetracycline resistance gene. Risk issues arise when there is potential for an antibiotic resistance gene to spread (from an introduced microorganism) to microbial pathogens that are controlled (in clinical, agricultural, or veterinary settings) by the antibiotic against which the resistance is active (Neu, 1992). Expert panels convened by both the EPA (EPA, 1989) and by Health Canada (1995) found that tetracycline resistance is among the least desirable resistance markers to include in microorganisms released to the environment. This finding was made based on clinical and veterinary use of major antibiotics, and on the transmissibility of the replicons carrying the resistances. The presence of this gene imbedded in two transposons carried by a conjugative plasmid increases the potential for it to spread to other taxa.

Health and ecological effects could also result from PAH breakdown products produced by Strain HK44 due to the introduced DNA. Also, such partially biodegraded PAH products could cause concern if produced by pseudomonads other than Strain HK44 following the transfer of degradative genes from Strain HK44 to these bacteria in the environment. Although available gene transfer data did not indicate this to be a likely scenario, the possibility remains that such a gene transfer could occur due to the nature of the genetic construct (for further details on these points, please see Appendix 3). If such degradative products were produced, any associated toxicity of these products could be offset by further degradation of these potentially toxic metabolites by other soil bacteria.

Further insight into the generation of byproducts resulting from catabolic degradation of xenobiotic wastes present in soils can be gained when the specific soils to be tested are considered, along with potential gene transfer mechanisms. The interactions of Strain HK44 with specific contaminants in the soils to be added to the lysimeters were undetermined since the nature of the contaminated soils to be treated in the lysimeters had not been decided. Following completion of the EPA risk assessment, an uncontaminated, nonsterile, loamy soil was selected and spiked with napthalene, phenanthrene, and anthracene. This soil was placed in the lysimeters for treatment with Strain HK44. Therefore, no toxic metabolites were expected from these three PAHs after degradation with HK44. If the *nah/sal* pathway was transferred to another microorganism that does not have the ability to degrade salicylate and its analogs, these intermediates would be present in the soils. However, degradation of these intermediates by other microorganisms present in the soils was thought to be likely. Microorganisms may generate toxic waste metabolites that are more water soluble and, therefore, have increased mobility as compared with the parent waste. However, this factor played little role in assessing overall risk of PAH metabolites due to the degree of physical containment provided by the lysimeter design.

Other contaminants could undergo partial degradation if present in test soils. However, none of these contaminants were present in the soils in the lysimeters or at the Y-12 site. Dibenzofuran, in the presence of strains carrying NAH7, is converted to a dead-end product 4-[2'-(3'-hydroxy)benzofuranyl]-2-keto-3-butenoic acid (Selifonov, et al., 1991). Napthalene-related compounds can be converted by pseudomonad dioxygenases to oxygenated products that on steric grounds would not be anticipated. Chapman (1978) cited data indicating that pseudomonads which initially convert napthalene to 1,2-*cis*-dihydrodiol encounter a related napthalene waste -- 1,5-dimethyl-napthalene -- it is a methyl substituent which is oxygenated to the primary alcohol and then converted to 1-methyl-5-napthoic acid with neither of the aromatic rings being oxidized. Chapman notes other studies in which acenapthene is converted by a napthalene-grown pseudomonad to 1-acenapthenol and then to 1-acenapthenone. The stability and toxicity of these compounds was not noted. All issues noted regarding toxic metabolites, while not of great concern for the proposed field test at ORNL, were noted as needing re-evaluation should Strain HK44 be used at other sites (with differing contaminants, containment, and soils).

Production, Application, Monitoring, and Disposal Characterization

Production of the cells for use in lysimeters was done using fermentors at the Oak Ridge National Laboratories adjacent to the Y-12 field test site. These fermentors had standard containment and spill mitigation procedures and equipment in place. All spent samples, and solid and liquid wastes, were autoclaved and/or chemically treated to eliminate viable cells. Air releases from fermentor off-gassing were to be vented through at least one filter. Descriptions of production, application, and disposal characterization of the ORNL field release are detailed in PMN PMN P95-1601 (University of Tennessee, 1995).

The cells were delivered from the fermentors to the Y-12 field site in secured carboys, and then released to contained lysimeters on the two-acre Y-12 site. This site is moderately sloped, has uncontaminated soils and sediments, is close to electrical power, and is reasonably secure.

The four lysimeters were originally designed for use in uranium leaching experiments connected with the disposal of uranium wastes generated by the Y-12 nuclear plant. The microorganisms were released to four 8-foot diameter by 10-foot deep lysimeters which are arrayed in a circle around a central core. Each lysimeter consists of a vertical 1/8 inch thick corrugated steel pipe which is fitted with a steel lid, rests on a concrete apron, and has a leachate collection system that empties into a 55-gallon drum. The core is large enough to allow researchers to enter and gather samples, store monitoring equipment, etc. The treatments were as follows: one lysimeter had PAH-contaminated soils only, one lysimeter had Strain HK44 in uncontaminated soils, and two lysimeters had both PAHs and Strain HK44 added.

Lysimeters were loaded with soil in a layered fashion, placing the soil containing HK44 cells between layers of clean soil. A Huntington loam soil with 1.3% organic carbon was used to prepare both clean, and PAH- and HK44-amended soil layers. Approximately 23 cm^3 of soil received the following final pre-testing concentrations of PAHs: 1,000 mg/kg napthalene, 100 mg/kg anthracene, and 100 mg/kg phenanthrene. Due to approximately 90% loss of PAHs prior to lysimeter loadings, on day 135 after test initiation additional anthracene and napthalene were added in 833 L Exxon Univolt 60 transformer oil was added via irrigation tubes directly above contaminated soils to re-establish approximate concentrations of 1,000 mg/kg napthalene and 100 mg/kg anthracene.

The 92-cm deep treatment zone of soil was sprayed with HK44 inoculum suspended in a saline solution, at the rate of approximately 4 L of cells (containing approximately 10^{11} bacteria) per 10 cm lift of soil. A 19-liter garden sprayer with an extended nozzle was used for the application. The application of the microorganism took approximately 12 h due to the volume of soil that was sprayed. Nutrients and air were added to the lysimeters as appropriate.

Strain HK44 can be detected by several techniques including a bioluminescence MPN procedure (detection limit approximately 10 cfu/g), agar plates with tetracycline and salicylate (detection limit 10^2 - 10^3 cfu/g), and by using *nah* and *sal* probes. Air monitoring during the application was done using selective media in either gravity plates or in one-stage Anderson air samplers. Details of the monitoring procedures can be found in the PMN submission, and in Ford, et al. (1999). Representatives of the EPA Regional office for Tennessee, and EPA Headquarters staff were on site during the release, as well as State and DOE safety officials.

All instruments, equipment, soils, and other samples were sanitized. In order to show the efficacy of hypochlorite inactivation, University of Tennessee provided data (as part of the PMN submission) that showed colonies on plates cultured with yeast extract/peptone/glucose were unable to form colonies after treatment with 1 - 2% hypochlorite.

Only skilled workers familiar with microbiological techniques were involved in the field test, and no workers with open cuts or sores were allowed on site. Gloves, and respirators to protect against organic vapors, were worn on advice from DOE on-site safety personnel.

Engineering and Exposure Assessments

Exposure assessment information included the exposures possible as a result of (1) the ORNL fermentation system that produced the HK44 cells needed for the field test, and (2) the field test itself. Information on the field test design, detection limits for Strain HK44, gene transfer information on Tn*4431* and pUTK21, proposals for worker protective gear, and sensitivity of Strain HK44 to hypochlorite. These items were already discussed in Sections 1.2. and 1.3.3. All of these issues, with the exception of gene transfer, were examined in the EPA engineering (Radian, 1995) and exposure (US EPA, 1995) assessments. For more detail on the overall process for EPA engineering assessments, please see Sayre, et al. (1994).

In addition to the information above, data on Strain HK44 and its ability to establish in a variety of nonsterile microcosms containing contaminated soils and sediments was provided to EPA (Sayler, 1995c). Contaminants added to the soil in these studies included napthalene alone, diesel fuel, and a mixture of PAHs and other organic contaminants. In napthalene-contaminated microcosms, the population of Strain HK44 increased over time with simultaneous degradation of napthalene. After introduction at approximately 10^4 cells/g, concentrations reached 10^7 cfu/g at Day 10, then declined to 10^4 - 10^5 cfu/g at Day 17 (with 4% of napthalene remaining) and less than 10^3 cfu/g after 6 months. The declining concentration of Strain HK44 with decreasing PAH concentrations is considered beneficial from a risk assessment standpoint since the microorganisms should decline in a similar fashion during field application.

Risk Assessment, and Regulatory, Conclusions for Strain HK44

The EPA concluded that the release of Strain HK44 at the ORNL Y-12 site did not pose an unreasonable risk to human health or the environment, as long as the release was conducted in accordance with the TSCA Section 5(e) Consent Order.

In the March 27, 1996 Consent Order, EPA and the submitter agreed to certain conditions that would govern the field testing of Strain HK44. Failure to comply with these conditions would have been a violation of TSCA section 15, and subjected the submitter to penalties (15 USC 2614 and 2615). Specifically, the Consent Order provided that Strain HK44 was only to be used at the Oak Ridge Y-12 site. Introduction of the Strain by means of a pesticide applicator that minimized spray drift of Strain HK44 was required. Sanitization of soils and other contaminated samples, equipment, and instrumentation was required. Such sanitization was considered effective when there was no colony forming units at the limit of detection, considered to by 10 cfu/gram of soil or liter of water. Routine monitoring in the area around the lysimeters was requested, particularly during periods when aerosol generation is more likely (such as during introduction of Strain HK44 into the contaminated soils, and the soil's subsequent introduction into the lysimeters).

In accordance with the Consent Order, quarterly reports on the status of the experiment generated for University of Tennessee and the Department of Energy were forwarded to EPA. Reports included operation evaluation of the lysimeters, operation evaluation of the monitoring equipment, analysis of data from sampling and monitoring, sampling schedule, and environmental safety and health evaluation (including accidents and injuries). Separate records of the progress of the field test were kept by the University of Tennessee for several topics including production volume, standard operating procedures, sampling information, routine monitoring activities for detection of Strain HK44, and effectiveness of sanitization techniques.

The Consent Order also identified three issues that required resolution prior to allowing the use of the same microorganism at any other site or under less stringent containment conditions. These issues would also be relevant to full-scale commercialization of Strain HK44 if the intent were to release it the many hazardous waste sites that contain PAHs. Since transfer of the tetracycline resistance to microbial pathogens could be a potential concern, data on the frequency of transfer of pUTK21 and Tn4431 should be examined. Second, the presence of persistent toxic metabolites may need to be addressed prior to commercialization. Finally, plant and animal pathogenicity concerns may need to be addressed in more detail prior to commercialization.

In addition to the EPA and USDA reviews, DOE conducted a NEPA review based on a checklist form supplied by the researchers conducting the field test. The DOE concluded that this field test qualified for a categorical exclusion from further NEPA review and consideration under 10 CFR 1021, Subpart D, Appendix B (La Grone, 1994). The exclusion under Appendix B, item B3.10 applies to small-scale research and development projects and small-scale pilot projects conducted (for generally less than two years) to verify a concept before demonstration actions, performed in an existing structure not requiring major modification.

The application of Strain HK44 to waste sites on a commercial scale will likely require regulatory coordination with other legal mandates. For example, on a Superfund site, there is generally an EPA Remedial Project Manager (RPM) in charge of the selection of the remedy, or remediation technology, used to clean up a site. The RPM also has nine criteria, as laid out under Superfund laws, used to direct the remedy selection process. One of the criteria to consider is the extent to which the remedy provides overall protection of human health and the environment. The TSCA review of HK44 provides considerations for application at the Y-12 site, but also provides considerations for concerns at other sites. For more on the Superfund risk assessment process, see Rock and Sayre (1999). The information in the TSCA risk assessment and consent order could be passed on for consideration by RPMs. Similar coordination with site managers could occur for other non-Superfund sites where RCRA (Resource Conservation and Recovery Act) and/or State considerations dominate site decisions.

Results from the Y-12 Field Test in Open Literature

Two recent articles in peer-reviewed journals, based on results from the 1996 Y-12 field test, provide insight into the performance and containment of Strain HK44. Ripp, et al. (2000) found that Strain HK44 was capable of real-time monitoring of bioavailable PAHs in soils. Sayler later noted that the detection limits for napthalene are in the low ppm range, and that the luminescence intensity was well correlated with napthalene concentrations (Sayler, 2000). Perhaps most importantly, Ripp et al. (2000) also noted that the study showed that it is possible to establish a recombinant bioremediation microorganism in a soil ecosystem over a prolonged period. Other findings by Ford, et al (1999) showed that although 10^{14} cells of Strain HK44 were spray-applied during the field test, selective agar plates and Anderson samplers only detected HK44 cells in a few cases. HK44 colonies were only found on 36 of 260 exposed plates, only 2 plates had more than 46 colonies, and no plates outside the 4-m range (from where the cells were applied) detected viable HK44 bacteria.

4.   Information and Data

As already noted, the information submitted to EPA by University of Tennessee in conjunction with the Department of Energy was that specified in the EPA's "Points to Consider" in the preparation and submission of TSCA premanufacture notices (PMNs) for microorganisms (EPA, 1994).

Information requirements are tailored in the Points to Consider guidance document to the particular type of biotechnology application: for example, different information requests are made for fermentation applications, as opposed to field tests. This information, submitted by the manufacturer is then reviewed by EPA's Office of Pollution Prevention and Toxics, with the resulting EPA risk assessment documents generated on which decisions are based (see Appendix 1 for example of risk assessment documents generated). Often, as in the case with the Strain HK44, additional data and information are requested. This can lead to extensions of the EPA review period. Outside literature, academicians, experts in other Agencies, and others are often consulted by the Agency in making its decision. In some cases, risk issues are brought to EPA Federal Advisory Committee Act committees (FACAs) for consideration. These committees consist largely of academicians. EPA has the legal authority and technical capacity to require or generate all data considered necessary.

5 and 6.   Mitigation and other management considerations, and monitoring

TSCA provides EPA with the authority to require any practical measure - including preventing commercialization - to prevent unreasonable risk. In the case of HK44, EPA's OPPT addressed concerns with the field test through the issuance of the TSCA 5(e) consent order. The conditions of this Order required monitoring, restricted use of the bacterium to one site, and mandated record-keeping and reporting to the Agency as detailed in Section 6 above. The Consent Order also identified issues for broader use of the bacterium at other sites for future consideration. For other biotechnology products reviewed under TSCA, additional conditions on production, distribution, marketing, use and disposal are or might be prescribed, including Significant New Use Rules (SNURs) to restrict additional uses of a microbial product (15 U.S.C. § 2604(a)(2)).

Prior to any further field tests, or commercialization, issues such as those raised in the risk assessment for the release at the Y-12 site would have to be considered.

7.   Enforcement and compliance

EPA has the legal authority to enforce TSCA, and has an enforcement/inspection program for TSCA in place that currently includes biotechnology products (15 U.S.C. § 2610 and §§ 2614-2616).

8.   Public involvement and transparency

All rulemakings concerning TSCA Biotechnology were conducted with public notice and comment pursuant to Administrative Procedures Act. EPA also has had public meetings and consulted with Agency/Government workgroups when developing its current biotechnology regulations in 40 CFR part 725. In some cases, the Agency consults its technical FACA committees on individual biotechnology product risks, although that was not deemed necessary for the review of Strain HK44.

Under TSCA sanitized versions of all notices received, rules/consent orders issued, and certain support documents (all of which have TSCA Confidential Business Information removed) are placed in a public docket for anyone to view. For more on TSCA confidentiality issues see 15 U.S.C. § 2613 and 40 CFR 725, Subpart C. The Agency also informs State and EPA Regional officials when field tests subject to TSCA are proposed in their area. Notification of TSCA reviews such as that of Strain HK44 are announced publicly in the Federal Register. The EPA's OPPT also has regular teleconferences to update all EPA's Regions on biotechnology activities. In the case of Strain HK44, both the State of Tennessee and EPA's Region IV Office were notified in advance of the field test by EPA Headquarters in Washington, D.C. EPA Headquarters and Regional representatives were present during the release of Strain HK44.

Other regulatory bodies involved in the HK44 release included the Department of Energy that sponsored development of the microorganism, and the USDA that conducted a review regarding the plant pest status of Strain HK44 under the Federal Plant Pest Act (FPPA), 7 U.S.C. §§ 150aa-150jj. Much of the information regarding the OPPT TSCA biotechnology program is available on the EPA website (www.epa.gov/opptintr/biotech).

Appendix 1: Characterization of the Recombinant Bacterium

Organism identification under TSCA consists of verifying the identity of the inserted DNA, site(s) of insertion, and the taxa used as major donors and recipients to construct the final GEOP. Strain HK44 consists of the recipient strain *P. fluorescens Strain 18H* which contains the 16kb plasmid pUTK21.

The recipient *Pseudomonas fluorescens Strain 18H* is an obligate aerobe which was originally isolated from a contaminated Manufactured Gas Plant soil, is resistant to ampicillin, and is able to degrade salicylate but not napthalene. Taxonomic identification of *Strain 18H* as a *Pseudomonas fluorescens Biovar II* was confirmed by Segal (1995).). The recipient Strain 18H which served as the recipient had an index of 0.394 for *P. chlororaphis* and on of 0.319 for *P. fluorescens* Biovar II. Strain 18H appears to be a transitional species between *P. chlororaphis* and *P. fluorescens* Biovar II. The DSM-German National Collection of Type Cultures accepted both strains as *P. fluorescens*. The Strain HK44 also produces the green fluorescing compound typical of the species (as opposed to the green pigment characteristic of *P. chlororaphis*), and therefore EPA agreed with the identification of Strain HK44 as a *P. fluorescens* Biovar II. Later Strain 18H was definitively identified as a *P. fluorescens* by 16srRNA analysis. According to the PMN submitter, the *ortho*-degradative pathway for salicylate degradation is chromosomally located, and there are two cryptic native plasmids in this strain that are also present in Strain HK44 (personal communication, EPA and PMN submitter).

Plasmid pUTK21 is derived from three sources: (1) the entire plasmid, except for the Tn4431 insert, comes from plasmid pKA1 found in a second Manufacture Gas Plant soil isolate *Pseudomonas fluorescens Strain 5R; (2)* Tn 4431 is comprised of genes from the bacterium *Vibrio fischeri Strain MJ-1* (now considered a *Photobacterium*) , which was isolated from the light organ of the fish *Monocentris japonicus* (Engebrecht, et al., 1983); Tn4431 also contains genes from (3) Tn5 and (4) *E. coli* Strain D1021 (Orskov & Orskov, 1973.

Verification of the final construct was provided in part by reference to King, et al. (1990) that documents development of Strain HK44, and by other data in the PMN submission (Sayler, 1995). EPA guidance includes a request for a detailed flow diagram that identifies all introduced DNA, vectors, and taxa used to develop the subject GEOP (see the OPPT APoints to Consider@ guidance document). The construction of pUTK21 was well described, and only a limited number of sequences were unidentified according to Sayre (1995), primarily nondegradative genes associated with the pKA1 backbone of plasmid pUTK21. Plasmid pKA1 is approximately 101 kb, and shares extensive homology with the well-described plasmid NAH7 in the 25 kb region which encodes the *nah* and *sal* pathways to the extent that these two pathways in pUTK21 and NAH7 can be considered homologous (Sanseverino, et al., 1993). However, NAH7 is only 83 kb (Yen and Serdar, 1988), and Herbes, et al. (1978) found significant differences in the restriction patterns of pKA1 as compared to NAH7 in the nondegradative portions of the plasmid.). Further details of the characterization and verification of pUTK21 can be found in Sayre (1995) and Tou (1995).

According to Sayre (1995) and King et.al (1990), Strain HK44 functions in the following manner. In the presence of napthalene, or the regulatory inducer salicylate, the pUTK21 bioluminescent reporter plasmid *lux* cassette produced visible light. The construct is intended to function as an indicator of bioavailable PAHs in soils so that the ability to degrade the PAHs using the microorganism can be assessed. For napthalene, the *nah* pathway present on pUTK21 degrades napthalene to salicylate, which then serves as an inducer for further napthalene degradation. Salicylate itself would normally then be degraded by the *sal* pathway genes present on pUTK21, except that the first gene in that pathway B *nahG* which encodes a salicylate hydrolase B has been inactivated by the insertion of transposon Tn4431 which contains the *lux* genes that lead to light production. According to the Premanufacture Notice (PMN) P95-1601 (Sayler, 1995a) submitted to EPA, translation stop codons in the two insertion sequences located on either end of the transposon prevent translation in all three reading frames. Therefore, there is no fusion protein resulting from *nahG* and *lux* genes, and there is no translation of the *sal* genes downstream of transposon Tn4431. The salicylate is, however, degraded further by an *ortho*-degradative pathway located on the chromosome of Strain HK44.

Appendix 2: EPA Risk Assessment Review Documents for Approval of Strain HK44 Release at the Y-12 Site

OPPT Risk Assessment Reports prepared for Biotechnology Submissions, with specific citations to Reports for This Bioremediation Field Release

Name of Report	Focus of Report
Taxonomy Report (Segal, 1995; 3 pp.)	Identifies genus and species of recipient microorganisms. May address donor microorganisms also
Chemistry Report (Tou, 1995; 9 pp.)	Identifies genetic manipulations made to construct intergeneric microorganism. May include a flow diagram for construction process and final construct illustration

Construct Analysis (Sayre, 1995; 22 pp.)	Identifies hazard and gene transfer issues associated with introduced DNA used to construct the intergeneric microorganism. Identifies any inserted DNA whose function is uncertain. May include a flow diagram for construction process and final construct illustration.
Ecological Hazard Assessment (McClung, 1995; 16 pp.)	Identifies potential environmental impacts of the recombinant microorganism and its products on environmental receptors such as aquatic and terrestrial vertebrates, invertebrates, and plants
Human Health Assessment (SRA Technologies, 1995; 12 pp.)	Identifies potential impacts of the recombinant microorganism and its products on human health. Pathogenic and toxic effects are considered.

Engineering Report (Radian, 1995; 23 pp.)	Identifies releases of microorganisms and their products to environmental media and estimates worker exposure to the subject microorganisms
Exposure Assessment (U.S. EPA, 1995)	Identifies concentrations of microorganisms in receiving air, water and soil
Risk Assessment (Broder, 1995; 15 pp.)	Balances hazard and exposure concerns to arrive at an overall determination for the field test

Appendix 3: Ability of Strain HK44 to Degrade PAHs, and Genetic Stability and Transfer of Introduced DNA Sequences

There was some uncertainty identified in the EPA construct analysis (Sayre, 1995) with regard to the substrate range of the degradative enzymes expressed by pUTK21, based on the lack of information on the full substrate range of NAH7. It is known that pUTK210-encoded enzymes are able to degrade the three-ring PAHs anthracene and phenanthrene to salicylate intermediates (Sanseverino, et al., 1993), which should be further degraded by the chromosomal *ortho*-degradative pathway of Strain HK44. Sayler (1995b) noted that compounds from napthalene to high molecular weight aromatics could be degraded by these enzymes, but not heavy tar residues. Hydroxylated and carboxylated intermediates could be expected from higher molecular weight PAHs, but other microbial populations present in soils are likely to further degrade these compounds. The issue of toxic metabolites that are generated from Strain HK44 is moot since pUTK21 would likely produce no different metabolites than pseudomonads which naturally bear pKA1, and the related NAH7, plasmids.

There is, however, a concern for salicylate-like metabolites if the *nah/sal* pathway of pUTK21 is transferred to other bacteria which may not bear the *sal* operon (Sayre, 1995). In this case, metabolites structurally analogous to salicylate may be produced in pseudomonads in the environment which receive the *nah/sal* pathway from HK44 via gene transfer. *P. fluorescens* Strain 5RL (donor of pUTK21 and original host for pKA1) does not have the *ortho*-degradative pathway and accumulated 1-hydroxy-2-napthoic acid and 2-hydroxy-3-napthoic acid from degradation of phenanthrene and anthracene, respectively (Menn, et al., 1993). Other pseudomonads in the environment which acquire the degradative genes from pUTK21 may also be unable to degrade salicylate analogs. Again, such intermediates are likely to be further degraded by other bacteria in the environment, since pseudomonads containing NAH7, or plasmids similar to pKA1 could mineralize all three compounds (Sanseverino, et al., 1993). Transfer of the *nah/sal* pathway could occur by conjugation since plasmid HK44 is a fully conjugative single copy plasmid (Sayler, 1995a). Transfer of the *nah/sal* pathway could also occur through mobilization of Tn4655-like transposon which may bracket the *nah/sal* pathway (as it does in NAH7). This assisted transposition could be aided by the Tn*1721* sequences present in Tn*4431*. Other gene transfer mechanisms are also theoretically possible.

Data relevant to assessing the stability of Strain HK44 and its ability to transfer pUTK21 and Tn*4431* were noted in Sayler (1995a). In nonselective chemostat experiments with Strain 18H, the Strain HK44 population experienced a 99% loss of the pUTK21 plasmid: 39 generations and a dilution rate of 0.086/hr resulted in 1.58×10^4 cfu/ml that retained the plasmid. The approximately 1×10^4 cfu/ml concentration was maintained for another 23 generations. Plasmid preparations showed that Tn*4431* remained stable in pUTK21, and all samples of isolates which lost pUTK21 were Tet[s] showing that the transposon did not insert into the chromosome.

REFERENCES

Ballows, A., W.J. Hauser, and H.J. Shadomy (eds), 1991, Manual of Clinical Microbiology, 5th edition, ASM, Washington, D.C.

Broder, M., 1995, Risk assessment for PMN P95-1601, Office of Pollution Prevention and Toxics, Washington, D.C., 15 pages.

Bullock, G., 1964, *Pseudomonadales* as fish pathogens. Devel. Industrial Microbiol., 5:101-108.

Canaday, C.H., J. E. Wyatt, and J.A. Mullins, 1991, Resistance in broccoli to bacterial soft rot caused by *Pseudomonas marginalis* and fluorescent *Pseudomonas* species. Plant Disease, 75:715-720.

Chapman, P., 1978, Degradation mechanics, in: Microbial degradation of pollutants in marine environments, USEPA, EPA-600/9-79-012, pp. 28-66.

Ford, C, G. Sayler, and R. Burlage. 1999. Containment of a genetically engineered microorganism during a field bioremediation application. Appl. Microbial Biotechnol., Vol 51, 397-400.

Health Canada, 1995, Workshop on the assessment of microorganisms containing antibiotic resistance genes - Ottawa, January 27-28, 1993, Health Canada.

King, M.,H., P.M. diGrazia, B. Applegate, R. Burlage, J. Sanseverino, P. Dunbar, F. Larimer, and G.S. Sayler, 1990, Rapid, sensitive bioluminescent reporter technology for napthalene exposure and biodegradation, Science, 249:778-780.

La Grone, J. November 14, 1994. Memorandum entitled ANational Environmental Policy Acti Categorical Exclusion Determination for Monitoring of Napthalene Biodegradation in Soil in Lysimeters, 2213X. Addressed to Martha Krebs, Director, Office of Energy Research, ER-1, HQ/FORS. 4 pp.

McClung, G., 1995, Ecological hazard assessment for PMN submission P95-1601, Office of Pollution Prevention and Toxics, Washington, D.C., 16 pages.

Menn, F., B. Applegate, and G. Sayler, 1993. NAH plasmid-mediated catabolism of anthracene and phenanthrene to napthoic acids, Appl. & Environm. Microbol., V59(6):1938-142.

Miller, S., 1980, Susceptibility of lettuce cultivars to marginal leaf blight caused by *Pseudomonas marginalis* (Brown 1918) Stevens 1925, New Zealand J. Experimental Agriculture, 8:169-171.

Neu, H., 1992, The crisis in antibiotic resistance, Science, 257:1064-1078.

Ohta, K., H. Morita, K. Mori, and M. Goro, 1976, Marginal blight of cucumber caused by a strain of *Pseudomonas marginalis* (Brown) Stevens, Ann. Phytopath. Soc. Japan, 42:197-203.

Orskov, I. And F. Orskov. 1973. Plasmid-determined hydrogen sulfide character in *Escherichia coli* and its relation to plasmid-carried raffinose fermentation and tetracycline resistance characters. J. Gen. Microbiol., 77:487-489.

OSTP. 1986. "Coordinated Framework for the Regulation of Biotechnology; Announcement of Policy and Notice for Public Comment@, Federal Register, Vol. 51, p. 23302.

Palleroni, N, 1984, Family I: *Pseudomonadaceae*, in: Bergey's Manual of Systematic Bacteriology, Volume 1, Williams and Wilkins, Baltimore, p. 156.

Ripp, S., et al. 2000. Controlled field release of a bioluminescent genetically engineered microorganism for bioremediation process monitoring and control. Environ. Sci & Technol, 34:846-853.

Rock, S. and P. Sayre. 1999. Phytoremediation of Hazardous Wastes: Potential Regulatory Acceptability, In: Environmental Regulation and Permitting, John Wiley & Sons, Inc., 33-42.

Sanseverino, J., B. Applegate, J. Henry King, and G. Sayler, 1993, Plasmid-mediated mineralization of napthalene, phenanthrene, and anthracene, Appl. & Environm. Microbiology, V59(6):1931-1937.

Sayler, G.S. 1995a. 14 June Premanufacture Notice for PMN P95-1601, The University of Tennessee, Knoxville, TN.

Sayler, G.S., 1995b, April 1 telephone conversation with EPA.

Sayler, G.S., 1995c, August 25 memorandum from to EPA from the University of Tennessse's Center for Environmental Biotechnology, Knoxville, TN.

Sayler, G.S. 2000. Speech given at the July 2000 Meeting of the International Society for Environmental Microbiology, Kyoto, Japan (abstract available only at this time, manuscript will be provided as part of ISEB 2000 proceedings).

Sayler, G.S. and P. Sayre, 1995, Risk assessment for recombinant pseudomonads released into the environment for hazardous waste degradation, in: Bioremediation: the Tokyo '94 Workshop, OECD, Paris, pp. 263-272.

Sayre, P., 1995, Construct analysis for PMN P5-1601. Office of Pollution Prevention and Toxics, Washington, D.C, 22 pages.

Sayre, P. 1997. Risk Assessment for a Recombinant Biosensor. Biotechnology in the Sustainable Environment (G. Sayer et al., eds.) Plenum Press, NY, 269-279.

Sayre, P., J. Burckle, G. Macek, and G. LaVeck. 1994. "Regulatory Issues for Bioaerosols". In Microbial Bioaerosols (B. Lighthart and J. Mohr, eds.). Chapman and Hall, New York, pp. 331-364.

Segal, M., 1995, P-95-1601 Recipient/donor identities, Office of Pollution Prevention and Toxics, Washington, D.C. 3 pages

Selifonov, S., A. Slepenkin, V. Adanin, M. Nefedova, and I. Starovoitov, 1991, Oxidation of dibenzofuran by pseudomonads harboring plasmids for napthalene degradation, Microbiology (Engl. Transl. MiKrobiologiya), V60:714-717. As cited in Menn, et al., 1993.

Shaw, J.J., L.G. Settles, & C.J. Kado, 1988, Transposon Tn*4431* mutagenesis of *Xanthamonas campestris pv. campestris*: characterization of a nonpathogenic mutant and cloning of a locus for pathogenicity, Molecular Plant-Microbe Interactions, 1:39-45.

Silver, S., et al. (eds.). 1990. *Pseudomonas*: Biotransformations, Pathogenesis, and Evolving Biotechnology. American Society for Microbiology, Washington, DC, 423 pages.

Tou, J., 1995, ETD/ICB biotechnology PMN chemistry report, Office of Pollution Prevention and Toxics, Washington, D.C. 9 pages.

Turner, V. and N.K. Van Alfen. 1983. Crown rot of alfalfa in Utah, Phytopath., 73:1333-1337.

U.S.D.A. 6 March 1996. Letter to Dr. Gary Sayler of University of Tennessee, 2 pages.

U.S. EPA. 1984. APoints to consider in the preparation and submission of TSCA premanufacture notices (PMNs) for microorganisms@, U.S. EPA, Office of Pollution Prevention and Toxics, Washington, D.C. [also see www.epa.gov/opptintr/biotech].

U.S. EPA. 1989, Summary of the Biotechnology Science Advisory Committee's subcommittee on antibiotic resistances, US EPA, Washington, D.C.

U.S. EPA. 1994a. Microbial Products of Biotechnology; Proposed Regulation under the Toxic Substances Control Act; Proposed Rule. Federal Register, Volume 59, Number 169, p. 45527.

U.S EPA. 1994b. Points to consider in the preparation and submission of TSCA premanufacture notices (PMNs) for microorganisms, U.S. EPA, Office of Pollution Prevention and Toxics, Washington, D.C. [also see www.epa.gov/opptintr/biotech]

U.S. EPA. 1997. Microbial Products of Biotechnology; Final Regulation under the Toxic Substances Control Act; Final Rule under TSCA for Biotechnology Regulation, Federal Register, Volume 62, Number 70, pp. 17909-17958.

Wright, P. and C. Hale, 1992, A field and storage rot of onion caused by *Pseudomonas marginalis*. New Zealand J. Crop and Horticul. Sci., 20:435-438.